SIGNING *Naturally*

TEACHER'S CURRICULUM GUIDE

TEACHER'S CURRICULUM GUIDE

Units 7–12

ELLA MAE LENTZ / KEN MIKOS / CHERI SMITH

San Diego, California

Published by DawnSignPress

ISBN: 978-1-58121-218-1

Printed in the United States of America

10 9 8 7 6 5 4 3 2

We dedicate this book to those who are first and foremost People of the Eye—the people to whom Nature has bestowed the eyes, minds, and souls to create and pass on this noble language for all to embrace, cherish, and celebrate.

May you forever show the world the importance of human diversity and listening to others through the human heart.

Contents

ACKNOWLEDGMENTS

Big waving hands to all those who have contributed to the creation and development of this book:

- Joe Dannis, owner of DawnSignPress, for his continued support.
- Rebecca Ryan, editor and associate producer, for all of her hard work, dedication, and occasional cheer leading while helping bring these materials to press.
- The team at DawnSignPress who worked diligently to make the new book and video look the best possible: especially Alfredo Sierra Jr., graphic artist; and Laura Harvey, video specialist.
- To Paddy Ladd, Nikki Norton and Nichole Smith for taking the time to give us thoughtful critiques on the culture notes.
- The Deaf Canadians who helped us get the signs for provinces right.
- To Iva Ikeda, for testing and giving feedback on our drafts.
- To all of the ASL teachers who took the time to give us feedback on the materials.
- The coordinators of Signing Naturally workshops for making it possible to meet and get input from teachers all over the country.
- Peter Freund whose artistic expertise provided the video design, and whose willingness to sit part time in the director's chair is very appreciated.
- Willie Smith for being our Facilities Engineer keeping everything running smoothly.
- Spankie and Vibolda for consenting to be our mascots.

PREFACE

We have learned that good lesson planning makes for effective teaching and more importantly, good learning. *Signing Naturally Teachers Curriculum Guide, Units 7–12* is a continuation of *Units 1–6*. Based on the feedback we have received from many dedicated and gifted teachers and our own teaching experience we continuing to improve our materials to maximize classroom learning. Like *Units 1–6* the student materials coordinate closely with instruction to review and reinforce language learned in the classroom.

Introduction

Signing Naturally, Units 7–12 is the second book in the series of curricular materials for the instruction of American Sign Language (ASL) as a second language. Teachers who have used *Signing Naturally, Units 1–6*, will find this book provides excellent materials to further the instruction of ASL with their students. The goal is to provide students with the skills to communicate in a wider array of situations, to further develop their language fluency and to advance their level of comprehension of ASL in culturally appropriate ways.

THE *SIGNING NATURALLY* CURRICULUM DESIGN APPROACH

According to the Standards for Foreign Language Learning provided by the American Council on the Teaching of Foreign Languages (ACTFL), *"all the linguistic and social knowledge required for effective human-to-human interaction is encompassed in those ten words 'Knowing how, when, and why to say what to whom.' Formerly, most teaching in foreign language classrooms concentrated on the how (grammar) to say what (vocabulary). While these components of language are indeed crucial, the current organizing principle for foreign language study is communication, which highlights the why, the whom, and the when. So, while grammar and vocabulary are essential tools for communication, it is the ability to communicate in meaningful and appropriate ways with users of other languages that is the ultimate goal of today's foreign language classroom."*

Meaningful and appropriate communication is reflected in the design of the *Signing Naturally* curriculum. The variety of lessons and activities in *Signing Naturally Units 7–12* are designed to help the language classroom and the language program meet the five areas of Communication, Cultures, Connections, Comparisons and Communities recommended by ACTFL.

In developing the curriculum, an approach that emphasized interpersonal communication and helped students achieve communicative competence was sought after. The functional-notional approach addresses both goals. Situations that predict everyday Deaf–hearing encounters are used to contextualize and give meaning to the function. The grammatical structures are determined by the function(s) introduced and the notions by the topic discussed in the lesson. Activities within the lessons are varied allowing students to use different strategies to practice what they've learned.

ENGLISH IN THE ASL CLASSROOM

The curriculum and workbook are designed with the assumption that the students in the classroom can read English. We take the position that ASL, the target language, should be used exclusively in the classroom.

The first reason is that it is culturally inappropriate to use voice in an ASL environment. Speaking eliminates the Deaf person, whether intentionally or not, from the communication around them. In the classroom, it is critical that the teacher, Deaf or hearing, maintain the culturally appropriate environment so that students develop the habit of signing, and not speaking, in Deaf–hearing situations.

The second reason is we believe that students can only become fluent by constantly using the target language. The more the student relies on English to understand ASL, the longer they will remain in the limbo of being unable to communicate in ASL. You cannot learn a language by speaking or listening to another language. No language is a direct translation of another, and concept formation is enhanced by full immersion. Students will not maximize learning ASL until they actually commit to using it as a living language. The only way to spur this on is to make the classroom a microcosm of the living world where all meaning is negotiated in the target language.

The teacher is crucial to the success of the ASL-only classroom. The more skilled the teacher, the more comfortable the student will feel. The teacher must have a repertoire of teaching strategies to conduct a successful immersion class. Lessons in *Units 7–12* are designed to offer teachers effective strategies for introducing and explaining signs, for engaging students in dialogue, and for implementing group activities without speaking or using English words to represent signs. The *Student Workbook* and videos reinforce and expand on classroom instruction by providing students with ASL examples, exercises, explanations, and other readings.

At the time of printing, there is not yet a standardized writing system for ASL, so written English is used to give instructions. However, it is not used to give English equivalents to ASL signs. For example, ASL vocabulary are introduced or reviewed with other signs, with pictures or English definitions rather than single word equivalents or glosses. A transcription system with glosses (see pages xxii–xxviii) are used to "represent ASL" in the Teacher's Curriculum Guide. Gloss is not to be shown to or used by students, but is used only in the Curriculum Guide to inform the teacher what to sign to the students or what students are expected to sign.

It is essential that you as the teacher understand and maintain this principle to maximize students' ASL learning.

THE ISSUE OF SIGN VARIATIONS

A common issue the ASL teacher faces is sign variations. For some concepts quite a few different signs are available, while for other concepts only one sign is used. We have chosen to handle this issue with these guiding principles:

- The most nationwide or commonly used sign is selected. Sometimes this means providing two or more variations.
- Initialized signs (a sign that directly represents an English word and is formed with the hand shape of the first letter) are not selected here if a more common non-initialized sign exists. The initialized signs that appear here are those already ingrained in the community and do not conflict with ASL linguistic or semantic rules.
- If the local sign is different from the one shown in the materials, we encourage you to teach the local sign in addition to the one introduced in the classroom.

To show teachers the signs or variation(s) that are used in the lesson, a picture of the sign appears on the page whenever a new gloss appears.

OVERVIEW OF TEACHER'S CURRICULUM SET

Signing Naturally, Teacher's Curriculum Guide, Units 7–12 set includes the following components:

- **Teacher's Curriculum Guide Units 7–12** (including Materials DVD Units 7–12)
- **Student Workbook** (including Student Video DVDs)

Teacher's Curriculum Guide

The Teacher's Curriculum Guide has a total of six units plus a Pre-Unit. Each unit has 10 to 14 detailed lessons that show you how to introduce, practice and review the material covered in the lesson. To help you organize, an overview of each lesson lists the approximate time it takes for the whole lesson and lists the goals and objectives, and which homework to assign.

The Pre-Unit, is designed to review *Signing Naturally Units 1–6*, such as vocabulary, phrases, skills and conversation behaviors. The Pre-Unit includes multiple activities that emphasize different skill areas, providing teachers the opportunity to assess students' current skills and knowledge and to determine what further review students' may need before starting *Units 7–12*.

Units 7–11 comprise several kinds of lessons: functional (conversational or narrative), skill building, comprehension, cultural and review. The **functional lessons** introduce vocabulary and key grammar structures through the use of key dialogues or narratives. **Skill building lessons** focus on practicing detailed language features that support students' general ASL production, such as various number types, expanded fingerspelling practice, space and semantic use of agreement or spatial verbs, and use of negation signs. The **comprehension lessons** use stories to expand students' skills to process and figure meanings from larger chunks of signed information. The **culture lessons** focus on behaviors and knowledge that enable students to act in appropriate linguistic and social ways, and to gain more cultural insight on the Deaf community. At end of each unit, a **review lesson** "Putting It All Together," provides students with opportunities to apply the language elements covered in the unit in new situations.

Unit 12 comprises 10 lessons covering different essential language elements to tell stories successfully. Even though Unit 12 can be taught by itself, we recommend that parts of the unit be taught in conjunction with other units so students can develop their storytelling skills over the course of the semester or year.

Finally, beginning on page xxix of this introduction are charts that provide an overview of all units, identifying for each lesson the language functions, grammar, vocabulary, conversational behaviors and student outcomes. These charts are useful in planning the course's syllabus.

Materials DVD

At the back of the curriculum guide is the Materials DVD. It has electronic files of all materials needed for use in the classroom. The majority of the files are PowerPoint slides that include dialogues, pictures, videos, and answer keys for homework follow-ups. A computer and a LCD/TV will be needed to use them, however they can be adapted to be used with overhead projectors or to print out to give to students or post on walls. In some units, there are also activity cards, handouts, and/or evaluation sheets that need to be printed and distributed to the students. Information about how and when to use the materials is found in each lesson.

Student Workbook (including Student Video DVDs)

The teacher's set comes with a complimentary copy of the *Student Workbook* including DVDs of videos demonstrating the ASL key phrases, dialogues, narratives and vocabulary covered in each lesson. Each lesson in the *Curriculum Guide* has a corresponding assignment in the *Student Workbook*. We also advise teachers to review the lesson's contents in the *Student Workbook* and the DVDs while preparing for the lesson.

ORGANIZATION OF EACH UNIT

Table of Contents. Each unit begins with a table of contents that lists the lessons by title. Titles in green indicate it's a core language lesson, (functional lessons, comprehension lessons, cultural lessons and unit review lesson) and titles in black indicate it's a skill building lesson (language leaning strategies, numbers, fingerspelling, grammar or semantic lessons).

The functional lessons (with the green titles) typically take one to one and a half hours to complete and skill lessons (black titles) take between twenty to forty five minutes to complete. The unit review lesson can take up to three hours if you choose to do all activities.

For the typical three-hour class session, we recommend teachers present one core language lesson (green title) and one or two skill lessons (black title), as time permits. For shorter class sessions, teachers can divide a core language lesson into two sessions. For example, teaching the "introduction" section one class session and the "practice" section of the lesson in the next class session and adding one skill lesson with the "practice" section.

The design is flexible enough to accommodate shorter or longer class sessions. Sample syllabi for typical semester-length and quarter-length classes are online at www.signingnaturally.com.

Overview

Each of the 10–14 lessons in a unit begins with an overview that lists the goals and objectives, the key language elements and vocabulary, length of the lesson (the amount of time given is based on a class size of 20 students), how to prepare, homework assignments, and where to find the materials for both the lesson and homework follow-up.

Each lesson is divided into three main activities—**Introduce**, **Practice** and **Homework**. The following is a basic description of each:

Introduce

Here, teachers are given instructions on how to present the new language structures and vocabulary. All instructional materials are provided to help the teacher introduce the lesson clearly and effectively.

Practice

The Practice section begins with a teacher demonstration followed by a series of student rehearsals that target language elements central to the dialogue.

At the end of this section, there is a list of specific language skills the students should be able to demonstrate. This list is useful in determining whether students have learned the information well enough to move on, or need more practice.

Homework
There is a homework assignment at the end of every lesson. Each homework number corresponds to the lesson's number. For example, after completing Lesson 7:1 in the *Teacher's Curriculum Guide* you would assign Homework 7:1 in the *Student Workbook.*

Homework activities vary. They include analyzing video segments, memorizing and rehearsing segments, answering questions, translating sentences, choosing the best answer, readings, and developing materials for classroom presentations.

These two other headings may also appear in the beginning of a lesson, **Warm Up**, and **Review**.

Warm Up
These activities are designed to provide students opportunities to practice specific skills that are not necessarily related to the lesson that follows.

Review
Review activities are designed to prepare students for the lesson that follows.

OTHER IMPORTANT ELEMENTS OF A LESSON
The following are titles that appear in the left margin in the teacher's curriculum guide.

Present
This indicates when you need to show certain materials such as images, videos or text (dialogues, lists, etc.) to the class using visual technology (primarily via PowerPoint). A reduced image of the materials appears in the lesson as a reference. The specific slide(s) needed for that section appears below **PRESENT** and can be found on the Materials DVD as Lesson Slides under that particular Unit. In a few cases, you will be asked to modify the slide. For example, to match the dates of the current month.

If, for some reason, you are unable to access technology to show the slide, you will need to create a transparency, or do it the good old fashioned way and use the board to write on or draw things!

Teacher to Teacher

In **Teacher to Teacher**, the authors speak directly to the teacher and share tips for teaching certain parts of the lesson, point out typical student mistakes, warn of difficulties that may occur during the lesson, or offer class management strategies to help the class run more smoothly.

Homework Follow-up

In **Homework Follow-up**, the goal is two pronged—one is to check student's answers and the other is to provide activities for expanded language practice.

Checking answers. In the back of *Student Workbook*, there is an **Answer Key** that provides the answers to some or all of the homework assignments. The other parts of the homework that are not in the **Answer Key** must be provided by the teacher. The Materials DVD provides those answers in **Follow-up Slides** for that lesson under that particular Unit. For example, if you teach the **Homework Follow-up** section at the end of Lesson 7:1 then slides for the homework answers and activities would be found in **Follow-up Slides 7:1**.

The quickest way is to just show the answers on the slides and have students correct their workbooks, or have fellow students correct their workbooks. But in order to provide more opportunities for language practice, you can:

Option 1: show the questions on the slide and ask students to sign the answers, then show the answers on slide to confirm

Option 2: instead of showing the answers on the slides, sign the questions and have students sign their answers.

Providing activities. In the *Student Workbook*, many homework assignments have a section titled "Assignment" in which students are asked to prepare or rehearse materials to present in class. In this case, the **Follow-up** section will also have activities designed for the assignment.

Don't forget to factor in the time needed for the **Homework Follow-up** activities when you prepare your lessons.

SPECIAL INFORMATION FOR UNIT 12

What is the goal of the unit?

Students will continue to build their storytelling skills, cumulating in adapting one of six fables from written English to ASL.

Although each fable has its own particular vocabulary and grammar elements, the overarching skills students will learn are:

- using role shift to show the character's manner, movements, thoughts and interaction with the environment or other characters in the story
- establishing and maintaining spatial agreement among characters and things in the environment
- using transitions and the accompanying non-manual signals to move the story along
- using eye contact to engage the listener.

How is the unit organized?

This Unit is organized differently from the other Units. Lessons 1–9 are based on five videotaped stories:

- **The Tailor** (Lessons 1)
- **My Favorite Leather Jacket** (Lesson 2)
- **One Fine Day** (Lessons 3–7)
- **The Lion and the Mouse** (Lesson 8 divided into several sessions)
- **The Fox and the Crow** (Lesson 9 divided into several sessions)

Lesson 10, the final lesson, focuses on preparing and evaluating students' ASL adaption of their assigned fables. The assigned fables are:

The Ant and the Grasshopper, Workbook pages 449–451
The Wolf and the Kid, Workbook pages 452–454
The Fox and the Stork, Workbook pages 455–457
The Dog and the Wolf, Workbook pages 458–460
The Scorpion and the Frog, Workbook pages 461–463
The Fox and the Goat, Workbook pages 464–466

Lessons 1–2

Lesson 1 focuses on students' understanding of the videotaped story **The Tailor** and the changes that were made to a garment. Lesson 2 focuses on students using key features of **The Tailor** with a different clothing item to create new stories, starting with the videotaped story **My Favorite Leather Jacket** as a model.

Lessons 3–7

These five lessons revolve around the videotaped story **One Fine Day**. The first lesson focuses on students' understanding of the story and each of the remaining four lessons emphasizes a different skill needed to re-tell this story effectively.

Lesson 8

This lesson focuses on adapting the fable **The Lion and the Mouse** from the English text. A model ASL adaptation is shown and analyzed after students have developed their own adaptation. It is recommended the lesson be divided into at least three class sessions.

Lesson 9

This lesson focuses on adapting the fable **The Fox and the Crow** from the English text. A model ASL adaptation is shown and analyzed after students have developed their own adaptation. It is recommended the lesson be divided into at least two class sessions.

Lessons 8 and 9 provide students with strategies to adapt fables from written English into ASL to use with their own assigned fables.

Evaluation Options for Lessons 1–9

We recommend that all stories be assigned and videotaped.

As a fluency assignment. We recommend students complete the self-evaluation form (see **Self-Evaluation** forms in **Materials DVD** under Unit 12), and then submit the form and video to you for evaluation and feedback. Grading can be as simple as "pass–fail" or as involved as assigning a letter grade (see **Evaluation** sheets in **Materials DVD** under Unit 12). In both case, it is recommended that you give feedback on the student's strengths and weaknesses.

As part of an exam. If you are grading the story as part of an exam, after filming, have students submit the video to you at the end of the exam.

In either case, if a student doesn't "pass," we recommend they be allowed extra time to work on the story, then to submit the story again. In this way, the student is still expected to develop the language skills needed to tell stories.

Lesson 10

This lesson focuses on students working in groups to adapt their assigned fables, applying storytelling and language features practiced in previous lessons. There are no model ASL versions, but there are worksheets in the *Student Workbook* that provide support and ideas on how to deal with the challenging parts of the fable. It is recommended this lesson be divided into five class sessions.

Session 1 (55–70 minutes) with focus on giving title, character descriptions and movements.

Session 2 (60–75 minutes) with focus on showing interactions with objects and other characters.

Session 3 (50–75 minutes) with focus on showing the character's thoughts and intentions, developing background to the story and translating the moral.

Session 4 and 5 (5–7 minutes per student) with focus on rehearsing and getting feedback from fellow students and presenting their fables as a final project.

Evaluating the Assigned Fables

Have the students tell their assigned fable. Film the student's presentation and complete the "Overall Comments" section of the evaluation based on the student's live presentation and then fill in the remaining sections of the evaluation after you review the student's presentation on videotape (see **12:10 Evaluation in the Materials DVD** under Unit 12).

When do I teach Unit 12 lessons?

We recommend you teach Unit 12 lessons along with the other units like this:

Lessons 1–2	toward the end of Unit 7
Lessons 3–7	toward the end of Unit 8
Lesson 8	along with Unit 9
Lesson 9	along with Unit 10
Lesson 10	along with Unit 11

PREPARING FOR CLASS

To prepare your lessons, we suggest you do the following:

1. Read the **Self-Assessment** located at end of the unit in the *Student Workbook* to get an overview of specific skills students will develop.
2. Check the **Preparation** section in the lesson overview.
   You may need to read **Grammar Notes** in *Student Workbook*, familiarize yourself with the contents of a video, or prepare materials from the **Materials DVD** under the folder for that Unit.
3. Read the lesson(s) thoroughly and check the **Lesson Slides** found in the **Materials DVD** and familiarize yourself with how to handle the materials in class.
4. Rehearse the lesson, especially in signing the key phrases or sentences.
5. Make note of the estimated length of the lesson (as well as the lengths of sections in it). As the lessons and objectives become more familiar, you will have a better idea of what areas may need more time and which are relatively simple for students to learn.
6. After you have gone through the curriculum at least once, feel free to add favorite activities or personal stories to enrich the lesson.

TRANSCRIPTION CONVENTIONS

At the time of this writing, a standardized writing system has not been established yet for ASL. We use this close approximation to the signing for you (not the students) to check or use in class. We hope this system shows you how a phrase or sentence should be signed. We advise you to rehearse before class to sign them as naturally and clearly as possible. Be sure your signing is consistent with the objectives of the lesson.

SYMBOLS USED TO WRITE ASL —

Symbol	Example	Explanation
WORD	SIGN	An English word in capital letters DEAF stands for an ASL sign (it is called a gloss). The meaning of the sign and the English word may not be the same.
fs-	fs-BOB fs-COKE	"fs-" represents a fingerspelled word.
#	#ALL #DO++	A pound sign (#) indicates a lexicalized sign.
-	OLD-1 LOOK-AT OPEN-DOOR	When the sign glosses are separated by a hyphen, they represent a single sign.
+	MOTHER+FATHER TIME+4	A plus sign between the sign glosses is used for both compound signs and contractions.
" "	"well" "what"	Quotation marks around lower-case words indicate a gesture-like sign.
! !	!HARD! !WRONG!	Exclamation marks are used for the emphatic form; the sign is stressed or emphasized.
++	DIFFERENT++ TEACH++	Plus markers after a gloss indicate repetitions of the sign. It is used for habitual or frequentative inflection as well as pluralization.
-cont.	CRY-cont.	The suffix "-cont." indicates continuous inflection of verbs.

Symbol	Example	Explanation
( )	(nod) (shake head) (name of city)	Words in parentheses depicting an action or movement indicates something is done without a manual sign. If the word(s) indicate a category, it means you or students should fill in with signs from that category
(wh)	(wh)3 (wh)TREE	The symbol "wh" in parentheses stands for the non-dominant (weak) hand and is used when the sign is made with the non--dominant hand.
(2h)	(2h)LCL*"doors open"*	(2h) stands for "two-handed" and is used when a commonly one-handed sign is made with both hands.
[(wh)SCL:1*"enter from left"*/WOMAN . . .]		Brackets with a back slash between two signs are used for two separate signs made at the same time; the "wh" symbol indicates which sign is made with the non--dominant hand.
BRING-here		A sign with spatial or locative information is shown in lower case and is attached to the sign gloss
all-LOOK-AT-her he-GIVE-TO-me		Lower case words before and after glosses for inflecting verbs indicate the subject and object of the verb.
IX	IX*"princess"*	Short for INDEX, IX indicates pointing and is used for third person pronouns (he, she, it, him, her). Specific referents are indicated by italicized words in quotation marks, immediately following the gloss.

Symbol	Example	Explanation
IX-loc	IX-loc *"under chair"*	IX-loc means "there" and is used to indicate the location of an object or place. Specific information is given in italics in quotation marks immediately after the sign gloss.
IX-dir	IX-dir *"upstairs"*	IX-dir is used when the pointing gives directions or traces a route to a place.
IX-thumb IX-index finger IX-midfinger IX-ring finger IX-pinkie		These signs are all used in the process of listing people or things on the non-dominant hand. Listing usually begins with the thumb.
POSS		POSS is used for the third-person possessive adjective.

SYMBOLS FOR NON-MANUAL BEHAVIORS —

Symbol	Example	Explanation
q	q YOU DEAF	Yes–no question. Brows are raised, head tilted forward slightly, starting just before the signs and continuing throughout the question.
whq	whq YOU LIVE WHERE	wh-word question. Brows are furrowed, head tilted forward slightly throughout the question.
nod	nod YES, ME LEARN+ER	Nodding with signs creates affirmative answers or statements.
neg	neg NOT-SEE	Shaking head with signs indicates the negation of the answer or statement.

Symbol	Example	Explanation
t (line under)	t: TREE, DCL*"describe . . ."* t: NOW, ME . . .	Topicalization (raised brows), reflects setting up the topic of the sentence or referring back to an established topic, sometimes functions as a transition to the next part in a narrative.
br (line under)	br: KNOW br: IX-loc*"top left square"*	Brow raise in conjunction with the sign is used to ensure the listener is following along.
t/q (line under)	t/q: WOMAN HAT, IX LIKE . . .	First part of a sentence when one confirms the listener knows who or what the subject is, before moving on to make a comment.
lf: MOTHER, rt: FATHER		Indicates where the signs should be made, in the left or right area of the signing space. The head and body should slightly lean toward that side. This is usually used when contrasting two persons/things.
cond (line under)	cond: WAIT++, ME NOT+LIKE . . .	Conditional clause—always the first part of a sentence.
when (line under)	when: . . . ME OLD-1, ME, . . .	When clause, similar to a conditional sentence, indicating whenever a certain thing happens, something else will happen.
rhet (line under)	rhet: DIFFERENT "what"	Rhetorical question is used to call attention to the information that follows it.

Symbol	Example	Explanation
rel cl	REMEMBER US-TWO PLAN rel. cl (activity), ...	Relative clause. Must have subject and verb but cannot stand alone as a sentence. It gives additional information about the noun. To sign a relative clause, raise brows, tilt head slightly back, and raise cheek and upper lip.
<rs: >	<rs:mother LOOK-AT*"mirror"* . . .>	Role shifting: the word following "rs:" indicates the person whose "role" the signer is assuming; the signer maintains the role until the closing brackets (>).

ADVERBIAL NON-MANUAL BEHAVIORS —

SIZE AND SHAPE

Symbol	Example	Explanation
oo	oo SMALL	abnormally small or thin
mm	mm SMALL MEDIUM	normal, average or ordinary
cha	cha LARGE	abnormally large or big

MANNER

Symbol	Example	Explanation
mm	mm ME WATCH . . .	relaxed, not stressed
struggling	struggling ICL*"trying to open lid"*	intense

SYMBOLS FOR CLASSIFIERS —

Symbol	Explanation
DCL" "	Descriptive classifier sign used to describe an object or a person. What is described is italicized and in quotation marks (i.e., DCL"*rolling hills*"). Sometimes referred to as size and shape specifiers or SASSes.
BPSASS" "	Bodypart size and shape specifiers used to describe parts of the body mainly on and around the face, i.e., BPSASS"very short hair"
LCL:_" "	Locative classifier sign representing an object in a specific place (and sometimes indicating movement). Handshape is given, followed by spatial or locative information italicized and in quotation marks (i.e., LCL:arm"*tree falling down,*" LCL:C"*gum on bench*").
SCL:_" "	Semantic classifier sign representing a category of nouns such as vehicle or person. Handshape is given, followed by information about specific movement italicized and in quotation marks (i.e., SCL:V"*struggling to get off bench*").
BCL" "	Body classifier sign in which the body "enacts" the verb of the sentence. Role shifting is usually required. Specific action is described in italics and quotation marks (i.e., BCL"*flap arms*").
ICL" "	Instrument classifier sign in which part of the body (usually the hands) manipulates an object (i.e., ICL"*typing,*" or ICL"*carry ax and lunch pail*").
BPCL:_" "	Bodypart classifier sign representing a specific part of the body doing the action. Handshape is often indicated and specific action is described in italics and quotation marks (i.e., (2h)BPCL:1"*step back,*" (2h)BP-CL:B"*shuffling*"). The (2h) stands for two-handed signs.
PCL:_" "	Plural classifier sign, indicating either specific number or non-specific number (i.e., PCL:V"*couple exit to right side*").

UNIT 7 —

UNIT 7	FUNCTIONS	GRAMMAR	VOCABULARY	STUDENT OUTCOMES	CONVERSATION BEHAVIORS
LESSON 7:1 Identifying Present People	Identify person by 1) body position, 2) appearance and/or 3) clothing	Body Classifiers (BCLs): describe arm position Bodypart Classifiers (BPCLs): describe leg positions Bodypart Classifiers (BPCLs): describe hair length, texture and style Descriptive Classifiers (DCLs): describe patterns Facial expressions ("oo," "mm," "cha," "ee," "puffed," "open mouth")	Height: TALL, SHORT-person Body type: SKINNY, SLENDER, BROAD-SHOULDERS, PLUMP Head and face: HEAD-WRAP, HAT, fs-SUN EYEGLASSES, MUSTACHE, BEARD Hair: BALD-TOP, (color)+HAIR	Identify person in room Add another description to confirm Ask to relay a message to the person	Ask to confirm: q THAT-ONE Confirm: !THAT-ONE!
LESSON 7:2 Fingerspelling: Clothing-Related Words	Spell words	Form and movement of certain letters	fs-PLASTIC, fs-SILK, fs-NYLON, fs-FUR, fs-WOOL, fs-COTTON, fs-SUEDE,etc.	Produce correct form and movement for clothing-related words	
LESSON 7:3 Numbers: Guess My Number	Guess a number	Review number forms and movement for numbers 1–100	THOUGHT-OCCUR, GUESS, LESS-THAN, MORE-THAN, IN-RANGE	Increase fluency in producing numbers 1–100	Confirm correct number
LESSON 7:4 Describing Personal Items	Describe an item and tell what kind of material it is made of	Descriptive Classifiers (DCLs) Instrument Classifiers (ICLs) Locative Classifiers (LCLs) Sequence for 1) describing tops 2) describing bags 3) describing eyeglasses	How Got Item: GIVE-TO-me, PRESENT-TO-me, BUY, TAKE-FROM-person, BIRTHDAY, VACATION, GARAGE fs-SALE, etc. Materials: FABRIC, METAL, GLASS, WOOD, etc. Type of Materials: REAL, FAKE, SEE-THROUGH, etc. Tops: SHIRT, DCL"T"+SHIRT, BLOUSE, COAT, etc. Items: PURSE, BACKPACK, EYEGLASSES Comments: PRETTY, STRANGE, fs-COOL, SWELL, etc.	Follow sequence to describe item Ask/tell what it is made of	Comment on item: • PRETTY • STRANGE • #COOL • SWELL • NEVER SEE • DIFFERENT • OLD+fs-FF • UGLY • LOUD-COLOR
LESSON 7:5 Translating Sentences with "Have" 1		Semantics	HAVE, MUST, FINISH, NONE, NOT-YET	Use appropriate signs to translate English sentences with "have" in them	
LESSON 7:6 Translating Sentences with "Drive To," "Take To" and "Pick Up"		Spatial agreement	Spatial verbs: GO-TO-location, DRIVE-TO-location, TAKE-FROM-location, DROP-OFF-location, PICK-UP-person, CARRY-TO-location	Correctly translating English sentences with spatial verbs and making sure the verbs show agreement with the locations that have been established for places	

UNIT 7 — *continued*

UNIT 7	FUNCTIONS	GRAMMAR	VOCABULARY	STUDENT OUTCOMES	CONVERSATION BEHAVIORS
LESSON 7:7 Numbers: Asking How Many	Ask/tell how many	Wh-question: whq HOW-MANY Review number forms and movement for numbers 1–100	Reactions to amount given: OH-I-SEE, !FEW!, !MANY!, WOW, !MADE-UP! YOU	Produce number correctly	Reactions: • OH-I-SEE • !FEW! • !MANY! • WOW • !MADE-UP! YOU
LESSON 7:8 Describing Lost Items	Describing item that is lost	Descriptive Classifiers (DCLs) Instrument Classifiers (ICLs) Sequence for 1) describing hats, tops and eyeglasses, 2) describing tops and coats 3) describing bags	HAT, SCARF	Follow sequence to describe item	Confirm item Express gratitude
LESSON 7:9 Numbers: Telling the Year	Sign year numbers	Year number forms (general) Years ending with –01 through –09 Years starting or ending with 10 through 15 Years with two zeros in the middle	YEAR+ONE-IN-PAST (2 variations) YEAR+TWO-IN-PAST YEAR+THREE-IN-PAST, etc. YEAR+ONE-IN-FUTURE YEAR+TWO-IN-FUTURE, etc.	Produce correct form and movement when expressing year numbers	
LESSON 7:10 Translating Sentences with "Have" 2		Semantics	HAVE, MUST, FINISH, NONE, NOT-YET	Use appropriate signs to translate English sentences with "have" in them	
LESSON 7:11 Cultural: Greeting and Leave-Takings	Greet others Say goodbyes		Greetings: "wave-hello," "salute-hi," HELLO Following up after greeting: (see page 115) Replying: (see page 116) Leave-takings: "wave-bye," BYE-BYE, "thumb-up," SEE-you LATER, etc.	Greet others Say goodbyes	Greetings: • making eye contact when greeting each other • acknowledging each other when passing by nodding Leave-takings: • making eye contact with individuals when saying goodbye
LESSON 7:12 Translating Sentences with "Drive To," "Take," and "Pick Up" 2		Spatial agreement	spatial verbs: • TAKE-FROM-location, GO-TO-location (or DRIVE-TO-location or DROP-OFF-location) • GO-TO-location, PICK-UP-person, DROP-OFF-location (or DRIVE-TO-location or CARRY-TO-location)	Correctly translating English sentences with spatial verbs and making sure the verbs show agreement with the locations that have been established for places	
LESSON 7:13 Comprehension: The Family Portrait	Re-tell story		USE, SAME-AS-arc, JOIN-me, BE-RELIEVED, PICTURE+ER, !TIME!, WAIT, DARK+BLUE, PROCEED/GO-AHEAD, etc.	Re-tell story	

UNIT 8 —

UNIT 8	FUNCTIONS	GRAMMAR	VOCABULARY	STUDENT OUTCOMES	CONVERSATION BEHAVIORS
LESSON 8:1 Making Requests	Explain situation, make request	q NOT-MIND (do favor)	Requesting: pleading/q NOT-MIND Declining: SORRY, HAVE PLAN, ME NOT-KNOW fs-HOW Verbs: (plane) TAKE-OFF, DROP-OFF-me, CONNECT, MISS (class), PLAN, etc. Nouns: TICKET, ADDRESS, BOSS, AIRPLANE, etc. Technology-related: SCANNER, INTERNET Time-related: RECENT Others: MIND-STUPID, fs-OT, THROUGH, MAYBE	First explain situation, then make request Decline, give reason Use pleading face when making the request Use regretful face when declining	
LESSON 8:2 Fingerspelling: Months	Ask/give month	Form and movement for fingerspelling months MONTH with numbers 1–9 incorporated	Months: fs-SEPT, fs-OCT, fs-NOV, fs-DEC, etc. Time-related: MONTH, NOW+MONTH, IN-PAST+MONTH, FUTURE+MONTH, (#)-MONTH+IN-PAST, etc. Seasons: AUTUMN, WINTER, SPRING, SUMMER	Produce correct form and movement for fingerspelling months Incorporate number with sign MONTH	
LESSON 8:3 Agreement Verbs 1	Relay information	Modify verb to agree with subject and object	TELL-TO, PHONE-TO, SEND/MAIL-TO, INFORM-TO, PAY-TO	Modify verb to agree with subject and object • "from me to you" • "from you to me" • "from someone to another"	
LESSON 8:4 Agreeing with Conditions	Explain situation, make request Agree with condition	Conditional clauses: • what must happen first • what is expected in return	Conditions: FIRST-THUMB, UNDERSTAND++ Agreeing: FINE++, TRUE/SURE, #OK, HAPPY Others: BUT, "but," IN-EXCHANGE	Explain situation, make request Agree with condition Integrate head nod and raised brows when stating the condition	Check if person q agrees: "well"
LESSON 8:5 Negations 1		Negative statements	Negations: NOT+FINISH, NOT+MUST, SHOULD+NOT, NONE, NOT+HAVE, "wave no," NOT-YET, NOT-WANT, FORBID, REFUSE, NOT+ALLOW,	Use correct word order when translating from English to ASL (establish time, location, topic, and end with negation)	
LESSON 8:6 Numbers: Giving Phone Numbers	Give phone numbers	Patterns for giving Identification number		Produce correct form and movement when giving phone numbers	

UNIT 8 — *continued*

UNIT 8	FUNCTIONS	GRAMMAR	VOCABULARY	STUDENT OUTCOMES	CONVERSATION BEHAVIORS
LESSON 8:7 **Asking for Advice 1**	Explain problem, ask for advice Give Advice	Sequence for explaining problem Conjunction: THOUGHT-OCCUR	Conjunction: THOUGHT-OCCUR Question: whq ME (2h)#DO++ Suggest: WHY+NOT Response: GOOD +IDEA Others: CREDIT-CARD	Explain problem using the conjunction THOUGHT-OCCUR before telling what happened Ask for advice Give Advice using WHY+NOT	Response: GOOD+IDEA
LESSON 8:8 **Asking for a Sign**	Ask for a sign (review of Unit 2, Skill 12 and Unit 3, Skill 15)			Use different strategies to ask for a sign	
LESSON 8:9 **Agreement Verbs 2**	Relay information	Modify verb to agree with subject and object	BAWL-OUT-TO, BOTHER-TO, TEASE-TO, BORROW-FROM, IGNORE-TO Other: LAPTOP	Modify verb to agree with subject and object • "from me to you" • "from you to me" • "from someone to another"	
LESSON 8:10 **Asking for Advice 2**	Explain problem, ask for advice Give Advice	Role shift to describe awkward conversations Sequence for incidents involving liquids Role shift to describe person doing something s/he was not supposed to do Element classifiers (ECLs) to describe spills Conjunction: !WRONG!	Conjunction: !WRONG! Food-related: HAMBURGER, fs-MUSTARD, SALAD, KETCHUP, KNIFE, FORK, etc. Verbs: BREAK, VOMIT, MEANING Nouns: GLASS, WEDDING (2h)alt.EAT++, SCHEDULE, WEDDING Others: QUOTE, CRACKED-on-iPad, AND	Explain problem using the conjunction !WRONG! before telling what happened Follow sequence for ECLS and role shift Ask for advice Give Advice using WHY+NOT	
LESSON 8:11 **Negations 2**		Negation Tag questions Word order: (location), topic, negation sign, tag question	Verbs: TAKE-UP, CANCEL, TOUCH, KNOW-THAT Nouns: MEAT, MONEY, HAWAII, TEST, LIST, SEMESTER, SOMEONE	Use correct word order when translating from English to ASL Integrate facial grammar and add tag questions	
LESSON 8:12 **Comprehension: The Candy Bar**	Re-tell story		GOING-TO, STOMACH-BOIL, BE-ANGRY, MESSED-UP-hair, COMB	Re-tell story Change details of the story	
LESSON 8:13 **Culture: Minimizing Interruptions**			Arriving late: SORRY LATE Leaving immediately: EXCUSE-ME	Interrupt politely to explain why you are late or have to leave early	Arriving late: • enter at the correct time • apologize and give reason • wait for teacher's nod before taking a seat Leaving immediately: • get up and move to the door at the right time • make eye contact with the teacher, then give brief explanation • wait for teacher's nod before leaving
LESSON 8:14 **Culture: Name Signs**				Apply principles of naming that are culturally appropriate	

UNIT 9 —

UNIT 9	FUNCTIONS	GRAMMAR	VOCABULARY	STUDENT OUTCOMES	CONVERSATION BEHAVIORS
LESSON 9:1 Discussing Neighborhoods	Narrate David's neighborhood	Rhetorical questions Locatives IX-dir, IX-loc, NEXT-TO, THUMB-loc"back"	Areas: DOWNTOWN "area", BUSINESS, MACHINE, FARM, etc. Neighborhoods: fs-APT, fs-LOFT, HOME "area" NEW++, MIXED, etc. Surroundings: ACROSS-FROM, NEXT-TO-right, etc. Comments about Neighbors: COLD, CHEERFUL, MAD-char, NOSEY People: YOUNG FAMILY, OLD+ER, ART+ER, WHITE +COLLAR, etc. Places Nearby: NEAR, FREEWAY, SWIMfs-POOL, HORSE fs-TRAIL, etc. Noise level: QUIET, NOISY Safety level: fs-SAFE, DANGEROUS, TRAFFIC, CLEAN, DIRTY, etc. Activity level: BORING, MANY, (2h)#DO-circle Cost of Living: CHEAP, EXPENSIVE Others: UP-TILL-NOW, LONG-AGO, CHANGE++(arc), DIVERSE, etc.	Repeat descriptions of neighborhood	
LESSON 9:2 Places in the Neighborhood			Places: fs-HYATT, 7-11, STARBUCKS, fs-ACE, etc. Government services/ facilities: POLICE, CITY fs-HALL, COURT+HOUSE, FIREFIGHTER, etc. Types of business: HOTEL, COFFEE HOUSE, FAST FOOD, EXERCISE, fs-RE (real estate)	Give signs for name and type of business	
LESSON 9:3 Numbers: Giving the Time	Give the time	Hour numbers Hour and minute numbers	Beginning and end verb pairs: START, FINISH, LEAVE-FROM, ARRIVE-TO Verbs: GET-UP, GET-IN-BED Wh-word question: TIME	Form clock numbers correctly	
LESSON 9:4 Describing Your Neighborhood	Narrate about own neighborhood	Rhetorical questions Locatives IX-dir, IX-loc, NEXT-TO, THUMB-loc"back"		Narrate about own neighborhood with emphasis on 1) using rhetorical question as a transition 2) maintaining spatial agreement when discussing neighbors	

UNIT 9 — *continued*

UNIT 9	FUNCTIONS	GRAMMAR	VOCABULARY	STUDENT OUTCOMES	CONVERSATION BEHAVIORS
LESSON 9:5 Giving Directions: Next to, Across From	Give directions to places located at or near corners	Signer's perspective Weak hand as reference point Horizontal map orientation Facial markers to tell how close/how far	CORNER-near right, CORNER-near left, CORNER-far right, CORNER-far left, NEXT-TO, ACROSS-FROM	Give directions to places using 1) KNOW 2) weak hand to maintain the location of the corner when signing NEXT-TO or ACROSS-FROM	
LESSON 9:6 Yes-No Questions 1		Topicalization Yes-No questions	Verbs: fs-FIX, IRON, TOUCH, DOWNLOAD Nouns: SPIDER, BUGS, FROG, INTERNET, PARIS Others: KNOW fs-HOW, MORE-THAN, EVERYDAY, EARLY, fs-EARLY, BE-AFRAID++	Translating yes-no questions following word order (time, location, topic, end with question)	
LESSON 9:7 Describing a Restaurant	Describe a restaurant	Descriptive classifiers (DCLs) to describe: 1) table/counter and seating arrangement 2) wall decorations 3) lighting Element classifiers to describe lighting	Ethnic restaurants: CHINA, JAPAN, THAI, INDIA, MEXICO, ITALY, FRANCE, etc. Opinions (price): EXPENSIVE, MEDIUM, REASONABLE, CHEAP Opinions (food): DELICIOUS, CHAMP, !GOOD!, FAIR/SO-SO, etc. Food and drinks: CHICKEN, FISH, fs-STEAK, fs-RICE, WINE, PASTA, SALAD, #BBQ, etc. Materials: WOOD, GLASS, METAL, etc. WH-word question: WHAT-KIND	Describe a restaurant using descriptive (DCLs), locative (LCLs) and element (ECLs) classifiers	
LESSON 9:8 Giving Directions: Where to Turn	Describe where to turn when giving directions	When clause	Distance: ALL-WAY-DOWN, END-STREET, (#) BLOCK-AWAY Intersection: INTERSECTION, CROSS-STREET Landmark: GO-PAST, LIGHT ECL"traffic stop light", etc. Where to turn: TURN-LEFT, TURN-RIGHT	Use when clause with landmarks, intersections, corners or places before telling where to turn Superimpose head nod(s) with BLOCK-AWAY++	
LESSON 9:9 Numbers: Giving the Time 2	Give the time	Hour numbers Hour and minute numbers	Wh-word question: TIME, DO++ Workbook vocab: SHOWER, BRUSH-TEETH, TAP-SHOULDER, GET-DRESSED, BATHE	Form clock numbers correctly	

UNIT 9	FUNCTIONS	GRAMMAR	VOCABULARY	STUDENT OUTCOMES	CONVERSATION BEHAVIORS
LESSON 9:10 Suggesting a Place to Eat	Suggest a restaurant	Transition: ONE WARNING	SUGGEST, WARNING	Use descriptive (DCLs), locative (LCLs) and element (ECLs) classifiers to describe restaurant environments Nod their head when listing food items Use raised brows with ONE WARNING	Comment
LESSON 9:11 Giving Directions: Perspective Shift	Give directions with perspective shift	Perspective shift	Workbook vocabulary: UMBRELLA, CERTIFICATE, ELECTRIC, TICKET, !BE-TICKETED!, FAST/SPEED, FULL, !FAR!	Use perspective shift to complete the directions	
LESSON 9:12 Yes-No Questions 2		Topicalization Yes-No questions	Verbs: MEET++, CAN, EXPERIENCE, TAKE-CARE-OF++, TO-NAME, Nouns: PEOPLE, EYES, POETRY, SNOWBOARDING, RABBIT, Others: !NEW!, FOREIGN/COUNTRY, FAMOUS	Translating yes-no questions following word order (time, location, topic, end with question)	
LESSON 9:13 Culture: Keeping Others Informed	Getting attention Getting permission Expressing gratitude		SORRY, MISS, BE-LATE	Informing teacher and others the reasons for their absences from and tardiness to class/events	Wave to get attention
LESSON 9:14 Comprehension: Stop the Traffic	Re-tell story		EMPTY++, !TRAFFIC!, GO-ACROSS, MELT/ DISSOLVE, TIME-arc+++, !RIGHT!	Re-tell story	

UNIT 10 —

UNIT 10	FUNCTIONS	GRAMMAR	VOCABULARY	STUDENT OUTCOMES	CONVERSATION BEHAVIORS
LESSON 10:1 **Giving Opinions about Tendencies**	Give Opinions Compare oneself with another	Temporal Aspect	Punctuality: TIME++, GO-TO++, LATE++, SKIP-WORK++ Approach to work: serious WORK-char, !PAY-ATTENTION!, COMPLETE++, etc. Relating to Others: QUIET++, BASHFUL++, TALK++, CHAT++, MEET++, AGREE-with++, BE-HONEST, LIE++, SHARE++, SELFISH++, etc. Others; TEND-TO, TRUST, EVADE, etc.	Give opinions by describing tendencies; Compare tendencies; Ask/Tell how two people are the same or different	Affirm; Negate
LESSON 10:2 **Numbers: Telling the Price 1**	Tell the Price	Money numbers for cents and dollars	money-related: DOLLAR, COST ask how much: whq COST HOW-MANY items: POPCORN, CANDY, RING, COUGH-MEDICINE, PENCIL, GUM, POSTAGE-STAMP, WHISTLE, etc.	Give price for different items; ask/tell cost	
LESSON 10:3 **Wh-word Questions 1**		Topicalization Wh-word question whq "what" HAPPEN	INVENT/CREATE	Translating wh-questions following word order (time, location, topic, end with question)	
LESSON 10:4 **Giving Opinions about Personal Qualities 1**	Give Opinions, Describe situation to support opinion	Predicate adjectives	Disposition: CHEERFUL, POLITE, STUCK-UP, RUDE++, SWEET, MEAN, MAD-char, HUMBLE/ MODEST, QUIET++, (2h)FUNNY-char, GOODY-TWO-SHOES, BIG-HEADED, etc. Dealing with others: OPEN-MINDED, WARM, STUBBORN, FLEXIBLE, etc. Good Sense/Foolish: GOOD+JUDGE, PEA-BRAINED	Give opinion, describe situation to support opinion Correct information, give explanation	Repeat what others said Correct information Respond
LESSON 10:5 **Numbers: Telling the Price 2**	Tell the Price	Money number for combinations of dollars and cents	SOUP, TOMATO, MILK, ONION, CHEESE, BANANA, BREAD, APPLE, BUTTER, ORANGE, PEANUT+BUTTER, EGG, SUGAR, JAM, LETTUCE, etc.	Ask/tell cost of item	

UNIT 10	FUNCTIONS	GRAMMAR	VOCABULARY	STUDENT OUTCOMES	CONVERSATION BEHAVIORS
LESSON 10:6 Giving Opinions about Personal Qualities 2	Give opinion about person by describing his personal qualities	Role shift to describe situation	Personal quality signs from 10:4	Describe person's personality by: • use at least three personal quality signs • use role shift to describe situations	
LESSON 10:7 Telling Where Items Are Located	Ask/tell where items are located	Topicalization Signer's perspective Reference points Non-manual signals for distance: "far away," "cs" LCLs and DCLs to describe parts of the kitchen	Household items: #TV ICL"use remote," MATCHES, SOAP, SCREWDRIVER, STAPLER, TOWEL, CAMERA, CANDLE, MAGAZINE, KNIFE, SCISSORS, etc. Kitchen appliances: fs-STOVE, fs-SINK, fs-OVEN, etc.	Tell where items are located by: • naming the room • naming appliance or part of room • specify location of item (use reference point)	
LESSON 10:8 Wh-word Questions 2		Topicalization Contrastive structure List across neutral space and nodding Wh-word question whq WHICH	COOL, WARM, LOVE, !THRILL!, EARN, USE-GUNS, SEND-TO, !MONEY!, WEATHER	Translating wh-questions following word order (time, location, topic, end with question)	Follow-up questions
LESSON 10:9 Comparing Personal Qualities	Compare two people's personal qualities	Conditional clause Contrastive structure	DISCUSS++, HURT, EUROPE, HIRE/INVITE, SUPPOSE, HAPPEN++	Ask "which" questions Give hypothetical situations Compare two people's personal qualities	
LESSON 10:10 Culture: Interrupting Others	Interrupt a conversation to deliver a short message		Interrupting: EXCUSE-me, INTERRUPT, SORRY, (wh)"hold on/wait" Resume conversation: (2h)GO-AHEAD, ANYWAY, NOTHING-TO-IT Distractions: FIRE RING/ALARM, SOMEONE YELL YOUR NAME #DOG BARK++ BABY CRY++ LIGHT ECL"flashing," etc.	Interrupting two people in a conversation Interrupting someone, ask to hold on and explain what is distracting Resuming conversation	Ask to hold on Apologize Resume conversation
LESSON 10:11 Comprehension: "Why the Owl Has Big Eyes"	Re-tell story		GOD, WORLD, BE-EXCEPTIONALLY-SKILLED	Re-tell story	

UNIT 10 — *continued*

UNIT 10	FUNCTIONS	GRAMMAR	VOCABULARY	STUDENT OUTCOMES	CONVERSATION BEHAVIORS
LESSON 10:12 Looking for a Misplaced Item	Tell narrative	Spatial Agreement Word Order: name object before using ICLS Instrument classifiers (ICLS) Role shifting with sign LOOK-AT	LOOK-AT	Tell narrative incorporating these language elements: • spatial agreement • word order: name object before using ICLS • word order: NONE used after each search segment • role shifting with LOOK-AT • thoughts • conclusion: end story with a reaction sign or comment	

UNIT 11 —

UNIT 11	FUNCTIONS	GRAMMAR	VOCABULARY	STUDENT OUTCOMES	CONVERSATION BEHAVIORS
LESSON 11:1 Discussing One's Knowledge and Abilities	Compare a person's knowledge of a subject matter to your own; Tell about an activity that you have become skilled at; Describe an unusual skill/ ability you possess; Tell someone what they should or should not do		Having knowledge/ability: BE-KNOWLEDGEABLE-IN, BE-SKILLED-IN, BE-EXCEPTIONAL-IN Lacking knowledge: ZERO-FOREHEAD, BE-MIND-STUPID Lacking ability: BE-INEPT, AWKWARD/CLUMSY, CAN'T Subjects: AMERICA fs-LIT, INTERPRETING, HISTORY, DEAF STUDIES, LINGUISTICS, etc. Others: MAJOR	Compare a person's knowledge of a subject matter to your own; Tell about an activity that you have become skilled at; Describe an unusual skill/ ability you possess; Tell someone what they should or should not do	
LESSON 11:2 Numbers Review 1	Give a number	Number types: cardinal, age, dollars, cents, clock, minutes, hours, days, weeks, months		Sign numbers quickly and accurately	
LESSON 11:3 Asking for Opinion about Someone	Ask/give opinion about a person		CONTACT-TO, BE-EXPERIENCED, (2h) PICK-UP++, BE-CREATIVE, TO-FLIRT, INVITE/ HIRE-person, TRANSFER-TO	Ask/give opinion about a person as a potential travel companion, roommate, employee, date, babysitter	ask follow up questions
LESSON 11:4 Describing Reactions	Ask a hypothetical question Tell how you would react or feel	Conditional clause	reactions: BE-THRILLED, BE-RELIEVED, JUMP-JOY, BE-SCARED, BE-LET-DOWN, etc. others: ELECTRIC, LAST++, RUN-OUT-OF, etc.	Ask hypothetical questions and give reactions	
LESSON 11:5 Fingerspelling: States and Provinces	Name a state/ province	fingerspelling patterns for states and provinces	States that are signed: ALASKA, ARIZONA, CALIFORNIA, etc. Provinces that are signed: ALBERTA, MANITOBA, etc. States/provinces with fingerspelled forms: fs-ALA, fs-ARK, fs-CONN, etc.	Give correct fingerspelling of name of state/ province	
LESSON 11:6 Making and Canceling Plans	Invite someone to join you Accept/decline invitation Explain why you need to cancel plans	Relative clause	Inviting: PLAN, JOIN-me Canceling: CANCEL Declining: BE-STUCK, CONFLICT, NOT-CARE-FOR Comments: SORRY, "shucks," (2h)PERFECT, (2h)LOOK-AT"forward" Signs for Thinking: THINK-ABOUT, IDEA, MULL-OVER, THOUGHT-OCCUR	Invite someone to join you Respond by accepting or declining Canceling plans Explain why Narrating about canceled plans	Acknowledge plans made previously Close conversation

UNIT 11 — *continued*

UNIT 11	FUNCTIONS	GRAMMAR	VOCABULARY	STUDENT OUTCOMES	CONVERSATION BEHAVIORS
LESSON 11:7 First and Last Time You Did Something	Ask/tell when was the last time someone did something Ask/tell how old someone was the first time s/he did something	When clauses Horizontal listing	LAST+TIME, FIRST-thumb+TIME, WHEN	Repeat information someone told you to another person Summarize results of survey using horizontal listing	
LESSON 11:8 Numbers Review 2	Tell the time, price or year	Number combinations for: • money, • clock • year		Give time, price or year using correct number combinations	
LESSON 11:9 Discussing Personal Goals	Narrate Personal Goals	Repeating for emphasis	Continents: WORLD, EUROPE, AFRICA, ASIA, AUSTRALIA, etc. Countries: COUNTRY, ENGLAND, FRANCE, SPAIN, MEXICO, ITALY, GERMANY, CHINA, etc. Time-related: BEFORE-EVENT Verbs: DIE, BE-GONE, SIX-FEET-UNDER, TRY, CHECKMARK, EXPERIENCE, TOUCH, VOLUNTEER, etc. Nouns: GOAL/AIM, LANGUAGE, DEGREE, (2h)THING	Narrate bucket list	
LESSON 11:10 Fingerspelling: States and Provinces 2	Name a state/ province	Fingerspelling patterns for states and provinces		Give correct fingerspelling of name of state/ province	
LESSON 11:11 Comprehension: Brother on the Roof	Re-tell story		Possible new signs: EXAGGERATE, SOMETHING/ SOMEONE, BE-GONE/DISAPPEAR, "shhh"	Re-tell story	
LESSON 11:12 Culture: ASL Student in the Community				Making appropriate decisions about: 1) whether to offer interpreting assistance to a Deaf person 2) when and where to use spoken language	
LESSON 11:13 Culture: Deaf Artist: Focus on Chuck Baird				Identify De'VIA artwork and describe how that artwork meets De'VIA criteria	

UNIT 12 —

UNIT 12	FUNCTIONS	GRAMMAR	VOCABULARY	STUDENT OUTCOMES	CONVERSATION BEHAVIORS
LESSON 12:1 "The Tailor" Understanding the Story	Retell the story	Descriptive classifiers (DCLs) Instrument classifiers (ICLs) Locative classifiers (LCLs) Transition	DECIDE, COLD, SMOOTH, SEW++, USE-cont, SCISSORS, WEAR-OUT, COMFORTABLE, [(wh) SCL:1 *"person"*/ SELF++]	Narrate the story	Engage the audience by maintaining eye contact
LESSON 12:2 "The Tailor" Telling One's Own Version	Narrate the story	Descriptive classifiers (DCLs) Locative classifiers (LCLs)	Removing: TAKE-AWAY, DROP-OFF-item Adding: PUT-ON, ADD-ON Reasons for change: UGLY, !NEW!, OLD-FASHION, fs-STYLE, TOO-PLAIN, FRILLY How feel about the change: BETTER, (2h)F *"perfect,"* BEAUTIFUL	Narrate the story – describing three changes to a clothing item	Engage the audience by maintaining eye contact
LESSON 12:3 "One Fine Day" Understanding the Story	Retell the story		FOX, THIRSTY, FULL, BE-ANGRY, COW, CHEW, GRASS, THANK-you, BE-READY++, FROM-NOW-ON	Narrate the story	Engage the audience by maintaining eye contact
LESSON 12:4 "One Fine Day" Character Placement	Retell the story	Spatial agreement to match placement of characters Sign orientation to reflect location and heights of the character		Retell placement of characters in story	Engage the audience by maintaining eye contact
LESSON 12:5 "One Fine Day" Conditional Sentence and Agreement Verbs with Role Shift	Retell the story	Role shift Conditional sentences Agreement verb "GIVE-TO" Spatial agreement		Rehearse agreement verbs in role shift	Engage the audience by maintaining eye contact
LESSON 12:6 "One Fine Day" Instrument Classifiers with Role Shift	Retell the story	Instrument classifiers (ICLs) with role shift Maintaining agreement among placement of characters Orienting eye gaze and signs to match the locations and heights of the characters		Rehearse role shift exchanges between characters in the story	Engage the audience by maintaining eye contact
LESSON 12:7 "One Fine Day" Story Cohesion	Retell the story			Narrate the story	Engage the audience by maintaining eye contact

UNIT 12 — *continued*

UNIT 12	FUNCTIONS	GRAMMAR	VOCABULARY	STUDENT OUTCOMES	CONVERSATION BEHAVIORS
LESSON 12:8 "The Lion and the Mouse"	Retell the story	Describing characters' movements, Describing character interacting with object Describing contact between characters Describing characters' movements, Describing character interacting with object Describing contact between characters	LION, MOUSE, LOOK-FOR, SLEEP, WAKE-UP, HUNGRY, ZOOM-AWAY, LATER-ON, ROPE, BE-STUCK, !HEAR!, (2h)YELL++, FLEE/ESCAPE, FROM-NOW-ON, BEST-FRIEND	Narrate the story following narrative structure	Engage the audience by maintaining eye contact
LESSON 12:9 "The Fox and the Crow"	Retell the story	Describing a character talking to itself Integrate reactions after each comment by other characters Object passing between characters	BE-EXCEPTIONALLY-SKILLED, FLATTER, SHAMPOO, WEIGHT-DECREASE, SUPPOSE, QUEEN, NAME-you, BE-LET-DOWN, SOMETHING/SOMEONE, BELIEVE, TO-TRUST	Narrate the story following narrative structure	Engage the audience by maintaining eye contact
LESSON 12:10 Telling Your Assigned Fable	Narrate the story	Movement of characters Interactions with objects and characters Two-person role shift Character's intentions and thoughts	BUG, FOX, BIRD, SCORPION, FROG, GOAT, #DOG, WOLF, BABY GOAT	Narrate the story following narrative structure	Engage the audience by maintaining eye contact

PRE-UNIT

Review Units 1–6

Lesson length: 360–480 minutes (6–8 hours)

LESSON GOAL

Students will review vocabulary, phrases, skills and behaviors they learned in *Signing Naturally Units 1–6*.

PREPARATION

Bring playing cards—one deck per group of 3–5 students (for Card Game "99" activity on page 11).

- make a set of **Questions 1–15** cards for each group of 3–4 students (for the **Questions to Ask** activity, pages 15–16)
- make copies of **Group A, B and C** handouts (for the cultural behavior skits, pages 19–21)

MATERIALS

Read **Introduction** pages xi–xlii

The following activities are designed to review vocabulary, grammar and cultural behaviors learned in *Units 1–6*. By reviewing language taught in *Units 1–6*, the teacher has the opportunity to informally assess the class' language skills and students have an opportunity to adjust to the teacher's signing style without the added stress of learning new materials. Total time for all activities will take between 6–8 hours. If teacher's schedule allows less time for review, the teacher will have to pick and choose activities to suit their classes.

REVIEW — *Names (Fingerspelling)*

45–55 minutes

Students review correct forms for fingerspelling names.

PRESENT
(LESSON SLIDES PRE-UNIT 1–4)

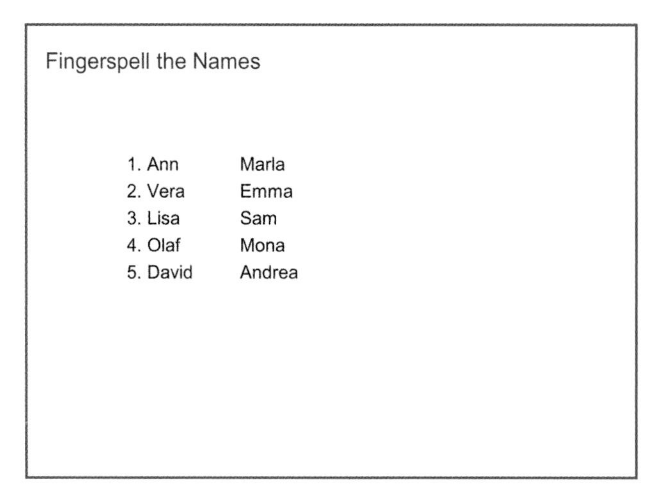

Fingerspell the Names
1. Ann Marla
2. Vera Emma
3. Lisa Sam
4. Olaf Mona
5. David Andrea

Call on a student to fingerspell the names in Row 1. Make sure their hand and arm positions are angled correctly. Correct handshape and movement, if needed. Then, have all students practice fingerspelling the names. Continue activity for the remaining rows in **Slides 1–4**.

Be sure students form the letters these ways:

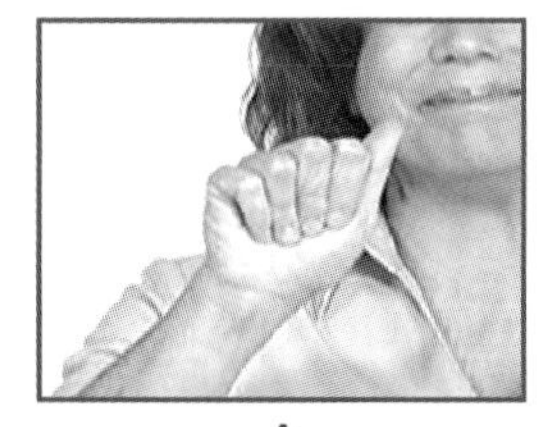
A

For ***"1. Ann Marla"*** (focus on the **letter** "A")
- the thumb is straight and flush to the hand
- fingers are not tucked in

E

For ***"2. Vera Emma"*** (focus on the **letter** "E")
- at least the index & middle fingers sit on the thumb
- the thumb does not overlap the fingers

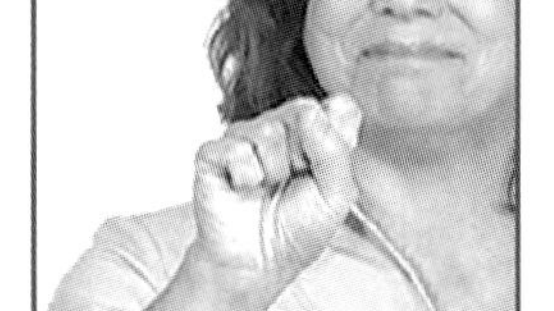
S

for ***"3. Lisa Sam"*** (focus on the **letter** "S")
- fingers are tucked in
- the thumb straps over the index and middle fingers in a "true fist"

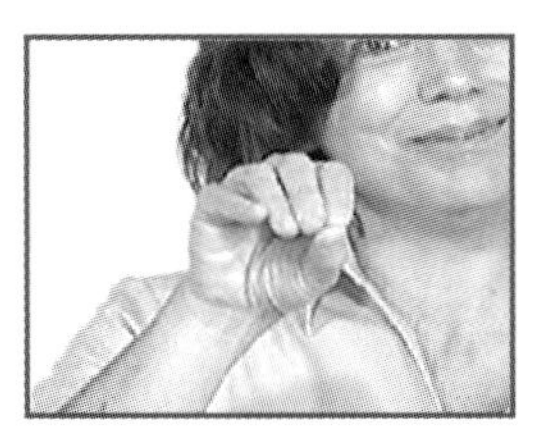
O

For *"4. Olaf Mona"* (focus on the **letter "O"**)
- the fingers make a "flat "O"

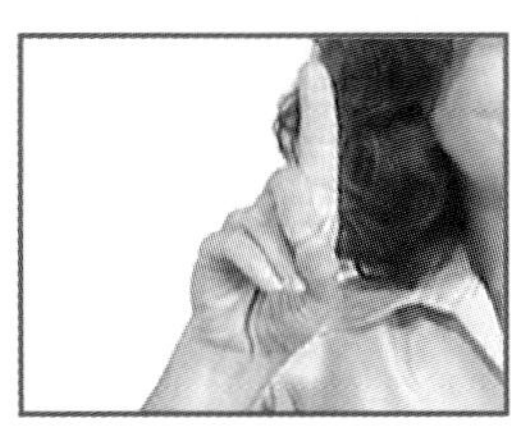
D

For *"5. David Andrea"* (focus on the **letter "D"**)
- middle finger and thumb make a flat "O"
- index finger extends upward
- ring and pinkie fingers softly curl downward toward the palm

Slide 2

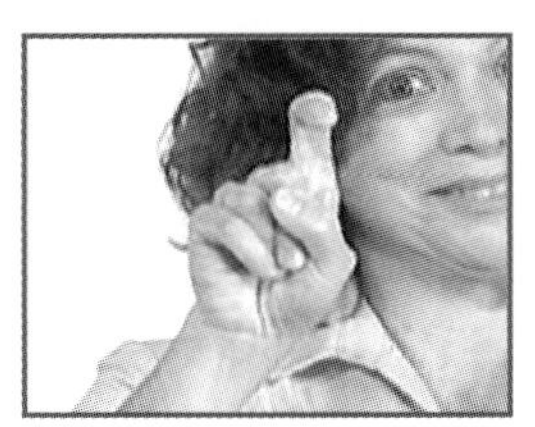
X

For *"6. Xavier Max Maxine"* (focus on the **letter "X"**)

letter "X" at the beginning of a name
- palm faces out

letter "X" in the middle or at the end
- palm faces to the side
- the hand tilts forward

Y

For *"7. Dylan Mary Yolanda Young"* (focus on the **letter "Y"**)

letter "Y" in the middle or at the end
- palm is oriented down

letter "Y"at the beginning
- the palm usually faces out

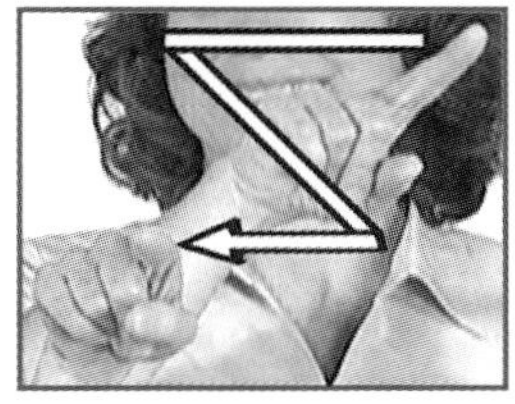
Z

For *"8. Zeke Hazel Luz"* (focus on the **letter "Z"**)

letter "Z" at the beginning
- after tracing "Z", hold the end position to spell the remaining letters

letter "Z" in the middle
- after tracing "Z", hold the end position to spell the remaining letters

letter "Z" at the end
- after tracing "Z", your hand position should be below the letters that precede it

Slide 3

P

For ***"9. Paolo Phil"*** (focus on the **letter "P"**)

- palm is facing down
- index finger is horizontal
- the middle finger is vertical

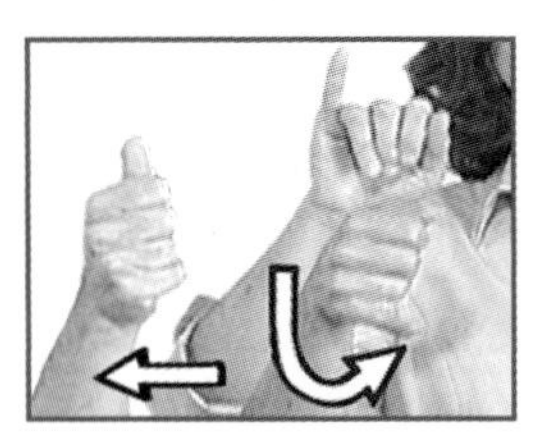
JA

For ***"10. Priscilla April"*** (focus on the **letters "PR"**)

- the palm of the "P" is oriented to the side
- the middle finger is horizontally pointed to the side

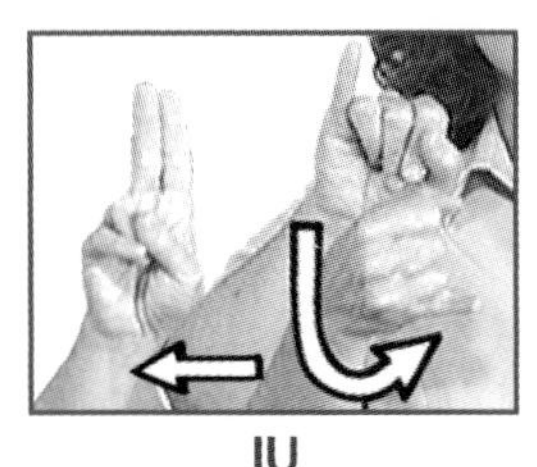
JU

For ***"11. Jay Jen Joe"*** and ***"12. Judy Jim"*** (focus on the **letter "J"**)

beginning with "Ja", "Je", and "Jo"

- the second letter (a, e, o) is formed at the final position of "J"

beginning with "Ju" and "Ji"

- the second letter (u, i) is formed at the final position of the with "J"
- and held as the hand rotates and faces forward

G

For ***"13. Gayle Craig"*** and ***"14. Hannah Holly Hope"*** (focus on the **letters "G"** and **"H"**)

- the hand positions pictured for **letters "G"** and **"H"** may vary depending on the letter that precedes or follows

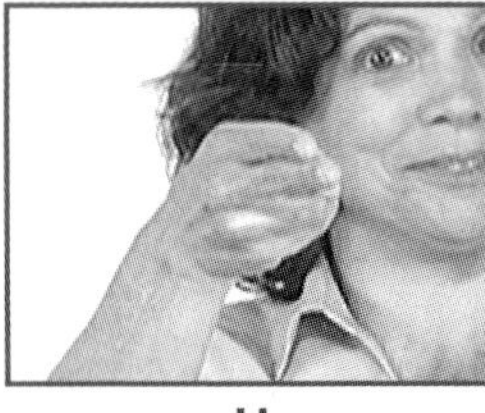
H

For ***"15. Cheryl Thomas Sheila Phyllis"*** (focus on **letters "CH," "TH," "SH,"** or **"PH"**)

- the letter "H" rolls towards the dominant side
- and ends up with palm upwards (i.e., the movement is similar to twisting a door knob to open a door)

Slide 4

For ***"16. Bobby Nikki Willy Barry"*** and ***"17. Will Bill Jill"*** (focus on **double letters "bb," "kk," "ll," and "rr"**)

- the letters are made with a bounce
- exception: If no letters follow "ll", the double letters move sideways. (Will, Bill, Jill)

For *"18. Bessie Quinn Wyatt"* and *"19. Cliff Eddie Emma"* (focus on **double letters "ss," "nn," "tt," "ff," "dd", "mm"**)

- the letters are made without a bounce

for *"20. Aaron Lee Cooper"* (focus on **double letters "aa," "ee," and "oo"**)

- the letters move sideways

Conclude. Have students spell their own first names. Check their letter movements, positions of hand, and arm position when spelling their names. Next class, take roll. Spell names at normal but deliberate pace. Once the students raise their hand, have them spell their name. Check for hand position and form.

REVIEW *Commands (Comprehension)*

10–20 minutes

Students demonstrate comprehension by following commands. Give different commands starting with identifying who, then telling person(s) what to do. Have the identified students follow the commands. For example:

t

T: YOU-all LIVE fs-APT, STAND.

S: (follow command)

t

T: YOU-all ALWAYS DRIVE-here SCHOOL, SIT.

S: (follow command)

t

T: YOU-all HEARING, SIT.

S: (follow command)

t

T: YOU-all WOMAN, STAND.

S: (follow command)

t

T: YOU-all USE/WEAR BROWN SHOES, SIT.

S: (follow command)

t

T: YOU-all HAVE OLD+EST BROTHER, JUMP.

S: (follow command)

Other ways to identify who:

- people who have a certain pet
- people who wear an item of a certain color
- people who prefer a certain drink/food
- people who live in a certain type of residence/city
- people who come to class a certain way
- people with a certain identity (gender, hearing/deaf, etc.)
- etc.

Other commands to use:
TURN-AROUND
DANCE

Add follow up questions. For example:

t when

T: YOU-all HAVE OLD+EST BROTHER, JUMP. FINISH,

t whq

you-TELL-me YOUR-all BROTHER HOW-OLD.

S: (jump, then tell their brother's age)

REVIEW *Categories (Vocabulary)*

15–20 minutes

Students review vocabulary by naming items belonging to a category.

PRESENT
(LESSON SLIDES
PRE-UNIT 5)

Name items that belong to the category.

Give a category sign. Have students name items from that category. For example:

t whq
T: COLOR DIFFERENT++, "what"
S: RED, WHITE, BLUE, BLACK, etc.

Continue activity with other categories:

t whq
T: (clothing) CLOTHES DIFFERENT++ "what"
S: SHIRT, SHOE, HAT, etc.

t whq
T: (people) PEOPLE DIFFERENT++ "what"
S: MAN, WOMAN, MOTHER, etc.

t whq
T: (leisure/activities) PEOPLE ENJOY (2h)DO++ "what"
S: TRAVEL, SHOPPING, RUN++, etc.

t whq
T: (pets) ANIMAL DIFFERENT++ "what"
S: BIRD, #DOG, CAT, etc.

t whq
T: (cities) CITY DIFFERENT++ "what"
S: fs-SF, OAKLAND, (name of local cities), etc.

t whq

T: (areas/districts) CITY "area" DIFFERENT++ "what"

S: DOWNTOWN, NEAR WATER, NEAR fs-PARK, etc.

t whq

T: (transportation) PEOPLE TRAVEL, HOW

S: CAR, BICYCLE, fs-BUS, etc.

t whq

T: (time signs) TIME SIGN DIFFERENT++, "what"

S: NOW/TODAY, WEDNESDAY, HOUR, etc.

t whq

T: (things in classroom) CLASS+ROOM HAVE "what"

S: CHAIR, TABLE, DOOR, etc.

t whq

T: (facilities) COLLEGE (or SCHOOL) HAVE "what"

S: BOOK+STORE, SODA-POP MACHINE, ELEVATOR, etc.

t whq

T: (chores) fs-CHORES DIFFERENT++ "what"

S: FLOOR ICL*"vacuum,"* CHILDREN TAKE-CARE-OF, CLOTHES WASH-CLOTHES, etc.

t whq

T: (errands) fs-ERRANDS DIFFERENT++ "what"

S: FOOD SHOPPING, FIND/PICK-UP CHILDREN, SEE DOCTOR, etc.

t whq

T: (holidays) VACATION SAME-AS CHRISTMAS, OTHER "what"

S: HALLOWEEN, THANKSGIVING, NEW+YEAR, etc.

REVIEW *Opposites (Vocabulary)*

20–30 minutes

Students review vocabulary by naming the opposites or signs commonly associated with given signs.

PRESENT
(LESSON SLIDES PRE-UNIT 6)

Give the opposite or a sign commonly associated with the sign.

Sign the first item in the pairs below, and have students give you the opposite (or a sign commonly associated with your sign). For example:

whq

T: OLD OPPOSITE IX-loc*"other side"* "what"

S: NEW

OLD	NEW
LEARN+ER	TEACH+ER
!EASY!	!HARD!
FORGET	REMEMBER
RIGHT	WRONG
neg NONE	HAVE
BLACK	WHITE
MARRY	DIVORCE
HUNGRY	FULL-STOMACH
SAME-AS	DIFFERENT
NOW++/TODAY	YESTERDAY

SPEAK	SIGN
KNOW	neg NOT-KNOW
DEAF	HEARING
cha LARGE	oo SMALL
WRITE	READ
MINUTE	HOUR
GET-ALONG	QUARREL
fs-HS	COLLEGE
NIGHT	DAY or MORNING
NOW+MONTH	IN-PAST MONTH
TEACH++	LEARN++
ANIMAL	PEOPLE
WIN	LOSE
RUN	WALK
PLAY	WORK
DETEST/VOMIT	LIKE
ECL*"light on"*	ECL*"light off"*
WORK	SCHOOL
OPEN-DOOR	CLOSE-DOOR
ALWAYS	NEVER
SHAPE	LETTER or NUMBER
SIT	STAND
fs-LOVE FADE-AWAY	FALL-IN-LOVE
DIED	LIVE
neg NOT-YET	FINISH

REVIEW *Cardinal Numbers 1–100*

20–30 minutes

Students review cardinal numbers 1 to 100 by playing card game "99."

Review 1–100. Have students count off 1 to 100. Make corrections as needed.

PRESENT
(LESSON SLIDES PRE-UNIT 7)

Card game "99"

Ace	= 1 or 11 points
K, Q, J	= 10 points
10	= minus 10 points
5	= minus 5 points
2	= no points, reverse turn
3-9	= face value

Play game. Give one set of playing cards to each group of three to five students.

Review the rules for "99."

- Deal three cards to each player and put the remaining cards in the center.
- At each turn, each player picks one card from the center pile, then chooses one card to discard.
- When a player discards a card, they declare the new total with the newly discarded card.
- However, if a "5" or a "10" card is discarded, the number is subtracted from the total.
- With a "2" card, the play is reversed.
- The goal is to add up to exactly "99," without going over. Otherwise, the player is eliminated.
- Whoever remains at the end wins.

Students play the game until each group has a winner.

REVIEW *Age Numbers*

10–15 minutes

Students practice giving ages, and orienting the number toward the person being referred to.

Have students line up from the youngest to the oldest.

Begin by giving your own age, then have the youngest person repeat your age then give their own age. The next student does the same. For example:

T: ME OLD+35.
S1: IX"*teacher*" OLD+35. ME OLD+21.
S2: IX"S1" OLD+21. ME OLD+22.
S3: IX"S2" OLD+22. ME OLD+22, S2-SAME-AS-me

Be sure when giving the previous person's age, students orient the number toward that person's location. Continue until all the students have had a turn.

REVIEW *Similarities and Differences*

30–40 minutes

Students practice asking wh-word questions and orienting signs toward the person being referred to.

PRESENT
(LESSON SLIDES PRE-UNIT 8)

Pick a person you don't know well. Get to know them. Find out five things you have in common and five ways you are different. Record the information on a chart like this:

Have in common	Differences
1.	1.
2.	2.
3.	3.
4.	4.
5.	5.

Give students a few minutes to find partners and conduct interviews.

When students are done, go around the room and have students tell you about their partner—one similarity and one difference.

Be sure students:

- point to and name their partner
- orient their signs toward the person they are referring to
- follow this structure:

IX*"person"* NAME (give name).
IX*"person"*, ME SAME-AS-person (tell what have in common).

rhet
IX*"person"*, ME DIFFERENT "what," IX*"person"* (name a difference),

neg
ME NOT (or NONE, or give the opposite).

REVIEW *Likes, Haves, Needs, Wants*

15–20 minutes

Students practice asking questions for a survey using these verbs LIKE, HAVE, NEED, and WANT.

PRESENT
(LESSON SLIDES PRE-UNIT 9)

Copy this chart. Then, survey three people and fill in the chart.

name	likes	haves	needs	wants
1.				
2.				
3.				

Before students start surveying, review the questions and have students copy:

whq
T: YOU NAME "what"

whq
YOU LIKE "what"

whq
YOU HAVE "what"

whq
YOU NEED "what"

whq
YOU WANT "what"

S: (copy)

Conclude. When surveys are done, ask each student to name one of the people they surveyed and tell what that person likes (or needs, wants, or has). For example:

rel cl ... t whq

T: YOU ASK-TO*"3 people"*, [(wh)3/IX*"one of three"*], WHO

S: (give person's name)

whq

T: IX*"person"* LIKE (or HAVE, NEED, WANT) "what"

S: (give information from the chart)

REVIEW *Questions to Ask*

30–40 minutes

Students practice signing yes–no and wh-word questions.

Questions 1–15

Make copies of Questions 1–15 cards (see **Materials**). Give each group of 3–4 students a set. Each student in the group pulls a card and asks the question, which everybody in the group will answer.

Conclude. When the groups are done, have each student ask you a question.

Be sure students:

- use correct facial grammar and word order when asking the questions. See *Teacher's Guide* below.

Teacher's Guide

#	QUESTIONS TO ASK
1	ask the person who she or he lives with and what their household duties are. t whq t whq YOU LIVE WITH WHO. POSS-all DUTY "what"
2	ask if the person exercises everyday q YOU EXERCISE EVERYDAY
3	ask what the person did last Saturday t whq IN-PAST SATURDAY, YOU (2h)#DO++

4	ask when the person does laundry t whq YOU CLOTHES WASH-CLOTHES, WHEN
5	explain you have one brother and one sister and you are the baby of the family. Then, ask if the person has brothers and sisters. ME HAVE ONE-left BROTHER-left, ONE-right SISTER-right. ME [(wh)3/IX-mid] nod q LAST. YOU HAVE BROTHER, SISTER, YOU
6	ask the person whom she or he is closest to t whq YOU BE-CLOSE-TO, WHO
7	ask the person if they want children in the future t q FUTURE, YOU WANT CHILDREN, YOU
8	ask the person how old she or he is whq HOW-OLD YOU
9	tell the person you need to see the teacher, ask where his or her office is located t nod t whq TEACH+ER, ME NEED SEE. POSS*"teacher"* fs-OFFICE, WHERE
10	ask the person what kind of residence she or he lives in t whq YOU LIVE HOUSE-left, fs-APT-right, WHICH
11	ask the person if she or he has a pet t q fs-PET, YOU HAVE
12	ask the person what is the sum of 23 + 3 whq 23-left PLUS 3-right, HOW-MUCH
13	ask if the person learned Spanish in high school t q IN-PAST fs-HS, YOU LEARN++ SPANISH, YOU
14	(name items in a category), ask what the category is t whq 1, 2, 3, 4, 5, 6, 7, 8, 9, 10, "trace circle around numbers," "what"
15	(point to an item or name and object), ask what color it is t whq BOOK IX*"book,"* COLOR "what"

REVIEW *Family Vocabulary and Possessive Pronouns*

30–40 minutes

Students practice family vocabulary and describing how family members are related using possessive pronouns.

PRESENT
(LESSON SLIDES PRE-UNIT 10)

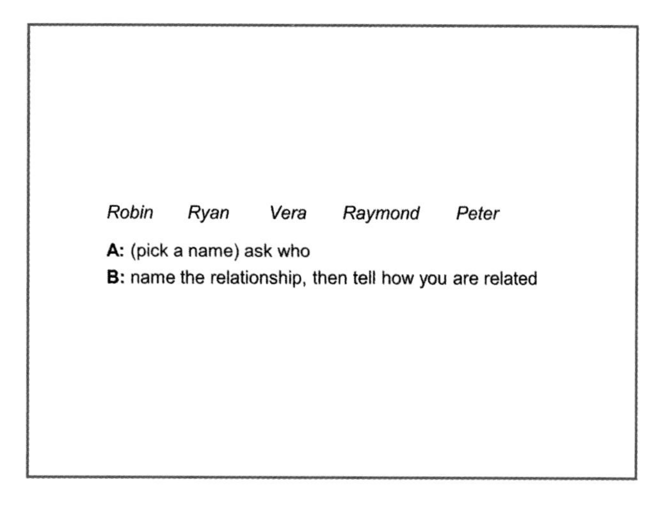
Robin Ryan Vera Raymond Peter
A: (pick a name) ask who
B: name the relationship, then tell how you are related

Replace the names on the slide with names from your family for the following relationships.

- a cousin
- a niece or nephew
- an in-law
- an aunt or uncle
- a grandparent or grandchild

Call a student to role play Signer A while you role play Signer B. For example:

A: fs-VERA WHO (whq)

B: MY MOTHER+LAW, MY WIFE, POSS*"wife"* MOTHER (t over MY WIFE)

S(All): (repeat B's line)

Repeat with another student. Have the student (as Signer A) pick a different name.

whq
A: fs-ROBIN WHO

t
B: MY COUSIN. MY MOTHER IX*"mother"* POSS*"mother"* SISTER IX*"mother's sister"* POSS*"mother's sister"* DAUGHTER.

S(ALL): (repeat B's line)

PRESENT
(LESSON SLIDES PRE-UNIT 11)

Robin *Ryan* *Vera* *Raymond* *Peter*

A: (pick a name) ask who

B: name the relationship, then tell how you are related

Instructions: Write names from YOUR family on a piece of paper for the following relationships:

- a cousin
- a niece or nephew
- an aunt or uncle
- a grandparent or grandchild

Pair off: Have students exchange papers and take turns asking about their partner's names.

REVIEW *Childhood Story (Narrating)*

20–30 minutes

Students practice retelling a childhood story.

Divide the class into three or four equal numbered groups. Have ONE student in each group tell the childhood story he or she developed for **Homework 6:17**. Be sure the other students in the group understand the story well enough to repeat it.

Re-Group. Select one student from each group to form a new groups. Have each student take turns retelling the story they saw.

REVIEW *Cultural Behaviors*

30–45 minutes

Students review cultural behaviors by developing skits to demonstrate appropriate behaviors.

Skits. Divide class into three groups (A, B or C) and give each member of the group a copy of the **Group A, B or C** handouts. (see **Materials**). Give the groups 10–15 minutes to develop skits to teach appropriate cultural behaviors.

Group A – Getting Others' Attention
Group B – Negotiating a Signing Environment
Group C – Maintaining a Clear Sightline

PRESENT
(LESSON SLIDES PRE-UNIT 12)

Getting Others' Attention
- waving
- tapping
- using an intermediary

When Group A is ready, call them to the front to present their skit(s). Then, review key behaviors.

For "**• *waving***"

- wave with one hand (that falls within the other person's field of vision)
- size of the wave corresponds to the distance between the waver and the other person

For "**• *tapping***"

- tap shoulder or upper arm gently but firmly two or three times

For *"• using an intermediary"*

- ask the intermediary using the sign TAP-SHOULDER-person in the direction of the person whose attention is desired
- the intermediary either taps or waves to get the other person's attention, then directs them to look at the signer

PRESENT
(LESSON SLIDES PRE-UNIT 13)

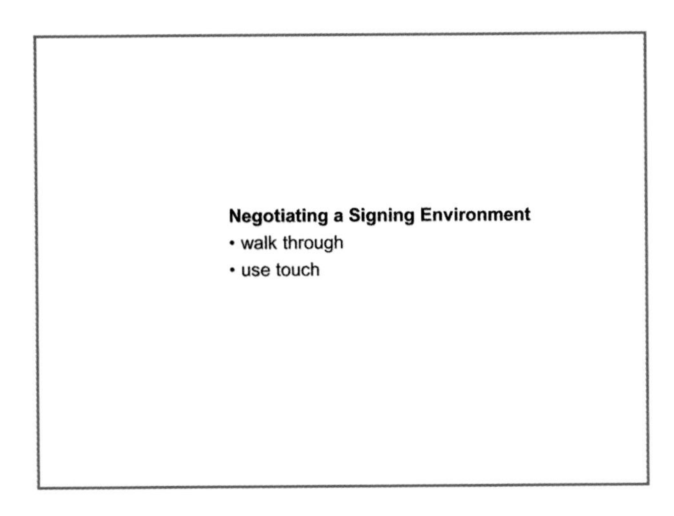
Negotiating a Signing Environment
• walk through
• use touch

When Group B is ready, call them to the front to present their skits. Then discuss and review key behaviors:

For *"• walk through"*

- pass quickly so the signers won't be interrupted
- don't hunch down or wait to be acknowledged by the signers
- as one passes through, she or he may sign EXCUSE-ME

For *"• use touch"*

- press someone's shoulder or upper back
- avoid tapping unless one wants to tell the person to move more than a few steps aside

PRESENT
(LESSON SLIDES PRE-UNIT 14)

Maintaining a Clear Sightline
Responsibilities of:
• the signer
• the listener in between the signer and another person
• the listener at the end of the row

When Group C is ready, call them to the front to present their skits. Then discuss and review key behaviors:

For ***"• the signer"***

- signer leans forward, stands up or moves to a place in front of the group so others can see him or her clearly

For ***"• the listener in between the signer and another person"***

- listener checks if others' sightlines are clear
- if needed, listener leans back, or moves chair back

For ***"• the listener at the end of the row"***

- listener first adjusts their position to see the signer better
- if this doesn't work, then listener presses the shoulder of the person blocking their view in the direction they need to move (don't tap the shoulder)

HOMEWORK

Tell students to read **Introduction** on workbook pages v–xiv.

NOTES:

UNIT 7

Describing People and Things

LESSON 7:1

Identifying Present People

Lesson length: 110–130 minutes

LESSON GOAL

Students will sign this dialogue:

Dialogue

A: Identify a person in the room[1]

B: Add another description to confirm[2]

A: Confirm[3], ask B to relay a message to that person

B: Relay the message

KEY PHRASES

q/t

[1] SEE (gender), (give one description)

q

[2] THAT-ONE

nod

[3] !THAT-ONE!

NOTIONS

Grammar

Identify a person

- Body Classifiers (BCLs)
- Body Part Classifiers (BPCLs)
- Body Part SASSes (BPSASSes)
- Descriptive Classifiers
  DCL*"clothing pattern"*
- Facial expressions
  ("oo," "mm," "cha," "ee," "puffed," "open mouth")

Vocabulary

body positions
BPCL *"legs positions"*

height
TALL
SHORT-person

body type
SKINNY
SLENDER
BROAD-SHOULDERS
PLUMP

appearance: head and face
HEAD-WRAP
HAT
fs-SUN+EYEGLASSES
MUSTACHE
BEARD

appearance: hair
(color)+HAIR
BALD-TOP or ECL:open8 *"bare head"*
BPSASS *"hair length, texture or style"*

describing patterns
DCL *"patterns"*

ask to confirm
q
THAT-ONE

confirm
!THAT-ONE!

PREPARATION

Review main points of the lesson in **Key Grammar: Identifying a Person**, *Student Workbook*, pages 4–5

MATERIALS

7:1 Lesson Slides
7:1 Follow-Up Slides

HOMEWORK 7:1

Student Workbook, pages 4–14

WARM UP *Spelling Names*

10 minutes

Tell each student to spell their name, then tell something about themselves that most students don't know.

INTRODUCE *Identify Person*

60 minutes

PRESENT
(LESSON SLIDE 7:1:1)

To point out a person in the room, you need to describe something that helps the listener locate the person quickly.

Identify person by describing one or two of these:

1. body position
2. appearance
3. clothing

Demonstrate by identifying several students in the room.
For example:

1. *body position*

   q/t
   T: SEE MAN IX-loc BCL*"crossed arms,"* ...

2. *appearance*

   T: SEE WOMAN IX-loc, EYEGLASSES
   q/t
   (2h)LCL:G*"glasses on top of head,"* ...

3. *clothing*

   q/t
   T: SEE WOMAN IX-loc BLUE COAT, ...

PRESENT
(LESSON SLIDE 7:1:2)

Body Position: Arms

Review by having students describe the arm positions in the slide.

1. BCL*"hands folded"*
2. BCL*"hands and arms stacked"*
3. BCL*"head resting on one hand"*
4. BCL*"head resting on both hands"*
5. BCL*"hands behind head"*
6. BCL*"crossed arms"*

PRESENT
(LESSON SLIDE 7:1:3)

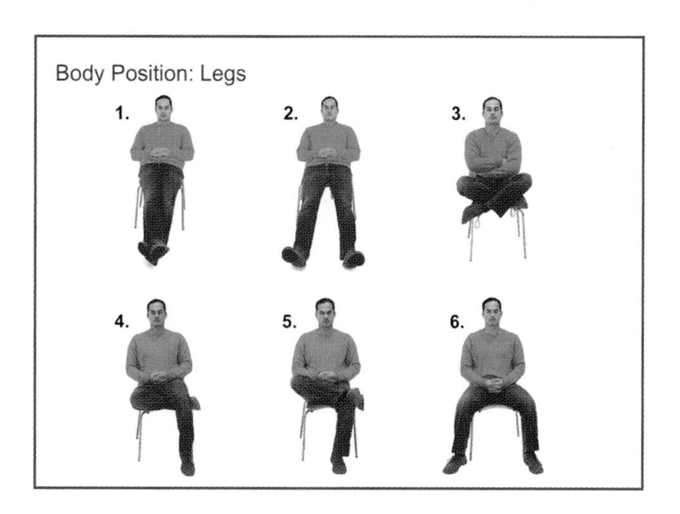

Body Position: Legs

Introduce classifiers to describe a person's leg positions.

BPCL*"sitting with legs crossed"*

BPCL*"sitting with legs outstretched"*

BPCL*"lotus sitting position"*

BPCL*"sitting with one foot tucked under the other leg"*

BPCL*"sitting with foot over knee"*

BPCL*"sitting with legs wide apart"*

PRESENT
(LESSON SLIDE 7:1:4)

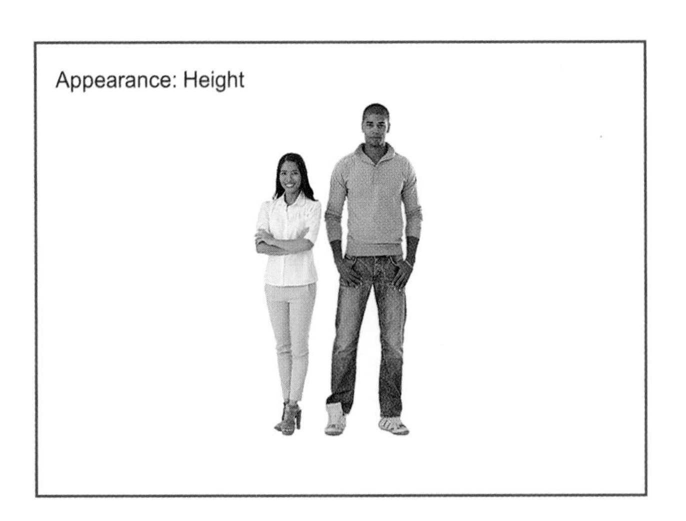

Appearance: Height

Introduce vocabulary to describe a person's height.

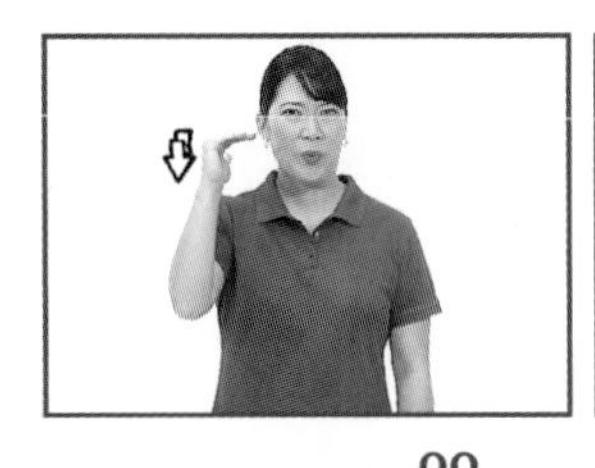

oo
SHORT-person

cha
TALL

PRESENT
(LESSON SLIDE 7:1:5)

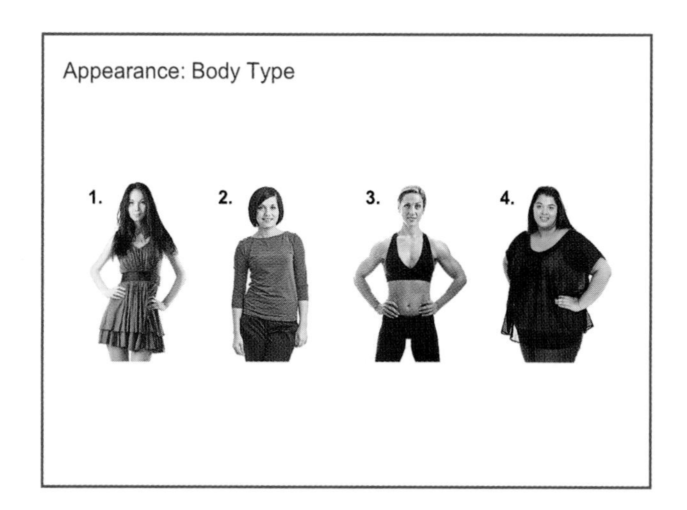

Appearance: Body Type
Introduce vocabulary to describe a person's body type.

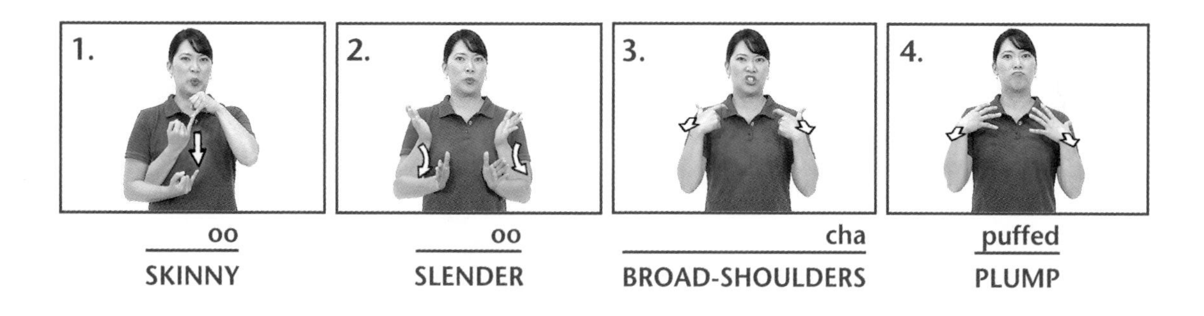

oo SKINNY	oo SLENDER	cha BROAD-SHOULDERS	puffed PLUMP

PRESENT
(LESSON SLIDE 7:1:6)

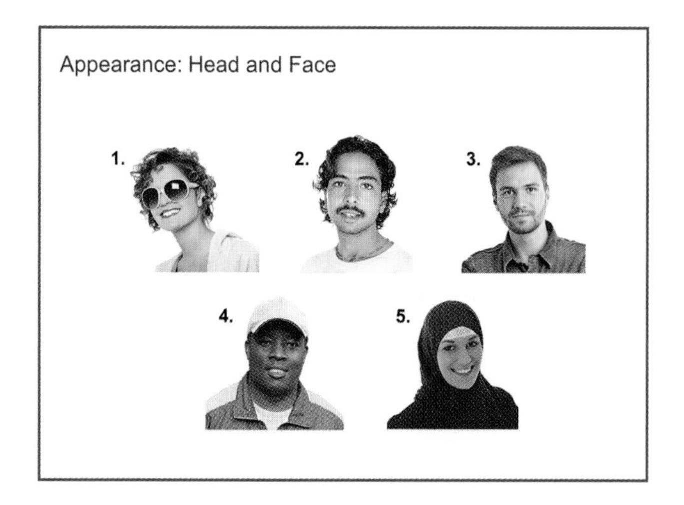

Appearance: Head and Face
Introduce vocabulary to describe the appearance of a person's head.

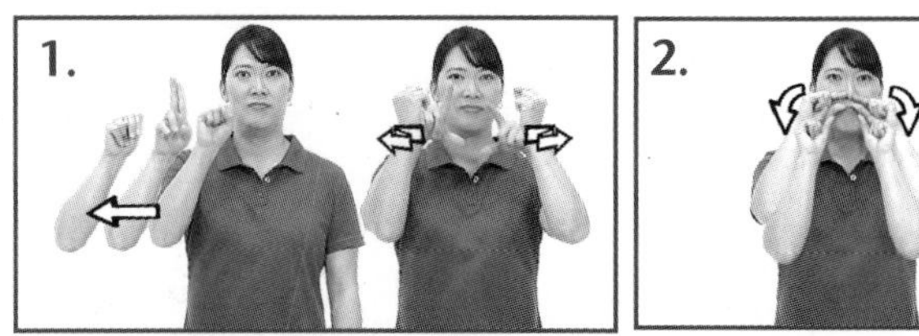

fs-SUN+EYEGLASSES

MUSTACHE

BEARD

HAT

HEAD-WRAP

PRESENT
(LESSON SLIDE 7:1:7)

Appearance: Hair

Introduce vocabulary and classifiers to describe a person's hair.

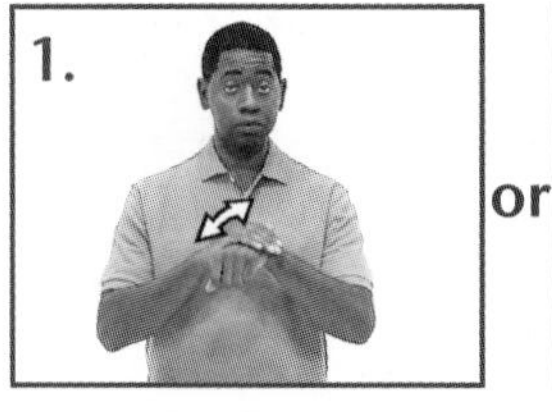

BALD-TOP

or

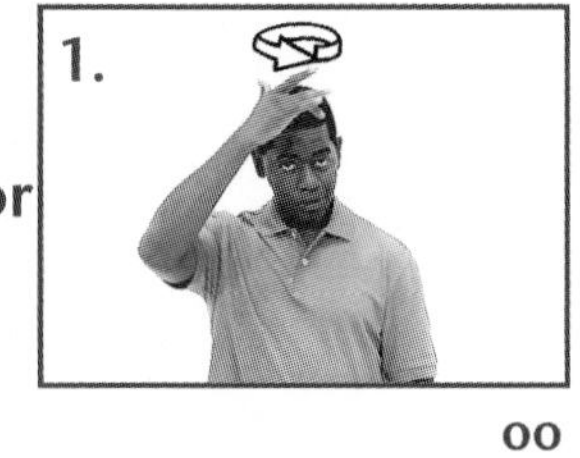

oo
ECL:open8 *"bare head"*

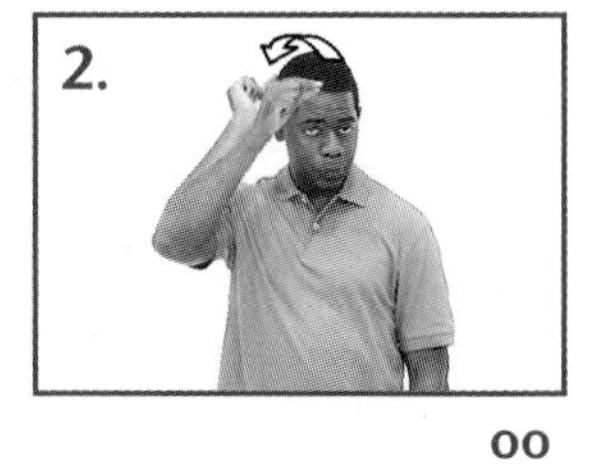

oo
BPSASS:G *"very short"*

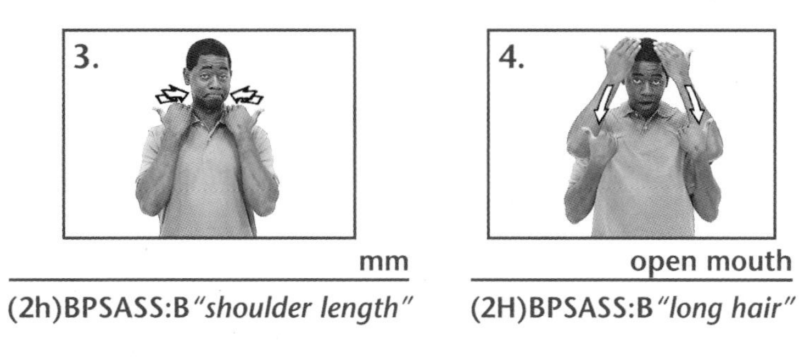

mm
(2h)BPSASS:B *"shoulder length"*

open mouth
(2H)BPSASS:B *"long hair"*

mm
(2h)BPSASS *"curly"*

ee
BPSASS *"frizzy"*

PRESENT
(LESSON SLIDE 7:1:8)

Continue introducing vocabulary and classifiers to describe a person's hair.

BPSASS *"bun"*

(2h)BPSASS *"pony tail"*

(2h)BPSASS *"pony tail"*

BPSASS:R*"large braid"*

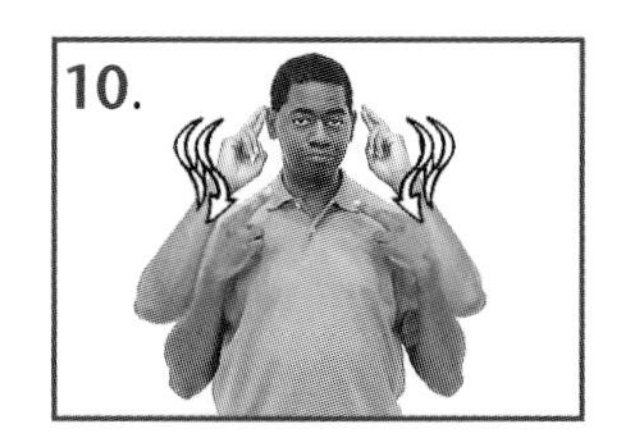

(2h)BPSASS:R*"dreads"*

!RED! HAIR

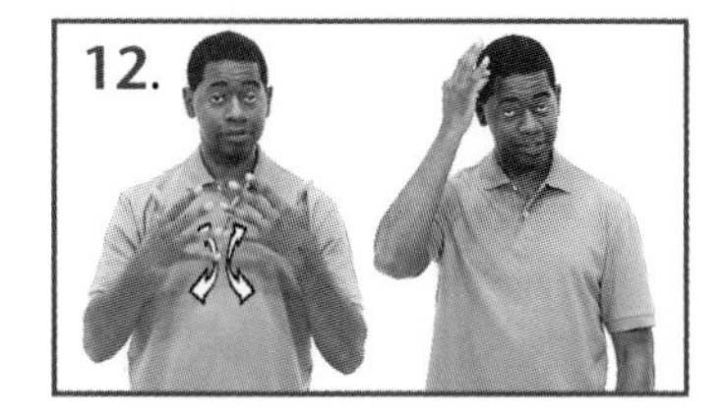

GRAY HAIR

PRESENT
(LESSON SLIDE 7:1:9)

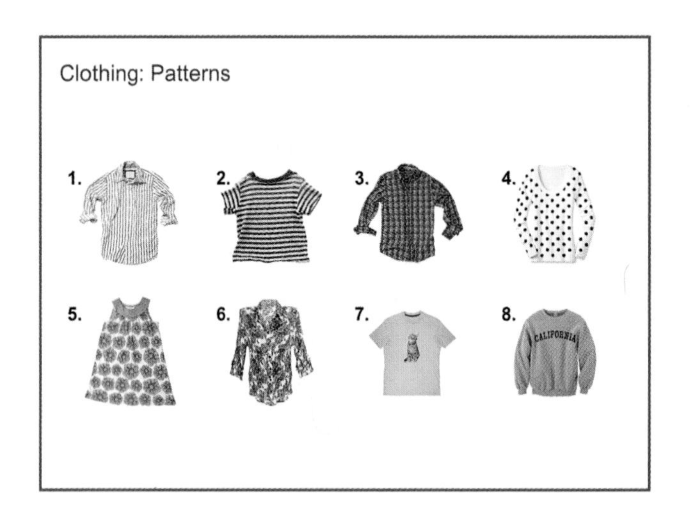

Clothing: Patterns

Introduce how to describe patterns on a person's clothes.

1. SHIRT, BLUE, WHITE **DCL:4*"vertical stripes"*** (oo)
2. SHIRT, BLACK, WHITE **DCL:4*"horizontal stripes"*** (oo)
3. SHIRT, RED, GRAY, **DCL:4*"plaid"*** (mm)
4. SHIRT, BLACK **(2h)altDCL:F*"dots"*** (mm)
5. SHIRT, FLOWER **(2h)altDCL:C*"flowers"*** (cha)
6. SHIRT, BLACK **(2h)altDCL:claw*"swirly"*** (mm)

7. SHIRT, PICTURE CAT **(2h)DCL:L*"picture on chest"***

8. SHIRT, NAME **(2h)DCL:bent L*"across chest"*** [(wh) DCL:bent L/IX-loc*"across chest"*] fs-CALIFORNIA

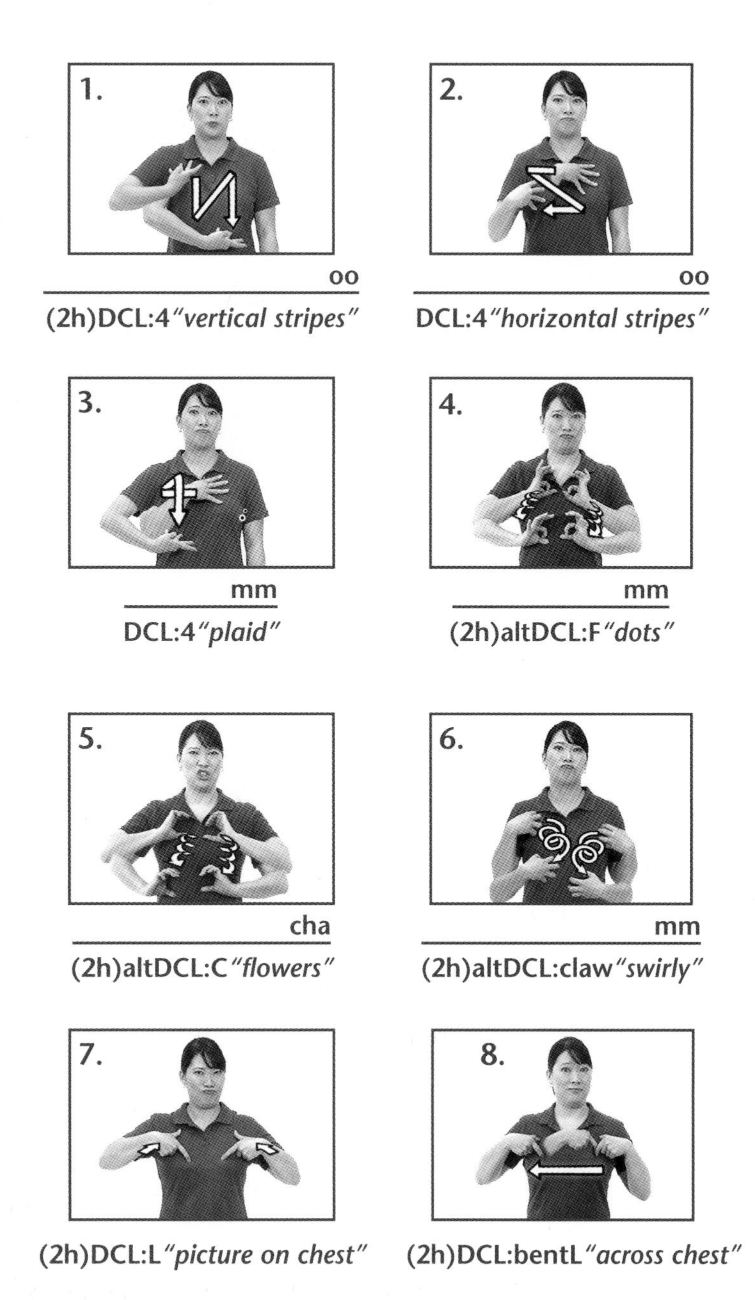

Review: Give a number between 1–8 and have students describe the shirt pattern shown on the slide.

PRACTICE 1 *Identify Person*

10–15 minutes

Students practice identifying the person concisely and confirming with THAT-ONE (nod).

PRESENT
(LESSON SLIDE 7:1:10)

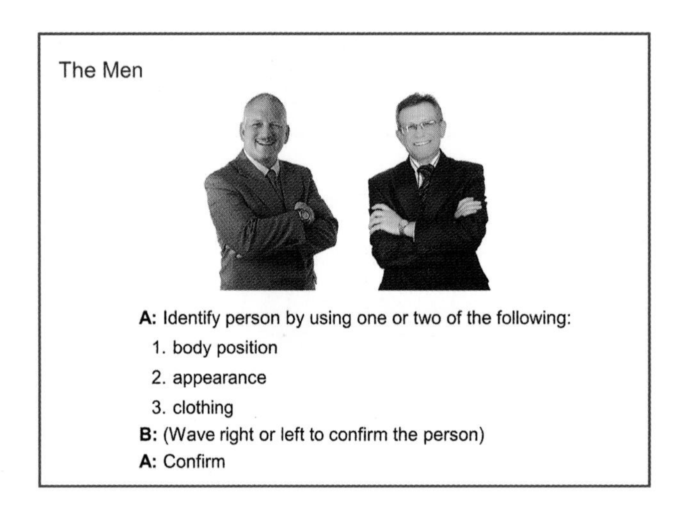

The Men
A: Identify person by using one or two of the following:
1. body position
2. appearance
3. clothing
B: (Wave right or left to confirm the person)
A: Confirm

Demonstrate Signer A's lines using description that distinguishes one man from the other, for example:

T: SEE MAN, GRAY HAIR BPSASS:G*"very short"* (q/t)

S: (wave left) (q)

T: (nod) THAT-ONE (nod)

Continue using different descriptions to distinguish one man from the other, and confirming with THAT-ONE.

Examples:

- black tie or red tie
- mustache or none

Have students role play Signer A.

Be sure students:

- identify person concisely by using only one description
- orient the sign SEE toward the person on the slide
- nod before and while signing THAT-ONE.

PRESENT
(LESSON SLIDE 7:1:11)

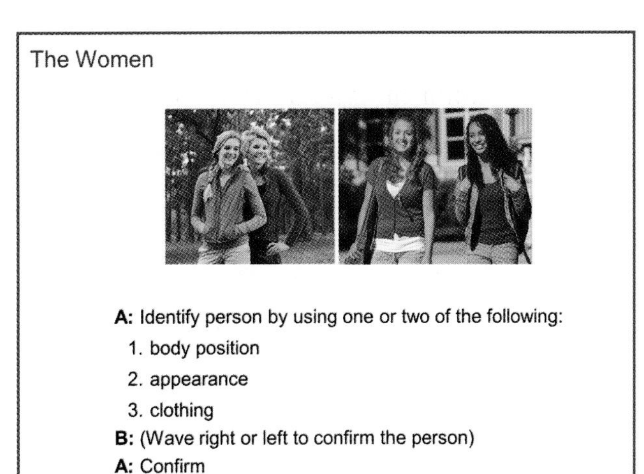
The Women
A: Identify person by using one or two of the following:
1. body position
2. appearance
3. clothing
B: (Wave right or left to confirm the person)
A: Confirm

Pair up students. Have them take turns being Signer A and identify a person in either picture.

PRACTICE 2 *Add Description to Confirm*

10–15 minutes

Students practice adding a description to confirm and asking

$\overline{\text{THAT-ONE}}^{\,q}$.

PRESENT
(LESSON SLIDE 7:1:12)

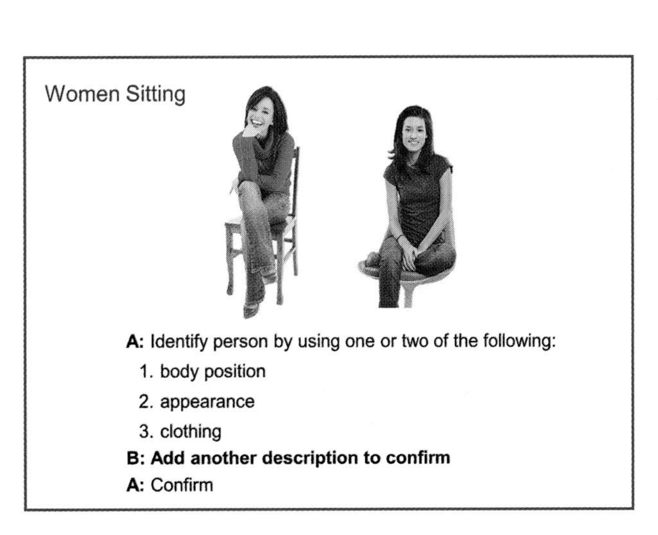
Women Sitting
A: Identify person by using one or two of the following:
1. body position
2. appearance
3. clothing
B: Add another description to confirm
A: Confirm

Have a student role play Signer A. Demonstrate Signer B's line by adding another description to confirm, for example:

q/t
S: SEE WOMAN, YELLOW SHIRT...

q
T: **SIT BPCL*"lotus sitting position,"* THAT-ONE**

nod
S: (nod) THAT-ONE

PRESENT
(LESSON SLIDE 7:1:13)

raise brows — *Ask to confirm*
nod — *Confirm*

Demonstrate the two different facial expressions with THAT-ONE and have students copy.

q / nod
T: THAT-ONE or (nod) THAT-ONE
S: (copy)

PRESENT
(LESSON SLIDE 7:1:14)

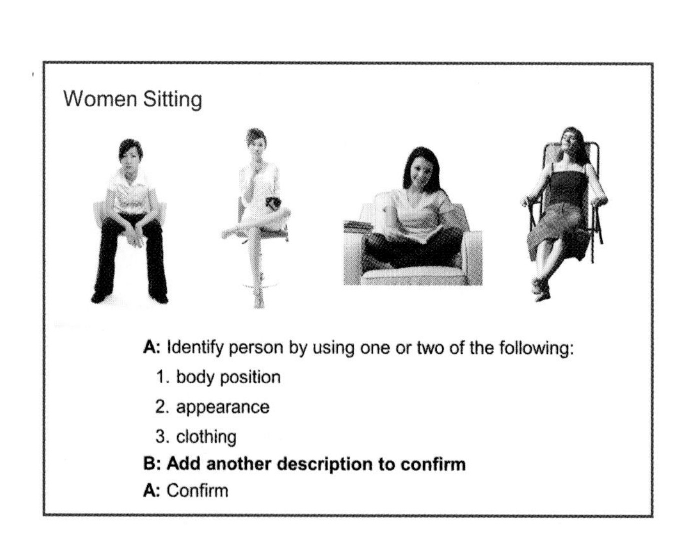
Women Sitting
A: Identify person by using one or two of the following:
1. body position
2. appearance
3. clothing
B: Add another description to confirm
A: Confirm

Pair up students. Have them take turns being Signer B and confirm by adding another description.

Be sure students:

- as Signer B raise brows while signing $\overline{\text{THAT-ONE}}^{\,q}$
- as Signer A nod before and while signing $\overline{\text{THAT-ONE}}^{\,nod}$.

TEACHER TO TEACHER

Students might sign YES to confirm. Be sure they use THAT-ONE instead.

HOMEWORK

Tell students to do **Homework 7:1** (*Student Workbook,* pages 4–14).

HOMEWORK FOLLOW-UP

30–45 MINUTES

PRESENT

(FOLLOW-UP SLIDES 7:1:1–10)

Minidialogue 1

1. How does David identify his uncle?
2. What additional information do Iva and David give to confirm they are talking about the same person?
3. What explanation does David give for his uncle's appearance?
4. How does Iva identify the second man?
5. What does Iva think of him?

Check students' answers to **Minidialogues 1** and **2**. See **Introduction** pages xviii–xix for different ways to check answers.

PRESENT
(FOLLOW-UP SLIDE 7:1:11)

A: Identify a person in the room
B: Add another description to confirm
A: Confirm, ask B to relay a message to that person
B: Relay the message

Students practice identifying a person and relaying a message.

You role play Signer A and ask a student to role play Signer B. ***For example:***

q/t
A: SEE WOMAN, GREEN SHIRT,...

q
B: SIT BPCL*"legs crossed,"* THAT-ONE

nod
A: (nod) THAT-ONE. YOU TELL-TO-person,

t
POSS*"person"* SHOES, ME !LIKE!

t
B: (to C) TEACH+ER IX*"teacher"* LIKE YOUR SHOES.

Repeat this line and have students copy:
For ***"A: ... ask B to relay message to that person"***

t
T: YOU TELL-TO-person, POSS*"person"* SHOES, ME !LIKE!
S: (copy)

Be sure students:

- use spatial agreement with IX*"third person"* or POSS*"third person"* and TELL-TO.

Do the dialogue again with a different student.

q/t
A: SEE MAN, MUSTACHE...

q
B: SHIRT DCL*"striped,"* THAT-ONE

nod
A: (nod) THAT-ONE. YOU TELL-TO-person,

t
POSS*"person"* BOOK, ME HAVE.

t
B: (to C) TEACH+ER IX*"teacher,"* YOUR BOOK
IX*"teacher"* HAVE.

Repeat this line and have students copy:
For ***"A: ... ask B to relay message to that person"***

t
T: YOU TELL-TO-person, POSS*"person"* BOOK,
ME HAVE.

S: (copy)

Be sure students:

- use spatial agreement with IX*"third person"* or POSS*"third person"* and TELL-TO.

Do the dialogue again with a different student.

q/t
A: SEE WOMAN, (2h)BPSASS:R*"dreads"*

cha q
B: SHIRT, FLOWER (2h)altDCL:C*"flowers,"* THAT-ONE

nod
A: (nod) THAT-ONE. YOU TELL-TO-person,

t
POSS*"person"* COAT, ME NEED.

B: (to C) TEACH+ER IX*"teacher"* NEED YOUR COAT.

Repeat this line and have students copy:

For ***"A: ... ask B to relay message to that person"***

t
T: YOU TELL-TO-person, POSS*"person"* COAT,
ME NEED.

S: (copy)

Be sure students:

- use spatial agreement with IX*"third person"* or POSS*"third person"* and TELL-TO.

> **NOTE:** In the relayed messages, we use Subject-Verb-Object word order but it's also acceptable to use the Object-Subject-Verb word order, for example:
>
> ____________t ______________________________nod
>
> YOUR BOOK, TEACH+ER IX*"teacher"* HAVE.

Group practice. Divide into small groups and have students take turns identifying students **outside** their group and relaying messages.

Correct as needed. Make note of what needs further practice.

Check to be sure students:

as Signer A

- nod before signing ~~confirm~~ THAT-ONE
- use verb agreement with TELL-TO
- use spatial agreement with IX*"third person"* or POSS*"third person"*

as Signer B

- raise brows when signing ~~q~~ THAT-ONE.

Present any corrections to the whole class to practice.

LESSON 7:2

Fingerspelling: Clothing-Related Words

Lesson length: 30–45 minutes

LESSON GOAL

Students will review the correct hand positions and movements to use when fingerspelling clothing-related words.

KEY SKILLS

Fingerspell the words correctly and comprehend the words in context

NOTIONS

Vocabulary

fingerspelled word list

fs-PLASTIC	fs-POLYESTER
fs-NYLON	fs-SIZE
fs-SILK	fs-STYLE
fs-COTTON	fs-CELL(phone)
fs-FUR	fs-SUIT
fs-WOOL	fs-TUX
fs-SUEDE	fs-WALLET
fs-FLEECE	fs-SUN EYEGLASSES
fs-GOLD	fs-BOOTS
fs-SILVER	fs-VEST
fs-COPPER	fs-BAG

PREPARATION

Review the fingerspelling forms on **Lesson Slides 7:2:1–22**.

MATERIALS

7:2 Lesson Slides
7:2 Follow-up Slides

HOMEWORK 7:2

Student Workbook, pages 14–16

INTRODUCE *Clothing-Related Words*

15–20 minutes

PRESENT

(LESSON SLIDES 7:2:1–22)

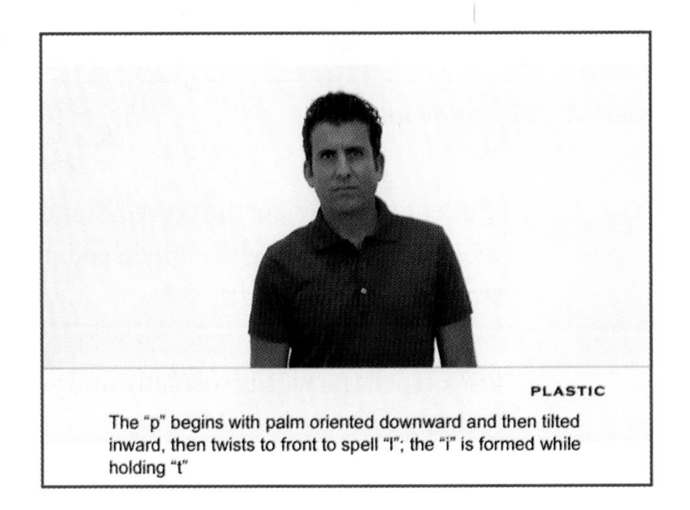

PLASTIC
The "p" begins with palm oriented downward and then tilted inward, then twists to front to spell "l"; the "i" is formed while holding "t"

Show video for "plastic." Have students copy. Check form. Repeat process for all words.

word list

plastic	suede	size	sun (eyeglasses)
nylon	fleece	style	boots
silk	gold	cell (phone)	vest
cotton	silver	suit	bag
fur	copper	tux	
wool	polyester	wallet	

PRACTICE *Clothing-Related Words*

15–20 minutes

Students practice fingerspelling clothing-related words using correct hand positions and movements.

PRESENT
(LESSON SLIDE 7:2:23)

Materials	Items	Metals
1. plastic	10. boots	16. gold
2. nylon	11. vest	17. silver
3. silk	12. suit	18. copper
4. cotton	13. tux	
5. fur	14. wallet	**Others**
6. wool	15. sunglasses	19. size
7. suede		20. style
8. fleece		21. cell phone
9. polyester		22. bag

Give a number from the list on the slide and have students fingerspell the word. For example:

T: NUMBER 19
S: fs-SIZE

Be sure students use:
- correct hand position
- correct movement.

Now, have students practice spelling the words on their own. Circulate and help where needed.

Conclude. Spell a word from the list. Have students give you the corresponding number.

HOMEWORK

Tell students to do **Homework 7:2** (*Student Workbook*, pages 14–16).

HOMEWORK FOLLOW-UP
5 MINUTES

PRESENT
(FOLLOW-UP SLIDE 7:2:1)

Materials	Items	Metals
plastic	boots	gold
Nylon	vest	silver
Silk	suit	copper
Cotton	tux	
Fur	wallet	**Others**
Wool	sunglasses	size
Suede		style
Fleece		cell phone
polyester		bag

ACTIVITY 1

Review by spelling a word from the list and asking students to spell the word above, below or next to it, for example:

t whq
T: fs-COTTON, [(wh)IX-loc*"cotton"*/IX-loc*"above"*], "what"
S: fs-SILK

ACTIVITY 2

Sign the sentences below and have students write down in English the fingerspelled words shown in bold.

t cond
1. CLOTHES **fs-COTTON**, WASH-MACHINE HOT WATER,
neg
"wave-no"(Don't wash clothes made of cotton with hot water.)

2. SOME **fs-PLASTIC** !HARD-SURFACE! SAME-AS METAL.
(Some plastic is as hard as steel.)

3. **fs-BOOTS** ICL*"put on boots"* !MUST! KEEP fs-FEET WARM.
(Boots are needed to keep your feet warm)

when
4. YOU USE **fs-SUIT**, YOU FACE !GOOD!.
(You look good in a suit.)

rhet
5. NOW+YEAR **fs-STYLE**, "what," PANTS DCL*"bell bottoms."*
(Bell bottomed pants are in style this year.)

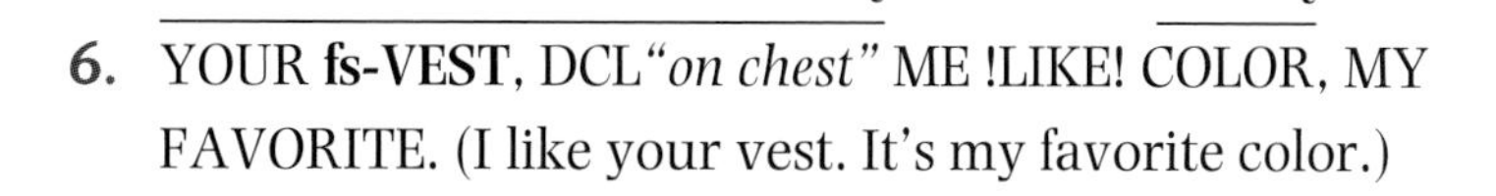

6. YOUR **fs-VEST**, DCL*"on chest"* ME !LIKE! COLOR, MY FAVORITE. (I like your vest. It's my favorite color.)

t

7. ME LOSE 20 WEIGHT. NOW ME **fs-SIZE** 6. (I've lost 20 pounds. I now wear a size 6.)

8. ME BUY **fs-SUN+EYEGLASSES** FOR fs-DOG. IX*"dog"* LIKE. (I bought sunglasses for my dog. He likes them.)

Check answers. Have students tell you what word was fingerspelled, then write the word on the board so the rest of class can confirm their answer.

ACTIVITY 3

Ask the following questions and have students answer by spelling a word from the list.

whq

T: (describes a boot) NAME "what"
S: fs-BOOT

T: MAN ICL*"take wallet from back pocket, open wallet"*

whq

NAME "what" [(wh)LCL:B*"wallet"*/IX-loc*"wallet"*]
S: fs-WALLET

whq

T: MAN PLAN MARRY, GET-DRESSED "what"
S: fs-TUX

t whq

T: IX-loc*"tag inside shirt,"* fs-S, fs-M, fs-L, "what"
S: fs-SIZE

t

T: FOOD SHOPPING, DCL*"bag"* [(wh)LCL:C*"bag"*/

t whq

FOOD ICL*"put food in bag,"* IX*"bag"*], "what"
S: fs-BAG

whq

T: UMBRELLA, MAKE FROM "what"
S: fs-NYLON

T: MAN GO-TO CHURCH, USE COAT, PANTS,

t

COLOR (2h)SAME-AS*"coat, pants,"* IX*"coats, pants"*

whq

NAME "what"

S: fs- SUIT

T: ANIMAL RABBIT, FOX, fs-CHINCHILLA POSS-all fs-HAIR

whq

NAME "what"

S: fs-FUR

whq

T: (describe cell phone) NAME "what"

S: fs-CELL PHONE

whq

T: (point to cotton shirt) MAKE FROM "what"

S: fs-COTTON

whq

T: (point to wool sweater) MAKE FROM "what"

S: fs-WOOL

t whq

T: (describe worm making thread) IX*"thread"* STRING "what"

S: fs-SILK

LESSON 7:3

Numbers: Guess My Number

Lesson length: 35–45 minutes

LESSON GOAL Students will review cardinal numbers 1–100.

KEY SKILLS Form cardinal numbers 1–100 correctly.

NOTIONS

Game phrases

A: ME THOUGHT-OCCUR ONE NUMBER, IN-RANGE 1-left, 100-right. NUMBER (t), YOU GUESS.

B: (number) (t), MORE-THAN (q) (or MORE-THAN (number) (q),)
or (number) (t), LESS-THAN (q) (or LESS-THAN (number) (q),)
or IN-RANGE (number)-left, (number)-right (q)

Confirm the number

A: [RIGHT] !THAT-ONE! (nod)

Game vocabulary

THOUGHT-OCCUR	LESS-THAN	IN-RANGE
GUESS	MORE-THAN	

Numbers
Cardinal 1–100

PREPARATION Review the number forms on pages 48–49

MATERIALS **7:3 Lesson Slides**

HOMEWORK 7:3 *Student Workbook*, pages 17–19

REVIEW *Cardinal Number Forms*

15–20 minutes

PRESENT
(LESSON SLIDE 7:3:1)

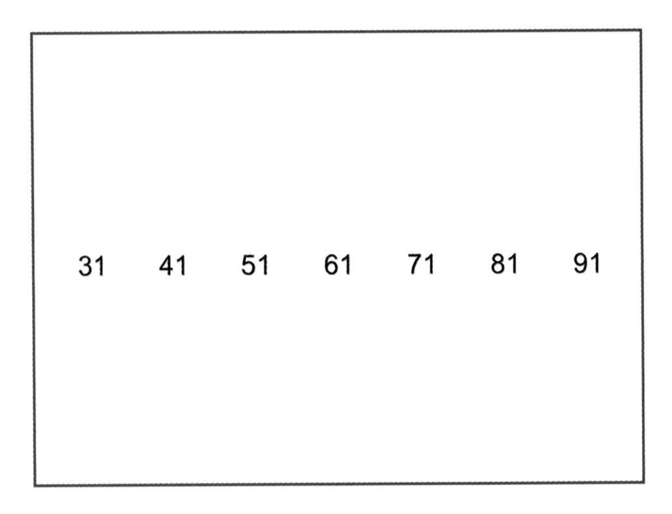

Have students sign the numbers. Make sure:

- sign the first digit of the number with the palm facing out
- move hand forward slightly while signing the second digit
- when signing the "1," the other fingers are closed in a fist, instead of making the letter "D."

PRESENT
(LESSON SLIDE 7:3:2)

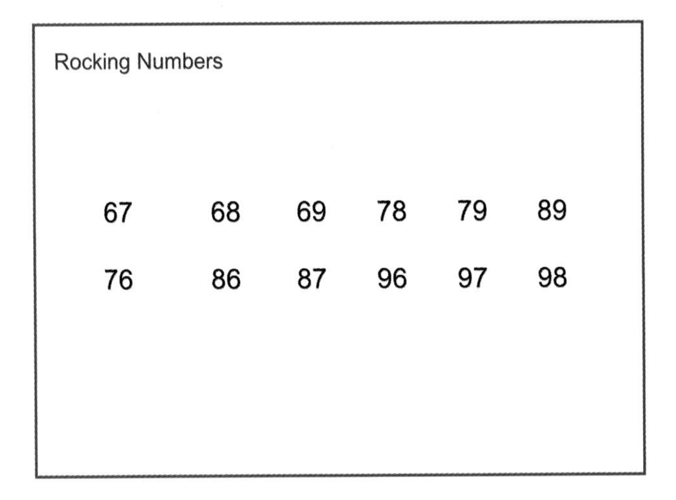

Have students sign the numbers.

For 67, 68, 69, 78, 79, 89, make sure:

- the wrist twists to the non-dominant side before giving the second (larger) digit.

For 76, 86, 87, 96, 97, 98, make sure:

- the wrist twists to dominant side before giving the second (smaller) digit.

PRESENT
(LESSON SLIDE 7:3:3)

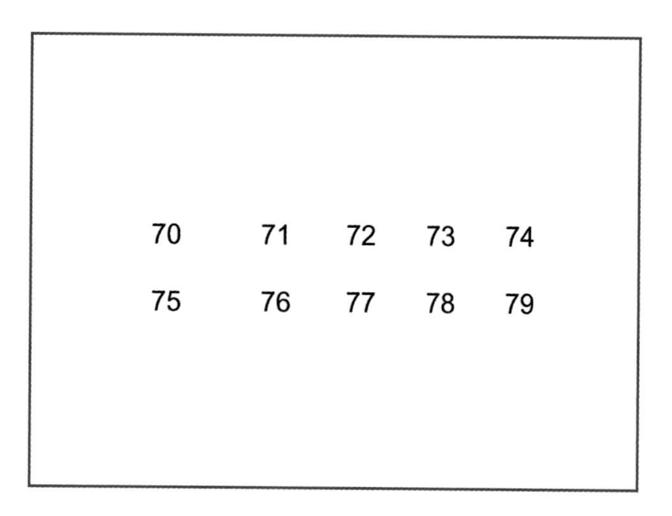

Have students sign the numbers in sequence to demonstrate their skills with different number forms. Make sure:

70—repeat number

71—second digit moves slightly forward; closed fist for the "1"

72, 73, 74, 75—move hand slightly forward to give the second digit

76—wrist twists toward the dominant side before giving the second (smaller) digit

78, 79—wrist twists toward non-dominant side before giving the second (larger) digit

77—palm faces down, hand moves sideways toward the dominant side for the second digit

INTRODUCE *Game: Guess My Number*

10-15 minutes

MORE-THAN

LESS-THAN

IN-RANGE

Activity. In this game players try to guess the number someone has in mind. Demonstrate the game.

q

T: WANT PLAY GAME. ME THOUGHT-OCCUR ONE

t

NUMBER, IN-RANGE 1-left, 100-right. NUMBER, YOU GUESS

S: (sign out numbers until they guess the right number)

nod

T: [RIGHT] !THAT-ONE!

Play again. Ask one student to think of a number, and you demonstrate the following phrases while guessing the number:

t q q

(number), **MORE-THAN** (or **MORE-THAN** (number)).

t q q

(number), **LESS-THAN** (or **LESS-THAN** (number)).

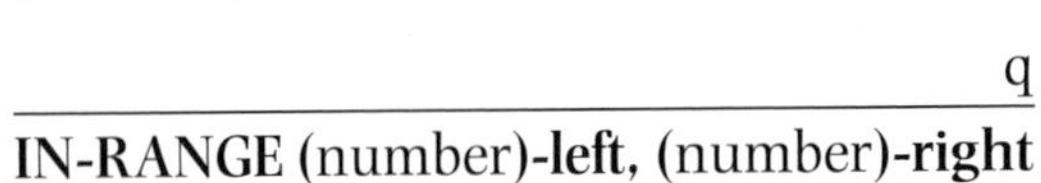

q

IN-RANGE (number)**-left,** (number)**-right**

PRACTICE *Play Game*

10–15 minutes

PRESENT

(LESSON SLIDE 7:3:4)

A: begin game
B: guess numbers
A: confirm when correct number is given

Sign the phrases and have students copy:

For ***"A: begin game"***

T: ME THOUGHT-OCCUR ONE NUMBER IN-RANGE

t

1-left, 100-right. NUMBER, YOU GUESS

S: (copy)

For ***"B: guess numbers"***

q q

T: (number) MORE-THAN, (or MORE-THAN (number)),

t q q

or (number) LESS-THAN, (or LESS-THAN (number)),

q

or IN-RANGE (number)-left, (number)-right

S: (copy)

For ***"A: confirm when correct number is given"***

nod

T: [RIGHT] THAT-ONE

S: (copy)

Group: Put students into groups of three or four. Students take turns thinking of a number and having the rest of the group guess the number.

HOMEWORK

Tell students to do **Homework 7:3** (*Student Workbook*, pages 17–19).

LESSON 7:4

Describing Personal Items

Lesson length: 160–200 minutes

LESSON GOAL

Students will sign this dialogue:

Dialogue

A: tell how you got the item
situation 1—inherited item
situation 2—received as a gift (for birthday or holiday)
situation 3—bought for an event or on a trip
situation 4—person didn't want item so it was given to me
situation 5—found it at garage sale or second hand store
situation 6—took it from someone

B: respond, ask what the item looks like [1]

A: describe (use the correct sequence for the item) [2], [3], [4]

B: ask what the item is made of [5]

A: tell kind of material; ask if B wants to see item

B: say yes

A: show item (picture on card)

B: comment

KEY PHRASES

whq (over FACE+SAME-AS "what")

[1] FACE+SAME-AS "what" [YOU] EXPLAIN

[2] ***Sequence: Describing tops and coats***

1) name item (give color, if only one)
2) describe neckline and sleeve length
3) describe pattern (name base color, then other color(s)
4) describe other details (pockets, snaps, sheer, beads, hood, zipper, fur trim, puffy)

[3] ***Sequence: Describing bags***

1) name item (give color if only one)
2) describe size/shape and its handle
3) describe details (pattern, fastener, zipper, pockets, flaps)
4) tell how it is handled or carried

[4] ***Sequence: Describing eyeglasses***

1) name item (give color if only one)
2) describe size and shape of lens
3) describe details

whq (over "what")

[5] MAKE FROM "what"

NOTIONS

Grammar

Descriptive Classifiers (DCLs)
Instrument Classifiers (ICLs)
Locative Classifiers (LCLs)

Vocabulary

how got item (phrases)

- (person) IX*"person"* GIVE-TO-me or PRESENT-TO-me (item)
- BIRTHDAY (or VALENTINE), IX*"person"* GIVE-TO-me (item)
- ME GO-TO VACATION (or name event), BUY (item)
- (item), (person) NOT-WANT, PRESENT-TO-me (neg over "(person) NOT-WANT")
- GO-TO GARAGE fs-SALE (or SECOND-HAND STORE), SEE (item), BUY
- (person) POSS*"person"* (item), ME TAKE-FROM-person

materials

FABRIC	WOOD
METAL	RUBBER
GLASS	LEATHER

type of materials

REAL (fur, leather, hair)	SEE-THROUGH
FAKE (fur, leather, hair)	DCL*"padded"*

tops

SHIRT	SWEATER/PULLOVER
DCL*"T"*+SHIRT	COAT
BLOUSE	fs-VEST

items

PURSE	EYEGLASSES
BACKPACK	

comments

PRETTY	DIFFERENT
STRANGE	OLD+fs-FF (old-fashioned)
fs-COOL	UGLY
SWELL	LOUD-COLOR
NEVER SEE	

PREPARATION

- Review main points of the lesson in **Key Grammar: Describing Personal Items (Coat and Tops, Bags and Eyeglasses)**, *Student Workbook*, pages 20–22.
- Make a set of **7:4 Item Cards** for each group of 4 students (for **Group Practice** activity, page 69)

MATERIALS

7:4 Item Cards
7:4 Lesson Slides
7:4 Follow-up Slides

HOMEWORK 7:4

Student Workbook, pages 20–34

INTRODUCE *Types of Materials*

10–15 minutes

FABRIC

Introduce sign **FABRIC.**

T: fs-COTTON, fs-WOOL, fs-NYLON, fs-POLYESTER,

rhet

THEY-ALL SIGN "what," **FABRIC.**

S: (repeat sign) FABRIC

t whq

T: YOUR *"student"* SHIRT, FABRIC, "what"

S: (fingerspell type of fabric)

METAL

Introduce sign **METAL.**

T: fs-GOLD, fs-COPPER, fs-SILVER, THEY-ALL SIGN

rhet

"what," **METAL.**

S: (repeat sign) METAL

t whq

T: METAL HERE IX-around-room, WHERE.

S: (point to metal objects or parts in the room)

GLASS

Introduce signs **GLASS**, **WOOD**, **RUBBER**, and **LEATHER**.

T: (point to items made of glass, for example, window, eyeglasses, lens on LCD projector), **GLASS.**

S: (repeat sign) GLASS

WOOD

T: (point to items made of wood, for example, table, door, floor), **WOOD.**

S: (repeat sign) WOOD.

RUBBER

T: (point to items made of rubber, for example, rubber bands, shoe soles, elastic), **RUBBER.**

S: (repeat sign) RUBBER

LEATHER

T: (point to items made of leather, for example, shoes, bags, belts, coats), **LEATHER.**
S: (repeat sign) LEATHER

Name or point to an item, ask what it's made of. For example:

              t   q
T: YOUR SHOE, LEATHER
S: YES (or #NO, IX*"shoes"* FABRIC)
                  t   q
T: (point to window), WOOD
S: #NO, IX*"window"* GLASS.

PRESENT
(LESSON SLIDE 7:4:1)

Introduce signs **REAL** and **FAKE.**

REAL

Identify person, and introduce the signs:

T: WOMAN, SHIRT DCL*"stripped shirt,"* POSS*"woman"* HAIR **REAL**

T: WOMAN, SHIRT PURPLE DCL*"chest,"* POSS*"woman"* HAIR **FAKE.**

FAKE

Identify eyes, have student sign FAKE or REAL.
                  t   whq
T: EYES "wave up," REAL, FAKE WHICH.
S: REAL

t / whq

T: EYES "wave down," REAL, FAKE WHICH

S: FAKE

Review. Ask students questions to review the signs. For example:

t / whq

T: SHOE IX*"shoe"* LEATHER REAL, FAKE WHICH

S: IX*"shoe"* LEATHER, FAKE

t / whq

T: EYEGLASS IX*"eyeglasses"* GLASS REAL, FAKE WHICH

S: IX*"eyeglasses"* GLASS, REAL

Do the same for METAL, WOOD and RUBBER.

INTRODUCE *Describing Tops*

45 minutes

PRESENT
(LESSON SLIDE 7:4:2)

Tops. Introduce the following signs:

SHIRT

DCL*"T"*+SHIRT

BLOUSE

PULLOVER

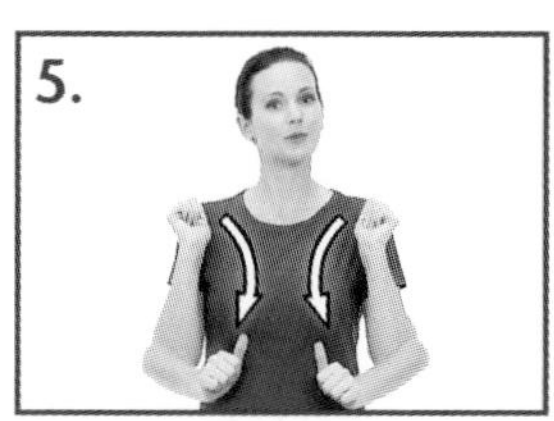

COAT

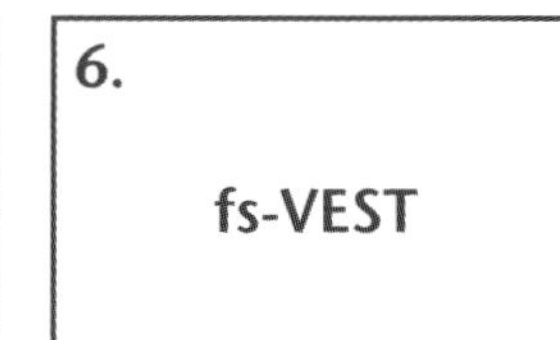

PRESENT
(LESSON SLIDE 7:4:3)

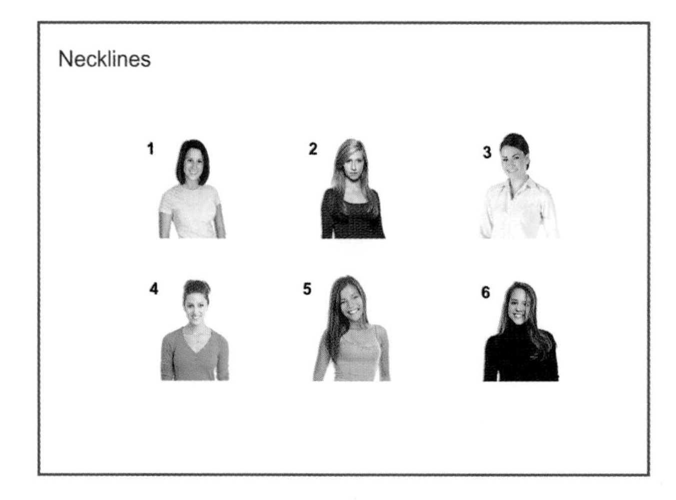

Necklines. Introduce how to describe various necklines.

DCL*"crew neck"*

DCL"scoop neck"

DCL*"collar"*

DCL*"V-neck"*

DCL*"spaghetti-straps"*

DCL*"turtleneck"*

PRESENT
(LESSON SLIDE 7:4:4)

Sleeve Lengths. Introduce how to describe various sleeve lengths.

1. SHIRT, **DCL*"long sleeve"***
2. SHIRT, **DCL*"3/4 sleeve"***
3. SHIRT, **DCL*"short sleeve"***
4. SHIRT, **DCL*"sleeveless"***

PRESENT
(LESSON SLIDE 7:4:5)

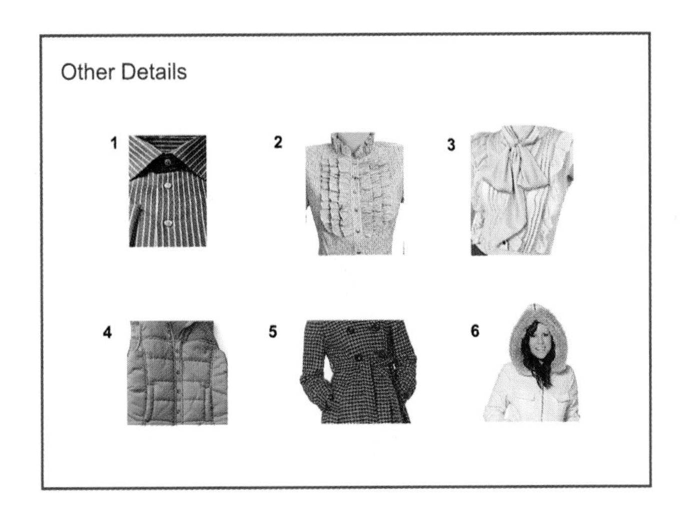

SEE-THROUGH

Other details. Introduce how to describe other details in shirts and coats.

1. DCL*"buttons down front"*
2. DCL*"ruffles on front"*
3. DCL*"bow on front"* SHIRT, **SEE-THROUGH**
4. DCL*"padded, puffy,"* ICL*"snap down front"*
5. ICL*"tie at waist"* BCL*"put both hands in side pockets"*
6. ICL*"zip up on front,"* ICL*"pull up hood,"* DCL*"fur trim"*

PRESENT
(LESSON SLIDE 7:4:6)

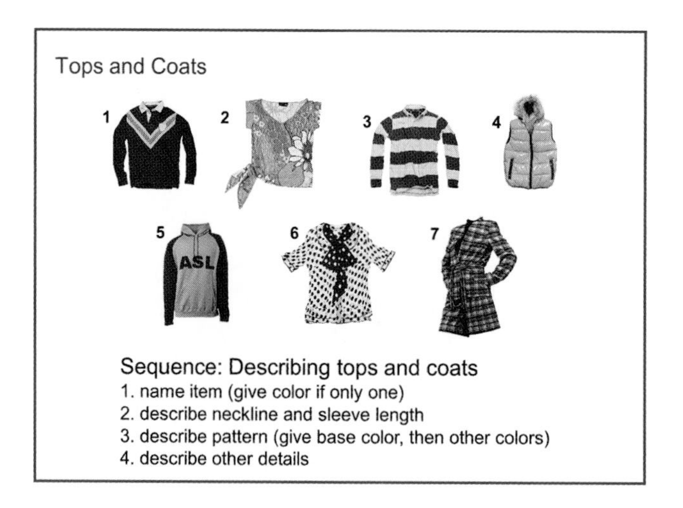

Demonstrate how to describe the clothes. Follow the sequence on the slide. Have students copy.

Picture 1

T: PULLOVER, DCL*"long sleeve"* WHITE DCL*"collar,"* DCL*"chest"* DARK BLUE, YELLOW DCL*"stripes in V-pattern across chest,"* LCL:C*"emblem on chest"*

S: (repeat description)

Picture 2

T: **BLOUSE DCL***"V-neckline,"* DCL*"very short sleeves"* FLOWER, DIFFERENT++ COLOR (2h)altDCL:C*"swirly design,"* ICL*"tie at waist"*

S: (repeat description)

Picture 3

T: **SHIRT, DCL***"long sleeves"* WHITE DCL*"collar,"* DCL*"chest"* GREEN, WHITE DCL*"wide stripes pattern"*

S: (repeat description)

Picture 4

T: **fs-VEST DCL***"sleeveless"* YELLOW DCL*"chest,"* ZIPPER-on-chest, DCL*"padded"* DCL*"hood"* fs-FUR DCL*"fur trim,"*

S: (repeat description)

Picture 5

T: **PULLOVER, DCL***"long sleeves"* DCL*"hood,"* DCL*"chest"* LIGHT-WEIGHT BLUE, DCL*"sleeve"* DARK BLUE, (2h)DCL:bentL*"across chest"* fs-ASL.

S: (repeat description)

Picture 6

T: **BLOUSE DCL***"elbow length sleeves,"* WHITE DCL*"chest,"* BLACK

t (over BOW-TIE"on front")

(2h)DCL:F*"dots on blouse,"* BOW-TIE*"on front"* BLACK, WHITE (2h)DCL:F*"dots on tie"*

S: (repeat description)

Picture 7

T: **COAT, DCL***"long sleeves,"* BLACK WHITE DCL:4*"plaid,"* TIE-at-waist, (2h)POCKET*"on sides"*

S: (repeat description)

Review. Have students pair up and take turns describing tops on the slide to each other. Have the partners confirm by giving the corresponding number.

INTRODUCE *Describing Bags*

30–40 minutes

PRESENT

(LESSON SLIDE 7:4:7)

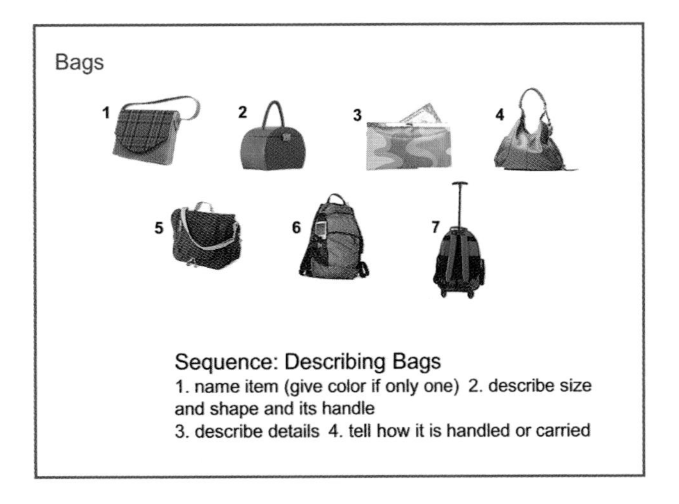
Bags
1
2
3
4
5
6
7
Sequence: Describing Bags
1. name item (give color if only one) 2. describe size and shape and its handle
3. describe details 4. tell how it is handled or carried

1. **Name item (give color if only one).** Introduce signs:

PURSE/BAG (1-5)

BACKPACK (6 AND 7)

2. **Describe size and shape, and handle.** Sign the following. Be sure descriptions are made in neutral space (in front of signer's body).
   1) DCL:openB*"square"* [(wh)DCL:G*"end of strap"*/ DCL:G*"long strap"*]
   2) DCL:openB*"dome"* [(wh) DCL:G*"end of strap"*DCL:G*"short strap"*]
   3) DCL:C*"long rectangle"*
   4) DCL:openB*"bowl-like"* [(wh) DCL:G*"end of strap"* DCL:G*"medium length strap"*]
   5) DCL:openB*"large rectangle"* [(wh) DCL:G*"end of strap/* DCL:G*"short strap"*], [(wh) DCL:G*"end of strap"*/ DCL:G*"long strap"*]
   6) DCL:openB*"upright rectangle"* [(wh) DCL:G*"end of strap on top"*/DCL:G*"short strap"*
   7) DCL:openB*"upright rectangle"* DCL:G*"handle"*

3. **Describe details.** Show how to describe details, such as zippers, pouches, clasps, fasteners, and patterns. Make sure the details are described in neutral space as opposed to describing clothes on the body.
   1) [(wh)LCL:B*"purse"*/LCL:B*"open/close flap"*], PINK, BLUE DCL:4*"plaid on flap"*
   2) [(wh)flatO*"fastener"*/LCL:U*"insert in fastener"*]
   3) (2h)ICL:flatO*"open/close purse"* PINK, ORANGE DCL:4"wavy"
   4) ICL*"open/close zipper on top"*
   5) [(wh)LCL:open B*"bag"*/LCL:open B*"open/close flap in front"* ICL*"zip open pocket on front"*
   6) ICL*"zip open different pocket and put in items,"* DCL*"side pouches,* ICL*"put in side pouches"*
   7) LCL:1*"wheels turning"*

4. **Tell how it is handled or carried.** Describe how bags are handled using classifiers.
   1) LCL:X*"put on shoulder"*
   2) ICL*"carry by the strap"*
   3) LCL:B*"put under arm"*
   4) LCL:X*"put on shoulder"*
   5) LCL:X*"put on shoulder"*

6) ICL*"put pack on back"*
7) ICL*"pull handle up and pull bag along"*

Now, demonstrate how to describe the bags following the sequence on the slide. Have students copy.

Picture 1

T: PURSE/BAG DCL:openB*"square"* [(wh)DCL:G*"end of strap"/* DCL:G*"long strap"* [(wh)LCL:B"purse"/LCL:B*"open and close flap"*], PINK, BLUE DCL:4*"plaid on flap,"* LCL:X*"put on shoulder"*
S: (repeat description)

Picture 2

T: PURSE/BAG RED, DCL:openB*"dome"*[(wh) DCL:G*"end of strap"/* DCL:G*"short strap"*] [(wh)flatO*"fastener"/* LCL:U*"insert in fastener"*] ICL*"carry by the strap"*
S: (repeat description)

Picture 3

T: PURSE/BAG, DCL:C*"long rectangle"* (2h)ICL:flatO*"open/close purse"* PINK, ORANGE DCL:4*"wavy"* LCL:B*"put under arm"*
S: (repeat description)

Picture 4

T: PURSE/BAG LEATHER, BROWN DCL:openB*"bowl-like"* [(wh) DCL:G*"end of strap"*/DCL:G*"medium length strap"*], ICL*"open/close zipper on top,"* ICL*"put strap over shoulder"*
S: (repeat description)

Picture 5

T: PURSE/BAG BLACK DCL:openB*"large rectangle"* [(wh) DCL:G *"end of strap*/DCL:G*"short strap"*], [(wh) DCL:G*"end of strap"/* DCL:G*"long strap"*], [(wh)LCL:open B*"bag"*/LCL:open B*"open/ close flap in front"* ICL*"zip open pocket on front"* LCL:X*"put on shoulder"*
S: (repeat description)

Picture 6

T: BACKPACK BLUE DCL:openB*"upright rectangle"* [(wh) DCL:G*"end of strap on top"*/DCL:G*"short strap"*], ICL*"zip open different pocket and put in items,"* DCL*"side pouches,"* ICL*"put in side pouches,"* ICL*"put pack on back"*

S: (repeat description)

Picture 7

T: **BACKPACK RED DCL:openB***"upright rectangle"* DCL:G*"handle"* ICL*"zip open different pocket and put in items,"* DCL"side pouches, ICL*"put in side pouches,"* LCL:1*"wheels turning,"* ICL*"pull handle up and pull bag along"*

S: (repeat description)

Review. Have students describe the bags. Pay attention to phrasing.

INTRODUCE *Describing Eyeglasses*

25–30 minutes

PRESENT

(LESSON SLIDE 7:4:8)

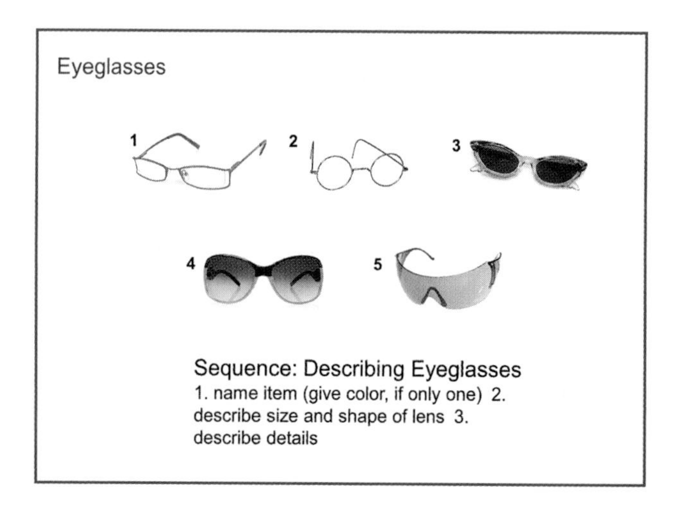

Eyeglasses
1
2
3
4
5
Sequence: Describing Eyeglasses
1. name item (give color, if only one) 2. describe size and shape of lens 3. describe details

1. **Name item (give color if only one).** Introduce signs:
   EYEGLASSES (1 and 2)
   fs-SUN+EYEGLASSES (3, 4 and 5)

2. **Describe size and shape of lens.** Show how to describe shapes of the lenses:
   1) DCL:G*"rectangular shaped"*
   2) DCL:I*"wire-rimmed"*
   3) DCL:G*"cat eye shaped"*
   4) DCL:bentL*"round shaped"*
   5) DCL:openB*"wrap around" (or* DCL:C*"wrap around")*

3. **Describe details.** Show how to describe details such as trim on edge, logo on frames.
   1) *(none)*
   2) *(none)*
   3) BROWN, YELLOW DCL*"mottled"*
   4) DCL:G*"top of frames" BLACK,*
      DCL:G*"bottom of frames"* YELLOW
   5) GREEN DCL:F*"emblem on sides"*

Now, demonstrate how to describe the eyeglasses following the sequence on the slide. Have students copy.

Picture 1

EYEGLASSES, RED DCL:G*"rectangular shaped"*

Picture 2

EYEGLASSES, METAL DCL:I*"wire-rimmed"*

Picture 3

fs-SUN+EYEGLASSES DCL:G*"cat eye shaped,"*
BROWN, YELLOW DCL*"mottled"*

Picture 4

fs-SUN+EYEGLASSES DCL:bentL*"round shaped"*
DCL:G*"top of frames"* BLACK, DCL:G*"bottom of frames"* YELLOW

Picture 5

fs-SUN+EYEGLASSES BROWN DCL:openB*"wrap around"*
(or DCL:C*"wrap around")*, GREEN DCL:F*"emblem on sides"*

Review. Have students describe the eyeglasses. Pay attention to phrasing.

PRACTICE *Describing Items*

30–40 minutes

Students will explain how they got an item and describe it using descriptive (DCL), locative (LCL) and instrument (ICL) classifiers.

PRESENT
(LESSON SLIDE 7:4:9)

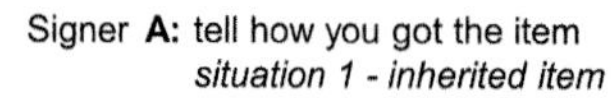

Signer **A:** tell how you got the item
situation 1 - inherited item
B: respond, ask what the item looks like
A: describe (use the correct sequence for the item)
B: ask what the item is made of
A: tell kind of material; ask if B wants to see item
B: say yes
A: show item (picture on card)
B: comment

Demonstrate Signer B's lines and have students copy:

For ***"B: ask what the item looks like"***

whq

T: FACE+SAME-AS "what" [YOU] EXPLAIN
S(all): (copy)

FACE+SAME-AS

For ***"B: ask what the item is made of"***

whq

T: MAKE FROM "what"
S(all): (copy)

EXPLAIN

For ***"B: comment"***
Begin by asking students what they think of the shirt on the slide. Make sure the following signs are introduced.

Using ***"situation 1—inherited item,"*** demonstrate the dialogue. Role play Signer A and have a student role play Signer B.

A: GRANDFATHER DIED, he-GIVE-me SHIRT !OLD!

whq

B: [SHIRT] FACE+SAME-AS "what"

A: YELLOW DCL*"long sleeved, long pointed collars,"* FLOWERS DCL*"on chest below collars,"* (2h)POCKETS, BUTTONS RED

whq

B: [SHIRT] MAKE FROM "what"

q

A: fs-SILK, YOU WANT SEE

nod

B: YES

A: (point to picture on slide)

B: (comment on item)

PRESENT
(LESSON SLIDE 7:4:10)

Signer **A:** tell how you got the item
situation 1 - inherited item
situation 2 - received as a gift (for birthday or holiday)
situation 3 - bought for event, trip
situation 4 - person didn't want item so it was given to me
situation 5 - found it at garage sale or second hand store
situation 6 - took it from someone
B: respond, ask what the item looks like
A: describe (use the correct sequence for the item)
B: ask what the item is made of
A: tell kind of material; ask if B wants to see item
B: say yes
A: show item (picture on card)
B: comment

Point to each situation and demonstrate how to sign the situation using the phrases listed below. Have students repeat.

For ***"situation 1: inherited item"***
(person) IX*"person"* GIVE-TO-me or **PRESENT-TO-me (item)**

For ***"situation 2: received as a gift (for birthday or holiday)"***
BIRTHDAY (or VALENTINE), (person) IX*"person"*GIVE-TO-me (item)

For ***"situation 3: bought for event, trip"***
ME GO-TO VACATION (or name event), BUY (item)

For ***"situation 4: person didn't want item so it was given to me"***

neg

(item), (person) NOT-WANT, PRESENT-TO-me

For ***"situation 5: found it at garage sale or second-hand store"***
**GO-TO GARAGE fs-SALE (or SECOND-HAND STORE),
SEE (item), BUY**

For ***"situation 6: took it from someone"***
(person) POSS*"person"* (item), ME TAKE-FROM-person

PRESENT-TO-ME

VALENTINE

VACATION

SECOND-HAND

Review: Point to different situations and have students sign the phrase for that situation.

Group Practice. Put students into groups of four. Give each group a set of **7:4 Item Cards** to use for the dialogue (see **Materials**). Separate the cards into three piles (one for the shirts, one for the bags, and one for the eyeglasses). Have students pick one card from each pile.

Have students in each group take turns being Signer A from **Slide 10** and do the following:

1. pick one of the three cards in their hand
2. pick a situation from the slide
3. pick another student in the group to role play Signer B
4. follow the dialogue on the slide
5. ask other members of the group to add their comments

Continue the activity until all cards are described using different situations.

EVALUATE

20–30 minutes

Call on students to demonstrate the dialogue.

Check to be sure students:

As Signer A:

- follow the correct sequence for the item and use appropriate phrasing when describing it

As Signer B:

whq

- sign FACE+SAME-AS fluently
- use a comment appropriate for the situation

HOMEWORK

Tell students to do **Homework 7:4** (*Student Workbook*, pages 20–34).

Also, tell them to bring the following items to the next class for **Lesson 7:8**.

- a shirt or jacket (with pattern or detail)
- a bag, for example, backpack or purse
- a pair of sunglasses, hat or scarf (with pattern or logo)

HOMEWORK FOLLOW-UP
10–15 MINUTES

PRESENT
(FOLLOW-UP SLIDES 7:4:1–24)

Minidialogue 1

1. How did Ursula get the item?
2. Draw and describe the item.
3. What is it made of?
4. What does Ursula think of it?

Check students' answers to **Minidialogues 1–4**. See **Introduction** pages xviii–xix for different ways to check answers.

LESSON 7:5

Translating Sentences with "Have" 1

Lesson length: 35–45 minutes

LESSON GOAL

Students will use the appropriate sign to translate English sentences with "have" in them.

KEY SKILLS

Determine which sign in ASL conveys the same meaning as the word "have" in the English sentence

NOTIONS

Vocabulary

HAVE
MUST
FINISH
NONE
NOT-YET

PREPARATION

Read and view **Translating Sentences with "Have,"** *Student Workbook*, pages 35–36.

MATERIALS

7:5 Lesson Slides
7:5 Follow-up Slides

HOMEWORK 7:5

Student Workbook, pages 35–38

INTRODUCE *Translating Sentences with "Have"*

20–30 minutes

PRESENT
(LESSON SLIDE 7:5:1)

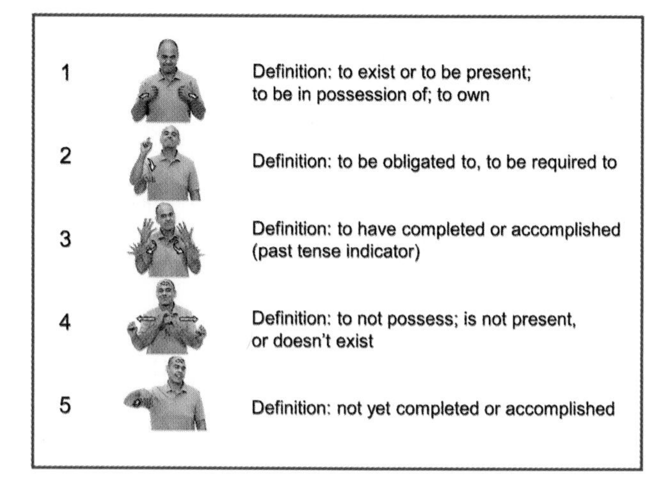

1
Definition: to exist or to be present; to be in possession of; to own
2
Definition: to be obligated to, to be required to
3
Definition: to have completed or accomplished (past tense indicator)
4
Definition: to not possess; is not present, or doesn't exist
5
Definition: not yet completed or accomplished

Review signs and give example sentences. Have each student create their own sentences using those signs.

1. **HAVE**
   T: ME HAVE #DOG
   S: (sign their own sentence using HAVE)

2. **MUST**
   T: ME MUST GO-TO SEE DOCTOR
   S: (sign their own sentence using MUST)

This time select students randomly to create their own sentences using the remaining signs.

3. **FINISH**
   T: ME FINISH EAT TIME-7.
   S: (sign their own sentence using FINISH)

4. **NONE**
   neg
   T: ME NONE WORK UP-TILL-NOW 7-MONTH
   S: (sign their own sentence using NONE)

5. **NOT-YET**

neg

T: ME NOT-YET FIND fs-APT.

S: (sign their own sentence using NOT-YET)

PRESENT
(LESSON SLIDE 7:5:2)

1. The hotel **has** a pool.

The "has" in this sentence means to exist or to be present.
It can also mean to be in possession of, or to own.

- Ask students which sign is similar to the definition. (***Answer:*** HAVE)

PRESENT
(LESSON SLIDE 7:5:3)

1. The hotel **has** a pool.

The "has" in this sentence means to exist or to be present.
It can also mean to be in possession of, or to own.

- Have students translate Sentence 1 using HAVE.

Possible translations:

1. HOTEL (or fs-HOTEL) **HAVE** SWIMMING+fs-POOL

t nod

2. SWIMMING+fs-POOL, HOTEL (or fs-HOTEL) **HAVE**

PRESENT
(LESSON SLIDES 7:5:4–5)

2. I **have to** go to work.

The "have to" in this sentence means to be obligated to, or to be required to.

Repeat the process: show **Lesson Slide 7:5:4**, ask what sign is similar to the definition then show **Lesson Slide 7:5:5** to confirm the answer.

Have students translate Sentence 2 using MUST.

Possible translations:
1. ME **MUST** GO-TO WORK.
2. ME **MUST** LEAVE-FOR WORK.

PRESENT
(LESSON SLIDE 7:5:6–7)

3. She **has written** two books.

The "has written" in this sentence means to have completed or to have accomplished.

Repeat process with **Lesson Slide 7:5:6** and **7:5:7**.
Have students translate Sentence 3 using FINISH.

Possible translations:

```
   ___________t  _______________________________nod
1. IX"man" MAN FINISH WRITE 2 BOOK, FINISH, IX"man."
   _____t  ___________________________nod
2. BOOK, IX"man" MAN FINISH WRITE 2.
```

PRESENT
(LESSON SLIDES 7:5:8–9)

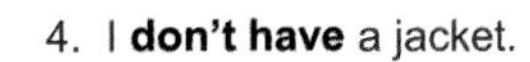

The "don't have" in this sentence means to not possess.
It can also mean item is not present, or doesn't exist.

Repeat process with **Lesson Slides 7:5:8** and **7:5:9**.
Have students translate Sentence 4 using NONE.

Possible translations:

```
   _____t  _______neg
1. COAT, ME NONE.
      __________neg
2. ME NONE COAT.
```

PRESENT
(LESSON SLIDES 7:5:10–11)

5. I **haven't** received the letter.

The "haven't" in this sentence means the action (receiving a letter) is not yet completed or accomplished.

Repeat process with **Lesson Slides 7:5:10** and **7:5:11**.

Have students translate Sentence 5 using NOT-YET.

Possible translations:

t / neg

1. LETTER, ME **NOT-YET** GET.

neg

2. ME **NOT-YET** GET LETTER.

PRACTICE

15 minutes

Students will translate sentences with "have" using the appropriate sign (HAVE, MUST, FINISH, NONE or NOT-YET).

PRESENT
(LESSON SLIDE 7:5:12)

1. I have to brush my teeth.
2. I haven't received your email.
3. I have the tickets.
4. I have no shoes.
5. I have already eaten.

Have students translate the sentences.

Possible translations:

t

1. ME **MUST** BRUSH-TEETH. or BRUSH-TEETH, ME **MUST**

t / neg

2. YOUR fs-EMAIL, ME **NOT-YET** GET. or

neg

ME **NOT-YET** GET YOUR fs-EMAIL.

t nod
3. ME **HAVE** TICKET. or TICKET, ME **HAVE**.

neg t neg
4. ME **NONE** SHOES. or SHOES, ME **NONE**.

t nod
5. ME **FINISH** EAT. or EAT, ME FINISH.

HOMEWORK

Tell students to do **Homework 7:5** (*Student Workbook*, pages 35–38).

HOMEWORK FOLLOW-UP

15 MINUTES

PRESENT

(FOLLOW-UP SLIDES 7:5:1–14)

ACTIVITY

Translating Sentences with "Have"

_____1. I have no money.
_____2. I have a car.
_____3. I already had cake.
_____4. I haven't told Jose.
_____5. I have to tell Jose.
_____6. I have told Jose.

Show **Follow-up Slide 7:5:1**, ask students for their answer for Sentence 1, then show **Follow-up Slide 2** to confirm the answer. Do the same for **Follow-up Slides 7:5:3–14**.

Then, divide class into groups of three. Have them translate the sentences into ASL. Go around, have students sign their translations.

Teacher's translation guide:

(D) **1.** I have no money.

t neg
MONEY ME NONE

(A) **2.** I have a car.

t nod
CAR ME HAVE

(C) **3.** I already had cake.

t nod
fs-CAKE ME FINISH EAT

(E) **4.** I haven't told Jose.

t neg
fs-JOSE, ME TELL IX*"Jose"* NOT-YET

(B) **5.** I have to tell Jose.

ME MUST TELL-TO fs-JOSE.

(C) **6.** I have told Jose.

ME FINISH TELL-TO fs-JOSE.

(A) **7.** I have a HDTV.

ME HAVE fs-HDTV.

(B) **8.** I have to buy a jacket.

t
JACKET, ME MUST BUY.

(C) **9.** I have done my homework.

t nod
HOMEWORK ME FINISH

(B) **10.** I have to call my mother

t
MY MOTHER ME MUST CALL-TO

(D) **11.** I don't have any ice cream.

t neg
ICE-CREAM, ME NONE

(E) **12.** I didn't have any ice cream.

t neg
ICE-CREAM, ME NOT-YET EAT, ME

LESSON 7:6

Translating Sentences with "Drive To," "Take" and "Pick Up" 1

Lesson length: 20–30 minutes

LESSON GOAL

Students will know how to translate sentences with "drive to," "take," or "pick up."

KEY SKILLS

- maintain spatial agreement in the translation
- add either TAKE-FROM or PICK-UP to DRIVE-TO, if there is a direct object
- add DROP-OFF, CARRY-TO, GO-TO, or DRIVE-TO to TAKE-FROM to indicate the person was transported.

NOTIONS

Vocabulary

spatial verbs
GO-TO-location
DRIVE-TO-location
TAKE-FROM-location
DROP-OFF-location
PICK-UP-person
CARRY-TO-location

PREPARATION

Read and view **Translating Sentences with "To Drive," "To Take," and "To Pick Up,"** *Student Workbook*, pages 39–42.

MATERIALS

7:6 Lesson Slides

HOMEWORK 7:6

Student Workbook, pages 39–44

INTRODUCE *"Drive to," "Take (someone) to"*

20–30 minutes

PRESENT
(LESSON SLIDE 7:6:1)

I drove to work.

She drove to work.

Ask students how to sign the first sentence. They may sign like this:

t
S: ME GO-TO-work WORK, CAR/DRIVE.

Show them another way to sign the sentence:

T: ME **DRIVE-TO-work** WORK.

DRIVE-TO

Ask students where is "work" located.
Answer: Where the sign DRIVE-TO ends.

Ask who is driving.
Answer: The signer.

Point out the movement for the sign DRIVE-TO must begin in the signer's location and end in the location for "work."

Ask students to sign the second sentence from **Slide 1**.

S: WOMAN IX*"woman"* she-DRIVE-TO-work WORK.

Be sure students:

- sign WOMAN, then IX*"woman"* to establish her location
- begin the movement of the sign DRIVE-TO in the location established for the woman ("she").

PRESENT
(LESSON SLIDE 7:6:2)

I drove her to work.

"her" is the direct object
in the sentence.

Explain that in English, the word "drive" can take a direct object, but in ASL, the sign DRIVE-TO can not take a direct object.

Demonstrate incorrect ways of handling the direct object in the sentence:

T: ME me-DRIVE-TO-work WOMAN WORK. (incorrect)

t (over: WOMAN IX-loc*"right"*)
T: WOMAN IX-loc*"right"* me-DRIVE-TO-work WORK. (incorrect)

Now, demonstrate the correct way to sign this sentence by adding a verb **TAKE-FROM** which can take the direct object. Have students repeat the sentences.

T: ME **TAKE-FROM-right, WOMAN, DRIVE-TO-left** WORK. (correct)
S: (repeat)

t (over: WOMAN IX-loc*"right"*)
T: WOMAN IX-loc*"right"* **ME TAKE-FROM-right, DRIVE-TO-left** WORK. (correct)
S: (repeat)

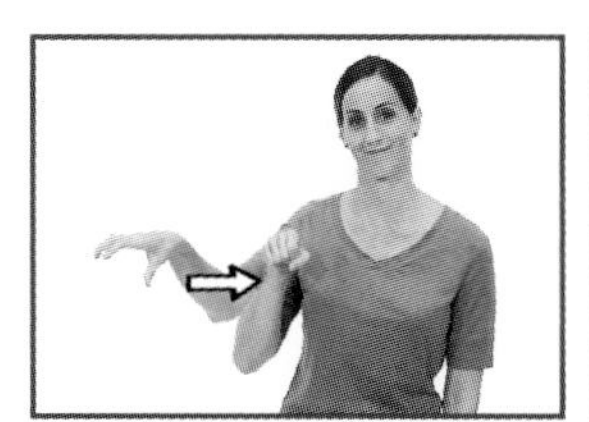
TAKE-FROM-right

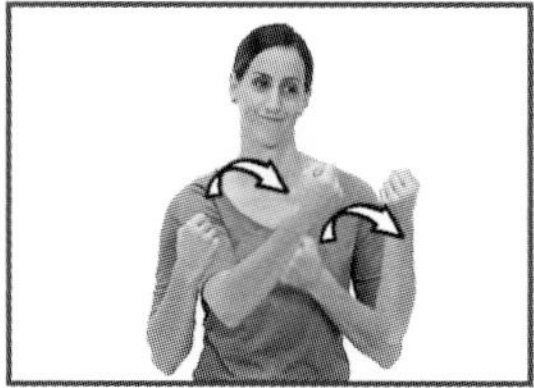
DRIVE-TO-left

Show other possible translations. Have students repeat.

T: WOMAN IX-loc*"right"* ME **TAKE-FROM-right, DROP-OFF-left** WORK.
S: (repeat)

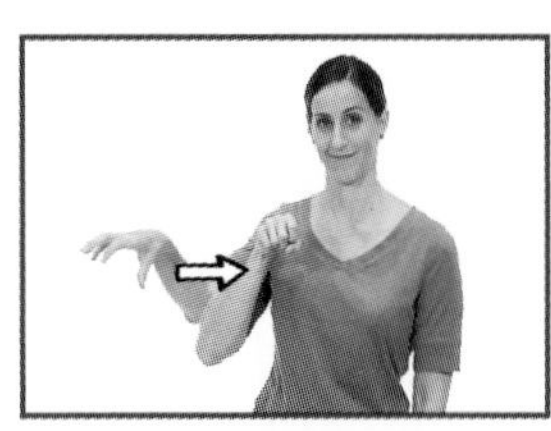
TAKE-FROM-right

DROP-OFF-left

T: WOMAN IX-loc*"right"* ME **TAKE-FROM-right, GO-TO-left** WORK.
S: (repeat)

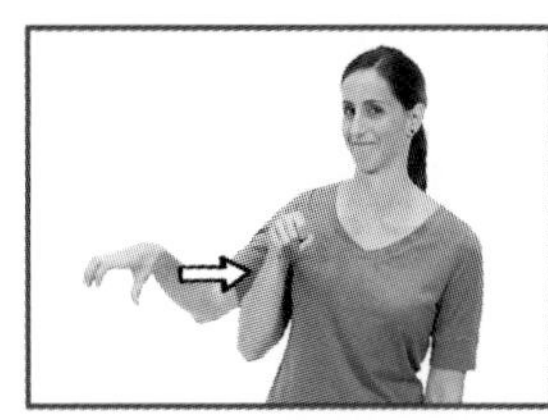
TAKE-FROM-right

GO-TO-left

PRESENT
(LESSON SLIDE 7:6:3)

I took her to school.

She took me to school.

In English the word **"took"** means both
1. getting the person and
2. transporting the person

Explain that, in ASL, the sign TAKE-FROM means getting someone only. It does not include transporting the person.

PRESENT
(LESSON SLIDE 7:6:5)

I picked him up at school and brought him home
(to where we live).

I picked him up from church and drove him to work.

Now ask students to sign these two sentences.

"I picked him up at school and brought him home (to where we live)."

t (over: ME GO-TO-school SCHOOL)

S: ME GO-TO-school SCHOOL, **PICK-UP-man** MAN,
CARRY-TO-here HOME.

Be sure students:

- begin and end the sign CARRY-TO-here to agree with locations of school and "here."

"I picked him up from church and drove him to work."

t (over: ME GO-TO-church CHURCH)

S: ME GO-TO-church CHURCH, **PICK-UP-man** MAN,
CARRY-TO-work WORK.

Be sure students:

- begin and end the sign CARRY-TO to agree with the locations of the church and work.

HOMEWORK

Tell students to do **Homework 7:6**
(*Student Workbook*, pages 39–44).

LESSON 7:7

Numbers: Asking How Many

Lesson length: 30 minutes

LESSON GOAL

Students will practice numbers 1–100, learn to ask questions to find out how many, and to react appropriately to the amount given.

KEY SKILLS

Form cardinal numbers 1–100 correctly

NOTIONS

Phrase

t (over: (item)) whq (over: YOU HAVE HOW-MANY)

(item) YOU HAVE HOW-MANY

Vocabulary

reactions to amount given

OH-I-SEE

!FEW! (with furrowed brow)

!MANY!

WOW (with open mouth)

!MADE-UP! YOU (with a smirk)

PREPARATION

Make cards from **7:7 Cards 1–100** (for **Activity** on page 89).

MATERIALS

7:7 Lesson Slides

7:7 Cards 1–100

HOMEWORK 7:7

Student Workbook, pages 45–46

REVIEW *Cardinal Numbers 1–100*

5–7 minutes

Review cardinal numbers 1–100 by going around the room and have students count off. Check and correct number forms.

INTRODUCTION *Reactions to Amount Given*

20–25 minutes

PRESENT
(LESSON SLIDE 7:7:1)

Reactions to the amount given that is…

- ordinary, common, expected
- less than expected
- more than expected
- unbelievable, ridiculous, outrageous

Select four students. Give each student one of these cards, **Card 2**, **Card 3**, **Card 10** or **Card 34**, to introduce different reactions.

For ***"ordinary, common, expected"***
Ask student with **Card 2**:

OH-I-SEE

t ______ whq ______
T: CAR YOU HAVE, HOW-MANY
S: (refer to card) 2 [CAR]
T: **OH-I-SEE**

Have all students repeat the sign OH-I-SEE.

For ***"less than expected"***
Ask student with **Card 3**:

!FEW!

t t

T: YOUR fs-ASL CLASS, LEARN+ER YOU HAVE,

whq

HOW-MANY

S: (refer to card) 3 [LEARN+ER]

T: **!FEW!** (with furrowed brow)

Have all students repeat the sign !FEW! (with furrowed brow).

!MANY!

For ***"more than expected"***
Ask student with **Card 10**:

t whq

T: #DOG YOU HAVE, HOW-MANY

S: (refer to card) 10 [#DOG]

T: **!MANY!** (and/or) **WOW** (with open mouth)

WOW

Have all students repeat the signs !MANY! and WOW.

For ***"unbelievable, ridiculous, outrageous"***
Ask student with **Card 34**:

!MADE-UP! YOU

t whq

T: CHILDREN YOU HAVE, HOW-MANY

S: (refer to card) 34

T: **!MADE-UP! YOU** (with a smirk)

Have all students repeat the sign !MADE-UP! YOU (with a smirk).

PRACTICE *Asking How Many and Reacting to Amount*

15–20 minutes

Students will practice asking how many, and the four reactions to the amount given.

PRESENT
(LESSON SLIDE 7:7:2)

A: Ask how many (of something) B has.
B: Give number (on your card).
A: React to the amount given that is...
- ordinary, common, expected
- less than expected
- more than expected
- unbelievable, ridiculous, outrageous

Have individual students role play Signer A and ask you the question. Give a number between 1 and 100 to elicit different reactions.

For example:

t whq
S1: CAT YOU HAVE, HOW-MANY
T: 12
S1: !MANY!

t whq
S2: EYES YOU HAVE, HOW MANY
T: 10
S2: !MADE-UP! YOU

Be sure students' questions follow this structure:

t whq
(item) YOU HAVE, HOW-MANY

Activity. Now, give each student two cards (one low number, one high number) from **7:7 Cards 1–100** (See **Materials**).

Have students mingle and follow the dialogue on the slide using appropriate reactions. After each conversation, have them trade cards and find new partners.

HOMEWORK

Tell students to do **Homework 7:7** (*Student Workbook*, pages 45–46).

LESSON 7:8

Describing Lost Items

Lesson length: 75–85 minutes

LESSON GOAL

Students will sign this dialogue:

Dialogue

Part 1 ***(A approaches B)***

A: tell what is lost, ask if B has seen it
B: say no, ask A to describe it
A: describe
B: tell A you will check

Part 2 ***(B returns without the item)***

B: add another description to confirm
A: confirm or correct
B: explain you will go get the item.

Part 3 ***(B returns with the item)***

B: ask if it is the correct item
A: confirm, express gratitude
B: respond

KEY PHRASES

Sequence: Describing hats, scarves and eyeglasses

1. name item (give color if only one)
2. describe basic size and shape
3. describe details

Sequence: Describing tops and coats

1. name item (give color, if only one)
2. describe neckline and sleeve length
3. describe pattern (name base color, then other colors)
4. describe other details (pockets, snaps, sheer, beads, hood, zipper, fur trim, puffy)

Sequence: Describing bags

1. name item (give color if only one)
2. describe size and shape and its handle
3. describe details (pattern, fastener, zipper, pockets, flaps)
4. tell how it is handled or carried

NOTIONS

Grammar

Descriptive Classifiers (DCLs):

- describe basic shape and size
- describe pattern and details

Vocabulary

HAT

SCARF

PREPARATION

- Review main points of the lesson in **Key Grammar: Describing Personal Items (Hats and Scarves),** *Student Workbook*, pages 47–48
- In **Homework 7:4 Assignment**, students were asked to bring the following items (for **Activity** on pages 98–99):
  - a shirt or jacket (with pattern or detail)
  - a bag, for example, backpack or purse
  - a pair of sunglasses (with pattern or logo)

In case students forget to bring their items, bring several of each item for them to use.

MATERIALS

7:8 Lesson Slides

7:8 Follow-up Slides

HOMEWORK 7:8

Student Workbook, pages 47–52

INTRODUCE *Describing Hats and Scarves*

45 minutes

PRESENT
(LESSON SLIDE 7:8:1)

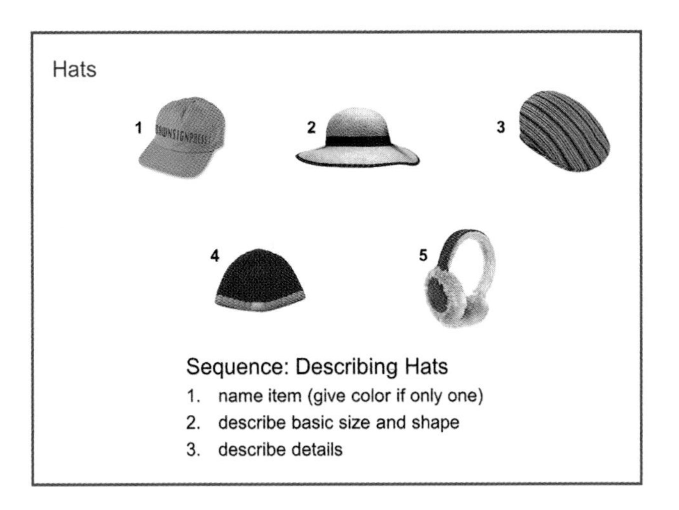
Hats
1
2
3
4
5
Sequence: Describing Hats
1. name item (give color if only one)
2. describe basic size and shape
3. describe details

HAT

1. **Name item (give color if only one).** Introduce signs:
   (1–4) HAT
   5) (none)

2. **Describe basic size and shape.** Sign the following. Be sure descriptions are made on the head.
   1) DCL*"dome of cap,"* LCL:B*"bill in front"*
   2) DCL*"dome of cap,"* LCL:openB*"wide brim"*
   3) DCL*"cap,"* (2h)DCL:openB->flat-O*"narrowing in front"*
   4) ICL*"pull over head,"* DCL*"dome of cap"*
   5) (2h)DCL:G*"strap over head,"* (2h)LCL:C*"muffs on ear"*

3. **Describe details.** Show how to describe details on hats. Make sure the details are described on the head as well.
   1) NAME (2h)DCL:G*"label across front of hat"*
   2) BLACK (2h)DCL:G*"trim around hat"*
   3) BLACK DCL:4*"stripes down the cap"*
   4) GRAY (2h)DCL:G*"trim around the cap"*
   5) FAKE fs-FUR

Now, demonstrate how to describe the hats following the sequence on the slide. Have students copy.

Picture 1

HAT BROWN, DCL*"dome of cap,"* LCL:B*"bill in front,"* NAME (2h)DCL:G*"label across front of hat"*

Picture 2

fs-STRAW HAT, DCL*"dome of cap,"* LCL:openB*"wide brim"* BLACK (2h)DCL:G*"trim around hat"*

Picture 3

HAT GRAY, DCL*"cap,"* (2h)DCL:openB->flat-O*"narrowing in front"* BLACK DCL:4*"stripes down the cap"*

Picture 4

HAT, BLACK ICL*"pull over head,"* DCL*"shape of cap"* GRAY (2h)DCL:G*"trim around the cap"*

Picture 5

BLACK, (2h)DCL:G*"strap over head,"* FAKE fs-FUR (2h)LCL:C*"muffs on ear"*

Review. Have students pair up and take turns describing hats on the slide to each other. Have the partners confirm the description by giving the corresponding number.

PRESENT
(LESSON SLIDE 7:8:2)

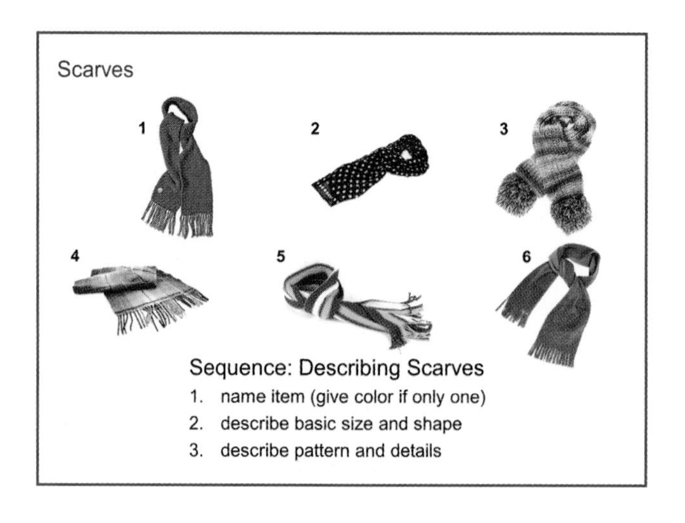
Scarves
1
2
3
4
5
6
Sequence: Describing Scarves
1. name item (give color if only one)
2. describe basic size and shape
3. describe pattern and details

SCARF

1. **Name item (give color if only one).** Introduce sign:
   (1–6) SCARF

2. **Describe basic size and shape.** Show how to describe the basic size and shape of the scarves. Be sure descriptions are made in neutral space.
   (1–4) (2h)DCL:C*"width and height of scarf"*

3. **Describe pattern and detail.** Show how to describe the pattern and details on the scarf. Make sure the details are described in neutral space as well.
   1) (2h)DCL:4*"fringes on both ends"*
   2) (2h)altDCL:F*"dots on scarf,"*
   3) (2h)DCL:C*"balls on ends,"*
   [(wh)DCL:C*"ball on end"*/DCL*"horizontal stripes on scarf"*]
   4) (2h)DCL:4*"fringes on both ends,"*
   [(wh) DCL:4*"fringes on one end*/DCL:4*"plaid on scarf"*
   5) (2h)DCL:4*"fringes on both ends,"*
   [(wh) DCL:4*"fringes on one end'*/
   DCL:G*"vertical stripes on scarf"*
   6) (2h)DCL:4*"fringes on both ends,"* (2h)DCL:C*"middle part"*
   GREEN, (2h)DCL:C*"end parts"* GRAY

Now, demonstrate how to describe the scarves following the sequence on the slide. Have students copy.

Picture 1

SCARF, BLUE (2h)DCL:C*"width and height of scarf,"*
(2h)DCL:4*"fringes on both ends"*

Picture 2

SCARF, BLACK (2h)DCL:C*"width and height of scarf,"* WHITE
(2h)altDCL:F*"dots on scarf,"* (2h)DCL:C*"end parts"* RED

Picture 3

SCARF (2h)DCL:C*"width and height of scarf,"*
(2h)DCL:C*"balls on ends,"* COLOR DIFFERENT++,
[(wh)DCL:C*"ball on end"*/DCL*"horizontal stripes on scarf"*]

Picture 4

SCARF, (2h)DCL:C*"width and height of scarf,"* (2h)DCL:4*"fringes on both ends,"* [(wh) DCL:4*"fringes on one end/* YELLOW, GREEN, WHITE DCL:4*"plaid on scarf"*]

Picture 5

SCARF (2h)DCL:C*"width and height of scarf,"* (2h)DCL:4*"fringes on both ends,"* [(wh) DCL:4*"fringes on one end/* PURPLE, WHITE DCL:G*"vertical stripes on scarf"*]

Picture 6

SCARF (2h)DCL:C*"width and height of scarf,"* (2h)DCL:4*"fringes on both ends,"* (2h)DCL:4*"fringes on both ends,"* (2h)DCL:C*"middle part"* GREEN, (2h)DCL:C*"end parts"* GRAY]

Review. Have students pair up and take turns describing scarves on the slide to each other. Have the partners confirm the description by giving the corresponding number.

PRACTICE *Describing Lost Items*

25–35 minutes

Students will describe items that are not present and confirm them.

PRESENT
(LESSON SLIDE 7:8:3)

Part 1 (**A** approaches B)
A: tell what is lost, ask if B has seen it
B: say no, ask A to describe it
A: describe
B: tell A you will check
Part 2 (**B** returns without the item)
B: add another description to confirm
A: confirm or correct
B: explain you will go get the item
Part 3 (**B** returns with the item)
B: ask if it is the correct item
A: confirm, express gratitude
B: respond

Tops and Coats (Round 1)

Review the sequence for describing a top or coat.

- name item (give color if only one)
- describe neckline and sleeve length
- describe pattern
- describe other details

Demonstrate both Signer A and B's lines. Have students copy.

Part 1 (A approaches B)

For ***"A: tell what is lost, ask if B has seen it"***

neg

T: ME LOSE JACKET. ME LOOK-FOR, CAN'T FIND.

q

YOU SEE IX-loc*"around."*

S: (copy)

For ***"B: say no, ask A to describe it"***

neg whq nod

T: NO++ FACE+SAME-AS "what," YOU DESCRIBE.

S: (copy)

For ***"A: describe"***

T: BLUE DCL*"chest,"* GREEN DCL*"sleeves"*

(2h)POCKET*"on front"* ZIPPER*"down front"*

S: (copy)

For ***"B: tell A you will check"***

T: ME GO-TO-location CHECK-location.

S: (copy)

Part 2 (B returns without the item)

For ***"B: add another description to confirm"***

q

T: YOUR JACKET HAVE ICL*"pull hood up"*

S: (copy)

For ***"A: confirm or correct"***

nod

T: YES, ICL*"pull hood up,"* YES.

S: (copy)

Part 3 (B returns with the item)

For ***"B: ask if it's the correct item"***

q

T: THAT-ONE

S: (copy)

For ***"A: confirm, express gratitude"***

nod

T: YES, THAT-ONE. THANK-YOU++

S: (copy)

For ***"B: respond"***

T: "pshaw" FINE++

S: (copy)

Now, put your top or coat out in the hallway or in a corner of the room and demonstrate the dialogue. Role play Signer A and have a student role play Signer B and find your item.

Activity. Collect students' tops and coats and place them out in the hallway or in a corner of the room (see **Preparation**). Pair up students and have them follow the dialogue to have their partners get their tops and coats.

Bags (Round 2)

Review the sequence for describing a bag.

- name item (give color if only one)
- describe size and shape and its handle
- describe details
- tell how it is handled or carried

Activity. Collect students' bags and place them out in the hallway or in a corner of the room (see **Preparation**). Have students change partners, and follow the dialogue to find their bags.

Hat, Scarf, Eyeglasses (Round 3)

Review the sequence for describing a hat, scarf or pair of sunglasses.

- name item (give color if only one)
- describe basic size and shape
- describe details

Activity. Collect students' hats, scarves or sunglasses, and place them out in the hallway or in a corner of the room (see **Preparation**). Have students change partners, and follow the dialogue to find their items.

EVALUATE

For each round, check to be sure all students:

- sign FACE+SAME-AS fluently
- orient the sign CHECK to the location of the item
- sign THAT-ONE with the correct non-manual signal
- follow the sequence to describe the item
- respond with "pshaw" FINE++.

HOMEWORK

Tell students to do **Homework 7:8** (*Student Workbook*, pages 47–52).

HOMEWORK FOLLOW-UP

35–45 MINUTES

Ask students to describe the item, then show slide to confirm. For example:

t whq
T: NUMBER 1 "what"
S: WHITE DCL*"baseball cap"*

PRESENT
(FOLLOW-UP SLIDE 7:8:1)

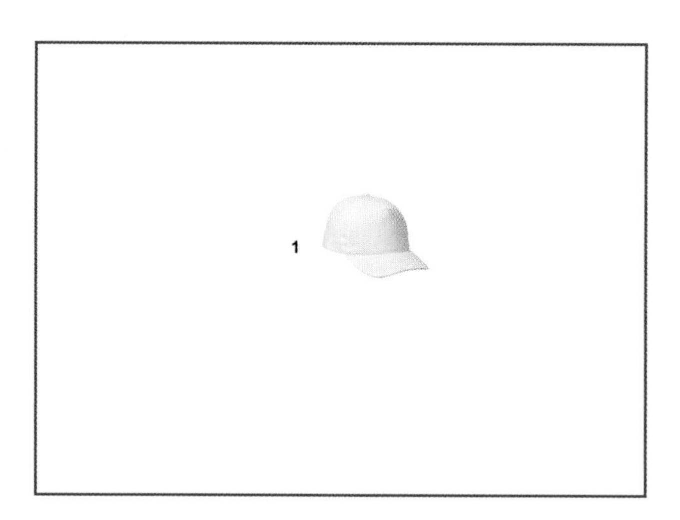

Then ask follow-up questions to get the other information given, for example:

whq (over GO-TO WHERE)

T: fs-AMBER GO-TO WHERE
S: fs-PARK

whq (over "what" HAPPEN "what")

T: "what" HAPPEN "what"
S: DCL*"strong wind blowing,"* HAT LCL:B*"fly off head and into river,"* WATER.

Show next slide to confirm the information.

PRESENT
(FOLLOW-UP SLIDE 7:8:2)

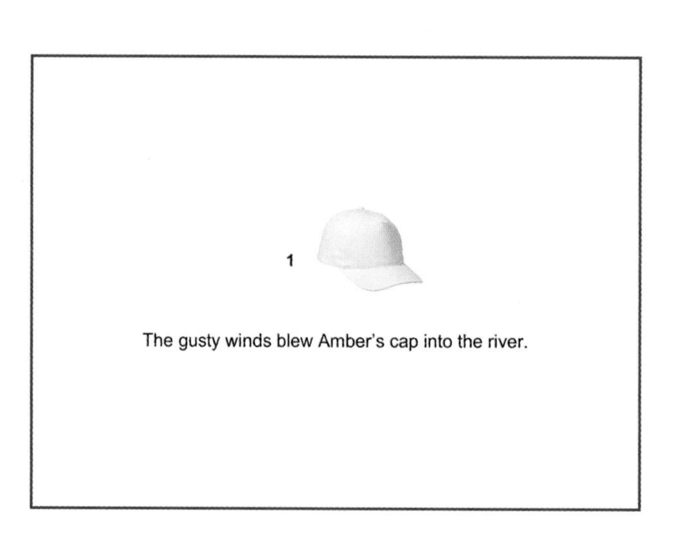

1
The gusty winds blew Amber's cap into the river.

Do the same for the remaining 11 items. (**Follow-up Slides 7:8:3–24**). Use the **Teacher's Guide** to develop your follow-up questions to get the other information given.

2 

Justin's nephew hid Justin's niece's handbag in the refrigerator.

3 

Suzanne's friend bought the briefcase. She didn't like it so she gave it to Suzanne.

4 

In July, JT went to San Francisco. He thought it was warm outside, so he put on a shirt. But when he went outside, it was cold and he didn't have a jacket with him.

5 

Amber found this hat in a trash can, tried it on, liked it, brought it home and washed it.

6 

For Christmas, Justin's Grandma gave him this t-shirt. He wears when working outdoors.

7 

Suzanne bought this scarf because the plaid pattern matched the pattern on her cousin's purse. Boy, was her cousin surprised when Suzanne gave it to her.

8 

Justin looked for but couldn't find his sister's jacket. He thought she might have left it at a friend's house. He called the friend. Sure enough, the jacket was there.

9 

Amber's sister bought this pair of sunglasses in Los Angeles so she could fit in.

10

One week after he purchased the sunglasses, JT put them on the passenger seat of his car. His friend sat on the seat and unknowingly crushed the sunglasses

11

Suzanne's aunt flew to San Francisco in July. At night, it was so cold she had to buy a jacket to stay warm.

12

Justin is surprised his uncle is a good knitter. He made that scarf.

LESSON 7:9

Numbers: Telling the Year

Lesson length: 35 minutes

LESSON GOAL

Students learn to sign year numbers.

KEY SKILLS

Basic year numbers

- give the first set of numbers
- shift your hand slightly to your dominant side
- then sign the second set of numbers

Years with 11–15

- the movement for numbers 11 through 15 (and 10) is not repeated
- for 13, 14, 15 flick fingers outward.

Years ending with 01–09

- when signing the second set of numbers, the palm faces out for numbers "0+1" through "0+5."

Years with two zero numbers in the middle

- give the first number
- slide the "0" handshape out from your dominant side
- give the final number (the palm faces out for numbers 1–5).

NOTIONS

Vocabulary

YEAR+ONE-IN-PAST (2 variations)
YEAR+TWO-IN-PAST
YEAR+THREE-IN-PAST
YEAR+FOUR-IN-PAST
YEAR+FIVE-IN-PAST

YEAR+ONE-IN-FUTURE
YEAR+TWO-IN-FUTURE
YEAR+THREE-IN-FUTURE
YEAR+FOUR-IN-FUTURE
YEAR+FIVE-IN-FUTURE

PREPARATION

Read and view **Numbers: Telling the Year** in *Student Workbook*, pages 53–54

Make sure to update **Lesson Slide 7:9:6** (see page 107)

MATERIALS

7:9 Lesson Slides
Exercise 1 (in *Student Workbook*, page 469)

HOMEWORK 7:9

Student Workbook, pages 53–56

INTRODUCE *Year Numbers*

15 minutes

PRESENT
(LESSON SLIDE 7:9:1)

Basic Year Numbers

1984	19+84
1992	19+92
1975	19+75

Demonstrate year numbers. Have students copy you.

Basic year numbers:

- give the first set of a year number, for example, "19"
- shift your hand slightly to the right (if you're right-handed)
- then sign the second set of numbers, for example, "84."

PRESENT
(LESSON SLIDE 7:9:2)

Years with Numbers 11 - 15

1911	19+**11**
1492	**14**+92
1913	19+**13**
1712	17+**12**

Years with 11–15:

- the movement for numbers 11 through 15 is not repeated at the beginning or the end of a number.
- for 13, 14, 15 flick fingers outward instead of inward.

PRESENT
(LESSON SLIDE 7:9:3)

Years Beginning with 20

2010	20+10
2011	20+11
2018	20+18
2030	20+30
2045	20+45

Years beginning with 20:

- in the first set of numbers ("20"), the movement is not repeated
- shift your hand slightly to your dominant side
- then sign the second set of numbers, for example, "10." The movement for the second set is also not repeated.

PRESENT
(LESSON SLIDE 7:9:4)

Years Ending with 01 - 09

1907	19+0+7
1801	18+0+1
1603	16+0+3

Years ending with 01– 09:

- give the first set of numbers, for example, "18"
- shift your hand slightly to your dominant side
- then sign the second set of numbers, for example, "0+1." The palm faces out for numbers "0+1" through "0+5."

PRESENT
(LESSON SLIDE 7:9:5)

Years with 00 in the Middle

2000 to 2009

Years with two zero numbers in the middle:

- give the number "2"
- slide the "0" handshape to your dominant side
- give the final number. The palm faces out for numbers 1–5.

PRESENT
(LESSON SLIDE 7:9:6)
(modify to indicate the last 5 years and the next 5 years. The slide is an example using 2014 as the present year)

Past	Present	Future
2008	2014	2015
2009		2016
2010		2017
2011		2018
2012		2019

Introduce these calendar time signs:

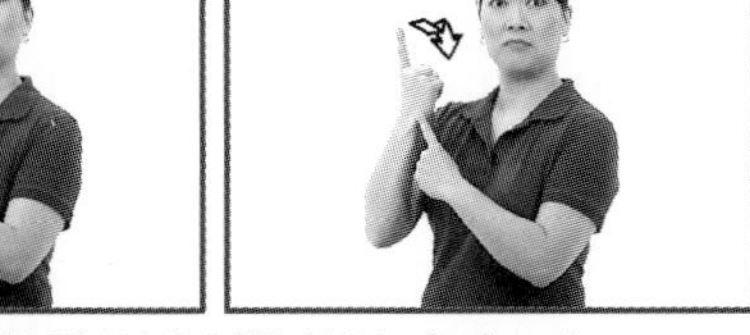

YEAR+ONE-IN-PAST (2 Variations)

YEAR+TWO-IN-PAST (2 Variations)

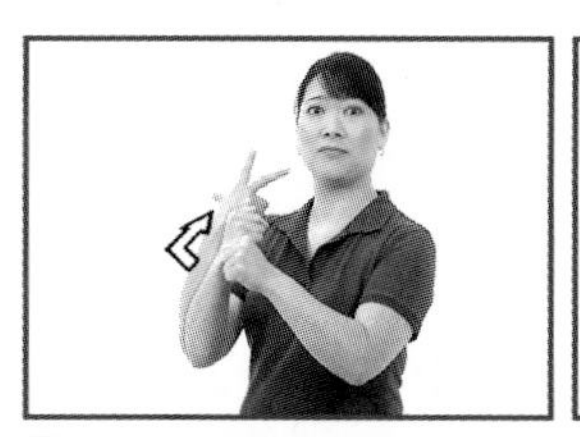

YEAR+THREE-IN-PAST (2 VARIATIONS)

YEAR+FOUR-IN-PAST (2 VARIATIONS)

YEAR+FIVE-IN-PAST (2 VARIATIONS)

YEAR+ONE-IN-FUTURE

YEAR+TWO-IN-FUTURE

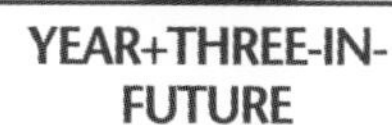

YEAR+THREE-IN-FUTURE

YEAR+FOUR-IN-FUTURE

YEAR+FIVE-IN-FUTURE

Review. Ask questions.
For example:

t whq
T: NOW+YEAR "what"
S: (give current year)

t whq
T: YEAR+ONE-IN-PAST YEAR "what"
S: (give year)

t whq
T: YEAR+THREE-IN-FUTURE YEAR "what"
S: (give year)

Now, have students practice the time signs. Ask different questions. For example:

t whq
T: (give the year number for next year), WHEN
S: YEAR+ONE-IN-FUTURE

t whq
T: (give the year number for two years ago), WHEN
S: YEAR+TWO-IN-PAST

Continue asking questions.

PRACTICE *Asking and Telling What Year*

20 minutes

Students will practice signing the correct form for a year number or a calendar time sign to answer questions in a survey.

EXERCISE 1: SURVEY

Have students open their *Student Workbook* to **page 469.** Review the questions before students do the survey.

For "*1. What year were you born?*"

t whq
T: YOU BE-BORN WHEN
S: (repeat)

For "*2. What year was the oldest member of your family born? Who?*"

t t t whq whq
T: YOUR FAMILY, OLD+EST PERSON, BE-BORN WHEN, WHO
S: (repeat)

For "*3. What year did you graduate from (pick one: high school, college)?*"

t whq
T: [fs-HS, COLLEGE] YOU GRADUATE , WHEN
S: (repeat)

For "*4. What year is your (pick one: car, motorcycle, bicycle)?*"

t whq
T: YOUR [CAR, MOTORCYCLE, BICYCLE], YEAR "what"

S: (repeat)

for "*5. What was the best year of your life?*"

t t whq
T: YOU BE-RAISED, !BEST! YEAR, "what"
S: (repeat)

Now, have each student survey four other students.

HOMEWORK

Tell students to do **Homework 7:9** (*Student Workbook*, pages 53–56).

HOMEWORK FOLLOW-UP
2–5 MINUTES

Discuss and give answer to the bonus question *"In 2069, Iva will be 100 years old, how old is she now?"*

1) first subtract 100 from 2069 to get Iva's birth year (1969)
2) then, subtract 1969 from the current year to get her age (For example, if the current year is 2014, the answer would be 45 years old.)

LESSON 7:10

Translating Sentences with "Have" 2

Lesson length: 30–40 minutes

LESSON GOAL

Students will use the appropriate sign to translate English sentences with "have" in them.

KEY SKILLS

Determine which sign in ASL conveys the same meaning as the word "have" in the English sentence

NOTIONS

Vocabulary

HAVE
MUST
FINISH
NONE
NOT-YET

MATERIALS

7:10 Lesson Slides
Exercise 2 (in *Student Workbook*, page 475)

HOMEWORK 7:10

Student Workbook, page 57

REVIEW

30–40 minutes

PRESENT
(LESSON SLIDE 7:10:1)

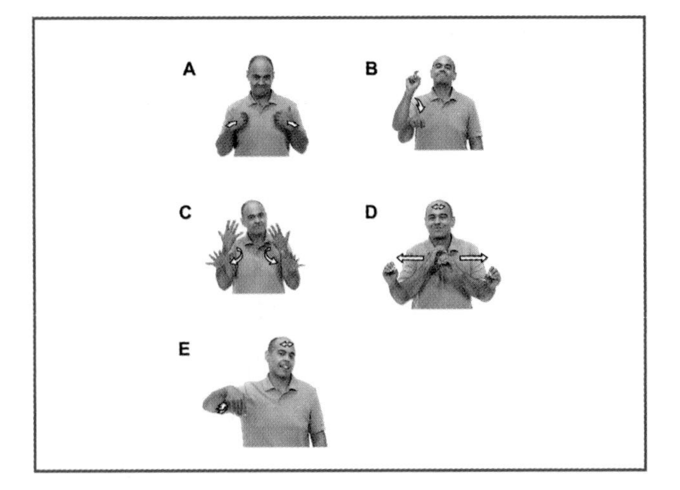

Review signs on the slide by having students create sentences using those signs.

Be sure students shake their heads when signing NONE and NOT-YET in their sentences.

EXERCISE 2 (page 475)

Now, ask students to open their *Student Workbook* and fill in the letters that represent the correct sign to use to translate "have" in each sentence. When students are done, check answers.

PRESENT
(LESSON SLIDES 7:10:2–21)

Exercise 2: Sentences with the word "have."

_____1. I don't have a plaid shirt.

Have students give their answer then confirm with the next slide. **Answer is D (NONE).**

Do the same with the rest of the sentences.

A **2.** My sister has three purses. **(HAVE)**
C **3.** Rita has already bought a dress. **(FINISH)**
E **4.** He hasn't seen that movie. **(NOT-YET)**
A **5.** I have sunglasses with orange frames. **(HAVE)**
B **6.** I have to call my doctor. **(MUST)**
B **7:** You have to tell her you're sorry. **(MUST)**
D **8.** The store doesn't have any leather jackets. **(NONE)**
E **9.** My daughter hasn't met her grandfather. **(NOT-YET)**
C, E **10.** I have bought the coat, but have yet to buy the hat. **(FINISH, NOT-YET)**

Pair Up. Have students translate the sentences.

When done, have students show their translations.

Teacher's translation guide:

t (over: SHIRT, DCL"plaid,") neg (over: ME NONE)
1. SHIRT, DCL*"plaid,"* ME NONE.

t (over: PURSE,)
2. PURSE, MY SISTER IX*"sister"* HAVE 3.

t (over: fs-RITA IX"Rita,")
3. fs-RITA IX*"Rita,"* FINISH BUY DRESS.

t (over: THAT-ONE MOVIE,) neg (over: NOT-YET SEE)
4. THAT-ONE MOVIE, IX*"man"* NOT-YET SEE.

t (over: fs-SUN+EYEGLASSES ORANGE DCL"frames,") nod (over: ME HAVE, ME)
5. fs-SUN+EYEGLASSES ORANGE DCL*"frames,"* ME HAVE, ME.

6. ME !MUST! PHONE-TO DOCTOR.

t (over: YOU)
7. YOU MUST TELL-her [YOU] SORRY.

t t neg
8. LEATHER JACKET, STORE IX*"store,"* NONE.

t neg
9. [MY] DAUGHTER IX*"daughter"* NOT-YET MEET POSS*"daughter"* GRANDFATHER.

t nod t neg
10. COAT, ME FINISH BUY. HAT, NOT-YET

HOMEWORK

Tell students to do **Homework 7:10** (*Student Workbook*, page 57).

LESSON 7:11

Culture: Greetings and Leave-takings

Lesson length: 45–65 minutes

LESSON GOAL

Students will practice culturally appropriate behaviors to greet others when they arrive at the classroom, and to say goodbye when they leave.

KEY BEHAVIORS

for Greetings

- making eye contact when greeting each other
- acknowledging each other when passing by nodding

for Leave-takings

- making eye contact with individuals when saying goodbye

NOTIONS

Greetings

"wave-hello"
"salute-hi"
HELLO

Following Up after Greeting

br
HOW YOU

whq
WHATS-UP

concerned-q
YOU FEEL BETTER, YOU

neg
NOT SEE-you UP-TIL-NOW

whq
WHERE YOU #BEEN

whq
WHERE YOU UP-TIL-NOW

Replying

FINE++ [THANK-YOU]

neg
NONE++, JUST-THE-SAME++

nod
YES, FEEL BETTER

Leave-takings

"wave-bye"

BYE-BYE

"thumb-up"

SEE-you LATER

SEE-you TOMORROW

MATERIALS **7:11 Lesson Slides**

HOMEWORK 7:11 *Student Workbook*, pages 58–62

INTRODUCE *Greetings*

5 minutes

PRESENT
(LESSON SLIDE 7:11:1)

Greetings

Greet everybody quickly as you enter the classroom.

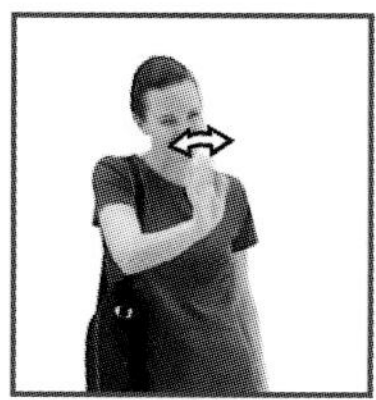
"wave-hello"

"salute-hi"

HELLO

Demonstrate how to greet everybody quickly as you enter a room. Introduce these greetings. Point out the importance of the "sweeping eye contact" as you move along and sign your greetings.

1. "wave-hello"
2. "salute-hi"
3. HELLO

PRACTICE *Greeting Everyone*

10–15 minutes

Students practice greeting everybody quickly as they enter the classroom.

Have half of the class leave the classroom and come in one by one. As students enter the class one by one, have them greet the class, starting with you, the teacher. After getting your "hello," the student is to greet everyone else while walking to their seat.

Switch with the other half, and continue until all students have had a chance to practice greeting.

Be sure students:

- use one of the three greetings
- use the "sweeping eye contact" with the greeting as they move to their seats.

INTRODUCE *Following Up after Greetings 1 and 2*

5 minutes

PRESENT
(LESSON SLIDE 7:11:2)

Following-up after Greetings 1

A & B: greet each other
A: **ask how is B**
B: **reply**
- **tell you are all right**
- **tell you are not all right**

A: respond

Review these phrases. Have students repeat.

For ***"A: ask how is B"***

br
T: HOW YOU
S: (repeat)

Point out:

- although "HOW" is a wh-word question sign, this phrase is usually signed with raised brows.

For ***"B: reply, tell you are all right"***
T: FINE++ [THANK-YOU]
S: (repeat)

For ***"B: reply, tell you are not all right"***
T: SO-SO or NOT FEEL GOOD or ME SICK
S: (repeat)

Point out:

- it is culturally acceptable to tell they are not all right rather than the typical "I'm fine."

Review. Pair students and have them go through the dialogue, alternating between the two replies for Signer B.

PRESENT
(LESSON SLIDE 7:11:3)

Following-up after Greetings 2

A & B: greet each other
A: **ask for an update**
B: reply
- **tell everything is the same**
- **tell about something recent that is not part of your routine**

A: respond

Introduce these phrases and have students copy:

WHATS-UP

For *"A: ask for an update"*

whq
T: WHATS-UP
S: (repeat)

NONE++,
JUST-THE-SAME++

For *"B: reply • tell everything is the same"*

neg
T: NONE++, JUST-THE-SAME++
S: (repeat)

For *"B: reply • tell about something recent that is not part of your routine"*
For example:
T: YESTERDAY, MY SISTER POSS*"sister"* HOUSE, ME HELP PAINT. ME !TIRED!

Point out:

- it is better to add an opinion about the unusual activity, like ME !TIRED!

Practice dialogue for ***"B: reply • tell everything is the same."*** You role play Signer A and call on different students to role play Signer B.

A: "wave-hello," "salute-hi" or HELLO
B: (greet)
whq
A: WHATS-UP
neg
B: NONE+++. JUST-THE-SAME++
A: OH-I-SEE

Practice dialogue for ***"B: reply • tell about something recent that is not part of your routine."*** You role play Signer A and call on different students to role play Signer B.

A: "wave-hello," "salute-hi" or HELLO
B: (greet)
whq
A: WHATS-UP
B: (fill in with their own information)
q
A: "wow" or REALLY or OH-I-SEE

Pair Practice. Have one student (B) remain sitting. Have the other student (A) approach B and begin a conversation. Switch roles and do the dialogue again.

Be sure students:

as Signer A:

- use a response appropriate for B's reply

as Signer B:

For ***"• tell about something recent that is not part of your routine":***

- describe an unusual event or activity
- end the description with an opinion.

INTRODUCE *Following Up after Greetings 3 and 4*

10 minutes

PRESENT
(LESSON SLIDE 7:11:4)

Following-up after Greetings 3

You know your classmate
has been sick.

A & B: greet each other
A: **ask about B's health**
B: **reply**
A: respond

Introduce phrases and have students copy:

For ***"A: ask about B's health"***

concerned-q
T: YOU FEEL BETTER, YOU
S: (repeat)

For ***"B: reply"***

nod ... neg
T: YES, FEEL BETTER or #NO, ME STILL NOT FEEL+GOOD;
neg
or #NO, ME STILL SICK
S: (repeat)

You role play Signer A and call on different students to role play Signer B and demonstrate different possible responses.

A: "wave-hello," "salute-hi" or HELLO
B: (greet)
q
A: YOU FEEL BETTER, YOU
B: (reply)
q
A: GOOD or REALLY or OH-I-SEE or SORRY

PRESENT
(LESSON SLIDE 7:11:5)

Following-up after Greetings 4

Your classmate has been absent for a while.

A & B: greet each other
A: **comment on absence to person**
- **you don't know well**
- **you know well**

B: explain absence
A: respond

UP-TILL-NOW

Introduce phrases and have students copy:

For "A comment on absence to person"

- ***"you don't know well"***

neg
T: **NOT SEE-you UP-TIL-NOW.**
S: (repeat)

- ***"you know well"***

whq
T: **WHERE YOU #BEEN.**
S: (repeat)

whq
T: **WHERE YOU UP-TIL-NOW.**
S: (repeat)

Practice. You role play Signer B and call on different students to role play Signer A and to practice the phrases for *"A: comment on absence."*

INTRODUCE *Leave-takings*

5–10 minutes

PRESENT
(SLIDE 7:11:6)

Leave-takings

Say goodbye as you leave the classroom.

"wave-bye"

"BYE-BYE"

"thumb-up"

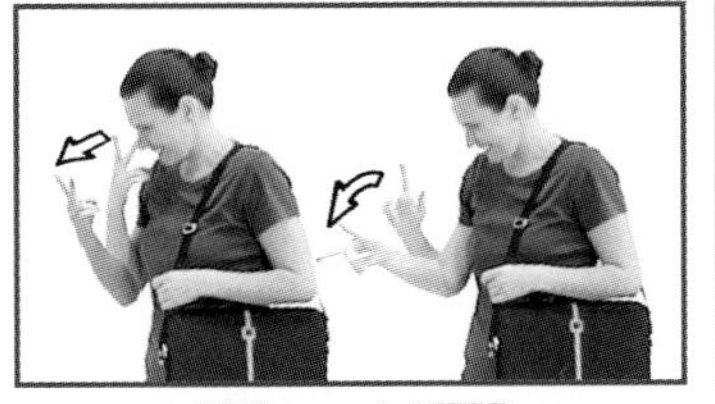
SEE-you LATER

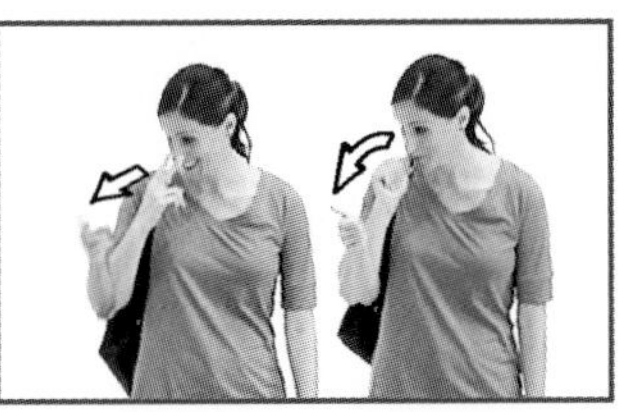
SEE-you TOMORROW
(or WEDNESDAY)

Introduce these phrases.

1. "wave-bye"
2. BYE-BYE
3. "thumb-up"
4. SEE-you LATER
5. SEE-you TOMORROW (or WEDNESDAY)

Then, demonstrate these phrases as you leave the classroom. Be sure you make eye contact with individuals as you say your goodbyes to them, and point that out.

PRACTICE *Signing Goodbye as One Leaves the Room*

5–10 minutes

Students practice using a "goodbye" phrase and making eye contact with individuals as they leave the classroom.

Have students, one by one, leave the classroom and practice signing goodbyes. Be sure they:

- use one of the phrases
- make eye contact with the students as they sign the goodbye phrase.

NOTE: Explain to students in the future class sessions, they are to greet each other as they arrive, and say goodbye to each other as they leave at end of class.

HOMEWORK

Tell students to do **Homework 7:11** (*Student Workbook*, pages 58–62).

Also, students are to observe greetings and leave taking in the Deaf event and compare those to their own culture. (See **Assignment**, *Student Workbook*, page 62.)

HOMEWORK FOLLOW-UP

Collect students' papers "Observations: Greetings and Leave-taking." Read and comment. (See **Assignment** in *Student Workbook*, page 62.)

LESSON 7:12

Translating Sentences with "Drive To," "Take" and "Pick Up" 2

Lesson length: 30–40 minutes

LESSON GOAL

Students will practice translating sentences with "drive to," "take," and "pick up."

KEY SKILLS

- maintain spatial agreement in the translation
- add either TAKE-FROM or PICK-UP to DRIVE-TO, if there is a direct object
- add DROP-OFF, CARRY-TO, GO-TO, or DRIVE-TO to TAKE-FROM to indicate the person was transported

NOTIONS

Vocabulary

Phrases

TAKE-FROM-location, DRIVE-TO-location
TAKE-FROM-location, DROP-OFF-location
TAKE-FROM-location, GO-TO-location
GO-TO-location PICK-UP-person, DROP-OFF-location
GO-TO-location PICK-UP-person, DRIVE-TO-location
GO-TO-location PICK-UP-person, CARRY-TO-location

MATERIALS

7:12 Lesson Slides
7:12 Follow-up Slides

HOMEWORK 7:12

Student Workbook, page 63

REVIEW "To Take or Pick Up" and "To Drive"

20 minutes

PRESENT
(LESSON SLIDE 7:12:1)

I drove to work.
I drove her to work.

Review
1. spatial agreement
2. lexical and grammatical differences

Spatial agreement. Point to *"I drove to work."* Ask students how to translate this sentence.

S: ME **DRIVE-TO-work** WORK.

Make sure students sign WORK in the same location as where DRIVE-TO ends.

Vary locations of the work place, for example, to student's left, right side, and in front and ask them to sign the sentence again.

Lexical and grammatical differences. Point to *"I drove her to work."* Have students translate this sentence, using various phrases. For example:

S: WOMAN IX*"right,"* ME **TAKE-FROM-right, DRIVE-TO-left** WORK.

Other possible phrases:

- TAKE-FROM-right, DROP-OFF-left
- TAKE-FROM-right, GO-TO-left
- GO-TO-right PICK-UP-woman, DROP-OFF-left
- GO-TO-right PICK-UP-woman, DRIVE-TO-left
- GO-TO-right PICK-UP-woman, CARRY-TO-left

TEACHER TO TEACHER

If needed, review "2. lexical and grammatical differences":
- ***The sign DRIVE-TO can not take a direct object as the English word "drive" can. Add sign TAKE-FROM, or PICK-UP to complete the translation.***
- ***The sign TAKE-FROM means getting someone only. It does not include transporting the person like the English "to take" does. Add sign DROP-OFF, CARRY-TO, GO-TO, or DRIVE-TO to indicate "transporting the person."***

Review. Have students sign the second sentence "I drove her to work" with the different phrases again. This time, vary the locations of the woman and workplace. For example:
- the woman on their left, and workplace on their right
- the woman on their left, and workplace in front of them.

Make sure the movement of the verb signs agree with the locations established for the signer, the woman, and workplace.

PRESENT
(LESSON SLIDES 7:12:2 AND 7:12:3)

1. My uncle drove to work.
2. My parents took me to church.
3. I dropped her off at work.
4. She took me to a restaurant.
5. My aunt drove me to the hospital.

Ask students to translate the sentences. Make sure they:
- maintain spatial agreements,
- add the verbs TAKE-FROM or PICK-UP to DRIVE-TO, if there is a direct object,
- add the verbs DROP-OFF, CARRY-TO, GO-TO, or DRIVE-TO to TAKE-FROM to indicate the person was transported.

Teacher's translation guide:

> **NOTE:** The other verb phrases can be used in the translation instead of the ones below.

1. *"My uncle drove to work."*
   MY UNCLE [IX*"uncle"*] DRIVE-TO*"work"* WORK.

2. *"My parents took me to church."*
   MOTHER+FATHER THEY-TWO TAKE-FROM-my location,
   GO-TO-church CHURCH.

3. *"I dropped her off at work."*
   ____________________t
   WOMAN IX*"woman,"* ME-TAKE-FROM-her location,
   DROP-OFF-work WORK.

4. *"She took me to a restaurant."*
   ___________________t
   WOMAN IX*"woman"* TAKE-FROM-my location,
   GO-TO-restaurant RESTAURANT.

5. *"My aunt drove me to the hospital."*
   ___________________t
   MY AUNT IX*"aunt"* TAKE-FROM-my location,
   DRIVE-TO-hospital, HOSPITAL.

6. *"Yesterday my dad drove to Dale's house."*
   YESTERDAY, MY FATHER IX*"father"* DRIVE-TO-house
   fs-DALE POSS*"Dale"* HOUSE.

7: *"I dropped him off at the train station."*
   _______________t
   MAN IX*"man,"* ME TAKE-FROM-his location,
   DROP-OFF-train-station TRAIN.

8. *"I brought the dog home from the veterinarian."*
   _______________________________t
   ME GO-TO-veterinarian fs-VET, PICK-UP-dog #DOG,
   CARRY-TO-home HOME.

9. *"My father took my son to school."*

t t

MY SON IX*"son,"* MY FATHER IX*"father,"* father-TAKE-FROM-son's location, DROP-OFF-school SCHOOL.

10. *"I will bring my mother to the party."*

t

MY MOTHER IX*"mother,"* ME IN-FUTURE PICK-UP-mother, mother-CARRY-TO-party PARTY.

HOMEWORK

Tell students to do **Homework 7:12** (*Student Workbook*, page 63). Have students sign their translations. Correct if needed.

HOMEWORK FOLLOW-UP
10–15 MINUTES

PRESENT
(FOLLOW-UP SLIDES 7:12:1–8)

Translate the following sentences:

1. My friend will take me home after school.

Teacher's translation guide:

NOTE: The other verb phrases can be used in the translation instead of the ones below.

1. *My friend will take me home after school.*
   when
   SCHOOL FINISH, MY FRIEND [IN–FUTURE] TAKE-FROM-my location DROP-OFF-home HOME.

2. *I drove four of my friends to see the show.*
   FRIEND, THEY-FOUR, ME TAKE-FROM-friends' location, DRIVE-TO-show PERFORMANCE.

3. I brought my mother home from the party.
   t
   MOTHER, IX-loc*"party"* PARTY, ME GO-TO-party PICK-UP-her, CARRY-TO-home HOME.

4. *Yesterday I took my niece to soccer practice.*
   YESTERDAY, MY NIECE IX*"niece"* ME TAKE-FROM-niece's location, GO-TO-practice SOCCER PRACTICE.

5. *When will you drive your family to San Francisco?*
   YOU TAKE-FROM-family's location FAMILY, DRIVE-TO fs-SF,
   whq
   WHEN

6. *We need to take the baby to the hospital.*
   t
   BABY, US-TWO MUST TAKE-FROM-baby's location, CARRY-TO-hospital HOSPITAL.

7. *My friend took me to the ballgame.*
   MY FRIEND COME-TO-here PICK-UP-me, DRIVE-TO-ballpark. BASEBALL GAME.

8. *My daughter wanted to come home, so I went and got her.*
   nod
   MY DAUGHTER WANT COME-TO-home HOME. FINE++ ME GO- TO-daughter's location PICK-UP-her CARRY-TO-here [HOME].

LESSON 7:13

Comprehension: The Family Portrait

Lesson length: 20–60 minutes

LESSON GOAL

Students will develop comprehension and production skills through the story **The Family Portrait**.

KEY SKILLS

For comprehension: Students will develop the ability to process larger chunks of information and figure out the meaning of a sign from context.

For production: Students will build fluency by re-telling the story or by asking questions about the story.

NOTIONS

Vocabulary

Possible new signs in the story

USE	DARK+BLUE
SAME-AS-arc	PROCEED/GO-AHEAD
BE-RELIEVED	PCL*"family members sitting together"*
!TIME!	NEXT+TIME
PICTURE+ER	MYSELF
WAIT	

PREPARATION

- View the story **The Family Portrait** on **Lesson Slide 7:13:1**.
- Decide which Comprehension and Production activities to use.

MATERIALS

7:13 Lesson Slides
7:13 Follow-up Slides

HOMEWORK 7:13

Student Workbook, pages 64–68

INTRODUCE *The Family Portrait*

5–10 minutes

PRESENT
(LESSON SLIDE 7:13:1)

Show the story. Then, do one of the options below.

Comprehension:

- quiz (page 132)
- answer questions (page 133)

Production:

- develop questions to ask (page 137)
- re-tell the story (page 137)
- change details of the story (page 137)

COMPREHENSION

15-30 minutes

Students will develop the ability to process larger chunks of information and figure out the meaning of a sign from context.

QUIZ (15–30 minutes)

Students write down the information given in the story. Collect papers and grade their papers using FC (full credit), PC (partial credit) or NC (no credit).

FC (full credit) = details are accurate and complete; one or two minor details may be missing, such as age of a grandchild

PC (partial credit) = sufficient details to show satisfactory comprehension of story, actions or cause and effect, but few significant details missing or incorrect, such as naming the mother instead of father doing the specific action

NC (no credit) = does not show sufficient comprehension of story, actions or cause/effect to follow along

Return the papers. Pair off "FC" with "PC" or "NC" students.

- Give the "FC" students a minute to read their own papers and review the story.
- Have the "PC" students ask the "FC" students questions to find out what they got wrong or missed and make corrections on their papers.
- Have the "FC" students sign the story so the "NC" students can rewrite their papers.

Check the "PC" or "NC" students' corrected papers.

ANSWER QUESTIONS (20–30 minutes)

First, pair off students and have them fill each other in on what happened in the story. If there is anything in the story they don't understand, have them ask other students to get clarification.

Then, ask the following questions:

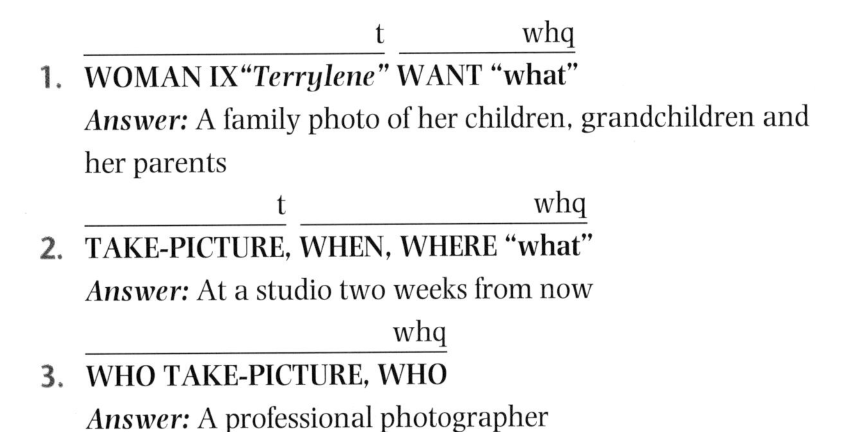

1. (t) (whq)
   WOMAN IX*"Terrylene"* WANT "what"
   Answer: A family photo of her children, grandchildren and her parents
2. (t) (whq)
   TAKE-PICTURE, WHEN, WHERE "what"
   Answer: At a studio two weeks from now
3. (whq)
   WHO TAKE-PICTURE, WHO
   Answer: A professional photographer

4. **WOMAN IX"*Terrylene*" WANT FAMILY IX-mult**
   USE CLOTHES,^t **FACE+SAME-AS "what"**^whq
   Answer: Blue jeans, black shirt, crew neck and long sleeved.

5. **!TIME! TAKE-PICTURE,**^t **FAMILY IX-mult USE "what"**^whq
   Answer:
   - Her mom was wearing a black turtleneck shirt.
   - Her father was wearing a dark blue shirt (he thought it was black).
   - Her middle daughter and son came dressed correctly.
   - Then she saw that her oldest daughter and her children dressed correctly. But the daughter's husband was wearing a black collared shirt with buttons.

7: **NEXT+TIME TAKE-PICTURE,**^t **WOMAN IX "Terrylene" (2h)#DO++**^whq
   Answer: Next time she will buy the shirts herself.

Show video again. Make sure students understand those possible new signs, and if needed, use one of the strategies below to explain the meaning.

- list things in a category
- give the opposite sign if known
- describe or act out situation
- give definition using familiar signs

signs	*definitions*
 USE	Definition: to wear; to have clothes on one's body
 SAME-AS-arc	Definition: to be similar, to be the same (everyone in the group dresses alike or have the same color shirt)

BE-RELIEVED

Definition:
reacting with feeling of relief from fear or worry; to be relieved

TIME!

Definition:
when the time came (to do something)

PICTURE+ER

Definition:
photographer: one who takes pictures

WAIT

Definition:
to wait; to stay in place for a while

DARK+BLUE

Definition:
dark blue

GO-AHEAD

Definition:
to proceed or carry on with an activity

PCL *"family members sitting together"*

Definition:
used to show arrangement of people during photo shoot

NEXT+TIME

Definition:
the next time

MYSELF

Definition:
me personally; myself

PRODUCTION

15 minutes

Students will build fluency by re-telling the story or by asking questions about the story.

After showing the video, and making sure students understand the story and all the signs, choose one of these activities:

- **DEVELOP QUESTIONS TO ASK** (20–30 minutes)
  Pair up students and assign one student to develop true or false questions and the other wh-word questions. Have them ask each other questions.

- **RE-TELL STORY** (15–20 minutes)
  Pair up students and have them repeat the story to each other.

- **CHANGE DETAILS OF THE STORY** (45–60 minutes)
  Pair up students and have them collaborate to change the details of the story. For example, change what everyone was supposed to wear, the reason for the portrait, who is in it, who wears the wrong thing, and the conclusion. Then, have students mingle and tell their versions of the story.

HOMEWORK

Tell students to do **Homework 7:13** (*Student Workbook*, pages 64–68).

HOMEWORK FOLLOW-UP
3–15 MINUTES

Review answers to **A Memorable Costume** (*Student Workbook*, page 64).

Option 1: show answers on **7:13 Follow-up Slides** and have students check their answers in *Student Workbook.*

Option 2: for more language practice, sign the questions from the *Student Workbook* and have students sign their answers.

For example:

"1. How old were Amber and her brother?"

t

T: fs-AMBER, POSS"*Amber*" BROTHER THEY-TWO

whq

HOW-OLD

Answer. Amber was 10–11 years old and her brother 7 or 8 years old.

"2. What traditionally happens at school for Halloween?"

t t whq

T: HALLOWEEN SCHOOL, IX"*school*" TEND-TO (2h)#DO++

Answer. The kids dressed up and marched in a Halloween parade. The ones with interesting, pretty costumes were given a blue ribbon.

"3. One Halloween, what did Amber and her brother want to be?"

t t whq

T: ONE-TIME, THEY-TWO WANT, DRESS "what"

Answer. They wanted to be a mouse.

"4. Explain what they did to make the costume."

t whq

T: THEY-TWO MAKE DRESS, THEY-TWO (2h)#DO++.

***Answer*—the head.** Consists of three balloons. One large one for the head, two small ones for the ears. Then they covered the balloon with paper mache. When the balloons were popped, the eyes were cut out, the mask was painted gray with white around the eyes, and black whiskers, and a smile.

the body—Gray exercise shirt (crew neck and long sleeve); pants (with drawstring); and tail is sewn onto the back of the pants.

"5. What did they win?"

whq

T: THEY-TWO WIN "what"

Answer. Nothing, but they had fun!

UNIT 7 REVIEW

Putting It All Together

Lesson length: 75–90 minutes

LESSON GOAL

Students will:

- practice describing differences in appearance, clothing, accessories, and body positions
- practice describing appearance, clothing, and accessories and giving additional information about them
- practice identifying a person
- comprehend commonly fingerspelled words and practice fingerspelling the words
- discuss memorable clothing items or accessories to review vocabulary and grammar practiced in this unit

NOTIONS

Vocabulary

vocabulary previously learned

PREPARATION

Make copies of **7UR Person A** and **Person B** (for **Find the Differences** on page 140)

MATERIALS

7UR Lesson Slides
7UR Person A and Person B
Exercise 3 (in *Student Workbook*, pages 485–486)

HOMEWORK

Student Workbook, page 69 (**Self-Assessment**)

PRACTICE *Find the Differences*

10 minutes

Students practice describing differences in appearance, clothing, accessories, and body positions.

Pair up students. Distribute **Person A** to half the class and **Person B** to the other half.

PRESENT
(LESSON SLIDE 7:UR:1)

Find the Differences

Without looking at your partner's picture, find the differences between the two pictures.

Be ready to describe the differences afterwards.

Demonstrate how to check for the differences and have students copy you.

T (for Person A): MY PICTURE, WOMAN HAT

DCL*"brimmed hat."* DCL:G*"trim around hat"* YOUR SAME-AS (q)

T (for Person B): #NO (neg), MY PICTURE WOMAN HAT

DCL*"beret cap,"* FLOWER (2h)altDCL:C*"flowers"*

Conclude. Call on students to tell you how their picture was different from their partners' picture. Demonstrate how to make the statement.

t

T: MY PICTURE, WOMAN HAT DCL*"beret cap."*

t

POSS PICTURE, WOMAN HAT DCL*"brimmed hat."*

Continue calling on students until all differences have been described.

Teacher's Guide

DIFFERENCES	PERSON A	PERSON B
1. hat	brimmed hat with band	beret cap with flowery pattern
2. hair	wavy/curly	straight
3. eyeglasses shape	round	cat-eye
4. jacket	pockets; sleeves not rolled up	no pockets; sleeves rolled up
5. blouse/shirt	swirly design; with bow	plain; scoop neck
6. scarf	no scarf	scarf
7. objects in hands	left hand holding handbag, right hand holding flowers	right hand holding handbag, left hand holding flowers
8. handbags	large hand-carrying strap purse	briefcase-style bag; short carrying handle
9. stickers on bags	New York and Miami	New York and California
10. pants	plaid	stripes
11. shoes	laced	slip-on

PRACTICE *Distinguishing Objects*

15–20 minutes

Students practice describing appearance, clothing, and accessories and giving additional information about them.

EXERCISE 3

Have students open *Student Workbook* to pages 485–486.

Pair off students and have them take turns identifying an item in each row, and giving additional information about the item. Their partner is to circle the item and record the information below the picture.

PRACTICE *Commonly Fingerspelled Words*

10 minutes

Students comprehend commonly fingerspelled words and practice fingerspelling the words.

Create sentences with fingerspelled words from **Lesson 7:2**, sign the sentences and have students write down the fingerspelled words. Some ideas to get you started:

- My shirts are all **cotton**.
- I can't wear **wool**. Makes me itch (scratch).
- I left my **wallet** on the train.
- My grandmother gave me her **fur** wrap. I don't want it.
- My shoe **size** is (give number).
- I need to buy a new **suit** for a wedding.
- My **vest** is reversible. One side is black **nylon** and the other side is red **silk**.

When done, have students fingerspell the words to you. Write the words on the board and check students' fingerspelling forms.

PRACTICE *Describing Memorable Items*

25–30 minutes

Students discuss memorable clothing items or accessories to review vocabulary and grammar practiced in this unit.

PRESENT
(LESSON SLIDE 7:UR:2)

Tell about a memorable clothing item or accessory.

Include the following:

- how you got the item
- description of item
- what the item is made of
- how often you use or wear it and where
- where the item is now or what happened to it

Group. Put students into groups of three or four. Have them take turns describing their memorable items.

HOMEWORK

Tell students to do **Homework** (*Student Workbook*, page 69).

NOTES:

UNIT 8

Making Requests and Asking for Advice

LESSON 8:1

Making Requests

Lesson length: 80–115 minutes

LESSON GOAL

Students will sign this dialogue:

Dialogue

A: explain situation, make request
B: decline, give reason

KEY PHRASES

q
NOT-MIND (do favor)

NOTIONS

Vocabulary

requesting

pleading/q
NOT-MIND

declining

neg
NOT-KNOW fs-HOW

verbs

(plane) TAKE-OFF
CONNECT
MISS (class)
PLAN
POSTPONE
WONDER
LAG-BEHIND (work)
CATCH-UP
USE
WAIT++
APPEAR
LOSE-object
LEAVE-ALONE

nouns

TICKET
PERFORMANCE
ADDRESS
BOSS
NEW-YORK
AIRPLANE/AIRPORT
FUNERAL

technology-related
PRINTER
SCANNER
INTERNET

time-related
RECENT

others

MYSELF	THROUGH
BE-MIND-STUPID	MAYBE
fs-OT	ALL-INCLUSIVE

PREPARATION Familiarize yourself with **Requests 1–6** on **Lesson Slides 8:1:2; 4; 6; 13; 15** and **17.**

MATERIALS **8:1 Lesson Slides**
8:1 Follow-up Slides

HOMEWORK 8:1 *Student Workbook*, pages 74–85

WARM-UP *Requests around the Classroom*

3–5 minutes

Introduce request sign:

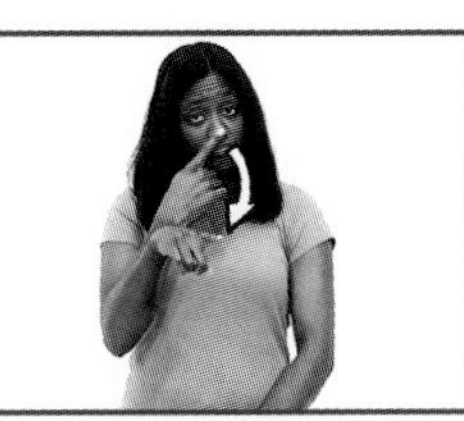

pleading/q
NOT-MIND

Request students do different things around the classroom using this request sign. Do the following:

pleading/q
T: (to S1) **NOT-MIND** DOOR IX*"door"* YOU OPEN-DOOR
S1: (opens door)

whq
T: (to all) ME TELL-TO-S1 "what"

pleading/q
S(all): **NOT-MIND** DOOR IX*"door"* YOU OPEN-DOOR

T: (to S2) **NOT-MIND**, CHAIR IX*"chair"* YOU
pleading/q
MOVE-TO *"different location"*
S2: (moves chair)

whq
T: (to all) ME TELL-TO-S2 "what"

S(all): **NOT-MIND**, CHAIR IX*"chair"* YOU
pleading/q
MOVE-TO *"different location"*

Do the same with other requests:
WINDOW, OPEN/CLOSE-WINDOW
LIGHT, ECL*"turn on/off lights"*
TABLE, MOVE-TO*"different location"*
DCL*"chalkboard,"* ICL*"erase board"*

INTRODUCE *Making Requests 1*

30–45 minutes

PRESENT

(LESSON SLIDES 8:1:1 AND 8:1:2)

A: Explain situation, make request
Request 1

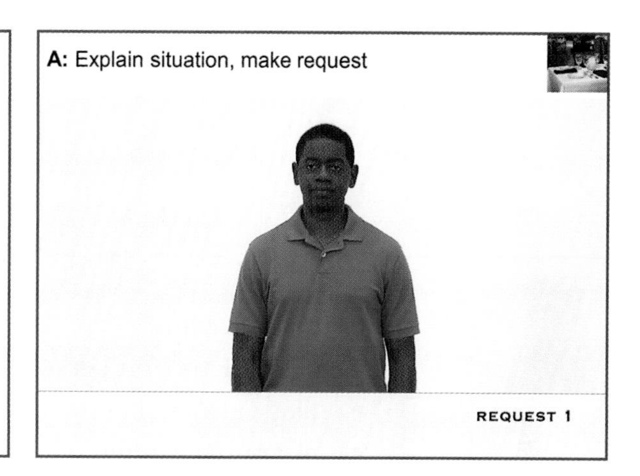
A: Explain situation, make request
REQUEST 1

PLAN

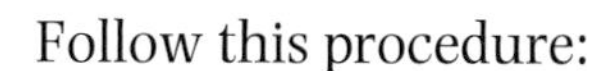

Follow this procedure:

- show picture on **Lesson Slide 8:1:1**
- play video on **Lesson Slide 8:1:2**
- clear up meanings of new signs (in bold below)
- have students practice **Request 1** (below).

BOSS

Request 1

Explain situation

REMEMBER TONIGHT US-TWO **PLAN**[1] LEAVE-FOR

q neg

EAT. (shake head). MY **BOSS** TELL-ME MUST WORK **fs-OT** 3-HOUR. "well"

POSTPONE

(make request) NOT-MIND YOU PHONE-TO-restaurant

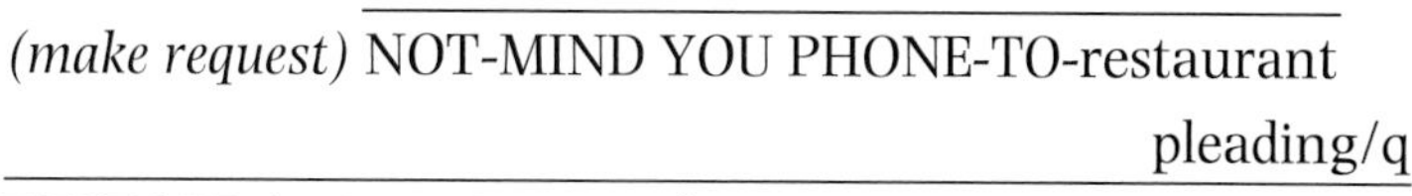

pleading/q

RESTAURANT **POSTPONE**[2] TOMORROW NIGHT, "well."

---

[1] To explain PLAN—make a schedule on board. Fill in some days with activities, leaving some days empty. Then contrast days you have plans (PLAN) with days nothing is planned (NONE PLAN).

[2] To explain POSTPONE—write on board today's date and appointment at 2:30. Then say you cannot go to your appointment today at 2:30. Introduce (POSTPONE) to change to tomorrow's date, same time (2:30).

PRESENT

(LESSON SLIDES 8:1:3–4)

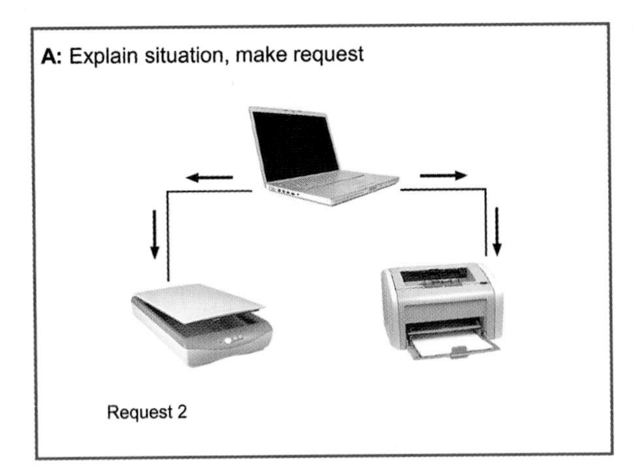
A: Explain situation, make request
Request 2

A: Explain situation, make request
REQUEST 2

Repeat procedure:

- show picture on **Lesson Slide 8:1:3**
- play video on **Lesson Slide 8:1:4**
- clear up meanings of new signs (in bold below)
- have students practice **Request 2** (below).

RECENT

PRINTER

Request 2

(explain situation) **RECENT**[3] BUY NEW, COMPUTER, **PRINTER, SCANNER**[4]. BUT ME MUST **MYSELF CONNECT++**[5]. "well" ME **BE-MIND-STUPID**[6].

(make request) NOT-MIND YOU COME-TO-here MY HOUSE HELP

pleading/q

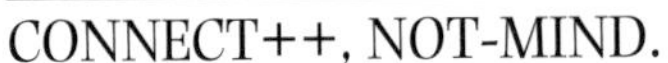

CONNECT++, NOT-MIND.

SCANNER

MYSELF

CONNECT++

BE-MIND-STUPID

[3] **To explain RECENT**—write on board "specified time sign" and "unspecified time sign" and compare two sentences, IN-PAST NIGHT TIME+11:45 ME SEE #DOG (specified), and RECENT ME SEE #DOG (unspecified). If needed give another pair of sentences, IN-PAST 19+40 GRANDMOTHER BE-BORN (specified), and LONG-AGO GRANDMOTHER BE-BORN (unspecified).

[4] **To explain SCANNER**—describe finding a picture you like, putting it in a scanner, pushing a button, and seeing the picture on the computer.

[5] **To explain CONNECT**—describe putting cords between the computer, printer and scanner.

[6] **To explain BE-MIND-STUPID (not knowing how to)**—Use Rubik's Cube as an example of something you can't figure out, therefore you are BE-MIND-STUPID.

PRESENT

(LESSON SLIDES 8:1:5–6)

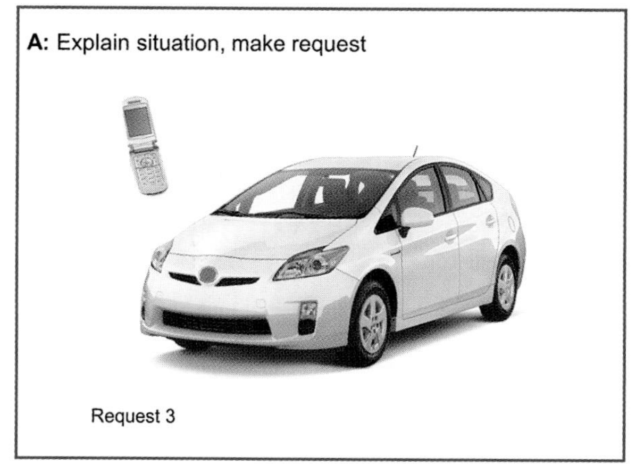
A: Explain situation, make request
Request 3

A: Explain situation, make request
REQUEST 3

Repeat procedure:

- show picture on **Lesson Slide 8:1:5**
- play video on **Lesson Slide 8:1:6**
- clear up meanings of new signs (in bold below)
- have students practice **Request 3** (below).

Request 3

(t over "MY fs-CELL+PHONE"; neg over "CAN'T+FIND")

(explain situation) MY fs-CELL+PHONE, CAN'T+FIND. ME THINK **LOSE-object**. PHONE IX*"phone"* HAVE PICTURE, **ADDRESS**[7], PHONE NUMBER **ALL-INCLUSIVE**[8]. ME MUST FIND. ME THINK **MAYBE** ME **LEAVE-ALONE** YOUR CAR.

(pleading/q over "NOT-MIND YOU GO-TO-car CHECK")

(make request) **NOT-MIND** YOU GO-TO-car CHECK

LOSE-object

ADDRESS

ALL-INCLUSIVE

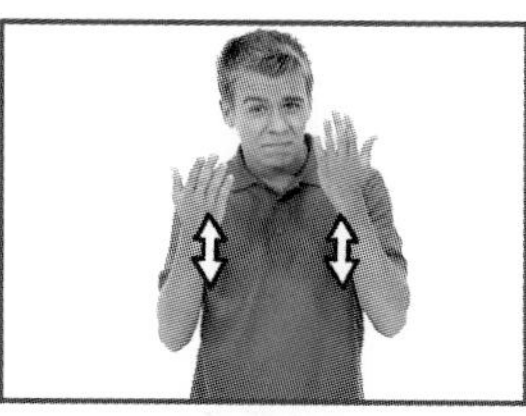

MAYBE

LEAVE-ALONE

---

[7] To explain ADDRESS—write several addresses on the board, point to them and sign ADDRESS.

[8] To explain ALL-INCLUSIVE—compare old cell phone with current cell phone. Old phone holds phone numbers only. Current cell phone holds phone numbers, pictures, videos, music, games, etc., (ALL-INCLUSIVE).

PRESENT
(LESSON SLIDE 8:1:7)

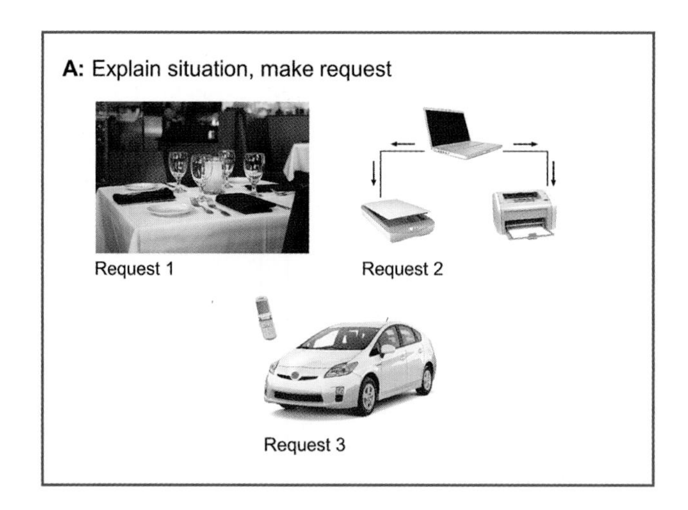
A: Explain situation, make request
Request 1
Request 2
Request 3

Review. Pair up students and have them practice signing **Requests 1–3** to each other.

PRACTICE *Declining Requests 1*

20 minutes

Students practice making and declining **Requests 1–3**.

PRESENT
(LESSON SLIDE 8:1:8)

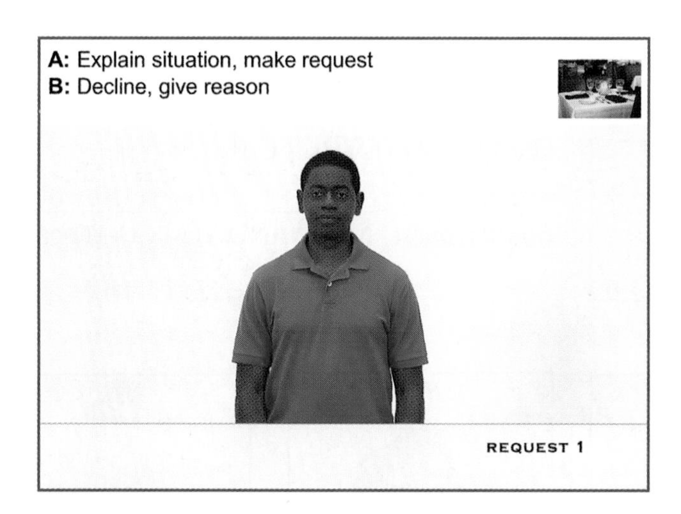
A: Explain situation, make request
B: Decline, give reason
REQUEST 1

Show **Request 1** video again. Role play Signer B to demonstrate the "decline" response below. Have students copy.

For ***"B: decline, give reason"***

regretful/neg

T: SORRY. CAN'T. MY fs-CELL+PHONE ME LEAVE-ALONE HOME.

S: (copy)

PRESENT
(LESSON SLIDE 8:1:9)

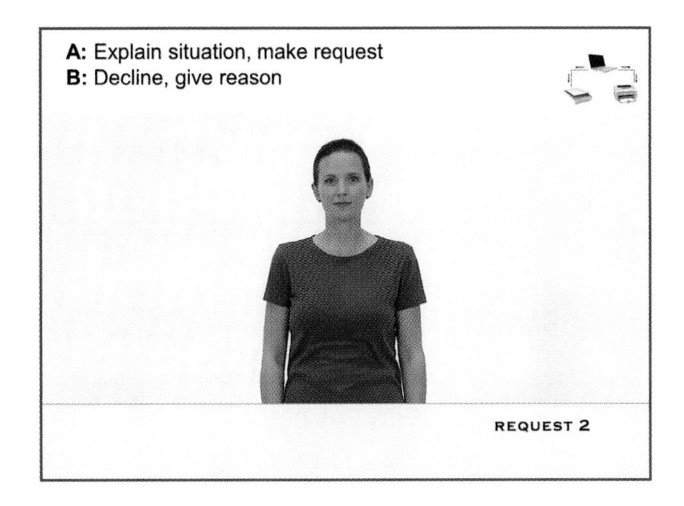
A: Explain situation, make request
B: Decline, give reason
REQUEST 2

Repeat procedure for **Request 2**.

For ***"B: decline, give reason"***

regretful/neg

T: SORRY. ME NOT-KNOW me-SAME-AS-you.

Now, have students give their own reasons for declining.

S: *(come up with reason for declining)*

PRESENT
(LESSON SLIDE 8:1:10)

A: Explain situation, make request
B: Decline, give reason
REQUEST 3

Repeat procedure for **Request 3**.

For ***"B: decline, give reason"***

regretful/neg

T: SORRY. CAN'T, MY FRIEND HAVE CAR KEY.

Have students give their own reasons for declining.

S: *(come up with reason for declining)*

PRESENT
(LESSON SLIDE 8:1:11)

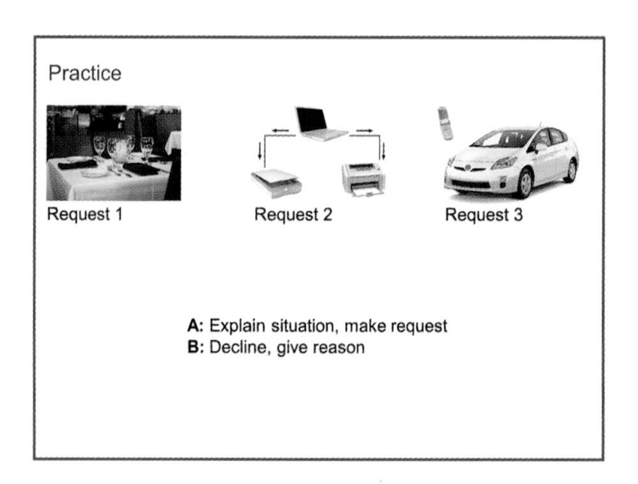
Practice
Request 1
Request 2
Request 3
A: Explain situation, make request
B: Decline, give reason

Mingle. Have students practice dialogue using **Requests 1–3**.

Check to be sure students:

As Signer A:

- sign request clearly
- use pleading expression when making the request

As Signer B:

- use regretful expression when declining.

INTRODUCE *Making Requests 2*

30–45 minutes

PRESENT
(LESSON SLIDES 8:1:12–13)

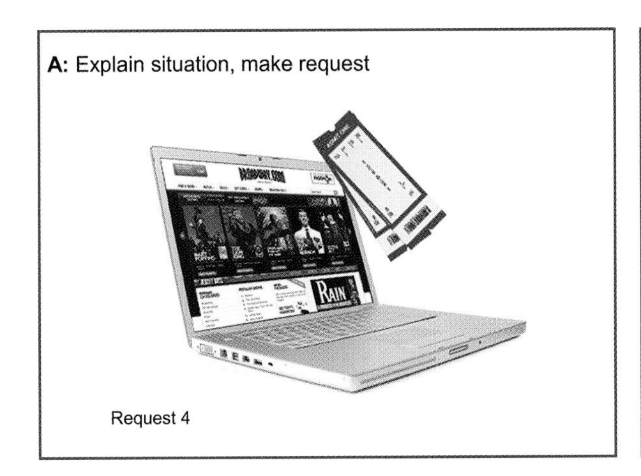
A: Explain situation, make request
Request 4

A: Explain situation, make request
REQUEST 4

Procedure:

- show picture on **Lesson Slide 8:1:12**
- play video on **Lesson Slide 8:1:13**
- clear up meanings of new signs (in bold below)
- have students practice **Request 4** (below).

NEW-YORK

PERFORMANCE

Request 4

(explain situation) ME PLAN GO-TO **NEW-YORK** SEE **PERFORMANCE**. ME WANT BUY **TICKET** NOW

neg

THROUGH INTERNET. ME **NOT-KNOW fs-HOW**.

pleading/q

(make request) NOT-MIND you-SHOW-me.

TICKET

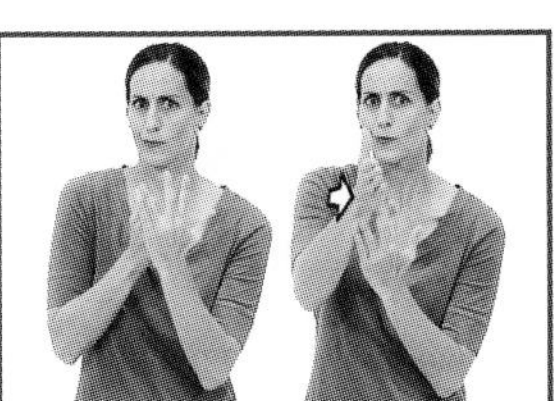
THROUGH

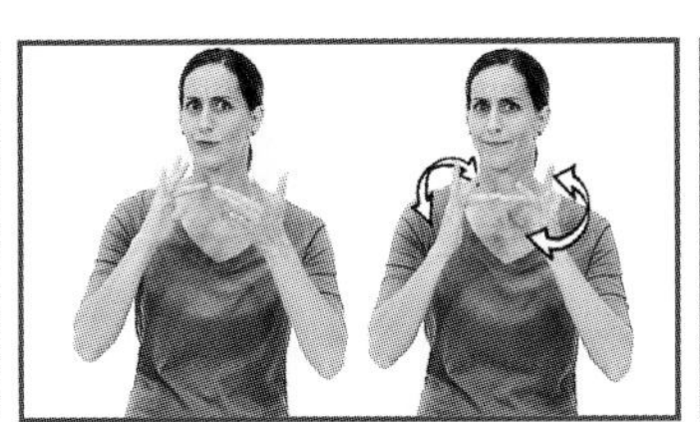
INTERNET

NOT-KNOW

PRESENT

(LESSON SLIDES 8:1:14–15)

A: Explain situation, make request
Request 5

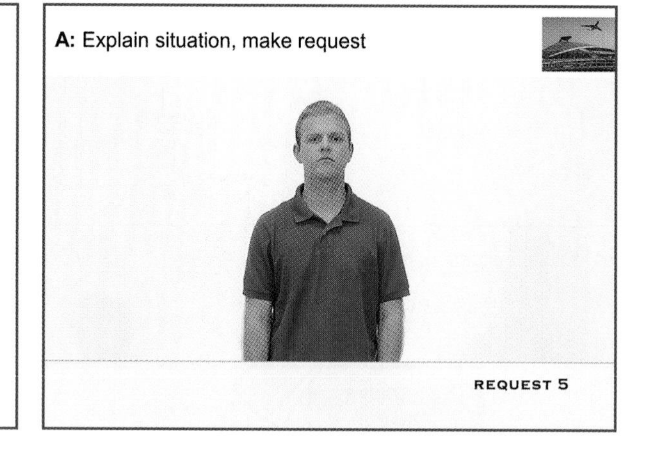
A: Explain situation, make request
REQUEST 5

AIRPLANE

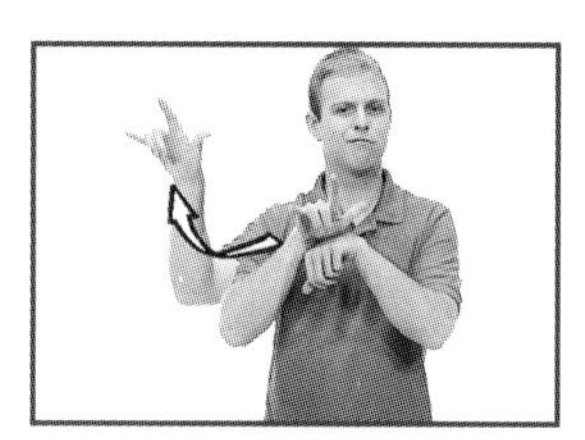
TAKE-OFF

WAIT-CONT

Repeat procedure:

- show picture on **Lesson Slide 8:1:14**
- play video on **Lesson Slide 8:1:15**
- clear up meanings of new signs (in bold below)
- have students practice **Request 5** (below).

Request 5

(explain situation) TIME+1 MY **AIRPLANE TAKE-OFF**.

neg

ME **WAIT-cont**. MY FRIEND IX*"friend"* NOT **APPEAR**.

(make request) ME **WONDER** YOU NOT-MIND

pleading/q

you-TAKE-FROM-my location, DROP-OFF-airport **AIRPLANE** YOU.

APPEAR

WONDER

PRESENT
(LESSON SLIDES 8:1:16–17)

A: Explain situation, make request
Request 6

A: Explain situation, make request
REQUEST 6

FUNERAL

MISS

LAG-BEHIND

CATCH-UP

Repeat procedure:

- show picture on **Lesson Slide 8:1:16**
- play video on **Lesson Slide 8:1:17**
- clear up meanings of new signs (in bold below)
- have students practice **Request 6** (below).

Request 6

(explain situation) MY UNCLE DIED, ME GO-TO **FUNERAL**. ME **MISS** CLASS ONE-WEEK. ME **LAG-BEHIND**.

pleading/q

(make request) NOT-MIND US-TWO PRACTICE SIGN, ME **CATCH-UP**. "well"

PRESENT
(LESSON SLIDE 8:1:18)

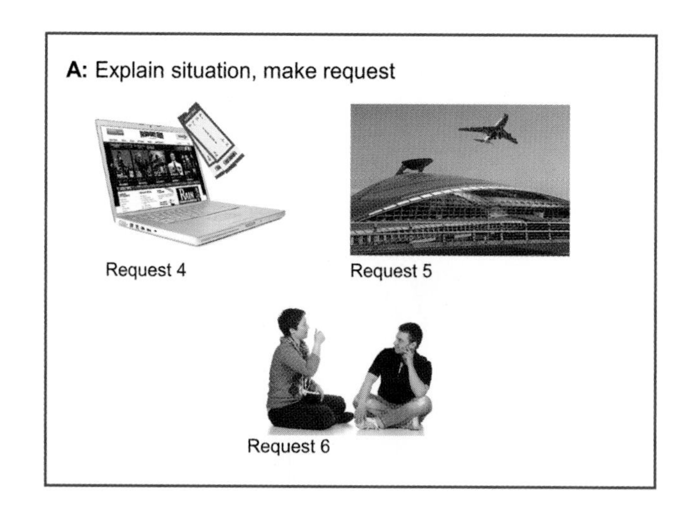
A: Explain situation, make request
Request 4
Request 5
Request 6

Review. Pair up students and have them practice signing **Requests 4–6** to each other.

PRACTICE *Declining Requests 2*

20 minutes

Students practice making and declining **Requests 4–6**.

PRESENT
(LESSON SLIDE 8:1:19)

A: Explain situation, make request
B: Decline, give reason
REQUEST 4

Show **Request 4** video again. Ask students to role play Signer B.

For *"B: decline, give reason"*
For example:

regretful/neg
S: SORRY, ME NOT-KNOW. me-SAME-AS-you.

PRESENT
(LESSON SLIDE 8:1:20)

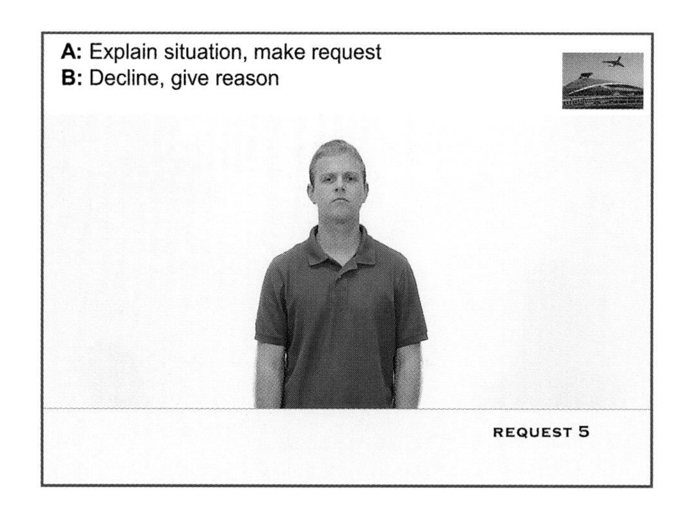
A: Explain situation, make request
B: Decline, give reason
REQUEST 5

USE

Repeat for **Request 5**.
For ***"B: decline, give reason"***
For example:

regretful/neg
S: SORRY. ME NONE CAR. HUSBAND TAKE-FROM-my location **USE**

PRESENT
(LESSON SLIDE 8:1:21)

A: Explain situation, make request
B: Decline, give reason
REQUEST 6

Repeat for **Request 6**.
For ***"B: decline, give reason"***
For example:

regretful/neg
S: SORRY, CAN'T. ME GO-TO CLASS NOW.

PRESENT
(LESSON SLIDE 8:1:22)

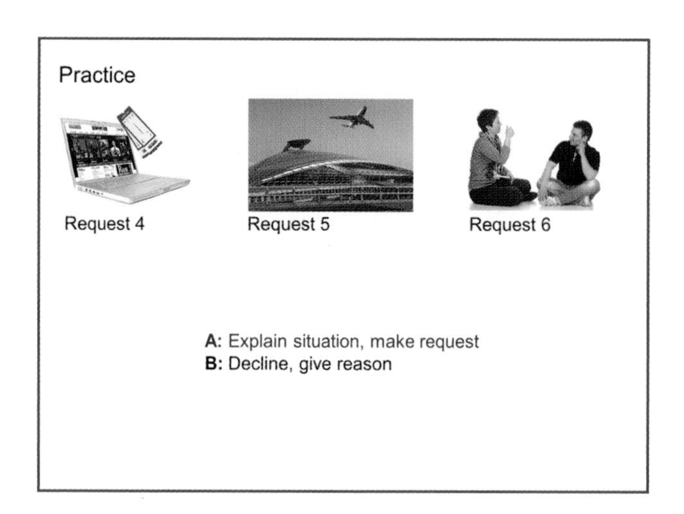

Practice
Request 4
Request 5
Request 6
A: Explain situation, make request
B: Decline, give reason

Mingle. Have students practice the dialogue using **Requests 4–6**.

Check to be sure students:

As Signer A:

- sign request clearly
- use pleading expression when making the request

As Signer B:

- use regretful expression when declining.

Any corrections should be presented to the whole group to practice.

HOMEWORK

Tell students to do **Homework 8:1**
(*Student Workbook*, pages 74–85).

Also, students are to create three requests of their own for **Lesson 8:4** (See **Assignment**, *Student Workbook*, page 81).

HOMEWORK FOLLOW-UP
10–15 MINUTES

PRESENT
(FOLLOW-UP SLIDES 8:1:1–27)

Minidialogue 1

Signer A
explain situation:

request made:

Signer B
reason for declining:

Check students' answers to **Minidialogues 1–6**.
See **Introduction** pages xviii–xix for different ways to check answers.

LESSON 8:2

Fingerspelling: Months

Lesson length: 50–65 minutes

LESSON GOAL Students will learn how to fingerspell the lexicalized forms for months.

KEY SKILLS Use the correct form and movement for each month.

NOTIONS

Vocabulary

Months (lexicalized forms)

fs-JAN	fs-APRIL	fs-JULY	fs-OCT
fs-FEB	fs-MAY	fs-AUG	fs-NOV
fs-MARCH	fs-JUNE	fs-SEPT	fs-DEC

Seasons

AUTUMN	SPRING
WINTER	SUMMER

Calendar Time Signs

MONTH
NOW+MONTH
IN-PAST+MONTH
IN-FUTURE+MONTH
(#)-MONTH+IN-PAST
(#)-MONTH+IN-FUTURE

YEAR+ONE-IN-FUTURE++
YEAR+TWO-IN-FUTURE++

PREPARATION Review the lexicalized forms on **Lesson Slides 8:2:1–12**.

MATERIALS
8:2 Lesson Slides
8:2 Follow-up Slides

HOMEWORK 8:2 *Student Workbook*, pages 86–93

INTRODUCE *Months*

10–15 minutes

PRESENT
(LESSON SLIDES 8:2:1–12)

Show video from **Lesson Slides 8:2:1–12**, introduce fingerspelling (lexicalized) patterns for the months, and have students copy.

- January: **fs-JAN**
  "A" begins with palm facing sideways
- February: **fs-FEB**
  "E" pulls back slightly, then moves forward to form "B"
- March: **fs-MARCH**
  "C" twists wrist (like turning a doorknob) to form "H"
- April: **fs-APRIL**
  "A" begins facing sideways position, then transitions to "P" and "R" in one continuous circular movement
- May: **fs-MAY**
  the hand moves downward to form "Y"
- June: **fs-JUNE**
  "U" is formed with palm facing inward and held as the hand rotates forward.
- July: **fs-JULY**
  "U" is formed with palm facing inward and as the hand rotates forward, it becomes "L"
- August: **fs-AUG**
  the palm of the hand faces sideways for "G"

- September: **fs-SEPT**
  "T" pulls back slightly
- October: **fs-OCT**
  "C" bounces slightly upward
- November: **fs-NOV**
  "O" pulls back slightly before moving forward for "V"
- December: **fs-DEC**
  "E" pulls back slightly before moving forward for "C"

INTRODUCE *Calendar Time Signs*

10–15 minutes

Introduce MONTH with numbers 1–9 incorporated.
Have students copy:

1–MONTH	6-MONTH
2–MONTH	7–MONTH
3–MONTH	8–MONTH
4–MONTH	9–MONTH
5–MONTH	

3-MONTH

Introduce MONTH with numbers 10 or above (number not incorporated in the sign and not repeated). Have students copy.

10 MONTH
11 MONTH
12 MONTH

10 MONTH

PRESENT
(LESSON SLIDE 8:2:13)

Signer **A:** Ask what month it is
B: Give month

Role play Signer A and ask students to role play Signer B.

t whq
T: NOW+MONTH "what"
S: (give month)

t whq
T: IN-PAST+MONTH "what"
S: (give month)

t whq
T: IN-FUTURE+MONTH "what"
S: (give month)

t whq
T: 2-MONTH+IN-PAST MONTH "what"
S: (give month)

t whq
T: 3-MONTH+IN-PAST MONTH "what"
S: (give month)

t whq
T: 3-MONTH+IN-FUTURE MONTH "what"
S: (give month)

Now, have students rehearse Signer A's lines.

t whq
T: (#)MONTH+IN-PAST MONTH "what"
S: (copy)

t whq
T: (#)MONTH+IN-FUTURE MONTH "what"
S: (copy)

Pair up. Have students follow the dialogue to practice both fingerspelling months and the calendar time signs.

INTRODUCE *Annuals and Seasons*

10–15 minutes

PRESENT
(LESSON SLIDES 8:2:14–16)

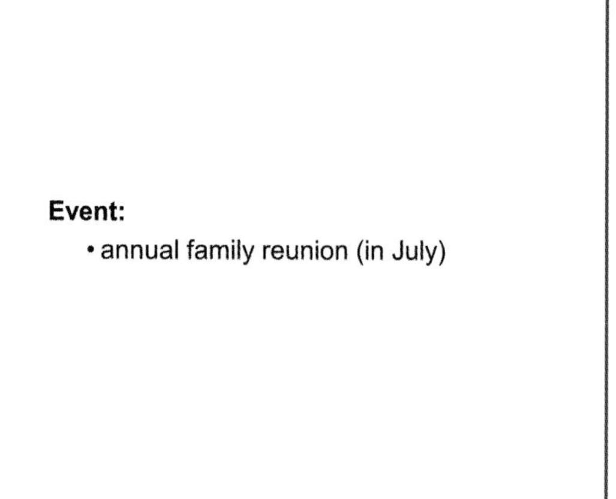
Event:
• annual family reunion (in July)

Introduce how to tell about events that occur annually:

YEAR+1-IN-FUTURE

YEAR+2-IN-FUTURE

t

T: **YEAR+1-IN-FUTURE++** fs-JULY, FAMILY GATHER++

S: (copy)

t

T: **YEAR+1-IN-FUTURE++** fs-AUG, ME GO-TO DOCTOR CHECK BODY

S: (copy)

t

T: **YEAR+2-IN-FUTURE++** fs-OCT, [fs-CELL] PHONE ME EXCHANGE++

S: (copy)

PRESENT
(LESSON SLIDE 8:2:17)

Tell what you do every year or two during a certain month.

Review. Have students tell you what they do every year or two during a certain month.

Check to be sure students use:

- correct word order: tell when (year, month) + activity
- correct forms for fingerspelling months.

PRESENT
(LESSON SLIDE 8:2:18)

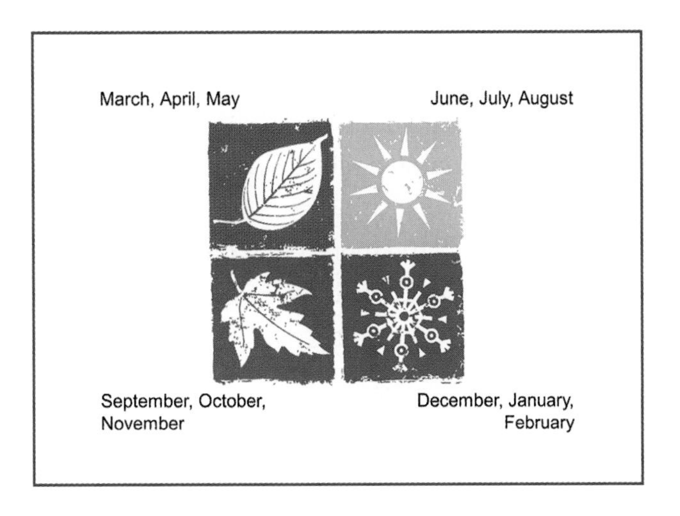

Introduce signs for seasons by pointing to each picture on the slide and sign **AUTUMN**, **WINTER**, **SPRING**, and **SUMMER**.

Ask students what their favorite season is and have them tell why.

t
T: AUTUMN, WINTER, SPRING, SUMMER, YOU FAVORITE
whq
WHICH
S: (tell which season and why)

Ask students what season they were born and spell the month. For example,

t
T: ME BE-BORN WINTER, MONTH fs-DEC.
whq
YOU BE-BORN WHEN
S: (tell season and month)

HOMEWORK

Tell students to do **Homework 8:2** (*Student Workbook*, pages 86–93).

Also, students are to develop five questions that require others to name a month. (See **Assignment**, *Student Workbook*, page 92).

HOMEWORK FOLLOW-UP
20 MINUTES

Spell the month and have students give you the spelling for the next or previous month, for example:

whq
T: fs-MAY, NEXT-TO-forward "what"
S: fs-JUNE
whq
T: fs-AUG, NEXT-TO-back "what"
S: fs-JULY

PRESENT
(FOLLOW-UP SLIDE 8:2:1)

Ask five questions that require your partner to name a month.

Pair up. Have students ask each other the five questions they developed for homework (See **Assignment**, *Student Workbook*, page 92).

Conclude. Call on one student to ask another student a question. Check the question form and the spelling of the month in the answer.

LESSON 8:3

Agreement Verbs 1

Lesson length: 40–50 minutes

LESSON GOAL

Students will learn to modify movement of the agreement verb to indicate the subject and the object of the sentence.

KEY SKILLS

Correctly modify movement and palm orientation of the verb to indicate the subject and object relationship.

NOTIONS

Vocabulary

Agreement Verbs

TELL-TO
PHONE-TO
SEND/MAIL-TO
INFORM-TO
PAY-TO

MATERIALS

8:3 Lesson Slides

HOMEWORK 8:3

Student Workbook, pages 94–98

INTRODUCE *Agreement Verbs*

10–15 minutes

PRESENT
(LESSON SLIDE 8:3:1)

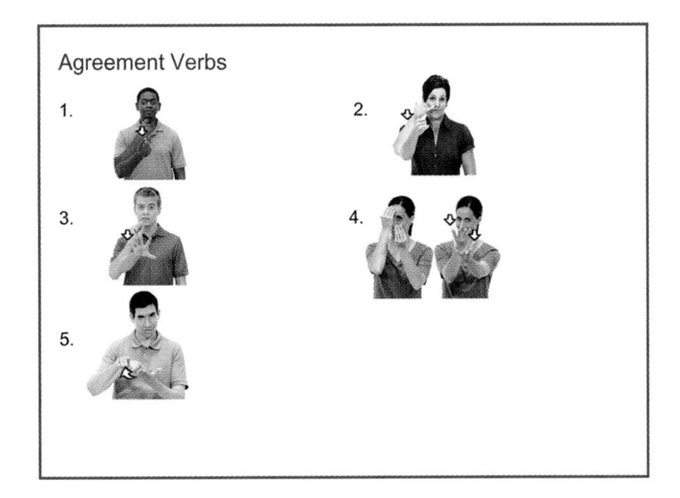

Review and introduce these verbs by showing and explaining the sign.

verb	*explanation*
1. **TELL-TO**	***act out:*** approach a student, tell him you like his shoes, then sign: rhet (over ME "what") ME "what" ME **TELL-TO-him** t (over POSS SHOE) POSS SHOE, ME LIKE.
2. **PHONE-TO**	***act out:*** punch number on your cell phone, put phone close to ear, talk to phone, then sign: rhet (over "what") ME "what" ME **PHONE-TO-person.**
3. **SEND-TO**	***act out:*** write on envelope, seal it, put stamp on envelope, put it in mailbox, then sign: rhet (over "what"), t (over LETTER) ME "what" LETTER, ME **SEND-TO-person.**

4. **INFORM-TO** ***act out:*** approach another student, remind him about the first student's shoes that you liked, tell him these shoes were bought in France and are pricey, then sign:

rhet

ME "what" ME **INFORM**-him

t

POSS *"first student"* SHOE ME LIKE, IX*"first student"* BUY IX-loc FRANCE, EXPENSIVE.

NOTE: **TELL-TO** and **INFORM-TO** have similar meaning, but **INFORM-TO** is used to give news, announcements, and warnings, but not to give instructions or commands.

5. **PAY-TO** ***act out:*** getting a bill, writing a check, putting it in an envelope and mailing it off, then sign:

rhet

ME "what" ME **PAY-TO-company**

PRESENT

(LESSON SLIDE 8:3:2–6)

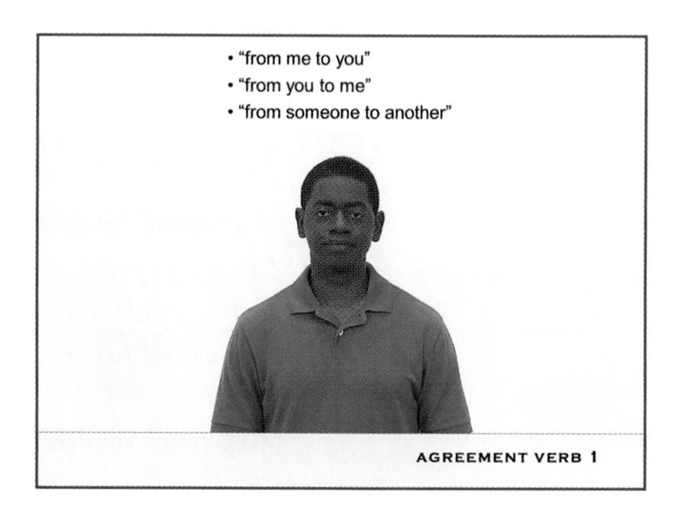
• "from me to you"
• "from you to me"
• "from someone to another"
AGREEMENT VERB 1

Show **Lesson Slides 8:3:2–6** and have students copy the signs. Check their movements when they sign:

- "from me to you"
- "from you to me"
- "from someone to another."

verb	things to check for
1. **TELL-TO**	index finger makes contact below the chin, but for "from you to me" the index finger makes contact *on the front* of the chin
2. **PHONE-TO**	for "from you to me" the sign makes contact on the side of the face, and ends on the chest
3. **SEND-TO**	at the end of the sign, the palm faces the receiver (direct object)
4. **INFORM-TO**	for "from you to me" and "someone to another," the movement of the sign bounces slightly back to the subject after contacting the forehead
5. **PAY-TO**	the back of the finger is oriented toward the receiver (direct object) at the time it contacts the palm of the other hand

NOTE: Make sure students make eye contact when talking to the person. When referring to the third person(s), they glance and/or shift their head in the direction of the person(s).

PRACTICE *Modifying Agreement Verbs*

15 minutes

Students will practice modifying movement of the verb to indicate the subject and the object of the sentence.

PRESENT
(LESSON SLIDE 8:3:7)

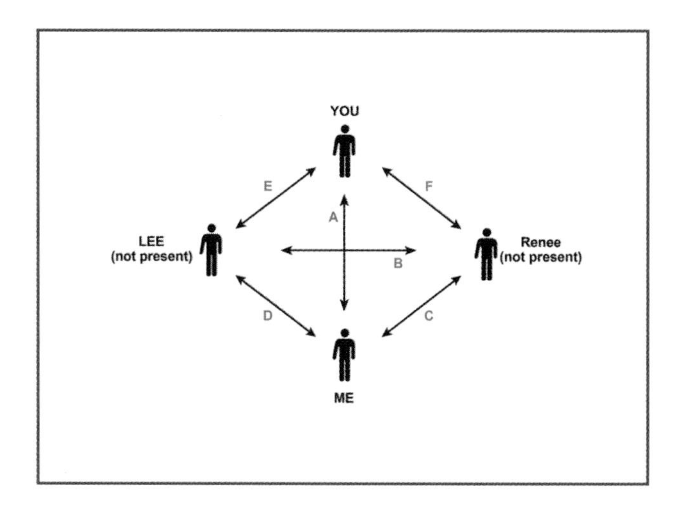

Call one student in front of you facing you. Demonstrate the activity by pointing to **Path A** on the diagram and sign to that student:

T: ME TELL-TO-you, YOU you-TELL-TO-me

Point to **Path B** and sign:

t

T: fs-RENEE*"right,"* fs-LEE*"left"* IX*"Lee"* left-TELL-TO-right; IX*"Renee"* right-TELL-TO-left.

Point to **Path C** and sign:

t

T: fs-RENEE, ME TELL-TO-right; IX*"Renee"* right-TELL-TO-me.

Repeat procedure for **Paths D**, **E** and **F**.

Whole class. Now, have students become "ME" on the diagram and have them sign to you, the teacher ("YOU" on the diagram). Give a verb sign and a path (**A** to **F**). Have them modify the verb to agree with the subject and the object in the path.

T: TELL-TO and fs-A *(path)*
S(all): me-TELL-TO-you, you-TELL-TO-me

T: PHONE-TO and fs-B *(path)*

t

S(all): fs-RENEE*"right,"* fs-LEE*"left"* IX*"Lee"* left-PHONE-TO-right; IX*"Renee"* right-PHONE-TO-left

T: INFORM-TO and fs-C *(path)*

t

S(all): fs-RENEE*"right,"* ME INFORM-TO-right; IX*"Renee"* right-INFORM-TO-me

T: PAY-TO and fs-D (path)

t

S(all): fs-LEE*"left,"* ME PAY-TO-left; IX*"Lee"* left-PAY-TO-me

T: LETTER SEND-TO and fs-E *(path)*

t

S(all): fs-LEE*"left,"* LETTER left-SEND-TO-you; YOU you-SEND-TO-left

T: BOX SEND-TO and fs-F *(path)*

t

S(all): fs-RENEE*"right,"* BOX right-SEND-TO-you; YOU you-SEND-TO-right

Be sure students:

- maintain eye contact with you while signing
- glance to the left when referring to Lee and to the right when referring to Renee
- spell "Lee" on the left, and "Renee" on the right
- modify movement of the verb (with the correct hand and palm orientation) to agree with the person.

PRACTICE *Two Agreement Verbs*

15-20 minutes

Students will practice modifying movements of two verbs to agree with the subject and the object of the sentence.

PRESENT
(LESSON SLIDE 8:3:8)

1. Lee told me that you have not paid him.
2. Renee told me you have not paid Lee.
3. You told me I have not paid Renee.

Remember Lee is on your left and Renee on your right.

Demonstrate ***"1. Lee told me that you have not paid him."***

t (over: YOU you-PAY-TO-left) neg (over: NOT-YET)

T: fs-LEE*"left"* **left-TELL-TO-me** YOU **you-PAY-TO-left** NOT-YET.

Pair up. Have students sign Sentences 2 and 3 to each other.

PRESENT
(LESSON SLIDE 8:3:9)

4. I told Renee class is cancelled, then she called Lee with the news.
5. You told me class is cancelled, then I called Renee with the news.
6. Lee told Renee class is cancelled, then Renee called you with the news.

Remember Lee is on your left and Renee on your right.

Demonstrate ***"4. I told Renee class is canceled, then she called Lee with the news."***

T: fs-RENEE*"right"* ME **INFORM-TO-right** CLASS CANCEL; IX*"Renee"* **right-PHONE-TO-left**, fs-LEE*"left"* **right-INFORM-TO-left**.

Pair up. Have students sign Sentences 5 and 6 to each other.

PRESENT
(LESSON SLIDE 8:3:10)

7. Renee sent me the book but you haven't paid her for it.
8. I sent you the book but Lee hasn't paid me for it.
9. Lee sent Renee the book but I haven't paid Lee for it.

Remember Lee is on your left and Renee on your right.

Demonstrate ***"7. Renee sent me the book but you haven't paid her for it."***

t
T: BOOK, fs-RENEE*"right"* IX*"Renee"* FINISH right-SEND-TO-me.

t neg
[BUT]YOU you-PAY-TO-right NOT-YET.

Pair up. Have students sign Sentences 8 and 9 to each other.

HOMEWORK

Tell students to do **Homework 8:3**
(*Student Workbook*, pages 94–98).

LESSON 8:4

Agreeing with Condition

Lesson length: 90–120 minutes

LESSON GOAL

Students will sign these dialogues:

Dialogue 1

A: explain situation, make request

B: agree with condition (what must happen first)[1]

Dialogue 2

A: explain situation, make request

B: agree with condition (what is expected in return)[2]

KEY PHRASES

nodding (over TRUE/SURE FINE++,) cond (over [BUT] FIRST-THUMB...)

[1] TRUE/SURE FINE++, [BUT] FIRST-THUMB...

nodding (over #OK, FINE++) cond (over "but" FIRST-THUMB...)

[1] #OK, FINE++ "but" FIRST-THUMB...

nod (over ME HAPPY (do something),) cond (over UNDERSTAND++ [IN-EXCHANGE])

[2] ME HAPPY (do something), UNDERSTAND++ [IN-EXCHANGE]

NOTIONS

Grammar

Conditional Clauses

- **what must happen first**

  cond (over [BUT or "but"] FIRST-THUMB...)

  [BUT or "but"] FIRST-THUMB...

- **what is expected in return**

  cond (over UNDERSTAND++ [IN-EXCHANGE])

  UNDERSTAND++ [IN-EXCHANGE]...

Conversation Behaviors

q (over "well")

"well"

Vocabulary

conditions

FIRST-THUMB

UNDERSTAND++

agreeing

TRUE/SURE

FINE++

#OK

HAPPY

others

IN-EXCHANGE

BUT

"but"

PREPARATION

In **Homework 8:1** students were asked to create three requests of their own for **Activity** on page 191. Make sure students are ready to sign them. (See **Assignment** *Student Workbook,* page 81.)

MATERIALS

8:4 Lesson Slides
8:4 Follow-up Slides

HOMEWORK 8:4

Student Workbook, pages 99–103

INTRODUCE *Agree with Condition (What Must Happen First)*

30–40 minutes

PRESENT
(LESSON SLIDE 8:4:1)

Request 1

Agree with condition (what must happen first)

1. express willingness (nod)
2. give condition (raise head and brows, shift to side)
3. tell what you will do ("when" clause, nod)
4. check if person agrees (raise brows, lean head forward, hold sign)

Ask a student to sign **Request 1** and you demonstrate the response.

S: REMEMBER TONIGHT US-TWO PLAN LEAVE-FOR
q neg
EAT. (shake head). MY BOSS TELL-ME MUST WORK

fs-OT 3-HOUR. "well" NOT-MIND YOU PHONE-TO-

restaurant RESTAURANT POSTPONE TOMORROW
pleading/q
NIGHT "well."

nodding cond
T: **TRUE/SURE, FINE++, BUT FIRST-THUMB ME** [MUST-right]
when
COPY-paper*"right,"* **FINISH*"right,"*** ME PHONE-TO-
nodding q
restaurant RESTAURANT **"well."**

TRUE/SURE

Repeat parts of the response and show variations. Have students copy.

FINE++

- For ***"1. express willingness (nod,)"*** be sure students nod heads throughout.

  nodding
  TRUE/SURE, FINE++
  nodding
  FINE++, TRUE/SURE
  nodding
  #OK, FINE++
  nodding
  FINE++, #OK

#OK

- For ***"2. give condition (raise head and brows, shift to side)"*** be sure students' brows are raised throughout the conditional clause.

  cond
  BUT FIRST-THUMB, ME [MUST-right] COPY-paper*"right"*
  cond
  or **"but" FIRST-THUMB,** ME [MUST-right] COPY-paper*"right"*

COPY-paper

BUT FIRST-THUMB

"but" FIRST-THUMB

- For ***"3. tell what you will do,"*** and ***"4. check if person agrees,"*** be sure students raise their brows for the when clause, and hold the sign "well." (q)

  when — nodding — q
  FINISH*"right,"* ME PHONE-TO-restaurant RESTAURANT **"well."**

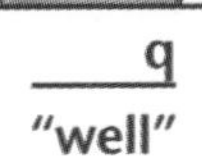
q
"well"

NOTE: FINISH should be signed in the same location as COPY-paper.

Now, have students practice the whole response.

nodding **cond**

S: **TRUE/SURE, FINE++, BUT FIRST-THUMB** ME [MUST-right]

when

COPY-paper*"right,"* **FINISH*"right,"*** ME PHONE-TO-

nodding q

restaurant RESTAURANT "well."

PRESENT
(LESSON SLIDE 8:4:2)

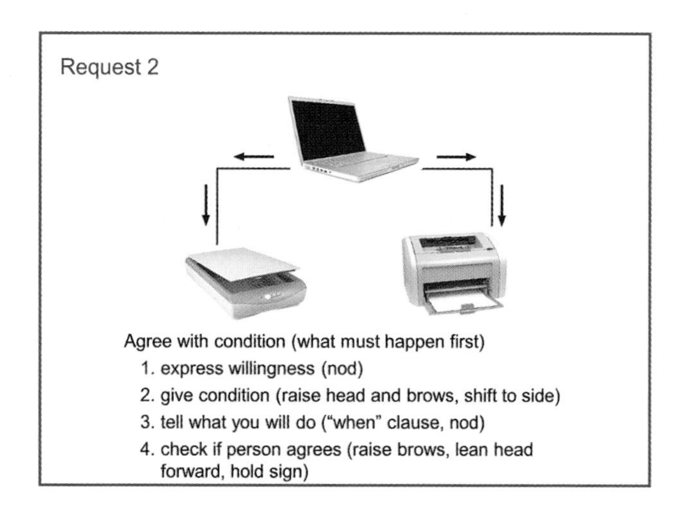

Request 2
Agree with condition (what must happen first)
1. express willingness (nod)
2. give condition (raise head and brows, shift to side)
3. tell what you will do ("when" clause, nod)
4. check if person agrees (raise brows, lean head forward, hold sign)

Repeat procedure. Ask a student to sign **Request 2.**
You demonstrate the response and have students copy.

S: RECENT BUY NEW, COMPUTER, PRINTER, SCANNER.
BUT ME MUST MYSELF CONNECT++. *"well"* ME

BE-MIND-STUPID. NOT-MIND YOU COME-TO-here

pleading/q

MY HOUSE HELP CONNECT++, NOT-MIND.

nodding cond

T: **#OK, FINE++ BUT FIRST-THUMB** MYSELF READ*"right"*

when **nodding** q

UNDERSTAND, ME GO-TO-house me-SHOW-you "well."

S(all): (copy)

PRESENT
(LESSON SLIDE 8:4:3)

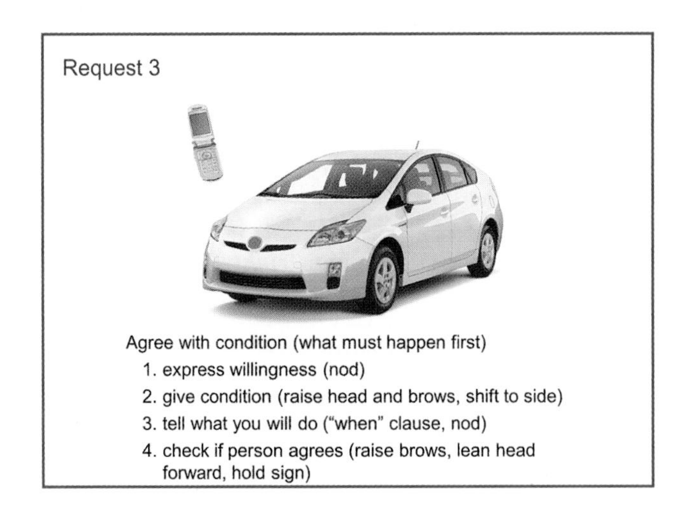
Request 3
Agree with condition (what must happen first)
1. express willingness (nod)
2. give condition (raise head and brows, shift to side)
3. tell what you will do ("when" clause, nod)
4. check if person agrees (raise brows, lean head forward, hold sign)

Repeat procedure. Ask a student to sign **Request 3.** You demonstrate the response and have students copy.

S: MY fs-CELL+PHONE (t), CAN'T+FIND (neg). ME THINK LOST. PHONE IX"*phone*" HAVE PICTURE, ADDRESS, PHONE NUMBER ALL-INCLUSIVE. ME MUST FIND. ME THINK MAYBE ME LEAVE-ALONE YOUR CAR. NOT-MIND YOU YOU GO-TO-car CHECK (pleading/q)

T: **FINE++, #OK** (nodding) **"but" FIRST-THUMB** ME GO-TO"*right*" MEETING. (cond) **FINISH"*right*,"** (when) ME GO-TO-car CHECK (nodding) "well." (q)

S(all): (copy)

PRESENT
(LESSON SLIDE 8:4:4)

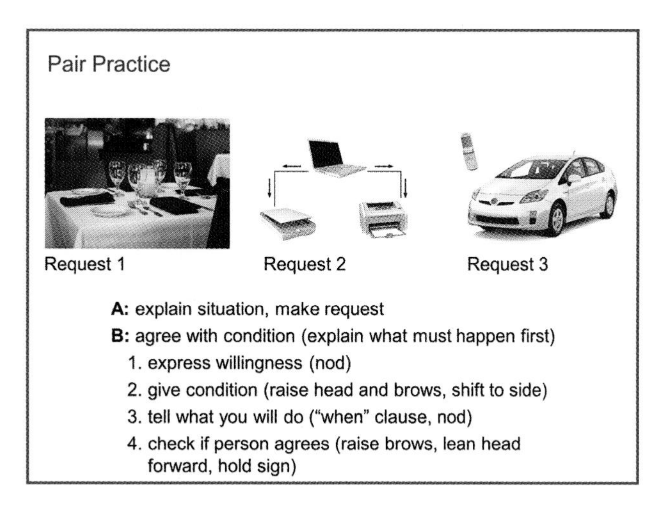
Pair Practice
Request 1
Request 2
Request 3
A: explain situation, make request
B: agree with condition (explain what must happen first)
1. express willingness (nod)
2. give condition (raise head and brows, shift to side)
3. tell what you will do ("when" clause, nod)
4. check if person agrees (raise brows, lean head forward, hold sign)

Review. Have students mingle and practice giving different responses to **Requests 1–3**. Be sure they:

- nod throughout the "express willingness" part
- raise brows when stating the condition
- raise brows for the when clause, and nod when telling what they will do.

INTRODUCE *Agree with Condition (What Is Expected in Return)*

30–40 minutes

PRESENT
(LESSON SLIDE 8:4:5)

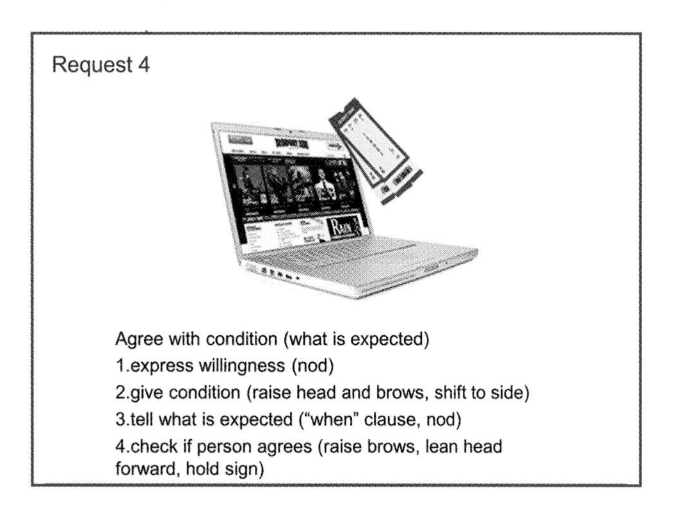
Request 4
Agree with condition (what is expected)
1.express willingness (nod)
2.give condition (raise head and brows, shift to side)
3.tell what is expected ("when" clause, nod)
4.check if person agrees (raise brows, lean head forward, hold sign)

Ask a student to sign **Request 4** and you demonstrate the response.

S: ME PLAN GO-TO NEW YORK SEE PERFORMANCE.
ME WANT BUY TICKET NOW THROUGH INTERNET

neg   pleading/q
ME NOT-KNOW fs-HOW. NOT-MIND you-SHOW-me.

nod   **cond**
T: ME **HAPPY** TEACH-you, **UNDERSTAND++**

q
IN-EXCHANGE, YOU BUY TICKET FOR+ME. "well"

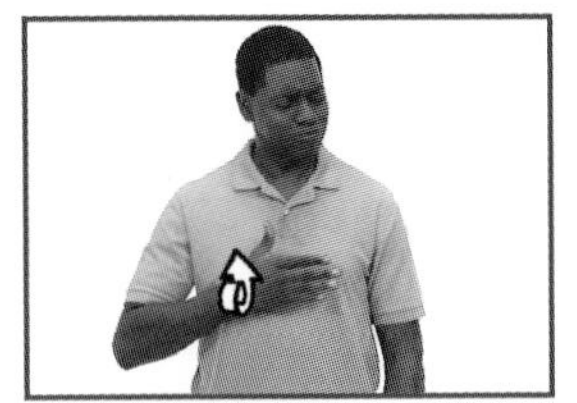

HAPPY

cond
UNDERSTAND++

Repeat parts of the response and have students copy:

- For ***"1. express willingness (nod),"*** be sure students nod heads throughout.

  nod
  ME **HAPPY** TEACH-you

- For ***"2. give condition (raise head and brows),"*** be sure students' brows are raised throughout the conditional clause.

  cond
  UNDERSTAND++

- For ***"3. tell what is expected,"*** and ***"4. check if person agrees"***

q
Be sure students raise brows, lean head forward for "well" and hold it.

q
IN-EXCHANGE, YOU BUY TICKET FOR+ME. **"well"**

IN-EXCHANGE

Now, have students practice signing the whole response.

nod   **cond**
S: ME **HAPPY** TEACH-you, **UNDERSTAND++**

q
IN-EXCHANGE, YOU BUY TICKET FOR+ME. "well"

PRESENT
(LESSON SLIDE 8:4:6)

Request 5

Agree with condition (what is expected)
1. express willingness (nod)
2. give condition (raise head and brows, shift to side)
3. tell what is expected ("when" clause, nod)
4. check if person agrees (raise brows, lean head forward, hold sign)

Repeat procedure. Ask a student to sign **Request 5** and you demonstrate the response.

S: TIME+1 MY AIRPLANE TAKE-OFF. ME WAIT++. MY FRIEND IX*"friend"* NOT APPEAR (neg). ME WONDER YOU NOT-MIND you-TAKE-FROM-my-location, DROP-OFF airport AIRPLANE YOU (pleading/q).

T: **HAPPY** me-TAKE-FROM-your location TAKE-you, DROP-OFF-airport AIRPLANE (nod) **UNDERSTAND++** IN-FUTURE+ MONTH ME FLY-TO VISIT DAUGHTER (**cond**), YOU [NOT-MIND] you-TAKE-FROM-my location, you-DROP-OFF-airport AIRPLANE (q). "well"

S(all): (copy)

PRESENT
(LESSON SLIDE 8:4:7)

Request 6

Agree with condition (what is expected)
1. express willingness (nod)
2. give condition (raise head and brows, shift to side)
3. tell what is expected ("when" clause, nod)
4. check if person agrees (raise brows, lean head forward, hold sign)

Repeat procedure. Ask a student to sign **Request 6** and you demonstrate the response.

S: MY UNCLE DIED, ME GO-TO FUNERAL. ME MISS CLASS ONE-WEEK. ME BE-BEHIND. NOT-MIND US-TWO PRACTICE SIGN. ME CATCH-UP. "well"
(pleading/q over: NOT-MIND US-TWO PRACTICE SIGN. ME CATCH-UP.)

T: FINE++ ME **HAPPY** me-HELP-you. **UNDERSTAND++**, MY ENGLISH PAPER, you-HELP-me TYPE. "well"
(nod over: FINE++ ME HAPPY me-HELP-you.; **cond** over: UNDERSTAND++,; t over: MY ENGLISH PAPER,; q over: you-HELP-me TYPE.)

S(all): (copy)

PRESENT
(LESSON SLIDE 8:4:8)

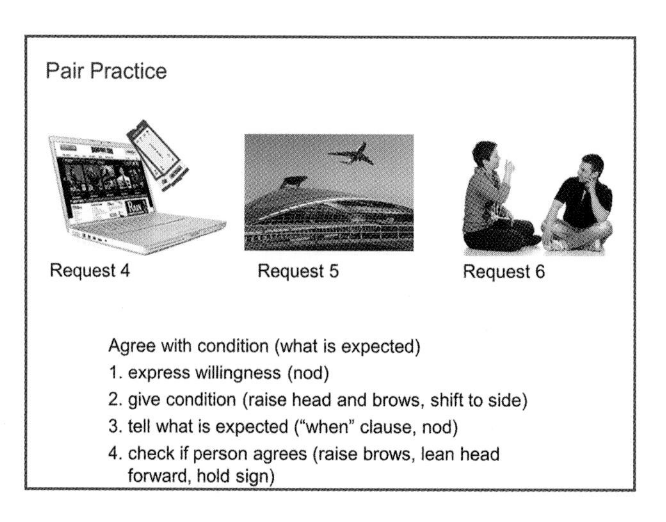
Pair Practice
Request 4
Request 5
Request 6
Agree with condition (what is expected)
1. express willingness (nod)
2. give condition (raise head and brows, shift to side)
3. tell what is expected ("when" clause, nod)
4. check if person agrees (raise brows, lean head forward, hold sign)

Review. Have students mingle and practice giving different responses to **Requests 4–6**. Be sure they:

- nod throughout the "express willingness" part
- raise brows when stating the condition with UNDERSTAND++
- raise brows, lean head forward for "well" (marked q) and hold it.

PRACTICE *Agree with Condition*

30–40 minutes

Students practice using conditional clauses with UNDERSTAND++ (marked cond) and BUT (or "but") FIRST-THUMB (marked cond) in responses to requests.

PRESENT

(LESSON SLIDE 8:4:9)

A: explain situation, make request
B: agree with condition (what is expected)

1. express willingness (nod)
2. give condition (raise head and brows, shift to side)
3. tell what you will do ("when" clause, nod)
4. check if person agrees (raise brows, lean head forward, hold sign)

You role play Signer A and sign **Request 1–3**. Call on students to role play Signer B, and give different responses using

cond
UNDERSTAND++

(If students need help with ideas for responses, here are some possible responses)

Responding to Request 1

nodding / **cond**

B: ME HAPPY PHONE-TO-restaurant, **UNDERSTAND++,**

q

ME USE YOUR PHONE "well"

Responding to Request 2

nodding / **cond**

B: TRUE/SURE, ME HAPPY SHOW-you, **UNDERSTAND++,**

q

IN-EXCHANGE YOU SHOW-TO-me HOW MAKE COOKIE. "well"

Responding to Request 3

nodding / **cond**

B: ME HAPPY LOOK-FOR FOR+YOU, **UNDERSTAND++,**

when

[ME] FIND, YOU you-TAKE-PICTURE-me, you-SEND-TO-

q

friend MY FRIEND. "well"

PRESENT
(LESSON SLIDE 8:4:10)

A: explain situation, make request
B: agree with condition (what must happen first)
1. express willingness (nod)
2. give condition (raise head and brows, shift to side)
3. tell what you will do ("when" clause, nod)
4. check if person agrees (raise brows, lean head forward, hold sign)

You role play Signer A and sign **Requests 4–6**.
Call on students to role play Signer B give a response using

cond

BUT (or "but") FIRST-THUMB

(If students need help with ideas for responses, here are some possible responses.)

Responding to Request 4

nodding

B: TRUE/SURE, FINE++, **BUT FIRST-THUMB** ME [MUST-right]

cond when nodding

FOOD, PICK-UP*"right"* FINISH*"right,"* ME SHOW-you #HOW.

Responding to Request 5

nodding

B: #OK, FINE++, **"but" FIRST-THUMB** ME [MUST-right] #DOG

cond

TAKE-FROM-dog's location LEAVE-FOR BATHROOM,

when

FINISH*"right"* ME TAKE-FROM-your location DROP-OFF-

nodding

airport AIRPLANE.

Responding to Request 6

nodding

B: FINE++, TRUE/SURE, **BUT FIRST-THUMB** ME [MUST-right]

cond when nodding

FEED*"right"*CHILDREN, FINISH, US-TWO PRACTICE SIGN.

PRESENT

(LESSON SLIDE 8:4:11)

A: explain situation, make request

B: agree with condition

- what must happen first

  or

- what is expected

ACTIVITY

Make sure the students have prepared their three requests. (See **Preparation**). Have students mingle, following the dialogue using the requests they created, and practice agreeing with the condition.

EVALUATE

Ask students to demonstrate the dialogue using their requests. Make notes of what needs further practice.

Check to be sure students:

as Signer A

- explain request clearly and give enough details to be compelling
- use the sign NOT-MIND (q)
- use pleading expression when making the request

as Signer B

- nod throughout the "express willingness" part
- raise brows when stating the condition with BUT FIRST-THUMB or UNDERSTAND++
- raise brows, lean head forward for "well" (q) and hold it.

Any corrections should be presented to the whole group to practice.

HOMEWORK

Tell students to do **Homework 8:4** (*Student Workbook*, pages 99–103).

Also, students are to create a response to each request in **Requests 1–4** using either way to "agree with condition." (See **Assignment**, *Student Workbook*, page 102).

HOMEWORK FOLLOW-UP
20 MINUTES

PRESENT
(FOLLOW-UP SLIDES 8:4:1–4)

Show video **Request 1** and have students sign their responses developed for homework (**Assignment**, *Student Workbook*, page 102).

Repeat procedure for remaining **Follow-up Slides 2–4**.

Summary of requests on video (for your reference)
Request 1: buy replacement ink for printer
Request 2: pay the other person, then be reimbursed later
Request 3: email me class notes for class that I missed
Request 4: show me how to download movies on my laptop

LESSON 8:5

Negations 1

Lesson length: 30–40 minutes

LESSON GOAL

Students will know how to translate English sentences using appropriate negation sign(s).

NOTIONS

Vocabulary

negations

NOT (NOT+FINISH, NOT+MUST, SHOULD+NOT)
NONE or NOT+HAVE
"wave no"
NOT-YET

NOT-WANT
FORBID or NOT+ALLOW
REFUSE

MATERIALS

8:5 Lesson Slides
8:5 Follow-up Slides

HOMEWORK 8:5

Student Workbook, pages 104–108

INTRODUCE *Negation Signs*

10 minutes

PRESENT

(LESSON SLIDE 8:5:1)

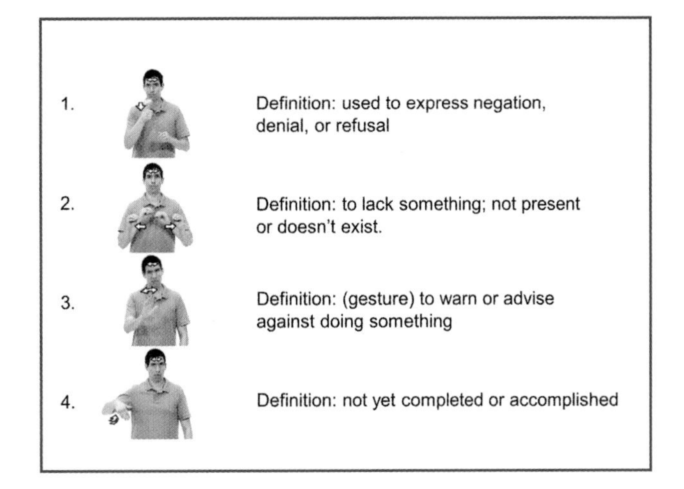

1.
Definition: used to express negation, denial, or refusal
2.
Definition: to lack something; not present or doesn't exist.
3.
Definition: (gesture) to warn or advise against doing something
4.
Definition: not yet completed or accomplished

Review signs and give example sentences. Have each student create their own sentences using those signs.

1. NOT

 t neg
 T: FOOD, ME NOT BRING-TO-here
 S: (sign their own sentence using NOT)

2. NONE

 neg
 T: MY MOTHER IX*"mother"* NONE COUSIN
 S: (sign their own sentence using NONE)

3. "wave no"

 t t neg
 T: MY PHONE NUMBER, you-GIVE-him "wave-no"
 S: (sign their own sentence using "wave-no")

4. NOT-YET

 t neg
 T: BUY TICKET, ME NOT-YET
 S: (sign their own sentence using NOT-YET)

PRESENT
(LESSON SLIDE 8:5:2)

5. Definition: to have no desire to; to have no interest in doing something

6. Definition: to prohibit; to forbid; to not allow

7. Definition: to refuse; not willing to

Introduce vocabulary by showing and explaining the sign. Then, have students copy the sign.

negation	*explanation*
5. NOT-WANT	***act out:*** you have an apple and an orange. You're considering which one to eat. Then sign:
	t APPLE IX*"apple"* ME WANT
	(act out: pick it up and eat it")
	t neg ORANGE IX*"orange"* ME NOT-WANT
	(act out: reject it)
	t ***contrast:*** WANT, OPPOSITE IX-loc*"other side"*
	neg **NOT-WANT**
6. FORBID	***show:*** Pull out your driver's license, and show it. Sign:
	t nod LICENSE IX*"license,"* ME CAN DRIVE
	neg/cond neg NONE LICENSE, DRIVE **FORBID**
	q ***ask:*** SMOKING HERE ALLOW, (shake head)
	neg **FORBID**

7. REFUSE *describe situation:* you encourage a child to eat vegetables. The more you plead, the worse he refuses (shakes his head, presses his lips closed). Then sign:

t t
BOY IX"*boy,*" VEGETABLE EAT IX"*boy*"

neg
REFUSE

PRACTICE *Translating Negative Sentences*

20–30 minutes

Students will identify time, location, topic and appropriate negation sign(s) to translate sentences.

PRESENT
(LESSON SLIDE 8:5:3)

1. I don't have your phone number.
2. My nephew won't eat peas.

Translating negative sentences
- establish time if specified (raise brows)
- establish location if specified (raise brows)
- name the topic (raise brows)
- end with a negation (shake head)

Be mindful there may be exceptions.

Help students analyze each sentence and prepare to translate it by asking:

- if the sentence has specific time information or location
- what is the topic
- what is the most appropriate negation sign or phrase.

For *"1. I don't have your phone number."*
Time: *none*
Location: *none*
Topic: *phone number*
Negation: NONE *or* NOT+HAVE

For *"2. My nephew won't eat peas."*
Time: *none*
Location: *none*
Topic: *nephew eating peas*
Negation: REFUSE

Demonstrate translations with the whole class. Have students copy you, paying attention to the facial expressions and phrasing.

Translation for 1:

YOUR PHONE NUMBER (t), ME **NONE**, ME (neg).

or

YOUR PHONE NUMBER (t), ME **NOT+HAVE**, ME (neg)

Translation for 2:

MY NEPHEW EAT fs-PEAS (t), IX*"nephew"* **REFUSE** (neg).

Pair up: Have students practice signing **Sentences 1** and **2** with each other.

PRESENT
(LESSON SLIDE 8:5:4)

3. There is no class Thursday.
4. Don't chew your nails.

Translating negative sentences
- establish time if specified (raise brows)
- establish location if specified (raise brows)
- name the topic (raise brows)
- end with a negation (shake head)

Be mindful there may be exceptions.

Repeat procedure.

For ***"3. There is no class Thursday."***
Time: *(this) Thursday*
Location: *none*
Topic: *class*
Negation: NONE
Translation:

                                        t   neg
IN-FUTURE+THURSDAY, CLASS **NONE**.

For ***"4. Don't chew your nails."***
Time: *none*
Location: *none*
Topic: *chewing nails*
Negation: "wave-no"
Translation:

                                        t   neg
CHEW-FINGERNAILS, **"wave no"**

Pair up: Have students practice signing **Sentences 3** and **4** with each other.

PRESENT
(LESSON SLIDE 8:5:5)

5. You can't smoke in restaurants.
6. I haven't met your mother.

Translating negative sentences
- establish time if specified (raise brows)
- establish location if specified (raise brows)
- name the topic (raise brows)
- end with a negation (shake head)

Be mindful there may be exceptions.

Repeat procedure.

For ***"5. You can't smoke in restaurants."***

Time: *none*

Location: *restaurant*

Topic: *smoking*

Negation: FORBID or NOT+ALLOW

Translation:

t t neg

RESTAURANT, SMOKING **FORBID**.

or

t t neg

RESTAURANT, SMOKING **NOT+ALLOW**.

For ***"6. I haven't met your mother."***

Time: *none*

Location: *none*

Topic: *meeting your mother*

Negation: NOT-YET

Translation:

t neg

YOUR MOTHER, ME MEET **NOT-YET.**

Pair up: Have students practice signing **Sentences 5** and **6** with each other.

PRESENT

(LESSON SLIDE 8:5:6)

7. Don't forget to bring your book.
8. I don't want Jack to come.

Translating negative sentences

- establish time if specified (raise brows)
- establish location if specified (raise brows)
- name the topic (raise brows)
- end with a negation (shake head)

Be mindful there may be exceptions.

Repeat procedure.

For "*7. Don't forget to bring your book.*"

Time: *none*

Location: *none*

Topic: *your book*

Negation: NOT

Translation:

t / neg

YOUR BOOK, BRING-here. **NOT** FORGET YOU

For "*8. I don't want Jack to come.*"

Time: *none*

Location: *none*

Topic: *Jack coming here*

Negation: NOT-WANT

Translation:

t / neg

fs-JACK COME-TO-here, ME **NOT-WANT**

Pair up: Have students practice signing **Sentences 7** and **8** with each other.

PRESENT
(LESSON SLIDE 8:5:7)

9. I didn't finish my homework.
10. These cookies are sugar free.

Translating negative sentences

- establish time if specified (raise brows)
- establish location if specified (raise brows)
- name the topic (raise brows)
- end with a negation (shake head)

Be mindful there may be exceptions.

Repeat procedure.

For ***"9. I didn't finish my homework."***
Time: *none*
Location: *none*
Topic: *homework*
Negation: NOT+FINISH
Translation:

t neg
HOME+WORK, ME **NOT+FINISH.**

For ***"10. These cookies are sugar free."***
Time: *none*
Location: *none*
Topic: *cookies*
Negation: NONE
Translation:

t neg
COOKIE IX-mult SUGAR **NONE.**

Pair up: Have students practice signing **Sentences 9** and **10** with each other.

PRESENT
(LESSON SLIDE 8:5:8)

11. You don't have to pay me back.
12. You should not read her mail.

Translating negative sentences

- establish time if specified (raise brows)
- establish location if specified (raise brows)
- name the topic (raise brows)
- end with a negation (shake head)

Be mindful there may be exceptions.

Repeat procedure.

For ***"11. You don't have to pay me back."***

Time: *none*

Location: *none*

Topic: *(money)*

Negation: NOT+MUST

Translation:

```
_______t                            _________neg
MONEY, YOU you-PAY-TO-me NOT+MUST
```

For ***"12. You should not read her mail."***

Time: *none*

Location: *none*

Topic: *her letter*

Negation: SHOULD+NOT

Translation:

```
________________t                  ____________neg
POSS-right LETTER, YOU READ SHOULD+NOT
```

Pair up: Have students practice signing **Sentences 11** and **12** with each other.

HOMEWORK

Tell students to do **Homework 8:5** (*Student Workbook*, pages 104–108).

HOMEWORK FOLLOW-UP

5–10 MINUTES

PRESENT

(FOLLOW-UP SLIDES 8:5:1–2)

1. I don't have your phone number.
2. My nephew won't eat peas.
3. There is no class Thursday.
4. Don't chew your nails.
5. You can't smoke in restaurants.
6. I haven't met your mother.

Have students sign the translations. Check word order, phrasing and facial expressions.

LESSON 8:6

Numbers: Giving Phone Numbers

Lesson length: 25–40 minutes

LESSON GOAL Students learn to sign phone numbers.

KEY SKILLS

- For area codes and the next 3 numbers, split the digits into a 1–2 pattern
- For the last four numbers, use a 2–2 pattern
- Except when the 2 middle digits are the same number, then all 4 numbers are signed as individual numbers.

PREPARATION Read and view **Numbers: Giving Phone Numbers** in *Student Workbook*, page 109

MATERIALS **8:6 Lesson Slides**

HOMEWORK 8:6 *Student Workbook*, pages 109–113

INTRODUCE *Phone Numbers*

10–15 minutes

PRESENT
(LESSON SLIDE 8:6:1)

Numbers 1-5

Cardinal (Counting)	**Identification** (phone, social security, house number, zip code, etc.)
orientation: palm in	orientation: palm out

Demonstrate cardinal and identification forms for numbers 1–5. Explain this lesson will focus on phone numbers.

PRESENT
(LESSON SLIDE 8:6:2)

Phone Numbers: Area Codes

510 925 415

408 707

559

Demonstrate number forms for signing area codes. Have students copy you.

For area codes, split the digits into a 1–2 pattern. For example:

- for 510, sign 5 (palm out), then 10 (don't shake the 10)
- for 925, sign 9, then 25 (movement is not repeated)
- for 415, sign 4, then 15 (use single movement)
- for 408, sign 4, then 0 and 8
- for 707, sign 7, then 0 and 7
- for 559, sign 5, then 59 or sign 5, then 5 and 9.

Ask students to sign the area codes in your surrounding area. Be sure they use the 1–2 pattern demonstrated above.

PRESENT
(LESSON SLIDE 8:6:3–8)

235-3104

225-3104

235-**3100**

235-**3114**

235-**1324**

235-**1115**

Introduce how to sign phone numbers. Have students copy.

235–3104 Split the first set of numbers into a 1–2 pattern and the second set into a 2-2 pattern, for example:
235—sign 2 (palm out) then 35
3104—sign 31, then 0 and 4 (palm out)

225–3104 Same patterns as above. However, there are two options for signing 225, for example:
225—sign 2, then 25 or sign 2, then 2 and 5

NOTE: It is incorrect to sign 22 then 5.

235–**3100** For 235, same pattern as above.
For 3100, sign 31, then 0 and 0.

235–**3114** For 235, same pattern as above. However, there are two options for signing 3114, for example:
sign 31, then 14 (single movement) or
sign 3, then 1, 1, and 4

NOTE: It is incorrect to sign 3, then 11, then 4.

235–**1324** For 235, same pattern as above.
For 1324, sign 13 (single movement), then 24

235–**1115** For 235, same pattern as above.
For 1115, sign 1, then 1, 1 and 5 (all palm out) or sign 11 (single movement), then 15 (single movement)

PRACTICE *Phone Numbers*

15–25 minutes

Students practice signing phone numbers correctly.

PRESENT
(LESSON SLIDE 8:6:9)

813-1670

642-1743

383-1207

960-7221

668-0844

512-4445

Pair up. Have students discuss how to sign the numbers. When ready, call on students to sign the numbers. Correct as needed.

Teacher's Guide

- **for 813–1670** 813—sign 8, then 13 (single movement)
  1670—sign 16, then 70 (single movement)
- **for 642–1743** 642—sign 6, then 42
  1743—sign 17, then 43
- **for 383–1207** 383—sign 3 (palm out), then 83
  1207—sign 12 (single movement), then 0, 7
- **for 960–7221** 960—sign 9, then 60 (single movement)
  7221—sign 7, then 2, 2, 1 (all palm out)
- **for 668–0844** 668—sign 6, then 6 , 8 (rocking movement would be awkward)
  0844—sign 0 then 8, then 44
- **for 512–4445** 512—sign 5 (palm out), then 12 (single movement)
  4445—sign 4, 4, 4, then 5 (all palm out)

PRESENT
(LESSON SLIDE 8:6:10)

Show video. Point out that Iva:

- starts with area code (707) on the non-dominant side, then pauses (with a nod)
- pauses, shifts slightly to the middle to give the next 3 digits (235), then pauses (with a nod)
- shifts again to the dominant side to give the final 4 digits (3104), then pauses (with a nod).

PRESENT
(LESSON SLIDE 8:6:11)

510-642-7339

415-559-8176

Have students take turns giving the phone numbers on the slide. Be sure they:

- start with area code on the non-dominant side, then pause (with a nod)
- pause, shift slightly to the middle to give the next 3 digits, then pause (with a nod)
- shift again to the dominant side to give the final 4 digits, then pause (with a nod)
- apply correct number patterns for 3 and 4 digit numbers.

Mingle. Have students mingle and get the phone number of their fellow students. Have students write the numbers down.

Conclude. Go around the room and have students give you their phone numbers. Check number patterns and placements.

HOMEWORK

Tell students to do **Homework 8:6** (*Student Workbook*, pages 109–113).

HOMEWORK FOLLOW-UP
5–10 MINUTES

Have student explain the purpose of each phone number. Be sure students use the vocabulary below in their explanations.

1. **411** to get the phone numbers of a restaurant, a company, or a friend who lives nearby

Vocabulary to include

#fs-CO (COMPANY)

2. **511** to get information about highway conditions, for example, accidents, highway repairs

Vocabulary to include

FREEWAY

PROBLEM

IMPROVE-cont

CAR-ACCIDENT

3. **611** to get phone company to identify and fix problems when you are unable to make a call from your landline phone or if there is a phone line breakdown

Vocabulary to include

PHONE (2h)LCL*"line"*

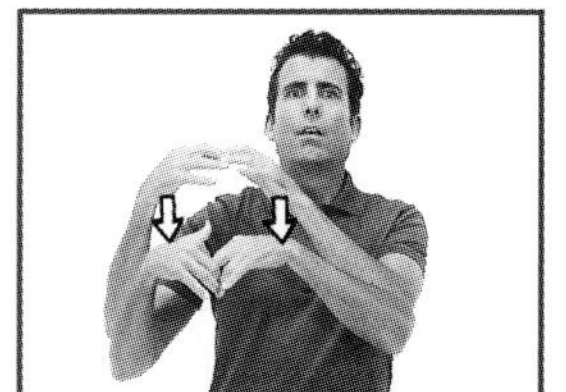

COLLAPSE/BREAKDOWN

4. 911 to call for assistance, for example, ambulance services if there is some kind of injury, death, an accident, a fall or difficulty breathing

Vocabulary to include

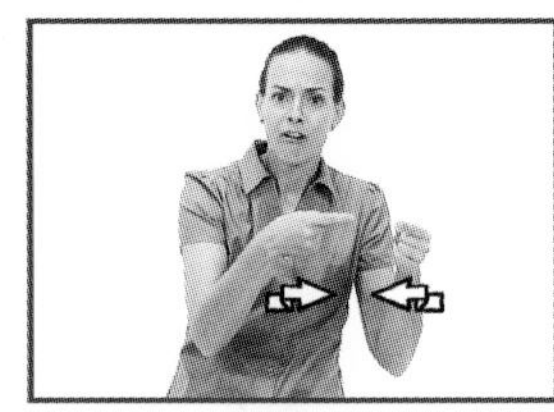

HURT

DIE

FALL-DOWN

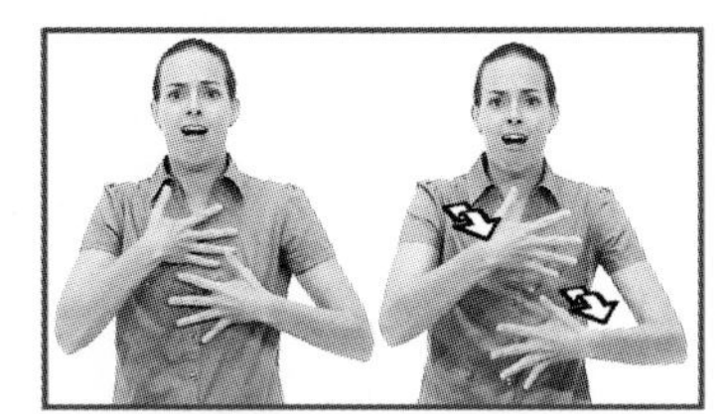

BREATHE (with difficulty)

EC:L*"ambulance lights flashing"*

HURRY

LESSON 8:7

Asking for Advice 1

Lesson length: 75–105 minutes

LESSON GOAL

Students will sign this dialogue:

KEY PHRASES

A: explain problem, ask for advice
- tell when
- explain situation
- tell what you forgot to do (use conjunction)[1]
- ask for advice[2]

B: give advice[3]

A: respond

conj
[1]ME (activity), !THOUGHT-OCCUR! ...

whq
[2]ME (2h)#DO++

[3]WHY+NOT [YOU] ...

NOTIONS

Grammar

Explaining problem (sequence)

- tell when
- explain situation
- tell what you forgot to do (use conjunction)
- ask for advice

Vocabulary

Conjunction

THOUGHT-OCCUR

Give advice

WHY+NOT

Response to advice

GOOD+IDEA

Others

MAKE/CREATE

LOCK-UP

CREDIT-CARD

NEXT-TO *"neighbor"*

PREPARATION

Review main points of the lesson **Conjunction: What You Forgot to Do** and **Asking for or Giving Advice**, *Student Workbook*, page 115

MATERIALS

8:7 Lesson Slides

8:7 Follow-up Slides

Exercise 1A and 1B (*Student Workbook*, pages 470 and 474)

HOMEWORK 8:7

Student Workbook, pages 114–119

INTRODUCE *Explain Problem, Ask for Advice*

45–60 minutes

PRESENT
(LESSON SLIDE 8:7:1)

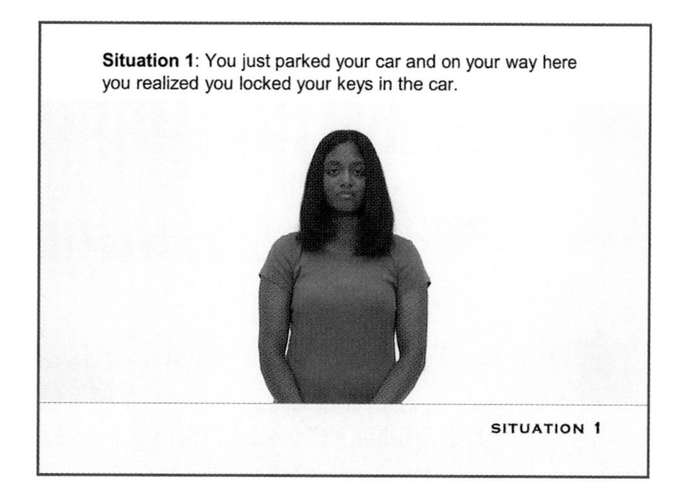
Situation 1: You just parked your car and on your way here you realized you locked your keys in the car.
SITUATION 1

Tell students to read the situation. Then, show video.

PRESENT
(LESSON SLIDE 8:7:2)

Situation 1: You just parked your car and on your way here you realized you locked your keys in the car.

Explain problem, ask for advice

- tell when
- explain the situation
- tell what you forgot to do (use conjunction)
- ask for advice

Repeat what Tonique signed in the video and have students copy.

For ***"• tell when"***

T: RECENT

S: (copy)

LOCK-UP"car"

For ***"• explain the situation"***

T: ME ARRIVE-here PARK-CAR*"on right."*
LOCK-UP***"car on right"***

S: (copy)

!THOUGHT-OCCUR!

For "• *tell what you forgot to do (use conjunction)*"

mm — conj

T: ME WALK, SCL:1*"coming from right"* **!THOUGHT-OCCUR!**

t

KEY, LEAVE-ALONE*"car on right,"* INSIDE CAR

S: (copy)

For "• *ask for advice*"

whq

T: ME (2h)#DO++

S: (copy)

Pair up. Have students rehearse the whole narrative.

S: RECENT ME ARRIVE-here PARK-CAR*"on right."*
LOCK-UP*"car on right"* ME WALK, SCL:1*"coming here"*

conj — t

!THOUGHT-OCCUR! KEY, LEAVE- ALONE*"car on right,"*

whq

INSIDE CAR. ME (2h)#DO++

Be sure students:

- show action before using conjunction, for example:

  conj

  WALK, SCL:1*"coming here"* !THOUGHT-OCCUR!

- name the object before explaining the problem, for example:

  t

  KEY, LEAVE-ALONE*"car on right"*

- modify verbs to agree with location, for example:
  (ME) PARK-CAR*"on right"*
  LOCK-UP*"car on right"*
  SCL:1*"coming from right"*
  LEAVE-ALONE*"car on right"*

PRESENT
(LESSON SLIDE 8:7:3)

Situation 2: This morning you put a kettle of water on the stove for tea, but forgot about it after you got dressed and left for work.

Explain problem, ask for advice

- tell when
- explain situation
- tell what you forgot to do (use conjunction)
- ask for advice

Ask questions to help students determine how to sign each part of the narrative:

For *"• tell when"*
T: (ask when it happened)
S: NOW MORNING

For *"• explain the situation"*
T: (ask what you want to make)
S: [MAKE] TEA

T: (ask how to make tea)
S: [(wh)LCL:C*"kettle"*/WATER POUR-*in-kettle*, ECL*"fill up"*] ICL:Y*"put kettle on burner"* ECL*"flames on burner"*

T: (ask what you do while water is boiling)
S: GET-DRESSED.

T: (ask how you go to work)
S: DRIVE, WALK or RIDE-IN #BUS

For *"• tell what you forgot to do (use conjunction)"*
T: (ask what is forgotten)
t
S: ECL*"flames on burner,"* #OFF

For *"• ask for advice"*
T: (ask how to ask for advice)
whq
S: ME (2h)#DO++

PRESENT
(LESSON SLIDE 8:7:4)

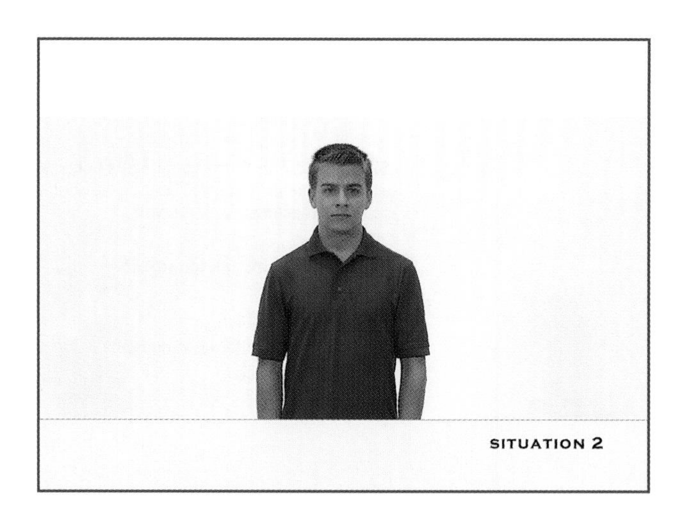

Pair up. Show Derrick signing the situation. Then, pair students up and have them rehearse the whole narrative.

MAKE

S: NOW MORNING, ME **MAKE** TEA, [(wh)LCL:C*"kettle,"*/WATER POUR-in-kettle, ECL*"fill up"*] ICL:Y*"put kettle on right burner"* ECL*"flames on right burner"* ME GET-DRESSED. FINISH, LEAVE-FOR WORK. DRIVE++, !THOUGHT-OCCUR! ME FORGET ECL*"flames on right burner"* #OFF-right. ME (2h)DO++

(non-manual markers: "when" over FINISH; "conj" over DRIVE++, !THOUGHT-OCCUR!; "t" over ECL*"flames on right burner"*; "whq" over ME (2h)DO++)

Be sure students:

- show action before using conjunction, for example:
  conj
  DRIVE++, !THOUGHT-OCCUR!
- name the object before explaining the problem, for example:
  t
  FORGET ECL*"flames on right burner,"* #OFF-right.
- modify verbs to agree with location, for example:
  ICL:Y*"put kettle on right burner"*
  ECL*"flames on right burner"*

PRESENT
(LESSON SLIDE 8:7:5)

Situation 3: Last night, you ate out. You paid with a credit card. On the way home, you realized you had forgotten your credit card.

Explain problem, ask for advice

- tell when
- explain situation
- tell what you forgot to do (use conjunction)
- ask for advice

Ask questions to help students determine how to sign each part of the narrative.

For "***• tell when***"

T: (ask when it happened)

S: IN-PAST NIGHT

For "***• explain the situation***"

T: (ask where you ate out)

S: RESTAURANT

CREDIT-CARD

T: (ask how you paid for meal)

S: **CREDIT-CARD**

T: (ask how you went home)

S: DRIVE, WALK or RIDE-IN #BUS

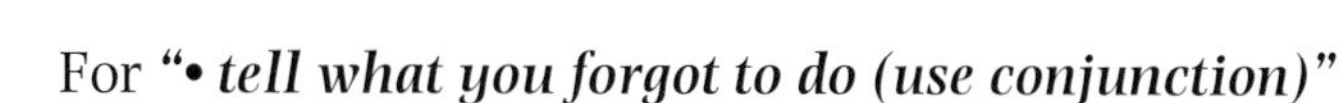
For "***• tell what you forgot to do (use conjunction)***"

T: (ask what is forgotten)

t

S: CREDIT-CARD, LEAVE-ALONE RESTAURANT

For "***• ask for advice***"

T: (ask how to ask for advice)

whq

S: ME (2h)#DO++

PRESENT
(LESSON SLIDE 8:7:6)

Pair up. Show Lauren signing the situation. Then, pair students up and have them rehearse the whole narrative.

S: IN-PAST NIGHT, ME GO-TO*"right"* RESTAURANT,

when: EAT++. FINISH, CREDIT-CARD ME GIVE-TO*"right"* (pause).

t: LEAVE-FOR*"left"* HOME, !THOUGHT-OCCUR! CREDIT-CARD,

whq: ME LEAVE-ALONE*"right"* ME (2h)DO++

Be sure students:

- show action before using conjunction, for example:

  conj: LEAVE-FOR*"left"* HOME, !THOUGHT-OCCUR!

- name the object before explaining the problem, for example:

  t: **CREDIT-CARD**, ME LEAVE-ALONE*"right"*

- modify verbs to agree with location, for example:

  restaurant on right
  - GO-TO*"right"*
  - GIVE-TO*"right"*
  - LEAVE-ALONE*"right"*

  home on left
  - LEAVE-FOR*"left"*

PRACTICE *Ask for or Give Advice*

30–45 minutes

Students will practice giving advice using WHY+NOT.

WARM UP

Sign these phrases and have students copy. Be sure they raise their brows when signing the conjunction.

mm / conj
T: ME WALK++, **!THOUGHT-OCCUR!** ME FORGET...
S: (copy)

mm / conj
T: ME READ++, **!THOUGHT-OCCUR!** ME FORGET...
S: (copy)

mm / conj
T: ME DRIVE++, **!THOUGHT-OCCUR!** ME FORGET...
S: (copy)

mm / conj
T: ME RIDE-BICYCLE++, **!THOUGHT-OCCUR!** ME FORGET...
S: (copy)

conj
T: ME LEAVE-FOR HOME, **!THOUGHT-OCCUR!** ME FORGET...
S: (copy)

conj
T: ME ARRIVE HOME, **!THOUGHT-OCCUR!** ME FORGET...
S: (copy)

PRESENT
(LESSON SLIDE 8:7:7)

Situation 1: You just parked your car and on your way here you realized you locked your keys in the car.

Signer A: explain problem, ask for advice
- tell when
- explain situation
- tell what you forgot to do (use conjunction)
- ask for advice

B: give advice
A: respond

Have a student role play Signer A and sign **Situation 1**. You demonstrate Signer B's line and give advice using **WHY+NOT**.

S1: (sign **Situation 1**)

T: **WHY+NOT** YOU PHONE-TO fs-AAA, TELL-TO
whq
COME-TO-here OPEN FOR+YOU.

For: ***"A: respond,"*** introduce phrase and have students copy.

nodding
T: **GOOD+IDEA**, ME PHONE-TO
S: (copy)

or

WHY+NOT (2 variations)

GOOD+IDEA

PRESENT
(LESSON SLIDE 8:7:8)

Situation 2: This morning you put a kettle of water on the stove for tea, but forgot about it after you got dressed and left for work.

Signer A: explain problem, ask for advice
- tell when
- explain situation
- tell what you forgot to do (use conjunction)
- ask for advice

B: give advice
A: respond

Repeat procedure. This time, have another student give different advice as well.

NEXT-TO*"neighbor"*

S1: (sign **Situation 2**)

T: **WHY+NOT** YOU PHONE-TO **NEXT-TO*"neighbor,"***

TELL-TO*"neighbor"* GO-TO*"your house"* ECL*"flames on*

whq
burner" ICL*"turn off"* #OFF, "well."

nodding
S1: GOOD+IDEA, ME PHONE-TO

whq
S2: (offer different advice) WHY+NOT...
S1: (respond) GOOD+IDEA...

PRESENT
(LESSON SLIDE 8:7:9)

Situation 3: Last night you ate out. You paid with a credit card. On the way home, you realized you had forgotten your credit card.

Signer A: explain problem, ask for advice
- tell when
- explain situation
- tell what you forgot to do (use conjunction)
- ask for advice

B: give advice
A: respond

Repeat procedure.

S1: (sign **Situation 3**)

T: **WHY+NOT** YOU PHONE-TO RESTAURANT, ASK-TO
whq
IX*"restaurant"* HAVE CREDIT-CARD

nodding
S1: GOOD+IDEA, ME PHONE-TO
whq
S2: (offer different advice) WHY+NOT...
S1: (respond) GOOD+IDEA, ...

EXERCISE 1A AND 1B

Assign half of the class **Exercise 1A** and the other half **Exercise 1B** (*Student Workbook*, page 470 and 474).

Have students with the same exercise sheet discuss among themselves how to sign the situations.

Pair Up. When ready, pair up students, one with **Exercise 1A** and the other with **Exercise 1B**. Have them take turns asking for advice. Have them follow the dialogue format on their exercise sheet.

Conclude. Have students sign one of the situations on their exercise sheets (use the **Teacher's Guide** below to check the translations). Then invite several students to give advice. Monitor WHY+NOT form. Continue until all four situations are signed.

Teacher's Guide

EXERCISE 1A

Ask for Advice 1: *This morning you were late for school so you rushed out of the house. On the way to class, you realized you forgot to give your dog his medicine. Ask for advice.*

- tell when: NOW MORNING

  when
- explain situation: ME GET-UP, TAKE-SHOWER, FINISH ME LOOK-AT-clock TIME, ME !LATE! ME HURRY-cont, GET-DRESSED, PACK-THINGS++, LEAVE-FOR SCHOOL.

  mm conj
- use conjunction: DRIVE++ !THOUGHT-OCCUR!

  t
- tell what you forgot to do: #DOG NEED MEDICINE, ME FORGET GIVE-TO-dog.

  whq
- ask for advice: ME (2h)DO++

Ask for Advice 2: *This morning as your cell phone was recharging, you got ready for work. When you arrived at work, you realized you forgot your cell phone. Ask for advice.*

- tell when: NOW MORNING

  t
- explain situation: MY fs-CELL PHONE, ME PLUG-IN, GET-READY++ FOR WORK (2h)DO++-cont.

  when

  PACK-THINGS, EAT, FINISH, ME LEAVE-FOR WORK.

- use conjunction: ME ARRIVE WORK,

  conj

  !THOUGHT-OCCUR!

t
- tell what you forgot to do: MY fs-CELL PHONE, ME LEAVE-ALONE HOME

whq
- ask for advice: ME (2h)DO++

EXERCISE 1B

Ask for Advice 3: *Last night you made a birthday cake for your classmate. This morning you were late and rushed out of the house. On the way to school you realized you forgot the cake. Ask for advice.*

- tell when 1: IN-PAST NIGHT

- explain situation 1: ME MAKE++ BIRTHDAY fs-CAKE (nod). ICL*"put cake aside."* ME SLEEP ALL-NIGHT

- tell when 2: NOW MORNING

- explain situation 2: ME GET-UP fs-LATE. ME HURRY GET-DRESSED, GET-IN CAR

ee conj
- use conjunction: DRIVE++ !THOUGHT-OCCUR!

- tell what you forgot to do: ME FORGET BRING-TO-here fs-CAKE

whq
- ask for advice: ME (2h)DO++

Ask for Advice 4: *This morning you let the dog out as you got ready for school. As soon as you got to school, it started to rain. You realized your dog is still outside. Ask for advice.*

- tell when: NOW MORNING

t
- explain situation: ME GET-UP. #DOG, EXIT, GO-AWAY

when
ME EAT, BRUSH-TEETH, GET-DRESSED, FINISH,
ME LEAVE-FOR SCHOOL

- use conjunction: ARRIVE SCHOOL, START RAIN (pause)
  ________________ conj
  !THOUGHT-OCCUR!

- tell what you forgot to do: ME FORGET LEAVE-ALONE #DOG EXIT

  ________ whq
- ask for advice: ME (2h)DO++

HOMEWORK

Tell students to do **Homework 8:7** (*Student Workbook*, pages 114–119).

HOMEWORK FOLLOW-UP
10–15 MINUTES

PRESENT
(FOLLOW-UP SLIDES 8:7:1–12)

Minidialogue 1

1. situation:
2. what was forgotten:
3. advice given:

Check students' answers to **Minidialogues 1–3**.
See **Introduction** pages xviii–xix for different ways to check answers.

LESSON 8:8

Asking for a Sign

Lesson length: 20 minutes

LESSON GOAL Students will review strategies to ask for a sign.

KEY SKILLS Strategies to ask for a sign

- list things in the category, ask for a sign
- use opposites, ask for a sign
- describe or act out, ask for a sign
- give definition

NOTIONS *Phrases*

1. (name several things in a category) SIGN "what" (whq over "what")
2. (give sign) OPPOSITE "what" (t over "(give sign)"; whq over "what")
3. (describe something or act something out) SIGN "what" (whq over "what")
4. (give definition) SIGN "what" (whq over "what")

PREPARATION Make copies of **8:8 What's the Sign** worksheets for each group of up to 14 students (for **Rounds 1–2** activity, page 230).

MATERIALS

8:8 Lesson Slides
8:8 Follow-up Slides
8:8 What's the Sign worksheets

HOMEWORK 8:8 *Student Workbook*, pages 120–121

REVIEW *Asking for a Sign*

10 minutes

PRESENT
(LESSON SLIDE 8:8:1)

Strategies to ask for a sign:

1. list things in the category
2. use opposites
3. describe or act out
4. give definition

Use the recommended strategies to ask students for the target signs below. After students give the sign, review the strategy used.

Target signs	*Strategy*
NUMBER	1
MAN	2
KEY	3
ENTER (room)	3
SISTER	4

PRACTICE *What's the Sign?*

10 minutes

Students practice strategies to ask for a sign.

PRESENT
(LESSON SLIDE 8:8:2)

Strategies to ask for a sign:

1. list things in the category
2. use opposites
3. describe or act out
4. give definition

***Activity**: Using the different strategies, get your partner to guess the sign for the item or concept listed on your worksheet.*

Set Up. Put students into even numbered groups, between 4–14 students in a group. Give each person in the group a different **What's the Sign** worksheet (See **Preparation**).

Give them a minute to look over their worksheets.

Now, divide each group into two rows and have students face one another. Indicate which row is A and B.

Round 1

Have students in Row A get their partners in Row B to guess their signs.

When Row A students are done with their lists, have Row B students give feedback to their partners on how to improve their strategies.

Round 2

Now have students in Row A shift to the right and do the list again with a new partner. This time their descriptions should improve based on the feedback they received. To make it more challenging, give a time limit for completing the list.

Now repeat the rounds with students in Row B doing their lists.

Wrap Up. Have students get you to guess the last word on their list. Make suggestions to help students be more effective.

HOMEWORK

Tell students to do **Homework 8:8** (*Student Workbook*, pages 120–121).

HOMEWORK FOLLOW-UP
15–20 MINUTES

PRESENT
(FOLLOW-UP SLIDE 8:8:1)

Describe the concept then ask for the sign.
Be sure to use the same strategy used by the signer on video.

Have students open their workbook to **Figure the Meaning**, (*Student Workbook*, page 121) and take turns describing the concept and asking for the sign.

After an adequate description by the student, show the sign.

Teacher's Guide

1. SCREWDRIVER

2. EUROPE

3. LICENSE

4. SMART

5. PLAIN

6. OVERSLEEP (sleep in)

7. BE-BROKE (no money)

8. BE-WORRIED

9. NOISY

10. HAND-MIXER

LESSON 8:9

Agreement Verbs 2

Lesson length: 25–35 minutes

LESSON GOAL Students will learn to modify movement of the agreement verb to indicate the subject and the object of the sentence.

KEY SKILLS Correctly modify movement and palm orientation of the verb to indicate the subject and object relationship.

NOTIONS

Vocabulary

Agreement Verbs

BAWL-OUT-TO
BOTHER-TO
TEASE-TO
BORROW-FROM
IGNORE-TO

Other

LAPTOP

MATERIALS **8:9 Lesson Slides**

HOMEWORK 8:9 *Student Workbook*, pages 122–125

INTRODUCE *Agreement Verbs 2*

10–15 minutes

PRESENT
(LESSON SLIDE 8:9:1)

Introduce these verbs by showing and explaining the sign.

verb	*explanation*
1. **BAWL-OUT-TO**	***explain:*** son takes car, but did not ask you. He arrives home. ***act out:*** with an angry expression, you bawl him out, saying he took the car without asking you, that he should know better, then sign: rhet ME "what." **me-BAWL-OUT-TO-him.**
2. **BOTHER-TO**	***act out:*** you tap your mother to get her attention. She tells you to wait. You keep tapping her until she says "What!?," then sign: rhet ME "what." **me-BOTHER-to-mom MOTHER.**

3. TEASE-TO *explain:* friend sitting across has a glass of beer. You have a glass of iced tea. They have the same color. While your friend is looking away, you switch the glasses. When your friend takes a sip and realizes you switched the glasses, you laugh, then sign:

rhet
ME "what." **me-TEASE-TO-friend.**

4. BORROW-FROM *act out:* approach student, say you need a pencil, ask if you can take his or her pencil and return it tomorrow, then sign:

rhet t
ME "what." POSS PENCIL, ME **me-BORROW-FROM-student.**

5. IGNORE *act out:* while typing on the computer, dog scratches you for attention. You brush dog aside. Dog keeps scratching you, you keep brushing it aside, then sign:

rhet
ME "what." **me-IGNORE-TO-dog.**

PRESENT

(LESSON SLIDES 8:9:2–6)

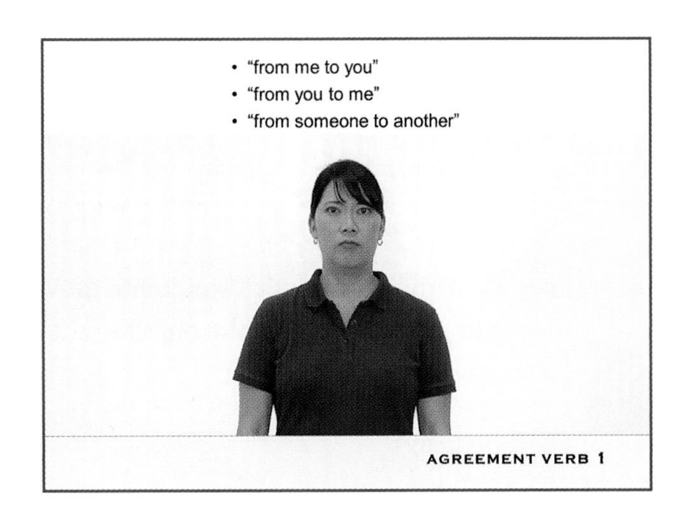

• "from me to you"
• "from you to me"
• "from someone to another"
AGREEMENT VERB 1

NOTE: Make sure students maintain eye contact when talking to the person, but when referring to the third person(s), they glance or shift head in the direction of the person(s).

Show video and have students practice the verb movements for each new sign. Check students' form for each of the following:

- "from me to you"
- "from you to me"
- "from someone to another"

	verb	*things to check for*
1.	**BAWL-OUT-TO**	fingers are directed toward the person being bawled out
2.	**BOTHER-TO**	the back of the weak hand is oriented toward the person being bothered
3.	**TEASE-TO**	the index finger on the dominant hand is oriented toward the person being teased
4.	**BORROW-FROM**	the movement of the sign begins at the person with the item and ends at the person who wants the item; the tips of the fingers always face the person who has the item at the beginning
5.	**IGNORE-TO**	the tip of the pinkie finger is directed at the person being ignored

PRACTICE *Two Agreement Verbs*

15–20 minutes

Students will practice modifying movements of two verbs to agree with the subject and the object of the sentence.

PRESENT
(LESSON SLIDE 8:9:7)

1. I was teasing Renee when she suddenly got angry and bawled me out.
2. Renee was teasing Lee when Lee suddenly got angry and bawled Renee out.
3. You were teasing Lee when Lee suddenly got angry and bawled you out.

Remember Lee is on your left and Renee on your right.

Demonstrate ***"1. I was teasing Renee when she suddenly got angry and bawled me out."***

t (over "fs-RENEE*"right"* IX*"Renee"*")

T: fs-RENEE*"right"* IX*"Renee"* ME **me-TEASE-TO-right++**, IX*"Renee"* !BE-ANGRY! **right-BAWL-OUT-TO-me.**

Pair up. Have students sign **Sentence 2** and **3** to each other.

PRESENT
(LESSON SLIDE 8:9:8)

4. Renee told me she borrowed Lee's laptop.
5. I told Lee you want to borrow his laptop.
6. Mind telling Lee I want to borrow his laptop?

Remember Lee is on your left and Renee on your right.

Demonstrate ***"4. Renee told me she borrowed Lee's laptop."***

LAPTOP

T: fs-RENEE*"right"* IX*"Renee"* right-TELL-TO-me fs-LEE*"left"* POSS*"Lee"* **LAPTOP**, IX*"Renee"* **right-BORROW-FROM-left.** (t)

Pair up. Have students sign **Sentence 5** and **6** to each other.

NOTE: For **Sentence 6**, make sure students use the sign NOT-MIND (q).

PRESENT
(LESSON SLIDE 8:9:9)

7. I know Lee's been bothering you. Just ignore him!
8. Renee's been bothering me. I can't ignore her.
9. Lee has been bothering Renee and

Remember Lee is on your left and Renee on your right.

Demonstrate ***"7. I know he's been bothering you. Just ignore him!"***

T: ME KNOW fs-LEE*"left"* IX*"Lee"* left-**BOTHER-TO** you++.
[YOU] **you-IGNORE-left.**

Pair up. Have students sign **Sentence 8** and **9** to each other.

HOMEWORK

Tell students to do **Homework 8:9** (*Student Workbook*, pages 122–125).

Also, students are to develop two narratives, each one using at least two agreement verbs that involve themselves and two other people (See **Assignment**, *Student Workbook*, page 123).

HOMEWORK FOLLOW-UP
(10–20 MINUTES)

Pair up. Have students take turns signing to each other the two narratives they developed for homework (**Assignment**, *Student Workbook*, page 123).

When done, have them switch partners and sign their narratives again.

Conclude. Call on students to sign one of their narratives to the class.

Be sure students:

- modify the movements of both verbs to agree among the three people in the narrative.

LESSON 8:10

Asking for Advice 2

Lesson length: 115–140 minutes

LESSON GOAL

Students will sign this dialogue:

A: explain problem, ask for advice
- tell when
- explain situation
- tell what unexpectedly happened (use conjunction)[1]
- ask for advice

B: give advice

KEY SKILLS

[1] (situation), !WRONG! (tell what happened) — "conj" marked over !WRONG!

NOTIONS

Grammar

Describing a spill (sequence)

1. tell what person/animal was doing
2. [name liquid], describe movement of liquid (element classifier)
3. tell where, describe how it lands (element classifier)

Describing an awkward conversation (sequence)

1. describe what you and another person were doing at the time
2. role shift other person asking or saying something uncomfortable or awkward
3. tell how you responded or reacted
4. tell other person's reaction

Describing what one's not supposed to do (sequence)

1. describe what went on before the incident
2. role shift to describe a person doing something she or he was not supposed to do

Element classifiers (ECLs) to describe spills

Vocabulary

Conjunction

!WRONG!

Food-related

HAMBURGER
fs-MUSTARD
SALAD
KETCHUP
KNIFE
FORK
SPOON
SALT+PEPPER
NAPKIN

Verbs

BREAK
VOMIT
MEANING

Nouns

GLASS
SCHEDULE
WEDDING (2h)alt.EAT++(wedding reception)

Others

QUOTE
CRACKED-*on-iPhone*
AND

PREPARATION

- Review main points of the lesson in **Conjunction: What Unexpectedly Happened** and **Explaining Situation**, *Student Workbook*, page 127–129

- Make from **8:10 Describe the Object** cards. (for **Activity** on page 242).

MATERIALS

8:10 Lesson Slides
8:10 Follow-up Slides
8:10 Describe the Object Cards
Exercise 2A and 2B (in *Student Workbook*, pages 476 and 480)

HOMEWORK 8:10

Student Workbook, pages 126–133

INTRODUCE *Describe the Object*

10–15 minutes

Set Up. Hand out the **8:10 Describe the Object** cards (see **Materials**) to ten students.

ACTIVITY

Have these students take turns describing the object on their cards to the class, WITHOUT using the sign for the object. After each has adequately described the object, you introduce the sign for it from the list below (these signs are needed for **Exercise 2**, used later in this lesson).

After you give the sign, ask students to give you at least two English equivalent words for the sign. Write the words on the board. For example:

1. HAMBURGER (burger, hamburger, ground beef, etc.)
2. fs-MUSTARD (mustard, yellow condiment, etc.)
3. SALAD (tossed salad, salad)
4. KETCHUP (red condiment, catsup, ketchup, etc.)
5. fs-RUG (mat, rug, carpet, etc.)
6. CHURCH (house of worship, chapel, church, etc.)
7. WEDDING (2h)alt.EAT++ (wedding reception, banquet, party, etc.)
8. KNIFE, FORK, SPOON (flatware, silverware, utensils, knives, forks and spoons, etc.)
9. SALT, PEPPER (seasonings, salt and pepper, etc.)
10. NAPKIN (cloth, towel, napkin, etc.)

INTRODUCE *Explain Situation, Incidents Involving Liquids*

40–45 minutes

PRESENT
(LESSON SLIDE 8:10:1)

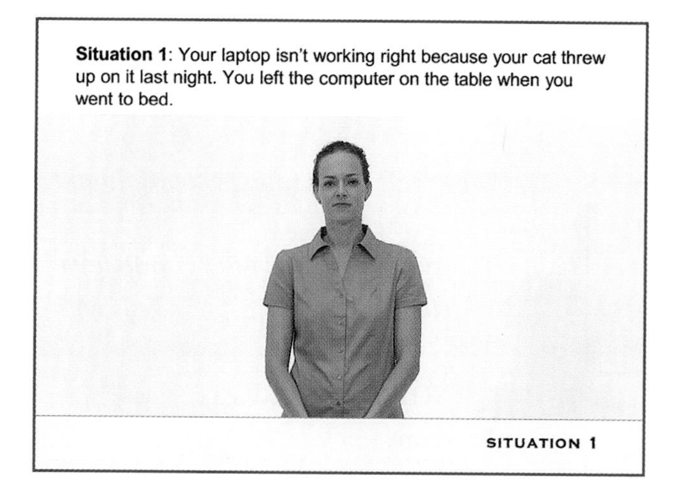

Tell students to read **Situation 1**, then show video.

PRESENT
(LESSON SLIDE 8:10:2)

Situation 1: Your laptop isn't working right because your cat threw up on it last night. You left the computer on the table when you went to bed.

Explain problem, ask for advice
- tell when
- explain the situation
- tell what unexpectedly happened (a spill)
- ask for advice

Repeat what Ursula signed for each part of the sequence and have students copy:

For "***• tell when***"
T: IN-PAST NIGHT
S: (copy)

For "**• *explain the situation***"

t

T: COMPUTER IX*"left,"* ME ICL*"open laptop(left)"*

when

TYPE++*"left."* FINISH, ME GO-AWAY*"right"* BED*"right."*
LCL:B*"laptop open(left)"* LEAVE-ALONE*"left."*

S: (copy)

!WRONG!

ECL*"vomit(left)"*

For "**• *tell what unexpectedly happened (a spill)***"

conj

T: **!WRONG!** CAT **ECL*"vomit(left)"*** **ECL*"spill on board (left)"*** NOW ICL*"press keys with difficulty(left)"* !HARD!

neg

NOT+WORK RIGHT.

S: (copy)

For "**• *ask for advice***"

whq

T: ME (2h)#DO++

S: (copy)

Pair up. Have students put the parts together and sign the incident.

t t

S: IN-PAST+NIGHT, COMPUTER IX*"left,"* ME ICL*"open laptop*

when

(left)" TYPE++*"left."* FINISH, ME GO-AWAY*"right"*

t

BED*"right."* LCL:B*"laptop open(left)"* LEAVE-ALONE*"left"*

conj

!WRONG! CAT ECL*"vomit(left)"* ECL*"spill on board(left)."*

neg

NOW ICL*"press keys with difficulty(left)"* !HARD! NOT+WORK

whq

RIGHT. ME (2h)#DO

Be sure students:

- name the topic/object, then describe action

  t
  COMPUTER IX*"left,"* ME ICL*"open laptop(left)"*
  TYPE++*"left"*

  t
  LCL:B*"laptop opened(left),"* LEAVE-ALONE*"left"*

- modify verbs to agree with location, for example:

  t
  COMPUTER IX*"left,"* ME ICL*"open laptop(left)"*
  TYPE++*"left"*

  t
  LCL:B*"laptop opened(left),"* LEAVE-ALONE*"left"*
  CAT ECL*"vomit(left)"* ECL*"spill on board(left)"*
  ICL*"press keys with difficulty(left)"*
  ME GO-AWAY*"right"* BED*"right"*

PRESENT
(LESSON SLIDE 8:10:3)

From Situation 1

- cat jumps on a table where laptop is
- cat throws up
- vomit splatters on the laptop

Describing a Spill

1. tell what person or animal was doing
2. name liquid, describe movement of liquid (element classifier)
3. tell where, describe how it lands (element classifier)

Determine when to use the conjunction.

Referring to **Situation 1**, have students repeat what was signed for each part of **Describing a Spill**.

For ***"1. tell what person or animal was doing"***

t t
S: TABLE, LCL:B*"laptop open(left)"* CAT (2h)SCL:V*"jumped onto the table"*

For ***"2. name liquid, describe movement of liquid (element classifier)"***

S: CAT ECL:5*"vomit(left)"*

For ***"3. tell where, describe how it lands (element classifier)"***

S: [LAPTOP] (2h)ECL:O→5*"spill on laptop keyboard(left)"*

Ask students where in **Situation 1** did the conjunction

conj
!WRONG! appear.

Answer:

conj
CAT (2h)SCL:V*"jumped onto the table"* **!WRONG!**
ECL:5*"vomit(left)"*...

PRESENT
(LESSON SLIDE 8:10:4)

Spill 1
- bouncing baby in front of you
- baby spits up
- spit up splatters on your shirt

Describing a Spill
1. tell what person or animal was doing
2. name liquid, describe movement of liquid (element classifier)
3. tell where, describe how it lands (element classifier)

Determine when to use the conjunction.

From **Spill 1**, ask students what should be signed for each part of **Describing a Spill**.

For ***"1. tell what person or animal was doing"***

S: BABY [ME] ICL*"bouncing baby in front of you"*

For ***"2. name liquid, describe movement of liquid (element classifier)"***

S: BABY ECL:5*"vomit outwardly"(front)*

For *"3. tell where, describe how it lands (element classifier)"*

S: [SHIRT] ECL:O→5*"splattered on front of shirt"*

Ask students where in the sequence they should use the

conj
conjunction **!WRONG!**

Answer:

conj
BABY [ME] ICL*"bouncing baby in front of you"* **!WRONG!** BABY ECL:5*"vomit outwardly (front)"...*

Pair Up. Have students put the parts together and sign the incident.

Be sure students:

- use the conjunction !WRONG! in the right place
- use element classifier that matches the liquid and its movement
- show where the liquid landed.

PRESENT
(LESSON SLIDE 8:10:5)

Spill 2

- eating hot dog
- mustard drips out
- mustard lands on your pants

Describing a Spill

1. tell what person or animal was doing
2. name liquid, describe movement of liquid (element classifier)
3. tell where, describe how it lands (element classifier)

Determine when to use the conjunction.

From **Spill 2**, ask students what should be signed for each part of **Describing a Spill**.

For *"1. tell what person or animal was doing"*

S: ME EAT HOT-DOG ICL*"holding hot dog to the mouth"*

For ***"2. name liquid, describe movement of liquid (element classifier)"***

S: YELLOW [or fs-MUSTARD] [(wh)ICL*"hold hot dog"*/ ECL:S→1*"drips down"*]

For ***"3. tell where, describe how it lands (element classifier)"***

S: PANTS [(wh)LCL:B*"pants"*/ECL:S→F*"lands on pants"*]

Ask students where in the sequence they should use the conjunction **!WRONG!**

Answer:

ME EAT HOT-DOG ICL*"holding hot dog to the mouth"*

conj t

!WRONG! YELLOW [or fs-MUSTARD]...

Pair Up. Have students put the parts together and sign the incident.

Be sure students:

- use the conjunction !WRONG! in the correct place
- use element classifier that matches the liquid and its movement
- show where the liquid landed.

PRESENT

(LESSON SLIDE 8:10:6)

Spill 3

- squeezing bottle of ketchup
- ketchup squirts out
- ketchup splatters on the wall

Describing a Spill

1. tell what person or animal was doing
2. name liquid, describe movement of liquid (element classifier)
3. tell where, describe how it lands (element classifier)

Determine when to use the conjunction.

From **Spill 3**, ask students what should be signed foe each part of **Describing a Spill**.

For ***"1. tell what person or animal was doing"***

```
 ________________t  ___________struggling
S: KETCHUP BOTTLE, ME  ICL"squeeze bottle"
```

For ***"2. name liquid, describe movement of liquid (element classifier)"***

S: [KETCHUP] [(wh)ICL*"hold bottle"*/ECL:S→1*"squirts"*]

For ***"3. tell where, describe how it lands (element classifier)"***

```
 ________t
S: fs-WALL [(wh)LCL:B"wall"/ECL:0→5"splatters on wall"]
```

Ask students where in the sequence they should use the conjunction **!WRONG!**

Answer:

```
                  ___________struggling  _____conj
KETCHUP BOTTLE, ME ICL"squeeze bottle" !WRONG!
[KETCHUP] [(wh)ICL"hold bottle"/ECL:S→1"squirts"]...
```

Pair Up. Have students put the parts together and sign the incident.

Be sure students:

- use the conjunction !WRONG! in the right place
- use element classifier that matches the liquid and its movement
- show where the liquid landed.

INTRODUCE *Explaining Situation—Awkward Conversations*

20–25 minutes

PRESENT
(LESSON SLIDE 8:10:7)

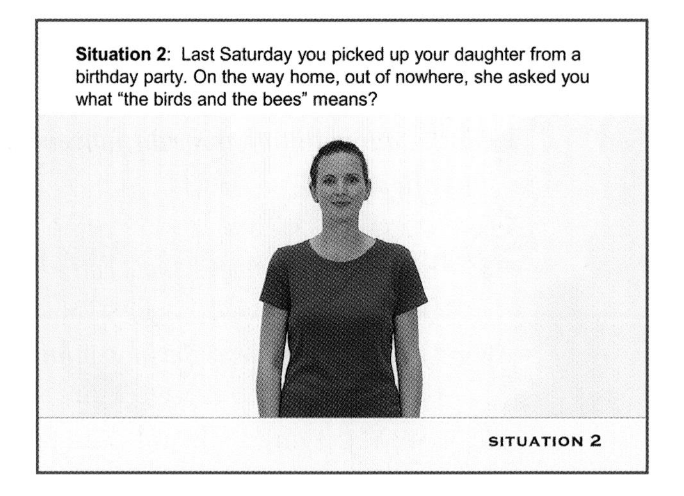
Situation 2: Last Saturday you picked up your daughter from a birthday party. On the way home, out of nowhere, she asked you what "the birds and the bees" means?
SITUATION 2

Tell students to read **Situation 2**, then show the video.

PRESENT
(LESSON SLIDE 8:10:8)

Situation 2: Last Saturday you picked up your daughter from a birthday party. On the way home, out of nowhere, she asked you what "the birds and the bees" means?

Explain problem, ask for advice

- tell when
- explain the situation
- tell what unexpectedly happened (awkward conversation)
- ask for advice

Repeat what Amber signed for each part of the sequence and have students copy:

For ***"• tell when"***

T: PAST+SATURDAY

S: (copy)

For “• *explain the situation*”

when
T: MY DAUGHTER GO-TO-right PARTY *“right.”* FINISH ME
GO-TO-right PICK-UP-her, BRING-TO-left HOME.
ME DRIVE++
S: (copy)

QUOTE

AND

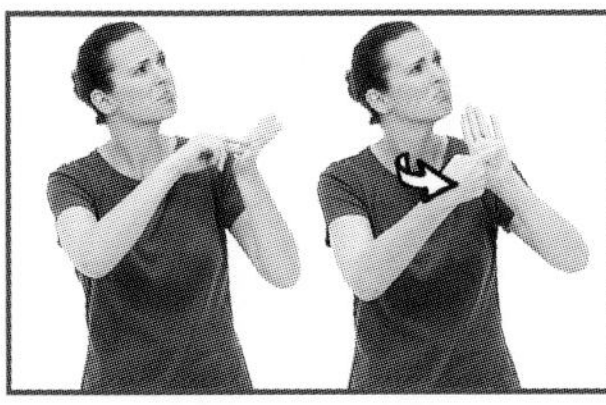

MEANING

For “• *tell what unexpectedly happened (awkward conversation)*”

conj
T: !WRONG! DAUGHTER she-ASK-TO-me <rs:daughter “hey”
whq
QUOTE BIRD **AND** fs-BEES **MEANING** “what”> <rs:me
q
ME TELL-TO-you LATER fs-OK> <rs:daughter FINE++>
S: (copy)

For “• *ask for advice*”

whq
T: ME (2h)#DO++
S: (copy)

Pair up. Have students sign the incident.

t
“pshaw” PAST+SATURDAY MY DAUGHTER
when
GO-TO-right PARTY *“right.”* FINISH ME GO-TO-right

PICK-UP-her, BRING-TO-left HOME. ME DRIVE++
conj
!WRONG! DAUGHTER she-ASK-TO-me <rs:daughter “hey”
whq
QUOTE BIRD AND fs-BEES **MEANING** “what”> <rs:me
q
ME TELL-TO-you LATER fs-OK> <rs:daughter FINE++>.
whq whq
ME (2h)#DO, ME TELL-TO-her “what”

Be sure students:

- use role shift to show the daughter's question and Amber's response.
- modify verbs to agree with location, for example:

GO-TO-right PARTY *"right."*
when
FINISH ME GO-TO-right PICK-UP-her *"right"*
BRING-TO-left HOME.

PRESENT
(LESSON SLIDE 8:10:9)

Awkward Conversation
While eating lunch in the cafeteria a person you don't particularly care for approaches you and begins chatting. Out of the blue, she or he asks you for a date on New Year's Eve. You say you will check your schedule and get back to her or him.

Describing Awkward Conversations
1. describe what you and another person were doing at the time
2. role shift other person asking or saying something uncomfortable or awkward
3. tell how you responded or reacted
4. tell other person's reaction

Determine when to use the conjunction.

From **Awkward Conversation** ask students what should be signed for each part of **Describing an Awkward Conversation.**

For ***"1. describe what you and another person were doing at the time"***
S: NOON, ME SIT EAT [MAN or WOMAN] SCL:1 *"approach me"* SIT, US-TWO CHAT++

For ***"2. role shift other person asking or saying something uncomfortable or awkward"***

S: IX ASK-TO-me <rs:person WANT US-TWO GO-TO NEW
q
YEAR fs-EVE PARTY>

SCHEDULE

For ***"3. tell how you responded or reacted"***
S: ME <rs:me (hesitant) ME CHECK **SCHEDULE**,
ME TELL-TO-you TOMORROW>

For ***"4. tell other person's reaction"***

S: <rs:person FINE++>

Ask students where in the sequence they should use the conjunction **!WRONG!**

Answer:

conj
US-TWO CHAT++ **!WRONG!** IX ASK-TO-me <rs:person
q
WANT US-TWO GO-TO NEW YEAR fs-EVE PARTY>...

Pair up. Have students sign the incident.

NOON, ME SIT EAT [MAN or WOMAN]
conj
SCL:1 *"approach me"* SIT, US-TWO CHAT++. **!WRONG!**

IX ASK-TO-me <rs:person WANT US-TWO GO-TO NEW
q
YEAR fs-EVE PARTY> ME <rs:me (hesitant) ME CHECK **SCHEDULE**, ME TELL-TO-you TOMORROW>
<rs:person FINE++>

Be sure students:

- use role shift to show the other person's question and "their" response
- match the locations of the people while role shifting
- use the conjunction !WRONG! in the correct place.

INTRODUCE *Explaining Situation, Something One's Not Supposed to Do*

20–25 minutes

PRESENT
(LESSON SLIDE 8:10:10)

Situation 3: This morning, your brother came over to visit and he showed you his new iPhone. When he left, he forgot his phone. While playing with the phone, it slipped out of your hands and fell to the floor. The touch screen cracked.

SITUATION 3

Tell students to read **Situation 3**, then show the video.

PRESENT
(LESSON SLIDE 8:10:11)

Situation 3: This morning, your brother came over to visit and he showed you his new iPhone. When he left, he forgot his phone. While playing with the phone, it slipped out of your hands and fell to the floor. The touch screen cracked.

Explain problem, ask for advice
- tell when
- explain the situation
- tell what unexpectedly happened (something one's not supposed to do)
- ask for advice

Repeat what Justin signed for each part of the sequence and have students copy.

For ***"• tell when"***
T: NOW+MORNING
S: (copy)

For *"• explain the situation"*

T: MY BROTHER right-COME-TO-here VISIT. IX*"brother"* right-SHOW-TO-me POSS !NEW! fs-I+PHONE !NICE! DCL*"rectangular, thin"* [(*wh*)ICL*"hold iPhone"*/ICL*"sweep over surface"* SWELL] (wh)ICL*"put iPhone on table."* US-TWO CHAT++. BROTHER LEAVE-FOR. *"ahh"* FORGET PHONE LEAVE-ALONE. *"shrug shoulders"* FINE++. ME WANT PLAY GAME. [(wh)ICL*"pick up iPhone from table"*/ICL*"type on touch screen"*]

S: (copy)

For ***"• tell what unexpectedly happened (something one's not supposed to do)"***

conj

T: **!WRONG!** [(wh)ICL*"hold phone"*/LCL:B*"iPhone slips from hands"]*

t

FLOOR [(wh)LCL:B*"floor"*/LCL:B*"iPhone hits floor"*] ME *"oh no"* [(wh)ICL*"pick up iPhone"*/**GLASS CRACKED-*on-iPhone*] BREAK.**

S: (copy)

For ***"• ask for advice"***

whq

T: ME (2h)#DO++

S: (copy)

GLASS

CRACKED-*on-iPhone*

BREAK

Pair up. Have students sign the incident.

> ________________t
> NOW+MORNING MY BROTHER right-COME-TO-here VISIT. IX*"brother"* right-SHOW-TO-me POSS !NEW! fs-I+PHONE !NICE! DCL*"rectangular, thin"* [(wh)ICL*"hold iPhone"*/ICL*"sweep over surface"* SWELL] (wh)ICL*"put iPhone on table."* US-TWO CHAT++.
> BROTHER LEAVE-FOR "ahh" FORGET PHONE LEAVE-ALONE. *"shrug shoulders"* FINE++. ME WANT PLAY GAME. (wh)ICL*"pick up iPhone from table"*/ICL*"type on*
> ________conj ____________________t
> *touch screen"*] !WRONG! [(wh)ICL*"hold phone"*/
> ______t
> LCL:B*"iPhone slips from hands"*] FLOOR
> [(wh)LCL:B*"floor"*/LCL:B"iPhone hits floor"] ME "oh no"
> [(wh)ICL*"pick up iPhone"*/GLASS CRACKED-*on-iPhone*]
> ____________whq
> BREAK. ME (2h)DO++

Be sure students:

- use role shift to show the person handling the phone
- describe handling of the iPhone in its location
- use the conjunction !WRONG! in the right place
- name the floor before showing the phone hitting it.

PRESENT
(LESSON SLIDE 8:10:12)

Not Supposed to Do
At Thanksgiving while family members sit around the table eating and chatting, you notice your nephew sneaking food to the dog under the table.

Describing What One's Not Supposed to Do
1. describe what went on before the incident
2. role shift to describe a person doing something she or he was not supposed to do

Determine when to use the conjunction.

From **Not Supposed to Do**, ask student what should be signed for each part of **Describing What One's Not Supposed to Do**.

For *"1. describe what went on before the incident"*

S: THANKSGIVING FAMILY SIT (2h)PCL:V*"seated around a table"* alt.EAT++, CHAT++

For ***"2. role shift to describe a person doing something she or he was not supposed to do"***

t t

S: ME SEE NEPHEW IX SIT. TABLE, #DOG SCL:V*"sits under table"* NEPHEW <rs:nephew he-LOOK-AT-dog, ICL*"take food from his plate and gives it to the dog several times"*> #DOG <rs:dog BPCL*"takes a bite each time"*>

Ask students where in the sequence they should use the conjunction.

Answer:

FAMILY SIT (2h)PCL:V*"seated around a table"* alt.EAT++,

conj

CHAT++. **!WRONG!** ME SEE NEPHEW IX SIT...

Pair up. Have students sign the incident.

FAMILY SIT (2h)PCL:V*"seated around a table"* alt.EAT++,

conj t

CHAT++. **!WRONG!** ME SEE NEPHEW IX SIT. TABLE,

t

#DOG SCL:V*"sits under table"* NEPHEW <rs:nephew he-LOOK-AT-dog, ICL*"take food from his plate and gives it to the dog several times"*> #DOG <rs:dog BPCL*"takes a bite each time"*>

Be sure students:

- use the conjunction !WRONG! in the correct place
- match the locations of the people while role shifting
- use role shift to show the other person's question and "their" response.

PRACTICE *Explain Problem, Ask for Advice*

40–45 minutes

EXERCISE 2A AND 2B

Assign half of the class **Exercise 2A** and the other half of the class **Exercise 2B** (*Student Workbook*, pages 476 and 480).

Have students with the same exercise sheet discuss among themselves how to sign the situations.

Pair Up. When ready, pair up students, one with **Exercise 2A** and the other with **Exercise 2B**. Have them take turns asking for advice. Have them follow the dialogue format on their exercise sheet.

Conclude. Have students sign one of the situations on their exercise sheets (use the **Teacher's Guide** below to check the translations). Then invite several students to give advice. Monitor their WHY+NOT form. Continue until all six situations are signed.

Teacher's Guide

EXERCISE 2A

Ask for Advice 1 (a spill): *You borrowed your sister's (or brother's) pants last night to go out to eat. As you were biting into a hamburger, mustard dripped onto the pants, leaving a yellow stain.*

- tell when: IN-PAST NIGHT
- explain situation: ME LEAVE-FOR EAT, $\overline{\text{NICE PANTS,}}^{\,t}$ $\overline{\text{ME NONE}}^{\,neg}$. ME BORROW BROTHER POSS PANTS. GO-TO RESTAURANT, [ORDER-TO] HAMBURGER. BRING-TO-here. ME ICL*"hold hamburger to mouth, bite"*

- tell what unexpectedly happened (use conjunction): !WRONG! YELLOW [or fs-MUSTARD] [(wh)ICL*"hold hamburger"*/ ECL:S→1*"drips down"*] PANTS [(wh)LCL:B*"pants"*/ ECL:S→F*"lands on pants"*]

  whq
- ask for advice: ME (2h)DO++

Ask for Advice 2 (an awkward conversation): *During a walk in the park with your niece yesterday, out of nowhere, your niece asked if she was adopted. You told her you would talk to her about it later.*

- tell when: YESTERDAY
- explain situation: NIECE US-TWO LEAVE-FOR fs-PARK, WALK...

  conj
- tell what unexpectedly happened (use conjunction): !WRONG!

  q

  NIECE ASK-TO-me <rs:niece "hey" ME BE-ADOPTED> <rs:me

  stumped q

  LOOK-AT-niece, ME TELL-TO-you LATER, fs-OK> <rs:niece #OK>.

  whq
- ask for advice: ME (2h)DO++

Ask for Advice 3 (not supposed to do): *Today at the restaurant where you work, while preparing food in the kitchen, you saw another employee who was preparing the salad accidentally flip the salad bowl onto the floor. Instead of throwing the ingredients away, he just put them back in the bowl.*

- tell when: NOW/TODAY

- explain situation: ME WORK IX-loc RESTAURANT, ME WORK++ ICL*"chopping, slicing vegetables,"* SEE OTHER WORK+ER IX*"worker"* MAKE SALAD, ICL*"breaking up lettuce and putting into a bowl"*

conj

- tell what unexpectedly happened (use conjunction): !WRONG! BOWL (2h)LCL:C*"flip over"* (2h)PCL:0→5*"contents of bowl spill out"* IX*"worker"* [(wh)LCL:C*"bowl"*/ICL*"put contents back into bowl, place bowl on table"*

whq

- ask for advice: ME (2h)DO+

EXERCISE 2B

Ask for Advice 4 (a spill): *Last Saturday, when you were house sitting for a friend and making your lunch, you had difficulty getting the ketchup out of the bottle when it suddenly gushed out and splashed on the white rug.*

t

- tell when: MY FRIEND IX GO-AWAY, POSS HOUSE, ME

  t

  TAKE-CARE-OF. IN-PAST SATURDAY [NOON]...

- explain situation: ME EAT, KETCHUP ME ICL*"pounding bottle."*...

conj

- tell what unexpectedly happened (use conjunction): !WRONG! [KETCHUP] [(wh)ICL*"hold bottle"*/ECL:S→5*"splatters outward"*]

  t

  fs-RUG !WHITE! "area" [(wh)LCL:B*"rug"*/ECL:0→5*"splatters on rug"*]

whq

- ask for advice: ME (2h)DO++

Ask for Advice 5 (an awkward conversation): *This morning during church service, your son, out of the blue, asked you if he had a brother. You told him to be quiet in church and that you would talk about it later. (His dad has another son the same age with another woman.)*

- tell when: NOW MORNING
- explain situation: SON, US-TWO GO-TO CHURCH, SIT, LOOK-AT-preacher

conj

- tell what unexpectedly happened (use conjunction): !WRONG!

  q

  SON he-ASK-TO-me <rs:son ME HAVE BROTHER.> ME LOOK-AT-him, <rs:me "shhh" CHURCH "shhh." ME TALK MORE LATER>

  whq

- ask for advice: ME (2h)DO++

Ask for Advice 6 (not supposed to do): *This afternoon you witnessed something improper at a wedding reception. You saw a guest at the next table putting silverware, salt and pepper shakers, and cloth napkins into her bag.*

- tell when: NOW AFTERNOON

  when

- explain situation: ME GO-TO WEDDING. WEDDING FINISH, ME GO-TO (2h)EAT++

  conj

- tell what unexpectedly happened (use conjunction): !WRONG! ME SEE TABLE NEXT-TO-ours WOMAN IX PURSE <rs:woman ICL*"open purse"* KNIFE, FORK, ICL*"put in purse"*

  shocked

  NAPKIN, SALT, PEPPER, ICL*"put in purse"*> ME LOOK-AT-her

  whq

- ask for advice: ME (2h)DO++

HOMEWORK

Tell students to do **Homework 8:10** (*Student Workbook*, pages 126–133).

Also, students are to create three "ask for advice" situations (See **Assignment**, *Student Workbook*, page 131).

HOMEWORK FOLLOW-UP
20–30 MINUTES

PRESENT
(FOLLOW-UP SLIDES 8:10:1–12)

Minidialogue 1

1. situation:
2. what happened:
3. advice given:

Check students' answers to **Minidialogues 1–3**. See **Introduction** pages xviii–xix for different ways to check answers.

ACTIVITY

Have students sign the three "ask for advice" situations they developed for homework to each other. (**Assignment**, *Student Workbook*, page 131)

Conclude. Have students sign one of their situations to the class and invite several students to give advice. Monitor students' WHY+NOT form.

Be sure students also:

For spills

- use the conjunction !WRONG! in the right place
- use element classifier that matches the liquid and its movement
- show where the liquid landed

For awkward conversations

- use role shift to show the other person's question and "their" response
- match the locations of the people while role shifting
- use the conjunction !WRONG! in the right place

For something one is not supposed to do

- use the conjunction !WRONG! in the right place
- match the locations of the people while role shifting
- use role shift to show the other person's question and "their" response.

LESSON 8:11

Negations 2

Lesson length: 50–65 minutes

LESSON GOAL

Students will translate English sentences with negation signs and tag questions.

KEY SKILLS

Integrate facial grammar with each part of the sentence

- establish location, if specified (raise brows and head)
- name topic (raise brows and head)
- end with a negation sign (shake head and furrow brows)
- add tag question (raise brows and lean head forward)

NOTIONS

Grammar

negation
tag questions

Vocabulary

Verbs

CANCEL
TOUCH
KNOW+THAT
TAKE-UP

Nouns

SEMESTER
SOMEONE
LIST
MEAT
MONEY
HAWAII
TEST

MATERIALS

8:11 Lesson Slides
8:11 Follow-up Slides

HOMEWORK 8:11

Student Workbook, pages 134–135

REVIEW *Negation Signs*

10 minutes

PRESENT
(LESSON SLIDE 8:11:1)

Review Negation Signs

Ask students to give negation signs they learned in **Lesson 8:5**

whq

T: [NEGATIVE] SIGN "what"

S: NOT (NOT+ALLOW, NOT+FINISH, NOT+MUST, SHOULD+NOT)

NONE
"wave-no"
NOT-YET
NOT-WANT
NOT-KNOW
FORBID
REFUSE

PRACTICE *Translating Negative Sentences*

20–30 minutes

Students will identify location, topic and appropriate negation sign(s) to translate sentences.

PRESENT
(LESSON SLIDE 8:11:2)

1. I have no money.
2. I don't eat meat.

Translating negative sentences
- establish location if specified (raise brows)
- name the topic (raise brows)
- end with a negation (shake head)

Help students analyze each sentence and prepare to translate it by asking:

- if the sentence has a specified location
- what is the topic
- what is the most appropriate negation sign or phrase.

For ***"1. I have no money."***
Location: *none*
Topic: *money*
Negation: NONE

For ***"2. I don't eat meat"***
Location: *none*
Topic: *meat*
Negation: NOT

MONEY

MEAT

Demonstrate translations with the whole class. Have students copy you, paying attention to the facial expressions and phrasing.

Translation for 1:

t / neg
MONEY, ME **NONE**.

Translation for 2:

t / neg
MEAT, ME **NOT** EAT, ME.

PRESENT
(LESSON SLIDE 8:11:3)

3. I didn't bring my USB.
4. I don't want to see the movie.

Translating negative sentences

- establish location if specified (raise brows)
- name the topic (raise brows)
- end with a negation (shake head)

Repeat procedure.

For ***"3. I didn't bring my USB."***
Location: *none*
Topic: *USB*
Negation: NOT

Translation:

 t   neg
fs-USB, ME **NOT** BRING [ME].

For ***"4. I don't want to see the movie."***
Location: *none*
Topic: *movie*
Negation: NOT-WANT

Translation:

 t   neg
MOVIE, ME **NOT-WANT** SEE [ME].

PRESENT
(LESSON SLIDE 8:11:4)

5. I don't know how to make coffee.
6. My parents don't allow smoking in the house.

Translating negative sentences
- establish location if specified (raise brows)
- name the topic (raise brows)
- end with a negation (shake head)

Repeat procedure.

For ***"5. I don't know how to make coffee."***
Location: *none*
Topic: *making coffee*
Negation: NOT-KNOW

Translation:

(t: MAKE COFFEE,) (neg: ME NOT-KNOW #HOW [ME].)

MAKE COFFEE, ME **NOT-KNOW** #HOW [ME].

For ***"6. My parents don't allow smoking in the house."***
Location: *parent's house*
Topic: *smoking*
Negation: NOT+ALLOW or FORBID

Translation:

(t: MY MOTHER+FATHER POSS HOUSE,) (neg: SMOKING NOT ALLOW.)

MY MOTHER+FATHER POSS HOUSE, SMOKING **NOT ALLOW**. (or FORBID)

PRESENT
(LESSON SLIDE 8:11:5)

1. I have no money.
2. I don't eat meat.
3. I didn't bring my USB.
4. I don't want to see the movie.
5. I don't know how to make coffee.
6. My parents don't allow smoking in the house.

Translating negative sentences
- establish location if specified (raise brows)
- name the topic (raise brows)
- end with a negation (shake head)

Pair up: Have students practice signing **Sentences 1–6** with each other.

Be sure students:
- for topic, raise brows and head
- for negation, shake head and furrow brows with negation sign.

Repeat procedure.

PRESENT
(LESSON SLIDE 8:11:6)

7. I have not been to Hawaii yet.
8. The teacher told me I don't have to take the test again.

Translating negative sentences
- establish location if specified (raise brows)
- name the topic (raise brows)
- end with a negation (shake head)

For ***"7. I have not been to Hawaii yet."***
Location: *none*
Topic: *Hawaii*
Negation: NOT-YET

Translation:

t neg
HAWAII, ME **NOT-YET TOUCH**.

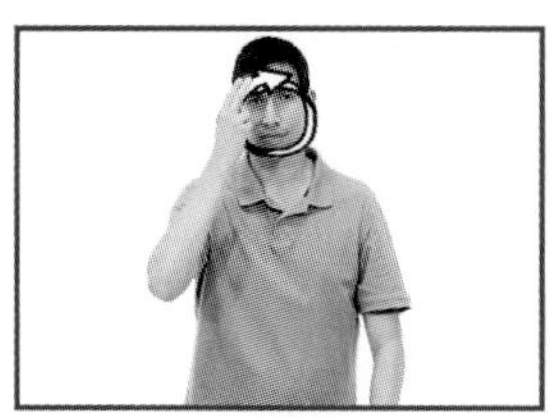

HAWAII

TOUCH

> **NOTE:** The sign TOUCH is used when referring to a destination or attraction. You can also use the sign GO-TO instead of TOUCH.

For ***"8. The teacher told me I don't have to take the test again."***
Location: *none*
Topic: *taking the test again*
Negation: NOT-MUST

Translation:

t
TAKE-UP TEST AGAIN, TEACH+ER IX-TELL-TO-me
neg
NOT+MUST

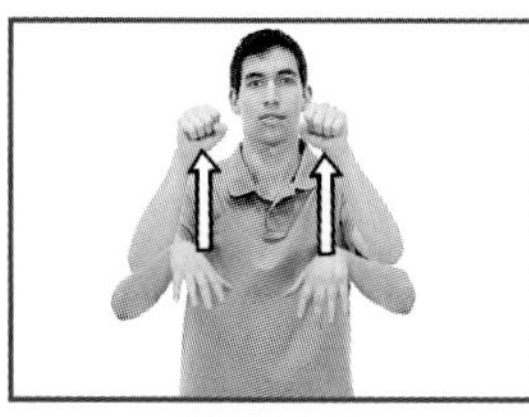

TAKE-UP

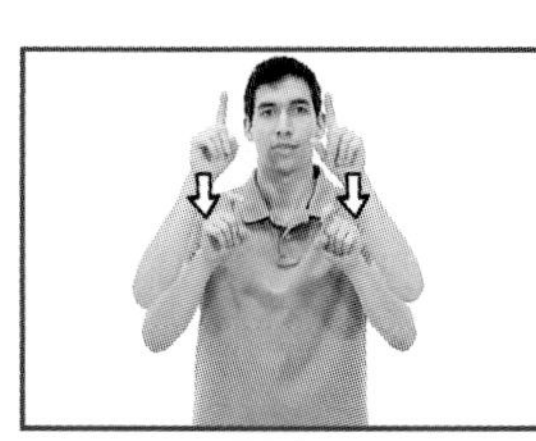

TEST

PRESENT
(LESSON SLIDE 8:11:7)

9. I have not received last semester's grades.

10. No one informed me that class was canceled.

Translating negative sentences
- establish location if specified (raise brows)
- name the topic (raise brows)
- end with a negation (shake head)

For ***"9. I have not received last semester's grades."***
Location: *none*
Topic: *last semester's grades*
Negation: NOT-YET

SEMESTER

Translation:

t ———— neg
IN-PAST **SEMESTER** fs-GRADES, ME **NOT-YET** GET.

For ***"10. No one informed me that class was canceled."***
Location: *none*
Topic: *class was canceled*
Negation: NONE

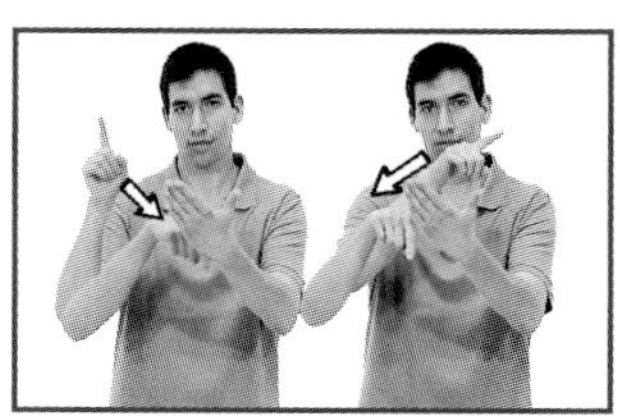
CANCEL

Translation:

t ———— neg
CLASS **CANCEL**, **NONE** INFORM-me

PRESENT
(LESSON SLIDE 8:11:8)

11. My name is not on the list.

12. The sign says "no eating or drinking."

Translating negative sentences

- establish location if specified (raise brows)
- name the topic (raise brows)
- end with a negation (shake head)

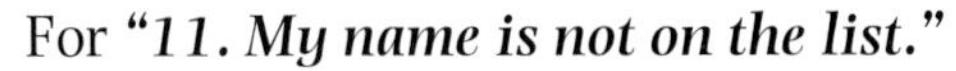

Repeat procedure.

For ***"11. My name is not on the list."***
Location: *list*
Topic: *my name*
Negation: NONE

LIST

Translation:

t t neg
LIST, MY NAME **NONE** [(wh)LCL:B*"list"*/IX-loc*"list"*].

For ***"12. The sign says 'no eating or drinking.'"***
Location: sign *(on wall)*
Topic: eating, *drinking*
Negation: FORBID (or NOT+ALLOW)

Translation:

t t **neg**
DCL*"sign"* IX-loc*"on wall,"* SAY EAT, DRINK **FORBID**
(or NOT+ALLOW)

PRESENT
(LESSON SLIDE 8:11:9)

7. I have not been to Hawaii yet.
8. The teacher told me I don't have to take the test again.
9. I have not received last semester's grades.
10. No one informed me that class was canceled.
11. My name is not on the list.
12. The sign says "no eating or drinking."

Translating negative sentences

- establish location if specified (raise brows)
- name the topic (raise brows)
- end with a negation (shake head)

Pair up. Have students practice signing **Sentences 7–12** with each other.

Be sure students:

- for topic, raise brows and head
- for negation, shake head and furrow brows with negation sign.

PRACTICE *Tag Questions*

20–30 minutes

Students practice ending sentences with a tag question.

PRESENT
(LESSON SLIDES 8:11:10–15)

Adding Tag Questions (raise brows and lean head forward)

1. I have no money. Do you?
2. I don't eat meat. Do you?

Demonstrate how to sign the sentences and tag questions. Have students copy.

t neg q

T1: MONEY, ME NONE. YOU HAVE, YOU

S: (copy)

t neg q

T2: MEAT, ME NOT EAT. YOU EAT, YOU

S: (copy)

Continue activity with the remaining sentences (on **Lesson Slides 8:11:11–15**).

Teacher's Translation Guide

3. I didn't bring my USB. Did you?

t neg q

fs-USB, ME BRING NOT. **YOU BRING, YOU**

4. I don't want to see the movie. Do you?

t neg q

MOVIE, ME NOT-WANT SEE. **YOU WANT SEE, YOU**

5. I don't know how to make coffee. Do you ?

t neg

MAKE COFFEE, ME NOT-KNOW #HOW. **YOU**

q

KNOW #HOW, YOU

6. My parents don't allow smoking in the house. Is it the same with your parents?

t

MY MOTHER+FATHER POSS HOUSE, SMOKING

neg q

NOT+ALLOW. **YOUR MOTHER+FATHER SAME-AS**

7. I have not been to Hawaii yet. Have you?

t neg q

HAWAII, ME NOT-YET TOUCH. **YOU FINISH TOUCH, YOU**

8. The teacher told me I don't have to take the test again. Do you have to?

t
TAKE-UP TEST AGAIN, TEACHER ix-TELL-TO-me

neg **q**
NOT+MUST. **YOU MUST, YOU**

9. I have not received last semester grades. Have you?

t neg
IN-PAST SEMESTER fs-GRADES, ME NOT-YET GET.

q
YOU FINISH GET, YOU

SOMEONE

10. No one informed me that class was canceled. Were you informed?

t neg
CLASS CANCEL, NONE INFORM-me.

q
SOMEONE INFORM-you

11. My name is not on the list. Is yours?

t t neg
LIST, MY NAME NONE [(wh)LCL:B*"list"*/IX-loc*"list"*].

q
YOUR NAME, [(wh)LCL:B*"list"*/IX-loc*"list"*]

12. The sign says "No eating or drinking." Did you know that?

t t neg
DCL*"sign"* IX-loc*"on wall,"* SAY EAT, DRINK FORBID

q
YOU KNOW+THAT, YOU

PRESENT
(LESSON SLIDE 8:11:16)

1. I have no money. Do you?
2. I don't eat meat. Do you?
3. I didn't bring my USB. Did you?
4. I don't want to see the movie. Do you?
5. I don't know how to make coffee. Do you?
6. My parents don't allow smoking in the house. Is it the same with your parents?

Pair up. Have students practice signing **Sentences 1–6** with each other.

Conclude. Go around the room and have students take turns signing one of the sentences. Correct facial grammar when needed.

Be sure students:

- for topic, raise brows and head
- for negation, shake head and furrow brows with negation sign
- for tag question, raise brows and lean head forward.

PRESENT
(LESSON SLIDE 8:11:17)

7. I haven't been to Hawaii. Have you?
8. The teacher told me I don't have to take the test again. Do you have to?
9. I have not received last semester grades. Have you?
10. No one informed me that class was canceled. Were you informed?
11. My name is not on the list. Is yours?
12. The sign says "No eating or drinking." Did you know that?

Repeat the procedure with **Sentences 7–12**.

Conclude. Go around the room and have students take turns signing one of the sentences. Correct facial grammar when needed.

HOMEWORK

Tell students to do **Homework 8:11** (*Student Workbook*, pages 134–135).

HOMEWORK FOLLOW-UP

10–15 MINUTES

PRESENT

(FOLLOW-UP SLIDES 8:11:1–2)

1. I have no money. Do you?
2. I don't eat meat. Do you?
3. I didn't bring my USB. Did you?
4. I don't want to see the movie. Do you?
5. I don't know how to make coffee. Do you?
6. My parents don't allow smoking in the house. Is it the same with your parents?

Have students sign the translations. Check word order, phrasing and facial expressions.

LESSON 8:12

Comprehension: The Candy Bar

Lesson length: 30–35 minutes

LESSON GOAL

Students will develop comprehension and production skills through the story **The Candy Bar**.

KEY SKILLS

For comprehension: Students will develop the ability to process larger chunks of information and figure out the meaning of a sign from context.

For production: Student will build fluency by re-telling the story or by asking questions about the story.

NOTIONS

Vocabulary

Possible new signs in the story

GOING-TO
STOMACH-BOIL
BE-ANGRY
MESSED-UP-hair
COMB

PREPARATION

- View the story **The Candy Bar** on **Lesson Slide 8:12:1**.
- Decide which **Comprehension** and **Production** activities to use.

MATERIALS

8:12 Lesson Slides
8:12 Follow-up Slides

HOMEWORK 8:12

Student Workbook, page 136–139

INTRODUCE *The Candy Bar*

5 minutes

PRESENT
(LESSON SLIDE 8:12:1)

Show the story. Then, do one of the options below.

Comprehension:

- quiz (page 280)
- answer questions (page 280)

Production:

- develop questions to ask (page 282)
- re-tell the story (page 282)
- change details of the story (page 282)

COMPREHENSION

15–30 minutes

Students will develop the ability to process larger chunks of information and figure out the meaning of a sign from context.

QUIZ (15–30 minutes)

Students write down the information given in the story.
Collect papers and grade their papers using FC (full credit), PC (partial credit) or NC (no credit).

FC (full credit) = details are accurate and complete; one or two *minor* details may be missing, such as buying the coffee

PC (partial credit) = sufficient details to show satisfactory comprehension of story, actions or cause/effect, but few significant details missing or incorrect, such as naming the other man as one eating up the first candy bar instead of the main character.

NC (no credit) = does not show sufficient comprehension of story, actions or cause/effect to follow along.

Return the papers. Pair off "FC" with "PC" or "NC" students.

- Give the "FC" students a minute to read their own papers to review the story.
- Have the "PC" students ask the "FC" students questions to find out what they got wrong or missed and make corrections on their papers.
- Have the "FC" students sign the story so the "NC" students can rewrite their papers.

Check the "PC" or "NC" student's corrected papers.

ANSWER QUESTIONS (20-30 minutes)

First, pair off students and have them fill each other in on what happened in the story. If there is anything in the story they don't understand, have them ask other students to get clarification.

Then, ask the following questions:

1. t (MAN) whq (GO-TO WHERE)
   MAN GO-TO WHERE
   Answer: To the airport.

t whq

2. **MAN GET TICKET, IX*"ticket agent"* TELL-TO-man "what"**
Answer. That the plane will be delayed.

whq

3. MAN IX*"man"* (2h)#DO++
Answer. Bought a newspaper, candy and coffee.

t when whq

4. **MAN SIT, ICL*"put down stuff,"* FINISH, NEXT "what"**
Answer. He saw a man sitting on his right take a bite of his candy.

5. **MAN HEAR IX*"loudspeaker"* AIRPLANE NOW READY**
when whq
SCL:ILY*"taking off,"* IX*"man"* (2h)#DO++
Answer. He picked up his bags and got on the plane.

t whq

6. **AIRPLANE SCL:ILY*"taking off,"* "what"+HAPPEN**
Answer. Man's hair was messy so he reached into his back pocket to get a comb. Instead, he found his candy bar!

Show video again. Make sure students understand these possible new signs. If needed, use one of the strategies below to explain the meaning.

- list things in a category (for category signs)
- give the opposite sign if known
- describe or act out situation
- give definition using familiar signs

GOING-TO

STOMACH-BOIL

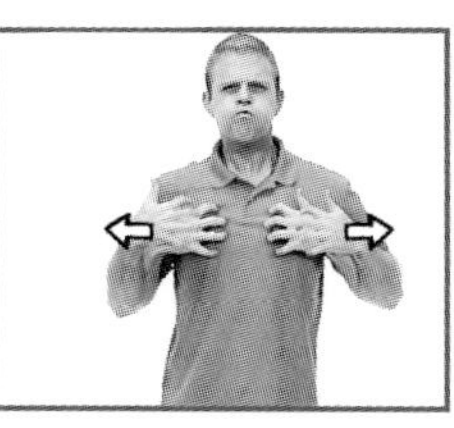
BE-ANGRY

MESSED-UP-hair

COMB

PRODUCTION

15 minutes

Students will build fluency by re-telling the story or by asking questions about the story.

After showing the video, and making sure students understand the story and all the signs, choose one of these activities:

- **DEVELOP QUESTIONS TO ASK** (20–30 minutes)
  Pair up students and assign one student to develop true or false questions and the other wh-word questions. Have them ask each other questions.

- **RE-TELL STORY** (15–20 minutes)
  Pair up students and have them tell each other the story.

- **CHANGE DETAILS OF THE STORY** (30–40 minutes)
  Pair up students and have them collaborate to change the details of the story. For example, change what the person is buying, add dialogue between the two characters, change what person is looking for, and the reason. Then, have students mingle and tell their versions of the story.

HOMEWORK

Tell students to do **Homework 8:12** (*Student Workbook*, pages 136–139).

HOMEWORK FOLLOW-UP
20–30 MINUTES

Pair up. Have students exchange their workbooks and discuss each other's summary of **The Motel Story**.

PRESENT
(FOLLOW-UP SLIDE 8:12:1)

S1: (tell "The Motel Story" from beginning to when the couple stopped at the motel)

S2: (continue until when the man went to the store)

S3: (continue until the end)

Then, put students in groups of three and have the students retell parts of the story to each other following instructions on the slide.

Conclude. Ask whole class why the story is funny.
Answer. The story shows that the Deaf man is conscious of how the hearing public responds to certain noises. He uses that to his advantage to find his Deaf wife.

LESSON 8:13

Culture: Minimizing Interruptions

Lesson length: 25–30 minutes

LESSON GOAL

Students will practice culturally appropriate behaviors to interrupt a class presentation minimally in order to explain their tardiness or need to leave.

KEY BEHAVIORS

For arriving late

- wait for an appropriate break in the presentation
- get the teacher's attention
- briefly apologize and explain the tardiness
- get teacher's permission before taking a seat

For leaving during class

- get up at the right time and move to the door
- get the teacher's attention
- briefly excuse self and explain why
- get teacher's permission before leaving the classroom

NOTIONS

Phrases

Arriving late

SORRY LATE (and give brief explanation).

Leaving immediately

[EXCUSE-ME] (and give brief explanation)

PREPARATION

Read and view **Minimizing Interruptions**, *Student Workbook*, pages 140–141

MATERIALS

8:13 Lesson Slides

HOMEWORK 8:13

Student Workbook, pages 140–141

INTRODUCE *Minimizing Interruptions*

10–15 minutes

PRESENT

(LESSON SLIDE 8:13:1)

Minimizing Interruptions

How do you minimize the interruption to the teacher's presentation if you arrive late or must leave class?

Considerations

1. the cultural value of keeping each other informed
2. the right time to interrupt
3. how to briefly apologize and excuse oneself, and get permission

Discuss the considerations:

For ***"1. the cultural value of keeping each other informed"***
It is important to try and keep people in your group informed whenever there is a change in the situation.

For ***"2. the right time to interrupt"***
Arriving late—The student should wait at the door or just outside the semicircle until an appropriate break in the teacher's presentation before they move forward and get the teacher's attention.

Leaving during class—The student should wait for an appropriate break in the teacher's presentation before getting up or getting the teacher's attention. If urgent, the student can get up and move toward the door and look at the teacher to get their attention.

SORRY LATE

EXCUSE-ME

For *"3. how to briefly apologize and excuse oneself, and get permission"*

Arriving late—When the teacher notices the student, the student should briefly apologize and explain their tardiness, using this phrase: **SORRY LATE**. After getting the teacher's permission, they can take their seat.

Leaving during class—After getting the teacher's attention, the student should briefly excuse themselves and explain why, using this optional sign: **[EXCUSE-ME]**. After getting the teacher's permission, the student can leave the room.

PRACTICE *Minimizing Interruptions*

15 minutes

Students practice interrupting, briefly apologizing for being late, excusing selves, and explaining to teacher why they are late or need to leave during class.

Set up. Divide class into two groups. Assign either **Arriving Late** or **Leaving During Class** to each group.

Arriving Late

Tell the **Arriving Late** group to role play. Have students leave the room and enter one at a time. You (the teacher) address the rest of the class as each student arrives late.

Check to be sure students:

- wait for an appropriate break in the presentation
- get the teacher's attention
- briefly apologize and explain the tardiness
- get teacher's permission before taking a seat.

Leaving During Class

Now, have the **Leaving During Class** group role play. Tell these students to leave the room one by one. Again, you (the teacher) address the class throughout this activity.

Check to be sure students:

- get up at the right time and move to the door
- successfully get your (the teacher's) attention
- briefly excuse themselves and explain why
- get your (the teacher's) permission before leaving the classroom.

Point out. In the event a student arrives late and is unable to get your attention, because you are either talking with a student or working with a group, the student should go ahead and take a seat. Likewise, if the student needs to leave and cannot get the teacher's attention, they should leave an explanation with a fellow classmate to deliver to the teacher when he or she is free.

HOMEWORK

Tell students to do **Homework 8:13** (*Student Workbook*, pages 140–141).

Also, students are to describe the "norm" for handling arriving late and leaving during class in spoken English classes and contrast this with how to conduct oneself in the ASL classroom. (See **Assignment**, *Student Workbook*, page 141)

HOMEWORK FOLLOW-UP
7–12 MINUTES

Ask students to compare the differences in handling "arriving late" and "leaving during class" behaviors (See **Assignment**, *Student Workbook*, page 141)

Teacher's Discussion Guide

	SPOKEN ENGLISH CLASSROOM	ASL CLASSROOM
arriving late	take a seat quietly; no need to tell teacher why *(goal is to minimize auditory distractions)*	wait for an appropriate break in the presentation, get the teacher's attention, briefly apologize and explain your tardiness, get permission before taking your seat *(goal is to minimize visual distractions)*
leaving early	leave quietly. Again, no need to inform the teacher.	wait for an appropriate break in the presentation, get the teacher's attention, briefly excuse yourself and explain why, get permission before leaving the class

LESSON 8:14

Culture: Name Signs

Lesson length: 40–55 minutes

LESSON GOAL Students will learn about two kinds of name signs—descriptive and arbitrary and how name signs are used in the community.

KEY SKILL apply the principles using handshape, location, contact point and movement to recognize properly made arbitrary name signs

PREPARATION

- Read **Cultural: Name Signs**, *Student Workbook*, pages 142–145
- Review **Lecture Notes** on pages 289–296 and 299–300 and think about how to sign the information
- View the story **Sam's Name Sign** on **Lesson Slide 8:14:6**

MATERIALS **8:14 Lesson Slides**

HOMEWORK 8:14 *Student Workbook*, pages 142–147

WARM UP — *How Names Are Given*

10–15 minutes

Ask students to describe how people come up with names for their babies, for example:

- named after their parents or other family members
- named after favorite actors
- named after people in the Bible
- names found in a book of baby names
- names picked because of how they sound.

Tell students Deaf parents usually give their child two names, one for the majority culture, for example, an English name (written or fingerspelled), and an ASL name sign.

LECTURE — *Arbitrary and Descriptive Name Signs*

25–35 minutes

PRESENT
(LESSON SLIDE 8:14:1)

Name Signs:

Arbitrary and Descriptive

Lecture Notes:
There are two kinds of name signs: Arbitrary and Descriptive.

An ***arbitrary*** name sign uses the first letter of the written name as basis for the name sign. For example, someone named Linda may get a name sign using the handshape "L," located somewhere on the body (forehead, shoulder, etc.) or in the neutral space (in front of the body).

A ***descriptive*** name sign usually focuses on a distinctive feature or characteristic of the person. For example,

- someone with dimples—BPSASS*"dimple"*
- someone who smiles or laughs a lot—"(1h)SMILE++"
- someone with long frizzy hair—BPSASS*"long frizzy hair"*
- someone who always wears short-sleeved shirts—DCL*"short sleeve"*

Traditionally, arbitrary name signs are considered more proper within the American Deaf community. However, currently there is a growing trend among Deaf parents to use descriptive name signs for their children.

PRESENT
(LESSON SLIDE 8:14:2)

How Arbitrary Name Signs Are Formed

Locations

- on head: single location
- on head: dual locations
- on torso: single location
- on torso: dual locations
- on non-dominant arm: single location
- on non-dominant arm: dual location
- in neutral space (front of body)

Locations

Point to places on the body where name signs are formed.

For ***"• on head: single location,"*** point to:

- the forehead
- the temple
- the cheek
- the chin (front or side)

For *"• **on head: dual locations,**"* point to:

- from forehead to chin
- from temple to cheek
- from dominant side to non-dominant side on chin
- from non-dominant side to dominant side on forehead

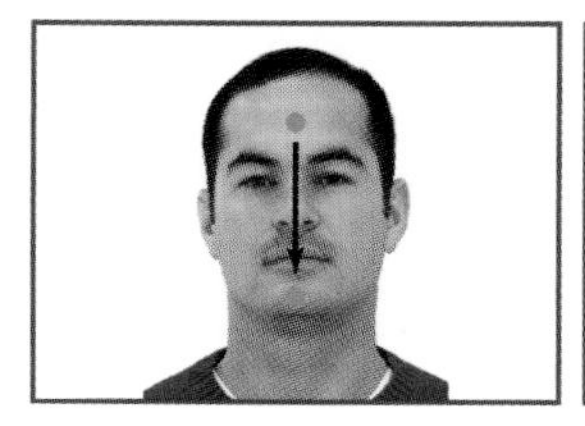 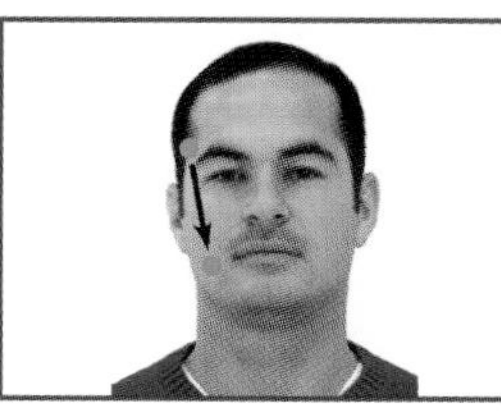  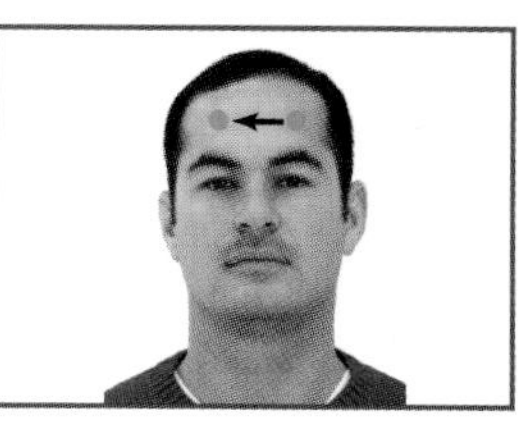

For *"• **on torso: single location,**"* point to:

- the non-dominant shoulder
- the chest

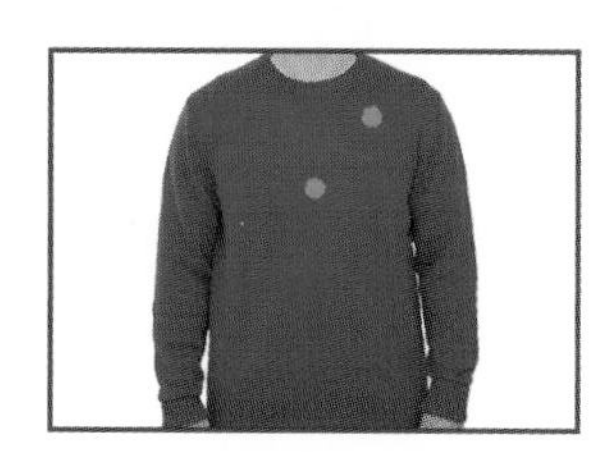

For *"• **on torso: dual locations,**"* point:

- from chest to tummy
- from non-dominant shoulder to dominant shoulder
- from non-dominant shoulder to waist on dominant side

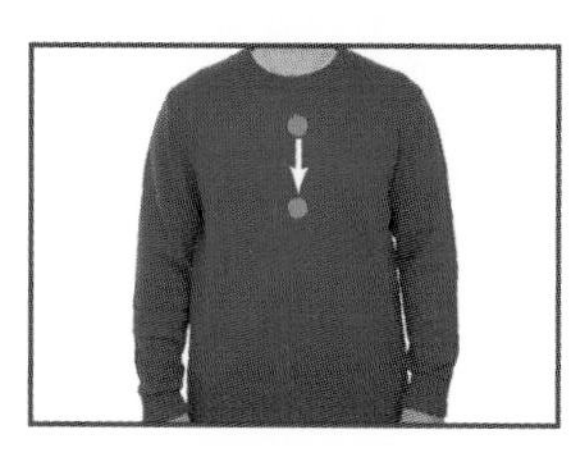 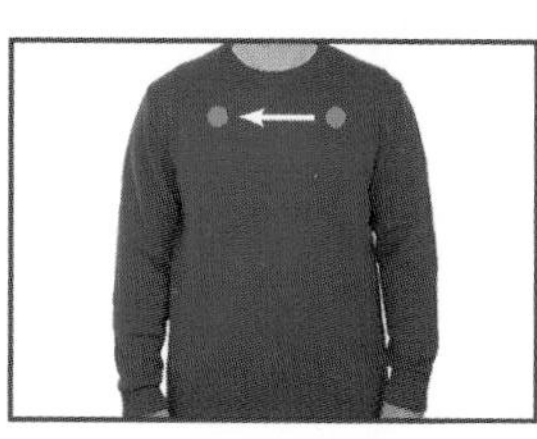 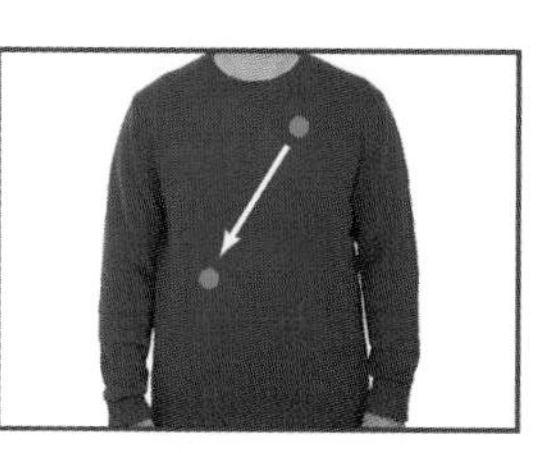

For *"• **on non-dominant arm: single location,**"* point to:

- the inner elbow
- the back of the hand
- the palm of the hand

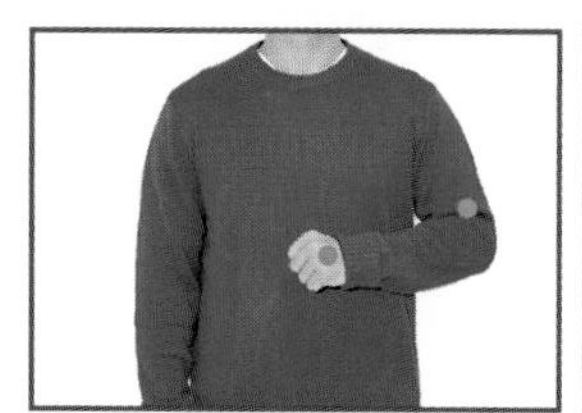 

For ***"• on non-dominant arm: dual locations,"*** point:

- from shoulder to inner elbow
- from shoulder to back of hand
- two locations on back of hand (from wrist to knuckles)
- two locations on palm of hand (from base of fingers to heel)

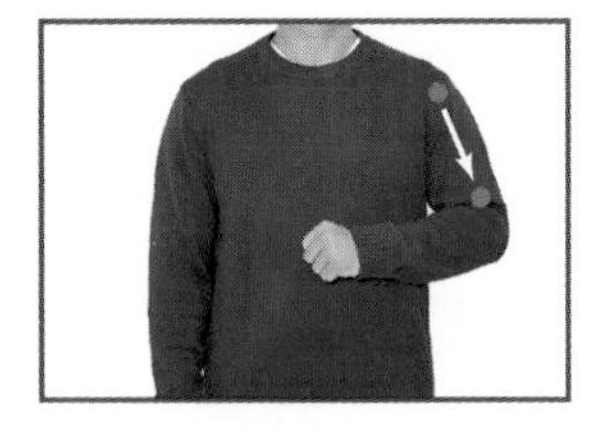 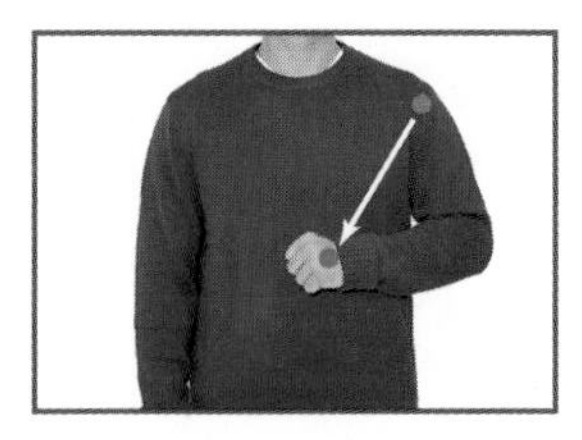 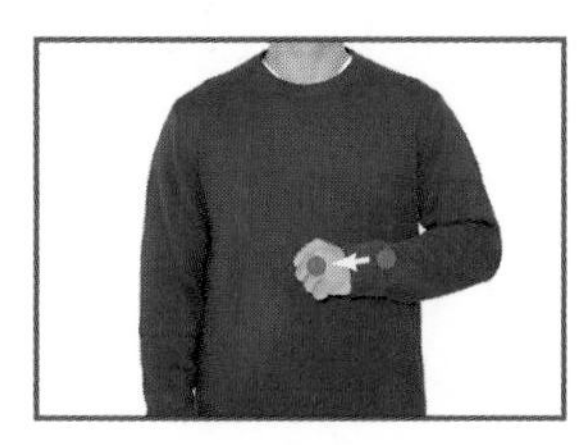 

For ***"• in neutral space (front of body),"*** shake hands:

- in area in front of signer's body (neck level)

PRESENT
(LESSON SLIDE 8:14:3)

How Arbitrary Name Signs Are Formed

Contact Points

- the radial side of hand, heel
- the tip(s) of finger or thumb
- the palm side of hand
- the ulnar side of hand
- no contact (in neutral space)

Contact Points

Point to where on the dominant hand contact is made with the location to form name signs.

For *"• the radial side of hand, heel "*

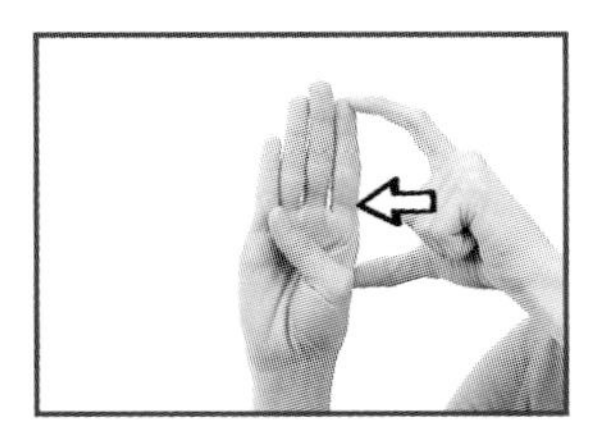

These letters use this contact point:
A, B, C, D, E, F, G, H, I, K, M, N, O, P, Q, S, T, U, V, W, X

Examples:
Point out: These letters do not use this contact point: J, L, R, Y, Z

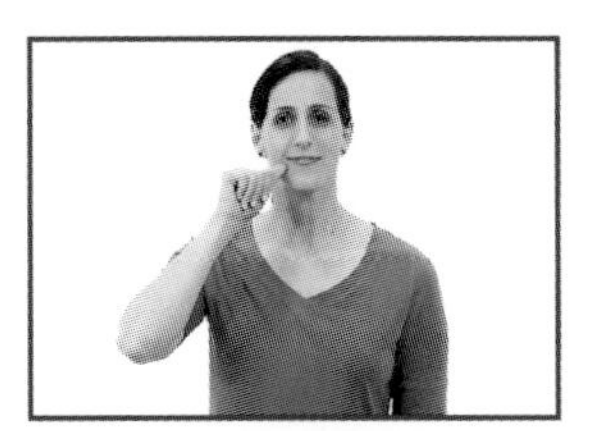

For *"• the tip(s) of finger or thumb "*

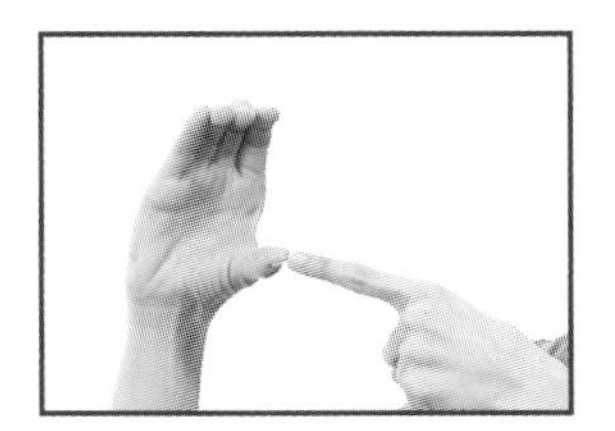

These letters use this contact point:
C, D, F, I, J, L, M, N, P, R, V, W, X, Y

Examples:

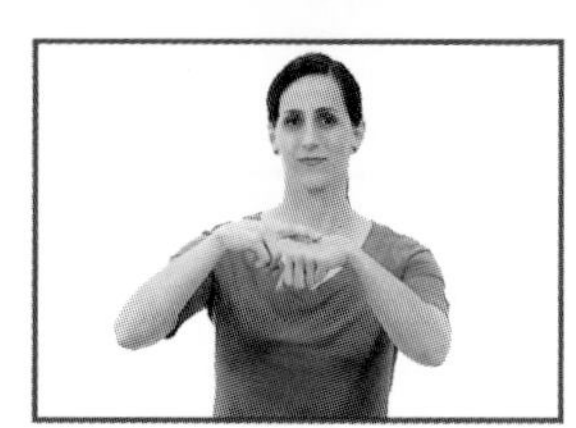

Point out. These letters do not use this contact point:
A, B, E, G, H, K, O, Q, S, T, U, Z

For ***"• the palm side of hand"***

These letters use this contact point:
A, E, L, Y

Examples:

Point out. This contact point cannot be used with any other letters.

For *"• the ulnar side of hand"*

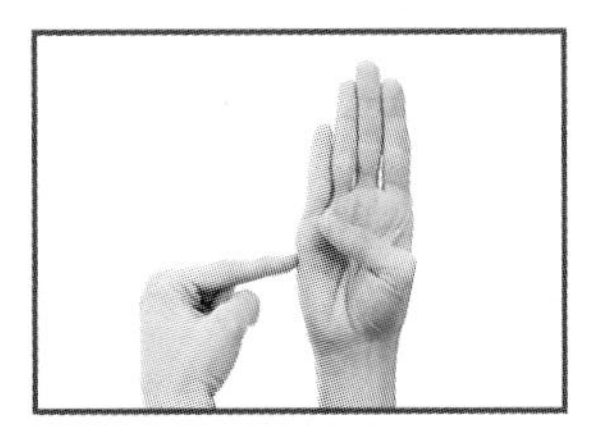

These letters use this contact point:
B, E, G, H, S

Example:

Point out. This contact point cannot be used with any other letters.

For *"• no contact (in neutral space)"*
All the handshapes in the manual alphabet use neutral space.

PRESENT
(LESSON SLIDE 8:14:4)

How Arbitrary Name Signs Are Formed

Locations
Contact Points
Movements
- tapping: single location
- tapping: dual locations
- shaking
- brushing

Movements
Demonstrate several name signs for each kind of movement.

For “• ***tapping: single location,***” demonstrate:

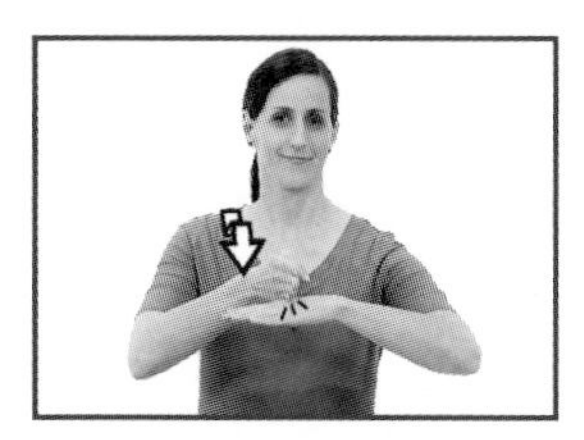

tap twice in same location

For “• ***tapping: dual locations,***” demonstrate:

tap once in each location

For “• ***shaking,***” explain:
Shaking is used for name signs made in neutral space.
Can shake all letters except “Z.”

For “• ***brushing,***” demonstrate:
Brushing can only be used for the letter “J.”

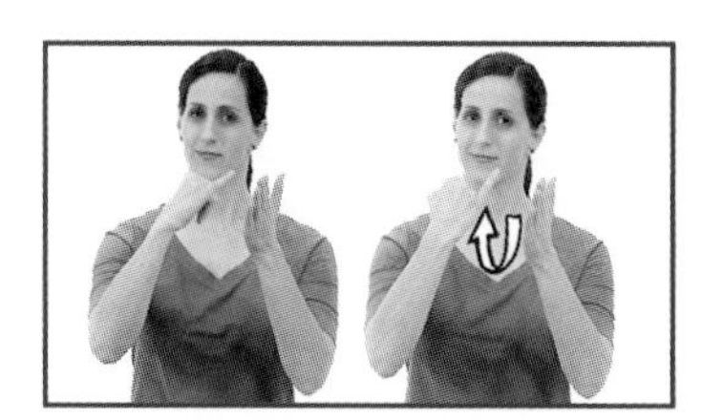

brushing

PRACTICE *Creating Name Signs*

25–35 minutes

Students apply the principles of forming name signs using handshape, location, contact point and movement.

PRESENT
(LESSON SLIDE 8:14:5)

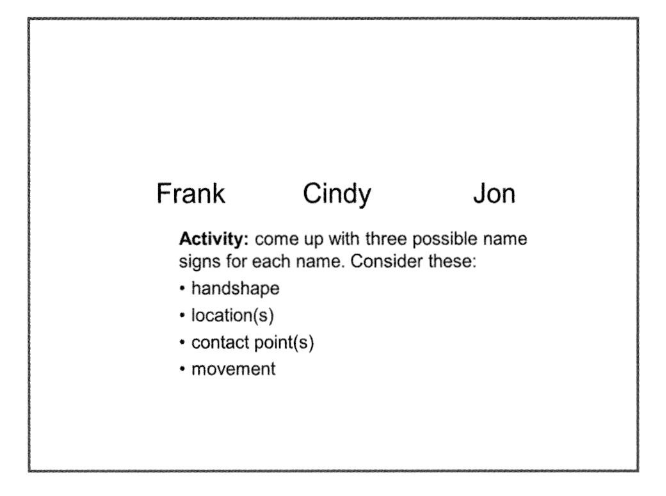

Frank Cindy Jon
Activity: come up with three possible name signs for each name. Consider these:
• handshape
• location(s)
• contact point(s)
• movement

Pair up. Have students confer with the student next to them to come up with three possible name signs for each name on the slide. Have students show you the name signs.

Be sure students:

- utilize the principles introduced for handshapes, locations, contact points, and movements.

PRESENT
(LESSON SLIDE 8:14:6)

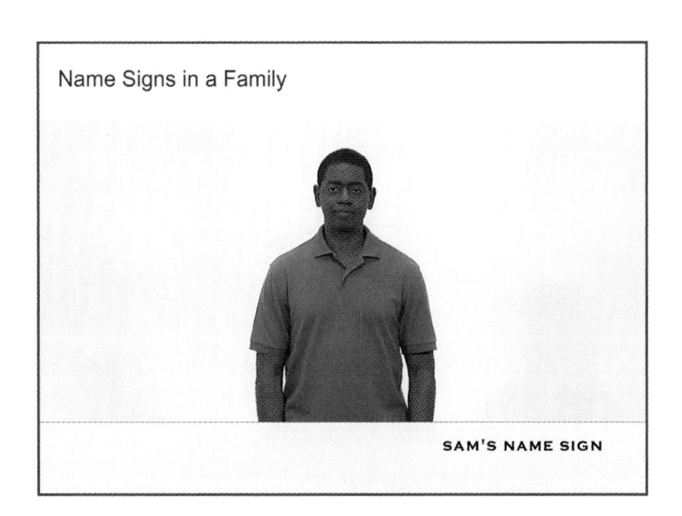

Show video about Sam's family names where the location is an important factor in determining the name signs for the children.

Then, ask the following questions:

whq

1. **BOY [(wh)4/IX-mult"*4 boys*"] NAME FINGERSPELL "what"**

   Answer:
   Steve, Ted, David and Sam (from oldest to youngest)

whq

2. **[(wh)4/IX-mult"*4 boys*"] NAME SIGN "what"**

   Answer:
   Steve: S-on-chin,
   Ted: T-on-chin,
   David: D-on-chin,
   Sam: S-on-chin*"side to other side"*

3. **FIRST-thumb FATHER THOUGHT-OCCUR [(wh)4/IX-pinkie]**

   neg whq

   NAME SIGN S-on-temple. MOTHER NOT+LIKE WHY

   Answer:
   The mother did not agree with the suggestion for Sam's name sign (S-on-temple) because all their children's name signs were supposed to be located on the chin.

4. **WHO THOUGHT-OCCUR NAME SIGN** S-on-chin*"side to other side,"*

   whq

   WHO

   Answer:
   Ted

Point out. Ted, a young boy at the time, understood the rules for forming name signs in order to make a suggestion that fit his mother's desire to have all name signs formed on the chin.

Optional. Give another example of a family whose name signs follow a pattern.

LECTURE *Getting a Name Sign*

25–35 minutes

PRESENT

(LESSON SLIDE 8:14:7)

How does a Deaf person get a name sign
if she or he does not have Deaf parents?

Lecture Notes:

For a child whose family does not sign: Upon enrollment at a Deaf school, teachers or dormitory counselors or houseparents may assign an arbitrary name sign to the child. Sometimes the child's peers may assign them a descriptive name sign.

As an adult: When an adult works with Deaf people, or moves to a new Deaf community, she or he may get a name sign. If they already have a name sign, they might get a new one. Those name signs tend to follow these patterns:

- in professional settings name signs are based on first letter of the last name
- for a newcomer who has the same name sign as someone in the community, their name sign is modified by adding a second handshape—usually the first letter of the last name, for example, "S" tapped on the chin becomes "S, G" on the chin
- if the person has a distinctive physical feature or behavior, a descriptive name sign may be given.

TEACHER TO TEACHER

We recommend you not give name signs to students. They should wait until they become a comfortable part of the Deaf community. Then, either their Deaf friend or co-worker will give them a name sign if needed.

PRESENT
(LESSON SLIDE 8:14:8)

When are name signs used?

Lecture Notes:

Explain name signs are mostly used to refer to the person not present or out of sight.

Let's say you wanted to get the attention of one person standing in a crowd or a group, it would be acceptable to use that person's name sign to signal to that person or others that you want to talk to him or her.

Name signs should not be used in direct address, that is, you would not use the person's name while talking to them.

Sometimes in introductions the person's name sign is added after fingerspelling their name.

PRESENT
(LESSON SLIDE 8:14:9)

1. What are the two types of name signs?
2. How are arbitrary name signs formed?
3. How would one get a name sign if one doesn't have Deaf parents?
4. When are name signs used?

Activity. First, have students write down their answers to the questions on **Lesson Slide 8:14:9**. Then put students into groups of 3–4 and have the groups discuss their answers.

When done, have everyone hand in their papers for you to review the answers.

HOMEWORK

Tell students to do **Homework 8:14** (*Student Workbook*, pages 142–147).

Also, students are to be prepared to tell how they got their names and the different names they go by, if any. (See **Assignment**, *Student Workbook*, page 147.)

HOMEWORK FOLLOW-UP
10–20 MINUTES

Return the groups' papers. (See **Activity**, page 301.) Discuss answers if needed.

Then, have students tell you how they got their English names and other names they go by, if any. (See **Assignment**, *Student Workbook*, page 147.)

UNIT 8 REVIEW

Putting It All Together

Lesson length: 80–95 minutes

LESSON GOAL

The student will:

- practice requesting that someone relay a message
- practice giving phone numbers
- create sentences incorporating negation signs and tag questions
- review fingerspelling for months

NOTIONS

Vocabulary

vocabulary previously learned

PREPARATION

Ask students to bring a picture of a person they know well—a family member or a friend. The picture should show the whole person or at least from the waist up (for **Request to Relay a Message** activity on page 303)

MATERIALS

8UR Lesson Slides

EXERCISE 3A, 3B and 3C

(*Student Workbook*, pages 488, 492 and 494)

HOMEWORK

Student Workbook, pages 148–149 (**Self-Assessment**)

PRACTICE *Request to Relay a Message*

20–25 minutes

Students practice requesting that someone relay a message.

PRESENT
(LESSON SLIDE 8:UR:1)

Dialogue

A: You are at a convention. Your meeting has gone over by 30 minutes and you are supposed to meet someone in the lobby now. Ask B to relay message (that you will be late)
B: agree, ask A to describe person
A: describe person (in your photo)
B: go get the picture, show it to A to confirm
- if confirmed, tell A you relayed the message
- if not, continue searching until you find the right photo

A: respond

Set up. Collect family or friend pictures from students. Spread out the pictures facing up on a table.

Pair Up. Have students take turns role playing Signer A.

PRESENT
(LESSON SLIDE 8:UR:2)

Discuss the person in your photo with your partner.

- how the person is related to you
- name of person
- age
- where she or he lives (and if you live with her or him)
- if friend, how long you have known her or him
- what the person does for a living

Conclude. Have students discuss the person in their photos according to the topics listed on **Lesson Slide 8:UR:2.**

PRACTICE *Phone Numbers*

20–25 minutes

Students practice giving phone numbers.

PRESENT

(LESSON SLIDE 8:UR:3–6)

Phone numbers

485-2906

Have students tell you how to sign the phone numbers. Correct as needed.

Teacher's Guide

- For 485-2906 — 485 – sign 4, then 85
  2906 – sign 29, then 0, then 6
- For 443-6119 — 443 – sign 4, then 43
  6119 – sign 61 then 19 or sign 6,1,1,9
- For 683-4445 — 683 – sign 6, then 83
  4445 – sign 4,4,4,5
- For 235-3100 — 235 – sign 2, then 35
  3100 – sign 31, then 0,0

PRESENT
(LESSON SLIDE 8:UR:7)

A: give name sign, ask for phone number
B: give phone number

EXERCISE 3A, 3B, 3C

Divide class into groups of three. Assign each student **Exercise 3A**, **3B** or **3C** (*Student Workbook*, pages 488, 492 and 494). Students take turns identifying the person by their name sign and asking for their phone number, for example:

	t	whq
S:	D-shake,	PHONE NUMBER "what"

Activity is over when students have filled in all the phone numbers on their exercise sheets.

PRACTICE *Negation*

30 minutes

Students review negation and tag questions by creating sentences.

PRESENT

(LESSON SLIDE 8:UR:8)

Review Negations

- name location (raise brows)
- identify the topic (raise brows)
- end with a negation (shake head)

Make a sentence using your assigned negation sign.

Show the negation sign FORBID, and make a sentence. For example.

t t neg

T: MY "area" SKATEBOARD, FORBID.

Repeat parts of the sentence.

For "*• name location (raise brows)*"

t

MY "area"

For "*• identify the topic (raise brows)*"

t

SKATEBOARD

For "*• end with a negation (shake head)*"

neg

FORBID

Now, give each student a negation sign from the list below. Have them make their own sentence using the sign and follow the sequence on the slide.

REFUSE	NONE	FORBID
NOT+FINISH	"wave-no"	NOT+ALLOW
MUST+NOT	NOT-YET	NOT-KNOW [#HOW]
SHOULD+NOT	NOT-WANT	

When students are ready, have students take turns signing their sentences.

Be sure students:

- follow the sequence
- use facial grammar (raise brows and shake head).

PRESENT
(LESSON SLIDE 8:UR:9)

Review Tag Questions

- add tag question (raise brows and lean head forward)

Demonstrate "tag question" by adding it to your sentence.

```
    __________t ______________t ______neg
T:  MY "area" SKATEBOARD, FORBID.
    ________________________q
    YOUR "area" SAME-AS
```

Point out there is a slight pause between the sentence and the tag question.

Now have students take turns signing their sentences with a tag question.

Be sure students:

- pause between the sentence and the tag question
- raise brows and lean head forward when signing the tag question.

PRACTICE *Fingerspelling Months*

10–15 minutes

Students practice fingerspelling months by answering questions.

Ask students the following questions:

t whq
T: AUTUMN, WHICH MONTH, WHICH
S: fs-SEPT, fs-OCT, fs-NOV

t
T: PEOPLE TEND-TO LEAVE-FOR VACATION WHICH
whq
MONTH, WHICH
S: fs-JUNE, fs-JULY, fs-AUG

t whq
T: PEOPLE TEND-TO MARRY WHICH MONTH, WHICH
S: fs-JUNE

t whq
T: PEOPLE PAY-TO fs-TAXES WHICH MONTH, WHICH
S: fs-APRIL

t whq
T: PEOPLE GO-TO SKIING, WHICH MONTH, WHICH
S: fs-JAN, fs-FEB

t whq
T: SCHOOL/CLASS FINISH, WHICH MONTH WHICH
S: fs-(month)

t whq
T: SCHOOL/CLASS START, WHICH MONTH WHICH
S: fs-(month)

t whq
T: PAST MONTH, WHICH MONTH WHICH
S: fs-(month)

t whq
T: CHRISTMAS, HANUKKAH, WHICH MONTH WHICH
S: fs-DEC

t whq
T: THANKSGIVING, WHICH MONTH WHICH
S: fs-NOV

t whq
T: HALLOWEEN, WHICH MONTH WHICH
S: fs-OCT

t whq
T: MOTHER DAY, WHICH MONTH WHICH
S: fs-MAY

t whq
T: FATHER DAY, WHICH MONTH WHICH
S: fs-JUNE

t whq
T: VALENTINE DAY, WHICH MONTH WHICH
S: fs-FEB

t whq
T: YOUR FAVORITE MONTH [YOUR,] WHICH
S: fs-(month)

Check form. Have students practice any corrections.

Spell the next month. You begin by naming the month. Point to a student and have him or her name the next month. Then point to another student and have him or her name the next month and so on.

NOTES:

UNIT 9

Describing Places

LESSON 9:1

Discussing Neighborhoods

Lesson length: 90 minutes

LESSON GOAL

Students will learn vocabulary and phrases to follow this narrative outline:

Narrative

1. tell where you live
   - kind of residence, and what city or district
   - for how long[1] and with whom
2. tell what your neighborhood is like
   - type of neighborhood/area[2]
   - what is nearby and convenient[3]
   - who lives in the neighborhood[4]
3. tell what is next to your residence[5]
4. tell what you like[6] and don't like about the area[7]
5. tell about your future plans[8]

KEY PHRASES

[1] UP-TILL-NOW (#) YEAR (or MONTH).

rhet

[2] "area" FACE+SAME-AS "what,"...

[3] [NEAR] IX-dir (place)
[NEAR] IX-loc (place)
(#) BLOCK-AWAY IX-loc (place)
(#) fs-MILE(S) IX-dir (place)

[4] [MY HOME] "area" HAVE MANY (group)...SOME (group).
[MY HOME] "area" MOST PEOPLE (group), FEW (group).
[MY HOME] "area" PEOPLE DIVERSE...(groups).

[5] ACROSS-FROM IX-loc, NEXT-TO-left IX-loc, NEXT-TO-right IX-loc, and THUMB-loc*"back"*

rhet

[6] ME LIKE "area" WHY...

t neg
[7] ONE, ME NOT+LIKE...

[8] ...STAY-here UNTIL (event).

NOTIONS

Grammar

Rhetorical Questions
Locatives (IX-dir, IX-loc, THUMB-loc*"back"* NEXT-TO, etc.)

Vocabulary

Areas
DOWNTOWN "area"
BUSINESS "area"
MACHINE "area" (industrial area)
HOME "area" (residential area)
FARM "area"
COUNTRY "area"
fs-HILLS, DCL*"rolling hills"*

Neighborhoods
fs-APT
fs-LOFT
fs-CONDO
HOME "area" NEW++ (newly constructed neighborhood)
HOME "area" OLD++ (older neighborhood)
HOME "area" (2h)alt.PCL*"mansion"*++

Surroundings
ACROSS-FROM
THUMB-loc*"back"*
NEXT-TO-right
NEXT-TO-left

Comments about neighbors
CHEERFUL
COLD
MAD-char
NOSEY

People in the neighborhood
YOUNG FAMILY
OLD+ER
ART+ER
WHITE+COLLAR
BLUE+COLLAR
PROFESSIONAL
RETIRED
BLACK (people) or
AFRICA+AMERICA or
AFRICA(face)+AMERICA
SPANISH (Latinos) or MEXICO
WHITE-FACE
INDIA (people)
ASIA (people)

Places nearby

NEAR	HORSE fs-TRAIL
FREEWAY SWIM fs-POOL	FARM++ fs-MARKET
ART fs-STUDIO	fs-FERRY LCL*"boat going out"*++

Noise level

QUIET	NOISY

Safety level

fs-SAFE	TRAFFIC
DANGEROUS	CLEAN
"area" TRAFFIC	DIRTY
(2h)ECL*"empty streets"*	SMELL STINKY

Activity level

BORING	MANY (2h)#DO-circle

Cost of living

EXPENSIVE	CHEAP

others

UP-TILL-NOW	DIVERSE
LONG-AGO	MOST
CHANGE++(arc)	SOME
PRETTY	FEW/SEVERAL
DIFFERENT++(arc)	

PREPARATION View **David's Neighborhood** in its entirety on **Lesson Slide 9:1:22**

MATERIALS **9:1 Lesson Slides**
9:1 Follow-up Slides

HOMEWORK 9:1 *Student Workbook*, pages 154–167

WARM UP *Know Everyone's Name*

10–15 minutes

Ask students if they know the names of everyone in the class. If they say no, then give them 5–7 minutes to learn the names of the students they are unsure of. Then quiz them to see if they really know the names. Ultimate challenge is to ask a student to tell you the names of everyone. (Be sure you know all the names as well!)

INTRODUCE *David's Neighborhood*

90 minutes

PRESENT
(LESSON SLIDE 9:1:1)

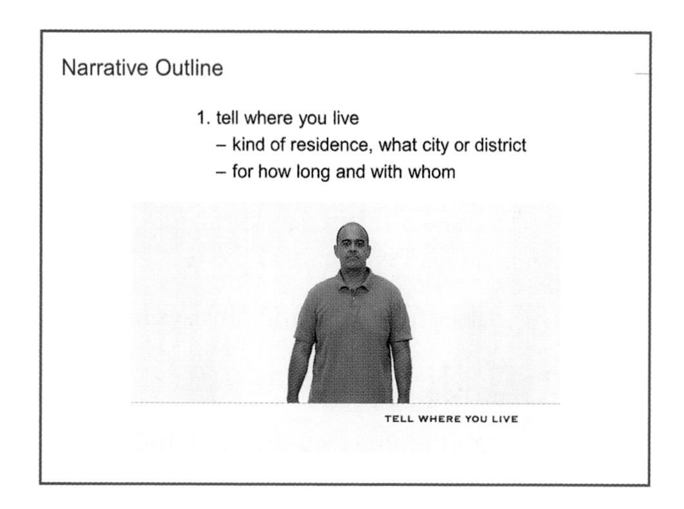

Narrative Outline
1. tell where you live
– kind of residence, what city or district
– for how long and with whom
TELL WHERE YOU LIVE

Show video **Tell Where You Live**, then ask:

whq

T: fs-DAVID IX*"David"* SIGN "what"

S: (IX*"David"*) LIVE fs-CONDO, IX-loc*"San Francisco"* #SF, (IX*"David"*) LIVE IX-loc*"upstairs"* 11+fs-TH FLOOR. **UP-TILL-NOW** 3+YEAR. (IX*"David"*) he-ALONE.

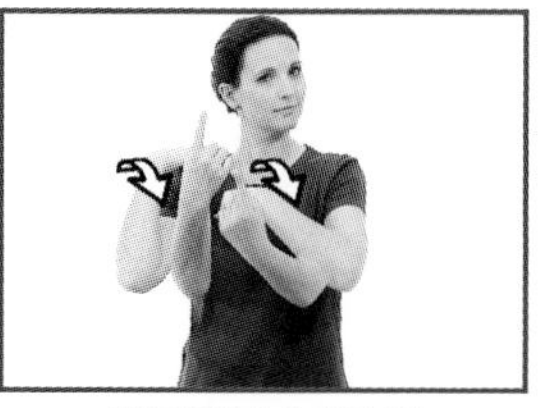

UP-TILL-NOW

Review. Have students follow the outline to tell about where they live.

S: ME LIVE (kind of residence), IX-loc (name city or district)
UP-TILL-NOW (#) YEAR (or MONTH).
ME LIVE (me-ALONE or WITH (person))

Be sure students:

- sign **UP-TILL-NOW**
- point with IX-loc before naming the location.

PRESENT
(LESSON SLIDES 9:1:2–10)

Introduce signs and phrases for neighborhood types and areas.

For **Slide 2**
Point to different areas in the picture and introduce:

DOWNTOWN "area"

MACHINE "area"
(industrial area with factories)

HOME "area"
(residential area)

For **Slide 3**

BUSINESS "area"

For **Slide 4**

MACHINE "area"
(industrial area with factories)

Show **Slides 5–10** then sign HOME "area" before introducing the new signs.

For **Slide 5**

OLD++

For **Slide 6**

NEW++

For **Slide 7** HOME "area" **fs-APT, fs-CONDO**

For **Slide 8**

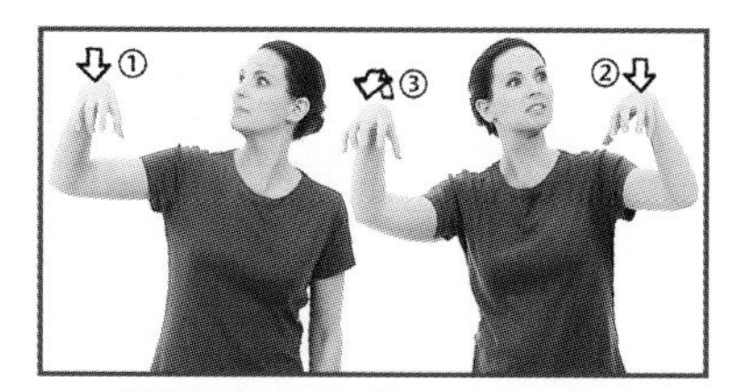

(2h)alt.PCL *"mansion"*++

For **Slide 9**

COUNTRY "area"

For **Slide 10**

FARM

PRESENT
(LESSON SLIDE 9:1:11)

2. tell what your neighborhood is like
– type of neighborhood or area
TYPE OF NEIGHBORHOOD OR AREA

Show video **Type of Neighborhood or Area**, then ask:

whq

T: fs-DAVID POSS "area" FACE+SAME-AS "what"

t

S: LONG-AGO, MACHINE+++(factories), NOW CHANGE+++,

t

fs-LOFTS, fs-CONDOS. DAY++ !MANY! PEOPLE TRAFFIC

t

GO-TO WORK. NIGHT, QUIET, ECL*"empty streets"*

Review. Have students tell about the type of neighborhood they live in. Introduce any new vocabulary students need. Demonstrate this rhetorical question. Have students copy and use it to tell about their neighborhoods.

rhet
T: [MY HOME] "area" FACE+SAME-AS "what"
S. (copy and describe their own neighborhood)

PRESENT
(LESSON SLIDE 9:1:12)

Introduce signs and phrases for what's nearby and convenient in the neighborhood.

SWIM fs-POOL
FARM+fs-MARKET
HORSE fs-TRAIL
fs-FERRY LCL*"boat going out"*++
BASEBALL
ART fs-STUDIO
FREEWAY

PRESENT

(LESSON SLIDE 9:1:13)

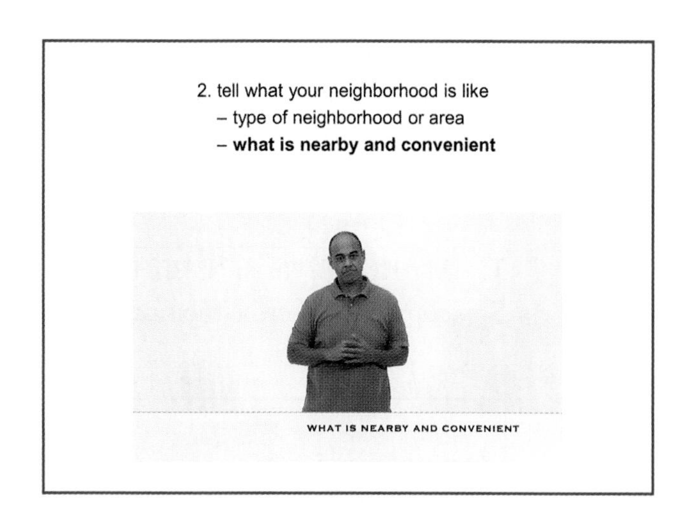

2. tell what your neighborhood is like
– type of neighborhood or area
– what is nearby and convenient
WHAT IS NEARBY AND CONVENIENT

Show video **What Is Nearby and Convenient**, then ask:

T: fs-DAVID HOME !MANY! NEAR IX-loc*"from here to there"*++
whq
"what"

Model the phrases to tell what's nearby and have students copy:
Examples:

T: NEAR **IX-dir** FARM+fs-MARKET
S: (copy)

T: NEAR **IX-loc***"right"* HORSE fs-TRAIL
S: (copy)

T: 2 **BLOCK-AWAY** IX-loc*"freeway"* FREEWAY
S: (copy)

T: 3 **fs-MILE(S)** IX-dir AIRPLANE
S: (copy)

Review. Have students tell what's nearby and convenient in their areas using one or more of these phrases. Introduce any new vocabulary students need.

- [NEAR] IX-dir (place)
- [NEAR] IX-loc (place)
- (#) BLOCK-AWAY IX-loc (place)
- (#) fs-MILE(S) IX-dir (place)

Be sure students:

- orient IX-dir, IX-loc, BLOCKS-AWAY and eye gaze in the direction of the places mentioned.

PRESENT
(LESSON SLIDE 9:1:14)

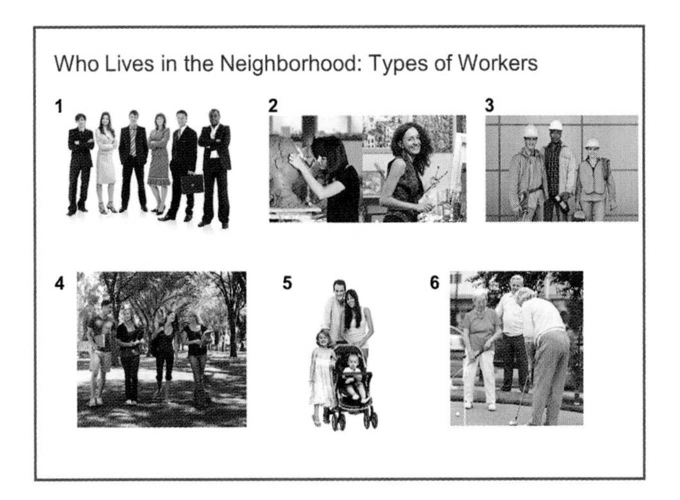

Introduce signs and phrases to tell who lives in the neighborhood:

PROFESSIONAL / WHITE+COLLAR (3 variations)

ARTIST **BLUE+COLLAR** **LEARN+ER**

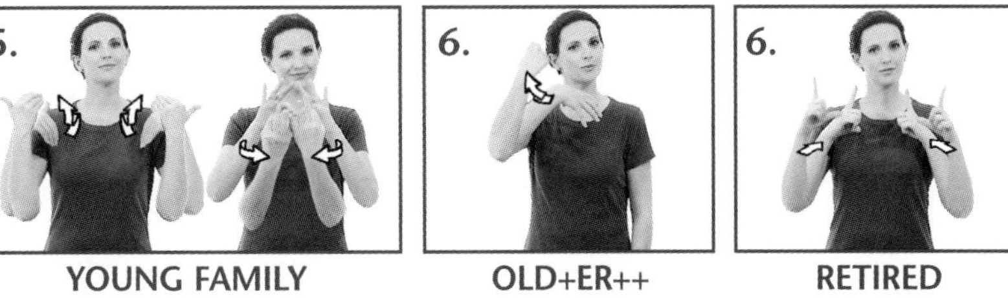

YOUNG FAMILY **OLD+ER++** **RETIRED**

PRESENT
(LESSON SLIDE 9:1:15)

Show slide and introduce signs and phrases to identify ethnic groups in the neighborhood:

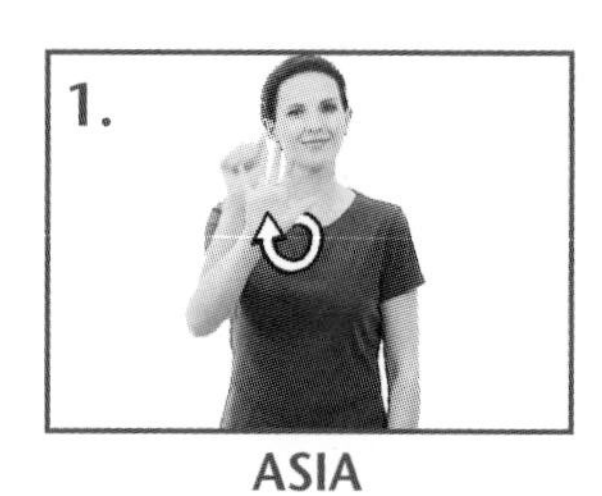

ASIA

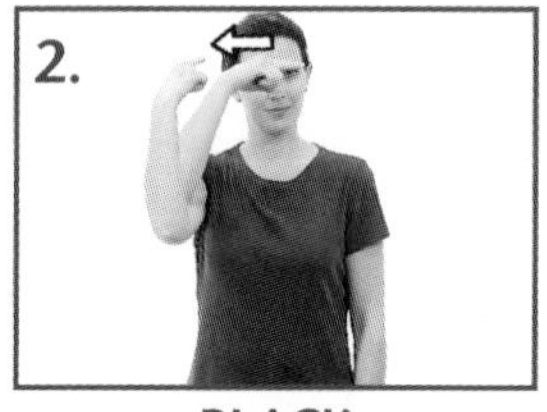

BLACK

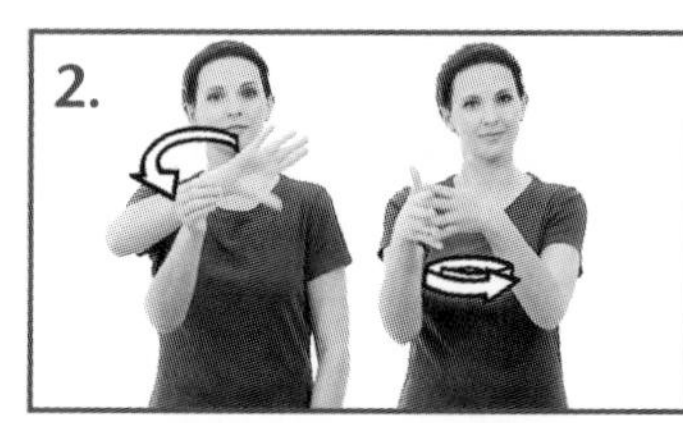

AFRICA+AMERICA

AFRICA(face)+AMERICA

(3 variations)

MEXICO

MEXICO

(2 variations)

INDIA

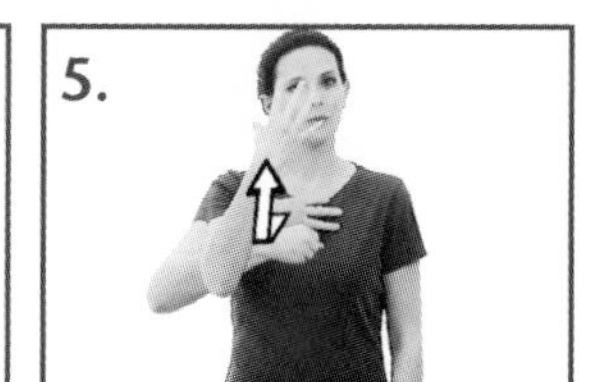

WHITE-FACE

PRESENT
(LESSON SLIDE 9:1:16)

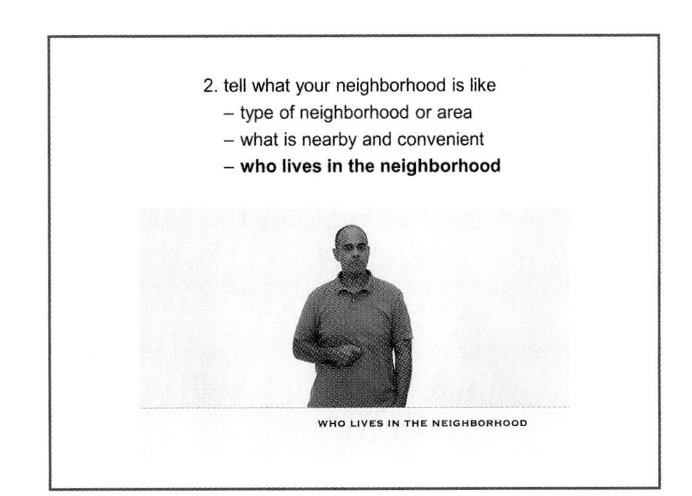

2. tell what your neighborhood is like
– type of neighborhood or area
– what is nearby and convenient
– who lives in the neighborhood
WHO LIVES IN THE NEIGHBORHOOD

MANY

SOME

MOST

FEW

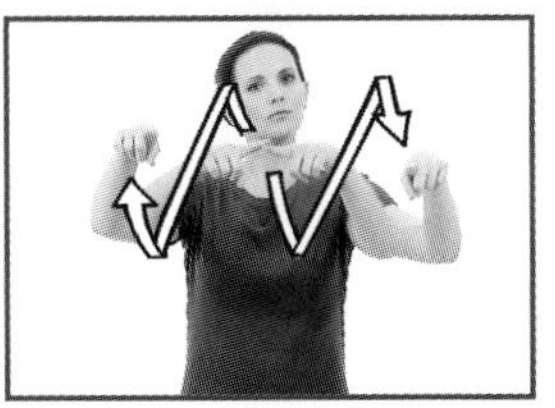
DIVERSE

Show video **Who Lives in the Neighborhood**, then ask:

whq

T: fs-DAVID HOME "area" PEOPLE "what"

S: "area" MOST PEOPLE, PROFESSIONAL, WHITE+COLLAR.

neg

IX-mult*"people"* MANY NONE CHILDREN.

Model the phrases to tell who lives in the neighborhood and have students copy you.

Examples:

T: [MY HOME] "area" HAVE **MANY** PEOPLE OLD+ER++, **SOME** YOUNG FAMILY

S: (copy)

T: [MY HOME] "area" **MOST** PEOPLE INDIA, **FEW** WHITE-FACE

S: (copy)

T: [MY HOME] "area" PEOPLE **DIVERSE** WHITE+COLLAR, BLUE+COLLAR, RETIRE, LEARN+ER

S: (copy)

TEACHER TO TEACHER

If students don't understand the sign MOST, SOME, FEW, you can draw a pie graph on the board and write "70% of people are white collar, 25% are blue collar, 5% are retired."

Review. Have students tell who lives in their neighborhood using one or more of these phrases. Introduce any new vocabulary students need.

- [MY HOME] "area" HAVE MANY (group)...SOME (group)
- [MY HOME] "area" MOST PEOPLE (group), FEW (group)
- [MY HOME] "area" PEOPLE DIVERSE...(groups)

Be sure students use contrastive structure or listing when naming more than one group.

PRESENT
(LESSON SLIDE 9:1:17)

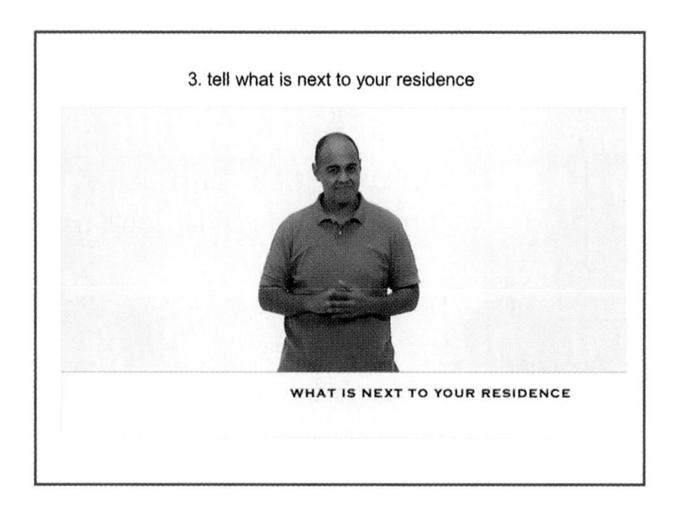

3. tell what is next to your residence
WHAT IS NEXT TO YOUR RESIDENCE

ACROSS-FROM-front

NEXT-TO

THUMB-loc"back"

Show video **What Is Next to Your Residence**, then ask:

T: fs-DAVID HOME ACROSS-FROM-front, NEXT-TO-right,
whq
NEXT-TO-left, THUMB-loc*"back"* "what"
S: **ACROSS-FROM-front** IX-loc fs-CONDO DCL*"high rise,"*
NEXT-TO-right "area" BASKETBALL,
NEXT-TO-left "area" fs-POOL SWIM,
THUMB-loc*"back"* PARKING "area."

PRESENT
(LESSON SLIDE 9:1:18)

What is next to your residence

- tell where and name facility or building
- add information about facility, building, or who lives there
- if you mention who lives there, give an opinion

Demonstrate how to tell what is next to your residence and have students copy.

For ***"• tell where and name facility or building"***

T: MY HOME, **ACROSS-FROM-front** IX-loc*"house"* HOUSE,
NEXT-TO-right "area" fs-APT,
NEXT-TO-left "area" SCHOOL,
THUMB-loc*"back"* fs-PARK
S: (copy)

For ***"• add information about facility, building, or who lives there"***

Repeat the sentences above and add more information.
T: MY HOME,
ACROSS-FROM-front IX-loc*"house"* HOUSE,
YOUNG FAMILY LIVE THERE.
NEXT-TO-right "area" fs-APT, **CHANGE-TO fs-CONDO**
NEXT-TO-left "area" SCHOOL, **fs-JRHS**
THUMB-loc*"back"* fs-PARK, **MANY TREE++.**

For ***"• if you mention who lives there, give an opinion"***
Introduce opinion vocabulary by using the sign in a sentence and then explaining the sign.

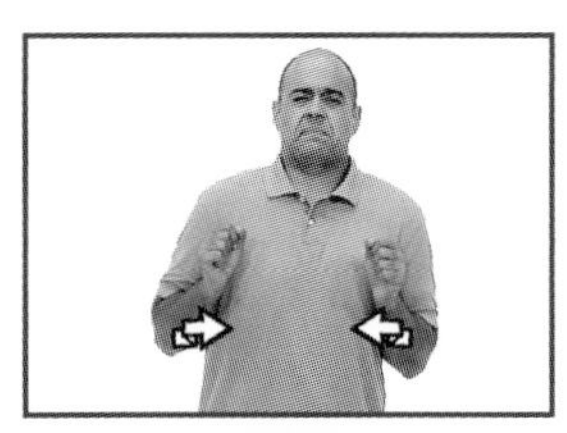

COLD

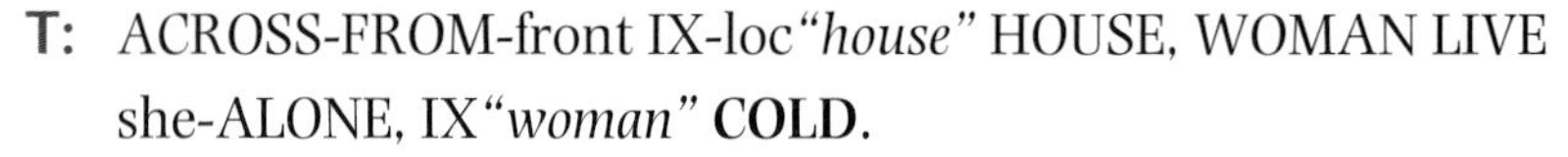

T: ACROSS-FROM-front IX-loc*"house"* HOUSE, WOMAN LIVE she-ALONE, IX*"woman"* **COLD**.

opinion	*explanation*
COLD	***act out:*** person snobbish, never says hello.

CHEERFUL

T: NEXT-TO-right "area" fs-APT, FAMILY RECENT MOVE-TO-right,
THEY-all **CHEERFUL**.

opinion	*explanation*
CHEERFUL	***act out:*** always say hello
	describe: smiles, likes to talk

MAD-char

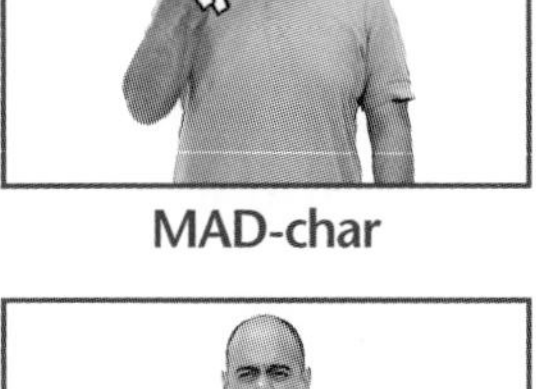

NOSEY

T: NEXT-TO-left "area" fs-CONDO, HUSBAND, WIFE LIVE IX-loc, THEY-TWO RETIRE. HUSBAND [TEND-TO] **MAD-char**, WIFE [TEND-TO] **NOSEY**

opinion	*explanation*
MAD-char	***act out:*** being a crabby person; shooing people away; wagging finger
NOSEY	***describe:*** peeking through the blinds or curtains, always staring at you and asking you too many questions about you or your visitors

Review. Have students tell what's next to their residences. Ask students, for at least one of the locations to add an opinion about the neighbor.

Be sure students:

- use these signs **ACROSS-FROM-front**, **NEXT-TO-right** "area," **NEXT-TO-left** "area," and **THUMB-loc*"back."***

PRESENT
(LESSON SLIDE 9:1:19)

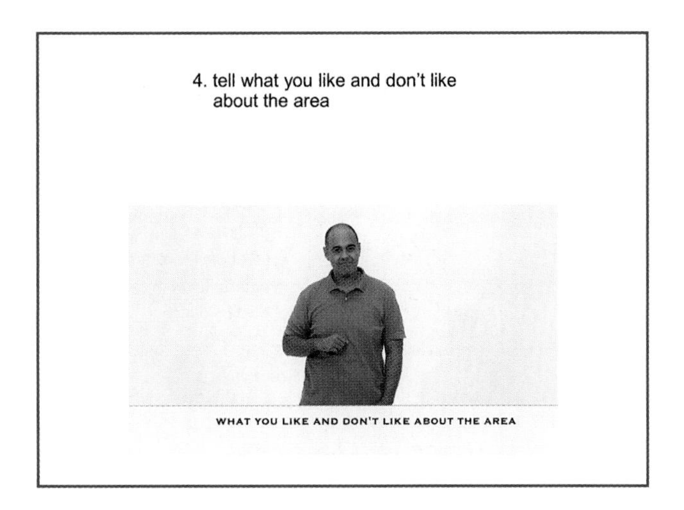

Show video **What You Like and Don't Like About the Area**, then ask:

whq (over WHY)
T: fs-DAVID IX*"David"* LIKE "area" WHY.
S: EASY IX-loc*"from here to there"*++, WALK++, SWELL.

t (over ONE); neg (over NOT LIKE); whq (over "what")
T: ONE, fs-DAVID IX*"David"* NOT LIKE "what"
S: EVERY-SATURDAY, EVERY-SUNDAY, RESTAURANT
rhet (over WHY); neg (over PEOPLE NOT GO-TO WORK)
IX-loc++ CLOSED++. WHY PEOPLE NOT GO-TO WORK.

PRESENT
(LESSON SLIDE 9:1:20)

What you like or don't like about the area

- noise level
- safety level
- traffic level
- level of cleanliness
- activity level
- cost of living

Introduce these signs:

noise level	*explanation*
QUIET	***describe:*** hear nothing; no cars driving by; no people talking, no music, no dogs barking

QUIET

NOISY	rhet (over "what,") ***sign:*** **[QUIET] OPPOSITE SIGN** "what," **NOISY.** ***describe:*** cars driving by and honking, dogs barking, sirens

NOISY

safety level	*explanation*
"area" fs-SAFE	***describe:*** children can play outside; no one will take them away; no break-ins

"area" fs-SAFE

DANGEROUS

safety level — *explanation*

DANGEROUS

sign: **[fs-SAFE],** OPPOSITE SIGN "what," **DANGEROUS**
describe: not safe area, children can't play outside; streets not well-lighted; break-ins

(2h)ECL*"empty streets"*

traffic level — *explanation*

(2h)ECL*"empty streets"* ***describe:*** no people or vehicles on the street

TRAFFIC

TRAFFIC

sign: [(2h)ECL*"empty streets"*]
rhet
OPPOSITE SIGN "what," **TRAFFIC**
describe: many people walking by and cars driving by

level of cleanliness — *explanation*

CLEAN

CLEAN

describe: no litter on streets, people sweeping streets; everything looks freshly painted; nothing is broken, for example, windows intact

DIRTY

DIRTY

sign: [CLEAN] OPPOSITE SIGN
rhet
"what," **DIRTY**
describe: streets and sidewalks littered with papers, garbage overflowing, smells bad **(SMELL STINKY)**

activity level — *explanation*

BORING

BORING

describe: nearby no stores, no movies; no fun; twiddling thumbs

MANY (2h)DO-circle

activity level	*explanation*
MANY (2h)DO	***sign:*** [BORING] OPPOSITE SIGN rhet "what," **MANY (2h)DO-circle** ***describe:*** go to stores, movies, restaurants, get together with friends, busy, fun

EXPENSIVE

cost of living	*explanation*
EXPENSIVE	***describe:*** paying for food, gas, lights keeps going up
CHEAP	***sign:*** [EXPENSIVE] OPPOSITE SIGN rhet "what" **CHEAP**

CHEAP

Review. Have students tell what they like or don't like about their areas. Introduce any new vocabulary students need. Have them use these phrases.

nod rhet
S: "area" ME LIKE, WHY...

t neg rhet
S: ONE, ME NOT LIKE "what"...

TEACHER TO TEACHER

When explaining why you like something, be sure to use the rhetorical question WHY instead of the sign BECAUSE.

PRESENT
(LESSON SLIDE 9:1:21)

5. tell about your future plans
FUTURE PLANS

Show video **Future Plans**, then ask:

whq

T: IX*"David"* SIGN "what"

S: IX*"David"* LIKE "area." IX*"David"* STAY-there **UNTIL** [IX*"David"*] RETIRE, MOVE-AWAY. MAYBE fs-FLA

UNTIL

Model the phrases to tell about future plans and have students copy you:

T: ME LIKE "area" ME PLAN STAY UNTIL ME GRADUATE.

S: (copy)

T: fs-RENT !CHEAP! ME STAY-here UNTIL ME FIND OTHER WORK.

S: (copy)

T: NOW ME LOOK-FOR OTHER fs-APT (or HOUSE), MOVE-AWAY.

S: (copy)

Review. Have students tell about their future plans using one or more of these phrases.

- ...ME LIKE "area" ME PLAN STAY-here **UNTIL** (event)
- ...(tell why) ME STAY-here **UNTIL** (event)
- ...ME LOOK-FOR OTHER (residence), MOVE-AWAY

PRESENT
(LESSON SLIDE 9:1:22)

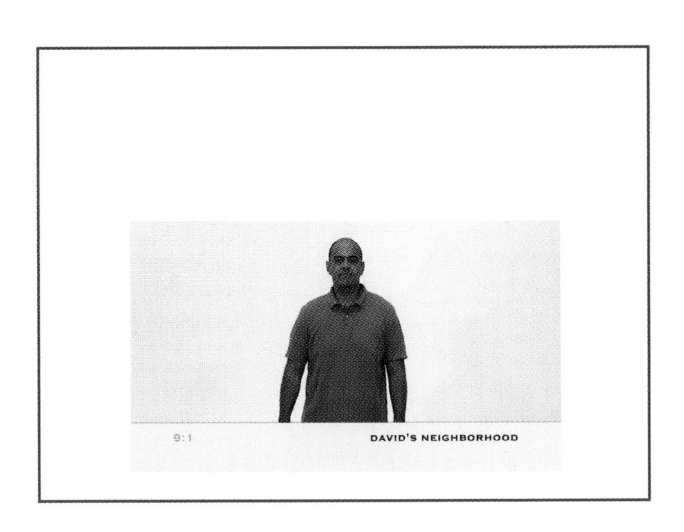

Conclude. Show the video **David's Neighborhood** in its entirety.

HOMEWORK

Tell students to do **Homework 9:1** (*Student Workbook*, pages 154–167).

HOMEWORK FOLLOW-UP
5–30 MINUTES

PRESENT
(FOLLOW-UP SLIDES 9:1:1–10)

Amber's Neighborhood

1. where Amber lives ______
   - kind of residence, what city or district ______
   - for how long and with whom ______

Check students' answers to **Amber's Neighborhood**. See **Introduction** pages xviii–xix for different ways to check answers.

LESSON 9:2

Places in the Neighborhood

Lesson length: 20–30 minutes

LESSON GOAL

Students learn vocabulary for names of and types of businesses in the neighborhood.

NOTIONS

Vocabulary

Places

fs-HYATT	fs-IKEA	fs-SAM'S-DELI
STARBUCKS	fs-AAA	fs-ABC LIQUOR
MCDONALD'S	fs-MACY'S	fs-ATT
fs-CURVES	7-11	fs-ADAMS FUNERAL
fs-REMAX	fs-ACE	DOLLAR STORE

Government services/facilities

fs-CITY fs-HALL	FIREFIGHTER
JUDGE+HOUSE	PARKING
POLICE	

Types of business

HOTEL	CAR INSURANCE	LIQUOR STORE
COFFEE HOUSE	fs-DEPT STORE	PHONE STORE
FAST FOOD	SMALL STORE, OPEN ALL-NIGHT	FUNERAL [HOME]
EXERCISE		CHEAP++, DISCOUNT
fs-RE (real estate)	fs-HARDWARE	
FURNITURE	SANDWICH	

PREPARATION

Optional. You can have students learn the vocabulary on their own in preparation for **Lesson 9:5**.

MATERIALS

9:2 Lesson Slides

HOMEWORK 9:2

Student Workbook, pages 168–173

INTRODUCE *Names and Types of Businesses*

20–30 minutes

PRESENT
(LESSON SLIDE 9:2:1)

Introduce signs for the stores and tell what they are.

HOTEL

Logo 1

T: IX-loc*"Hyatt logo"* **fs-HYATT**, IX*"Hyatt"* **HOTEL**.

Logo 2

T: IX-loc*"Starbucks logo"* **STARBUCKS**, IX*"Starbucks"* **COFFEE HOUSE**.

STARBUCKS

COFFEE HOUSE

Logo 3

T: IX-loc*"McDonald's logo"* **MCDONALD'S**, IX*"McDonald's"* **FAST FOOD**.

MCDONALDS

FAST FOOD

EXERCISE

Logo 4

T: IX-loc*"Curves logo"* **fs-CURVES**, IX*"Curves"* **EXERCISE.**

Review the signs for the stores and the types of stores they are.

PRESENT
(LESSON SLIDE 9:2:2)

Introduce signs for the stores and tell what they are.

FURNITURE

Logo 5

T: IX-loc*"RE/MAX logo"* **fs-REMAX**, IX*"RE/MAX"* **fs-RE.**

Logo 6

T: IX-loc*"IKEA logo"* **fs-IKEA**, IX*"IKEA"* **FURNITURE.**

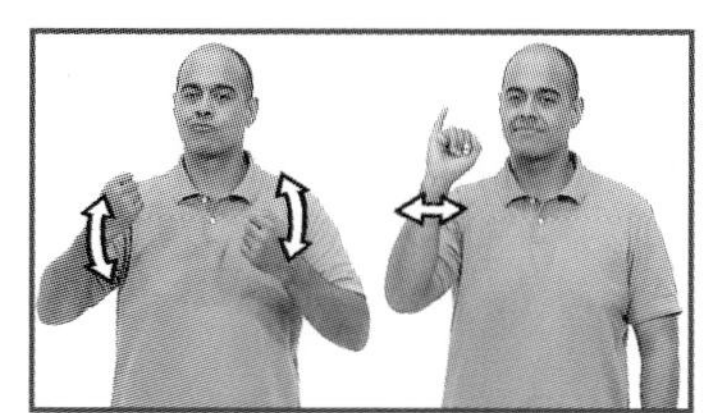
INSURANCE

Logo 7

T: IX-loc*"AAA logo"* **fs-AAA**, IX*"AAA"* **CAR INSURANCE.**

Logo 8

T: IX-loc*"Macy's logo"* **fs-MACYS**, IX*"Macy's"* **fs-DEPT STORE.**

> **NOTE:** Be sure to twist the letter "s" at the end of "Macy's." This movement is commonly used when the printed name is followed by an apostrophe and an "s."

Review the signs for the stores and types of stores.

PRESENT

(LESSON SLIDE 9:2:3)

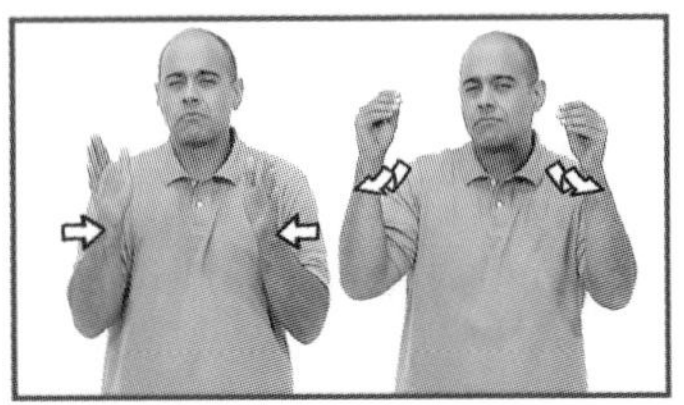
SMALL STORE

OPEN ALL-NIGHT

Introduce signs for the stores and tell what they are.

Logo 9

T: IX-loc*"7-11 logo"* 7-11, IX*"7-11"* **SMALL STORE, OPEN ALL-NIGHT.**

Logo 10

T: X-loc*"ACE logo"* **fs-ACE**, IX*"ACE"* **fs-HARDWARE.**

SANDWICH

LIQUOR STORE

Logo 11

T: IX-loc*"Sam's Deli logo"* **fs-SAM'S DELI**, IX*"Sam's Deli"* **SANDWICH.**

Logo 12

T: IX-loc*"ABC logo"* **fs-ABC**, IX*"ABC Liquor"* **LIQUOR STORE.**

Review the signs for the stores and the types of stores.

PRESENT
(LESSON SLIDE 9:2:4)

Introduce signs for the stores and to tell what they are.

PHONE STORE

Logo 13

T: IX-loc*"AT&T logo"* **fs-ATT**, IX*"AT&T"* **PHONE STORE**.

FUNERAL [HOME]

Logo 14

T: IX-loc*"Adams logo"* **fs-ADAMS**, IX*"Adams"* **FUNERAL [HOME]**.

Logo 15

T: IX-loc*"Dollar logo"* **DOLLAR STORE**, IX*"Dollar Stores"*

DOLLAR STORE

CHEAP++

DISCOUNT

CHEAP++, DISCOUNT.

Review the signs for the stores and the types of stores.

PRESENT
(LESSON SLIDE 9:2:5)

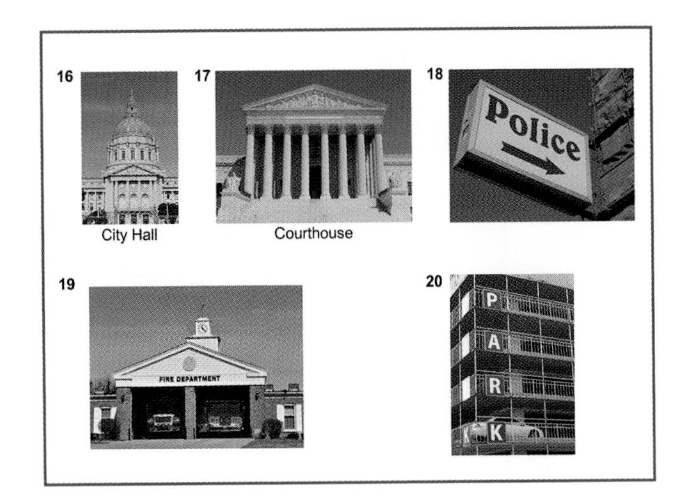

Introduce signs for local government services.

Photo 16
T: IX-loc*"city hall"* **fs-CITY fs-HALL.**

Photo 17
T: IX-loc*"courthouse"* **JUDGE+HOUSE.**

JUDGE+HOUSE

Photo 18
T: IX-loc*"police"* **POLICE.**

POLICE

Photo 19
T: IX-loc*"fire station"* **FIREFIGHTER.**

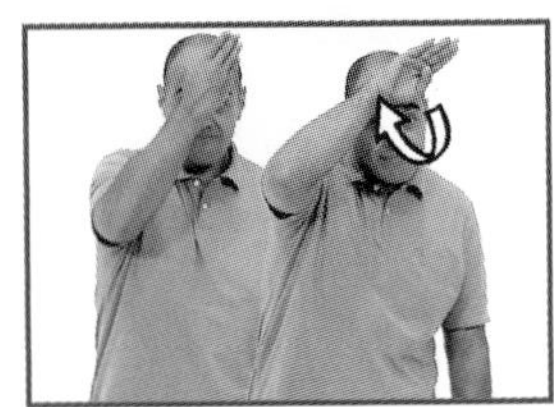
FIREFIGHTER

Photo 20
T: IX-loc*"garage"* **PARKING.**

PARKING

Review. Go over **Lesson Slides 9:2:1–5** again. This time, ask students to give signs for the name and type of each business.

HOMEWORK

Tell students to do **Homework 9:2** (*Student Workbook*, pages 168–173).

LESSON 9:3

Numbers: Giving the Time 1

Lesson length: 30–40 minutes

LESSON GOAL

Students will learn to sign clock numbers and use them to discuss schedules.

KEY SKILLS

Hour Numbers

On the hour 1:00–9:00

- tap index finger on the wrist before giving the number
- move the hand outward and shake the hand
- have the palm face out for numbers 1–5

On the hour for 10:00 to 12:00

- tap index finger on the wrist before giving the number
- numbers 10–12 can be repeated or have a single movement

Hour and Minute Numbers

For the hour part:

- tap index finger on the wrist before giving the hour number
- hours 1–9 the hand is not shaken and hours 10–12 the number is not repeated

For the minutes part:

- before giving minute number, the hand moves slightly to the side
- palm faces out for minutes :01–:09
- minutes :10–:15 and :20, it is best to use an emphatic and singular movement, but repeated movement is acceptable
- minutes :30, :40 and :50 these numbers use an emphatic and singular movement only

NOTIONS

Vocabulary

beginning–end verb pairs

START	LEAVE-FROM
FINISH	ARRIVE-TO

Verbs

GET-UP
GET-IN-BED

Wh-word question

whq
TIME

PREPARATION

Read and view **Numbers: Giving the Time 1** (*Student Workbook*, page 174)

MATERIALS

9:3 Lesson Slides
9:3 Follow-up Slides
Exercise 1 (*Student Workbook*, page 471)

HOMEWORK 9:3

Student Workbook, pages 174–176

INTRODUCE *Hour Numbers*

7–10 minutes

PRESENT

(LESSON SLIDES 9:3:1–12)

Clock Numbers

1:00	4:00	7:00	10:00
2:00	5:00	8:00	11:00
3:00	6:00	9:00	12:00

Demonstrate clock number forms 1:00 to 9:00. Students copy.

T: (point to "1:00"), TIME+1
S(all): (copy)

Point out:

- the index finger taps the wrist
- the hand moves outward before the number is given,
- the palm faces out and the hand is shaken for numbers 1–9.

Demonstrate clock numbers 10:00, 11:00 and 12:00.

T: (point to "10:00"), TIME+10
S(all): (copy)

Point out:

- the index finger taps the wrist
- the hand moves outward before the number is given
- the number 10–12 can either be repeated or have a single movement.

Review. Point to numbers on **Slide 9:3:12** and have students sign the numbers.

INTRODUCE *Hour and Minute Numbers*

7–10 minutes

PRESENT
(LESSON SLIDES 9:3:13–24)

Clock Numbers

1:05	4:20	7:35	10:50
2:10	5:25	8:40	11:55
3:15	6:30	9:45	12:30

Demonstrate hour and minute combination for 1:05–12:30.

T: (point to “1:05”) 1:05
S: (copy)

Point out:
For the hour:

- the index finger taps the wrist before giving the hour number
- for hours 1–9 the hand is not shaken, and for the hours 10–12 the number is not repeated

For the minutes:

- before giving minute number, the hand moves slightly to the side
- the palm faces out for minutes :01–:09
- for minutes :10–:15 and :20, it is best to use an emphatic and singular movement, but repeated movement is acceptable
- for :30, :40 and :50 these numbers use an emphatic and singular movement only.

Review. Point to numbers on **Slide 9:3:24** and have students sign the numbers.

Continue until all students have a chance to sign hour–minute combinations.

PRACTICE *Telling What Time*

15–20 minutes

PRESENT

(LESSON SLIDE 9:3:25)

Beth's Schedule

9:30-12:30 – ASL class

12:30-1:30 – lunch

3:00-10:00 – work

Ask class the following questions. Encourage students to sign the part of the day after giving the time.

START TIME

FINISH TIME

t when whq

T: fs-BETH, POSS*"Beth"* fs-ASL CLASS **START TIME**

S: TIME+9:30 [MORNING]

t when whq

T: [CLASS] **FINISH TIME**

S: TIME+12:30 [NOON]

t whq

T: [CLASS] HOW-MANY HOUR

S: 3-HOUR

t when whq

T: IX*"Beth"* EAT **START TIME**

S: TIME+12:30

t when whq

T: [EAT] **FINISH TIME**

S: TIME+1:30

t when whq

T: IX*"Beth"*WORK **START TIME**

S: TIME+3:00 [AFTERNOON]

t when whq

T: IX*"Beth"* WORK **FINISH TIME**

S: TIME+10:00 [NIGHT]

Continue asking questions until students are signing clock numbers correctly.

PRESENT
(LESSON SLIDE 9:3:26)

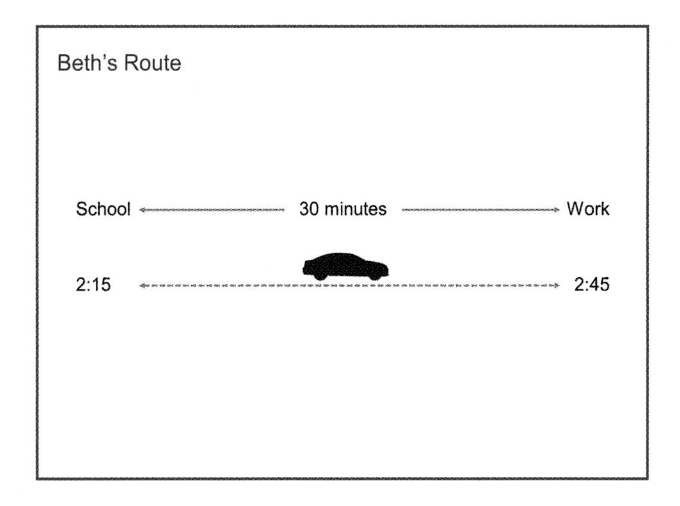

Ask the following questions.

LEAVE-FROM

ARRIVE-TO

t — when — whq

T: fs-BETH, **LEAVE-FROM** SCHOOL TIME
S: TIME+2:15 AFTERNOON

t — when — whq

T: IX*"Beth"* **ARRIVE-TO** WORK TIME
S: TIME+2:45 AFTERNOON

NOTE: Be sure LEAVE-FROM begins in one location and ARRIVE-TO ends in the other location.

T: SCHOOL IX-loc*"left,"* WORK IX-loc*"right"*

whq

DRIVE-TO*"from school to work,"* HOW-MANY MINUTE
S: 30 MINUTE

PRESENT
(LESSON SLIDE 9:3:27)

NAME OF STUDENT	1	2	3
1. get up			
2. go to bed			
3. left home today			
4. arrived at school today			
5. start work (typically)			
6. finish work (typically)			
7. do ______ (name activity)			

EXERCISE 1

Review questions on the exercise sheet **What Time?** (*Student Workbook*, page 471) before beginning the activity.

GET-UP

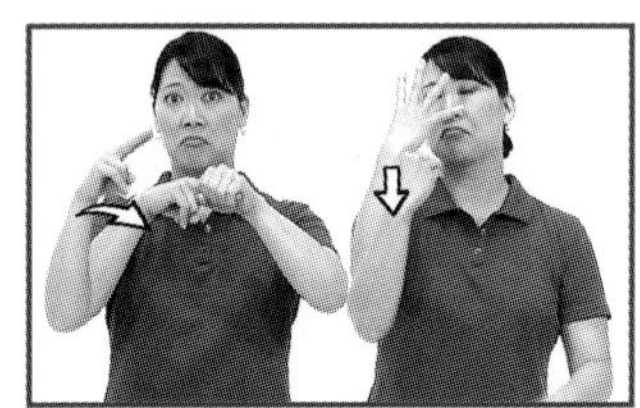
GET-IN-BED SLEEP

For "*1. get up*"

when whq
T: YOU **GET-UP**, TIME
S: (copy)

For "*2. go to bed*"

when whq
T: YOU **GET-IN-BED SLEEP**, TIME
S: (copy)

For "*3. left home today*"

when whq
T: TODAY/NOW YOU LEAVE-FROM HOME, TIME
S: (copy)

For "*4. arrived at school today*"

when whq
T: TODAY/NOW YOU ARRIVE-TO SCHOOL, TIME
S: (copy)

For "*5. start work (typically)*"

t when whq
T: WORK YOU [TEND-TO] START TIME
S: (copy)

For *"6. finish work (typically)"*

t when whq

T: WORK YOU [TEND-TO] FINISH TIME

S: (copy)

For *"7. do _______ (name activity)"*

Have students brainstorm different activities to ask about. For example,

t when whq

S: NOW+NIGHT YOU EAT TIME

Mingle. Have students interview three students and write down the times in their workbook.

HOMEWORK

Tell students to do **Homework 9:3** (*Student Workbook*, pages 174–176).

HOMEWORK FOLLOW-UP

5–30 MINUTES

PRESENT

(FOLLOW-UP SLIDES 9:3:1–7)

Fill in the Time

	Activity or Place	Time 1	Time 2
1.			
2.			
3.			
4.			
5.			
6.			

Check students' answers. See **Introduction** pages xviii–xix for different ways to check answers.

LESSON 9:4

Describing Your Neighborhood

Lesson length: 70–85 minutes

LESSON GOAL

Students will use this outline to describe their neighborhoods.

Narrative

1. tell where you live
   - kind of residence, and what city or district
   - for how long[1] and with who
2. tell what your neighborhood is like
   - type of neighborhood and area[2]
   - what is nearby and convenient[3]
   - who lives in the neighborhood[4]
3. tell what is next to your residence[5]
4. tell what you like[6] and don't like about the area[7]
5. tell about your future plans[8]

KEY PHRASES

[1] UP-TILL-NOW (#) YEAR (or MONTH)

rhet

[2] "area" FACE+SAME-AS "what,"...

[3] [NEAR] IX-dir (place)
[NEAR] IX-loc (place)
(#) BLOCK-AWAY IX-loc (place)
(#) fs-MILE(S) IX-dir (place)

[4] [MY HOME] "area" HAVE MANY (group)...SOME (group)
[MY HOME] "area" MOST PEOPLE (group), FEW (group)
[MY HOME] "area" PEOPLE DIVERSE...(groups)

[5] ACROSS-FROM IX-loc, NEXT-TO-left IX-loc NEXT-TO-right IX-loc, and THUMB-loc *"back"*

nod rhet
[6] ME LIKE "area" WHY,...

t neg whq
[7] ONE, ME NOT+LIKE, "what"

[8] ...STAY-here UNTIL (event)

NOTIONS

Grammar

Rhetorical Questions

Locatives (IX-dir, IX-loc, THUMB-loc*"back,"* NEXT-TO, etc.)

PREPARATION

- Read and view **Key Grammar: Using Rhetorical Questions**, **Learn the Narrative** and **Assignment**, (*Student Workbook*, pages 178–183)
- Make copies of **9:4 Evaluation** (for **Homework Follow-up**)

MATERIALS

9:4 Lesson Slides
9:4 Evaluation
Exercise 2 (*Student Workbook*, page 477)

HOMEWORK 9:4

Student Workbook, pages 177–183

REVIEW *Amber's Neighborhood*

40–45 minutes

PRESENT
(LESSON SLIDE 9:4:1)

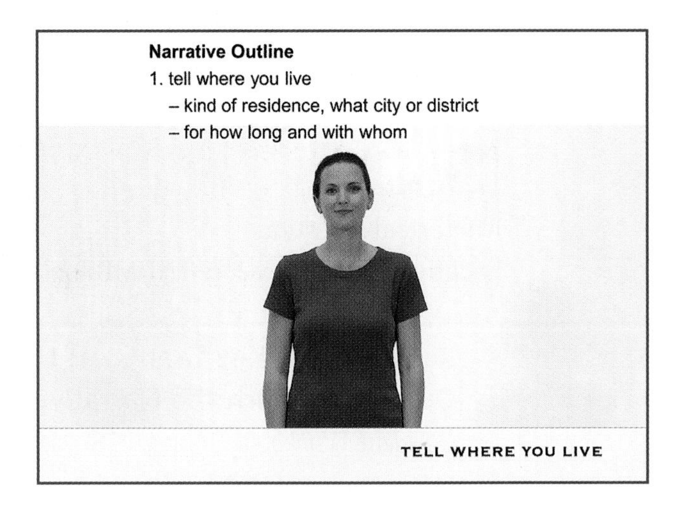

Narrative Outline
1. tell where you live
– kind of residence, what city or district
– for how long and with whom
TELL WHERE YOU LIVE

Show video **Tell Where You Live**, then ask:

whq (over: fs-AMBER IX"Amber" SIGN "what")

T: fs-AMBER IX"*Amber*" SIGN "what"

S: IX"*Amber*" LIVE fs-APT IX-loc OAKLAND, NEAR BERKELEY. IX"*Amber*" LIVE UP-TILL-NOW 7+YEAR. LIVE WITH POSS HUSBAND, ONE #DOG

Rehearse. Have students rehearse this phrase:

T: **LIVE UP-TILL-NOW 7+YEAR**

S: (repeat)

PRESENT
(LESSON SLIDE 9:4:2)

2. tell what your neighborhood is like
– type of neighborhood and area
TYPE OF NEIGHBORHOOD OR AREA

Show video **Type of Neighborhood and Area**, then ask:

whq

T: fs-AMBER POSS "area" **FACE+SAME-AS "what"**

S: POSS*"Amber"* HOME "area" fs-APT, HOUSE MIXED. MOST HOUSE OVER-LIMIT 100+YEAR OLD. POSS*"Amber"* fs-APT IN LARGE HOUSE, IX*"house"* BUILD 19+06, "wow" OLD

Rehearse. Have students rehearse the rhetorical question and emphasize the facial grammar (raised brows).

rhet

T: **MY HOME "area" FACE+SAME-AS "what"...**

S: (repeat)

PRESENT

(LESSON SLIDE 9:4:3)

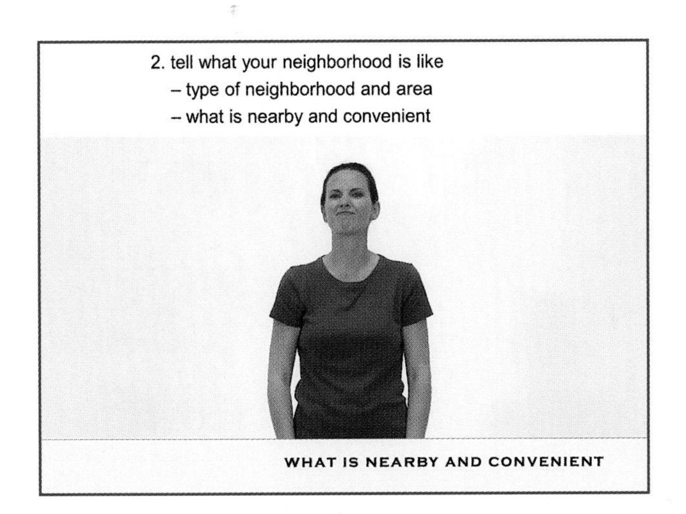
2. tell what your neighborhood is like
– type of neighborhood and area
– what is nearby and convenient
WHAT IS NEARBY AND CONVENIENT

Show video **What Is Nearby and Convenient**, then ask:

whq

T: IX*"Amber"* HOME NEAR "what"

S: ONE BLOCK-AWAY, "row," DIFFERENT+++ STORE, IX-loc*"left"* COFFEE STORE, (shift right) FOOD STORE, "well" MANY+ DIFFERENT++ RESTAURANT IX-loc++, "well" CLOTHES STORE, "well" SHOE+STORE, #DOG STORE, "well" fs-PO, ICE-CREAM, MOVIE, VARIOUS-THINGS, ONE fs-MILE IX-loc*"from here to there (right)"* BIG, ART COLLEGE

Rehearse. Have students rehearse these phrases.

T: **ONE BLOCK-AWAY**, "row" DIFFERENT+++ STORE

S: (copy)

T: **ONE fs-MILE IX-loc***"from here to there (right)"* BIG, ART COLLEGE
S: (repeat)

T: **NEAR IX-dir** FARM+fs-MARKET
S: (repeat)

T: **NEAR IX-loc*"right"*** FREEWAY
S: (repeat)

Be sure students orient eye gaze and these signs in the direction of the places mentioned: **BLOCK-AWAY, IX-dir, IX-loc**

PRESENT
(LESSON SLIDE 9:4:4)

Show video **Who Lives in the Neighborhood**, then ask:

whq
T: fs-AMBER HOME "area" PEOPLE "what"
S: POSS*"Amber"* HOME "area" HAVE !MANY! COLLEGE LEARN+ER, ART+ER, SOME YOUNG FAMILY

Rehearse. Have students rehearse these phrases.

T: "area"HAVE !MANY! COLLEGE LEARN+ER, ART+ER, SOME YOUNG FAMILY
S: (repeat)

T: "area" MOST PEOPLE ASIA, FEW MEXICO
S: (repeat)

T: "area" PEOPLE DIVERSE, WHITE+COLLAR, BLUE+COLLAR, LEARN+ER, ART+ER, DIVERSE
S: (repeat)

Be sure students use contrastive structure or listing when naming two or more groups.

PRESENT
(LESSON SLIDE 9:4:5)

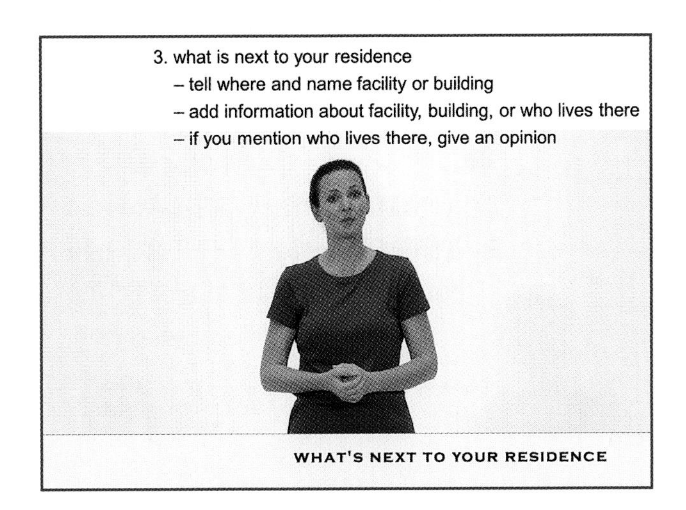

3. what is next to your residence
– tell where and name facility or building
– add information about facility, building, or who lives there
– if you mention who lives there, give an opinion
WHAT'S NEXT TO YOUR RESIDENCE

Show video **What Is Next to Your Residence**, then ask:

T: fs-AMBER HOME ACROSS-FROM-front, NEXT-TO-right,
NEXT-TO-left, THUMB-loc*"back"* "what" (whq)
S: ACROSS-FROM-front IX-loc "area" SCHOOL, fs-JRHS
NEXT-TO-right IX-loc*"right,"* fs-APT, PEOPLE LIVE
IX-loc*"right,"* NOT-KNOW WHO
NEXT-TO-left HOUSE IX-loc*"left,"* OLD WOMAN
IX*"woman,"* MAD-char
THUMB-loc*"back,"* CHURCH

Rehearse. Have students add information, change the information or add opinions about neighbors in these phrases. For example:

T: ACROSS-FROM-front IX-loc "area" SCHOOL, fs-JRHS
S: ACROSS-FROM-front IX-loc "area" SCHOOL, ELEMENTARY (or DEAF-SCHOOL, !LARGE!, FRANCE)

T: NEXT-TO-right IX-loc*"right,"* fs-APT, PEOPLE LIVE IX-loc*"right,"* NOT-KNOW WHO
S: NEXT-TO-right IX-loc*"right,"* fs-APT, PEOPLE LIVE IX-loc*"right,"* **THEY-all CHEERFUL** (or LEARN+ER, MOST WORK MACHINE*"factory"*)

T: NEXT-TO-left HOUSE IX-loc*"left,"* OLD WOMAN IX*"woman"* MAD-char
S: NEXT-TO-left HOUSE IX-loc*"left,"* OLD WOMAN IX*"woman"* **NOSEY** (or COLD, CHEERFUL, LIVE she-ALONE)

T: THUMB-loc*"back,"* CHURCH
S: THUMB-loc*"back,"* CHURCH, BEAUTIFUL FRILLY (or CUTE SMALL, ASIA PEOPLE GO-TO*"church"*)

PRESENT
(LESSON SLIDE 9:4:6)

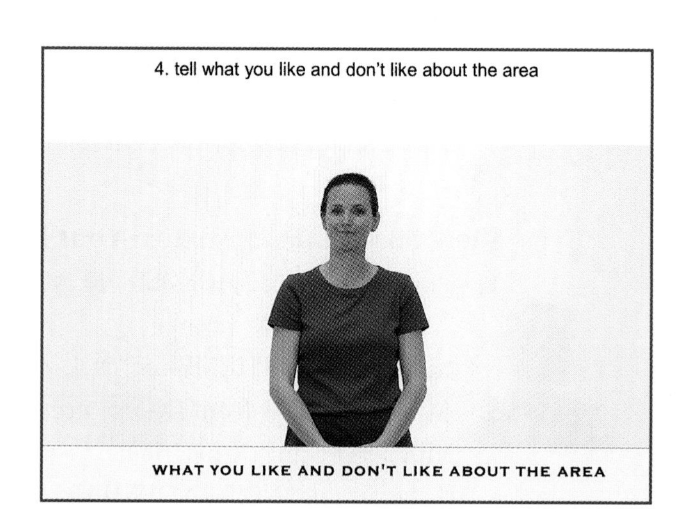

Show video **What You Like and Don't Like About the Area**, then ask:

(whq over: fs-AMBER LIKE "area" WHY)
T: fs-AMBER LIKE "area" WHY
S: NEAR IX-loc*"from here to there"*++, CAN WALK, IX*"Amber"* NOT+NEED DRIVE. MORNING, IX*"Amber"* GET-UP, IX-dir*"right"* WALK, IX-dir*"right."* COFFEE, READ NEWSPAPER.
(when over: BUY FOOD)
BUY FOOD, WALK(left) IX-dir*"left"* BUY++ FOOD.

when
NIGHT, IX*"Amber"* THEY-TWO HUSBAND, WANT LEAVE-FOR EAT, MOVIE, THEY-TWO CAN WALK

when
IX-dir*"front"* RESTAURANT, EAT FINISH, GO-TO*"right"* MOVIE.

when / when
FINISH, IX-dir*"left"* ICE-CREAM, FINISH, GO-TO HOME.

when
SUNDAY, HAVE FARM+fs-MARKET, IX*"Amber"* WALK IX-loc*"from here to there"* BUY++ FOOD

neg / whq
T: fs-AMBER NOT+LIKE "what"

t / neg
S: ONE, IX*"Amber"* NOT+LIKE, SCHOOL ACROSS-FROM IX-loc

when
CHILDREN, FINISH SCHOOL, PAPER, FOOD (2h)alt.DROP-OFF-street. IX*"Amber"* MUST ICL*"put trash in bag"*++, CLEAN++.

Rehearse. Have students rehearse these rhetorical questions. Emphasize the facial grammar.

nod / rhet
T: "area" ME LIKE, WHY, !MANY! NEAR IX-loc*"from here to there"*++, EASY WALK++

S: (repeat)

t / neg / rhet
T: ONE, ME NOT+LIKE "what," "area" EXPENSIVE

S: (repeat)

PRESENT
(LESSON SLIDE 9:4:7)

5. tell about future plans
FUTURE PLANS

Show video **Future Plans**, then ask:

whq

T: IX*"Amber"* SIGN "what"

S: IX*"Amber"* NOT MOVE-AWAY, IX*"Amber"* LIKE POSS*"Amber"* HOME "area," IX*"Amber"* STAY-there.

Rehearse. Have students change your phrase to tell about future plans.

T: ME LIKE "area." ME STAY-there UNTIL ME RETIRE

S: ME LIKE "area." ME STAY-there UNTIL ME...(GRADUATE, GET NEW WORK, MARRY)

when

T: ME LIVE IX*"house"* HOUSE SEVERAL MORE YEARS, FINISH ME MOVE-TO HOUSE ONE-STORY, EASY SCL:V*"walk around"*

S: ME LIVE IX*"house"* HOUSE...(6-MONTHS MORE, 1 MORE

when

YEAR, UNTIL ME GRADUATE), FINISH ME MOVE-TO... (fs-SF, fs-APT, COUNTRY "area")

PRACTICE *Narrative*

30–40 minutes

Students practice narrating about a neighborhood with emphasis on using transitions to move from one part of the narrative to another.

PRESENT
(LESSON SLIDE 9:4:8)

Narrative Outline
1. tell where you live
   - kind of residence, what city or district
   - for how long and with whom
2. tell what your neighborhood is like
   - type of neighborhood and area
   - what is nearby and convenient
   - who lives in the neighborhood
3. what is next to your residence
4. tell what you like and don't like about the area
5. tell about future plans

EXERCISE 2 (*Student Workbook*, page 477).
Have students pair up and discuss how to sign the narrative based on the information in the exercise.

When done, call on students to sign segments of the narrative. Correct if necessary.

Teacher's Guide

1. Tell where you live
   - ***live in a loft in Berkeley***
   - ***for the past 8 months, with 2 roommates***

   ME LIVE fs-LOFT IX"*loc*" BERKELEY. UP-TILL-NOW 8-MONTH ME LIVE WITH 2 ROOMMATE.

2. Tell what your neighborhood is like
   - ***an industrial area with some buildings converted into lofts***
   - ***freeway nearby which provides easy access to work and school***
   - ***mostly artists and blue collar workers live in the area***

   rhet
   [MY HOME] "area" FACE+SAME-AS "what," MACHINE "area" SOME CHANGE++ fs-LOFT.

   NEAR IX-dir"*around the corner*" FREEWAY,
   NEAR IX-dir"*right*" WORK,
   IX-dir"*left*" SCHOOL.

   [MY HOME] "area" MOST ART+ER. SAME-AS, !MANY! WORK BLUE+COLLAR.

3. Tell what's next to your residence
   - *across from*—***house; nice, friendly couple lives there***
   - *on your right*—***liquor store, noisy outside the store***
   - *on your left*—***house; nosey artist lives there***
   - *behind*—***furniture factory***

t

ACROSS-FROM-front IX-loc HOUSE, HUSBAND, WIFE LIVE IX-loc*"house,"* THEY-TWO NICE, CHEERFUL

NEXT-TO-right IX-loc*"right"* LIQUOR STORE. NOISE++ PEOPLE EXIT, STAND++ CHAT++

NEXT-TO-left HOUSE, IX-loc*"left"* ONE ART+ER LIVE IX-loc*"left"* IX*"artist"* ALWAYS NOSEY++

THUMB-loc*"back"* MACHINE/FACTORY MAKE FURNITURE

4. Tell what you like and don't like about the area
   - *like—**cheap rent***
   - *don't like—**parking is difficult***

nod rhet

"area" ME LIKE WHY fs-RENT !CHEAP!

t neg rhet

ONE, ME NOT+LIKE "what," PARKING, !HARD! FIND SCL:3*"driving around the block several times"*

5. Tell your future plans

   —stay until you graduate from college, then move to a quieter area.

...BUT "area" CHEAP, NEAR SCHOOL. ME STAY-here

when

UNTIL ME GRADUATE. FINISH, MOVE-TO QUIET "area"

Pair up. Have students take turns signing the whole narrative to each other.

Conclude. Call a few students to sign the narrative to the whole class. Give feedback as needed.

Be sure students:

- use rhetorical questions as transitions
- maintain spatial agreement when discussing neighbors.

HOMEWORK

Tell students to do **Homework 9:4** (*Student Workbook*, pages 177–183).

Also, students are to develop a narrative about their neighborhood (See **Assignment**, *Student Workbook*, page 183).

HOMEWORK FOLLOW-UP
45–90 MINUTES

Have students present their own narratives about their neighborhood (See **Assignment**, *Student Workbook*, page 183).

Two ways to approach this:

1. ***As fluency practice.*** Have students get into groups and tell about their neighborhoods to each other. Conclude by calling on several students to share their narratives with the whole class.

   Be sure students:
   - use rhetorical question as a transition
   - maintain spatial agreement when discussing neighbors
   - include new phrases and vocabulary.

2. ***As preparation for quiz.*** If you want to use this narrative as a production quiz, have students present their narratives. Give feedback to help them develop fuller and richer narratives before videotaping their final versions. Rate with **9:4 Evaluation** (see **Materials**).

NOTE: If you have a large class, divide class and focus on one group at a time.

LESSON 9:5

Giving Directions: Next to, Across from

Lesson length: 45–60 minutes

LESSON GOAL

Students will give directions to places located at or near the corner.

KEY SKILLS

- take the signer's perspective to determine which corner
- use horizontal map orientation to give directions
- raise brows when establishing reference point
- use weak hand to maintain the place
- use "cs" to tell how close and "tilt head up" to tell how far

NOTIONS

Grammar

Signer's perspective
Weak hand as reference point
Horizontal map orientation
Facial markers to tell how close or how far

Phrases

- **from a corner**

  ___________t ____________________
  KNOW (place), CORNER-near left/right
  ___t/cs (or tilt head up) _______________bounce
  [(wh)CORNER/IX-loc+, NEXT-TO-left/right
  __________nod
  IX-loc*"place"*] (name place)

- **across from a place**

  ______________________t
  KNOW (place) IX-loc*"place,"* ACROSS-FROM-place
  ____________nod
  IX-loc*"other place"* (name that place)

Vocabulary

basic directions

CORNER-near right, CORNER-near left, CORNER-far right, CORNER-far left

NEXT-TO

ACROSS-FROM

PREPARATION Read and view **Giving Directions: Next To, Across From** (*Student Workbook*, pages 184–188)

MATERIALS **9:5 Lesson Slides**

HOMEWORK 9:5 *Student workbook*, pages 184–188

REVIEW *Names and Types of Businesses*

8–10 minutes

PRESENT
(LESSON SLIDES 9:5:1–5)

Review the signs for the stores and the types of stores.

T: NUMBER 1, "what" (whq)
S: IX-loc*"Hyatt logo"* **fs-HYATT**, IX*"Hyatt"* **HOTEL.**

T: NUMBER 2, "what" (whq)
S: **STARBUCKS**, IX*"Starbucks logo"* **COFFEE HOUSE.**

T: NUMBER 3, "what" (whq)
S: IX-loc*"McDonald's logo"* **MCDONALD'S**, IX*"McDonald's"* **FAST FOOD.**

T: NUMBER 4, "what" (whq)
S: IX-loc*"Curves logo"* **fs-CURVES**, IX*"Curves"* **EXERCISE.**

Repeat procedure for **Lesson Slides 9:5:2–5.**

Logo 5: fs-REMAX, IX*"RE/MAX"* fs-RE.

Logo 6: fs-IKEA, IX*"IKEA"* FURNITURE.

Logo 7: fs-AAA, IX*"AAA"* CAR INSURANCE.

Logo 8: fs-MACYS, IX*"Macy's"* fs-DEPT STORE.
(Be sure to twist the letter "s" at the end of "Macy's")

Logo 9: 7-11, IX*"7-11"* SMALL STORE, OPEN ALL-NIGHT.

Logo 10: fs-ACE, IX*"ACE"* fs-HARDWARE.

Logo 11: fs-SAM'S DELI, IX*"Sam's Deli"* SANDWICH.

Logo 12: fs-ABC, IX*"ABC Liquor"* LIQUOR STORE.

Logo 13: fs-ATT, IX*"AT&T"* PHONE STORE.

Logo 14: fs-ADAMS, IX*"Adams"* FUNERAL [HOME].

Logo 15: DOLLAR STORE, IX*"Dollar Stores"* CHEAP++, DISCOUNT.

Photo 16: fs-CITY fs-HALL.

Photo 17: JUDGE+HOUSE.

Photo 18: POLICE.

Photo 19: FIREFIGHTER.

Photo 20: PARKING.

INTRODUCE *The Four Corners*

10–12 minutes

PRESENT
(LESSON SLIDE 9:5:6)

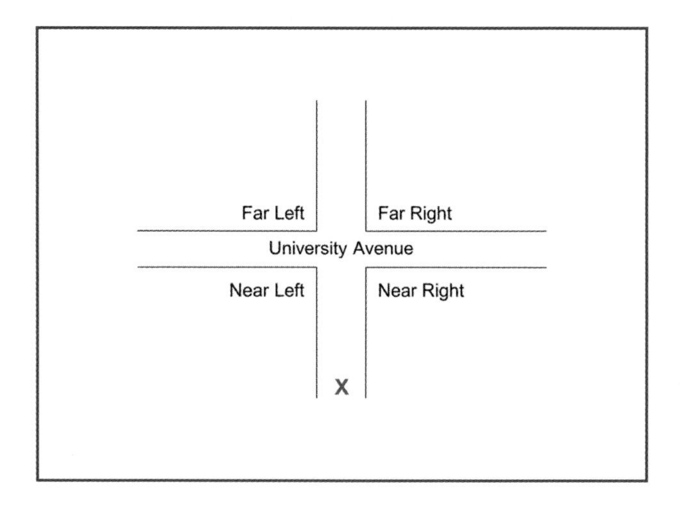

Demonstrate how to identify the four corners using horizontal map orientation[1]. Have students copy.

For ***"far left"***

tilt head up

T: CORNER-far left

nod

[(wh)CORNER/IX-loc+]

S: (copy)

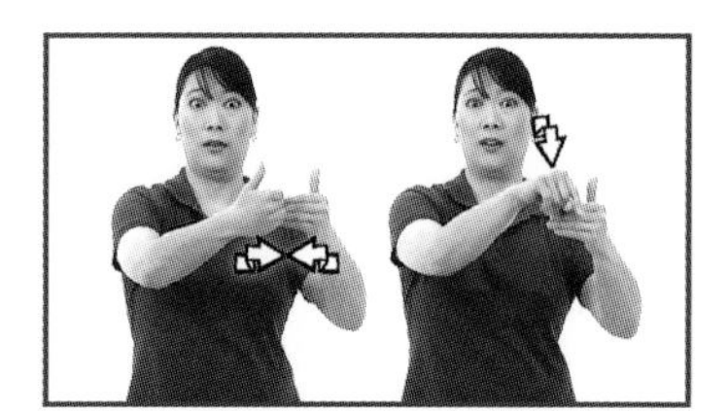

CORNER-far left

For ***"far right"***

tilt head up

T: CORNER-far right

nod

[(wh)CORNER/IX-loc+]

S: (copy)

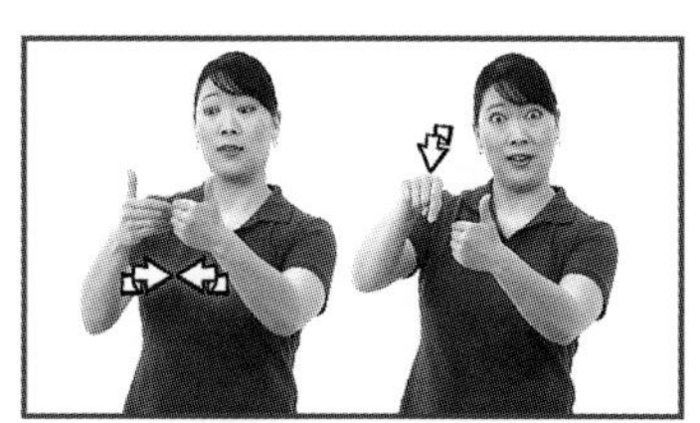

CORNER-far right

[1] Horizontal map orientation requires the signer to describe the area "with a street view" as opposed to "reading a map."

For ***"near left"***

T: **CORNER*"near left"*** (cs)
[(wh)CORNER/IX-loc+] (nod)

S: (copy)

CORNER-near left

For ***"near right"***

T: **CORNER*"near right"*** (cs)
[(wh)CORNER/IX-loc+] (nod)

S: (copy)

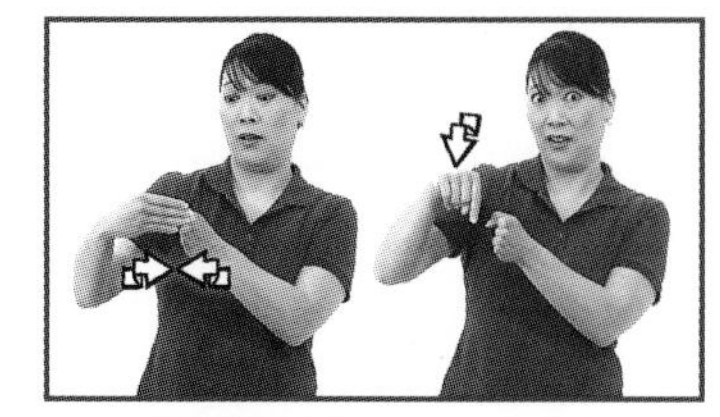

CORNER-near right

Be sure students:

- form the sign CORNER correctly for all four corners
- use horizontal map orientation
- use facial expressions "cs" and "tilt head up" to imply corner being near or further away
- use weak hand to maintain the location of the corner
- nod when using [(wh)CORNER/IX-loc*"corner"*].

PRESENT
(LESSON SLIDE 9:5:7)

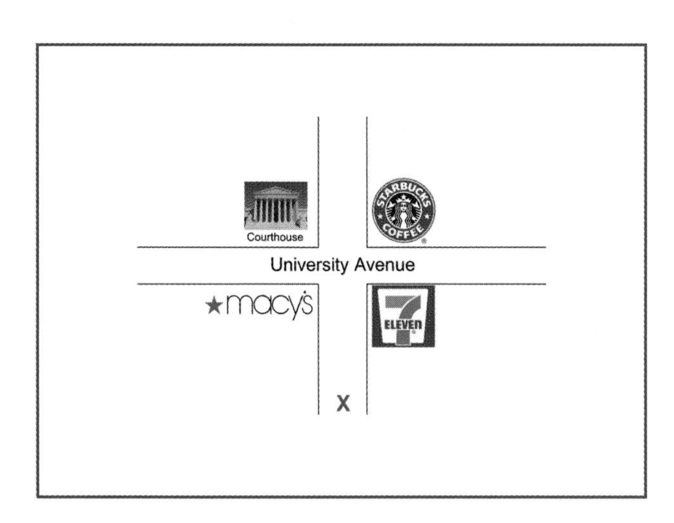

Now, ask students to tell where each business is located.

whq

T: JUDGE+HOUSE WHERE

tilt head up ______ nod

S: CORNER-far left [(wh)CORNER/IX-loc+]

whq

T: STARBUCKS WHERE

tilt head up ______ nod

S: CORNER-far right [(wh)CORNER/IX-loc+]

whq

T: 7-11 STORE WHERE

cs ______ nod

S: CORNER-near right [(wh)CORNER/IX-loc+]

whq

T: fs-MACY'S WHERE

cs ______ nod

S: CORNER-near left [(wh)CORNER/IX-loc+]

Continue until everyone has a chance to give a location.

INTRODUCE *From the Corner*

10–15 minutes

PRESENT

(LESSON SLIDE 9:5:8)

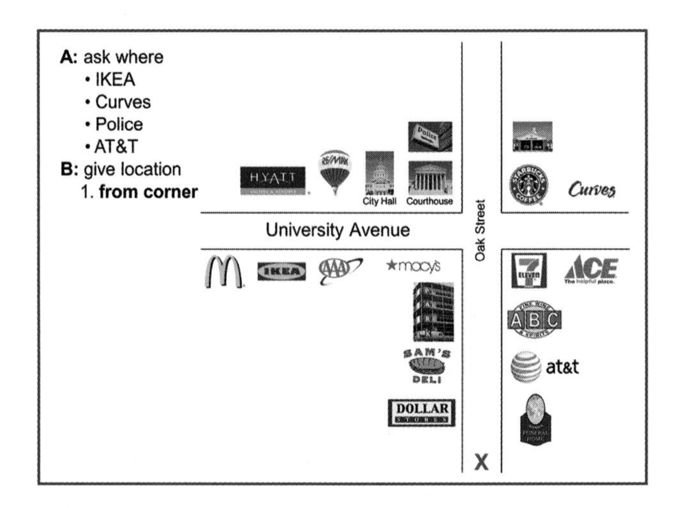

Have students sign Signer A's line and ask you where these places (IKEA, Curves, police, and AT&T) are located.

As Signer B demonstrate establishing a corner as the reference point, then signing NEXT-TO and IX-loc+. Have students copy.

whq
S1: fs-IKEA WHERE

t t/cs
T: **KNOW** fs-MACYS, CORNER-near left **[(wh)CORNER/IX-loc+,**
bounce bounce nod
NEXT-TO*"left,"* NEXT-TO*"left,"* IX-loc*"IKEA"*] fs-IKEA
S(all): (copy)

whq
S2: fs-CURVES WHERE

t t/tilt head up
T: **KNOW** STARBUCKS CORNER-far right **[(wh)CORNER/IX-loc+,**
bounce nod
NEXT-TO*"right,"* IX-loc*"Curves"*] fs-CURVES
S(all): (copy)

whq
S3: POLICE WHERE

t
T: **KNOW** JUDGE+HOUSE CORNER-far left **[(wh)CORNER/**
t/tilt head up bounce nod
IX-loc+, **NEXT-TO*"forward,"* IX-loc*"Police"*]** POLICE
S(all): (copy)

whq
S4: fs-ATT PHONE STORE, WHERE

t t/cs
T: **KNOW** 7-11, CORNER-near right **[(wh)CORNER/IX-loc+,**
bounce bounce nod
NEXT-TO*"behind,"* NEXT-TO*"behind"* IX-loc*"AT&T"*] fs-ATT
S(all): (copy)

Review. Ask where these places (Remax, ACE Hardware, Sam's Deli, and the firehouse) are located and have students tell where using **CORNER** and **NEXT-TO**. For example:

whq
T: fs-REMAX, WHERE

t
S: **KNOW** JUDGE+HOUSE CORNER-far left **[(wh)CORNER/**

t/tilt head up — bounce — bounce — nod
IX-loc+, **NEXT-TO*"left,"*** **NEXT-TO-left IX-loc*"Remax"*]**
fs-REMAX.

Be sure students:

- use KNOW when naming the business on the corner (raise brows)
- use weak hand to maintain the location of the corner when signing NEXT-TO (with head bounce) and IX-loc+ (with head nod) to give location.

INTRODUCE *Across from Another Place*

10–15 minutes

PRESENT
(LESSON SLIDE 9:5:9)

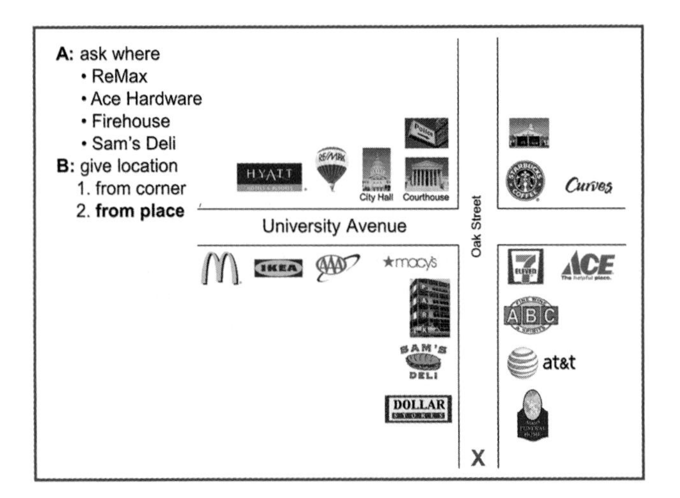

Have students sign Signer A's line and ask you where these places (ReMax, Ace Hardware, Firehouse, and Sam's Deli) are located.

As Signer B, demonstrate giving locations by naming another business as the reference point, then signing ACROSS-FROM and IX-loc+. Have students copy.

whq

S: fs-REMAX, WHERE

t

T: **KNOW** fs-IKEA [(wh)IX-loc*"IKEA,"* **ACROSS-FROM-front**

nod

IX-loc*"ReMax"* fs-REMAX

S(all): (copy)

nod

ACROSS-FROM-front IX-loc

whq

S: fs-ACE [STORE], WHERE

t

T: **KNOW** fs-CURVES IX-loc*"Curves,"* **ACROSS-FROM-behind**

nod

IX-loc*"Ace"* fs-ACE

S(all): (copy)

nod

ACROSS-FROM-behind IX-loc

whq

S: FIREHOUSE, WHERE

t

T: **KNOW** POLICE (wh)IX-loc*"Police,"* ***"left"*ACROSS-**

nod

FROM-right IX-loc*"Firehouse"* FIREHOUSE

S(all): (copy)

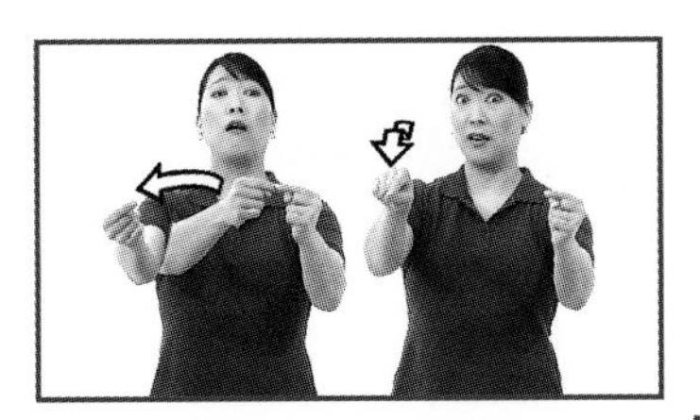

nod
left-ACROSS-FROM-right IX-loc

whq
S: SANDWICH STORE (or fs-SAM's-DELI), WHERE

t
T: **KNOW** fs-ATT STORE IX-loc*"AT&T,"* **right-ACROSS-**

nod
FROM-left (wh)IX-loc*"Sam's Deli"* fs-SAM'S-DELI

S(all): (copy)

nod
right-ACROSS-FROM-left IX-LOC

Be sure students:

- use KNOW when naming the the other business (raise brows)
- use weak hand to maintain the location of the other business when signing ACROSS-FROM and IX-loc+ (with head nod) to give location.

PRACTICE *Tell Where*

10–12 minutes

PRESENT

(LESSON SLIDE 9:5:10)

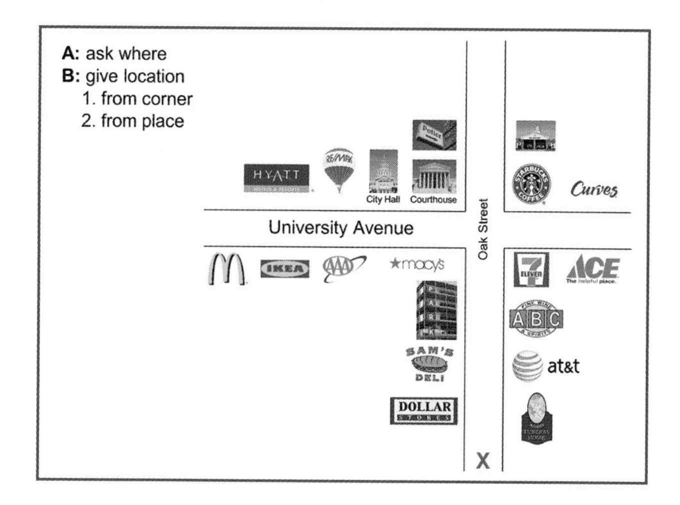

Pair up. Have students take turns asking each other where places are located using both "from corner" and "from place."

Be sure students:

For ***"from corner"***

- use KNOW when naming the business on the corner (raise brows)
- use weak hand to maintain the location of the corner when signing NEXT-TO (with head bounce) and IX-loc+ (with head nod) to give location

For ***"from place"***

- use KNOW when naming the other business (raise brows)
- use weak hand to maintain the location of the other business when signing ACROSS-FROM and IX-loc+ (with head nod) to give location.

HOMEWORK

Tell students to do **Homework 9:5** (*Student Workbook*, page 184–188).

LESSON 9:6

Yes–No Questions 1

Lesson length: 45–60 minutes

LESSON GOAL

Students will translate yes-no questions.

KEY SKILLS

Translating the question

- establish time if specified (raise brows)
- establish location if specified (raise brows)
- name the topic (raise brows)
- ask yes-no question (raise brows, tilt head forward, hold last sign)

NOTIONS

Grammar

topicalization
yes-no question

Vocabulary

Verbs	*Nouns*
fs-FIX	SPIDER
IRON	BUGS
TOUCH	FROG
DOWNLOAD	INTERNET
	PARIS

Others

KNOW fs-HOW	BE-AFRAID++
MORE-THAN	EARLY
EVERYDAY	fs-EARLY

MATERIALS

9:6 Lesson Slides
9:6 Follow-up Slides

HOMEWORK 9:6

Student Workbook, pages 189–192

REVIEW *Identifying the Topic*

7–10 minutes

PRESENT
(LESSON SLIDES 9:6:1–12)

Identify the topic in each question.

1. Do you like coffee?
2. Do you know how to fix a car?
3. Do you like to iron clothes?
4. Have you tried Thai food?
5. Do you read a newspaper daily?

Have students open their workbooks to **Yes–No Questions** on page 189 and underline the topic(s) in each question.

When done, ask students to tell you what they underlined, then confirm students' answers with **Lesson Slides 9:6:2–6**. For example:

whq

T: SENTENCE ONE, [fs-TOPIC] "what"
S: COFFEE
T: (show **Lesson Slide 9:6:2** to confirm)

Do the same for **Questions 6–10** (**Lesson Slides 9:6:7–12**).

Teacher's Guide

question	*topic*
Question 1	COFFEE
Question 2	**fs-FIX** CAR
Question 3	CLOTHES **IRON**
Question 4	fs-THAI FOOD

IRON

PARIS

DOWNLOAD++

EARLY

Question 5 NEWSPAPER

Question 6 BOOK

Question 7 **PARIS** IX-loc*"Paris"* FRANCE

Question 8 MUSIC **DOWNLOAD++**

Question 9 **SPIDER**-lf, **BUG**-mid, **FROG**-rt

SPIDER

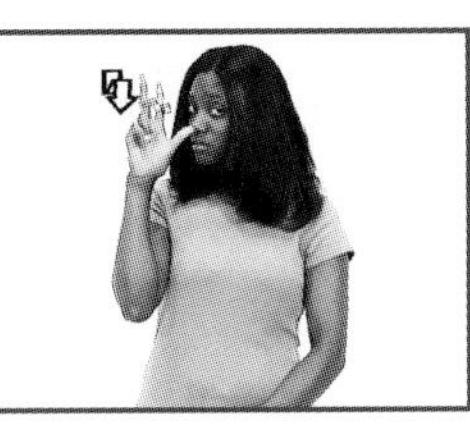

BUG

FROG

Question 10 MORNING GET-UP **EARLY** [or **fs-EARLY**]

PRACTICE *Translating Yes–No Questions*

35–45 minutes

Students practice integrating the topic and facial grammar to translate yes–no questions.

PRESENT
(LESSON SLIDES 9:6:13–14)

Translating yes-no questions

- establish time if specified (raise brows)
- establish location if specified (raise brows)
- name the topic (raise brows)
- ask question (raise brows, tilt head forward, hold last sign)

1. Do you like coffee?
2. Do you know how to fix a car?
3. Do you like to iron clothes?
4. Have you tried Thai food?
5. Do you read a newspaper daily?

Demonstrate the translations and have students copy.

1. ***Do you like coffee?***

t q

T: COFFEE, YOU LIKE YOU

S(all): (copy)

Be sure students:

- raise brows and head with the topic
- raise brows and tilt head forward and hold the last sign (YOU) with the yes–no question.

Repeat procedure for the remaining questions.

Teacher's Translation Guide

2. ***Do you know how to fix a car?***

t q

fs-FIX CAR, YOU **KNOW fs-HOW**, YOU

NOTE: It is best to fingerspell H-O-W when signing this phrase "KNOW fs-HOW." When asking wh-word question or using rhetorical question that involves the sign HOW, there are two ways to sign it. One is repeated on the dominant hand. The other is not repeated.

HOW++

used to ask how something is done, YOU COME TO CLASS HOW++, MAKE COFFEE HOW++

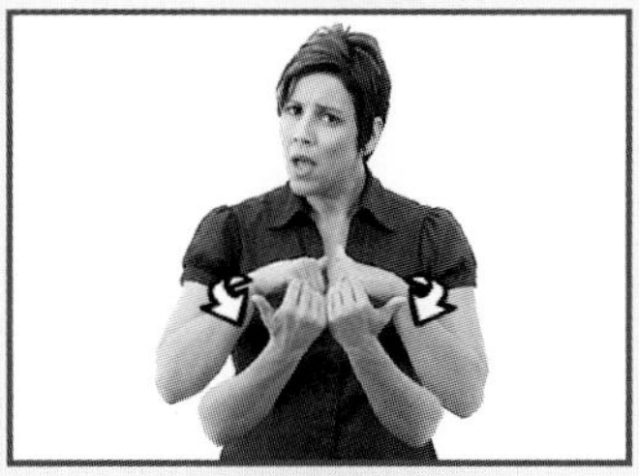

HOW

used in commonly borrowed English phrases like, HOW YOU, HOW KNOW

3. *Do you like to iron clothes?*

t q

CLOTHES IRON, YOU LIKE, YOU

4. *Have you tried Thai food?*

t q

fs-THAI FOOD, YOU FINISH TRY, YOU

EVERYDAY

5. *Do you read a newspaper daily?*

t q

NEWSPAPER, YOU READ++ **EVERYDAY**, YOU

NOTE: EVERYDAY, even though it is a time sign, it is not signed in the beginning because it doesn't refer to a specific day or time, but to a routine.

6. *Do you have more than 100 books?*

t q

BOOK, YOU HAVE **MORE-THAN** 100, YOU

TOUCH

7. *Have you been to Paris?*

t

PARIS IX-loc*"Paris"* FRANCE, YOU FINISH **TOUCH**

q

[or GO-TO], YOU

8. *Do you know how to download music off the Internet?*

t t q

INTERNET, MUSIC DOWNLOAD++, YOU KNOW fs-HOW, YOU

NOTE: INTERNET is the specified location where one downloads music, thus it is signed in the beginning.

BE-AFRAID++

9. *Are you afraid of spiders, bugs or frogs?*

t q

SPIDER-lf, BUG-mid, FROG-rt, **YOU BE-AFRAID++**, YOU

10. *Do you like to get up early?*

t q

MORNING GET-UP EARLY [or fs-EARLY], YOU LIKE, YOU

PRESENT
(LESSON SLIDE 9:6:15)

This practice consists of three rounds.

Round 1: focus on word order and sign articulation
Round 2: focus on facial grammar
- raise brows for topic
- raise brows, tilt head forward, hold last sign (for yes–no question)

Round 3: focus on fluency (phrasing)

Pair Up. Have students take turns signing the questions in their workbooks (page 189) according to the instructions for each round.

HOMEWORK

Tell students to do **Homework 9:6** (*Student Workbook*, pages 189–192).

HOMEWORK FOLLOW-UP
30–40 MINUTES

PRESENT
(FOLLOW-UP SLIDES 9:6:1–2)

Elaborating on Answers

1. Do you like coffee?
2. Do you know how to fix a car?
3. Do you like to iron clothes?
4. Have you tried Thai food?
5. Do you read a newspaper daily?

Elaborating on Answers
Have students sign the questions to you (the teacher). Demonstrate how to elaborate on answers. For example:

For **Question 1**:

______t ____________q
S: COFFEE, YOU LIKE, YOU

_______________nod ____________cond
T: YES, ME LIKE COFFEE, UNDERSTAND++ WITH LIQUOR

or

neg
T: #NO, ME VOMIT COFFEE, ME PREFER TEA.

Continue for all 10 questions.

Mingle. Have students mingle asking each other questions and elaborating on their answers.

Wrap Up. ***(optional)*** Ask students the questions to see how well they elaborate on their answers.

LESSON 9:7

Describing a Restaurant

Lesson length: 90–115 minutes

LESSON GOAL

Students will sign this dialogue:

Dialogue

A: ask if B has been to a certain restaurant[1]

B: say yes

A: ask what it looks like[2]

B: describe[3]

A: ask what kind of food is served

B: tell what is served

A: ask if food is good, and if it's expensive

B: give opinion

KEY PHRASES

t / q

[1] (restaurant), YOU FINISH TOUCH, YOU

whq

[2] FACE+SAME-AS "what"

[3] (descriptive and locative classifiers to describe the interior of a restaurant)

NOTIONS

Grammar

- Descriptive (DCLs) and Locative (LCLs) classifiers to describe:
  - tables and counter and seating arrangement
  - wall decorations
  - lighting
- Element (ECLs) classifiers to describe lighting

Vocabulary

Ethnic restaurants

CHINA	JAPAN	THAI
ITALY	FRANCE	GREECE

INDIA	MEXICO
AMERICA	VEGETABLE

Opinions: price

EXPENSIVE	MEDIUM
REASONABLE	CHEAP

Opinions: food

DELICIOUS	FAIR/SO-SO	DETEST/VOMIT
#OK	pout GOOD++	YUCK
CHAMP		GAG
!GOOD!	LOUSY	

Food and Drinks

#PIZZA	fs-FF(french fries)	SUSHI
SANDWICH	FISH	DESSERT
HAMBURGER	SHRIMP	BEER
PASTA	CHICKEN	WINE
SALAD	STEAK/MEAT	ALCOHOL
#BBQ	fs-RICE	

Materials

WOOD	fs-CEMENT
GLASS	ROCK/STONE
METAL	RED+BRICK
STUCCO	

Wh-word question

WHAT-KIND

Others

BAR	HOME+MAKE
VARIOUS-THINGS	INTERESTING

PREPARATION Read and view **Key Grammar: Descriptive, Locative and Element Classifiers** (*Student Workbook*, pages 194–196)

MATERIALS **9:7 Lesson Slides**

HOMEWORK 9:7 *Student Workbook*, pages 193–209

INTRODUCE *Kinds of Restaurants*

15–20 minutes

PRESENT
(LESSON SLIDES 9:7:1–3)

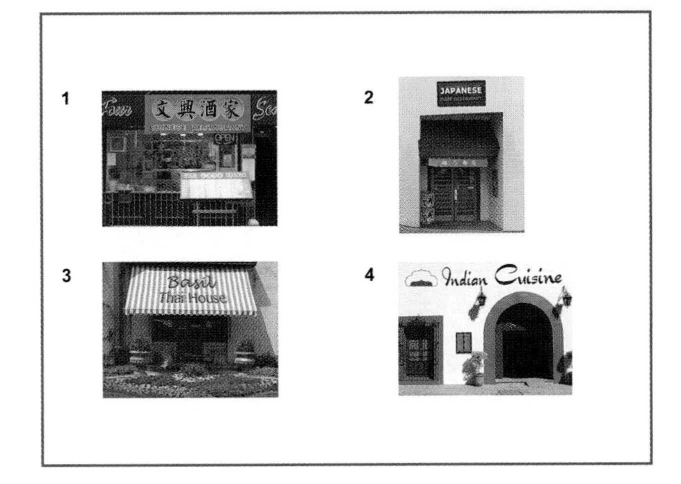

Introduce signs for different kinds of restaurants:

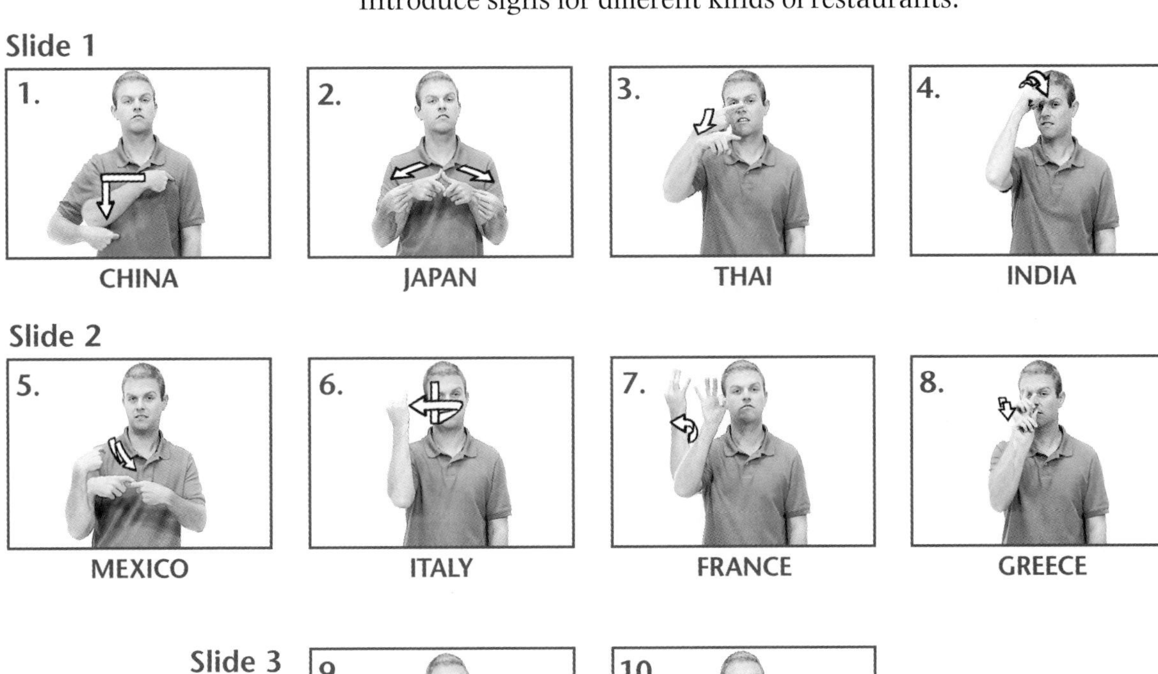

Slide 3

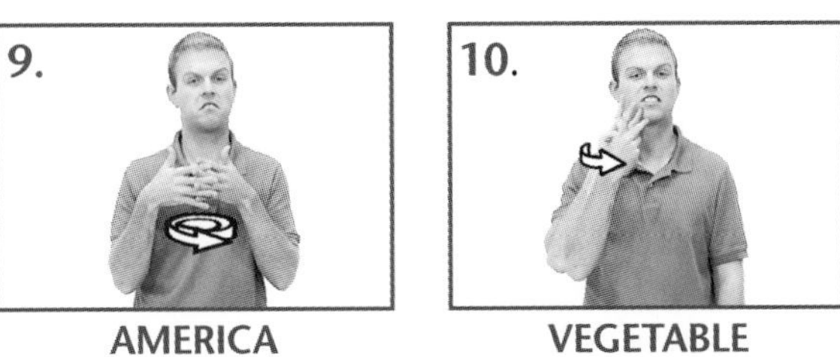

Review. Show the slides again, ask students to give you signs for each kind of restaurant.

PRESENT
(LESSON SLIDE 9:7:4)

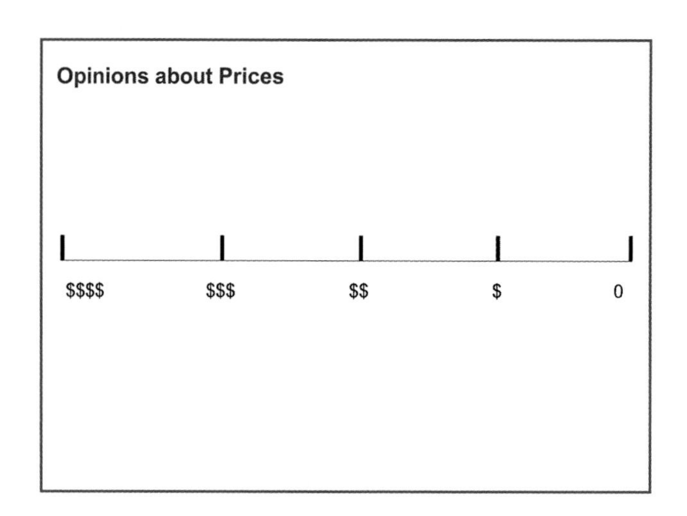

Introduce signs for giving opinions about prices:

$$$$ = !EXPENSIVE!
$$$ = MEDIUM EXPENSIVE
$$ = REASONABLE
$ = CHEAP
0 = fs-FREE

!EXPENSIVE!

MEDIUM EXPENSIVE

REASONABLE

CHEAP

PRESENT
(LESSON SLIDE 9:7:5–10)

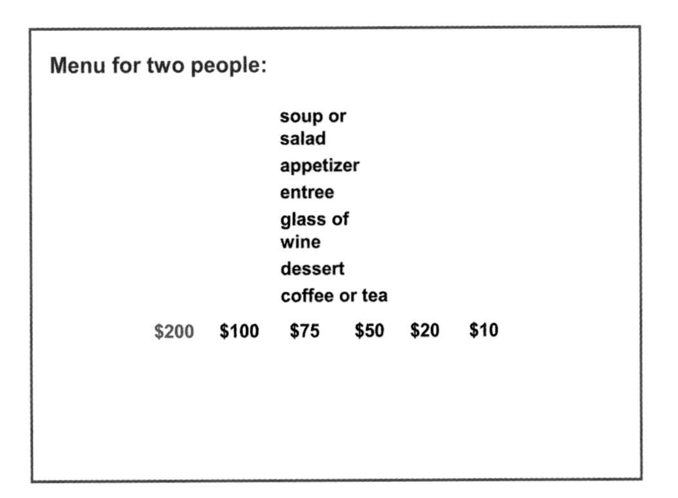

Menu for two people:
soup or salad
appetizer
entree
glass of wine
dessert
coffee or tea
$200 $100 $75 $50 $20 $10

Ask students to give opinions about the prices, for example,

T: FOOD IX-loc *"menu"* (t) 200 DOLLAR, EXPENSIVE, CHEAP WHICH (whq)

S: (give opinion)

Show **Lesson Slides 9:7:6–10** with different prices for the same menu. Repeat, asking students for their opinions on the price.

PRESENT
(LESSON SLIDE 9:7:11)

DELICIOUS
(variation 1)

DELICIOUS
(variation 2)

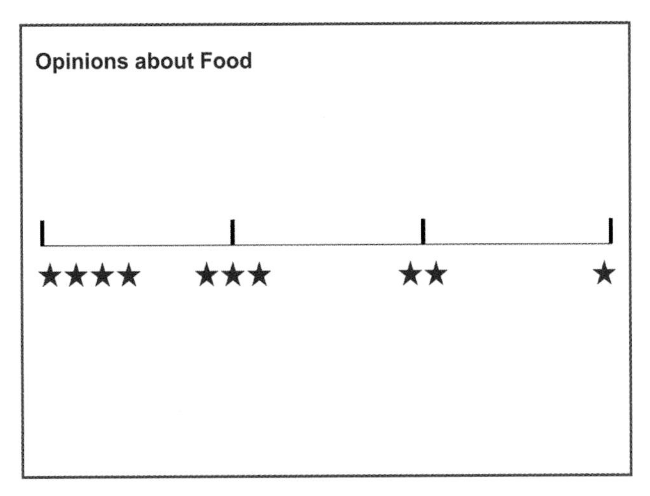

Introduce signs for giving opinions about food:

★ ★ ★ ★ = DELICIOUS (2 variations), CHAMP

★ ★ ★ = !GOOD!

★ ★ = SO-SO (pout), GOOD++ (pout), #OK++

★ = LOUSY, DETEST, YUCK and GAG

Review. Point to different sets of stars and have students give sign(s) for opinions about food.

INTRODUCE *Describing Restaurants*

60–75 minutes

PRESENT
(LESSON SLIDE 9:7:12)

Ask students:

T: IX"*Benihana*"(t), YOU-all FINISH TOUCH YOU(q)

S: YES, FINISH TOUCH(nod) or #NO, NOT-YET TOUCH(neg)

WHAT-KIND

whq
T: RESTAURANT **WHAT-KIND**
S: JAPAN

t whq
T: IX-loc*"Benihana,"* EXPENSIVE, CHEAP WHICH
S: (give opinion)

t q
T: IX-loc*"Benihana,"* FOOD DELICIOUS
S: (give opinion)

PRESENT
(LESSON SLIDE 9:7:13)

Show video **Describe Environment 1**, then ask:

t whq
T: RESTAURANT ENTER, "area" FACE-SAME-AS "what"
S: ENTER RESTAURANT

- HAVE **TABLE (2h)LCL:B*"several tables around room"***

  t
- IX-lox*"table in front"* **TABLE, PEOPLE SIT (2h) V*"around table"***

  t
- **MIDDLE IX-loc*"middle of table"*** DCL***"rectangular stovetop"*** COOK++.

PRESENT
(LESSON SLIDES
9:7:14–16)

Introduce LCLs and DCLs to describe placement of tables in restaurants. Emphasize eye gaze when referring to the location(s). Have students copy.

For **Slide 14**

T: TABLE (2h)DCL:bent-L*"round tables randomly placed around"*

S: (copy)

For **Slide 15**

T: TABLE (2h)LCL:B*"rectangular tables in rows"*

S: (copy)

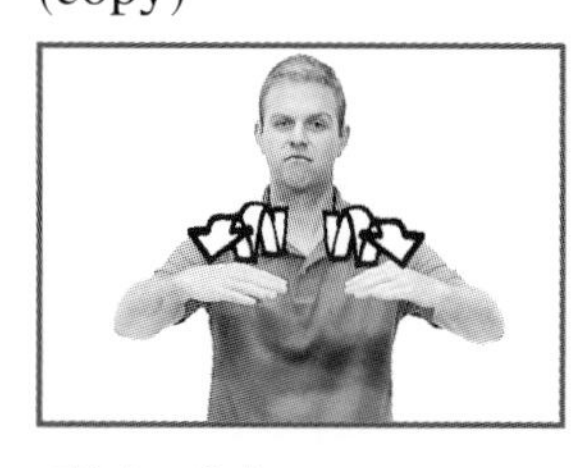

For **Slide 16**

T: TABLE (2h)alt.LCL:B*"tables randomly placed around"*

S: (copy)

NOTE: The LCL:B *"object with flat surface"* classifier usually represents objects that are either rectangular or square. However, if there is a mix of differently shaped objects in the same area, for example, rectangle, square or round tables, then (2h) altLCL:B can represent the general placement of tables in the area.

PRESENT
(LESSON SLIDES 9:7:17–21)

Introduce how to specify seating arrangements in restaurants using SCL:V*"seating arrangement."* Emphasize eye gaze when referring to location(s) of chairs. Have students copy.

For **Slide 17**

T: BAR (2h)DCL:C*"shape of counter,"* CHAIR (2h)SCL:V*"seats along counter"*

S: (copy)

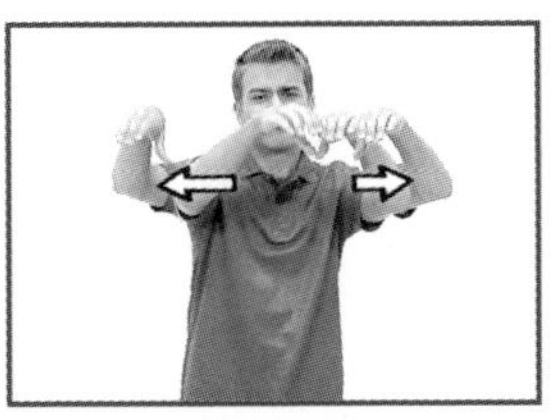

(2h)DCL:C*"shape of counter"*

(2h)SCL:V*"seats along counter"*

For **Slide 18**

T: SMALL TABLE IX-loc*"alongside right wall"*++, (2h)SCL:V*"two seats per table"*

S: (copy)

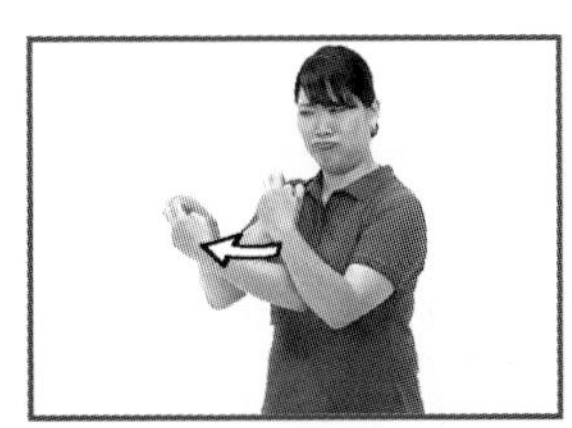

(2h)SCL:V*"two seats per table"*

For **Slide 19**

T: TABLE (2h)DCL:C*"long rows of tables"*++, CHAIR (2h)SCL:V*"seats on both sides of tables"*++

S: (copy)

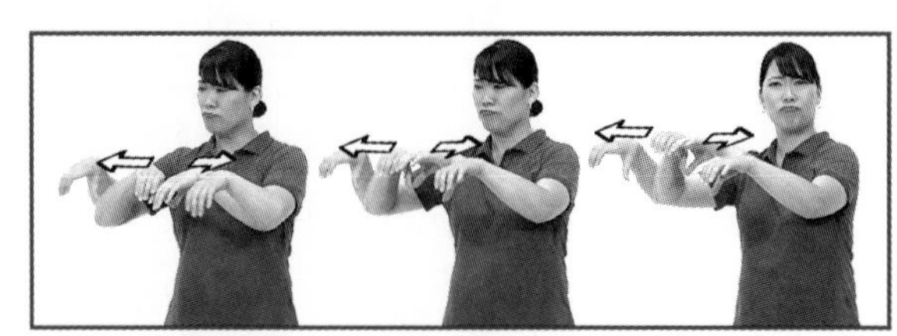

(2h)DCL:C*"long rows of tables"*++

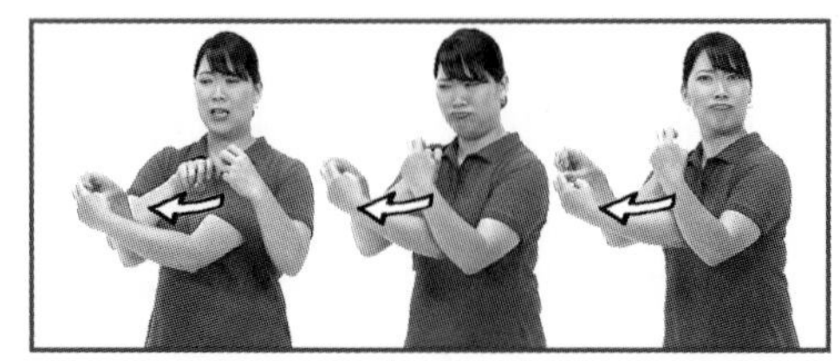

(2h)SCL:V*"seats on both sides of tables"*++

For **Slide 20**

T: TABLE (2h)DCL:bent-L*"large round table"* CHAIR (2h)SCL:V*"seats around the table"*

S: (copy)

(2h)DCL:bent-L*"large round table"*

(2h)SCL:V*"seats around the table"*

For **Slide 21**

T: TABLE (2h)DCL:C*"long table in middle of room"* CHAIR (2h)SCL:V*"seats on both sides of the table"*

S: (copy)

(2h)DCL:C*"long table in middle of room"*

(2h)SCL:V*"seats on both sides of the table"*

PRESENT
(LESSON SLIDE 9:7:22)

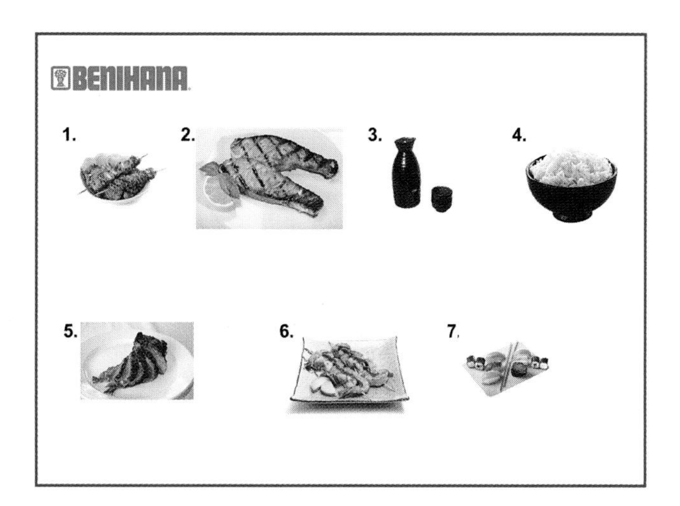

Introduce signs:

1. **CHICKEN**
2. **FISH**
3. JAPAN **WINE** fs-SAKE
4. fs-RICE
5. fs-STEAK
6. **SHRIMP**
7. **SUSHI**

1.
CHICKEN

FISH

WINE

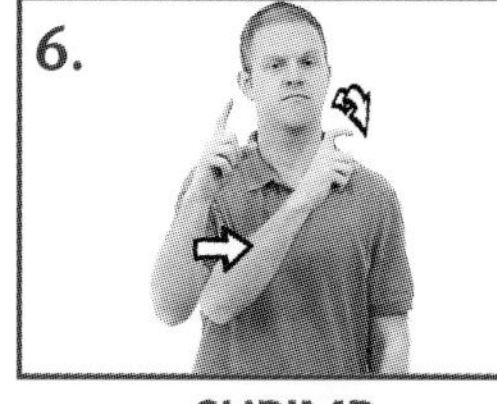

SHRIMP

SUSHI

Review. Give numbers from the slide and ask students to give signs for the items.

PRESENT
(LESSON SLIDE 9:7:23)

Ask students:

T: IX-*"Hard Rock Cafe,"* YOU-all FINISH TOUCH YOU (t: IX-"Hard Rock Cafe,"; q: YOU-all FINISH TOUCH YOU)

S: YES, FINISH TOUCH or #NO, NOT-YET TOUCH (nod: YES, FINISH TOUCH; neg: #NO, NOT-YET TOUCH)

T: RESTAURANT WHAT-KIND (whq)

S: AMERICA [FOOD]

T: IX-loc*"Hard Rock Cafe,"* EXPENSIVE, CHEAP WHICH (t: IX-loc"Hard Rock Cafe,"; whq: EXPENSIVE, CHEAP WHICH)

S: (give opinion)

T: IX-loc*"Hard Rock Cafe,"* FOOD DELICIOUS (t: IX-loc"Hard Rock Cafe,"; q: FOOD DELICIOUS)

S: (give opinion)

PRESENT
(LESSON SLIDE 9:7:24)

Show video **Describe Environment 2**, then ask:

T: RESTAURANT, "area" FACE+SAME-AS (t: RESTAURANT, "area"; whq: FACE+SAME-AS)

S: [RESTAURANT] IX-loc*"restaurant"* NICE, LARGE. HAVE BAR AND fs-GIFT-SHOP. (t: [RESTAURANT] IX-loc"restaurant")

- OUTSIDE, !WHITE! DCL*"shape of restaurant building."* (wh)LCL:C*"placed on left of restaurant,"* GUITAR (wh)DCL*"large guitar on left of restaurant building"*

- ENTER (2h)*"all over"* TABLE (2h)LCL:B*"scattered around the room"* (t: TABLE)

- IX-loc*"back of room"* BAR, DCL*"long bar table,"* CHAIR (2h)SCL:V*"chairs at bar"*

- (2h)DCL:B*"walls around room"* DIFFERENT++ PICTURE

- (2h)LCL:B*"pictures hung on walls"* "what" FAMOUS MUSIC+ER, PERFORM+ER, DIFFERENT++, (2h)LCL:B*"pictures hung on walls"* SAME-AS RECORD (2hLCL:L*"records on wall."* SOME IX-loc*"on wall"*++ FAMOUS MUSIC+ER POSS*"musician"* COAT/JACKET (2h)LCL:X*"hung up"*+++, GUITAR (2h)LCL:G*"guitars hung up"*+++, **INTERESTING.** (rhet: "what")

INTERESTING

PRESENT
(LESSON SLIDE 9:7:25)

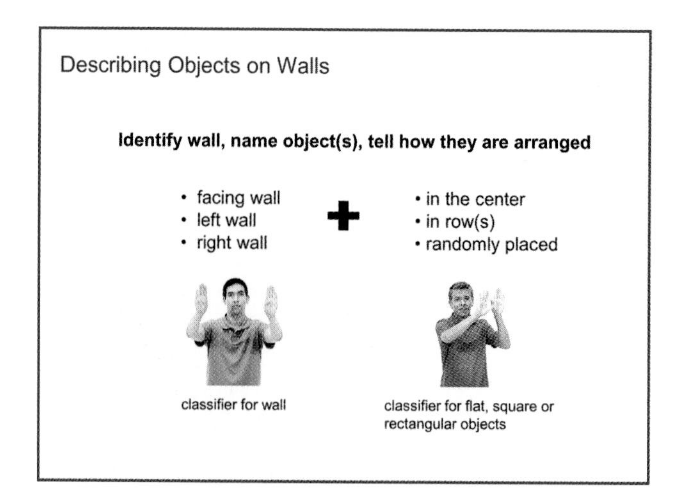

Demonstrate "identify wall." Have students copy.

T: (point to "facing wall"), (2h)DCL:B*"facing wall"*
S: (copy)

T: (point to "left wall"), (2h)DCL:B*"left wall"*
S: (copy)

T: (point to "right wall"), (2h)DCL:B*"right wall"*
S: (copy)

Demonstrate adding "name object(s), tell how they are arranged" for square or rectangular objects using LCL:B. Emphasize eye gaze when referring to location(s) of the object(s). Have students copy.

For ***"facing wall"+"in the center"***

T: (2h)DCL:B*"facing wall,"* PICTURE LCL:B*"picture in center of facing wall"*
S: (copy)

For ***"facing wall"+"in row(s)"***

T: (2h)DCL:B*"facing wall,"* PICTURE (2h)LCL:B*"pictures in row(s)"*
S: (copy)

For ***"facing wall"+"randomly placed"***

T: (2h)DCL:B*"facing wall,"* PICTURE (2h)alt.LCL:B*"pictures randomly placed"*
S: (copy)

Review. Name either "left wall" or "right wall" and name a square or rectangular object like a PAINTING. Have students describe one of the arrangements of object(s) listed on slide.

T: (2h)DCL:B*"left wall"* (or (2h)LCL:B*"right wall"*), PAINTING...
S1: (2h)DCL:B*"left wall,"* PAINTING LCL:B*"in the center of left wall"*
S2: (2h)DCL:B*"left wall,"* PAINTING (2h)LCL:B*"in row(s) on left wall"*
S3: (2h)DCL:B*"left wall,"* PAINTING (2h)altLCL:B*"randomly placed on left wall"*

Continue with naming other objects (CERTIFICATE and MIRROR) and have students describe their arrangement on either the left or right wall.

PRESENT
(LESSON SLIDE 9:7:26)

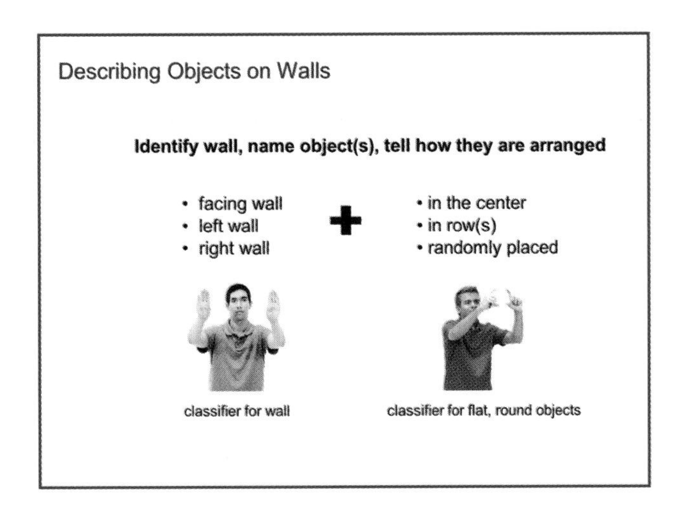

Demonstrate adding "name object(s), tell how they are arranged" for round-shaped objects using (2h)LCL:bentL. Have students copy.

For ***"facing wall"+"in the center"***

T: (2h)DCL:B*"facing wall,"* RECORD (2h)LCL:L*"record in center of facing wall"*
S: (copy)

For ***"facing wall"+"in row(s)"***

T: (2h)DCL:B*"facing wall,"* RECORD (2h)LCL:L*"records in row(s)"*
S: (copy)

For ***"facing wall"+"randomly placed"***

T: (2h)DCL:B*"facing wall,"* RECORD (2h)alt.LCL:L*"records randomly placed"*
S: (copy)

Review. Name either "left wall" or "right wall" and name a round-shaped object like a CLOCK. Have students describe one of the arrangements of objects listed on the slide.

T: (2h)DCL:B*"left wall"* (or (2h)LCL:B*"right wall"*), CLOCK...
S1: (2h)DCL:B*"left wall,"* CLOCK (2h)LCL:L*"in the center of left wall"*
S2: (2h)DCL:B*"left wall,"* CLOCK (2h)LCL:L*"in row(s) on left wall"*
S3: (2h)DCL:B*"left wall,"* CLOCK (2h)altLCL:L*"randomly placed on left wall"*

Continue with other objects (PLATE, etc.) and have students describe their arrangement on either the left or right wall.

PRESENT
(LESSON SLIDE 9:7:27)

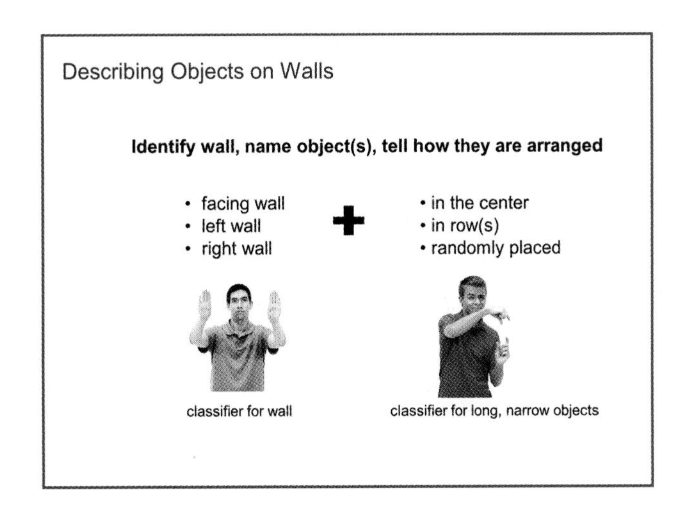

Demonstrate "name object(s), tell how they are arranged" for long, narrow objects using (2h)LCL:G. Have students copy.

For ***"facing wall"+"in the center"***

T: (2h)DCL:B*"facing wall,"* GUITAR (2h)LCL:G*"guitar in center of facing wall"*
S: (copy)

For ***"facing wall"+"in row(s)"***

T: (2h)LCL:B*"facing wall,"* GUITAR (2h)LCL:G*"guitar in row(s)"*
S: (copy)

For ***"facing wall"+"randomly placed"***

T: (2h)DCL:B*"facing wall,"* GUITAR (2h)alt.LCL:G*"guitar randomly placed"*
S: (copy)

Review. Name either "left wall" or "right wall" and name a long narrow object like fs-OAR. Have students describe one of the arrangements of object(s) listed on the slide.

T: (2h)DCL:B*"left wall"* (or (2h)LCL:B*"right wall"*), fs-OAR...
S1: (2h)DCL:B*"left wall,"* fs-OAR (2h)LCL:G*"in the center of left wall"*
S2: (2h)DCL:B*"left wall,"* fs-OAR (2h)LCL:G*"in row(s) on left wall"*
S3: (2h)DCL:B*"left wall,"* fs-OAR (2h)altLCL:G*"randomly placed on left wall"*

Continue with naming other objects (SKI, SWORD, etc.) and have students describe their arrangement on either the left or right wall.

PRESENT
(LESSON SLIDE 9:7:28)

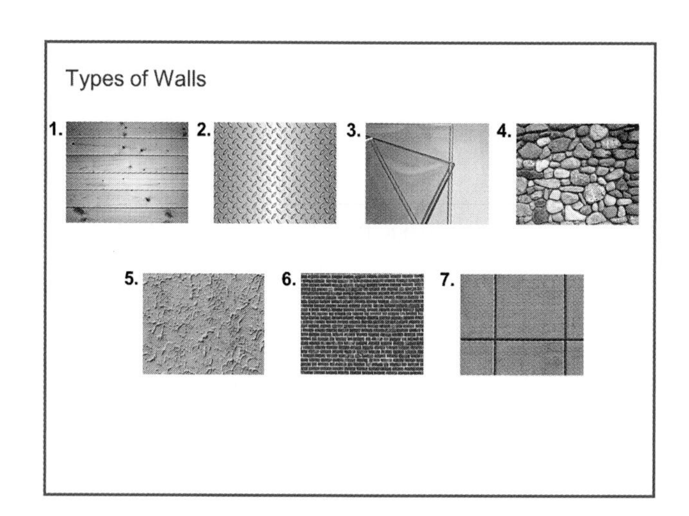

Introduce signs:

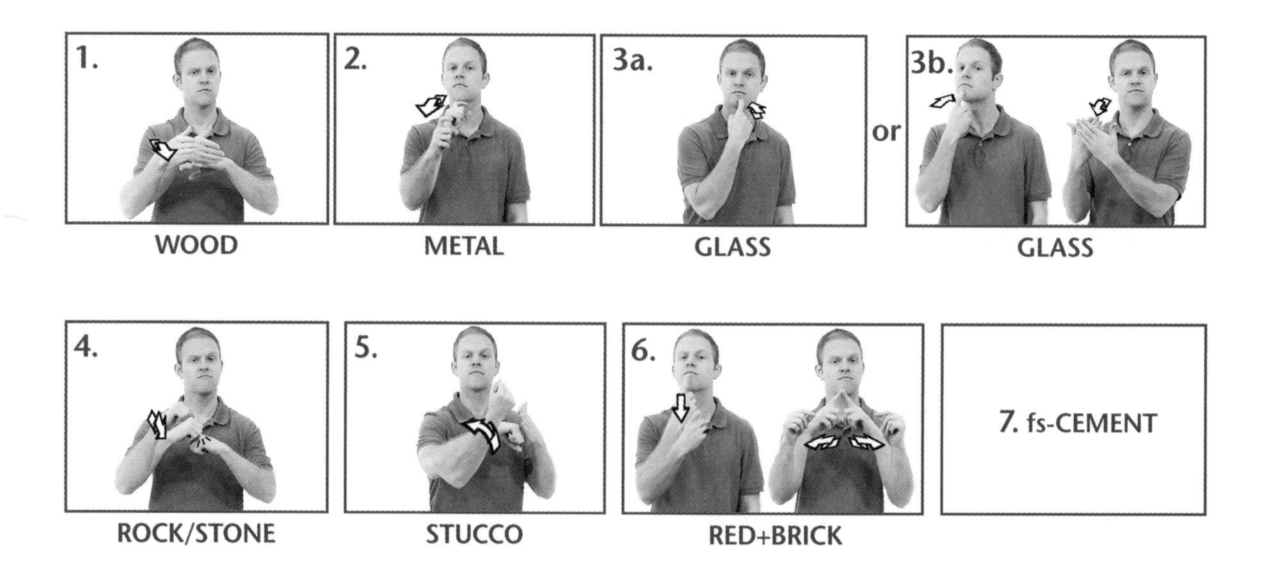

Demonstrate how to describe types of walls and have students copy:

T: (2h)DCL:B*"wall,"* WOOD "all over wall"
(2h)DCL:B*"wall,"* METAL "all over wall"
(2h)DCL:B*"wall,"* GLASS "all over wall"
(2h)DCL:B*"wall,"* ROCK/STONE (2h)LCL:C*"rocks"* "all over wall"
(2h)DCL:B*"wall,"* STUCCO "all over wall"
(2h)DCL:B*"wall,"* RED+BRICK "all over wall"
(2h)DCL:B*"wall,"* fs-CEMENT "all over wall"

S(all): (copy)

PRESENT
(LESSON SLIDE 9:7:29)

Introduce signs:

PASTA

SALAD

HAMBURGER

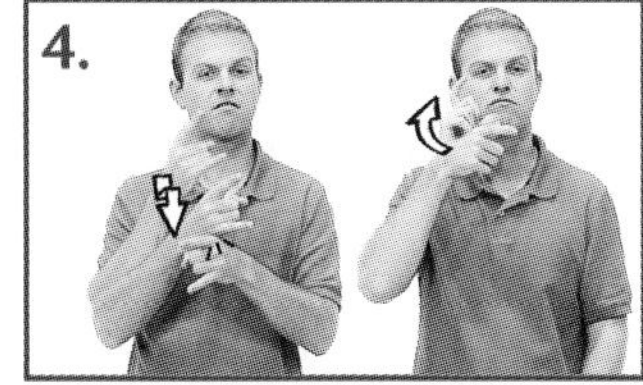

ALCOHOL DRINK

WINE

MEAT

SANDWICH

DESSERT

BEER

10. #BBQ
11. fs-FF (french fries)
12. fs-FAJ (fajitas)

Review. Give numbers from the slide and ask students to give signs for the items.

PRESENT
(LESSON SLIDE 9:7:30)

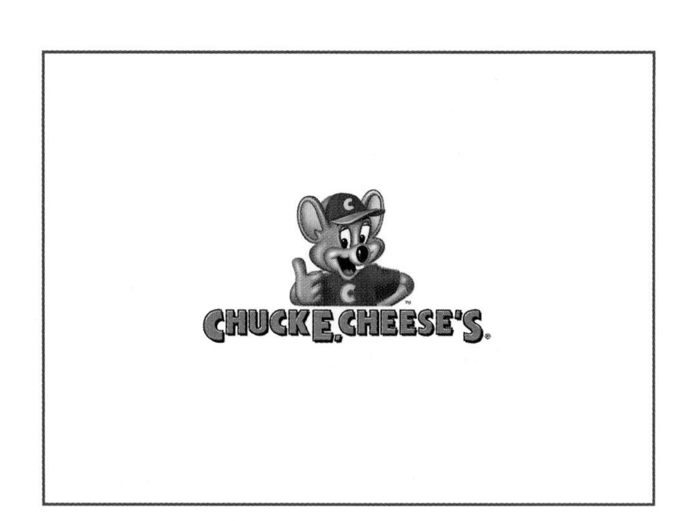

Ask students:

q

T: IX*"Chuck E. Cheese's,"* YOU-all FINISH TOUCH YOU

nod neg

S: YES, FINISH TOUCH or #NO, NOT-YET TOUCH

whq

T: RESTAURANT WHAT-KIND

S: FOR CHILDREN

t whq

T: IX-loc*"Chuck E. Cheese's,"* EXPENSIVE, CHEAP WHICH

S: (give opinion)

t q

T: IX-loc*"Chuck E. Cheese's,"* FOOD DELICIOUS

S: (give opinion)

PRESENT
(LESSON SLIDE 9:7:31)

whq

T: RESTAURANT, IX NAME "what"
S: fs-CHUCK-E-CHEESE

Point out the initial "E" is signed as a single circular movement and the "'s" is not fingerspelled.

Show video **Describe Environment 3**, then ask:

t whq

T: RESTAURANT, "area" FACE+SAME-AS
S: RESTAURANT, ENTER TWO (wh)"area"-left or right.

t

- "area"-right EAT, LARGE. **TABLE (2h)LCL:C*"rows of tables"*** CHAIR (2h)LCL:V*"two rows of chairs at each table"*++.
- **fs-WALL (2h)LCL:B*"center wall"* HAVE fs-PUPPETS, IX-loc++*"3 on wall"* LIGHT ECL*"beam on one section"*** (2h)BPCL:fist*"2 puppet heads bobbling"* SING, PERFORM, (2h)BPCL:fist*"2 puppet heads bobbling."* **(2h)ECL*"lights off."***
- **ECL*"lights beam on next section"*** (wh)BPCL:fist*"1 puppet head bobbling"* BPCL*"mouths open and close"*++ (2h)ECL*"lights off."*
- ECL*"lights beam on next section"*++ DIFFERENT++.
- "area"-left GAME "wow" PCL*"hordes of"* GAME.

PRESENT
(LESSON SLIDE 9:7:32)

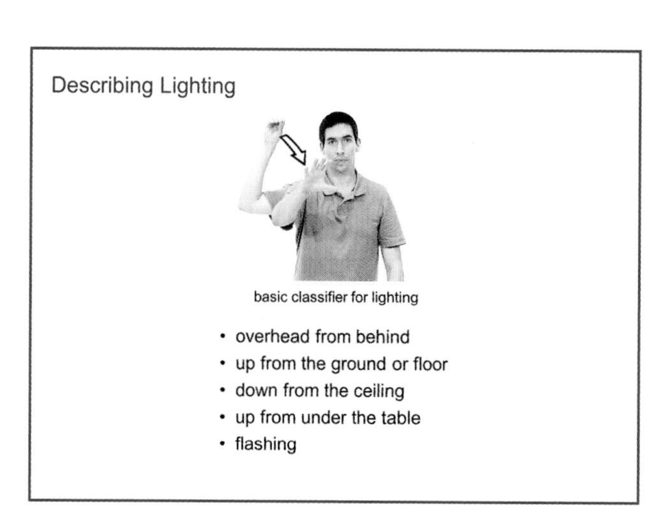

Describing Lighting
basic classifier for lighting
• overhead from behind
• up from the ground or floor
• down from the ceiling
• up from under the table
• flashing

Demonstrate describing lighting using ECL*"light."* Emphasize eye gaze when referring to location(s) of the light(s).

For *"overhead from behind"*
T: LIGHT *"lighting overhead from behind"*

Now, have students describe the remaining lighting arrangements listed on the slide with ECL*"light."*

S: LIGHT ECL*"light"* (describe each lighting arrangement)

PRESENT
(LESSON SLIDE 9:7:33)

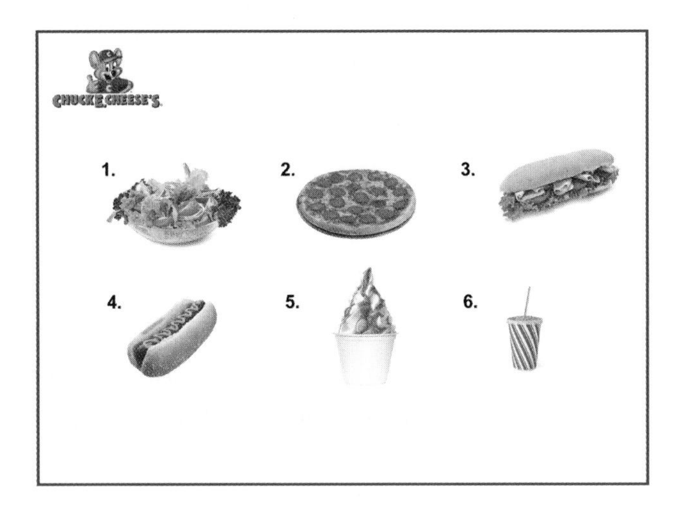

Ask students to give the signs for each of the food items:

1. SALAD
2. #PIZZA (MEAT, VEGETABLE)
3. SANDWICH
4. HOT-DOG
5. ICE-CREAM
6. SODA-POP

PRACTICE *Describing Restaurants*

15–20 minutes

Students practice describing restaurants and discussing food the restaurants serve.

PRESENT

(LESSON SLIDE 9:7:34)

Describing Restaurants

A: ask if B has been to a certain restaurant
B: say yes
A: ask what it looks like
B: describe, include:
- table or counter and seating arrangement
- wall decorations
- lighting

A: ask what kind of food is served
B: tell what is served (use listing)
A: ask if food is good, and if it's expensive
B: give opinion

Demonstrate Signer A's lines for Benihana. Have students copy:

For ***"A: ask if B has been to a certain restaurant"***

t q
T: fs-BENIHANA, YOU **FINISH TOUCH**, YOU
S: (copy)

For ***"A: ask what it looks like"***

whq
T: FACE+SAME-AS "what"
S: (copy)

For ***"A: ask what kind of food is served"***

whq whq
T: FOOD **WHAT-KIND** or FOOD "what"
S: (copy)

For ***"A: ask if food is good, and if it's expensive"***

q
T: FOOD !GOOD!, !EXPENSIVE!
S: (copy)

Demonstrate Signer B's line *"tell what is served (use listing)"* for Benihana, Hard Rock Cafe and Chuck E. Cheese's. Have students copy. Be sure students nod with each item:

For ***"B: tell what is served (use listings)"***

Benihana

nod nod nod nod nod

T: JAPAN FOOD, SUSHI, CHICKEN, FISH, fs-STEAK, fs-RICE, VARIOUS-THINGS.

S(all): (copy)

Hard Rock Cafe

nod nod nod nod

T: AMERICA FOOD, HAMBURGER, fs-FF, CHICKEN, SALAD, VARIOUS-THINGS.

S(all): (copy)

Chuck E. Cheese's

nod nod nod

T: FOOD VARIOUS-THINGS, #PIZZA, SALAD, PASTA.

S(all): (copy)

Pair Up. Have students write down the names of their two favorite restaurants on a slip of paper.

Now, have students exchange slips of paper (with names of restaurants) with their partners. Have them take turns asking each other about one of the restaurants listed on their papers. Repeat activity with different partners.

Conclude. Call student up to demonstrate the dialogue. Remember all corrections are made for the whole class to practice.

Be sure students:

- use descriptive (DCLs), locative (LCLs) and element (ECLs) classifiers to describe:
  - tables and counter and seating arrangement
  - wall decorations
  - lighting
- nod their head when listing food items.

HOMEWORK

Tell students to do **Homework 9:7** (*Student Workbook*, pages 193–209).

LESSON 9:8

Giving Directions: Where to Turn

Lesson length: 30–40 minutes

LESSON GOAL

Students will describe where to turn using different references.

KEY SKILLS

- use "when" clause when identifying landmarks, intersections, corners or places before telling where to turn
- use single movement for ALL-WAY-DOWN
- superimpose head nod(s) with BLOCK-AWAY
- use left hand to sign TURN-LEFT and right hand to sign TURN-RIGHT

NOTIONS

Grammar

"when" clause

Phrases

- when
(distance) ALL-WAY-DOWN GO-PAST (place),
nod
TURN-LEFT/RIGHT

- (distance+landmark) (#) BLOCK-AWAY, CORNER,
when nod
IX-loc*"(place)"* (name place), TURN-LEFT/RIGHT

- (distance+intersection) ALL-WAY-DOWN, INTERSECTION,
when nod
CROSS-STREET, (name of street), TURN-LEFT/RIGHT

Vocabulary

Distance	*Landmark*
ALL-WAY-DOWN	GO-PAST
END-STREET	LIGHT ECL*"traffic stop light"*
(#) BLOCK-AWAY	

Intersection	*Where to Turn*
INTERSECTION	TURN-LEFT
CROSS-STREET	TURN-RIGHT

PREPARATION Read and view **Giving Directions: Where To Turn** (*Student Workbook*, pages 210–211)

MATERIALS **9:8 Lesson Slides**

HOMEWORK 9:8 *Student Workbook*, pages 210–212

INTRODUCE *Distance, Landmark(s) or the Intersection*

12–15 minutes

PRESENT
(LESSON SLIDES 9:8:1–8)

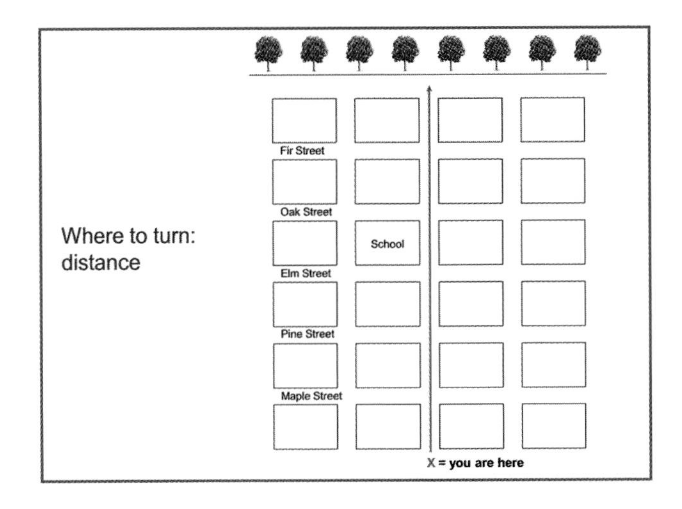

Introduce signs and phrases for telling where to turn by referring to distance, landmark(s) or the intersection. Have students copy.

For **Slide 1** (distance)

T: ALL-WAY-DOWN, END-STREET

S(all): (copy)

NOTE: The movement for ALL-WAY-DOWN is not repeated.

ALL-WAY-DOWN, END-STREET

END-STREET

For **Slide 2** (distance)

T: ONE BLOCK-AWAY, TURN-LEFT (nod over TURN-LEFT)

S(all): (copy)

NOTE: Make sure students superimpose head nod with BLOCK-AWAY and use their left hand to sign TURN-LEFT.

ONE BLOCK-AWAY

TURN-LEFT

For **Slide 3** (distance plus landmark)

T: ALL-WAY-DOWN FOUR BLOCK-AWAY++,

when nod

GO-PAST SCHOOL, TURN-RIGHT

S(all): (copy)

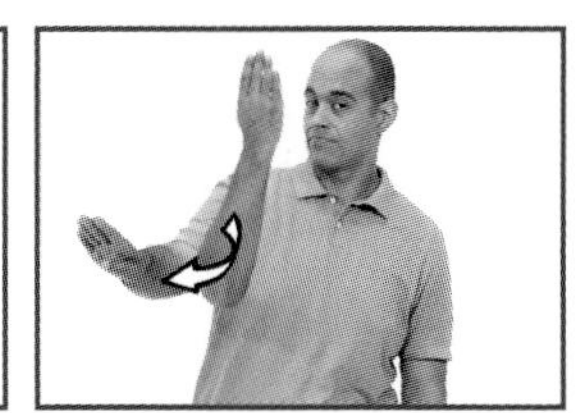

GO-PAST **TURN-RIGHT**

NOTE: Make sure students raise brows for the "when" clause, and use their right hand to sign TURN-RIGHT.

LIGHT
ECL*"traffic stop light"*

For **Slide 4** (distance plus landmark)

when

T: ALL-WAY-DOWN, **LIGHT ECL*"traffic stop light,"***

nod

TURN-RIGHT

S(all): (copy)

For **Slide 5** (distance plus landmark)

T: TWO BLOCK-AWAY+, **CORNER*"near left,"***

when nod

IX-loc"7-11" fs-7-11, TURN-LEFT

S(all): (copy)

INTERSECTION

CROSS-STREET

For **Slide 6** (distance plus intersection)

T: ALL-WAY-DOWN, **INTERSECTION, CROSS-STREET**,

when nod

fs-FIR-ST, TURN-LEFT

S(all): (copy)

For **Slide 7** (distance plus landmark)

when

T: ALL-WAY-DOWN, GO-PAST LIGHT ECL*"traffic stop light,"*

ONE BLOCK-AWAY, **CORNER*"far right,"* IX-loc*"Starbucks"***

when nod

STARBUCKS, TURN-RIGHT

S(all): (copy)

For **Slide 8** (distance plus intersection)

T: THREE BLOCK-AWAY, INTERSECTION, CROSS-STREET,

when nod

fs-ELM-ST, TURN-RIGHT

S(all): (copy)

Review. Show **Lesson Slides 9:8:1–8** again, and have students practice signing the phrases.

PRACTICE *Telling Where to Turn*

20–25 minutes

Students practice telling where to turn within city blocks by referring to the distance, intersection, or landmarks.

PRESENT

(SLIDES 9:8:9–14)

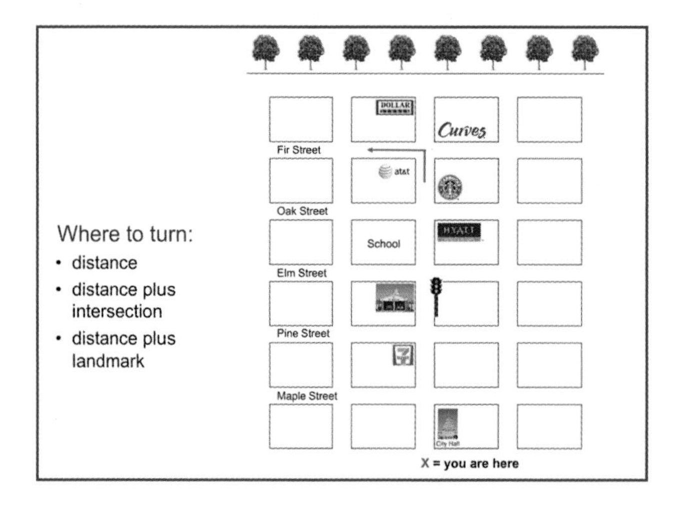

For each slide, have 2–3 students sign different ways to tell where to turn, using distance, landmark or intersection as reference.

For example:

For **Slide 9**

S1: (distance) ALL-WAY-DOWN, FIVE BLOCK-AWAY+++,

nod

TURN-LEFT

S2: (distance plus landmark) ALL-WAY-DOWN, CORNER*"near left"*

when nod

IX-loc*"AT&T"* PHONE STORE, TURN-LEFT

S3: (distance plus intersection) ALL-WAY-DOWN, INTERSECTION,

when nod

CROSS-STREET, fs-FIR-ST, TURN-LEFT

Repeat for **Lesson Slides 9:8:10–14**. Encourage students to use the following vocabulary:

- **distance:** ALL-WAY-DOWN, END-STREET, (#) BLOCK AWAY,
- **intersection:** INTERSECTION, CROSS-STREET
- **landmark:** GO-PAST, LIGHT ECL*"traffic stop light,"* (name of business)
- **where to turn:** TURN-LEFT, TURN-RIGHT.

Be sure students:
- use single movement for ALL-WAY-DOWN
- superimpose head nod(s) with BLOCK-AWAY
- use their left hand to sign TURN-LEFT and right hand to sign TURN-RIGHT
- use "when" clause when identifying landmarks, intersections, corners or places before telling where to turn.

HOMEWORK

Tell students to do **Homework 9:8** (*Student Workbook*, pages 210–212).

LESSON 9:9

Numbers: Giving the Time 2

Lesson length: 35–45 minutes

LESSON GOAL Students will practice clock number forms and asking wh-word questions about daily routines.

KEY SKILLS sign clock numbers correctly

NOTIONS

Grammar

(activity) $\overline{\text{TIME}}^{\text{whq}}$

$\overline{\text{(specific time)}}^{\text{t}}$ $\overline{\text{(who) DO++}}^{\text{whq}}$

Vocabulary

SHOWER
BRUSH-TEETH
TAP-SHOULDER, "get up"
GET-DRESSED
TAKE-BATH

MATERIALS

9:9 Lesson Slides
9:9 Follow-up Slides

HOMEWORK 9:9 *Student Workbook*, pages 213–215

REVIEW *Clock Numbers*

10–15 minutes

PRESENT
(LESSON SLIDES 9:9:1–24)

Review Clock Numbers

3:15

For each slide, have students sign the clock number. Make sure students use correct forms:

hour numbers 1:00–9:00

- the index finger taps the wrist
- the hand moves outward before the number is given,
- the palm faces out and the hand is shaken for numbers 1–9

hour numbers 10:00–12:00

- the index finger taps the wrist
- the hand moves outward before the number is given
- the number 10–12 can either be repeated or have a single movement

hour and minute combinations:

For the hour:

- the index finger taps the wrist before giving the hour number
- for hours 1–9 the hand is not shaken, and for the hours 10–12 the movement is not repeated

For the minutes:

- after giving the hour number, move hand slightly to the side
- the palm faces out for minutes :01–:09
- for minutes :10–:15 and :20, a singular movement is best, but it is acceptable if movement is repeated
- for :30, :40 and :50, the movement is not repeated.

PRACTICE *Asking and Responding with Clock Number*

15–20 minutes

Students practice clock numbers and daily routine vocabulary.

PRESENT
(LESSON SLIDE 9:9:25)

A: ask what Tanya does at a certain time
B: give time

Tanya's Schedule

6:15	gets up, exercises	**4:15**	leaves work, buys groceries
6:45	showers, dresses	**5:10**	arrives home
7:00	wakes the children	**6:30**	family eats dinner
7:20	children eat breakfast	**7:00**	children watch TV
7:40	children go to school	**8:30**	children take a bath
8:00	goes to work	**9:00**	children in bed
8:25	arrives work	**9:05**	showers and brushes teeth
12:30	eats lunch with friend	**9:40**	checks email
10:00	watches the news	**11:00**	in bed

Ask what Tanya does at certain times, and have students answer. For example:

t (over "6:15 MORNING,") whq (over "WOMAN (2h)#DO++")
T: 6:15 MORNING, WOMAN (2h)#DO++
S: GET-UP, EXERCISE

Ask other questions and introduce if needed, these activity signs:

SHOWER
BRUSH-TEETH
TAP-SHOULDER, "get up"
GET-DRESSED
TAKE-PATH

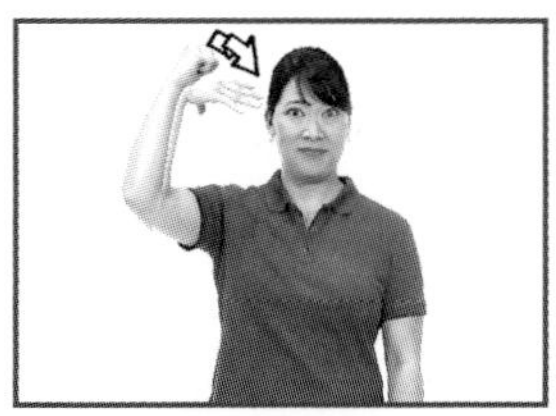

SHOWER

BRUSH-TEETH

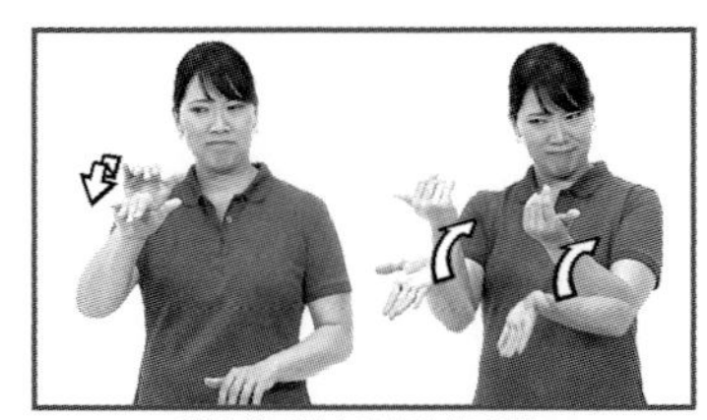

TAP-SHOULDER
"get up"

GET-DRESSED

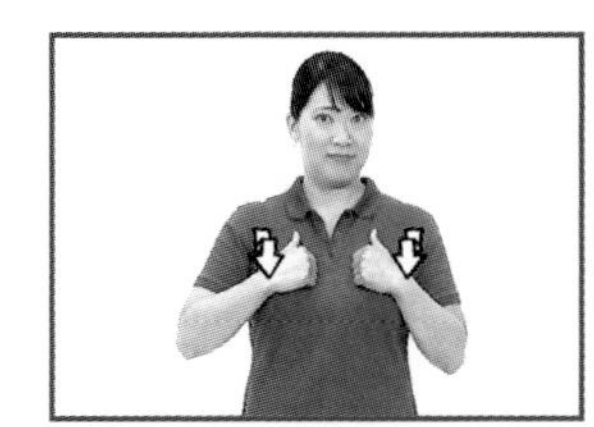

TAKE-BATH

Pair Up. Have students take turns asking what Tanya does at a certain time. Be sure students give time using correct clock number form and end with the wh-word question $\overline{\text{(2h)DO++}}^{\text{whq}}$.

PRESENT
(LESSON SLIDE 9:9:26)

A: ask what time Tanya does an activity
B: give time

Tanya's Schedule

6:15	gets up, exercises	**4:15**	leaves work, buys groceries
6:45	showers, dresses	**5:10**	arrives home
7:00	wakes the children	**6:30**	family eats dinner
7:20	children eat breakfast	**7:00**	children watch TV
7:40	children go to school	**8:30**	children take a bath
8:00	goes to work	**9:00**	children in bed
8:25	arrives work	**9:05**	showers and brushes teeth
12:30	eats lunch with friend	**9:40**	checks email
10:00	watches the news	**11:00**	in bed

Ask what time Tanya does an activity in random order. Check student's clock number forms. For example:

whq

T: NIGHT, WOMAN (or fs-TANYA) FAMILY EAT, TIME

S: 6:30

whq

T: WOMAN (or fs-TANYA) LEAVE-FOR WORK, TIME

S: 8:00 [MORNING]

Pair Up. Have students take turns asking each other what time Tanya does different activities. Be sure students name activity first, then ask TIME. (whq)

Conclude. With a faster signing pace, ask students what time Tanya does at certain activities.

HOMEWORK

Tell students to do **Homework 9:9** (*Student Workbook*, pages 213–215).

Also, students are to create five questions to ask what time. (**Assignment**, *Student Workbook*, page 215).

HOMEWORK FOLLOW-UP
20–30 MINUTES

PRESENT
(FOLLOW-UP SLIDES 9:9:1–3)

The Number 11
cardinal: 11
age: 11 years old
year: 2011 (20 and 11 are not repeated)
clock: 7:11 (hand moves slightly to the side)

The Number 13
cardinal: 13
age: 13 years old
year: 2013 (20 and 13 are not repeated)
clock: 8:13 (hand moves slightly to the side)

Number Tune Up. Have students sign the numbers on **Slides 1–3**.

Be sure students:

- use the correct number forms for the four different types for numbers 11, 13, 15, 20 and 30.

Five Questions
Put students into groups and allow them to ask each other their five questions (See **Assignment**, *Student Workbook*, page 215).

Be sure students:

- name activity, then ask $\overline{\text{TIME}}^{\text{whq}}$ with furrowed brows and leaning head leaned forward
- use correct clock number form when answering

Conclude by having each student ask one of their questions to either you or another student.

LESSON 9:10

Suggesting a Place to Eat

Lesson length: 50–65 minutes

LESSON GOAL

Students will sign this dialogue:

Dialogue

A: explain reason; ask to suggest a restaurant[1]

B/C: each suggest a place, elaborate on the following:

- description of the environment
- what people do there
- kind of food served
- opinions (prices, food and atmosphere)
- one drawback[2]

A: explain preference

B/C: comment on A's choice

A: reply

KEY PHRASES

whq

[1] (explain reason), YOU SUGGEST "what"

or

q

(explain reason), ANY RESTAURANT "area" GOOD

or

whq

(explain reason), GOOD RESTAURANT WHERE

t

[2] ONE WARNING,...

NOTIONS

Grammar

transition

t

ONE WARNING

Vocabulary

SUGGEST WARNING

MATERIALS

9:10 Lesson Slides
9:10 Follow-up Slides

HOMEWORK 9:10

Student Workbook, pages 216–221

INTRODUCE *Suggesting a Restaurant*

30–40 minutes

PRESENT
(LESSON SLIDE 9:10:1)

Describe environment
• table and seating arrangement

Review. Have students describe the environment at Benihana from **Lesson 9:7**.

S: ENTER RESTAURANT

- HAVE TABLE (2h)LCL:B*"several tables around room"*
 t
- IX-lox*"table in front"* TABLE, PEOPLE SIT (2h) V*"around table"*
 t
- MIDDLE IX-loc*"middle of table"* DCL*"rectangular stovetop"* COOK++

PRESENT
(LESSON SLIDE 9:10:2)

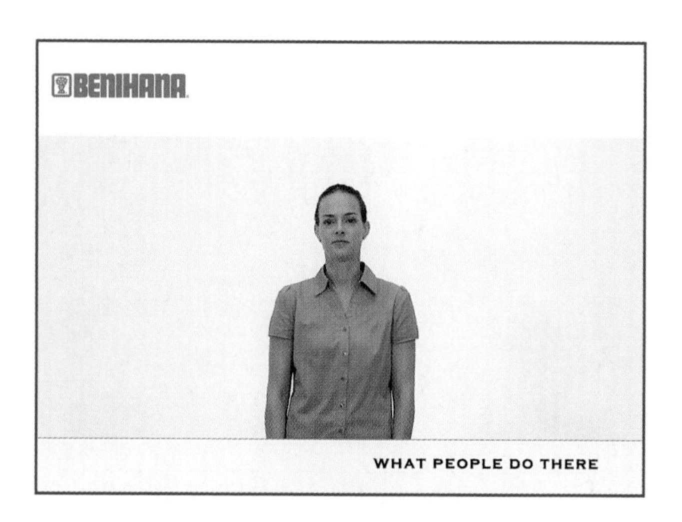

Show video **What People Do There**, then ask:

whq

T: PEOPLE IX-loc*"restaurant"* (2h)#DO

S: IX*"cook"* COOK+ER BRING-TO-here FOOD, FISH, CHICKEN, fs-STEAK, COOK !IX-loc*"there"*!

COOK GIVE SMALL PERFORMANCE. ICL*"chop food quickly"* fs-OR KNIFE ICL*"toss in air"* (2h)alt.LCL:1 *"twirl knives up in air."* fs-OR FOOD [(wh)ICL*"hold knife"*/IX-loc*"food on knife"* ICL*"flip food up in air"* (2h)alt.LCL:1 *"food twirl up in air,"* LCL:1 *"lands in chef's upper pocket"* fs-OR HAT DCL*"chef's hat"* FOOD (2h)alt.LCL:1 *"food twirl up in air,"* LCL:1 *"food lands on top of hat."*

PRESENT
(LESSON SLIDE 9:10:3)

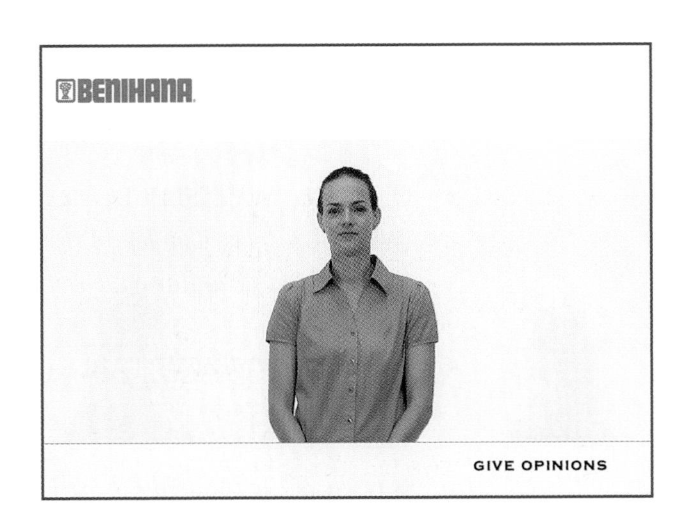

Show video **Give Opinions**, then ask:

t whq

T: RESTAURANT, WOMAN IX*"Ursula"* LIKE *"what"*

S: #FUN, FOOD !GOOD!

Then, ask what is the drawback:

whq

T: **ONE WARNING** *"what"*

S: TABLE MUST 8 PEOPLE (2h)SCL:V*"around table."* OTHER PEOPLE (2h)SCL:V*"more people seated to the right."*

neg

IX-they YOU NOT-KNOW WHO, THEY STRANGE+ER

ONE WARNING

PRESENT
(LESSON SLIDE 9:10:4)

Hard Rock
CAFE
Describe environment
• table or counter and seating arrangement
• wall decorations

Review. Have students describe the environment at Hard Rock Cafe from **Lesson 9:7**.

(t over [RESTAURANT] IX-loc"restaurant")
S: [RESTAURANT] IX-loc*"restaurant"* NICE, LARGE. HAVE BAR AND fs-GIFT-SHOP.

- OUTSIDE, !WHITE! DCL*"shape of restaurant building,"* (wh)LCL:C*"placed on left of restaurant,"* GUITAR (wh)DCL*"large guitar on left of restaurant building"*
- (t over TABLE) ENTER (2h)*"all over"* TABLE (2h)LCL:B*"scattered around the room"*
- X-loc*"back of room"* BAR, DCL*"long bar table,"* CHAIR (2h)SCL*"chairs at bar"*
- (2h)LCL:B*"walls around room"* DIFFERENT++ PICTURE
- (rhet over "what") (2h)LCL:B*"pictures hung on walls"* "what" FAMOUS MUSIC+ER, PERFORM+ER, DIFFERENT++, (2h)LCL:B*"pictures hung on walls"* SAME-AS RECORD (2h)LCL:L*"records on wall."* SOME IX-loc*"on wall"*++ FAMOUS MUSIC+ER POSS*"musician"* COAT/JACKET (2h)LCL:X*"hung up"*+++, GUITAR (2h)LCL:G*"guitars hung up"*+++, INTERESTING.

PRESENT
(LESSON SLIDE 9:10:5)

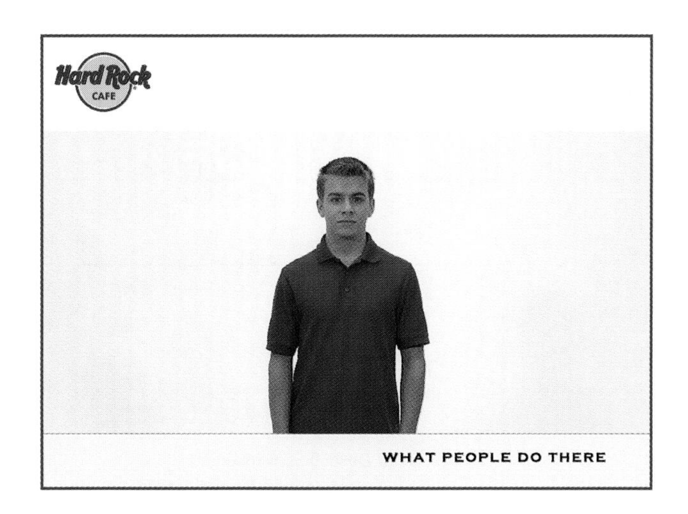

Show video **What People Do There**, then ask:

whq

T: PEOPLE IX-loc*"restaurant"* (2h)#DO

S: PEOPLE... (2h)alt.EAT++, DRINK, CHAT, (2h)LOOK-AT*"around on walls"* DIFFERENT++ PICTURE. IX*"gift shop"* fs-GIFT STORE, CAN BUY DCL*"cup/mug"* DRINK, DCL"T"+SHIRT, HAT, DIFFERENT++.

PRESENT
(LESSON SLIDE 9:10:6)

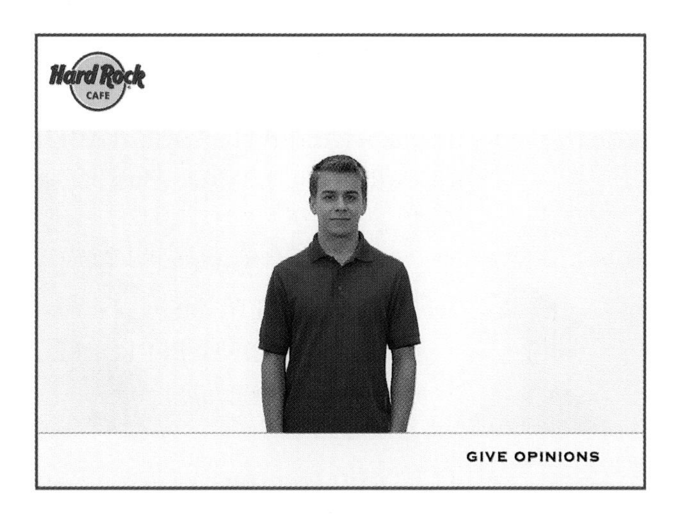

Show video **Give Opinions**, then ask:

whq

T: MAN IX*"man"* LIKE RESTAURANT "what"

S: IX*"restaurant"* RESTAURANT, INTERESTING. GOOD FOR YOUR FRIEND, EXIT CITY COME-TO*"here,"* TAKE-FROM*"friend"* GO-TO EAT. FOOD DELICIOUS.

Ask what is the drawback:

                                        whq
T: ONE WARNING *"what"*

S: PCL:4*"long line"* WAIT++

PRESENT

(LESSON SLIDE 9:10:7)

Describe environment
- table or counter and seating arrangement
- wall decorations
- lighting

Review. Have students describe the environment at Chuck E. Cheese from Lesson **9:7**.

S: RESTAURANT, ENTER TWO (wh)"area"-left, "area"-right.

            t
- "area"-right EAT, LARGE. TABLE (2h)LCL:C*"rows of tables"* CHAIR (2h)LCL:V*"two rows of chairs at each table"*++.
- fs-WALL (2h)LCL:B"wall" HAVE fs-PUPPETS, IX-loc++*"3 on wall"* LIGHT ECL*"beam on one section"* (2h)BPCL:fist*"2 puppet heads bobbling"* SING, PERFORM, (2h)BPCL:fist*"2 puppet heads bobbling."* (2h)ECL*"lights off."*
- ECL*"lights beam on next section"* (wh)BPCL:fist*"1 puppet head bobbling"* BPCL*"mouths open and close"*++ (2h)ECL*"lights off."*
- ECL*"lights beam on next section"*++ DIFFERENT++.

            t
- "area"-left, GAME "wow" PCL*"hordes of"* GAME.

PRESENT
(LESSON SLIDE 9:10:8)

Show video **What People Do There**, then ask:

whq

T: PEOPLE IX-loc*"restaurant"* (2h)#DO

S: BIRTHDAY PARTY, CAN HOST/ADOPT IX-loc*"there."*

TABLE (2h)GRAB*"table"* PCL*"people seated around table"* CELEBRATE, (2h)alt.EAT, WATCH PERFORM.

CHILDREN LIKE "area"-left GAME, PCL*"flock-to (left)"* (2h)PLAY-cont. ICL*"use joystick, shooting, hammering"* VARIOUS-THINGS. TICKET [(wh)LCL:B*"machine"*/ LCL:H*"strip of tickets"* DCL*"strip of tickets"* (2h)ICL*"get tickets and hand over (right)"* GET fs-PRIZE.

PRESENT
(LESSON SLIDE 9:10:9)

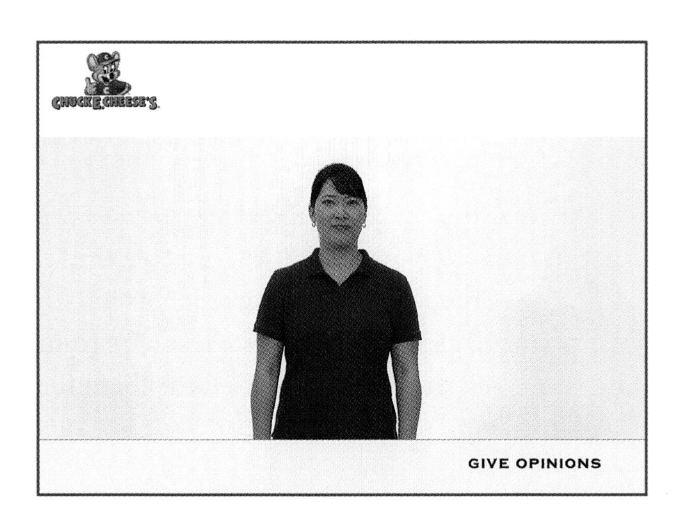

Show video **Give Opinions**, then ask:

whq

T: WOMAN IX*"woman"* LIKE RESTAURANT "what"

S: !GOOD! FOR CHILDREN GO-TO-restaurant ENJOY. #FUN. (2h)#DO-circle

Ask what is the drawback.

whq

T: ONE WARNING "what"

S: !NOISY! ICL*"use joystick"* (2h)BPCL:fist*"2 puppet heads bobbling"* MUSIC, ECL*"lights flashing"* (2h)BPCL*"eyes darting"* "wow"

PRACTICE *Suggest a Restaurant*

20–25 minutes

Students practice suggesting restaurants appropriate for different groups.

PRESENT

(LESSON SLIDE 9:10:10)

Activity

Groups 1 and 2 – restaurant for *kids*
Groups 3 and 4 – restaurant to take *friends*.
Groups 5 and 6 – restaurant for an *anniversary*.

Instructions: Decide on a restaurant to recommend and the information to share about each category listed below:

- description of the environment
- kind of food served
- what people do there
- opinions (prices, food, and atmosphere)
- one drawback

You can make up or embellish parts – but the information must be believable.

Group. After dividing students into the six groups, give them 10–15 minutes to decide on the restaurant and to develop the information they will share about the restaurant.

PRESENT
(LESSON SLIDE 9:10:11)

A: explain reason; ask to suggest a restaurant
(for young kids, for friends or to celebrate an anniversary)
B/C: each suggest a place, elaborate on the following:
- description of the environment
- what people do there
- kind of food served
- opinions (prices, food ,and atmosphere)
- one drawback

A: explain preference
B/C: comment on A's choice
A: reply

Demonstrate Signer A's first line ***"A: explain reason, ask to suggest a restaurant."*** Have students copy.

For ***"for young kids"***

SUGGEST

T: TOMORROW MY DAUGHTER POSS *"daughter"* BIRTHDAY, ME WANT TAKE-FROM-daughter's location LEAVE-FOR
whq
RESTAURANT, **YOU SUGGEST "what"**
S(all): (copy)

Have students brainstorm reasons to take young kids out to eat. For example:

- want to treat them
- don't feel like cooking
- celebrate their birthday
- don't have time to cook; in a hurry.

For ***"for friends"***

T: MY FRIEND EXIT CITY, COME-TO-here VISIT, ME WANT TAKE-FROM-friend's location LEAVE-FOR EAT,
q
ANY RESTAURANT "area" GOOD
S(all): (copy)

Have students brainstorm reasons to take friends out to eat. For example:

- out of town friends visiting
- host a small group function
- celebrate special occasions (birthdays, promotions, achievements).

For ***"to celebrate an anniversary"***

neg

T: MY FRIEND NONE SMOKE-CIGARETTE 1 YEAR, ME WANT CELEBRATE, TAKE-FROM-friend's location LEAVE-FOR

whq

FANCY RESTAURANT. **GOOD RESTAURANT WHERE**

S(all): (copy)

Have students brainstorm reasons to go out to eat to celebrate an anniversary. For example:

- dating for 6 months, 1 year, 5 years
- wedding
- celebrate abstinence (quitting smoking, drinking, sweets).

Rehearse Drawbacks. Have students review the drawbacks. Be sure students raise brows

t

with **ONE WARNING.**

From ***Benihana:***

t **whq**

T: fs-BENIHANA IX*"Benihana"* ONE WARNING, "what"

t

S1: ONE WARNING, PEOPLE (2h)SCL:V*"more people seated to the right."* IX-they STRANGE+ER

S(all): (repeat)

From ***Hard Rock Cafe:***

t

T: fs-HARDROCK-CAFE, IX*"Hard Rock Cafe"* ONE WARNING,

whq

"what"

t

S2: ONE WARNING, PCL:4*"long line"* WAIT++

S(all): (repeat)

From ***Chuck E. Cheese's:***

t

T: fs-CHUCK-E-CHEESE'S, IX*"Chuck E. Cheese's"* ONE WARNING,

whq

"what

t

S3: ONE WARNING, NOISY! ECL*"lights flashing"*
(2h)BPCL*"eyes darting"*

S(all): (repeat)

PRESENT
(LESSON SLIDE 9:10:12)

A: explain reason; ask to suggest a restaurant
(for young kids, for friends, or to celebrate an anniversary)

B/C: each suggest a place, elaborate on the following:

- description of the environment
- what people do there
- kind of food served
- opinions (prices, food, and atmosphere)
- one drawback

A: explain preference

B/C: comment on A's choice

A: reply

Instructions. In the new groups, when role playing Signer A:

- the person from Group 1 or 2 is to ask where to take friends
- the person from Group 3 or 4 is to ask where to go for an anniversary
- the person from Group 5 or 6 is to ask where to take kids.

Re-Group. Form new groups with three students in each (one person from Groups 1 or 2, one person from Groups 3 or 4 and one person from Groups 5 or 6). Have each student take turns role playing Signer A.

Conclude. Call students up to demonstrate the dialogue.

Be sure students:

- use descriptive (DCLs), locative (LCLs) and element (ECLs) classifiers to describe restaurant environments
- nod their head when listing food items
- use raised brows with ONE WARNING (t).

HOMEWORK

Tell students to do **Homework 9:10** (*Student Workbook*, pages 216–221).

HOMEWORK FOLLOW-UP
20–25 MINUTES

PRESENT
(FOLLOW-UP SLIDES 9:10:1–23)

Minidialogue 1

1. Who does Suzanne want to take out to eat?

Check students' answers to **Minidialogues 1–3**. See **Introduction** pages xviii–xix for different ways to check answers.

LESSON 9:11

Giving Directions: Perspective Shift

Lesson length: 50–70 minutes

LESSON GOAL

Students will use perspective shift to complete the directions.

KEY SKILLS

- use left hand for TURN-LEFT and right hand for TURN-RIGHT
- use perspective shift
- end with "IX-loc*"that one"* superimposed with "cs" expression

NOTIONS

Grammar

Perspective shift

Phrases

when
ALL-WAY-DOWN, END-STREET, TURN-LEFT/RIGHT,

bounce t
(shift perspective) (#) BLOCK-AWAY, CORNER

nod
IX-loc*"that-one"* (name place).

PREPARATION

Read and view **Giving Directions: Perspective Shift**, *Student Workbook*, pages 222–223

MATERIALS

9:11 Lesson Slides

Exercise 3 (Italian and Greek) (*Student Workbook*, pages 489 and 493)

HOMEWORK 9:11

Student Workbook, pages 222–226

INTRODUCE *Perspective Shift*

30–40 minutes

PRESENT
(LESSON SLIDE 9:11:1)

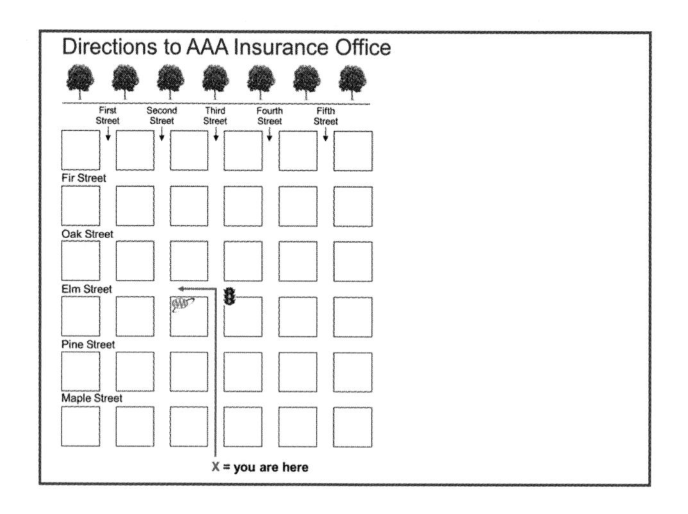

Give partial directions to AAA and ask which corner it is on.

T: ALL-WAY-DOWN, THREE BLOCK-AWAY, INTERSECTION,
when
CROSS-STREET, fs-ELM, TURN-LEFT; **(shift perspective)**,
t whq
ONE BLOCK-AWAY. fs-AAA, CORNER WHICH
(then show next slide)

PRESENT
(LESSON SLIDE 9:11:2)

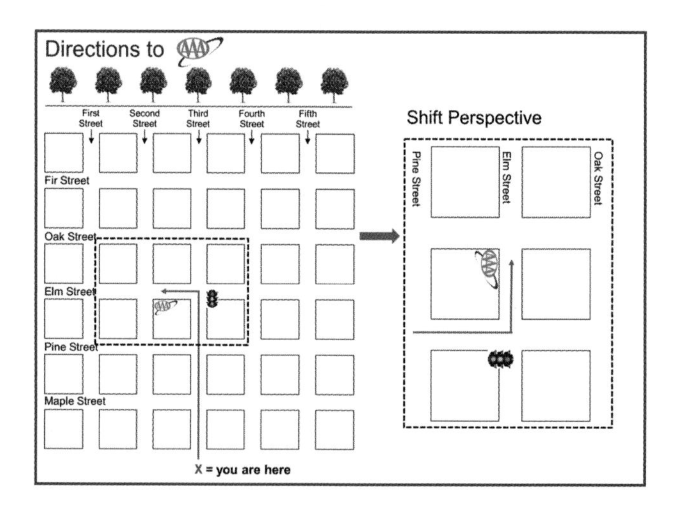

Introduce perspective shift. Tell students to imagine themselves looking down Elm Street. Now, ask which corner again.

t whq
T: fs-AAA, CORNER WHICH
S: CORNER*"near left"*

TEACHER TO TEACHER

If a student is struggling to identify which corner, assign them a student who understands perspective shift to help them during this session.

Then demonstrate giving directions with perspective shift. Have students copy.

T: ALL-WAY-DOWN, THREE BLOCK-AWAY, INTERSECTION,
when
CROSS-STREET, fs-ELM, TURN-LEFT; **(shift perspective)**,
t
ONE BLOCK-AWAY, CORNER*"near left"* IX-loc*"that-one"*
nod
fs-AAA.
S(all): (copy)

Be sure students:

- use single movement for ALL-WAY-DOWN
- superimpose head nod(s) with BLOCK-AWAY
- use "when" clause (raise brows) when identifying intersections before telling where to turn
- use left hand to sign TURN-LEFT
- use perspective shift
- end with IX-loc*"that one"* superimposed with "cs" expression.

PRESENT
(LESSON SLIDE 9:11:3)

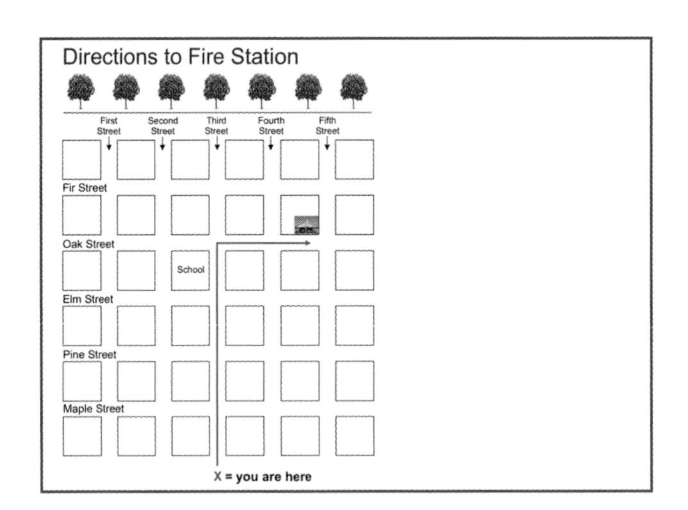

Give partial directions to the fire station on the map and ask which corner it is on.

when (over GO-PAST SCHOOL); cs (over TURN-RIGHT)

T: ALL-WAY-DOWN, GO-PAST SCHOOL, TURN-RIGHT, **(shift perspective)**, TWO BLOCK-AWAY+

t (over FIREFIGHTER); whq (over CORNER WHICH)

FIREFIGHTER, CORNER WHICH (then show next slide)

PRESENT
(LESSON SLIDE 9:11:4)

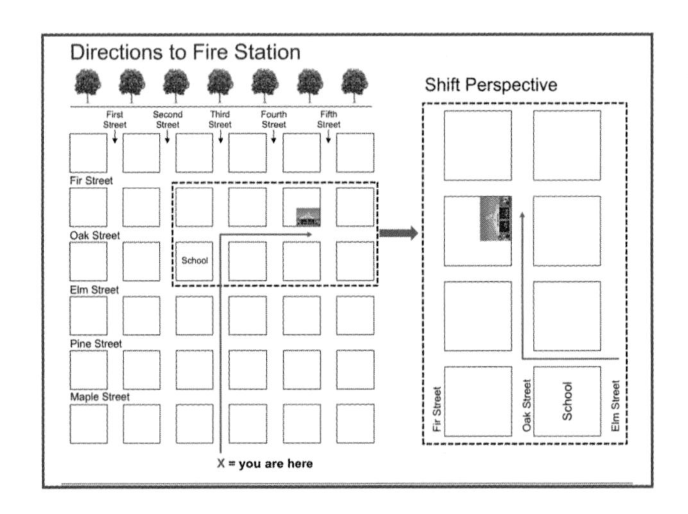

Tell students to imagine themselves looking down Oak street. Now, ask which corner again.

t (over FIREFIGHTER); whq (over CORNER WHICH)

T: FIREFIGHTER, CORNER WHICH

S: CORNER *"near left"*

Demonstrate giving directions with perspective shift.
Have students copy.

when cs
T: ALL-WAY-DOWN, GO-PAST SCHOOL, TURN-RIGHT,

t
(shift perspective), TWO BLOCK-AWAY+, CORNER*"near left"*

nod
IX-loc*"that-one"* FIREFIGHTER.

S(all): (copy)

Be sure students:

- use right hand to sign TURN-RIGHT
- use perspective shift
- end with IX-loc*"that one"* superimposed with "cs" expression.

PRESENT
(LESSON SLIDE 9:11:5)

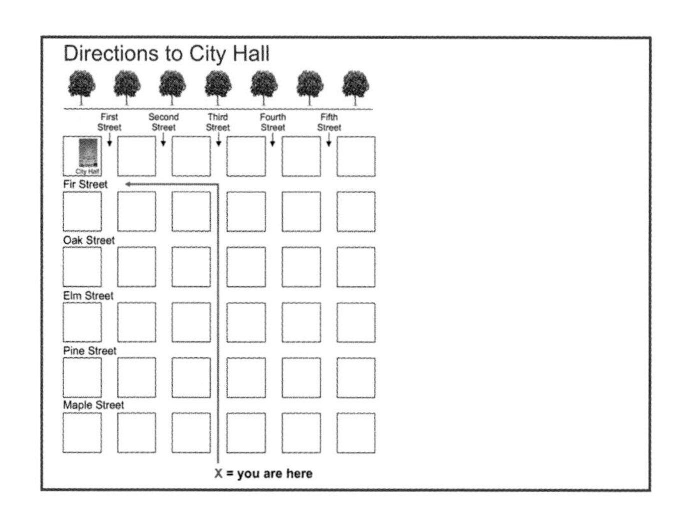

Give partial directions to City Hall on the map and ask which corner it is on.

when
T: ALL-WAY-DOWN, INTERSECTION, CROSS-STREET, fs-FIR, TURN-LEFT, **(shift perspective)** TWO BLOCK-AWAY+,

t whq
fs-CITY-HALL, CORNER WHICH (then show next slide)

PRESENT

(LESSON SLIDE 9:11:6)

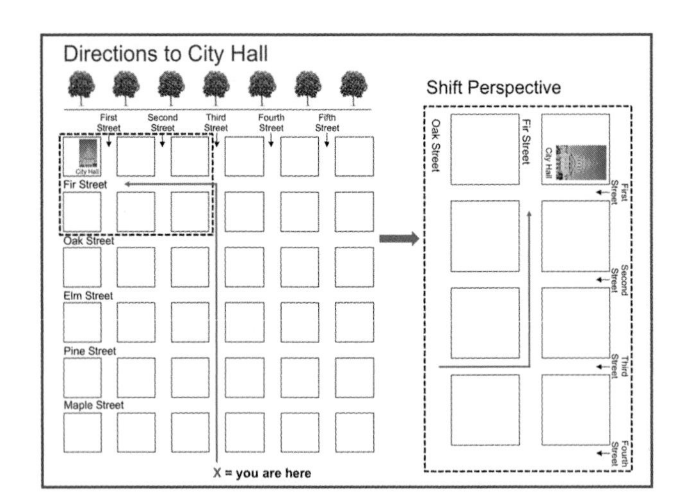

Tell students to imagine themselves looking down Fir Street. Now, ask which corner again.

t (over "fs-CITY-HALL,") whq (over "CORNER WHICH")

T: fs-CITY-HALL, CORNER WHICH

S: CORNER *"far right"*

Demonstrate giving directions with perspective shift. Have students copy.

when (over "INTERSECTION, CROSS-STREET, fs-FIR,")

T: ALL-WAY-DOWN, INTERSECTION, CROSS-STREET, fs-FIR, TURN-LEFT, **(shift perspective)**, TWO BLOCK-AWAY+

t (over "CORNER "far right"") nod (over "IX-loc "that-one" fs-CITY-HALL.")

CORNER *"far right"* IX-loc *"that-one"* fs-CITY-HALL.

S(all): (copy)

Be sure students:

- shift perspective to complete the directions
- end with IX-loc *"that one"* superimposed with "cs" expression.

PRESENT
(LESSON SLIDES 9:11:7–11)

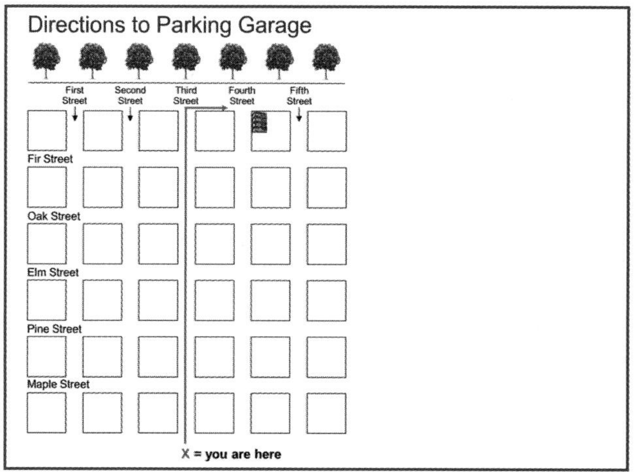

For **Lesson Slides 9:11:7–11**, have students give directions using perspective shift without the aid of the close up map. Be sure students identify the correct corner when giving the location.

For **Slide 7** (parking garage)

whq
T: PARKING WHERE

when
S: ALL-WAY-DOWN, END-STREET, TURN-RIGHT,

t
(shift perspective), ONE BLOCK-AWAY, CORNER *"far right"*

nod
IX-loc *"that-one"* PARKING

For **Slide 8** (courthouse)

whq
T: JUDGE+HOUSE WHERE

S: ONE BLOCK-AWAY, TURN-RIGHT, **(shift perspective)**,

t
ONE BLOCK-AWAY, CORNER *"far left"* IX-loc *"that-one"*

nod
JUDGE+HOUSE .

For **Slide 9 (7–11)**

whq

T: 7-11 WHERE

when

S: TWO BLOCK-AWAY, INTERSECTION, CROSS-STREET, fs-PINE , TURN-LEFT, **(shift perspective)**, ONE BLOCK-AWAY,

t nod

CORNER*"near left"* IX-loc*"that-one"* 7-11.

For **Slide 10** (police station)

whq

T: POLICE WHERE

when

S: ALL-WAY-DOWN, INTERSECTION, CROSS-STREET, fs-OAK TURN-RIGHT, **(shift perspective)**, TWO BLOCK-AWAY,

t nod

CORNER*"near right"* IX-loc*"that-one"* POLICE.

For **Slide 11** (Curves)

whq

T: fs-CURVES WHERE

S: ALL-WAY-DOWN, [THREE BLOCK-AWAY++], LIGHT

when

ECL*"traffic stop light,"* TURN-RIGHT **(shift perspective)**,

t

ONE BLOCK-AWAY, CORNER*"near left"* LIQUOR STORE,

nod nod

IX-loc*"that one"* NEXT-TO-left IX-loc*"Curves"* fs-CURVES.

Be sure students:

- use "when" clause when identifying ABC liquor store on the near *left* corner before telling that Curves is next to it.

Continue with **Slide 11** (IKEA)

whq

T: fs-IKEA WHERE

S: ALL-WAY-DOWN, [THREE BLOCK-AWAY++], LIGHT

when

ECL*"traffic stop light,"* TURN-RIGHT, **(shift perspective)**,

ONE BLOCK-AWAY, CORNER*"far left"* MCDONALDS,

when nod
IX-loc*"that one"* NEXT-TO*"front"* IX-loc*"IKEA"* fs-IKEA.

Be sure students:

- use "when" clause (raise brows) when identifying McDonald's on the *far left* corner before telling that IKEA is next to it.

PRACTICE *Giving Directions Using Perspective Shift*

20–30 minutes

Students practice giving directions and shifting their perspective to tell where a place is located.

PRESENT

(LESSON SLIDE 9:11:12)

Signer A: tell what you need, ask if you can find it around here
Signer B: name place, ask if acceptable
A: confirm, ask where
B: give directions
A: (write name of the location on the map)

EXERCISE 3

Italian and Greek

Pair off students. Assign one person **Exercise 3—Italian** (*Student Workbook*, page 489) and the other **Exercise 3—Greek** (*Student Workbook*, page 493).

Demonstrate the activity. Role play Signer A and pick a student to role play Signer B.

T (as A): ME HAVE PARKING TICKET, ME MUST PAY-TO.
whq
NEAR "area" WHERE
q
S (as B): JUDGE+HOUSE FINE++

nod whq
T (as A): YES. WHERE
S (as B): (give directions based on the map)
T (as A): (write name in the location on the map in the *Student Workbook*)

Have students do the activity. When done, have them check each other's workbooks to confirm their answers.

Be sure students:

- use single movement for ALL-WAY-DOWN.
- superimpose head nod(s) with BLOCK-AWAY
- use "when" clause (raise brows) when telling where to turn
- use left hand for TURN-LEFT and right hand for TURN-RIGHT
- use perspective shift
- end with IX-loc*"that one"* superimposed with "cs" expression

HOMEWORK

Tell students to do **Homework 9:11** (*Student Workbook*, pages 222–226).

LESSON 9:12

Yes–No Questions 2

Lesson length: 50–60 minutes

LESSON GOAL

Students will translate yes-no questions and elaborate on the answer when responding to the question.

KEY SKILLS

Translating the question

- establish time if specified (raise brows)
- establish location if specified (raise brows)
- name topic (raise brows)
- ask yes-no question (raise brows, tilt head forward, hold last sign)

NOTIONS

Grammar

topicalization
yes-no question

Vocabulary

Verbs	*Nouns*
MEET++	PEOPLE
EXPERIENCE	POETRY
TAKE-CARE-OF++	RABBIT
TO-NAME	EYES
CAN	SNOWBOARDING

Others

!NEW!
FOREIGN/COUNTRY
FAMOUS

MATERIALS

9:12 Lesson Slides

HOMEWORK 9:12

Student Workbook, pages 227–229

REVIEW *Identifying the Topic*

7–10 minutes

PRESENT

(LESSON SLIDES 9:12:1–11)

Identify the topic in each question.

1. Do you like meeting new people?
2. Do you like foreign films?
3. Have you ever tried eating raw fish?
4. Have you ever experienced raising a rabbit?
5. Do you write poetry?

Have students open their workbooks to **Yes–No Questions 2** on page 227 and underline the topic(s) in each question.

When done, confirm students' answers with **Lesson Slides 9:12:2–11** for all nine questions and introduce translations for the topics. For example:

For **Question 1**

T: (show **Lesson Slide 9:12:2** to confirm), **MEET++ NEW PEOPLE**

S: (copy)

Teacher's Guide

question	*topic*
Question 1	**MEET++ NEW PEOPLE**
Question 2	**FOREIGN/COUNTRY MOVIE**
Question 3	EAT fs-RAW FISH
Question 4	**RABBIT TAKE-CARE-OF++** DCL*"from small to big"*
Question 5	**POETRY**
Question 6	(1) COMPUTER, (2) PICTURE
Question 7	**EYES**
Question 8	**SNOWBOARDING**
Question 9	PAINTER+ER **FAMOUS**

MEET++ !NEW! PEOPLE

FOREIGN/COUNTRY

RABBIT TAKE-CARE-OF++

POETRY

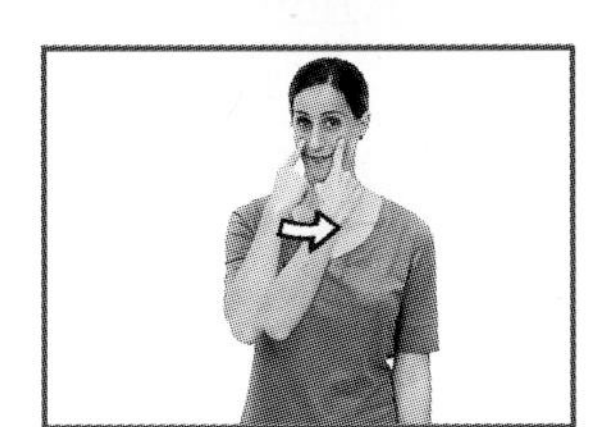
EYES

SNOWBOARDING

FAMOUS

PRACTICE *Translating Yes–No Questions*

35–45 minutes

Students practice integrating the topic and facial grammar to translate yes–no questions.

PRESENT
(LESSON SLIDES 9:12:12–13)

Translating yes-no questions

- establish time if specified (raise brows)
- establish location if specified (raise brows)
- name the topic (raise brows)
- ask question (raise brows, tilt head forward, hold last sign)

1. Do you like meeting new people?
2. Do you like foreign films?
3. Have you ever tried eating raw fish?
4. Have you ever experienced raising a rabbit?
5. Do you write poetry?

Demonstrate the translation and have students copy.

1. ***Do you like meeting new people?***

t q

T: MEET++ !NEW! PEOPLE, YOU LIKE, YOU
S(all): (copy)

Be sure students:

- raise brows and head with the topic
- raise brows and tilt head forward and hold the last sign (YOU) with the yes-no question.

Repeat procedure for the remaining questions.

Teacher's translation guide

2. ***Do you like foreign films?***

t q

FOREIGN/COUNTRY MOVIE, YOU LIKE, YOU

3. ***Have you ever tried* <u>*eating raw fish*</u>*?***

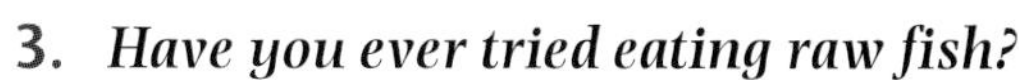

t q
EAT fs-RAW FISH, YOU FINISH TRY, YOU

4. ***Have you ever experienced* <u>*raising a rabbit*</u>*?***

t
RABBIT TAKE-CARE-OF++ DCL*"from small to big,"* YOU

q
FINISH **EXPERIENCE**, YOU

EXPERIENCE

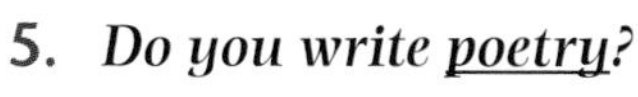

5. ***Do you write* <u>*poetry*</u>*?***

t q
POETRY, YOU WRITE, YOU

6. ***Do you know how to scan* <u>*pictures*</u> *into the* <u>*computer*</u>*?***

t t q
COMPUTER, PICTURE TO-SCAN, YOU KNOW fs-HOW, YOU

7. ***Can you cross* <u>*your eyes*</u>*?***

t q
EYES BPCL:1*"cross eyes,"* CAN YOU

8. ***Have you ever tried* <u>*snowboarding*</u>*?***

t q
SNOWBOARDING, YOU FINISH EXPERIENCE, YOU

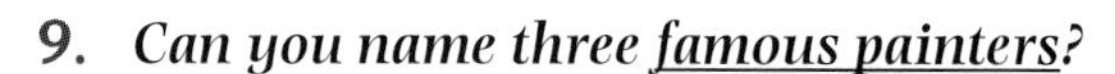

9. ***Can you name three* <u>*famous painters*</u>*?***

t q
PAINT+ER FAMOUS **TO-NAME++** THREE, **CAN** YOU

TO-NAME

CAN

Review. Have students take turns asking you the questions. When answering, be sure to elaborate on your answer.

For example:

t q
S: MEET++ !NEW! PEOPLE, YOU LIKE, YOU
T: YES, SOMETIMES ME LIKE MEET++, MOST TIME, ME PREFER me-ALONE.

Mingle. Now have students mingle asking each other the questions and elaborating on their answers.

HOMEWORK

Tell students to do **Homework 9:12** (*Student Workbook*, pages 227–229).

Also, students are to pick five questions and change the topics to make new questions (**Assignment**, *Student Workbook*, page 227).

HOMEWORK FOLLOW-UP
15–30 MINUTES

Five New Questions. Have students take turns signing their new questions (See **Assignment**, *Student Workbook*, page 227).

Have other students answer the questions. Remind (or help) them to elaborate on their answers.

Be sure students:

- raise brows and head with the topic
- raise brows and tilt head forward and hold the last sign (YOU) with the yes-no question
- elaborate on their answers.

LESSON 9:13

Culture: Keeping Others Informed

Lesson length: 35–40 minutes

LESSON GOAL

Students will practice culturally appropriate behaviors to inform the teacher (and others) the reasons for their absences from and tardiness to class or events.

KEY BEHAVIORS

- getting attention
- getting permission
- being prepared to explain
- when to start
- expressing gratitude

NOTIONS

Phrases

1. ***You were absent from the last class.***

   rhet

   IN-PAST (day of last class), ME CLASS MISS, WHY, (give reason), SORRY.

2. ***You will leave class early.***

   when

   ME INFORM-you TODAY (time), ME MUST LEAVE, (give reason).

3. ***You are late to class.***

   SORRY, ME BE-LATE. (give reason) SORRY.

4. ***You will be absent from the next class.***

   t neg

   IN-FUTURE (date), ME CAN'T COME-TO-here CLASS, ME [MUST] (give reason)

Vocabulary

SORRY
MISS
BE-LATE

PREPARATION	Read and view **Keeping Others Informed**, *Student Workbook*, pages 230–231
MATERIALS	**9:13 Lesson Slides**
HOMEWORK 9:13	*Student Workbook*, pages 230–231

INTRODUCE *Explaining Absences and Tardiness*

20–25 minutes

PRESENT

LESSON SLIDE 9:13:1)

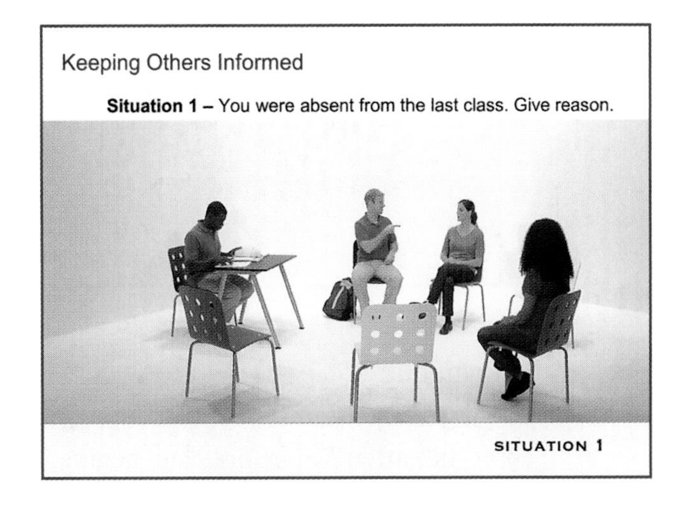

Keeping Others Informed
Situation 1 – You were absent from the last class. Give reason.
SITUATION 1

Point out:

- **getting attention.** As soon as Amber enters the classroom she gets Melvin's (teacher's) attention to inform him of her absence from a previous class (instead of quietly taking her seat which would be the norm in a hearing classroom)
- **getting permission.** Only *after* getting permission from the teacher, Amber takes her seat.

Have students give other reasons for missing a class.
Be sure they follow this structure:

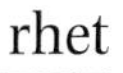

rhet

S: IN-PAST (day of last class), ME CLASS **MISS**, WHY, (give reason), **SORRY**.

MISS

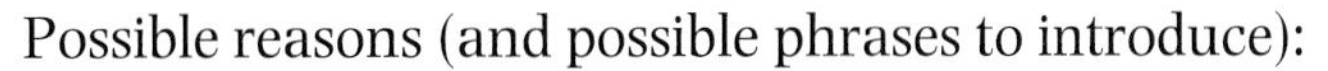

Possible reasons (and possible phrases to introduce):

- illness (!SICK!)
- had to work (!MUST! WORK)
- car trouble (CAR BREAKDOWN)
- can't find a babysitter (CAN'T FIND BABY+TAKE-CARE-OF).

PRESENT
(LESSON SLIDE 9:13:2)

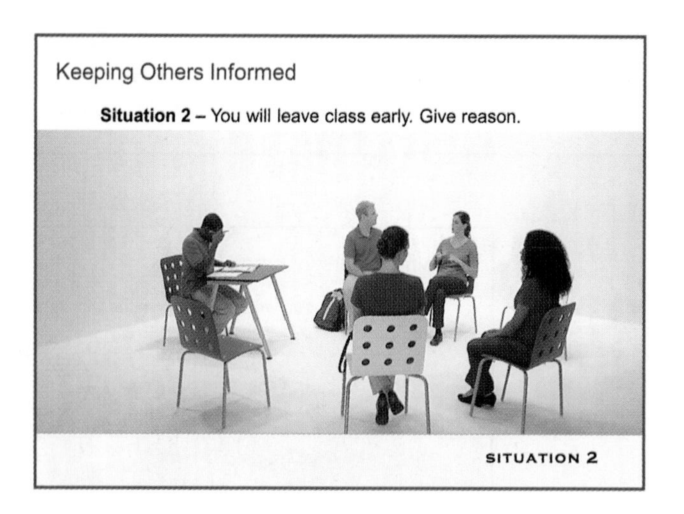

Keeping Others Informed
Situation 2 – You will leave class early. Give reason.
SITUATION 2

Point out:

- **getting attention.** Lauren approaches Melvin (teacher) to get his attention before class begins.
- **expressing gratitude.** Lauren thanks Melvin for allowing her to leave class early.

Have students give other reasons for leaving class early
Be sure they follow this structure:

when
S: ME INFORM-you TODAY (time), ME MUST LEAVE, (give reason).

Have students give other reasons for leaving class early.
Possible reasons (and possible phrases to introduce):

- need to pick up child (MUST PICK-UP SON)
- need to attend a meeting (MEETING)
- need to go to work (!MUST! WORK)
- not feeling well (NOT FEEL+GOOD).

PRESENT
LESSON SLIDE 9:13:3)

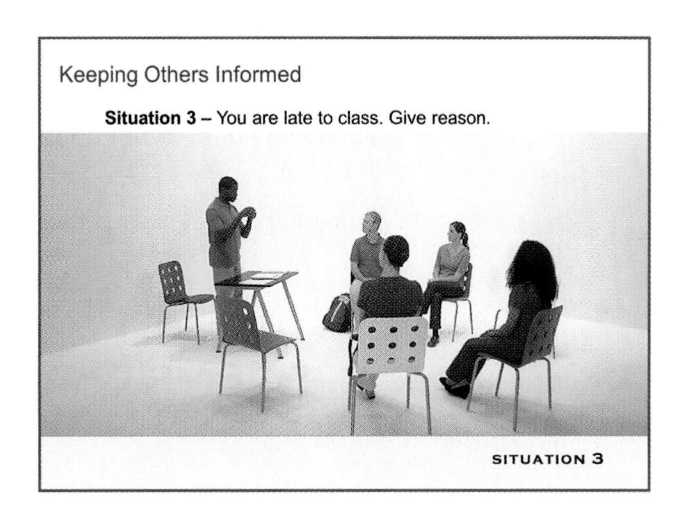

Point out:

- **being prepared to explain.** JT watching Melvin (teacher), ready to explain why he was late after he got the teacher's attention. Had Melvin not noticed him, JT would have sat down.

Have students give other reasons for arriving to class late.
Be sure they follow this structure:

S: SORRY, ME **BE-LATE.** (give reason) SORRY.

Have students give other reasons for arriving to class late.

Possible reasons (and possible phrases to introduce):

- missing the bus (MISS #BUS)
- stuck in traffic ((2h)PCL:5 *"slow stop and go traffic"*)
- being picked up late (FRIEND LATE, PICK-UP-me)
- having a flat tire (fs-TIRE FLAT-TIRE).

PRESENT
LESSON SLIDE 9:13:4)

Point out:

- **when to start.** Suzanne begins her explanation as soon as Melvin (teacher) notices her approaching him.

Have students give other reasons for not coming to next class.

Be sure they follow this structure:

t — neg

S: IN-FUTURE (date), ME CAN'T COME-TO-here CLASS, ME [MUST] (give reason).

Have students give other reasons for not coming to next class. Possible reasons and possible phrases to introduce:

- flying out of town [FLY-TO (place)]
- having an appointment [APPOINTMENT]
- need to take someone somewhere else [TAKE-FROM-person's location, DROP-OFF-place or GO-TO-place].

PRACTICE *Explaining Tardiness or Absences*

20–30 minutes

Students will practice culturally appropriate behaviors to inform the teacher the reasons for their absences or tardiness.

PRESENT
(LESSON SLIDE 9:13:5)

Keeping Others Informed

Situation 1
You were absent from the last class. Give reason.

Situation 2
You will leave class early. Give reason.

Situation 3
You are late to class. Give reason.

Situation 4
You will be absent from the next class. Give reason.

Divide the class into four groups. Assign each group a situation. Give the groups a few minutes to brainstorm the reasons and rehearse their assigned situations.

When ready, call one student at a time to role play their situation with you. To give students added attention-getting practice, vary what you do when they approach you, such as:

- reading a book
- talking to another student
- using your pager/Smart phone
- grading papers.

Be sure students follow these structures:

Situation 1

rhet (over WHY)

S: IN-PAST (day of last class), ME CLASS MISS, WHY, (give reason), SORRY.

Situation 2

when (over ME INFORM-you TODAY (time))

S: ME INFORM-you TODAY (time), ME MUST LEAVE-FROM, (give reason).

Situation 3

S: SORRY, ME BE-LATE. (give reason) SORRY.

Situation 4

t (over IN-FUTURE (date)); neg (over ME CAN'T COME-TO-here CLASS)

S: IN-FUTURE (date), ME CAN'T COME-TO-here CLASS, ME [MUST] (give reason)

HOMEWORK

Tell students to do **Homework 9:13** (*Student Workbook*, pages 230–231).

LESSON 9:14

Comprehension: Stop the Traffic

Lesson length: 30–35 minutes

LESSON GOAL

Students will develop comprehension and production skills through the story **Stop the Traffic**.

KEY SKILLS

For comprehension: Students will develop the ability to process larger chunks of information and figure out the meaning of a sign from context.

NOTIONS

For production: Student will build fluency by re-telling the story or by asking questions about the story.

Vocabulary

Possible new signs in the story:

EMPTY++	!TRAFFIC!
GO-ACROSS	MELT/DISSOLVE
TIME-arc+++	!RIGHT!

PREPARATION

- View the story **Stop the Traffic** on **Lesson Slide 9:14:1**.
- Decide which **Comprehension** and/or **Production** activities to use.

MATERIALS

9:14 Lesson Slides
9:14 Follow-up Slides

HOMEWORK 9:14

Student Workbook, pages 232–237

INTRODUCE *Stop the Traffic*

5 minutes

PRESENT
(LESSON SLIDE 9:14:1)

Show the story. Then, do one of the options below.

Comprehension:

- quiz (page 453)
- answer questions (page 454)

Production:

- develop questions to ask (page 456)
- re-tell the story (page 456)
- change details of the story (page 456)

COMPREHENSION

15–30 minutes

Students will develop the ability to process larger chunks of information and figure out the meaning of a sign from context.

QUIZ (15–30 minutes)

Students write down the information given in the story. Collect papers and grade their papers using FC (full credit), PC (partial credit) or NC (no credit).

FC (full credit) = details are accurate and complete; one or two minor details may be missing, such as what gender Suzanne's baby was.

PC (partial credit) = sufficient details to show satisfactory comprehension of story, actions or cause/effect, but few significant details missing or incorrect, such as why the car was parked off-campus rather than at the faculty lot on-campus or that the person was in a hurry that day

NC (no credit) = does not show sufficient comprehension of story, actions or cause/effect to follow along.

Return the papers. Pair off "FC" with "PC" or "NC" students.

- Give the "FC" students a minute to read their own papers to review the story.
- Have the "PC" students ask the "FC" students questions to find out what they got wrong or missed and make corrections on their papers.
- Have the "FC" students sign the story so the "NC" students can rewrite their papers.

Check the "PC" or "NC" students' corrected papers.

ANSWER QUESTIONS (20-30 minutes)

First, pair off students and have them fill each other in on what happened in the story. If there is anything in the story they don't understand, have them ask other students to get clarification.

Then, ask the following questions:

1. t whq whq
WOMAN PARK WHERE, WHY
Answer. On the street in a residential area. Because parking at the college garage is expensive.
2. when whq
WOMAN WALK GO-TO SCHOOL, PROBLEM "what"
Answer. One street is very busy. She has to wait at the corner until there are no cars approaching, then make a run for it.
3. t
SUMMER, WOMAN IX"*Suzanne*" WALK GO-ACROSS EASY,
whq
WHY
Answer. She was pregnant. When drivers saw a pregnant woman standing at the corner, they stopped to let her cross.

when

4: WOMAN GIVE-BIRTH FINISH, GO-ACROSS STREET, EASY,

whq

HARD, WHICH

Answer. Hard.

t

5: ONE+DAY, WOMAN BE-LATE GIVE-TO TEST, "what"

whq

HAPPEN

Answer. She took off her jacket, stuffed it under her shirt to make her look pregnant. Sure enough, all the cars stopped to let, "the pregnant woman" cross.

t whq

6: WOMAN ARRIVE CLASS LATE, HOW-MANY MINUTE

Answer. One minute late.

Show video again. Make sure students understand these possible new signs. If needed, use one of the strategies below to explain the meaning.

- list things in a category (for category signs)
- give the opposite sign if known
- describe or act out situation
- give definition using familiar signs

EMPTY++ (available)

!TRAFFIC!

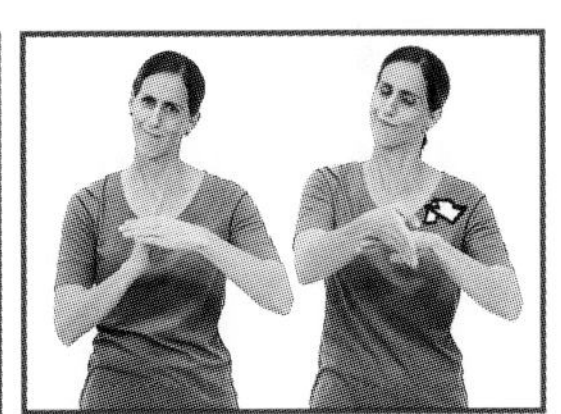

GO-ACROSS

MELT/DISSOLVE

TIME-ARC+++ (pressed for time)

!RIGHT! (as expected, sure enough, I was right)

PRODUCTION

15 minutes

Students will build fluency by re-telling the story or by asking questions about the story.

After showing the video, and making sure students understand the story and all the signs, choose one of these activities:

- **DEVELOP QUESTIONS TO ASK** (20–30 minutes)
  Pair up students. Tell one student to develop true or false questions and the other wh-word questions. Have them ask each other questions.

- **RE-TELL STORY** (15–20 minutes)
  Pair up students and have them tell each other the story.

- **CHANGE DETAILS OF THE STORY** (30–40 minutes)
  Pair up students and have them collaborate to change the details of the story. For example, change the job, the reason for the hurry, or how the traffic was stopped. Then, have students mingle and tell their versions of the story.

HOMEWORK

Tell students to do **Homework 9:14** (*Student Workbook*, pages 232–237).

HOMEWORK FOLLOW-UP

Review answers to **The Hitchhiker** (*Student Workbook*, pages 232–233).

Option 1: show answers on **Follow-up Slides 9:14:1–19** and have students check their answers in workbook.

Option 2: for more language practice, sign the questions from the workbook and have students sign their answers. For example:

For "*1. Describe the hitchhiker.*"

t whq

T: MAN HITCHHIKE FACE+SAME-AS "what"

Answer: A bald headed man with a bushy beard, wearing a plaid shirt and carrying a backpack.

For "*2. Describe the driver.*"

t whq

T: DRIVE+ER FACE+SAME-AS "what"

Answer: A man with a crewcut and wearing a white shirt with a bowtie; he is Deaf.

For "*3. How did the hitchhiker and the driver communicate with each other?*"

t t

T: HEARING MAN, DEAF MAN, THEY-TWO

whq

COMMUNICATE HOW

Answer: Using gesturing and paper and pen.

For "*4. Where did the hitchhiker want to go?*"

t whq

T: MAN HITCHHIKE WANT GO-TO WHERE

Answer: Las Vegas

For "*5. What did the driver see in the rearview mirror?*"

t

T: DRIVE+ER <rs:driver LOOK-AT-mirror MIRROR>,

whq

SEE "what"

Answer: Patrol car lights, flashing sirens.

For "*6. Why was he pulled over?*"

t whq

T: CAR (2h)SCL:3*"cars being pulled over"* WHY

Answer: He was driving too fast (90 mph).

For "*7. How did they communicate?*"

t t whq

T: POLICE, DRIVE+ER THEY-TWO COMMUNICATE HOW++

Answer: By gesturing.

For "*8. What did the driver and the cop say to each other?*"

T: POLICE, DRIVE+ER THEY-TWO SAY "what" (t: POLICE; t: DRIVE+ER; whq: "what")

Answer: After realizing the driver was Deaf, the cop told him to slow down and observe the speed limit. To which the driver said "sure thing."

For "*9. What was the hitchhiker's reaction?*"

T: HEARING MAN IX"*hitchhiker*" RESPOND/ANSWER HOW++ (t: HEARING MAN IX"*hitchhiker*"; whq: HOW++)

Answer: He was astonished that the driver was excused.

For "*10. Why did the two switch places?*"

T: HEARING, DEAF THEY-TWO (2h)SCL:V"*switch places*" WHY (t: HEARING; t: DEAF; whq: WHY)

Answer: The driver got tired and wanted to sleep.

For "*11. How fast was the second driver going when stopped by the policeman?*"

T: HEARING MAN IX"*hitchhiker*" FAST+++ POLICE (2h)SCL:3"*cars being pulled over.*" MAN DRIVE HOW-MANY fs-MPH (t: HEARING MAN IX"*hitchhiker*"; whq: HOW-MANY fs-MPH)

Answer: He was speeding...at 90 mph.

For "*12. When the second driver was stopped by the police, what did he plan to do?*"

T: POLICE (2h)SCL:3"*cars being pulled over*" HEARING MAN IX"*hitchhiker*" PLAN "what" (whq: "what")

Answer: Pretend he is deaf.

For *"13. Why did his plan not work?"*

t

T: MAN IX*"hitchhiker"* PLAN NOT SUCCEED, (FAIL or

whq

BREAKDOWN) WHY

Answer: When the cop used ASL with the hitchhiker, he couldn't respond.

For *"14. What did he get?"*

t whq

T: MAN IX*"hitchhiker"* GET "what"

Answer: A speeding ticket.

For *"15. What can we learn from this story?"*

whq

T: YOU LOOK-AT-story STORY, YOU LEARN "what"

Possible Answer: It doesn't pay to pretend to be someone you are not. It doesn't pay to lie. It is not a good idea to try to fool the cops.

UNIT 9 REVIEW

Putting It All Together

Lesson length: 95–130 minutes

LESSON GOAL

The student will practice:

- translating and asking yes-no questions
- understanding the fingerspelling of names of places
- clock numbers, question forms and descriptions.

NOTIONS

Vocabulary

vocabulary previously learned

MATERIALS

9UR Lesson Slides

Exercise 4 (*Student Workbook*, page 496)

Exercise 5A and **5B** (*Student Workbook*, pages 498–499)

HOMEWORK

Student Workbook, page 238 (**Self-Assessment**)

PRACTICE *Yes–No Questions*

20-30 minutes

Students practice translating and asking yes–no questions.

PRESENT
(LESSON SLIDE 9:UR:1)

Write questions beginning with the following:

1. Have you been to (place)...?
2. Have you ever tried (eating a certain food or doing a certain activity)...?
3. Do you know how to...?
4. Do you like to...?
5. Can you (name a skill or activity)...?
6. Do you have more than (number of something)...?

Translate the questions into ASL—remember to begin with the topic, then state the question.

When students are done writing their questions, put them into small groups to ask each other their questions in ASL. Everyone in the group is to give an elaborated answer to all questions asked.

Conclude. Have students ask you one of their questions. Give elaborated answers.

Be sure students:

- raise head and brows to name the topic
- lean head forward and raise brows to ask the question.

PRACTICE *Write the Names*

30–40 minutes

Students practice understanding the fingerspelling of names of places.

PRESENT
(LESSON SLIDES 9:UR:2–11)

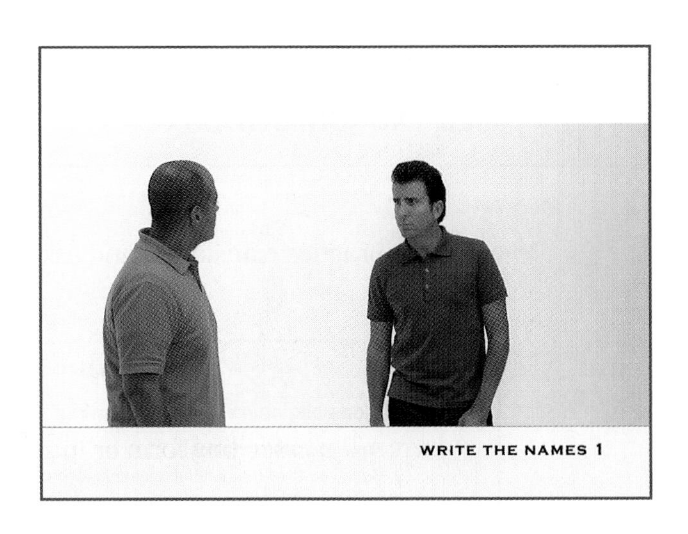

EXERCISE 4: WRITE THE NAMES.

Show video **Write the Names 1**. Continue with **Slides 2–11** and have students write in answers (*Student Workbook*, page 496).

Explain any signs in the videos that students may not be familiar with, for example, **FREQUENT-TO, !STRONG!** (coffee), and **JOIN-IN**.

PRESENT
(LESSON SLIDES 9:UR:12–21)

Write the Names

Topic	Names	
1. grocery store	Whole Foods	Safeway

Show **Slides 12–21** to confirm answers then have students fingerspell the names. Correct their forms if needed.

Conclude. Ask students which store or place they frequent in a category.

- grocery stores
- furniture stores
- gas stations

FREQUENT-TO

- exercise facilities
- clothes stores
- restaurants

Correct fingerspelling form or introduce sign for the store or place, if any. For example:

t (over CLOTHES+STORE) whq (over WHICH)

T: CLOTHES+STORE, YOU **FREQUENT-TO**, WHICH
S: (tell which)
T: (correct fingerspelling form or introduce sign for the store)

PRACTICE *Does the Alibi Hold Up?*

45–60 minutes

Students practice clock numbers, question forms and descriptions.

EXERCISE 5A AND 5B

Assign half of the class **Exercise 5A: Investigators** and the other half **Exercise 5B: Suspects** (*Student Workbook*, pages 498–499).

Have them pair off within the group and follow instructions in the workbook. They are to deal with this situation:

A crime had occurred three days ago between 8 A.M. and 6 P.M. Someone had broken into a house in the neighborhood and stole a valuable painting.

Give the pairs 10–15 minutes to prepare.

The pairs of suspects are to create a *detailed accounting* of their activities together on the day of the crime to avoid being accused of the crime. Encourage pairs of suspects to predict questions that the investigators might ask them and to have answers ready for them.

The pairs of investigators are to develop *detailed questions* to find discrepancies in the suspects' accounting of the day they spent together. Encourage pairs of investigators to come up with questions that may uncover discrepancies in their answers.

Interviews. When done, combine pairs of investigators with pairs of suspects to make groups of four. Have one of the investigators interview one of the suspects and the other investigator interview the other suspect separately. Give them 10–15 minutes for the interviews.

Review. After the interview, have each pair of investigators get together to compare notes on their suspects to find any discrepancies in their answers. Likewise, have each pair of suspects get together to discuss how the interviews went.

Conclude. Reconvene the class and have investigators share the discrepancies they found. Then have the whole class vote on the pair of suspects who they think is most suspicious, meaning, the pair with the most discrepancies.

HOMEWORK

Tell students to do **Homework 9:UR** (*Student Workbook*, page 238).

UNIT 10

Giving Opinions About Others

LESSON 10:1

Giving Opinions about Tendencies

Lesson length: 75–105 minutes

LESSON GOAL

Students will sign these dialogues:

Dialogue A

A: tell about your tendency, ask if it is the same for B[1]

B: respond

- affirm, tell that it is the same for you[2]
- negate, tell how you are different[3]

Dialogue B

A: tell about tendency of someone you know, ask if it is the same for the person B knows[1]

B: respond

- affirm, tell that it is the same for B's person[2]
- negate, tell how B's person is different[3]

KEY PHRASES

[1] ME (or person) TEND-TO (describe tendency when doing something)

q (over: YOU (or person) SAME-AS)

YOU (or person) SAME-AS

nodding (over: YES, ME (or person) SAME-AS)

[2] YES, ME (or person) SAME-AS

neg (over: #NO)

[3] #NO, ME (or person) TEND-TO (describe opposite tendency or behavior)

NOTIONS

Grammar

temporal aspect

Vocabulary

Punctuality

being on time	*attendance*
TIME++	GO-TO++
LATE++	SKIP-WORK++

Approach to Work

hardworking	*completion of tasks*
serious WORK-char	COMPLETE++
th (2h)alt.PLAY++	th POSTPONE++

focused

serious
!PAY-ATTENTION!

th
LOOK-AT-up-cont

Level of Accountability

responsibility	*carefulness*
GOOD BE-RESPONSIBLE++	serious BE-CAREFUL
neg NOT+BE-RESPONSIBLE++	th (2h)BE-CARELESS

organized/orderly	*money matters*
IN-GEAR++	GOOD MONEY+EXCHANGE
MESSED-UP	BE-BROKE++

Relating to Others

extrovert/introvert	*supportive*
QUIET++	mm SUPPORT++
BASHFUL++	CRITICIZE/CORRECT++
TALK++, CHAT++, MEET++	

encouraging

mm
ENCOURAGE
mm
BE-POSITIVE++
(2h)alt.INSULT
BE-NEGATIVE++

amiable/agreeable

GET-ALONG-WITH
AGREE-with++
DISAGREE++
COMPLAIN++

directness

STRAIGHT-TALK-TO
VAGUE-TALK-TO

honesty

BE-HONEST
LIE++

sharing

mm
SHARE++
SELFISH++

respect one's privacy

RESPECT-TO
NOSE-IN++

respect one's things

LEAVE-ALONE++
th
TOUCH++

others

TEND-TO
TRUST
EVADE++
FLICK-SHOULDER++
!CLEAN!
th
(2h)alt."pshaw"
MINGLE

PREPARATION Review main points of the lesson in **Key Grammar: Temporal Aspect**, *Student Workbook*, pages 242–243

MATERIALS **10:1 Lesson Slides**
10:1 Follow-up Slides

HOMEWORK 10:1 *Student Workbook*, pages 242–251

INTRODUCE *Describing Tendencies*

30–40 minutes

PRESENT
(LESSON SLIDE 10:1:1)

Use temporal aspect to describe
a person's tendency.

Introduce adding **temporal aspect** to a sign to describe a person's tendency. For example, demonstrate this sentence using this sign **GO-TO** (without temporal aspect):

T: **TODAY, MAN IX*"man"* GO-TO CLASS.**

Now, add temporal aspect (repeated movement) to GO-TO to describe a person's tendency to always arrive on time. For example:

T: **MAN IX*"man"* GO-TO++ CLASS, NEVER MISS.**

PRESENT
(LESSON SLIDES 10:1:2–3)

punctuality
- being on time
- **attendance**

rhet

Use situations and 'OPPOSITE "what"' to introduce signs with temporal aspect indicated by "++," "-cont," and "-char."

being on time	*explanation*
ON-TIME++	Person always comes to class by 9:00 A.M. and is never late. Introduce: PERSON IX*"person"* **TIME++**.
LATE++	OPPOSITE "what" (rhet) **LATE++**.

ON-TIME++

LATE++

attendance	*explanation*
GO-TO++	Person always comes to class and never misses a class. Introduce: PERSON IX*"person"* **GO-TO++**.
SKIP-WORK++	OPPOSITE "what" (rhet) **SKIP-WORK++**.

GO-TO++

SKIP-WORK++

PRESENT

(LESSON SLIDES 10:1:4–6)

approach to work and activities

- hardworking (or diligent)
- completion of tasks
- **focused**

WORK-char

hardworking (or diligent)	*explanation*
serious **WORK-char**	Person doesn't stop work until she or he is finished. Work isn't boring to him or her. She or he enjoys working. Introduce: serious PERSON IX*"person"* **WORK-char**.

(2h)alt.PLAY++

th **(2h)alt.PLAY++**	rhet th OPPOSITE "what" **(2h)alt.PLAY++**.

NOTE: Facial expressions add meaning to the sign, helping to convey more specifically the attitude and intention of the person described. Be sure students integrate the appropriate facial expressions with the new signs.

COMPLETE++

POSTPONE++

completion of tasks	*explanation*
COMPLETE++	Every time the boss assigns the person a task, she or he always finish it by the due date. Introduce: PERSON IX"person" **COMPLETE++**.
th **POSTPONE++**	rhet th OPPOSITE "what" **POSTPONE++**.

PAY-ATTENTION++

focused

serious
PAY-ATTENTION++

explanation

Person is always focused on the task, ignores others who try to get his or her attention, ignores all other distractions. Introduce: PERSON IX*"person"*
serious
PAY-ATTENTION++.

LOOK-AT-up-cont

th
LOOK-AT-up-cont

rhet th
OPPOSITE "what" **LOOK-AT-up-cont.**

PRESENT
(LESSON SLIDES 10:1:7–10)

level of accountability
- responsibility
- carefulness
- organized and orderly
- **money matters**

BE-RESPONSIBLE++

responsibility
BE-RESPONSIBLE++

explanation
When the person is given a task, you know she or he will complete it in time. You do not need to watch or remind him or her. This person will not forget the task, will not ignore it. Introduce: PERSON IX*"person"*
BE-RESPONSIBLE++, YOU CAN **TRUST** IX*"person."*

neg
NOT+RESPONSIBLE

rhet neg
OPPOSITE "what" **NOT+RESPONSIBLE** PERSON IX*"person"* **EVADE++**,
th
FLICK-SHOULDER, (2h)alt."pshaw."

BE-CAREFUL

carefulness

serious
BE-CAREFUL

explanation

Two girls are coloring a picture. One girl is careful, making sure she colors within the lines. Introduce:

serious
GIRL IX*"careful one"* **BE-CAREFUL.**

(2h)BE-CARELESS

th
(2h)BE-CARELESS

The other girl is not as careful...she colors outside of the lines. Introduce:

th
GIRL IX*"careless one"* **(2h)BE-CARELESS.**

organized and orderly

IN-GEAR++

explanation

Person arranges and organizes files, and they're easy to find. Introduce: PERSON IX*"person"* GOOD **IN-GEAR++**, ICL*"straighten up paper,"* **!CLEAN!**

IN-GEAR++

MESSED-UP++

MESSED-UP++

Person leaves paper scattered around and doesn't put them in files. Introduce:

th
PERSON IX*"person"* **(2h)alt."pshaw,"** TEND-TO ICL*"throw things around"* **MESSED-UP++.**

money matters

GOOD MONEY +EXCHANGE++

explanation

Person is responsible with money, careful with money, always pay bills. At end of month, has some money left. Introduce: PERSON IX*"person"* **GOOD MONEY+EXCHANGE++**

GOOD MONEY+EXCHANGE++

BE-BROKE++

BE-BROKE++

rhet
OPPOSITE "what" **BE-BROKE++** PERSON IX*"person"* CAN'T PAY fs-BILLS.

Review. Give a sign, and ask students to give the opposite. For example,

whq
T: TIME++, OPPOSITE "what"
S: LATE++

Repeat procedure with the signs below.

signs	***opposites***
GO-TO++	SKIP-WORK++
serious WORK-char	th (2h)alt.PLAY++
COMPLETE++	th POSTPONE++
serious PAY-ATTENTION++	th LOOK-AT-up-cont
BE-RESPONSIBLE++	neg NOT+RESPONSIBLE
serious BE-CAREFUL	th (2h)BE-CARELESS
IN-GEAR++	MESSED-UP++
GOOD MONEY+EXCHANGE++	BE-BROKE++

INTRODUCE *Describing Tendencies 2*

30–40 minutes

PRESENT
(LESSON SLIDES 10:1:11–19)

relating to others
- extrovert or introvert
- supportive
- encouraging
- honest
- direct
- amiable and agreeable
- sharing
- respects one's privacy
- **respects one's things**

TALK++

CHAT++

MEET++

MINGLE

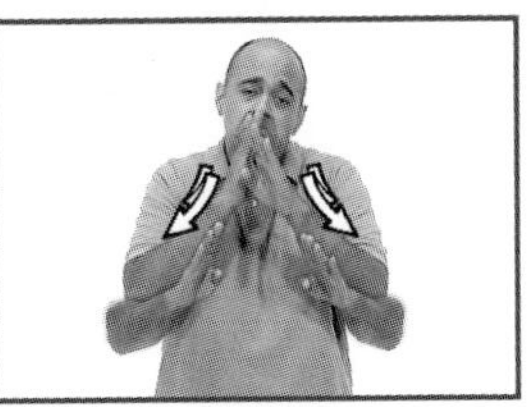
QUIET++

BASHFUL

extrovert or introvert	*explanation*
TALK++, CHAT++ **MEET++, MINGLE**	Person who likes to meet people and have conversations. Introduce: PERSON IX*"person"* **TALK++, CHAT++, MEET++, MINGLE.**
QUIET++ **BASHFUL**	rhet: OPPOSITE "what" PERSON **QUIET++**, SIT, MAYBE **BASHFUL.**

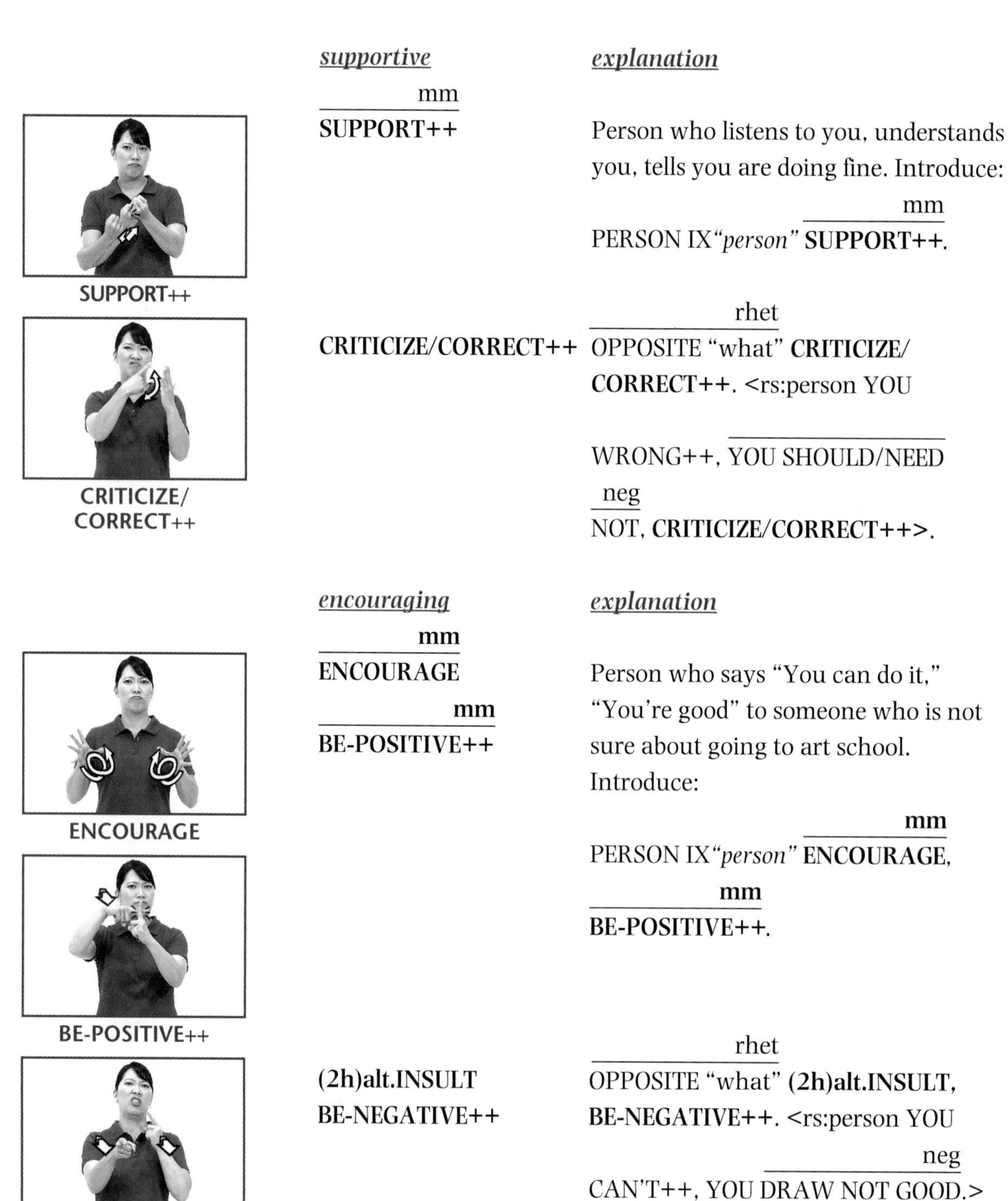

SUPPORT++

CRITICIZE/
CORRECT++

ENCOURAGE

BE-POSITIVE++

INSULT

BE-NEGATIVE++

supportive

mm
SUPPORT++

explanation

Person who listens to you, understands you, tells you are doing fine. Introduce:

mm
PERSON IX*"person"* **SUPPORT++.**

CRITICIZE/CORRECT++

rhet
OPPOSITE "what" **CRITICIZE/CORRECT++.** <rs:person YOU WRONG++, YOU SHOULD/NEED

neg
NOT, **CRITICIZE/CORRECT++**>.

encouraging

mm
ENCOURAGE

mm
BE-POSITIVE++

explanation

Person who says "You can do it," "You're good" to someone who is not sure about going to art school. Introduce:

mm
PERSON IX*"person"* **ENCOURAGE,**

mm
BE-POSITIVE++.

(2h)alt.INSULT
BE-NEGATIVE++

rhet
OPPOSITE "what" **(2h)alt.INSULT, BE-NEGATIVE++.** <rs:person YOU

neg
CAN'T++, YOU DRAW NOT GOOD.>
IX*"person"* **(2h)alt.INSULT, BE-NEGATIVE++.**

BE-HONEST

honest

BE-HONEST

explanation

A boy took Mommy's ring. She asks him if he took the ring. He says yes, he did. Introduce: BOY IX*"boy"* **BE-HONEST**.

LIE++

LIE++

Again, the boy took Mommy's ring. This time, he denied taking the ring. Introduce: BOY IX*"boy"* **LIE**.

cond
AGAIN, AGAIN, IX*"boy"* LIE++.

For "• *direct*"

STRAIGHT-TALK-TO

STRAIGHT-TALK-TO

When asked what she or he thinks of the hair color (dyed red), person responds to person with the dyed hair "I don't like the color." Introduce: PERSON IX*"person"* **STRAIGHT-TALK-TO**.

VAGUE-TALK-TO

VAGUE-TALK-TO

rhet
OPPOSITE "what" VAGUE-TALK-TO.

amiable and agreeable

EASY GET-ALONG-WITH
AGREE-with++

explanation

Two roommates live together. They never quarrel. They are fine with what the other person does or wants to do. Introduce: THEY-TWO **[EASY] GET-ALONG-WITH, AGREE-with++**.

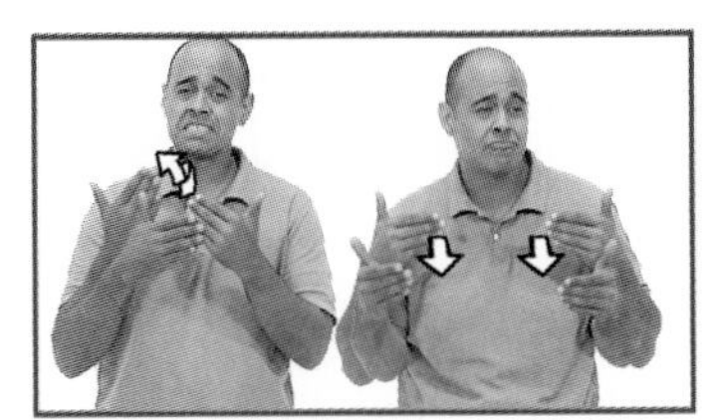

EASY GET-ALONG-WITH

AGREE-with++

DISAGREE++

COMPLAIN++

DISAGREE++
COMPLAIN++

They get another roommate. Turns out the new roommate doesn't like the house rules. Disagrees with the assigned tasks. Introduce: PERSON IX*"person"* **DISAGREE++**. He does not like and constantly criticizes the neighbors, the noise, and roommates' messes. Introduce: PERSON IX*"person"* **COMPLAIN++.**

sharing

explanation

SHARE++

mm
SHARE++

Person who always lets others use his things (car, camera, computer), or gives you half of his sandwich, for example.

mm
PERSON IX*"person"* **SHARE++.**

SELFISH++

SELFISH++

rhet
OPPOSITE "what," **SELFISH++.**

RESPECT-TO*"person"*

respects one's privacy
RESPECT-TO*"person"*

explanation

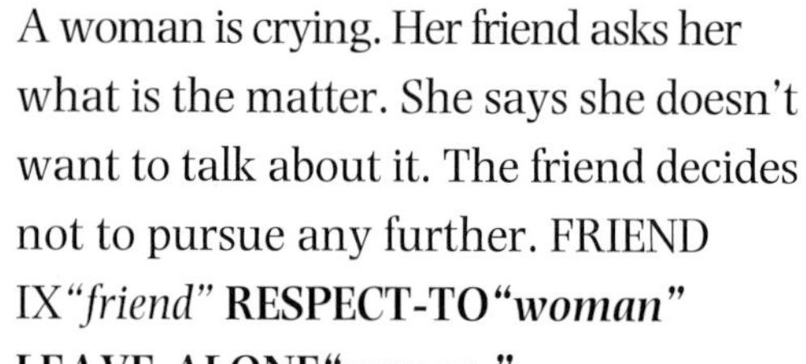
A woman is crying. Her friend asks her what is the matter. She says she doesn't want to talk about it. The friend decides not to pursue any further. FRIEND IX*"friend"* **RESPECT-TO*"woman"* LEAVE-ALONE*"person."***

NOSE-IN++

NOSE-IN++

rhet
OPPOSITE "what,"
NOSE-IN++, (2h)alt.ASK-TO++
neg
NONE RESPECT-TO.

respects one's things	*explanation*
LEAVE-ALONE++	Two girls visit their aunt's house. One girl sits, asks before touching things, asks permission before taking a piece of candy from a bowl. Introduce: GIRL IX*"girl"* **LEAVE-ALONE++, RESPECT-TO.**
th **TOUCH++**	The other girl is not as respectful. She takes candy from the bowl, touches things on the table without permission. th GIRL IX*"other girl"* **TOUCH++,** neg **TAKE-FROM++, NONE RESPECT-TO.**

LEAVE-ALONE++

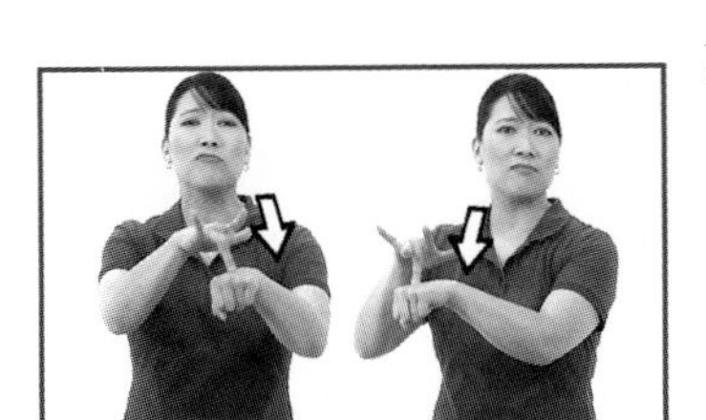
TOUCH++

Review. Give a sign, and ask students to give the opposite. For example,

t whq
T: QUIET++, BASHFUL, OPPOSITE "what"
S: TALK++, CHAT++, MEET++, MINGLE

Repeat procedure with the signs below.

signs	*opposites*
mm SUPPORT++	CRITICIZE/CORRECT++
mm ENCOURAGE, mm BE-POSITIVE++	(2h)alt.INSULT, BE-NEGATIVE++
BE-HONEST	LIE++
STRAIGHT-TALK-TO	VAGUE-TALK-TO
[EASY] GET-ALONG-WITH, AGREE-with++	DISAGREE++, COMPLAIN++

mm SHARE++	SELFISH++
RESPECT-TO	NOSE-IN++
LEAVE-ALONE++	th TOUCH++

PRACTICE *Comparing with Someone Else*

15–25 minutes

Students practice describing tendencies using temporal aspects.

PRESENT
(LESSON SLIDE 10:1:20)

Compare yourself with your partner.

A: tell about your tendency, ask if it is the same for B
B: respond
- *affirm, tell that it is the same for you*
- *negate, tell how you are different*

Demonstrate the dialogue by calling up one student to role play Signer B. You role play Signer A.

when
A: ME GO-TO-arc PARTY, ME **TEND-TO** QUIET++, BASHFUL.
q
YOU SAME-AS

nodding
B: (affirm) YES, me-SAME-AS-you

or neg
B: (negate) #NO, ME TEND-TO TALK++, CHAT++, MEET++

Have the whole class rehearse Signer A's line. Be ready to explain TEND-TO if students don't know the sign.

Call another student to role play Signer B. Demonstrate the dialogue again with different signs.

A: PEOPLE (2h)alt.ASK-TO-me++, (when) ME THINK "what," (whq) SUPPOSE ME NOT AGREE, (cond) ME **TEND-TO** RESPOND/ANSWER, VAGUE-TALK-TO, YOU SAME-AS (q)

B: (affirm) YES, ME SAME-AS (nodding)

or

B: (negate) #NO, (neg) ME TEND-TO STRAIGHT-TALK-TO

Have the whole class rehearse Signer A's line.

Group. Put students in groups of three. Have each person take turns role playing Signer A and asking the question. Have the two others answer the question.

Be sure students:

- use temporal aspect to describe the tendency
- integrate facial expressions with the sign
- use the sign SAME-AS without using verb agreement (orienting sign to agree with the person).

PRESENT

(LESSON SLIDE 10:1:21)

Compare two other people.

A: tell about a tendency of someone you know, ask if it is the same for a person B knows

B: respond

- *affirm, tell that it is the same for the person you know*
- *negate, tell how the person you know is different*

Demonstrate the dialogue by calling up one student to role play Signer B. You role play Signer A.

A: MY MOTHER TEND-TO POSTPONE++,

q

YOUR MOTHER SAME-AS

nodding

B: (affirm) YES, MY MOTHER SAME-AS

or neg

B: (negate) #NO, MY MOTHER TEND-TO COMPLETE++

Have the whole class rehearse Signer A's line.

Call another student to role play Signer B. Demonstrate the dialogue again with different signs.

A: MY BOSS TEND-TO ENCOURAGE++, SUPPORT++, YOUR

q

BOSS SAME-AS

nodding

B: (affirm) YES, MY BOSS SAME-AS

or neg

B: (negate) #NO, MY BOSS NOT SUPPORT++, ALWAYS CRITICIZE++, BE-NEGATIVE++

Have the whole class rehearse Signer A's line.

Group. Again, put students in groups of three. Have each person take turns role playing Signer A and asking the question. Have the two others answer the question.

Be sure students:

- use temporal aspect to describe the tendency
- integrate facial expressions with the sign
- use the sign SAME-AS without using verb agreement (orienting sign to agree with the person).

HOMEWORK

Tell students to do **Homework 10:1** (*Student Workbook*, pages 242–251).

Also, students are to define six English words using signs they have learned, opposite signs and describing behavior or situations to illustrate the tendency (See **Assignment**, *Student Workbook*, page 245).

HOMEWORK FOLLOW-UP
30–45 MINUTES

PRESENT
(FOLLOW-UP SLIDES 10:1:1–9)

Minidialogue 1

1. Why does John suggest to David they trade roommates?

2. Why do you think David responds the way he does?

Check students' answers to **Minidialogues 1–3**. See **Introduction** pages xviii–xix for different ways to check answers.

PRESENT
(FOLLOW-UP SLIDE 10:1:10)

Define these English words:

1. cautious
2. unreliable
3. friendly
4. trustworthy
5. tidy
6. bashful

Strategies to use:

- explain the meaning of the word by using signs you have learned
- use opposite signs to emphasize what the word is not
- describe behavior or a situation to illustrate the tendency.

Group. Put students in groups of three, and have each student take turns defining a word on the slide (See **Assignment**, *Student Workbook*, page 245).

Conclude. Call on students to define a word for you.

Teacher's Guide

1. ***cautious***

[PERSON] BE-CAREFUL INVESTIGATE/CHECK
nod
(2h)alt.LOOK-AT, !DECIDE!

2. ***unreliable***

[PERSON] TELL-TO-me IX*"person"* IN-FUTURE COME-TO-here, ME WAIT-cont. IX*"person"* NOT+COME-TO-here. IX*"person"* ALWAYS SKIP-WORK++. IX*"person"*
neg
NOT BE-RESPONSIBLE++.

3. ***friendly***

[PERSON] LIKE TALK++, CHAT++, MEET++ PEOPLE, EASY GET-ALONG-WITH, IX*"person"* NICE, EASY LIKE.
neg
NOT+AFRAID. IX*"person"* CHEERFUL.

4. ***trustworthy***

PERSON IX*"person"* GOOD RESPONSIBLE++, ME CAN TRUST, ME ASK-TO-person HELP, IX*"person"* IN-FUTURE HELP-me,

neg

ME TELL-TO-person SOMETHING, NOT-WANT OTHER PEOPLE KNOW, IX*"person"* IN-FUTURE NOT TELL-person-arc++.

5. ***tidy***

PERSON ALWAYS !CLEAN!, GOOD IN-GEAR++, (look into dresser, see things are neatly stacked),

neg

NEVER MESSED-UP. IX*"person"* !CLEAN!

6. ***bashful***

t cond

PERSON IX*"person"* QUIET++, MEET++ NEW PEOPLE, IX*"person"* AFRAID++. IX*"person"* BASHFUL.

LESSON 10:2

Numbers: Telling the Price 1

Lesson length: 35–45 minutes

LESSON GOAL Students learn to sign money numbers (cents or dollars).

KEY SKILLS Correct sign formation for cents. (*See* pages 252–254.)
Correct sign formation for dollars. (*See* page 254.)

NOTIONS

Vocabulary

money-related	***ask how much***
DOLLAR	whq
COST	COST HOW-MANY

items	
POPCORN	PENCIL
COUGH+MEDICINE	RUBBER+ERASE
POTATO+fs-CHIPS	DEER STATUE
CANDY	SHOE+STRING
RING	ICL"*spray*" SMELL
POSTAGE-STAMP	GUM
MOVIE TICKET	WHISTLE
MAGNIFYING-GLASS	DCL"T"+SHIRT

PREPARATION Read and view **Numbers: Telling the Price** in *Student Workbook* pages 252–254.

MATERIALS
10:2 Lesson Slides
10:2 Follow-up Slides
Exercise 1 (in *Student Workbook*, page 472)

HOMEWORK 10:2 *Student Workbook*, pages 252–258

INTRODUCE *Cents*

15–20 minutes

PRESENT
(LESSON SLIDES 10:2:1–7)

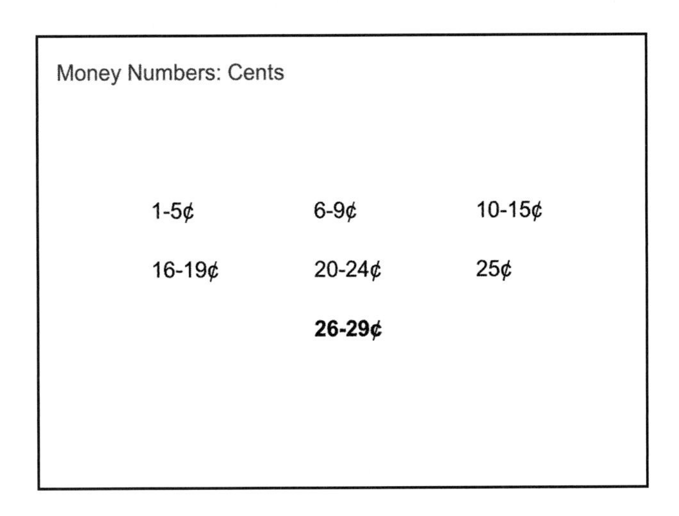

Money Numbers: Cents
1-5¢
6-9¢
10-15¢
16-19¢
20-24¢
25¢
26-29¢

Demonstrate money number forms for cents.
Have students copy you.

For **Slide 1 (1–5¢)**

T: **ONE-CENT, TWO-CENT, THREE-CENT, FOUR-CENT, FIVE-CENT**

S(all): (copy)

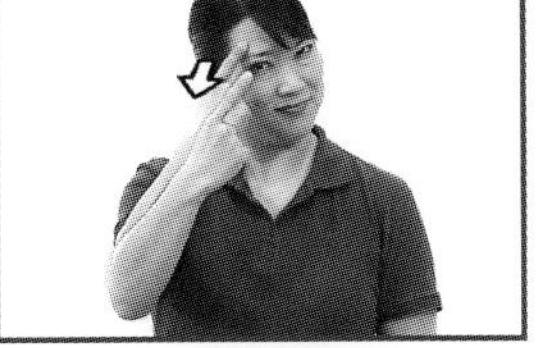
ONE-CENT

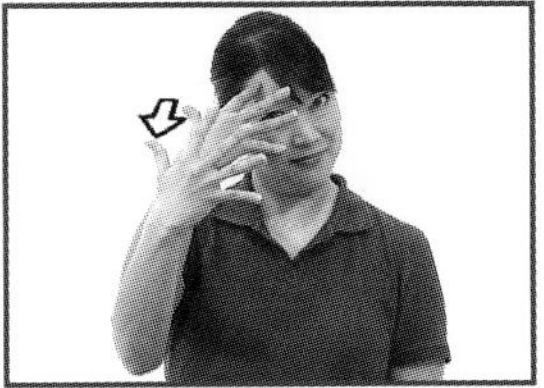
FIVE-CENT

Point out:

- the palm faces in
- the tip of the index finger touches the forehead
- the handshape for the cent number is formed at the forehead and remains the same as the hand moves outward.

SEVEN-CENT

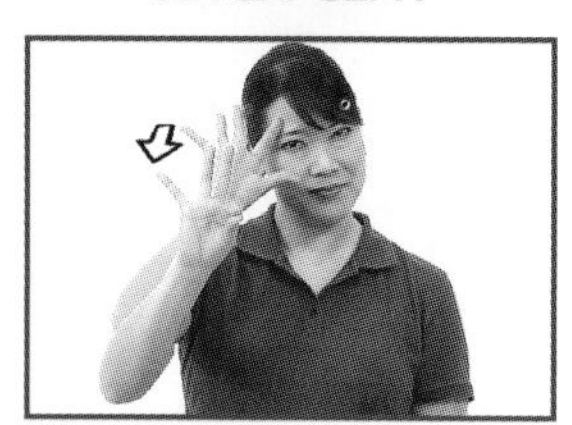
NINE-CENT

Continue introducing number forms for cents for **Lesson Slides 10:2:2–7**.

For **Slide 2 (6–9¢)**

T: SIX-CENT, SEVEN-CENT, EIGHT-CENT, NINE-CENT

S(all): (copy)

Point out:

- the palm faces out
- the side of the index finger touches the forehead
- the handshape for the cent number is formed at the forehead and remains the same as the hand moves outward
- for 9¢, the handshape is modified at the beginning and the side of the index finger contacts the forehead.

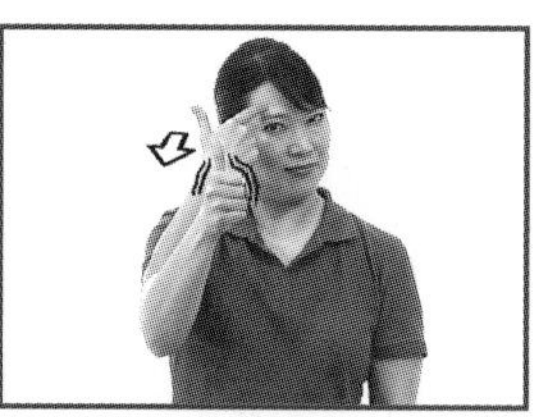
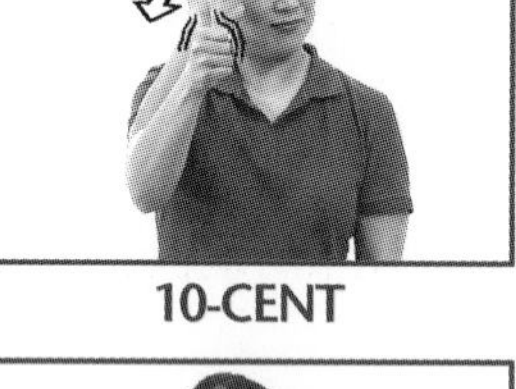
10-CENT

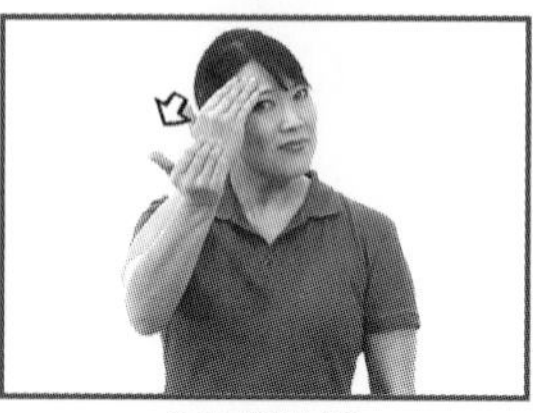
15-CENT

For **Slide 3 (10–15¢)**

T: 10-CENT, 11-CENT, 12-CENT, 13-CENT, 14-CENT, 15-CENT

S(all): (copy)

Point out:

- for 10¢, begin with the "L" handshape, the palm facing in, at the forehead and end with the number 10 as the hand moves outward
- for 11–15¢, the handshape for the cent number is formed at the forehead and remains the same as the hand moves outward
- the tips of the fingers that form the numbers 11–15 touch the forehead.

18-CENT

For **Slide 4 (16–19¢)**

T: 16-CENT, 17-CENT, 18-CENT, 19-CENT

S(all): (copy)

Point out:

- begin with the "L" handshape, the palm facing in, with the tip of the index finger touching the forehead
- as you twist the hand, the palm faces out to form the number 16–19.

20-CENT

For **Slide 5 (20–24¢)**

T: 20-CENT, 21-CENT, 22-CENT, 23-CENT, 24-CENT

S(all): (copy)

Point out:

- begin with the "L" handshape, the palm facing out, with the tip of the index finger touching the forehead
- as the hand moves outward, form the number 20–24.

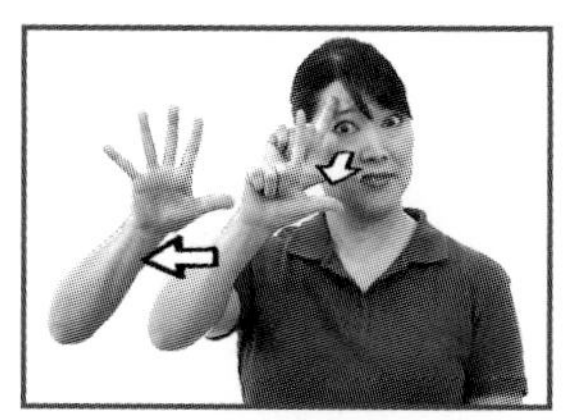
25-CENT (variation 1)

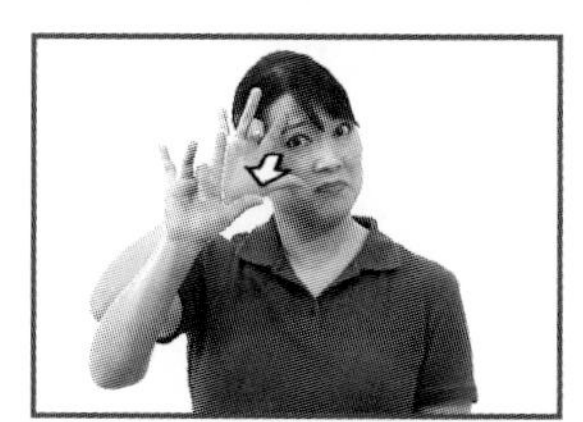
25-CENT (variation 2)

For **Slide 6 (25¢)**

T: 25-CENT (2 variations)

S(all): (copy)

Point out:

- **for variation 1**, begin with the "L" handshape, the palm facing out, with the tip of the index finger touching the forehead and the hand moves outward to form the number 25.
- **for variation 2**, begin with the "5" handshape, the palm facing out, with the side of the index finger touching the forehead and as the hand moves outward, the middle finger wiggles to form the variation for number 25.

For **Slide 7 (26–29¢)**

T: 26-CENT, 27-CENT, 28-CENT, 29-CENT,

S(all): (copy)

Point out:

- **they are formed with the same principles as for cent numbers 21–24¢.**

Review. Point to a set of cents on the slide and have students sign the numbers in that set. For example:

T: (point to 6–9¢)

S: SIX-CENT, SEVEN-CENT, EIGHT-CENT, NINE-CENT

PRESENT
(LESSON SLIDES 10:2:8–11)

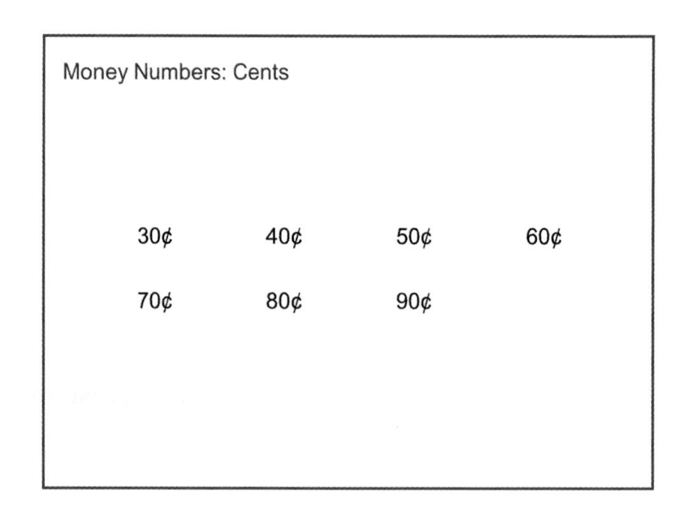

Money Numbers: Cents
30¢
40¢
50¢
60¢
70¢
80¢
90¢

Continue procedure for **Lesson Slides 10:2:8–11.**

For **Slide 8 (30–90¢)**
T: 30-CENT, 40-CENT, 50-CENT, 60-CENT, 70-CENT, 80-CENT, 90-CENT
S(all): (copy)

Point out for multiples of 10:
- for the first digit 3, 4, 5, 6, 7, or 8, the palm faces out, with the side of the index finger touching the forehead
- for the first digit 9, the handshape is modified at the beginning and the side of the index finger contacts the forehead
- as the hand moves outward, form the number 30–90 (repeat the number twice).

For **Slide 9 (33–99¢)**
T: 33-CENT, 44-CENT, 55-CENT, 66-CENT, 77-CENT, 88-CENT, 99-CENT
S(all): (copy)

Point out for multiples of 11:
- for the first digit 3, 4, 5, 6, 7, or 8, the palm faces out, with the tip of the index finger touching the forehead
- for the first digit 9, the handshape is modified at the beginning and the side of the index finger contacts the forehead
- as the hand moves outward, form the number 33–99 (don't forget to bounce the number sideways to the dominant side).

For **Slide 10 (67–89¢)**

T: 67-CENT, 68-CENT, 69-CENT, 78-CENT, 79-CENT, 89-CENT

S(all): (copy)

Point out for rocking numbers 67–89:

- for the first digit 6, 7, or 8, the palm faces out, with the side of the index finger touching the forehead
- as your hand moves outward, form the number. After the first digit (smaller number) twist up to the second digit (larger number).

For **Slide 11 (76–98¢)**

T: 76-CENT, 86-CENT, 87-CENT, 96-CENT, 97-CENT, 98-CENT

S(all): (copy)

Point out for rocking numbers 76–98:

- for the first digit 7, 8, or 9, the palm faces out, with the side of the index finger touching the forehead
- as your hand moves outward, form the number. After the first digit (larger number) twist down to the second digit (smaller number).

PRESENT
(LESSON SLIDES 10:2:12–23)

Money Numbers: Cents

77¢	87¢	76¢
50¢	67¢	44¢
89¢	33¢	98¢
90¢	40¢	**78¢**

Review. Show **Lesson Slides 10:2:12–23** and have students sign the numbers.

INTRODUCE *Dollars*

3–5 minutes

PRESENT
(LESSON SLIDES 10:2:24–25)

Money Numbers: Dollars

$1.00 – $9.00

$10.00

Demonstrate money number forms for dollars. Have students copy you.

For **Slide 24 ($1–9)**

T: **ONE-DOLLAR, TWO-DOLLAR, THREE-DOLLAR, FOUR-DOLLAR, FIVE-DOLLAR, SIX-DOLLAR, SEVEN-DOLLAR, EIGHT-DOLLAR, NINE-DOLLAR**

S(all): (copy)

Point out:

- the palm faces out
- twist the hand in a sweeping arc ending up with the palm facing in.

For **Slide 25 ($10.00)**

T: **TEN DOLLAR**

S(all): (copy)

Point out:

- the movement for number 10 is not repeated
- end with the sign for DOLLAR.

Review. Have students take turns signing a number.

PRACTICE *What Is the Price?*

15–20 minutes

Students practice understanding and signing money numbers.

PRESENT
(LESSON SLIDES 10:2:26–29)

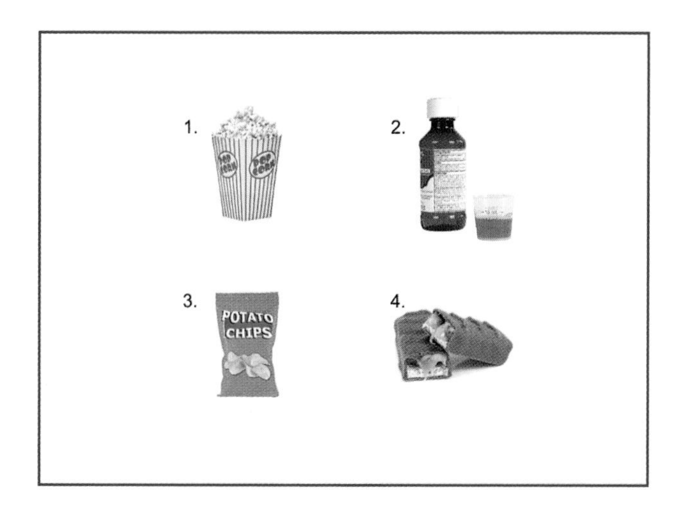

Introduce signs:

For **Slide 26**

POPCORN

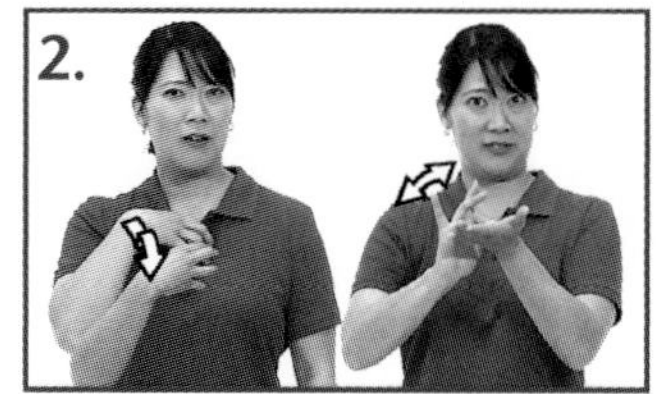

COUGH+MEDICINE

POTATO+fs-CHIPS

CANDY

For **Slide 27**

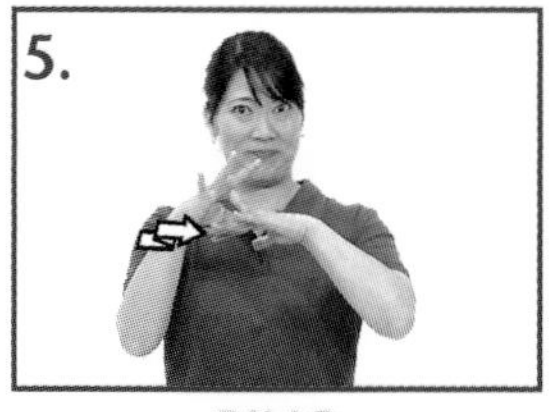

RING

POSTAGE-STAMP

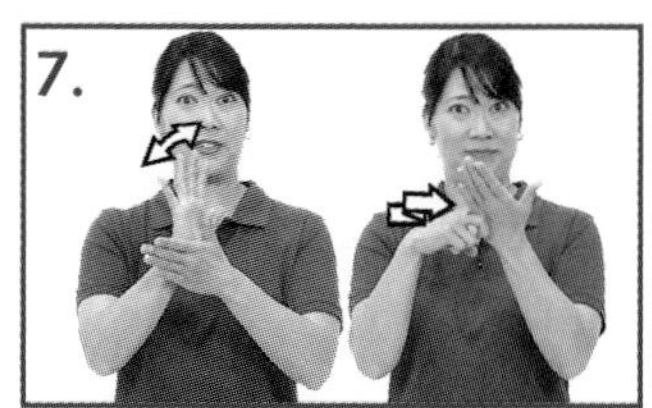

MOVIE TICKET

MAGNIFYING-GLASS

For **Slide 28**

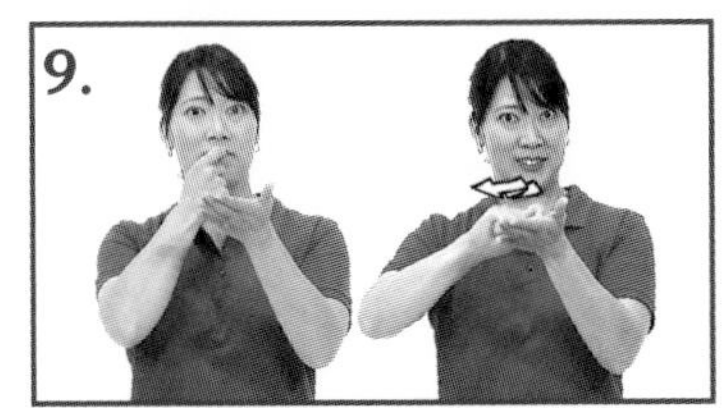

PENCIL

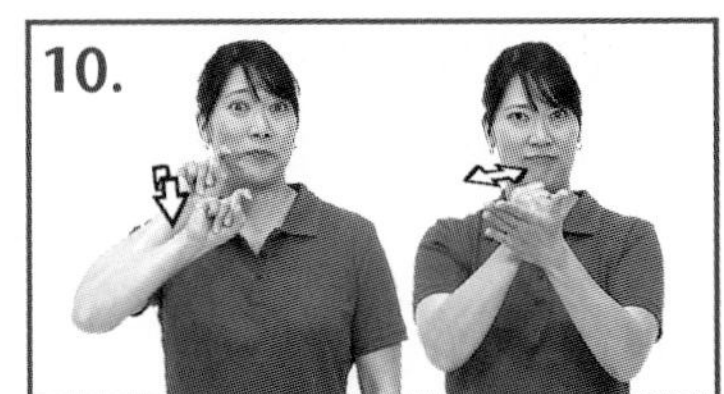

RUBBER+ERASE

DEER STATUE

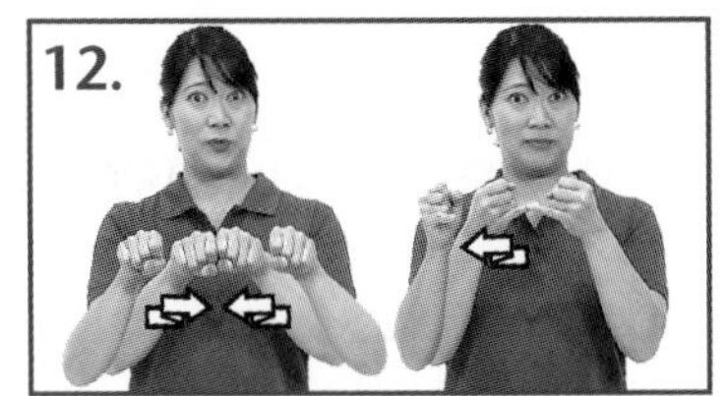

SHOE+STRING

For **Slide 29**

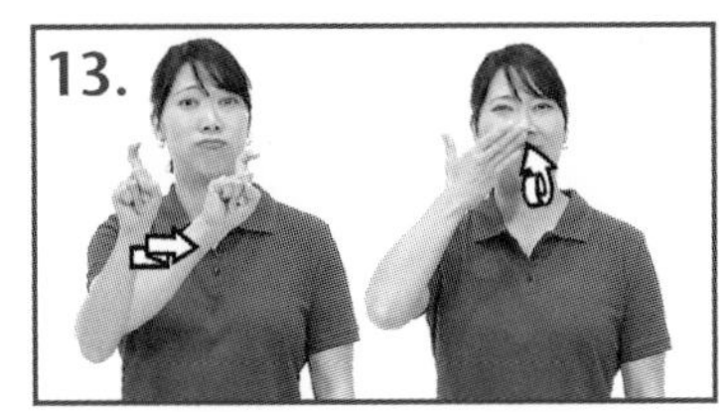

ICL*"spray"* SMELL

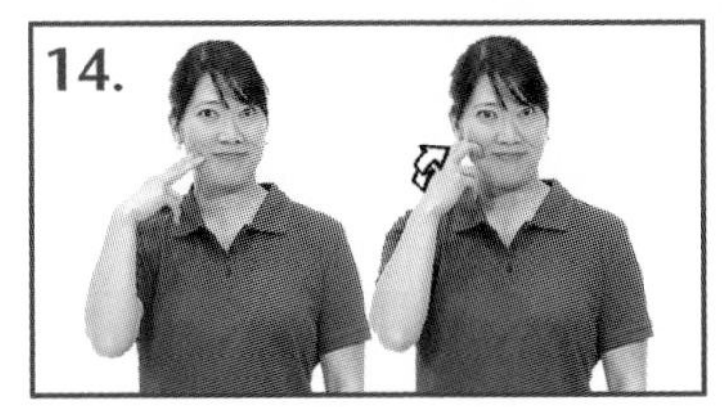

GUM

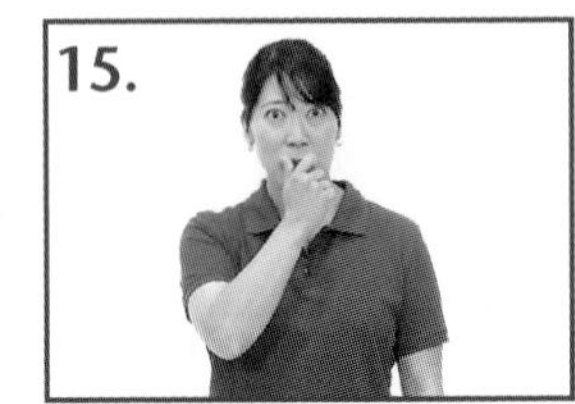

WHISTLE

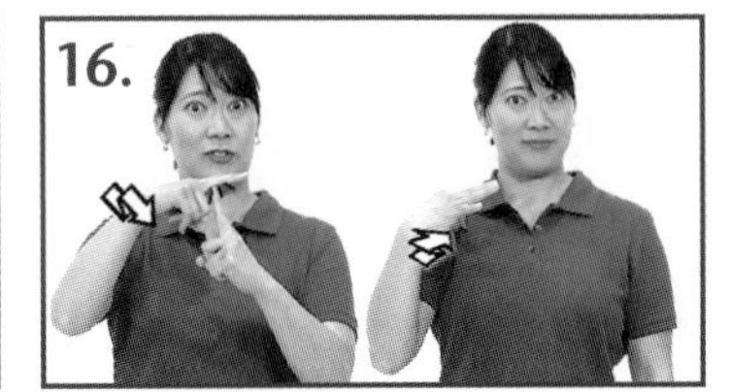

DCL"T"+SHIRT

EXERCISE 1

(*Student Workbook*, page 472)

Have students open their workbook to page 472. Sign the sentences below that include an item and its price. Have students fill in the blanks.

Gum (3¢)

t

T: BUY fs-ABC GUM, **COST 3-CENT.**

T-shirt ($1 and $10)

T: ME BUY DCL"T"+SHIRT, WHITE, ONE-DOLLAR. BORING. ICL*"dye shirt"* ORANGE. ME SELL **TEN DOLLAR.**

COST

Movie ticket ($3)

T: MOVIE TICKET, ME BUY THROUGH INTERNET, COST **THREE-DOLLAR.**

Potato chips (70¢)

t

T: POTATO+fs-CHIPS, fs-BAG SMALL, COST **70-CENT.**

Pencils (10¢ and 99¢)

cond cond

T: PENCIL, BUY 1, **TEN-CENT.** BUY 10, COST **99-CENT.**

Cough medicine ($2)

t

T: COUGH+MEDICINE, ONE ICL*"pour into spoon and put spoon in mouth,"* COST **TWO-DOLLAR.**

Postage stamp (29¢)

T: IN-PAST 19+91, POSTAGE-STAMP, COST **29-CENT.** !CHEAP!

Candy (40¢)

T: CANDY DCL*"candy bar"* [(wh)DCL*"candy bar"*/ICL*"cut in half"* IX*"one piece,"* **40-CENT**]

Deer statue (66¢)

T: ME GO-TO SECOND-HAND STORE, FIND DEER STATUE, !OLD! ME BUY **66-CENT**.

Whistle (87¢)

neg

T: COLLEGE "area" NOT+fs-SAFE, BOOK+STORE IX*"bookstore"* NOW SELL WHISTLE COST **87-CENT**.

Air freshener (79¢)

grimace

T: CAR, ME SPILL MILK. ONE-WEEK LATER-ON, SMELL. ME GO-TO BUY ICL*"spray"*+SMELL, COST **79-CENT**.

Popcorn (96¢)

when

T: ME GO-TO SCHOOL PLAY. HALFTIME, IX*"school"* SELL FOOD DIFFERENT++. IX POPCORN, **96-CENT**, ME BUY.

Eraser (8¢)

T: ME GO-TO fs-GARAGE-SALE, SEE RUBBER+ERASE COST **EIGHT-CENT**, ME BUY.

Magnifying glass (68¢)

q

T: YOU NEED MAGNIFYING-GLASS. YOU GO-TO ONE-DOLLAR+STORE. NOW IX*"store"* SELL+++ **68-CENT**.

Ring (25¢)

T: DCL*"bubble gum machine"* **25-CENT** ICL*"drop quarter in machine, turn crank"* LCL:S-1 *"object drops to bottom"* IX*"ring"* RING fs-PLASTIC. BEAUTIFUL, ME ICL*"put ring on my finger."*

Shoelaces (15¢)

T: ME LOOK-FOR-cont SHOE+STRING. HARD FIND.

neg

ME GO-TO SHOE STORE, IX*"store"* NONE. BUT SHOE ICL*"untie one lace and dangle it"* ONE, GIVE-TO-me. ME PAY-TO **15-CENT**.

PRESENT
(LESSON SLIDE 10:2:30)

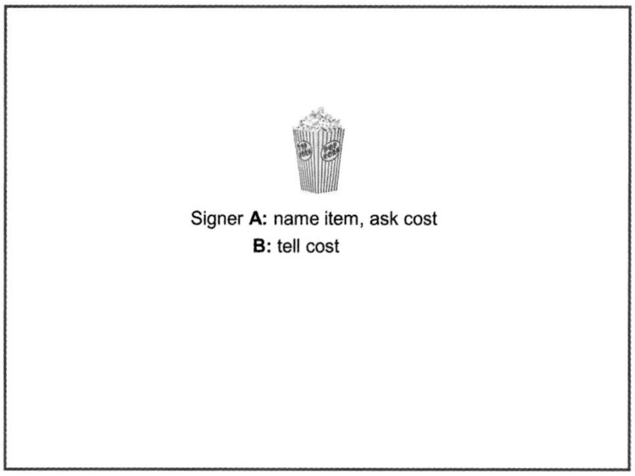

Conclude. Have students practice the question form to check their answers.

Begin by demonstrating Signer A's line. Have students copy. For example:

For ***"A: name item, ask cost"***

t (over POPCORN) whq (over COST HOW-MANY)
T: POPCORN, **COST HOW-MANY**
S(all): (copy)

Pair Up. Have students confirm their answers by asking each other the price of the items in **Exercise 1**. Have them check with you if there are any disagreements.

HOMEWORK

Tell students to do **Homework 10:2** (*Student Workbook*, pages 252–258).

HOMEWORK FOLLOW-UP
3–10 MINUTES

PRESENT
(FOLLOW-UP SLIDES 10:2:1–2)

How Much?

Item	Amount
1. box of bandages	$5.00
2. light bulb	$0.39
3. post-it notes	$0.99
4. bottle of water	$1.00
5. mascara	$0.89
6. stick deodorant	$7.00

Check students' answers for **How Much?** See **Introduction** pages xviii–xix for different ways to check answers.

LESSON 10:3

Wh-word Questions 1

Lesson length: 30–40 minutes

LESSON GOAL Students will translate wh-word questions.

KEY SKILLS

Translating the question

- establish time if specified (raise brows)
- establish location if specified (raise brows)
- name the topic (raise brows)
- ask wh-word question (furrow brows, tilt head forward, hold last sign)

NOTIONS

Grammar

topicalization
wh-word question

Vocabulary

INVENT/CREATE

whq
"what" HAPPEN

MATERIALS

10:3 Lesson Slides
10:3 Follow-up Slides

HOMEWORK 10:3 *Student Workbook*, page 259–260

REVIEW *Identifying the Topic*

30–40 minutes

PRESENT
(LESSON SLIDES 10:3:1–12)

Identify the topic of the question.

1. How much does a baseball hat cost?
2. What is the number that comes after 67?
3. What activities do you have to do in the next few days?
4. Why is talking not allowed in class?
5. How do you get money from an ATM?

Have students open their workbooks to **Wh-Word Questions** on page 259 and underline the topic(s) in each question.

When done, ask students to tell you what they underlined, then confirm students' answers with **Lesson Slides 10:3:2–6**. For example:

                                                          whq
T: SENTENCE ONE, [fs-TOPIC] "what"
S: BASEBALL HAT
T: (show Slide 2 to confirm)

Do the same for **Questions 6–10** (**Lesson Slides 10:3:7–12**).

Teacher's Guide

question	*topic*
Question 1	BASEBALL HAT
Question 2	NUMBER
Question 3	MUST fs-DO (no specific sign for "activities")
Question 4	TALK
Question 5	MONEY
Question 6	MOTHER-left, FATHER-right
Question 7	LIGHT ICL"*screw bulb*"
Question 8	GALLAUDET, CLERC
Question 9	TWO COLOR

Question 10

t — nod — nod

DAY WEEK, [(wh)LCL:B*"week"*/MONDAY, TUESDAY,

nod — nod — nod — nod — nod

WEDNESDAY, THURSDAY, FRIDAY, SATURDAY, SUNDAY]

PRACTICE Translating Wh-word Questions

35–45 minutes

Students practice integrating the topic and facial grammar to translate wh-word questions.

PRESENT
(LESSON SLIDES 10:3:13–14)

1. How much does a baseball hat cost?
2. What is the number that comes after 67?
3. What activities do you have to do in the next few days?
4. Why is talking not allowed in class?
5. How do you get money from an ATM?

Translating wh-word questions

- establish time if specified (raise brows)
- establish location if specified (raise brows)
- name the topic (raise brows)
- ask question (furrow brows, tilt head forward, hold last sign)

Demonstrate the translations and have students copy.

1. ***How much does a baseball hat cost?***

t — whq

T: BASEBALL HAT COST HOW-MANY
S(all): (copy)

Be sure students:

- raise brows and head with the topic and location
- furrow brows and tilt head forward and hold the last sign with the wh-word question.

Repeat procedure for the remaining questions.

Teacher's Translation Guide

2. ***What is <u>the number</u> that comes after 67?***

q/t (over: YOU KNOW NUMBER 67)

YOU KNOW NUMBER 67, NEXT-TO IX"number"

t (over: NUMBER) whq (over: "what")

NUMBER "what"

> **NOTE:** "YOU KNOW NUMBER 67" *(after 67)* functions like a location, thus it is signed in the beginning.

3. ***What <u>activities</u> do you have to do in the next few days?***

t (over: NEXT-FEW-DAYS) t (over: YOU MUST fs-DO) whq (over: "what")

NEXT-FEW-DAYS, YOU MUST fs-DO, "what"

> **NOTE:** NEXT-FEW-DAYS is a specified range time, thus it is signed in the beginning. The phrase MUST fs-DO refers to "activities" so it functions as the topic.

4. ***Why is <u>talking</u> not allowed in class?***

t (over: CLASS) t (over: TALK) neg (over: !FORBID!) whq (over: WHY)

CLASS, TALK, !FORBID!, WHY

> **NOTE:** CLASS is the specified location, thus it is signed in the beginning.

5. ***How do you get <u>money</u> from an ATM?***

t (over: fs-ATM) t (over: MONEY TAKE-OUT) whq (over: HOW)

fs-ATM, MONEY TAKE-OUT HOW

> **NOTE:** fs-ATM is the specified location, thus it is signed in the beginning.

6. *Who are you closer to—your mom or your dad?*

t ... whq

MOTHER-left, FATHER-right, YOU BE-CLOSE-TO, WHICH

INVENT/CREATE

7. *Who invented the light bulb?*

t ... whq

LIGHT ICL*"screw bulb,"* **INVENT/CREATE** WHO

8. *What happened when Gallaudet and Clerc arrived in America?*

t ... t ... when

AMERICA, GALLAUDET-right, CLERC-left, THEY-TWO ARRIVE,

whq

"what" HAPPEN

whq

"what" HAPPEN

> **NOTE:** In student's video the sentence is translated differently—the location is not signed first because it is embedded in a "when" clause and therefore not topicalized.
>
> t
>
> GALLAUDET-right, CLERC-left, THEY-TWO ARRIVE
>
> when ... whq
>
> AMERICA, FROM-NOW-ON **"what" HAPPEN**

9. *What two colors make green?*

t

TWO COLOR (2h)ICL*"pour contents of two vessels into one,"*

when ... nod

MIX-UP, BECOME GREEN, [(wh)2/IX-index, IX-mid,

whq

COLOR "what"]

10. *Which day of the week do you like best?*

t ... nod ... nod

DAY WEEK, [(wh)LCL:B*"week"*/MONDAY, TUESDAY,

nod ... nod ... nod ... nod ... nod

WEDNESDAY, THURSDAY, FRIDAY, SATURDAY, SUNDAY,

whq

IX-mult YOU LIKE BEST], WHICH.

PRESENT
(LESSON SLIDE 10:3:15)

This practice consists of three rounds.

Round 1: focus on word order and sign articulation
Round 2: focus on facial grammar
- raise brows for topic
- furrow brows, tilt head forward, hold last sign for the wh-word question

Round 3: focus on fluency (phrasing)

Pair Up. Have students take turns signing the questions in their workbooks for each round.

HOMEWORK

Tell students to do **Homework 10:3** (*Student Workbook*, pages 259–260).

HOMEWORK FOLLOW-UP
15–20 MINUTES

PRESENT
(FOLLOW-UP SLIDE 10:3:1)

1. How much does a baseball hat cost?
2. What is the number that comes after 67?
3. What activities do you have to do in the next few days?
4. Why is talking not allowed in class?
5. How do you get money from an ATM?
6. Who are you closer to, your mom or your dad?
7. Who invented the light bulb?
8. What happened when Gallaudet and Clerc arrived in America?
9. What two colors make green?
10. Which day of the week do you like best?

Call on each student to ask another student one of the questions. Encourage students to elaborate on their answers when appropriate.

LESSON 10:4

Giving Opinions about Personal Qualities 1

Lesson length: 90–100 minutes

LESSON GOAL

Students will sign this dialogue:

Dialogue

Scene 1
A: (to B) tell about C[1]
B: ask why A thinks that way
A: describe situation to support opinion[2]
B: respond, state will check with C

Scene 2
B: (to C) repeat what A told you about C
C: respond, ask why
B: repeat A's situation
C: correct information, give explanation[3]
B: respond

Scene 3
B: (to A) tell what you found out
A: respond

KEY PHRASES

q/t (over SEE (person))
[1] SEE (person), (person) (give opinion with predicate adjective)
[2] (person) (describe situation using verbs with temporal aspect)

neg (over "wave-no")
[3] "wave-no" !MISUNDERSTAND! (correct misperception)

NOTIONS

Grammar
predicative adjectives

Vocabulary
Disposition

pleasant	*polite*
CHEERFUL	POLITE
STUCK-UP	RUDE++

kind
SWEET
MEAN

temperament
MAD-char

modest
HUMBLE/MODEST
BIG-HEADED
(2h)alt.TALK++
BOASTFUL

goody-goody
GOODY-TWO-SHOES
TROUBLE++
MISCHIEVOUS

humor
(2h)FUNNY-char
QUIET++

imposing discipline
STRICT/STERN
HEART+SOFT

cool
NEAT/COOL
STRANGE/ODD

active
(2h)DO++arc
th
LAID-BACK

anxious or carefree
BE-WORRIED
mm
LAID-BACK

temperament
SWEET
MAD-char

Dealing with Others

tolerance
OPEN-MINDED
(2h)alt.UNDERSTAND
NARROW-MINDED
STUBBORN
FLEXIBLE
ACCEPT++

affectionate
WARM
COLD

patience
GOOD BEAR-WITH
neg
NONE BEAR-WITH

intellectual ability
SMART
neg
NOT+SMART

good sense or foolish	**courage**
GOOD+JUDGE	BRAVE
PEABRAINED	BE-AFRAID++

others
CRY++
LAUGH++
MISUNDERSTAND

PREPARATION

- Review main points of the lesson in **Predicative Adjectives**, *Student Workbook*, page 262.
- Review the situations used to introduce the predicative adjectives on pages 509–518.

MATERIALS

10:4 Lesson Slides
10:4 Follow-up Slides

HOMEWORK 10:4

Student Workbook, pages 261–270

INTRODUCE *Personal Qualities 1*

30 minutes

PRESENT
(LESSON SLIDES 10:4:1)

Describing Personal Qualities

In English, these types of adjectives can be used:
- attributive adjectives in noun phrases
  "The friendly dog is eating."
- predicative adjectives
  "The dog is friendly."

In ASL, **only** predicative adjectives are used

Introduce the differences between **attributive adjectives** and **predicative adjectives** to describe one's personal qualities.

In English, the personal quality ("friendly") can be a part of a noun phrase and comes before the noun ("dog") as an attributive adjective, or as a predicative adjective, which comes after the subject ("the dog is friendly").

However when describing personal qualities in ASL, only predicative adjectives are used and are signed **after** naming the subject. Demonstrate the following ASL example:

t (over #DOG IX"dog")
T: #DOG IX"dog" CHEERFUL.

PRESENT
(LESSON SLIDES 10:4:2–12)

disposition
- pleasant
- polite
- kind
- temperament
- modest
- goody-goody
- humor
- imposing discipline
- cool
- active, on the go
- **anxious or carefree**

Use situations to introduce the signs (predicative adjectives) that describe personal qualities.

pleasant	*explanation*
CHEERFUL	Person who is always smiling, positive, likes meeting people. Introduce: PERSON IX*"person"* **CHEERFUL.**
STUCK-UP	Person who is cold, doesn't like meeting people, looks down at other people. Introduce: PERSON IX*"person"* **STUCK-UP.**

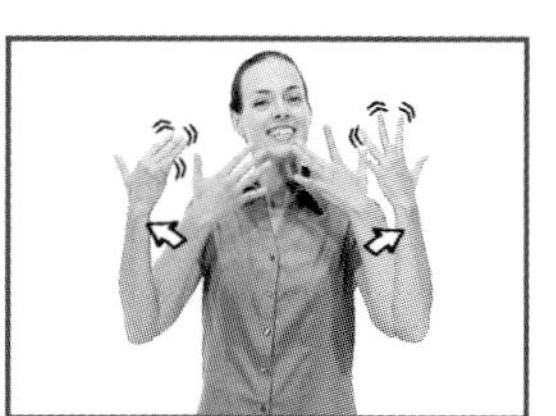

CHEERFUL

STUCK-UP

polite	*explanation*
POLITE	Person shows respect to the elderly by opening doors or giving up their seat on the bus. If conversation with others is boring, person still pays attention. Introduce: PERSON IX*"person"* **POLITE.**
RUDE++	Person talks in class interrupting teacher, cuts in a line, puts feet up on furniture when visiting someone. Introduce: PERSON IX*"person"* **RUDE++.**

POLITE

RUDE++

kind	*explanation*
SWEET	Person is nice, helpful, giving (generous), sharing, never complaining. Introduce: PERSON IX*"person"* **SWEET.**
MEAN	Person is not nice, not helpful, selfish, critical of others. Introduce: PERSON IX*"person"* **MEAN.**

SWEET

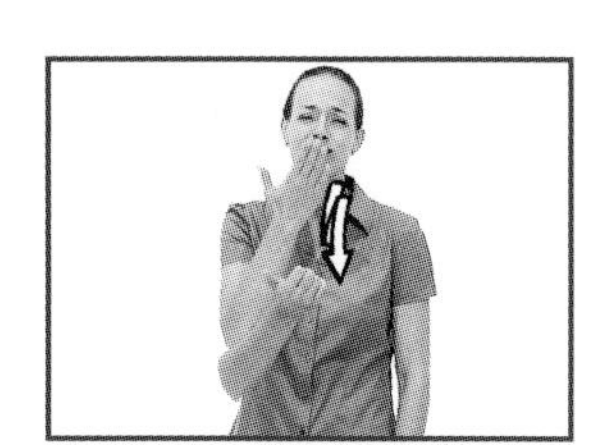

MEAN

temperament	*explanation*
SWEET	Person is positive, friendly, encouraging. Introduce: PERSON IX*"person"* **SWEET.**
MAD-char	Person is not friendly, negative, complaining. Introduce: PERSON IX*"person"* **MAD-char.**

SWEET

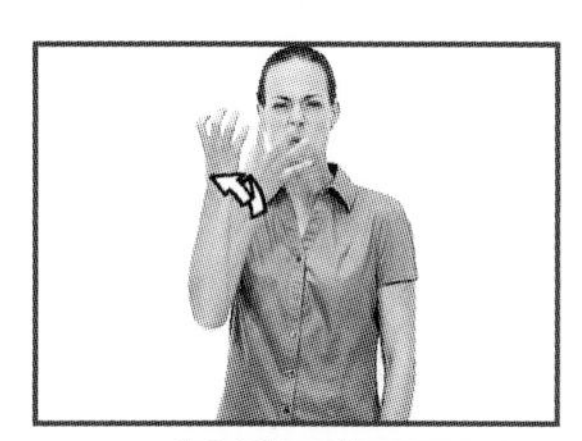

MAD-char

modest	*explanation*
HUMBLE/MODEST	Person who, even though they may be richer or more famous than others, sees others as equals, respects others and works with them. Introduce: PERSON IX*"person"* **HUMBLE/MODEST.**
BIG-HEADED	Person thinks they are number 1, better than others, loves attention ((2h)alt.ME++). Introduce: PERSON IX*"person"* **BIG-HEADED, (2h)alt.TALK++, BOASTFUL.**

HUMBLE/MODEST

BIG-HEADED

BOASTFUL

goody-goody	*explanation*
GOODY-TWO-SHOES	Person who is good, follows rules, is not a problem for parents or teachers. Person is easy to discipline and never gets into trouble. Introduce: PERSON IX*"person"* **GOODY-TWO-SHOES.**
TROUBLE++	Person breaks rules and constantly gets into trouble, gets disciplined or suspended. Introduce PERSON IX*"person"* **TROUBLE++.**
MISCHIEVOUS	Person plays pranks, teases others. Introduce PERSON IX*"person"* **MISCHIEVOUS.**

GOODY-TWO-SHOES

TROUBLE++

MISCHIEVOUS

humor	*explanation*
(2h)FUNNY-char	Person says funny things, likes to see people laugh, not shy, talkative. Introduce: PERSON IX*"person"* **(2h)FUNNY-char.**
QUIET++	OPPOSITE "what," (rhet) **QUIET++** Person prefers watching others talk.

(2h)FUNNY-char

QUIET++

STRICT/STERN

imposing discipline

STRICT/STERN

explanation

Mother tells teenage child to be home by 10 P.M. They get home late, Mother grounds them for a week. Introduce: MOTHER IX*"mother"* **STRICT/STERN.**

HEART+SOFT

HEART+SOFT

Teenage child arrives home past the curfew not once, but often. Each time the child begs for forgiveness, and the mother forgives. Introduce: MOTHER IX*"mother"* **HEART+SOFT.**

NEAT/COOL

cool

NEAT/COOL

explanation

Person is easy to like, easy to get along with, friendly, fun. Introduce: PERSON IX*"person"* **NEAT/COOL.**

STRANGE/ODD

STRANGE/ODD

Person talks and acts different. His conversation makes others feel uncomfortable. Introduce: PERSON IX*"person"* **STRANGE/ODD.**

(2h)DO++arc

active, on the go

(2h)DO++arc

explanation

Person doesn't like to sit and relax, must be on the go at all times. Introduce: PERSON IX*"person"* WORK++, **(2h)DO++arc.**

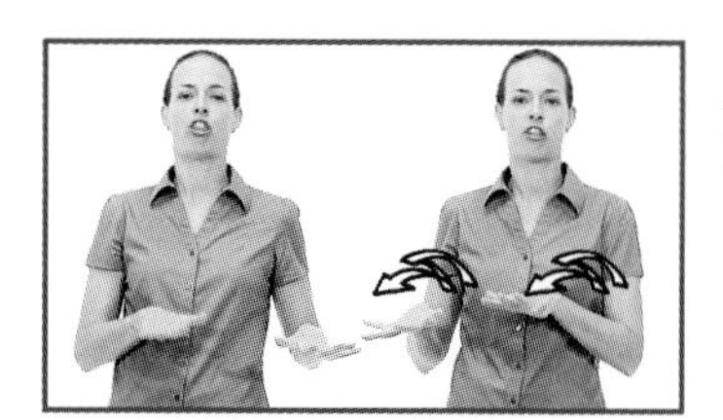
LAID-BACK(th)

th

LAID-BACK(th)

Person is in no hurry, sits down and takes things slowly (like a sloth). Introduce:

th

PERSON IX*"person"* **LAID-BACK(th).**

BE-WORRIED

LAID-BACK

anxious or carefree	*explanation*
BE-WORRIED	Two people are planning a party for next month. One person is constantly asking the other if they have finished buying, ordering, or calling, because the person thinks maybe the store will run out of items. Introduce: PERSON IX*"person"* **BE-WORRIED.**
mm **LAID-BACK**	The other person is nonchalant and carefree, as if nothing fazes him or her. Introduce: PERSON IX*"person"* mm **LAID-BACK or (2h)"pshaw"++.**

Review. Give a sign, and ask students to give the opposite, for example,

t whq
T: CHEERFUL, OPPOSITE "what"
S: STUCK-UP

Repeat procedure with the signs below.

signs	*opposites*
POLITE	RUDE++
SWEET	MEAN or MAD-char
HUMBLE/MODEST	BIG-HEADED, [(2h)alt,TALK++, BOASTFUL]
GOODY-TWO-SHOES	TROUBLE++ or MISCHIEVOUS
(2h)FUNNY-char	QUIET++
STRICT/STERN	HEART+SOFT
NEAT/COOL	STRANGE/ODD
(2h)DO++arc	th LAID-BACK
WORRIED	mm LAID-BACK

INTRODUCE *Personal Qualities 2*

30 minutes

PRESENT
(LESSON SLIDES 10:4:13–15)

dealing with others
- tolerance
- affectionate
- **patience**

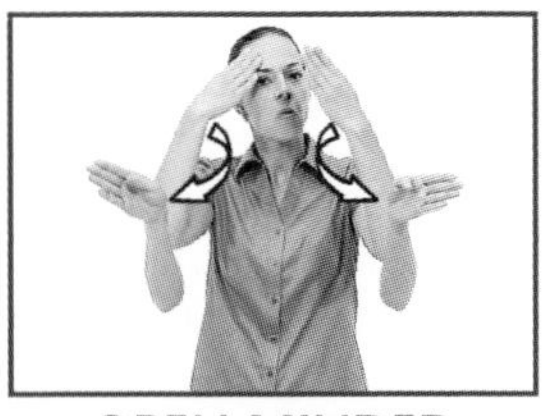
OPEN-MINDED

(2h)alt.
UNDERSTAND

ACCEPT

FLEXIBLE

Continue introducing other predictive adjectives that describe personal qualities using situations.

tolerance	*explanation*
OPEN-MINDED	Person is presented with a new way of thinking that contradicts his or her beliefs. But person is open to it, listens, and allows discussion on the topic. Introduce: PERSON IX*"person"* **OPEN-MINDED, (2h)alt.UNDERSTAND, ACCEPT** NEW IDEA, **FLEXIBLE.**

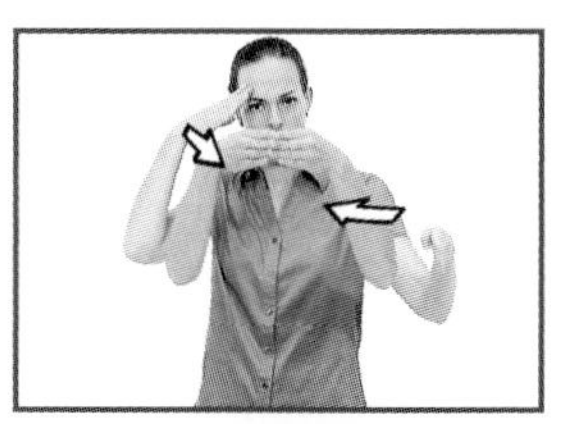
NARROW-MINDED

STUBBORN

NARROW-MINDED — Person is not willing to listen, not open to new ideas, is stubborn and doesn't allow discussion. Introduce: PERSON IX*"person"* **NARROW-MINDED, STUBBORN,** HARD CHANGE MIND, HARD ACCEPT NEW IDEA.

affectionate	*explanation*

WARM

WARM — Person hugs others, wrap their arms around others and holds other people's hands, shows emotions, (says "ILY," for example.) Introduce: PERSON IX*"person"* **WARM**, CHEERFUL.

COLD

COLD — Person keeps his or her distance from others, is reserved, doesn't express feelings. Introduce: PERSON IX*"person"* **COLD**, STUCK-UP.

patience	*explanation*

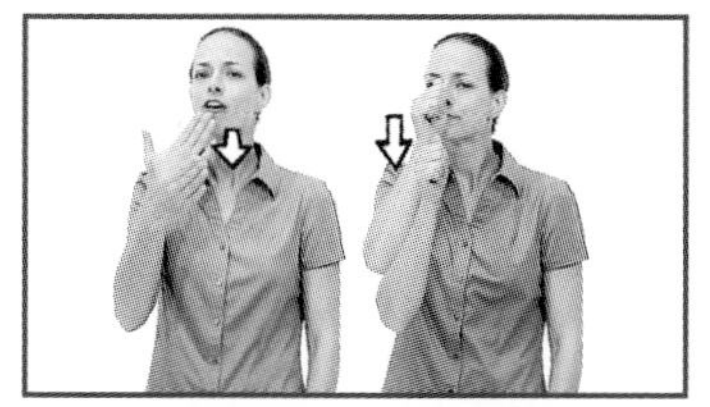
GOOD BEAR-WITH

GOOD BEAR-WITH — Driver is behind a slow-moving car. Driver doesn't pass or honk, driver waits until the car up front moves out of the way. Introduce: CAR/DRIVE+ER IX*"driver"* **GOOD BEAR-WITH.**

NONE BEAR-WITH

neg
NONE BEAR-WITH — Driver is behind a slow moving car. Honks the horn, tailgates, flashes headlights, passes the car at the first opportunity. Introduce: PERSON IX*"person"* **NONE BEAR-WITH** (neg).

PRESENT
(LESSON SLIDE 10:4:16)

intellectual ability

SMART

NOT+SMART

intellectual ability	*explanation*
SMART	Person who learns fast, picks up on things quickly. Introduce: PERSON IX*"person"* **SMART**.
neg **NOT+SMART**	Person who has difficult time learning. Introduce: PERSON IX*"person"* neg **NOT+SMART**.

PRESENT
(LESSON SLIDE 10:4:17)

good sense or foolish

good sense or foolish	*explanation*
GOOD+JUDGE	Before making a big decision, person carefully considers several things, asks around, does some research, then makes the right decision. Introduce: PERSON IX*"person"* **GOOD+JUDGE.**
PEABRAINED	Person makes a hasty decision, without carefully considering several things. Makes a poor decision. Introduce: PERSON IX*"person"* **PEABRAINED.**

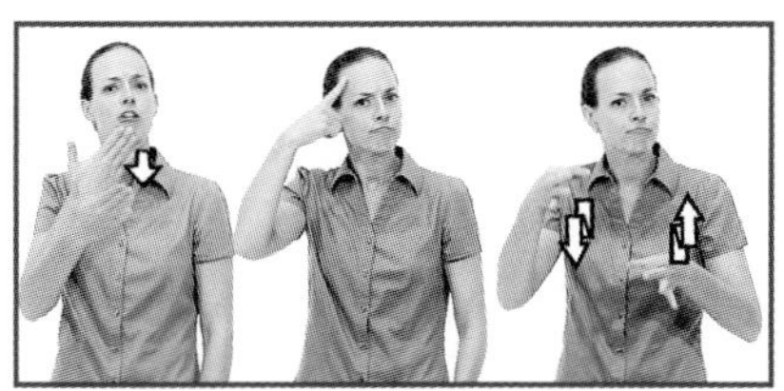

GOOD+JUDGE

PEABRAINED

PRESENT
(LESSON SLIDE 10:4:18)

courageous

courageous	*explanation*
BRAVE	Person takes action in the face of danger, for example, rescuing someone from a burning car or house. Introduce: PERSON IX*"person"* **BRAVE.**
BE-AFRAID++	(rhet over OPPOSITE "what,") OPPOSITE "what," **BE-AFRAID++**, BIRD-char(chicken).

BRAVE

BE-AFRAID++

Review. Give a sign, and ask students to give the opposite. For example,

	t	whq
T:	WARM,	OPPOSITE "what"
S:	COLD	

Repeat procedure with the signs below.

signs	*opposites*
OPEN-MINDED, (2h)alt.UNDERSTAND FLEXIBLE	NARROW-MINDED, [STUBBORN, HARD ACCEPT NEW IDEA]
GOOD BEAR-WITH	neg NONE BEAR-WITH
SMART	neg NOT+SMART
GOOD+JUDGE	PEABRAINED
BRAVE	BE-AFRAID++
FLEXIBLE	STUBBORN

PRACTICE *Discussing Others' Personal Qualities*

30–40 minutes

Students practice describing others' personal qualities.

PRESENT
(LESSON SLIDE 10:4:19)

MISUNDERSTAND

Show video, then ask these comprehension questions:

whq

T: WHY fs-URSULA THINK fs-ZACK MEAN, WHY

S: IX*"Zack,"* (2h)alt.INSULT-TO-left IX*"friend"* CRY++

t whq

T: fs-JOHN ASK-TO-Zack, fs-ZACK TELL-TO-John "what"

S: fs-URSULA **MISUNDERSTAND.** fs-ZACK IX*"Zack"* TEASE-TO-friend. IX*"friend"* LAUGH, CRY*"tears down cheeks"* LAUGH-teeth

NOTE: To define MISUNDERSTAND, tell students it means NOT+UNDERSTAND, HAVE WRONG IDEA.

PRESENT

(LESSON SLIDE 10:4:20)

Scene 1

- **A**: (to B) tell about C
- **B**: ask why A thinks that way
- **A**: describe situation to support opinion
- **B**: respond, state will check with C to see if it's true

Scene 2

- **B**: (to C) repeat what A told you about C
- **C**: respond, ask why
- **B**: repeat A's situation
- **C**: correct information, give explanation
- **B**: respond

Scene 3

- **B**: (to A) tell what you found out
- **A**: respond

Repeat the lines from **Conversation 2** on the video to demonstrate the dialogue. Stand in different locations when doing lines for Signers A, B or C. Have students copy.

Scene 1

For ***"A: (to B) tell about C"***

q/t

T: (as Signer A) SEE fs-ZACK IX*"Zack."* IX*"Zack"* !MEAN!

S(all): (copy)

For ***"B: ask why A thinks that way"***

whq

T: (as Signer B) WHY YOU THINK, WHY

S(all): (copy)

For ***"A: describe situation to support opinion"***

T: (as Signer A) POSS*"Zack"* FRIEND, IX*"friend,"* IX*"Zack,"* (2h)alt.INSULT-TO-friend. IX*"friend"* CRY++. IX*"Zack"* MEAN

S(all): (copy)

For ***"B: respond, state will check with C"***

q

T: (as Signer B) REAL/TRUE. ME LETS-SEE ASK-TO-Signer-C,

q

#OK

S(all): (copy)

Scene 2

For ***"B: (to C) repeat what A told you about C"***

T: (as Signer B) IX*"A"* TELL-TO-me YOU !MEAN! YOU

S(all): (copy)

For ***"C: respond, ask why"***

q whq

T: (as Signer C) ME MEAN. WHY

S(all): (copy)

For ***"B: repeat A's situation"***

T: (as Signer B) IX"A" SAY YOU, IX*"friend"* FRIEND, YOU <rs:C ASL-TALK, (2h)alt.INSULT-TO>, "well"

S(all): (copy)

For ***"C: correct information, give explanation"***

T: (as Signer C) "wave-no" **!MISUNDERSTAND!** YOU "wow"

neg

ME (2h)alt.INSULT-TO-friend++, NOT. ME me-TEASE-TO-friend++ IX*"friend"* LAUGH++, !LAUGH-teeth!, CRY++, FINISH++ ("that's all")

S(all): (copy)

For ***"B: respond"***

T: (as Signer B) !OH-I-SEE! IX*"A"* **MISUNDERSTAND.** ME TELL-TO-A

S(all): (copy)

Scene 3

For ***"B: (to A) tell what you found out"***

T: (as Signer B) YOU **MISUNDERSTAND**. IX*"friend"* FRIEND (t), IX*"Zack"* TEASE-TO-her++. IX*"friend"* LAUGH++, CRY++, LAUGH-teeth, !THAT-ONE!

S(all): (copy)

For ***"A: respond"***

T: (as Signer A) OH-I-SEE. ME WRONG

S(all): (copy)

Rehearse. Put students into groups of three and have them take turns playing all three roles in the dialogue. Provide coaching or show video again when needed.

Activity. Keep students in the same groups of three. Have them determine who will be Signer A, B and C. Then, assign a sign from this list to each group and have them develop dialogues based on the sign:

MISCHIEVOUS	MAD-char	BIGHEADED
MEAN	STUCK-UP	COLD
BE-WORRIED	STRICT	NARROW-MINDED
ODD/STRANGE	STUBBORN	PEABRAINED

Monitor to make sure the descriptions and explanations are adequate and make sense for these parts of the dialogue:
"A: describe situation to support opinion" (line 3)
"C: correct information, give explanation" (line 8)

Conclude. When ready, call each group up front to demonstrate their dialogue.

Be sure students:

- descriptions and explanations are adequate and make sense for the assigned personal quality sign.

HOMEWORK

Tell students to do **Homework 10:4** on (*Student Workbook*, pages 261–270).

HOMEWORK FOLLOW-UP
10–15 MINUTES

PRESENT
(FOLLOW-UP SLIDES 10:4:1–11)

Minidialogue 1

1. What was Iva's initial opinion about John and what situation did she describe to support the opinion?

2. What explanation does John give to Tonique that corrected Iva's misperception of him?

Check students' answers to **Minidialogues 1–3**. See **Introduction** pages xviii–xix for different ways to check answers.

LESSON 10:5

Numbers: Telling the Price 2

Lesson length: 35–50 minutes

LESSON GOAL

Students learn to sign money numbers combining dollars and cents.

KEY SKILLS

- after giving the dollar amount, the cent part of the number doesn't begin at forehead
- when cent part is .01–.09, add ZERO and palm faces out
- when cent part is .10–.15, use singular movement
- when cent part is a multiple of 10, like .20 or .90, use singular movement.
- if cent part is either .25 or .50, use singular movement, palm faces in or out

NOTIONS

Vocabulary

SOUP	TOMATO	BACON
MILK	ONION	HOT-DOG
CHEESE	BANANA	CEREAL
BREAD	APPLE	fs-YOGURT
BUTTER	ORANGE	TEA
EGG	PEANUT+BUTTER	ICE-CREAM
SUGAR	JAM	COOKIE
LETTUCE	fs-MAYO	fs-FF
		CRACKERS

PREPARATION

Read and view **Numbers: Telling the Price 2** in *Student Workbook* pages 271.

MATERIALS

10:5 Lesson Slides
10:5 Follow-up Slides
Exercise 2A, **2B**, and **2C** (*Student Workbook*, pages 478, 481 and 483)

HOMEWORK 10:5

Student Workbook, pages 271–276

REVIEW *Cents and Dollars*

5 minutes

Students review money number forms for cents and dollars.

PRESENT
(LESSON SLIDES 10:5:1–3)

4¢	9¢	12¢	17¢	21¢	25¢
33¢	50¢	69¢	77¢	80¢	97¢
$1	$5	$6	$10		

Ask students to sign the numbers on **Slides 1–3**.

Be sure students:

- form each number correctly (see **Lesson 10:2**, pages 252–254 for guidelines).

INTRODUCE *Combining Dollars and Cents*

20–25 minutes

PRESENT
(LESSON SLIDE 10:5:4)

Dollar and Cent Combinations

$4.28 $8.44 $2.78 $9.76 $3.19

BANANA

Demonstrate the first number ($4.28):
T: FOUR-DOLLAR+28

Ask students what is the difference between this combined number form and the dollar and cent numbers they reviewed in **Lesson 10:2**.

Answer.
In combinations, the cent part of the number doesn't begin at the forehead.

Now, have students sign the rest of the numbers on the slide.

S: ($8.44) EIGHT-DOLLAR+44
($2.78) TWO-DOLLAR+78
($9.76) NINE-DOLLAR+76
($3.19) THREE-DOLLAR+19

PRESENT
(LESSON SLIDE 10:5:5)

Dollar and Cent Combinations

$1.09 $2.08 $3.07 $4.06 $5.05 $6.04
$7.03 $8.02 $9.01 $10.09

Demonstrate the first pairs of numbers:

T: ($1.09) **ONE-DOLLAR+ZERO+NINE**
($6.04) **SIX-DOLLAR+ZERO+FOUR*"palm out"***

Point out:

- ZERO is added and the palm faces out for the cent part .09 and .04.

Now have students take turns signing the pairs of numbers. For example:

S1: ($2.08) **TWO-DOLLAR+ZERO+EIGHT**
($7.03) **SEVEN-DOLLAR+ZERO+THREE*"palm out"***

S2: ($3.07) **THREE-DOLLAR+ZERO+SEVEN**
($8.02) **EIGHT-DOLLAR+ZERO+TWO*"palm out"***

S3: ($4.06) **FOUR-DOLLAR+ZERO+SIX**
($9.01) **NINE-DOLLAR+ZERO+ONE*"palm out"***

S4: ($5.05) **FIVE-DOLLAR+ZERO+FIVE*"palm out"***
($10.09) **TEN-DOLLAR+ZERO+NINE**

Point out:

- for $10.09, the TEN-DOLLAR part is made with a singular movement and there is no separate sign for DOLLAR before signing ZERO+NINE (.09)

PRESENT
(LESSON SLIDE 10:5:6)

Dollar and Cent Combinations

$1.10	$3.12	$5.14
$2.11	$4.13	$6.15

Demonstrate the first pair of numbers:

T: ($1.10) **ONE-DOLLAR+TEN*"single movement"***
($2.11) **TWO-DOLLAR+ELEVEN*"single movement"***

Point out:

- for the cent part .10 and .11, a singular movement is best, but repeated movement is acceptable.

Now have students take turns signing the pairs of numbers. For example:

S1: ($3.12) **THREE-DOLLAR+TWELVE*"single movement"***
($4.13) **FOUR-DOLLAR+THIRTEEN*"single movement"***

S2: ($5.14) **FIVE-DOLLAR+FOURTEEN*"single movement"***
($6.15) **SIX-DOLLAR+FIFTEEN*"single movement"***

PRESENT
(LESSON SLIDE 10:5:7)

Dollar and Cent Combinations

$1.20	$2.30	$3.40	$4.50
$5.60	$6.70	$7.80	$8.90

Demonstrate the first pair of numbers:

T: (for $1.20) **ONE-DOLLAR+20*"single movement"***
(for $5.60) **FIVE-DOLLAR+60*"single movement"***

Point out:

- for cent numbers that are multiples of 10, for example, .20 or .90, use a singular movement.

Now have students take turns signing the pairs of numbers. For example:

S1: (for $2.30) **TWO-DOLLAR+30*"single movement"***
(for $6.70) **SIX-DOLLAR+70*"single movement"***

S2: (for $3.40) **THREE-DOLLAR+40*"single movement"***
(for $7.80) **SEVEN-DOLLAR+80*"single movement"***

S3: (for $4.50) **FOUR-DOLLAR+50*"single movement"***
(for $8.90) **EIGHT-DOLLAR+90*"single movement"***

PRESENT
(LESSON SLIDE 10:5:8)

Dollar and Cent Combinations

$7.25 $3.50

Demonstrate the two ways to sign the cent part of the numbers. Have students copy:

T: (for $7.25) **SEVEN-DOLLAR+25*"singular+palm out"***
SEVEN-DOLLAR+25*"singular+palm in"*

S: (copy)

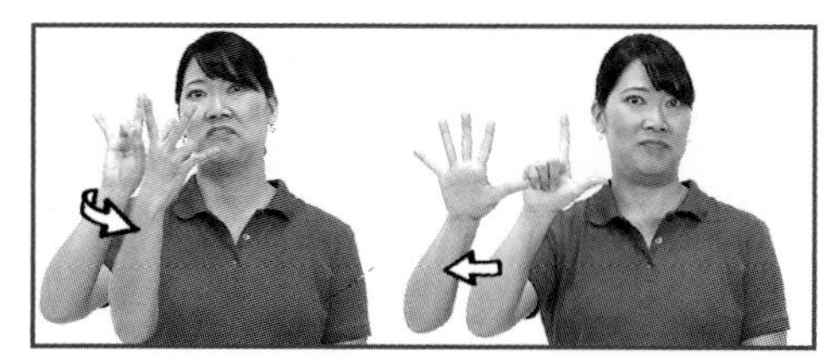

SEVEN-DOLLAR+25*"singular+palm out"* SEVEN-DOLLAR+25*"singular+palm in"*

T: (for $3.50) **THREE-DOLLAR+50*"singular+palm out"***
THREE-DOLLAR+50*"singular+palm in"*

S: (copy)

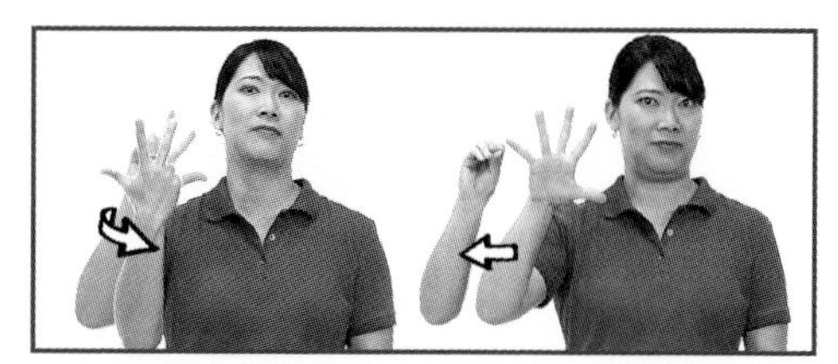

THREE-DOLLAR+50*"singular+palm out"*

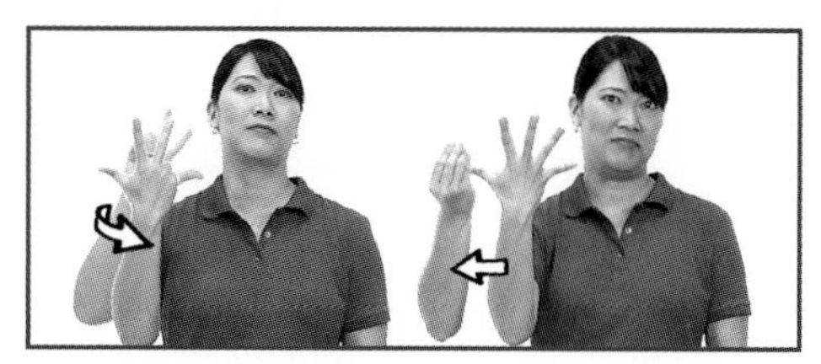

THREE-DOLLAR+50*"singular+palm in"*

Point out:

- the cent part (.25 and .50) uses a singular movement and the palm faces either in or out.

PRESENT
(LESSON SLIDES 10:5:9–44)

Dollar and Cent Combinations

$1.03

Review. Show **Lesson Slides 10:5:9–44** to review all kinds of combinations. Have students sign the numbers.

PRACTICE *What Is the Price?*

12–20 minutes

Students practice understanding and signing money numbers.

PRESENT
(LESSON SLIDE 10:5:45–47)

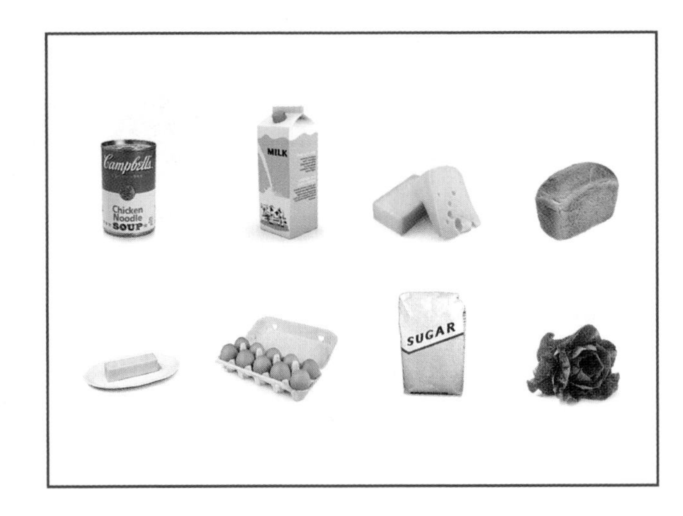

Introduce signs and have students copy:

For **Slide 45**

SOUP

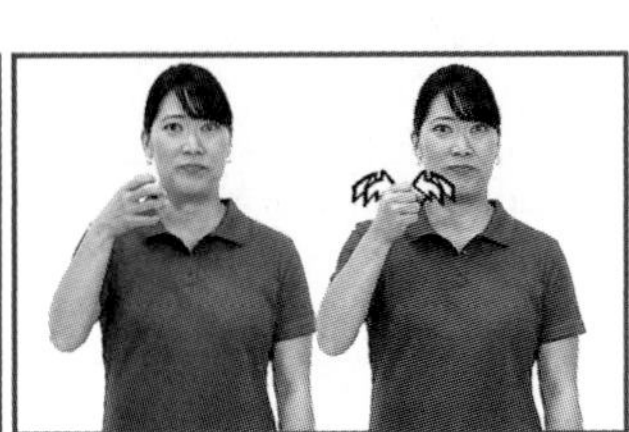
MILK

CHEESE

BREAD

BUTTER

EGG

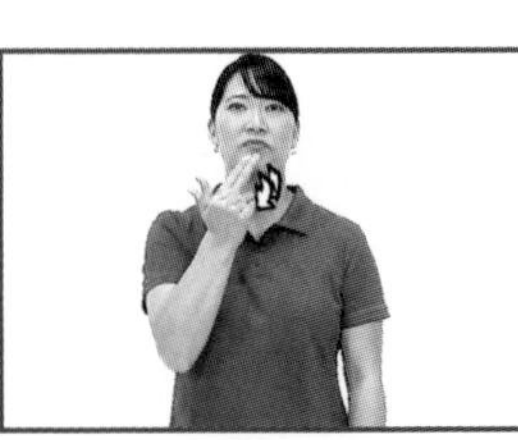
SUGAR

LETTUCE

For **Slide 46**

For **Slide 47**

PRESENT
(LESSON SLIDE 10:5:48)

A: name item, ask cost
B: tell cost

EXERCISE 2A, 2B, AND 2C

Divide class into groups of three. Assign each student **Exercise A, B** or **C** (*Student Workbook*, pages 478, 481 and 483). Each **Exercise** sheet has prices for 8 of the items. Students take turns asking their partners to get prices for the remaining items, for example,

t (over BREAD), whq (over COST HOW-MANY)
S: BREAD, COST HOW-MANY

Activity is over when they have all the prices filled in on the sheets.

Be sure students:

- raise brows and head with the topic and location
- furrow brows and tilt head forward and hold the last sign with the wh-word question
- sign the correct form for the dollar and cents combinations.

HOMEWORK

Tell students to do **Homework 10:5** (*Student Workbook*, pages 271–276).

Also, students are to bring in six items all under the price of $10.00 to class (See **Assignment**, *Student Workbook*, page 273).

HOMEWORK FOLLOW-UP
30–45 MINUTES

PRESENT
(FOLLOW-UP SLIDES 10:5:1–2)

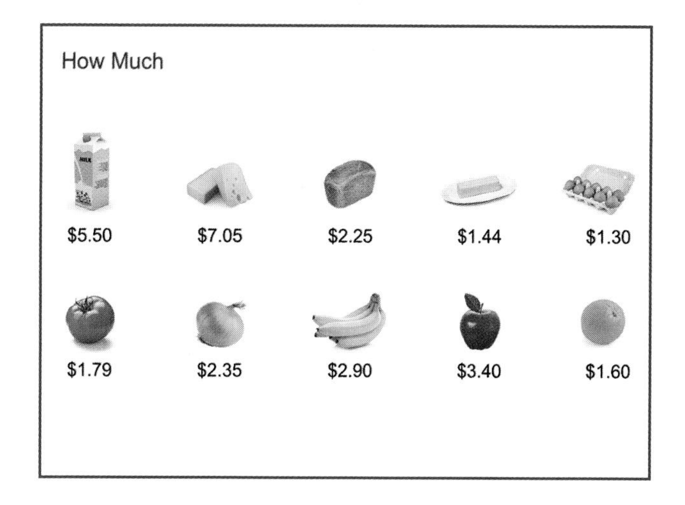

Check students' answers to **How Much**. See **Introduction** pages xviii–xix for different ways to check answers.

ACTIVITY

Divide class into groups of four to five students each. Each student shows their group an item they brought to class (See **Assignment**, *Student Workbook*, page 273), and asks the group to guess how much it costs. After several guesses, the student reveals the actual cost.

Conclude. Have each student show you an item they may not know the sign for. Give the sign for the item, then ask the student how much it costs.

LESSON 10:6

Giving Opinions about Personal Qualities 2

Lesson length: 50–70 minutes

LESSON GOAL Students will sign this dialogue:

KEY SKILLS

Dialogue

A: (pick a name), ask who

B: explain relationship and how met him or her

A: ask if B likes him or her, ask why

B: reply, describe person

- use at least three personal quality signs
- use role shift to describe situation(s)

A: comment or ask further questions

B: reply

NOTIONS

Grammar

role shift to describe situation(s) involving the person discussed

Vocabulary

personal quality signs from **Lesson 10:4**

PREPARATION Review main points of the lesson in **Using Role Shift to Describe Situation**, *Student Workbook* page 277.

MATERIALS **10:6 Lesson Slides**

HOMEWORK 10:6 *Student Workbook*, pages 277–280

REVIEW — *Vocabulary for Personal Qualities*

35–45 minutes

Review signs for personal qualities by describing situations or behaviors without using the signs themselves. Have students guess the sign. Then, repeat the description with the sign itself and have students copy.

For **SMART**

T: IX*"person"* STUDY++ fs-A*"on test"*++, LEARN FAST,

whq

(2h)PICK-UP FAST. IX*"person"* "what"

S: SMART

T: PERSON IX*"person"* SMART, IX*"person"* STUDY++ fs-A*"on test"*++, LEARN FAST, (2h)PICK-UP FAST

S(all:) copy

neg

For **NOT+SMART**

T: IX*"person"* HARD LEARN, SLOW UNDERSTAND, MUST

whq

TELL++ AGAIN++. IX*"person"* "what"

neg

S: NOT+SMART

T: (repeat description using the sign)

S(all): (copy)

For **GOOD+JUDGE**

T: IX*"person"* MAKE GOOD DECIDE++, BE-CAREFUL

(2h)alt.LOOK-AT DECIDE, BE-RESPONSIBLE++. IX*"person"*

whq

"what"

S: GOOD+JUDGE

T: (repeat description using the sign)

S(all): (copy)

For **PEABRAINED**

T: IX*"person"* NOT+THINK BE-CAREFUL, BAD+JUDGE, BAD

whq

+DECIDE, (2h)alt.WRONG. IX*"person"* "what"

S: PEABRAINED

T: (repeat description using the sign)

S(all): (copy)

For **BE-AFRAID++**

t

T: IX*"person"* EASY BE-WORRIED, MEET NEW PEOPLE, EVADE++,

t neg

PROBLEM NOT+BE-COMFORTABLE EVADE++. IX*"person"*

whq

"what"

S: BE-AFRAID++

T: (repeat description using the sign)

S(all): (copy)

For **BRAVE**

neg

T: IX*"person"* BE-AFRAID++ NOT. IX*"person"* SEE BOY DCL*"small,"* OTHER BOY DCL*"tall, big shoulders"* big-boy-(2h)alt.INSULT-TO-kid. IX*"person"* (2h)SCL:1*"person approaches the bully"* <rs:person TELL-TO-bully !FINISH!

neg

LEAVE-ALONE-kid>. IX*"person"* BE-AFRAID++ NOT.

whq

IX*"person"* "what"

S: BRAVE

T: (repeat description using the sign)

S(all): (copy)

For **HUMBLE/MODEST**

T: IX*"person"* (2h)SAME-AS-all, EVERYDAY, THINK #ALL

neg

EQUAL-arc, NOT BIG-HEADED, NOT STUCK-UP.

whq

IX*"person"* "what"

S: HUMBLE/MODEST

T: (repeat description using the sign)

S(all): (copy)

For **BIG-HEADED**

T: IX*"person"* THINK IX BETTER THAN #ALL. <rs:person (2h)alt.TALK++, (2h)alt.ME++, BOASTFUL, ME KNOW++>.

whq

IX*"person"* "what"

S: BIG-HEADED

T: (repeat description using the sign)

S(all): (copy)

For **CHEERFUL**

T: IX*"person"* HAPPY+FACE, SMILE++, SWEET, BE-POSITIVE,

whq

WARM. IX*"person"* "what"

S: CHEERFUL

T: (repeat description using the sign)

S(all): (copy)

For **STUCK-UP**

neg

T: IX*"person"* COLD, NOT+CHEERFUL, LOOK-DOWN*"on others,"*

whq

REJECT*"others"*++. IX*"person"* "what"

S: STUCK-UP

T: (repeat description using the sign)

S(all): (copy)

For **POLITE**

T: IX*"person"* NICE, SWEET, RESPECT-TO OTHER PEOPLE.

whq

IX*"person"* "what"

S: POLITE

T: (repeat description using the sign)

S(all): (copy)

For **RUDE++**

neg

T: IX*"person"* NOT+POLITE, (2h)alt.INSULT++, BOTHER++.

t neg

PEOPLE POSS*"people"* THINGS, NOT+RESPECT-TO.

whq

IX*"person"* "what"

S: RUDE++

T: (repeat description using the sign)

S(all): (copy)

For SWEET

t

T: IX*"person"* HEART+SOFT, OTHER PEOPLE, IX*"person"* HELP,

whq

SUPPORT++, SHARE++. IX*"person"* "what"

S: SWEET

T: (repeat description using the sign)

S(all): (copy)

For MEAN

neg

T: IX*"person"* NOT+NICE, SELFISH+, (2h)alt.INSULT++,

whq

CRITICIZE/CORRECT++. IX*"person"* "what"

S: MEAN

T: (repeat description using the sign)

S(all): (copy)

For MAD-char

neg

T: IX*"person"* NOT+CHEERFUL. ALWAYS COMPLAIN++,

whq

BE-NEGATIVE++. IX*"person"* "what"

S: MAD-char

T: (repeat description using the sign)

S(all): (copy)

For GOODY-TWO-SHOES

T: IX*"person"* RESPECT-TO, GOOD+BOY [or GOOD +GIRL],

t neg whq

ANGEL DCL*"halo"* TROUBLE++ NEVER. IX*"person"* "what"

S: GOODY-TWO-SHOES

T: (repeat description using the sign)

S(all): (copy)

For **TROUBLE++**

t

T: IX*"person"* BAD+BOY [or BAD+GIRL], RULE "pshaw,"

whq

MISCHIEVOUS++. IX*"person"* "what"

S: TROUBLE++

T: (repeat description using the sign)

S(all): (copy)

For **2h)FUNNY-char**

t

T: IX*"person"* LIKE TEASE, NARRATE, PEOPLE LAUGH++.

whq

IX*"person"* "what"

S: (2h)FUNNY-char

T: (repeat description using the sign)

S(all): (copy)

For **STRICT/STERN**

neg

T: IX*"person"* NOT HEART+SOFT. IX*"person"* !MANY! ,

cond neg

RULE+++ MUST FOLLOW-rule. NOT FOLLOW-rule,

whq

IX*"person"* BAWL-OUT++. IX*"person"* "what"

S: STRICT/STERN

T: (repeat description using the sign)

S(all): (copy)

For **HEART+SOFT**

neg

T: IX*"person"* SWEET, NOT+STRICT/STERN, ALLOW++.

whq

IX*"person"* "what"

S: HEART+SOFT

T: (repeat description using the sign)

S(all): (copy)

For **NEAT/COOL**

T: IX*"person"* OPEN-MINDED, EASY GET-ALONG-WITH, #FUN.

whq
IX*"person"* "what"

S: NEAT/COOL

T: (repeat description using the sign)

S(all): (copy)

For **STRANGE/ODD**

T: IX*"person"* DIFFERENT. SAME-AS-arc, ONE*"that person"* FACE

whq
DIFFERENT, TALK DIFFERENT. IX*"person"* "what"

S: STRANGE/ODD

T: (repeat description using the sign)

S(all): (copy)

For **(2h)DO++arc**

serious neg whq
T: IX*"person"* WORK-char, NOT+LAID-BACK. IX*"person"* "what"

S: (2h)DO++arc

T: (repeat description using the sign)

S(all): (copy)

For **LAID-BACK**

t neg t neg
T: IX*"person"* BE-WORRIED, NOT, HURRY, NOT. <rs:person

whq
PLENTY TIME>. IX*"person"* "what"

S: LAID-BACK

T: (repeat description using the sign)

S(all): (copy)

For **BE-WORRIED**

neg
T: IX*"person"* THINK++, (2h)alt.MULL-OVER, CAN'T SLEEP,

whq
TOSS-TURN. IX*"person"* "what"

S: BE-WORRIED

T: (repeat description using the sign)

S(all): (copy)

For **OPEN-MINDED**

T: IX*"person"* (2h)alt.UNDERSTANDING, ACCEPT++. SOMEONE

t neg

DIFFERENT, STRANGE/ODD, IX*"person"* NOT BE-AFRAID.

whq

IX*"person"* "what"

S: OPEN-MINDED

T: (repeat description using the sign)

S(all): (copy)

For **NARROW-MINDED**

T: IX*"person"* STUBBORN, HARD CHANGE MIND, HARD

whq

ACCEPT NEW IDEA. IX*"person"* "what"

S: NARROW-MINDED

T: (repeat description using the sign)

S(all): (copy)

For **GOOD+BEAR-WITH**

neg t

T: IX*"person"* NOT COMPLAIN, WAIT-cont, FINE++, ACCEPT,

whq

BE-POSITIVE++. IX*"person"* "what"

S: GOOD+BEAR-WITH

T: (repeat description using the sign)

S(all): (copy)

For **NONE+BEAR-WITH**

t neg

T: IX*"person"* WAIT-cont, NOT+LIKE. SCL:V*"sit restlessly,"*

whq

COMPLAIN++. IX*"person"* "what"

S: NONE+BEAR-WITH

T: (repeat description using the sign)

S(all): (copy)

PRACTICE *Describing a Person*

15–25 minutes

Students use personal quality vocabulary and role shift to describe situation(s) involving the person being discussed.

PRESENT
(LESSON SLIDE 10:6:1)

Give your partner two names:

- one person you like
- one person you are not fond of

A: (pick a name), ask who
B: explain relationship and how you met him or her
A: ask if B likes him or her, ask why
B: reply, describe person
- use at least three personal quality signs
- use role shift to describe situation(s)

A: comment or ask further questions
B: reply

Demonstrate dialogue by calling up a student to role play Signer A and you role play Signer B. Give the student the names of two people you know, for example, Ethan and Emily.

whq
A: fs-ETHAN, WHO

B: US-TWO MEET fs-HS, US-TWO PLAY TENNIS, US-TWO SHARE+ER

q whq
A: YOU LIKE IX*"Ethan,"* YOU. (after B replies "yes") WHY

For "*• use at least three personal quality signs*"

B: IX*"Ethan"* SWEET, NICE, POLITE, GOODY-TWO-SHOES. IX*"Ethan"* BE-RAISED FARM

serious
IX*"Ethan"* GOOD BE-RESPONSIBLE, WORK-cont,

when
IX*"Ethan"* SMART. MEET NEW PEOPLE, IX*"Ethan"* LITTLE-BIT SHY. ME PLAY TENNIS, IX*"Ethan"* ALWAYS SUPPORT++, ENCOURAGE++

For "• *use role shift to describe situation(s)*"

B: (describe this with role shift—whenever I miss a tennis ball, he runs up behind me and hits the ball, doesn't get mad, says it's fine)

q
A: YOU SEE-him UP-TO-NOW

nod
B: YES, ME SEE IX"*Ethan*" FROM-TIME-TO-TIME

Pair up students and have them go through the dialogue taking turns asking about the two people their partners named.

Be sure students:

- use role shift to describe their situation(s)
- name at least three personal qualities for the person discussed.

HOMEWORK

Tell students to do **Homework 10:6** (*Student Workbook*, pages 277–280).

Also, students are to describe two people they know using one of the four personal qualities (BIG-HEADED, SWEET, PEA-BRAINED, or GOODY-TWO-SHOES).

HOMEWORK FOLLOW-UP
25–30 MINUTES

ACTIVITY

Divide class into groups of 4–5 students. Each student takes turns describing two people they know (See **Assignment**, *Student Workbook*, page 277).

For each of the two persons described, be sure students:

- use one of these personal quality signs (BIGHEADED, SWEET, PEABRAINED or GOODY-TWO-SHOES)
- follow this narrative sequence and use role shift:
  - give name of person
  - tell how you know this person
  - tell if you like or don't like the person
  - tell why, describe the person
    - use at least three personal quality signs
    - use role shift to describe situation(s).

LESSON 10:7

Telling Where Items Are Located

Lesson length: 50–60 minutes

LESSON GOAL

Students will sign this dialogue:

Dialogue

A: ask where

B: tell where

- name the room (raise brows)
- name furniture or appliance, or part of room (raise brows)
- specify location of item (use reference point)

A: respond

KEY SKILLS

sequence to tell where items are located

• name the room (raise brows)

q/t, t

KITCHEN, ENTER

• name furniture or appliance, or part of the room (raise brows)

t

IX-loc*"furniture/appliance or part of room"* (name it)

• specify location of item (use reference point)

[(wh)DCL or LCL*"furniture or appliance or part of room"*/

nod

IX-loc*"specific location"*] (item)

NOTIONS

Grammar

topicalization

signer's perspective

reference points

non-manual signals for distance: "far away," "cs"

classifiers

LCL:B*"flat objects"* (cabinet doors, table, stove)
LCL:C*"upright object"* (oven, refrigerator, dishwasher)
(2h)DCL*"long flat object"* (table)
ICL*"open drawers, doors"*

Vocabulary

household items

#TV ICL*"use remote"*	NEEDLE+STRING
MATCHES	CANDLE
SOAP	NAIL-CLIPPERS
HEADACHE+MEDICINE	MAGAZINE
SCREWDRIVER	KNIFE
STAPLER	SCOTCH-TAPE
TOWEL	SCISSORS
CAMERA	DICTIONARY

kitchen appliances

fs-STOVE
fs-SINK
fs-OVEN
fs-REF
fs-DW

PREPARATION Read and view **Telling Where Items Are Located** in *Student Workbook*, page 281.

MATERIALS **10:7 Lesson Slides**
Exercise 3 (*Student Workbook*, page 490)

HOMEWORK 10:7 *Student Workbook*, pages 281–286

REVIEW *Household Items and Kitchen Appliances*

20 minutes

PRESENT
(LESSON SLIDES 10:7:1–4)

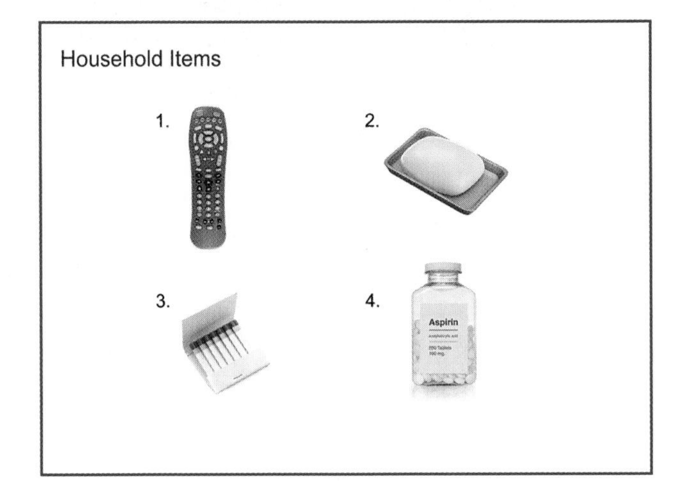

Introduce these signs for household items:

For **Slide 1**

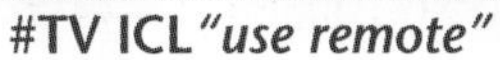

#TV ICL*"use remote"*

SOAP

MATCHES

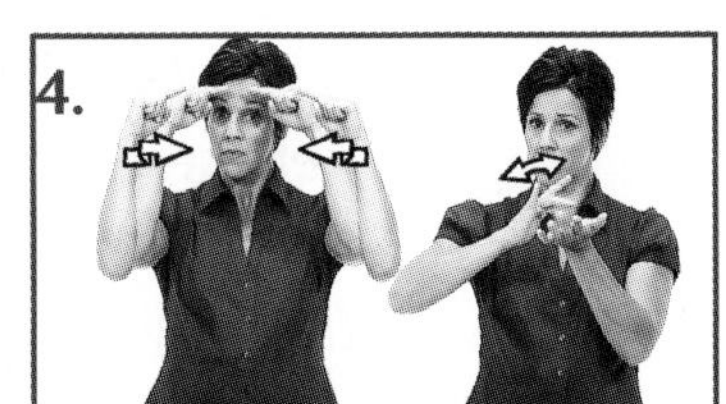

HEADACHE+MEDICINE

For **Slide 2**

SCREWDRIVER

KNIFE

SCISSORS

NEEDLE+STRING

For **Slide3**

NAIL-CLIPPERS

DICTIONARY

STAPLER

CAMERA

For **Slide4**

CANDLE

SCOTCH-TAPE

TOWEL

MAGAZINE

Review. Describe each object by either giving a definition or a situation without using the sign for the object. Have students give you the sign, for example:

Dictionary

(neg: NOT-KNOW; rhet: ME DO++)

T: ME SEE WORD, NOT-KNOW. ME DO++. ME GET BOOK

(whq: READ. IX"book" "what")

ICL"*turn pages*" FIND WORD, READ. IX"*book*" "what"

S: DICTIONARY

Continue until all signs are reviewed.

PRESENT
(LESSON SLIDE 10:7:5)

Introduce the following signs for appliances and classifiers to indicate their locations and general appearance:

appliances/furniture	*classifiers*
1) fs-OVEN	LCL:C*"upright object (left)"* or (2h)ICL*"pull open oven doors (left)"*
2) fs-REF	LCL:C*"upright object (left)"*
3) SHELVES	DCL*"shelves (front upper left)"*
4) fs-DW	LCL:C*"small upright object (front lower left)"*
5) fs-SINK	DCL*"bowl"* IX*"bowl (front)"*
6) fs-CABINET	ICL*"open door(s) (front upper right)"* LCL:B*"open door(s) (front upper right)"*
7) fs-STOVE	DCL*"stovetop"* or LCL:B*"stove (right)"*
8) DRAWER (1h or 2h)	ICL*"open drawer(s) (right)"*
9) fs-COUNTER	(2h)DCL:C*"long flat object (left, front and right)"*
10) TABLE	LCL:B*"flat object (front center)"* or (2h)DCL:C*"long flat object" (front center)*

DRAWER

Review. Describe location for each appliance in the slide and have student give the sign for it. For example:

q/t t

T: KITCHEN, ENTER, "wave left" LCL:C*"oven (left),"*

whq

(2h)ICL*"open double oven doors (left)"* IX*"oven"* "what"

S: fs-OVEN

q/t t far away

T: KITCHEN, ENTER, IX-dir*"sink"* *(front)* DCL*"bowl"* IX-loc*"bowl*

whq

(front)" "what"

S: fs-SINK

Continue until all the appliances and parts of the kitchen have been described and named.

INTRODUCE *Sequence To Tell Where Items Are Located*

15–20 minutes

PRESENT

(LESSON SLIDE 10:7:6)

X
Tell where
• name the room (raised brows)
• name furniture or appliance, or part of room (raised brows)
• specify location of item (use reference point)

Demonstrate how to tell where the **matches** are located. *(The matches are in the third drawer to the right of the stove—see the red "X.")*

For "• ***name the room (raised brows)***"

q/t t
T: KITCHEN, ENTER
S(all): (copy)

Make sure students raise brows when naming the kitchen.

For "• ***name furniture or appliance, or part of the room (raised brows)***"

t
T: IX-loc"*stove (right)*" fs-STOVE, LCL:B"*stove top (right)*"
S(all): (copy)

Make sure students raise brows when naming the stove.

For "• ***specify location of item (use reference point)***"
T: **[(wh)LCL:B"*stove top*"/IX-loc"*drawer on right side*"]**
t t
DRAWER, FIRST, SECOND, THIRD, ICL"*pull drawer open*"]
[(wh)IX-loc"*inside drawer*"/ICL"*hold drawer open*"]
nod
MATCHES, IX-loc"*the drawer*"
S(all): (copy)

Make sure students establish the location of the stove on their weak hand before indicating the location of the next object, the drawer and the matches.

NOTE: Perspective shift (see **9:11**) may be used by shifting your point of view as if you are standing in front of the furniture or appliance when describing the item.

Now have students sign the whole thing:

q/t t
S: KITCHEN, ENTER
t
IX-loc"*stove (right)*" fs-STOVE, LCL:B"*stove top (right)*"
[(wh)LCL:B"*stove top*"/IX-loc"*drawer on right side*"]
t
DRAWER, FIRST, SECOND, THIRD, ICL"*pull drawer open*"]
[(wh)IX-loc"*inside drawer*"/ICL"*hold drawer open*"]
nod
MATCHES, IX-loc"*the drawer.*"

PRESENT
(LESSON SLIDE 10:7:7)

Tell where
- name the room (raised brows)
- name furniture or appliances, or part of room (raised brows)
- specify location of item (use reference point)

Demonstrate how to tell where the **nail clippers** are located.
(The nail clippers are on the bottom shelf to the left of the windows—see the red "X.")

For "• ***name the room (raised brows)***"

q/t t
T: KITCHEN, ENTER
S(all): (copy)

Make sure students raise brows when naming the kitchen.

For "• ***name furniture or appliance, or part of the room***"

t t
T: IX-loc*"windows (front)"* WINDOW IX*"window"*
S(all): (copy)

Make sure students raise brows when naming the window and the counter.

For "• ***specify location of item***"
T: **[IX-loc*"window (front)"*/(wh)IX-loc*"shelves (left)"*]** SHELVES.

t
FIRST SHELF **[(wh)LCL:B*"shelf (left)"*/IX-loc*"on the shelf"*]**

nod
NAIL-CLIPPER IX-loc*"the shelf"*
S(all): (copy)

Make sure students use reference point when specifying location of shelves and nail clipper (on the shelf).

Now have students sign the whole thing:

q/t t t

S: KITCHEN, ENTER, IX-loc*"windows (front)"* WINDOW,
[IX-loc"*window (front)*"/(wh)IX-loc"*shelves (left)*"] SHELVES.

t

FIRST SHELF **[(wh)LCL:B"*shelf (left)*"/IX-loc"*on the shelf*"]**

nod

NAIL-CLIPPER IX-loc*"the shelf"*

PRESENT
(LESSON SLIDE 10:7:8)

Tell where
• name the room (raised brows)
• name furniture or appliances, or part of room (raised brows)
• specify location of item (use reference point)

Demonstrate how to tell where the **magazine** is located.
(The magazine is in the cabinets above the ovens—see the red "X.")

For "• ***name the room (raised brows)***"

q/t t

T: KITCHEN, ENTER
S(all): (copy)

Make sure students raise brows when naming the kitchen.

For "• ***name furniture or appliance, or part of the room***"

cs t

T: "wave left" [fs-OVEN], LCL:C*"double oven (left)"* IX-loc*"cabinets*

t

above the oven (left)" [fs-CABINET], (2h)LCL:B*"open doors (left)"*
S(all): (copy)

Make sure students use "cs" to indicate the oven is close to the entry point, and to raise brows when naming the oven and the cabinets.

For "• ***specify location of item***"

T: **[(wh)LCL:B*"door"*/IX-loc*"left side of cabinet"*]**

nod: MAGAZINE

S(all): (copy)

Make sure students use reference point when specifying location of magazine (inside the cabinet).

Now have students sign the whole thing:

S: [KNOW] KITCHEN (q/t), ENTER (t), "wave left" fs-OVEN,
LCL:C*"double oven (left)"* (t) IX-loc*"cabinets above the oven (left)"*
[fs-CABINET] (t), (2h)LCL:B*"open doors (left),"* **[(wh)LCL:B*"door"*/**
IX-loc*"left side of cabinet"*] MAGAZINE (nod)

PRACTICE *Telling Where an Item Is Located*

15–20 minutes

Students practice the sequence for telling where an item is located.

PRESENT
(LESSON SLIDE 10:7:9)

A: ask where
B: tell where
- name the room (raise brows)
- name furniture or appliances, or part of room (raise brows)
- specify location of item (use reference point)

A: (write the number for the item in that location)

EXERCISE 3

(*Student Workbook*, page 490).

Pair students up and have them decide which row of items **Items 1–8** or **Items 9–16** they will use and decide where an item is kept by putting a number in the location. When ready, have them follow the dialogue to locate each others' items.

Be sure students:

- follow the sequence to tell where
- raise brows when naming locations
- maintain weak hand as reference point when specifying location of an item.

HOMEWORK

Tell students to do **Homework 10:7** (*Student Workbook*, pages 281–286).

LESSON 10:8

Wh-word Questions 2

Lesson length: 35–40 minutes

LESSON GOAL Students will translate questions about choices using WHICH.

KEY SKILLS

Translating the question

- name the topic (raise brows)
- name the choices (contrastive structure)
- end with wh-word question: WHICH (furrow brows, tilt head forward, hold last sign)

NOTIONS

Grammar

Contrastive structure
List across neutral space and nodding

Vocabulary

Wh-word question
WHICH

Others

COOL	!THRILL!	EARN
WARM	USE-GUNS	!MONEY!
LOVE	SEND-TO	WEATHER

MATERIALS

10:8 Lesson Slides
10:8 Follow-up Slides

HOMEWORK 10:8 *Student Workbook*, pages 287–289

INTRODUCE *Describing the Choices*

15–20 minutes

Have students open their workbooks to **Wh-Word Questions 2** on page 287, draw a circle around the topic, and underline the choices in each question.

PRESENT
(LESSON SLIDES 10:8:1–9)

1. Do you prefer cool or warm weather?

Focus on the underlined choices in each question and demonstrate how to sign the choices using contrastive structure. Introduce signs in bold. Have students copy.

For **Slide 1**

     left   right
T: **COOL, WARM**
S: (copy)

COOL

WARM

Do the same for **Slides 2–9**.

For **Slide 2**

    lf   rt
CAT, #DOG

For **Slide 3** ***(more than two choices)***

lf / mid / rt

(2h)FUNNY, **LOVE/HUG** STORY, **THRILL USE-GUN++**

LOVE

!THRILL!

USE-GUNS

For **Slide 4**

TABLE [(wh)LCL:B*"table"*/SCL:V*"sit at table"*]

lf

(2h)alt.ICL:A*"use forks putting food in mouth,"* SIT WATCH

rt

#TV, [(wh)ICL*"hold plate"*/ICL*"use fork putting food in mouth"*

For **Slide 5**

lf / rt

SCL:V*"on back,"* SCL:V*"on side"*

SEND-TO

For **Slide 6**

lf / rt

fs-EMAIL **SEND-TO-left**, USE-VIDEOPHONE CHAT

EARN

!MONEY!

For **Slide 7**

lf / rt

SAVE/STORE, SPEND-MONEY++

For **Slide 8**

lf / rt

EARN !MONEY! BUT VOMIT, EARN SMALL, BUT ENJOY, #FUN

For **Slide 9** ***(more than two choices)***

lf / mid / rt

SWEET, SMART, BEAUTIFUL

PRACTICE *Translating the Questions*

35–40 minutes

Students practice asking WHICH questions (wh-word), using contrastive structure and listing.

PRESENT
LESSON SLIDE
10:8:10–12)

1. Do you prefer warm or cool weather?
2. Do you prefer cats or dogs?
   (topic is implied: type of pets)
3. Do you prefer romantic, comedy, or action films?

Translating the Question

- name the topic *(raise brows)*
- name the choices *(contrastive structure)*
- end with wh-word question
  (furrow brows, tilt head forward, hold last sign)

Demonstrate the translations and have students copy.

WEATHER

1. ***Do you prefer warm or cool weather?***

t lf rt whq
T: **WEATHER**, YOU PREFER, COOL, WARM, WHICH
S(all): (copy)

Be sure students:

- raise brows when naming the topic
- establish and orient their signs for the first choice toward their non-dominant side, then orient their signs toward their dominant side for the second choice
- furrow brows and tilt head forward when signing WHICH at the end of the sentence.

Teacher's Translation Guide

NOTE: Add "fs-PET" to name the implied topic.

2. ***Do you prefer cats or dogs?***

t lf rt whq
fs-PET, YOU PREFER, CAT, #DOG, WHICH

NOTE: Since there are three choices, put the three choices in sequence across the neutral space in front. Be sure to nod with each choice.

3. ***Do you prefer comedy, romance or action films?***

lf mid

MOVIE, YOU PREFER, (2h)FUNNY++, **LOVE** STORY,

rt whq

!THRILL! USE-GUNS, WHICH

4. ***Do you prefer to eat at table or in front of TV?***

t t

EAT, YOU PREFER, TABLE [(wh)LCL:B*"table"/SCL:V"sit at table"*]

lf

ICL:A*"use forks to eat,"* #OR SIT WATCH #TV, [(wh)ICL*"holding*

rt whq

bowl/plate"/ICL*"putting food in mouth,"* WHICH

NOTE: Use #OR to clearly separate the choices.

5. ***Do you prefer to sleep on your back or on your side?***

t lf

SLEEP, YOU PREFER, (wh)LCL:B*"bed"*/SCL:V*"lie on back,"*

rt whq

(wh)LCL:B*"bed"*/ SCL:V*"lie on side,"* WHICH

6. ***Do you prefer to get in touch with Deaf people by email or videophone?***

t

YOU CONTACT DEAF PEOPLE, YOU PREFER fs-EMAIL,

rt whq

SEND-TO, #OR USE-VIDEOPHONE CHAT, WHICH

NOTE: Use #OR to clearly separate the two choices.

7. ***Do you prefer to save or spend money?***

t lf rt

MONEY, YOU PREFER, SAVE/STORE, SPEND-MONEY++,

whq

WHICH

8. ***Do you prefer to work at a job you hate but get paid a lot of money or a job that's fun but doesn't pay well?***

t lf

WORK, YOU PREFER, **EARN !MONEY!** BUT VOMIT, #OR EARN

rt whq

SMALL, BUT ENJOY, #FUN, WHICH

NOTE: Use #OR to clearly separate the choices.

NOTE: Since there are three choices, put the three choices in sequence across the neutral space in front. Be sure to nod with each choice.

9. ***Do you prefer to be with a person who is kind, beautiful or intelligent?***

t: PERSON YOU BE-STEADY-WITH, YOU PREFER, SELF

lf: SWEET,

mid: SMART,

rt: BEAUTIFUL,

whq: WHICH

HOMEWORK

Tell students to do **Homework 10:8** (*Student Workbook*, pages 287–289).

HOMEWORK FOLLOW-UP
20–25 MINUTES

PRESENT
(FOLLOW-UP SLIDE 10:8:1)

1. Do you prefer cool or warm weather?
2. Do you prefer cats or dogs?
3. Do you prefer comedy, romance or action films?
4. Do you prefer to eat at a table or in front of the TV?
5. Do you prefer to sleep on your back or on your side?
6. Do you prefer to get in touch with Deaf people by email or videophone?
7. Do you prefer to save or spend money?
8. Do you prefer to work at a job you hate but get paid a lot of money or a job that's fun but doesn't pay well?
9. Do you prefer to be with a person who is kind, beautiful or intelligent?

Call on each student to sign one of the questions to you. Be sure students:

- raise brows when naming the topic
- use contrastive structure for two choices by orienting their signs for the first choice toward their non-dominant side, and orienting their signs toward their dominant side for the second choice
- use listing for three choices by sequencing them across the neutral space in front and nod with each choice

- furrow brows and tilt head forward when signing WHICH at the end of the sentence.

Follow-up questions. Now ask students one of the questions. After students answer, ask follow-up questions. For example:

t lf rt whq
T: WEATHER, YOU PREFER, COOL, WARM, WHICH
S: [ME PREFER] WARM
whq
T: WHY
S: WARM, ME CAN LEAVE-FOR fs-BEACH, SWIM, WALK
t whq
T: fs-BEACH, YOU PREFER WHICH
S: fs-MALIBU-BEACH
T: SWELL

Mingle. Have students mingle and ask each other questions along with a couple of follow-up questions.

LESSON 10:9

Comparing Personal Qualities

Lesson length: 35–45 minutes

LESSON GOAL

Students will sign this interview.

Dialogue

A: ask who are the two people B chose[1]

B: name two people you know well—introduce them:

- their names
- how they are related to you
- what they look like
- what they do
- their ages
- etc.

A: ask "which" questions
"which is more..."[2]
"which is better..."[3]

B: reply, give reason and give examples

A: give a hypothetical situation, ask who B would pick or prefer[4]

B: reply, explain why

A: respond

KEY PHRASES

t whq
[1] TWO PEOPLE, [YOU] PICK-left, PICK-right, WHO

whq
[2] WHICH (wh)IX-left, IX-right MORE SWEET WHICH

whq
[3] WHICH (wh)IX-left, IX-right BETTER BE-GEARED WHICH

cond
[4] SUPPOSE (situation), WHICH (wh)IX-left, IX-right YOU PREFER

whq
(wh)IX-left, IX-right WHICH

NOTIONS	***Grammar*** contrastive structure conditional clause
	Vocabulary DISCUSS++ EUROPE HIRE/INVITE SUPPOSE HURT HAPPEN++
PREPARATION	Read and view key language elements in **Learn the Interview**, *Student Workbook*, pages 290–293.
MATERIALS	**10:9 Lesson Slides** **10:9 Follow-up Slides**
HOMEWORK 10:9	*Student Workbook*, pages 290–296

INTRODUCE *Discuss Two People*

20–30 minutes

PRESENT

(LESSON SLIDE 10:9:1)

Show **Interview Part 1** and ask comprehension questions to elicit the information about the two people being compared:

TOPICS	PERSON 1	PERSON 2
names	Tia	Kim
relationship	older sister	younger sister
ages	44	38
marital status	married, 2 children	not married, no children
occupation	doctor	lawyer
appearance	black hair, brown eyes, light-skinned, pretty	black hair, brown eyes, slightly-darker-skinned, pretty

Be sure students remember that the **older sister is on Iva's left** and the **younger sister on her right** before they view the next video segment.

PRESENT
(LESSON SLIDE 10:9:2)

Show **Interview Part 2** and ask comprehension questions:

Ask which one is more friendly.

T: WHICH (wh)IX-left, IX-right MORE CHEERFUL, WHICH (wh)IX-left, IX-right [whq]

S: **IX-right** (nod), MORE CHEERFUL, IX-right++.
SOCIALIZE, CHAT, LIKE, IX-right.
IX-left (shake head) QUIET-char, LITTLE-BIT STUCK-UP,
"well" QUIET++, POSS-left

Ask which one is more responsible.

T: WHICH (wh)IX-left, IX-right MORE BE-RESPONSIBLE, WHICH (wh)IX-left, IX-right [whq]

S: BOTH !GOOD! BE-RESPONSIBLE.
IX-right !GOOD! BE-RESPONSIBLE.
IX-left (shake head) IN-PAST *"long ago"* AVOID+++,
(2h)alt."pshaw." NOW [t], IX-left MARRY, HAVE
CHILDREN, IX-left BE-RESPONSIBLE

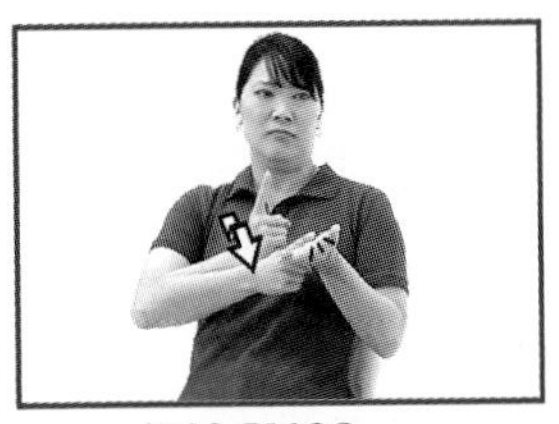
DISCUSS++

Ask which one is funnier.

T: WHICH (wh)IX-left, IX-right MORE (2h)FUNNY, WHICH
whq
(wh)IX-left, IX-right

S: **IX-left** MORE (2h)FUNNY. QUIET-char, BUT REAL/SURE SELF-left (2h)FUNNY. IX-left NARRATE, PEOPLE LOOK-AT-left LAUGH-teeth.
IX-right (shake head), LIKE DISCUSS++. IX-right

HIRE/INVITE

Ask which one is more organized.

T: WHICH (wh)IX-left, IX-right BETTER BE-GEARED++, WHICH
whq
(wh)IX-left, IX-right

t
S: WORK, BOTH !GOOD! BE-GEARED++,
t
POSS-left, POSS-right HOME, MESSED-UP+++.
IX-left SMART. IX-left **HIRE/INVITE** WOMAN WORK CLEAN
IX-right (shake head) TRY++ CLEAN++, STILL MESSED-UP++, "pshaw"

HURT

Ask which one is more honest.

T: WHICH (wh)IX-left, IX-right MORE HONEST, WHICH
whq
(wh)IX-left, IX-right

S: BOTH HONEST.
IX-right STRAIGHT/DIRECT
neg
IX-left(shake head) VAGUE-TALK, NOT-WANT **HURT** FEEL, IX-left VAGUE-TALK.

Ask which one has better judgement.

T: WHICH (wh)IX-left, IX-right BETTER THINK+JUDGE, WHICH

whq

(wh)IX-left, IX-right

S: BOTH !GOOD! THINK+JUDGE

PRESENT
(LESSON SLIDE 10:9:3)

EUROPE

HAPPEN++

SUPPOSE

Show **Interview Part 3** and ask these questions:

Ask what advantages each person has when traveling in Europe.

whq

T: TRAVEL **EUROPE**, IX-left GOOD, IX-right GOOD "what"

S: IX-left MORE (2h)FUNNY-char **HAPPEN++**, #FUN, IX-right GOOD GEAR-WITH

Ask which sister students would choose to travel with in Europe.

cond t

T: **SUPPOSE** YOU TRAVEL EUROPE, TWO SISTER,

whq whq

YOU PICK WHICH, WHY

S: (share their own preference for which sister and explain why)

PRACTICE *Preparing for the Interview*

15 minutes

Students practice questions in preparation for the interview.

PRESENT
(LESSON SLIDE 10:9:4)

A: ask who are the two people B chose
B: name two people you know well and describe them: - their names - how they are related to you
- what they look like
- what they do
- their ages
- etc.

A: ask "which" questions
"which is more..."
"which is better..."
B: reply, give reasons and give examples
A: give a hypothetical situation, ask who B would pick or prefer
B: reply, explain why
A: respond

Demonstrate Signer A's questions. Have students copy.

For *"A: ask who are the two people B chose"*

t whq
T: Two PEOPLE, YOU PICK-left, PICK-right, WHO
S(all): (copy)

For *"A: ask "which" questions" (which is more...?)*

whq
T: WHICH (wh)IX-left, IX-right MORE SWEET, WHICH
S(all): (copy)

For *"A: ask "which" questions" (which is better...?)*

whq
T: WHICH (wh)IX-left, IX-right BETTER+JUDGE, WHICH
S(all): (copy)

Point out that only three signs are appropriate to ask with "which is better...?" BE-GEARED, JUDGE, and MONEY EXCHANGE.

For *"A: give a hypothetical situation, ask who B would pick or prefer"*

cond

T: **SUPPOSE** (situation), WHICH (wh)IX-left, IX-right YOU

whq

PREFER (wh)IX-left, IX-right WHICH

S(all): (copy)

Assign Roles. Assign **Interviewer 1** to half of the class and **Interviewer 2** to the other half prepare for next class. See **Homework** below.

HOMEWORK

Tell students to do **Homework 10:9** (*Student Workbook*, pages 290–296).

HOMEWORK FOLLOW-UP
45 MINUTES

Also, students are to prepare information about two people they know well and to create interview questions as **Interviewer 1** and **Interviewer 2**.

PRESENT
(FOLLOW-UP SLIDE 10:9:1)

Interviews

Partners will interview each other following this dialogue. Feel free to take turns being A and B for each question before moving on. For example both partners ask about the two people the other chose and so on.

A: ask who are the two people B chose

B: name two people you know well and describe them

A: ask 6 to 8 questions to compare the two people

B: reply, give reasons and give examples

A: give a hypothetical situation, ask who B would pick or prefer

B: reply, explain why

A: respond

Pair up students assigned as **Interviewer 1** with those assigned as **Interviewer 2**, and have them take turns interviewing each other (See **Assignment**, *Student Workbook*, page 293).

Conclude. Have students (as Signer A) take turns asking you (as Signer B) a question from their interviews.

Be sure students:

- use contrastive structure to refer to the two people when asking the "which" questions
- begin the hypothetical situation with SUPPOSE.

LESSON 10:10

Culture: Interrupting Others

Lesson length: 50–70 minutes

LESSON GOAL

Students will practice culturally appropriate behaviors to interrupt conversations, and to resume the conversations.

KEY SKILLS

Interrupting others' conversations

- approach and lean over when waving to get attention
- once acknowledged by both, explain the interruption
- apologize to Signer A after Signer B leaves

Interrupting someone signing to you

- sign (wh)"hold on/wait" and wait for Deaf person (or teacher) to acknowledge the interruption before breaking eye contact
- give an explanation of the distraction
- resume or end conversation appropriately

NOTIONS

Phrases

Resuming Conversation

"pshaw"-(explain distraction), GO-AHEAD

"pshaw"-(explain distraction), NOTHING-TO-IT, ANYWAY, (resume talk)

Vocabulary

Interrupting

EXCUSE-me

INTERRUPT

SORRY

(wh)"hold on/wait"

Resume Conversation

(2h)GO-AHEAD

ANYWAY

NOTHING-TO-IT

Distractions

- FIRE RING/ALARM
- PHONE RING/ALARM
- #DOG BARK++
- BABY CRY++
- LIGHT IX-loc*"light"* ECL*"flashing"*
- SCL:3*"vehicle pass by"* ECL*"sirens flashing"*
- CAR ICL*"horn honking"*
- SOMEONE OUTSIDE YELL++
- TELL-all AIRPLANE, PLANE-TAKE-OFF POSTPONE
- TELL-all BUILDING NOW BE-CLOSED

PREPARATION Make a copy of **10:10 Distraction Cards** (for dialogue practice, page 579–581)

MATERIALS **10:10 Lesson Slides**
10:10 Distraction Cards

HOMEWORK 10:10 *Student Workbook*, pages 297–301

INTRODUCE *Interrupting Others' Conversation*

5–7 minutes

PRESENT
(LESSON SLIDE 10:10:1)

INTERRUPT TO DELIVER A MESSAGE

Show video **Interrupt to Deliver a Message**.

Point out:

- Derrick leaning over and extending his hand to get Melvin and Terrylene's attention
- as soon as Melvin and Terrylene look at Derrick, he signs **EXCUSE-me INTERRUPT *"so-sorry"***
- Terrylene acknowledging Derrick by signing "well"
- after Melvin leaves the room, Derrick signs **SORRY** to Terrylene for the interruption
- after Terrylene responds, Derrick leaves the room.

EXCUSE-me INTERRUPT *"so-sorry"*

SORRY

PRACTICE *Interrupting Others' Conversations*

15–20 minutes

Students practice interrupting others' conversation.

PRESENT
(LESSON SLIDE 10:10:2)

Signers **A & B**: (conversing casually)
C: (get A and B's attention), interrupt
A & B: (acknowledge C)
C: deliver message to B
B: respond to C, say goodbye to A (exit)
C: apologize to A
A: respond

Demonstrate Signer C's lines. Have students copy:

For ***"C: (get A and B's attention), interrupt"***

apologetic
T: (lean over) "hey" **EXCUSE-me INTERRUPT-you, "so-sorry"**
S: (copy)

For ***"C: deliver message to B"***
T: YOUR FRIEND IX-loc*"back there"* WAIT
S: (copy)

For ***"C: apologize to A"***
apologetic
T: **SORRY [INTERRUPT]**
S: (copy)

You role play Signer C. Have two students be Signers A and B and demonstrate the dialogue in front of class.

Line Up. Now, you become Signer A and the student role playing Signer A becomes Signer C. Have rest of class form a line behind Signer C.

When done with the dialogue, have Signer C take Signer B's place and Signer B goes to the back of the line. The next person in line becomes Signer C.

The activity is over when every student has had a chance to role play Signer C.

Be sure students as Signer C:

- approach and lean over when waving to get attention
- once acknowledged by both, explain the interruption
- apologize to Signer A after Signer B leaves.

INTRODUCE *Interrupting Someone Signing to You*

10–15 minutes

PRESENT

(LESSON SLIDE 10:10:3)

Show video **Ask to Hold On 1**.

Point out:

- Lauren signs **(wh)"hold on/wait"** with her weak hand to interrupt Suzanne, then tells what is distracting her (Suzanne's name being called on the public address system)

- Suzanne pauses, looks and nods at Lauren to acknowledge the interruption before Lauren looks away and explains the distraction.

(wh)"hold on/wait"

Discuss: Whenever there is a distraction, the listener should inform the signer by signing **(wh)"hold on/wait"** and wait for him or her to acknowledge the interruption before breaking eye contact. Breaking eye contact without forewarning and an explanation is considered rude.

PRESENT
(LESSON SLIDE 10:10:4)

"pshaw"

GO-AHEAD

Show video **Ask to Hold On 2.**

Point out:

- Lauren signs **(wh)"hold on/wait"** with her weak hand to interrupt JT, then tells what is distracting her (a car horn honking)
- JT pauses, looks at Lauren and slightly nods to acknowledge the interruption before Lauren looks away
- after checking the distraction and explaining further, Lauren asks JT to resume conversation **("pshaw" GO-AHEAD)**

PRESENT
(LESSON SLIDE 10:10:5)

Distractions

- fire alarm
- phone ringing
- dog barking
- baby crying
- flashing light(s)
- sirens blaring
- car horn honking
- someone outside shouting
- announcement that the plane is delayed
- announcement that the building is closing

Introduce signs for distractions by using them in sentences with (wh)"hold on/wait." Have students copy. For example:

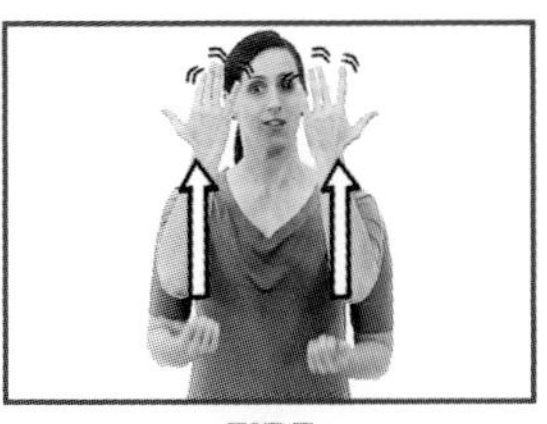
FIRE

For ***"• fire alarm"***

T: **(wh)"hold on/wait,"** HEAR IX*"location of noise"* **FIRE RING/ALARM.**
S: (copy)

Do the same with the rest of the distractions.

RING/ALARM

For ***"• phone ringing"***
PHONE RING/ALARM

BARK++

For ***"• dog barking"***
#DOG **BARK++**

For ***"• baby crying"***
BABY CRY++

For ***"• flashing light(s)"***
LIGHT IX-loc*"light"* ECL*"flashing"*

ECL*"sirens flashing"*

For ***"• sirens blaring"***
SCL:3*"vehicle pass by"*
ECL*"sirens flashing"*

ICL*"horn honking"*

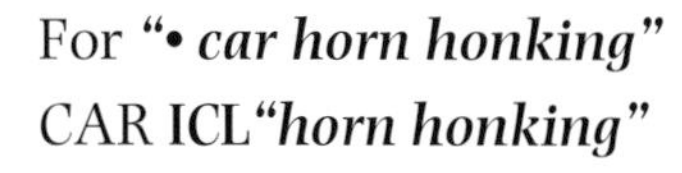

For "• *car horn honking*"
CAR **ICL*"horn honking"***

OUTSIDE

For "• *someone outside shouting*"
SOMEONE **OUTSIDE YELL++**

For "• *announcement that the plane is delayed*"
TELL-all AIRPLANE, PLANE-TAKE-OFF POSTPONE

For "• *announcement that the building is closing*"
TELL-all **BUILDING** NOW BE-CLOSED

YELL++

TELL-all

BUILDING

PRACTICE *Interrupting Someone Signing to You*

20–30 minutes

Students practice interrupting someone signing to them, asking them to hold on, explaining what is distracting, and resuming the conversation.

PRESENT
(LESSON SLIDE 10:10:6)

Situation: at A's home

Signer **A**: talk about something
(while A talks, student with a card distracts B)
B: ask to hold on
A: (pause)
B: explain distraction
A: check distraction, resume conversation

NOTHING-TO-IT

ANYWAY

NOTE: Explain NOTHING-TO-IT means NOT IMPORTANT, NOT MUST PAY-ATTENTION.

Ask a student to use a smart phone or flashlight to flash light behind you (as Signer A) to demonstrate the last line *"A: check distraction, resume conversation"* for "light flashing." Have students copy.

T (as A): (looks back, checks light) **"pshaw"-light, NOTHING-TO-IT, ANYWAY,** (resume talk)
S: (copy)

Pass out **10.10 Distraction Cards (Situation: in A's home)** to four students (See **Materials**). Tell the student with Card 1 to distract Signer B with the noise on their card.

Role play Signer A and call up a student without a card to role play Signer B and handle the distraction made by the student with the card.

Continue calling up students to be Signer B, until all four **Distraction Cards (Situation: in A's home)** are done. Pass on the cards to four other students and repeat procedure.

Be sure students as Signer B:
- sign (wh)"hold on/wait" and wait for Signer A to acknowledge the interruption before breaking eye contact
- give an explanation of the distraction
- resume or end conversation appropriately.

PRESENT
(LESSON SLIDE 10:10:7)

Situation: at B's workplace

Signer
A: talk about something
(while A talks, student with a card distracts B)
B: ask A to hold on
A: (pause)
B: explain and check distraction, ask A to resume conversation

Again, ask a student to use a smart phone or flashlight to flash light in front of you (as Signer B) to demonstrate the last line *"B: explain and check distraction, ask A to resume conversation"* for "light flashing" in the following locations. Have students copy.

T (as B): (wh)"hold on/wait" LIGHT IX-loc*"light"* ECL*"flashing"* (looks in direction of the flashing light, then to Signer A) **"pshaw"-light, GO-AHEAD**
S: (copy)

Pass out the **10.10 Distraction Cards (Situation: at B's workplace)** to four students (See **Materials**). Tell the student with Card 1 to distract Signer B with the noise on their card.

Call up a student without a card to role play Signer B and handle the distraction made by the student with the card while you role play Signer A.

Continue calling up students to be Signer B, until all four **Distraction Cards (Situation: at B's workplace)** are done. Pass on the cards to other students and repeat procedure until all students have had a chance to be Signer B.

Be sure students as Signer B:
- sign (wh)"hold on/wait" and wait for Signer A to acknowledge the interruption before breaking eye contact
- give an explanation of the distraction
- resume or end conversation appropriately.

PRESENT
(LESSON SLIDE 10:10:8)

Situation: at an airport

Signer
A: talks about something
B: (distracted by public announcement), ask A to hold on
A: (pause)
B: explain distraction (A's plane leaving soon)
A or B: respond to distraction, resume (or end) conversation

Divide class into groups of four and have them brainstorm what to say for the last line *"A or B: respond to distraction, resume (or end) conversation."* When done, call a pair from each group up front to demonstrate the dialogue.

Be sure students as Signer B:

- sign (wh)"hold on/wait" and wait for Signer A to acknowledge the interruption before breaking eye contact
- give an explanation of the distraction
- resume or end conversation appropriately.

PRESENT
(LESSON SLIDE 10:10:9)

Situation: in a public place
(theatre, restaurant, or a shopping mall)

Signer
A: talks about something
B: (distracted by public announcement) ask A to hold on
A: (pause)
B: explain distraction (building closing)
A or B: respond to distraction, resume (or end) conversation

Return students to their groups to brainstorm the last line for this situation. When done, call out the other pair from each group to front to demonstrate the dialogue.

Be sure students as Signer B:

- sign (wh)"hold on/wait" and wait for Signer A to acknowledge the interruption before breaking eye contact
- give an explanation of the distraction
- resume or end conversation appropriately.

HOMEWORK

Tell students to do **Homework 10:10** (*Student Workbook*, pages 297–301).

LESSON 10:11

Comprehension: Why the Owl Has Big Eyes

Lesson length: 30–50 minutes

LESSON GOAL Students will develop comprehension and production skills through the story **Why the Owl Has Big Eyes**

KEY SKILLS **For comprehension:** Students will develop the ability to process larger chunks of information and figure out the meaning of a sign from context

For production: Student will build fluency by re-telling the story or by asking questions about the story

NOTIONS *Vocabulary*

Possible new signs in the story:

GOD

WORLD

BE-EXCEPTIONALLY-SKILLED

PREPARATION

- View the story **Why the Owl Has Big Eyes** on **Lesson Slide 10:11:1**
- Decide which **Comprehension** and **Production** activities to use for the lesson

MATERIALS **10:11 Lesson Slides**

10:11 Follow-up Slides

HOMEWORK 10:11 *Student Workbook*, page 303–304

INTRODUCE *Why the Owl Has Big Eyes*

5–7 minutes

Introduce these signs before showing the video story:

GOD

sign	*explanation*
GOD	PERSON IX-loc*"up there"* IX*"God"* MAKE TREE, ANIMAL, PEOPLE. rhet SIGN "what" **GOD**
WORLD	DCL*"world"* [(wh)IX-loc NORTH AMERICA, IX-loc*"down"* SOUTH AMERICA, IX-loc*"to right"* ENGLAND, FRANCE, SPAIN IX*"here and there"* t rhet DCL*"world"* SIGN *"what."* **WORLD**
BE-EXCEPTIONALLY-SKILLED	(wh)!ONE-person! KNOW fs-HOW MAKE, FIX, IX-mult*"others"* CAN'T. [(wh)!ONE-person!/**BE-EXCEPTIONALLY-SKILLED**]

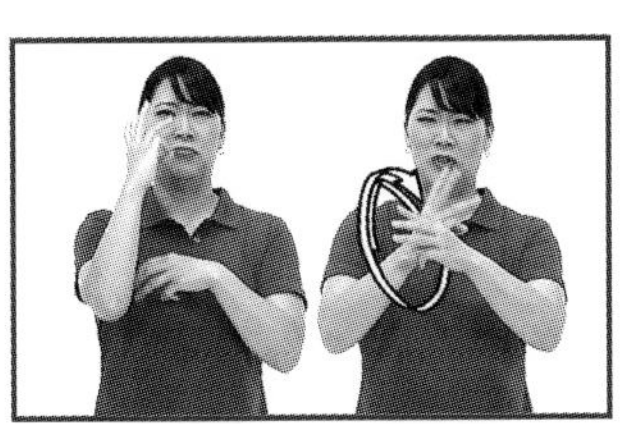

WORLD

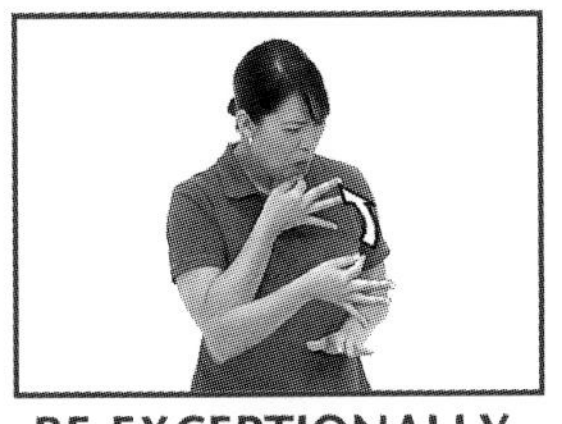

BE-EXCEPTIONALLY-SKILLED

PRESENT

(LESSON SLIDE 10:11:1)

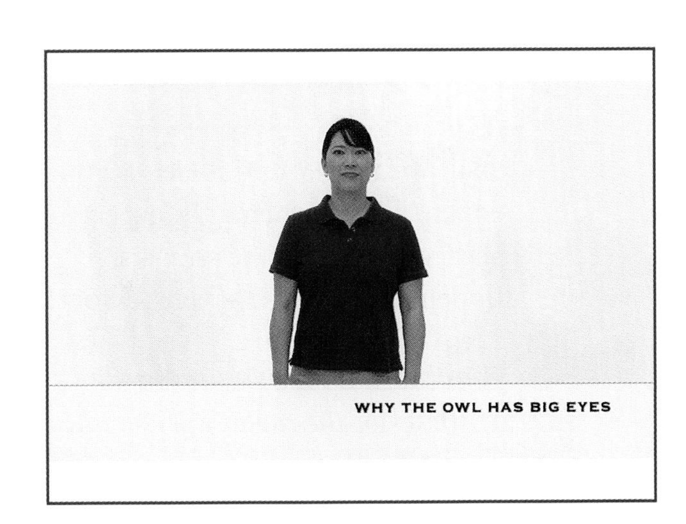

Show the story. Then, do one of the options below.

Comprehension:

- quiz (page 584)

Production:

- develop questions to ask (page 586)
- re-tell the story (page 586)

COMPREHENSION

15–20 minutes

Students will develop the ability to process larger chunks of information and figure out the meaning of a sign from context.

QUIZ (15–30 minutes)

PRESENT
(LESSON SLIDE 10:11:2)

Why the Owl Has Big Eyes

1. Describe the rabbit's personality and what he looked like originally.
2. Describe what the rabbit wanted to look like and why.
3. Describe what the rabbit ended up looking like and why.
4. Describe what the owl wanted to look like.
5. Describe how the Creator changed the owl and what explanations the Creator gave for making the changes.
6. Why did the owl end up with big eyes?

Show the video. Have students write the answers to questions on the slide and submit the papers to you to grade. Return graded papers and discuss the answers.
Optional: show answers on **Lesson Slides 10:11:3–9**.

Teacher's Discussion Guide

1. ***Describe the rabbit's personality and what he looked like originally.***
   Answer. The rabbit had short ears and his short front and rear legs caused him to inch along. He was shy, easily frightened and always worrying.

2. ***Describe what the rabbit wanted to look like and why.***
   Answer. Long ears to hear better, long front and rear legs to run faster, claws to fight off others.

3. ***Describe what the rabbit ended up looking like and why.***
   Answer. Long ears and long back legs but short front legs that caused the rabbit to hop. The rabbit was so frightened by how God changed the owl that he took off before God was finished with him.

4. ***Describe what the owl wanted to look like.***
   Answer. Long neck, long beak, red breast, and golden crest on top of head.

5. ***Describe how the Creator changed the owl and what explanations the Creator gave for making the changes.***
   Answer.
   - pressed its beak to make it short and hooked
   - pushed its head down so it has no neck
   - squeezed its body to make its eyes big and round
   - rolled its body in the dirt to make it brown with black spots
   - God made the changes because the owl was stubborn and arrogant and didn't do what God asked.

6. ***Why did the owl end up with big eyes?***
   Answer. With big eyes, the owl could only be awake during the night and couldn't watch God do His or Her work.

PRODUCTION

20–25 minutes

Students will build fluency by re-telling the story or by asking questions about the story.

After showing the video, and making sure students understand the story and all the signs, choose one of these activities:

- **DEVELOP QUESTIONS TO ASK** (20–30 minutes)
  Pair up students and assign one student to develop true or false questions and the other wh-word questions. Have them ask each other questions.

- **RE-TELL STORY** (25–30 minutes)
  Pair up students and have them fill each other in on what happened in the story. If there is anything in the story they don't understand, have them ask other students to get clarification. If students are still unable to get clarification, have them ask you (the teacher), or you show the video story again to get the answer.

HOMEWORK

Tell students to do **Homework 10:11** (*Student Workbook*, page 302–304).

HOMEWORK FOLLOW-UP
3–15 MINUTES

Review answers to **A Lesson Learned** (*Student Workbook*, page 302).

Option 1: show answers on the **Follow-up Slides 10:11:1–7** and have students check their answers in their workbook.

Option 2: for more language practice, sign the questions from the workbook and have students sign their answers.
For example:

For ***"1. Describe the family"***

t / whq

T: FAMILY, IX"*mult*" FACE+LIKE "what"
Answer. A deaf couple with a three-year-old daughter Melvin has known since birth.

For *"2. Why did the father ask Melvin to babysit?"*

T: **FATHER ASK-TO-Melvin fs-MELVIN <rs:father NOT-**

q whq

MIND TAKE-CARE DAUGHTER>. WHY

Answer. The father had to work overtime (mother was already at work).

For *"3. What did Melvin teach the little girl and why?"*

whq whq

T: **fs-MELVIN TEACH-TO-girl "what." WHY**

Answer. How to stand up on the chair to turn the lights on and off because he got tired of doing it for her.

For *"4. After Melvin left, what happened during the night?"*

when whq

T: **fs-MELVIN LEAVE-FOR, ALL-NIGHT "what" HAPPEN**

Answer. The parents got little sleep because the girl kept turning on the lights during the night to ask to brush her teeth, to ask to have a story read, and she continued this way throughout the night turning on the lights to ask for something.

For *"5. Why is the title 'A Lesson Learned' appropriate for this story?"*

t whq

T: **TITLE fs-A LESSON LEARN, !RIGHT! WHY**

Answer. The little girl learned to turn on/off the lights by herself, but Melvin learned teaching a child independent skills may not always be a good idea, especially a three-year-old.

LESSON 10:12

Looking for a Misplaced Item

Lesson length: 40–45 minutes

LESSON GOAL

Students will sign this narrative from their storyboards:

Narrative

I. Background

II. Body

  A. the search (at least three searches)[1]

  B. the discovery

III. Conclusion

NOTIONS

Grammar

[1] ***Language elements to describe the search:***

- **rationale for search (transition)**
  (tell why you thought to search in that place)
- **spatial agreement**
  (set up location, match movements to location)
- **word order** (name object before describing how you handled it)
- **role shift** (show yourself searching)
- **conclude the search** (with the sign NONE)

Others

SCL:1*"moving from location to location"*

ICL*"handling object"*

LOOK-AT (moving head and eye gaze together with this sign)

PREPARATION

- Read **Key Language Elements** and **Assignment**, *Student Workbook*, page 309–310.
- Make copies of **10:12 Evaluation** for **Homework Follow-up**)

MATERIALS

10:12 Lesson Slides

10:12 Follow-up Slides

10:12 Evaluation

HOMEWORK 10:12

Student Workbook, pages 305–310

INTRODUCE *Language Elements for Narrative*

25–30 minutes

PRESENT
(LESSON SLIDE 10:12:1)

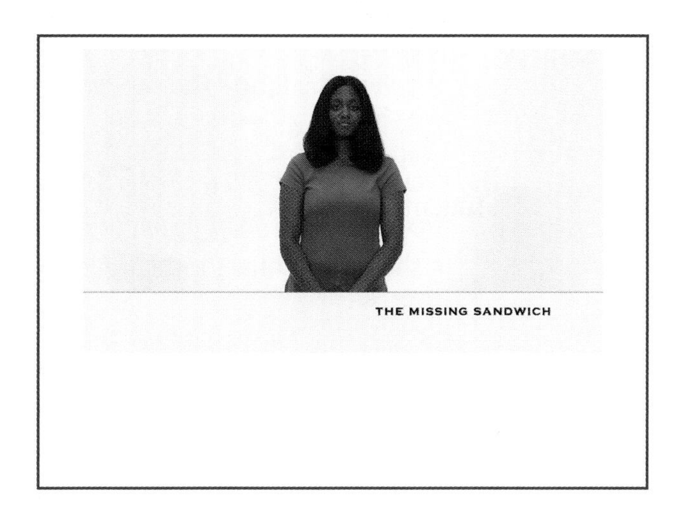

Show the video **The Missing Sandwich** and ask the following comprehension questions.

t whq whq
1. WOMAN IX*"woman"* GO-TO WHERE. IX*"woman"*. BUY "what."
   Answer. Grocery store to buy eggs, butter, milk, bread, toilet paper and a sandwich.

when whq
2. WOMAN IX*"woman"* ARRIVE HOME, IX*"woman"* (2h)DO++
   Answer. She put the food away and worked in her home office.

when whq
3. NOON, "what" HAPPEN
   Answer. Tonique became hungry so she went to get her sandwich but couldn't find it.

t whq
4. IX*"woman"* LOOK-FOR SANDWICH, LOOK-FOR WHERE
   Answer. In the kitchen (refrigerator, counter and table), in the car trunk and in the bathroom (upper and lower cabinets).

neg
5. IX*"woman"* LOOK-FOR++, CAN'T FIND SANDWICH,
   whq
   IX*"woman"* WOMAN (2h)DO++
   Answer. Made something else for lunch then returned to work.

whq / who

6. DOOR, KNOCK*"on door"* WHO. IX*"person at door"* WANT "what"

Answer. The newspaper boy asking to be paid.

t / whq

7. WOMAN IX"woman" GO-TO GET MONEY, "what" HAPPEN

Answer. She found the sandwich in her purse.

when / whq

8. WOMAN IX*"woman"* FIND SANDWICH, IX*"woman"* (2h)DO++

Answer. Paid the newspaper boy and put the sandwich in the refrigerator for the next day.

whq

9. WOMAN IX*"woman"* FEEL "what"

Answer. Felt stupid (BE-DISGUSTED, PEABRAINED).

PRESENT

(LESSON SLIDE 10:12:2)

Show video **Search 1: The Kitchen** and explain these language elements. Point out how Tonique incorporated the elements for **Search 1**. Demonstrate and have students copy:

For ***"• rationale for search (transition)"***
(narrator shares her thought that leads to the search in that particular location, usually starting with THOUGHT-OCCUR)

T: ALL-MORNING, NOON, ME THOUGHT-OCCUR SANDWICH

S: (copy)

For **"• *spatial agreement*"**
(narrator matches the movement to established location using SCL:1"moving from location to location" or signs like GO-TO, ENTER)

T: ME **SCL:1"*walk from left side (office) to front*"** KITCHEN
S: (copy)

For **"• *word order*"**
(narrator names an object in the search then describes how she handles it)

t
T: **fs-REF, (wh)ICL"*open refrigerator door*"**
S: (copy)

For **"• *role shift*"**
(narrator role shifts to show herself searching using LOOK-AT, her eye gaze matching the movement with the sign)

T: <rs:narrator [(wh)ICL"*hold refrigerator door*"/
LOOK-AT"*through refrigerator*"] >
S: (copy)

For **"• *conclude the search*"**
(narrator ends the search with the sign NONE.)

neg
SANDWICH **NONE**

Continue with other rights from **Search 1: The Kitchen.**

The refrigerator (2nd time):
T: ME AGAIN++,<rs:narrator **(2h)alt.LOOK-AT**"*around inside refrigerator,*" **(2h)alt.ICL**"*moving things, opening drawers*">,
neg
NONE
S: (copy)

The counter:
T: (wh)ICL"*close refrigerator door,*" DCL"*counter on left side,*"
neg
<rs:narrator ME **LOOK-AT**"*all over counter on left*">, **NONE**
S: (copy)

The table:

T: TABLE, <rs: self ME LOOK-AT*"table in front left"*>,

neg

NONE

S: (copy)

PRESENT

(LESSON SLIDE 10:12:3)

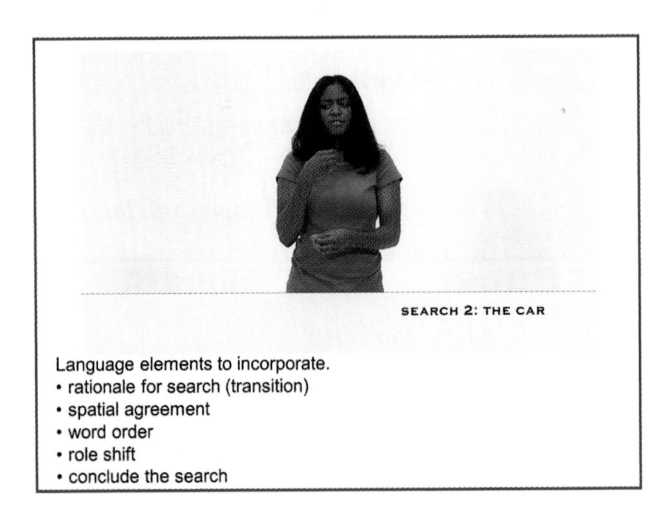

Show video **Search 2: The Car** and point out how Tonique incorporated the elements for **Search 2**. Demonstrate and have students copy.

For **"• *rationale for search (transition)*"**

T: "hmm" ME **THOUGHT-OCCUR** MAYBE CAR IX*"car on right"* ME (2h)PUT-AWAY*"bags from car to house,"* sandwich-FALL-OUT*"of the bag"*

S: (copy)

For **"• *spatial agreement*"**

T: ME **(wh)GO-TO-car***"on right"*

S: (copy)

For **"• *role shift*"**

T: <rs:narrator ICL*"open trunk,"* [(wh)ICL*"hold trunk door"*/ **ME LOOK-AT***"around trunk"*]

S: (copy)

For “• *conclude the search*”

neg

T: **NONE** SANDWICH. “hmm”

S: (copy)

PRESENT
(LESSON SLIDE 10:12:4)

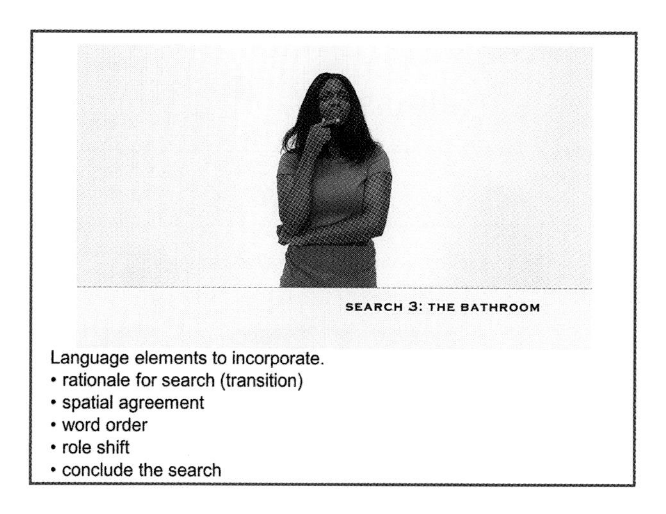

Show video **Search 3: The Bathroom** and point out how Tonique incorporated the elements for **Search 3**. Demonstrate and have students copy:

For “• *rationale for search (transition)*”

T: **THOUGHT-OCCUR**, MAYBE WRONG, ME (wh)PUT-IN-left TOILET+PAPER, MAYBE (nod)

S: (copy)

For “• *spatial agreement*”

T: ME **ENTER**-left BATHROOM

S: (copy)

For “• *word order and role shift*”

T: ME <rs:narrator ICL*“open top cabinet,”* [(wh)ICL*“hold cabinet door”*/**LOOK-AT***“inside top cabinet”*]>

S: (copy)

T: <rs:narrator ICL*“close top cabinet doors,”* ICL*“open bottom cabinet doors,”* [(wh)ICL*“hold cabinet door”*/ **LOOK-AT***“inside bottom cabinet”*]>

S: (copy)

For *"• conclude the search"*

neg
T: NONE (after checking each cabinet)
S: (copy)

PRACTICE *Narrating from a Storyboard*

25–30 minutes

PRESENT
(LESSON SLIDE 10:12:5)

Practice using the storyboard to retell **The Missing Sandwich**. Begin with **I. Background**. Point to picture(s). Repeat parts from the video and have students copy.

For **Picture 1**

T: YESTERDAY, ME THOUGHT-OCCUR, NEED
nod
FOOD+SHOPPING. [(wh)THUMB-UP/IX-thumb], EGG,
nod nod nod
[(wh)L/IX-index] BUTTER, [(wh)3/IX-mid] MILK, BREAD,
nod
[(wh)5/IX-pinky] TOILET+PAPER. IX-right STORE HAVE !DELICIOUS! SANDWICH
S: (copy)

For **Pictures 2–4**

T: ME GO-TO STORE, COLLECT-right-arc, SANDWICH, PUT-IN*"pile"* PAY-TO-left*"cashier"*

S: (copy)

For **Picture 5**

T: ICL*"push cart"* CAR ICL*"open trunk,"* ICL*"take from cart, into trunk,"* ICL*"shut trunk"* GET-IN*"car,"* DRIVE-cont

S: (copy)

For **Picture 6**

when

T: ARRIVE HOME ICL*"open trunk,"* ICL*"put away grocery bags from car to house"* FOOD. HOUSE ICL*"put away bags."*

S: (copy)

For **Picture 7**

T: FINISH, ME GO-TO-left WORK, (nod) HAVE HOME fs-OFFICE HAVE. ME WORK*"left"*-cont ALL-MORNING

S: (copy)

PRESENT

(LESSON SLIDE 10:12:6)

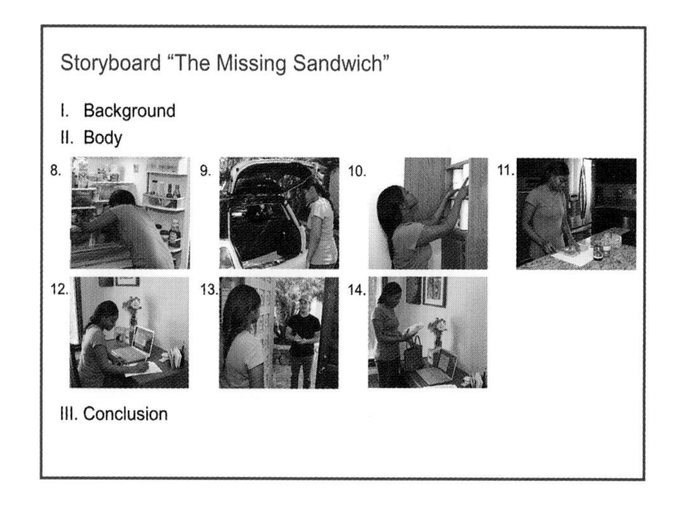

Continue with the **II. Body** and **III. Conclusion**.

For **Picture 8**

t t

T: NOON, ME THOUGHT-OCCUR SANDWICH, ME
SCL:1 ***"walk from left side (office) to front"*** KITCHEN.
fs-REF, (wh)ICL*"open refrigerator door"*
<rs:narrator [(wh)ICL*"hold refrigerator door"*/

neg

LOOK-AT*"through refrigerator"*] > SANDWICH **NONE**.

ME AGAIN++, <rs:narrator **(2h)alt.LOOK-AT***"around inside refrigerator,"* **(2h)alt.ICL***"moving things, opening drawers"*>,

neg

NONE

(wh)ICL*"close refrigerator door,"* DCL*"counter on left side,"*

neg

<rs:narrator ME **LOOK-AT***"all over counter on left"*>, **NONE**.
TABLE, <rs: self ME **LOOK-AT***"table in front left"*>,

neg

NONE.

S: (copy)

For **Picture 9**

T: "hmm" ME **THOUGHT-OCCUR** MAYBE CAR
IX*"car on right"* ME (2h)PUT-AWAY*"bags from car to house,"*
sandwich-FALL-OUT*"of the bag"*
ME (wh)**GO-TO-car*"on right,"*** <rs:narrator ICL*"open trunk,"*
[(wh)ICL*"hold trunk door"*/**ME LOOK-AT***"around trunk"*]

neg

NONE SANDWICH. "hmm"

S: (copy)

For **Picture 10**

T: **THOUGHT-OCCUR**, MAYBE WRONG, ME (2h)PUT-IN-left TOILET+PAPER, MAYBE (nod) ME **ENTER**-left BATHROOM. ME <rs:narrator ICL*"open top cabinet,"* [(wh)ICL*"hold cabinet door"*/

neg

LOOK-AT*"inside top cabinet"*]> **NONE**.

<rs:narrator ICL*"close top cabinet doors,"* ICL*"open bottom cabinet doors,"* [(wh)ICL*"hold cabinet door"*/LOOK-AT*"inside*

neg

bottom cabinet"]> **NONE**

S: (copy)

For **Pictures 11 and 12**

T: "well" TIME, ME HUNGRY. ME GO-TO KITCHEN.

when

MAKE-cont, EAT. FINISH, ME MUST GO-TO WORK, ME LAG-BEHIND. ME GO-TO, WORK-cont

S: (copy)

For **Picture 13**

when

T: HEAR KNOCK*"to me."* ME (wh)GO-TO, (wh)LCL:B*"open door,"* "oh" IX*"outside door"* NEWSPAPER BOY, IX*"boy"* WANT ME PAY-TO-him

S: (copy)

For **Picture 14**

T: <rs:narrator ME *"hold on/wait,"* ME IX*"purse"* PURSE, "hold on/ wait."> ME GO-TO ME <rs:narrator ICL*"open purse, look in"*>

th

(sheepish) IX-loc*"in purse"* SANDWICH. ME BE-DISGUSTED

For **III. Conclusion**

when

T: MONEY, ME purse-GIVE-TO-boy-right. FINISH, SANDWICH ME (2h)ICL*"pick up,"* [(wh)ICL*"hold sandwich"*/GO-TO] KITCHEN, fs-REF, ME [(wh)ICL*"open ref door"*/ICL*"put sandwich in"*] (wh)ICL*"ref door closed."* (cross arms) IN-FUTURE EAT IX*"sandwich"* TOMORROW.

"well" ME PEA-BRAINED, NOT LOOK-AT*"left"* PURSE,

neg

NOT ME. PEA-BRAINED, "well"

S: (repeat)

Pair Up. Have students sign the story to each other.

Be sure students:

- use THOUGHT-OCCUR when sharing the thought that leads to the search in that particular location
- use spatial agreement where they place the locations below and match movements to locations using SCL:1 or signs like GO-TO, ENTER
  - house and office on the left
  - kitchen in front
  - car and front door on right
  - bathroom just left of front
- for word order, name objects before describing how they handle them
- role shift and use LOOK-AT to show themselves searching, with their eye gaze matching the movement of the sign

  neg
- end each unsuccessful search with NONE
- conclude the story using the signs BE-DISGUSTED and PEABRAINED.

HOMEWORK

Tell students to do **Homework 10:12** (*Student Workbook,* pages 305–310).

Also, students are to prepare their own storyboards and be ready to narrate their own stories about something they lost or misplaced (See **Assignment**, *Student Workbook,* pages 309–310).

HOMEWORK FOLLOW-UP
35–90 MINUTES

Have students turn in their storyboards and present their **Misplaced Item** stories (See **Assignment**, *Student Workbook,* pages 309–310).

Two ways to approach this:

As fluency practice. Have students get into groups and tell their stories to each other. Conclude by calling on several students to share their stories with the whole class.

Be sure students:

- begin each search with transition THOUGHT-OCCUR
- for each search, set up location and match movements to the location
- keep locations constant throughout the story
- name objects before describing how they are handled
- use role shift to show the person searching
- end each search with NONE
- sign a reaction sign upon discovering the misplaced item, for example, BE-DISGUSTED or PEA-BRAINED.

As a quiz. If you want to use this story as a production quiz, have students videotape their stories and present the videos to you with the storyboards. Rate with **10:12 Evaluation** (See **Materials.**)

UNIT 10 REVIEW

Putting It All Together

Lesson length: 85–120 minutes

LESSON GOAL

The student will:

- practice using temporal aspects, predicative adjectives and role shifting
- practice defining the signs for personal qualities and tendencies
- practice locating items in the house and creating sentences with #ALL (or ALL), MOST, MANY, SOME, SEVERAL, NONE.
- practice money number forms and vocabulary for food and household items

NOTIONS

Vocabulary

vocabulary previously learned

PREPARATION

- Make a copy of **10UR Tendencies and Personal Qualities, Activity Sheets 1–8** for each group of 8–16 students (for **Tendencies and Personal Qualities** practice on page 602). Further instructions are on page 602.

- Make copies of **10UR Seller's List** for one-third of the students and **10UR Buyer's List** for the remaining students (for **The Best Price** practice on page 606).

MATERIALS

10UR Lesson Slides
10UR Tendencies and Personal Qualities, Activity Sheets 1–8
10UR Seller's List
10UR Buyer's List

HOMEWORK

Student Workbook, page 311 (**Self-Assessment**)

PRACTICE *Reflections of Oneself*

15–30 minutes

Students practice using temporal aspects, predicative adjectives and role shift to explain why they think someone may choose or favor a particular thing.

Divide the class into groups of four.

Call one group out of the room and have them tell you their **favorite colors**. Explain to them:

- the class will guess who likes what color and discuss why
- to keep a straight face and not reveal the truth until all groups have shared their guesses and reasons.

When done, have that group come back into the room and stand at the front. Name the four favorite colors then have the other groups discuss which color matches which person and explain why.

After all groups have shared their guesses and reasons, the four students then give the answers and explain why.

Repeat procedure with the other groups.

You can use different topics such as:

- favorite animals
- which animals they would like to be
- dream jobs
- types of car they own.

NOTE: This is a fun activity and it makes for good discussion because the groups' decisions are often very wrong.

PRACTICE *Tendencies and Personal Qualities*

30–40 minutes

Students practice defining the signs for personal qualities and tendencies.

PRESENT
(LESSON SLIDE 10:UR:1)

Tendencies and Personal Qualities

Instructions for Row A (then Row B).
On your activity sheet, there are eight signs and definitions related to tendencies and personal qualities. Give clues without using the sign itself to get your partner in the other row to guess the sign. You have two minutes to do all eight signs.

Set Up. Divide the class into groups with 8–16 students. Have each group form two rows (A and B) with the same number of students in both rows. Pass out copies of the **Tendencies and Personal Qualities Activity Sheets 1–8** to students in Row A. (See **Materials**). Give students some time to read and think about the information on their sheets

NOTE: There are eight different **Tendencies and Personal Qualities** activity sheets. Make enough copies for the rows. For example, if there are four students in Row A, make copies of Sheets 1–4, if five students, copy Sheets 1–5 and so on up to eight. Make sure that all students in Row A have a different sheet.

ROUND 1

Have Row A students give the clues for the signs on their activity sheets and Row B students guess the signs.

After two minutes, students in Row A give their activity sheets to their partners in Row B.

ROUND 2

Now have students in Row A shift to the right so they are across from a new partner. This time, students in Row B give the clues from the activity sheets and their new partners in Row A guess the signs.

After two minutes, Row B students give activity sheets to partners in Row A and then move to their right.

ROUNDS 3–8

The activity can be repeated up to eight rounds, with Rows A and B passing sheets back and forth and shifting to their right.

PRACTICE *Telling Where Items Are Kept*

15–20 minutes

Students practice locating items in the house and creating sentences with **#ALL (or ALL), MOST, MANY, SOME, SEVERAL, NONE.**

PRESENT
(LESSON SLIDE 10:UR:2)

Places in and around the house

Review or introduce signs for rooms and places in a home where things may be kept.

LIVING-ROOM	fs-ATTIC
BED+ROOM	THUMB-loc*"back"*+fs-YARD
EAT+ROOM	**GARAGE**
BATHROOM	**CLOSET**
BASEMENT	DRESSER (DRAWERS)

Assign each student a sign from the list below.

- DICTIONARY
- MATCHES
- HEADACHE+MEDICINE
- SCREWDRIVER
- STAPLER
- POSTAGE-STAMP
- CAMERA
- KNIFE
- #TV ICL*"use remote"*
- SCISSORS
- NEEDLE+STRING
- CANDLE
- NAIL-CLIPPERS
- MAGAZINE
- TOWEL
- SCOTCH-TAPE

PRESENT
(LESSON SLIDE 10:UR:3)

A: ask if B has item at home
B: respond
A: if yes, ask where B keeps it
B: tell where
- name the room (raise brows)
- name furniture or appliance, or part of room (raise brows)
- specify location of item (use reference point)

Demonstrate lines and have students copy:

For "***A: ask if B has item at home.***"

t (over YOUR HOME), q (over YOU HAVE (item))
A: YOUR HOME, YOU HAVE (item)

For ***"B: respond"***

nod

B: YES, HAVE

For ***"A: if yes, ask where B keeps it."***

whq

A: PUT-IN, WHERE

For ***"B: tell where"***

t

B: BED+ROOM, (specify exact location)

Then have all students circulate and write down where the item is kept by others.

When done, have students summarize their findings by using quantifier vocabulary: **#ALL (or ALL), MOST, MANY, SOME, SEVERAL, NONE**. For example:

SCISSORS

whq

S: SCISSORS, ME ASK-TO*"all"* PUT-IN WHERE. !MANY! BATHROOM, SOME KITCHEN, SEVERAL BED+ROOM,

neg

NONE LIVING-ROOM

PRACTICE *The Best Price*

25–30 minutes

Students practice money number forms and vocabulary for food and household items.

Distribute copies of **Seller's List** to one third of the class (See **Materials**). Have them follow instructions and assign prices to 12 items. Then, have them position themselves as "stores" in different parts of the room.

Distribute copies of **Buyer's List** to the remaining students (See **Materials**). Have them follow instructions and buy as many items as possible with $10.00. Have them "shop" for 20 minutes.

Conclude. Have students report how many items they bought and how much they spent. The student with the most items for the least amount of money wins!

HOMEWORK

Tell students to do **Homework** (*Student Workbook*, page 311).

UNIT 11

Discussing Plans and Goals

LESSON 11:1

Discussing One's Knowledge and Abilities

Lesson length: 95–120 minutes

LESSON GOAL

Students will use target vocabulary to describe one's knowledge and abilities.

KEY PHRASES

Compare a person's knowledge of a subject matter to your own

t (over "(subject)")
(subject) IX*"person"* (having knowledge), (subject) ME (lacking knowledge)

Tell about an activity that you have become skilled in

t (over "(activity/skill)"), t (over "IN-PAST"), t (over "NOW")
(activity/skill) IN-PAST ME AWKWARD/CLUMSY, NOW BE-SKILLED-IN

Describe an unusual skill/ability you (or someone/animal you know) possess

ME BE-EXCEPTIONAL-IN, (describe skill) ME BE-EXCEPTIONAL-IN.

If someone lacks a certain ability or talent to do something, explain what they should or should not do

cond (over "[SUPPOSE] IX"person" BE-INEPT (skill/talent)")
[SUPPOSE] IX*"person"* BE-INEPT (skill/talent), IX*"person"* SHOULD [NOT] (activity).

NOTIONS

Vocabulary

Having knowledge/ability

BE-KNOWLEDGEABLE-IN
BE-SKILLED-IN
BE-EXCEPTIONAL-IN

Lacking knowledge
ZERO-FOREHEAD
BE-MIND-STUPID

Lacking ability
BE-INEPT
AWKWARD/CLUMSY
CAN'T

Subjects
AMERICA fs-LIT
INTERPRETING
HISTORY
DEAF STUDIES
SCIENCE
LINGUISTICS
MATH
MEDICINE
PSYCHOLOGY
LAW
POLITICS
COUNSELING
SOCIOLOGY
ARCHITECTURE
ENGINEERING
ECONOMICS
INFORM++ TECHNOLOGY or fs-IT
BUSINESS

Others
MAJOR

PREPARATION

Familiarize yourself with sentences used to introduce key vocabulary about one's knowledge and abilities on pages 612–616.

MATERIALS

11:1 Lesson Slides

HOMEWORK 11:1

Student Workbook, pages 316–322

INTRODUCE *Areas of Study*

20–30 minutes

PRESENT
(LESSON SLIDES 11:1:1–4)

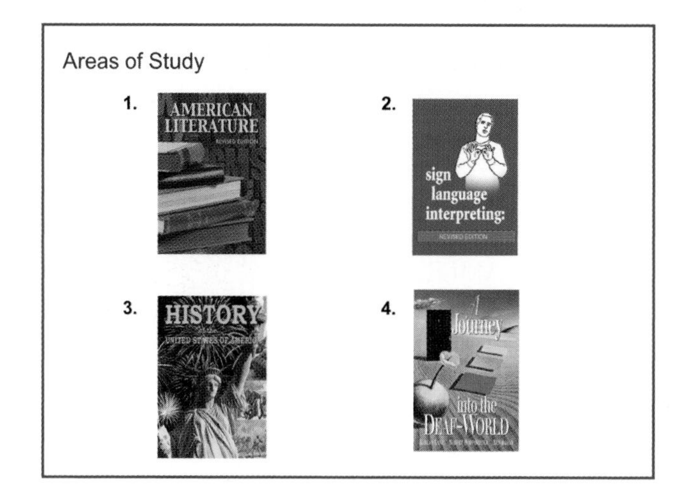

Introduce signs for areas of study:

For **Slide 1**

1. AMERICA fs-LIT (optional: fs-ASL fs-LIT, FRANCE fs-LIT)
2. **INTERPRETING**
3. **HISTORY** (optional: AMERICA HISTORY, WORLD HISTORY, EUROPE HISTORY, DEAF HISTORY)
4. DEAF **STUDIES** (optional: WOMAN STUDIES, ENVIRONMENT STUDIES, AFRICA+AMERICA STUDIES)

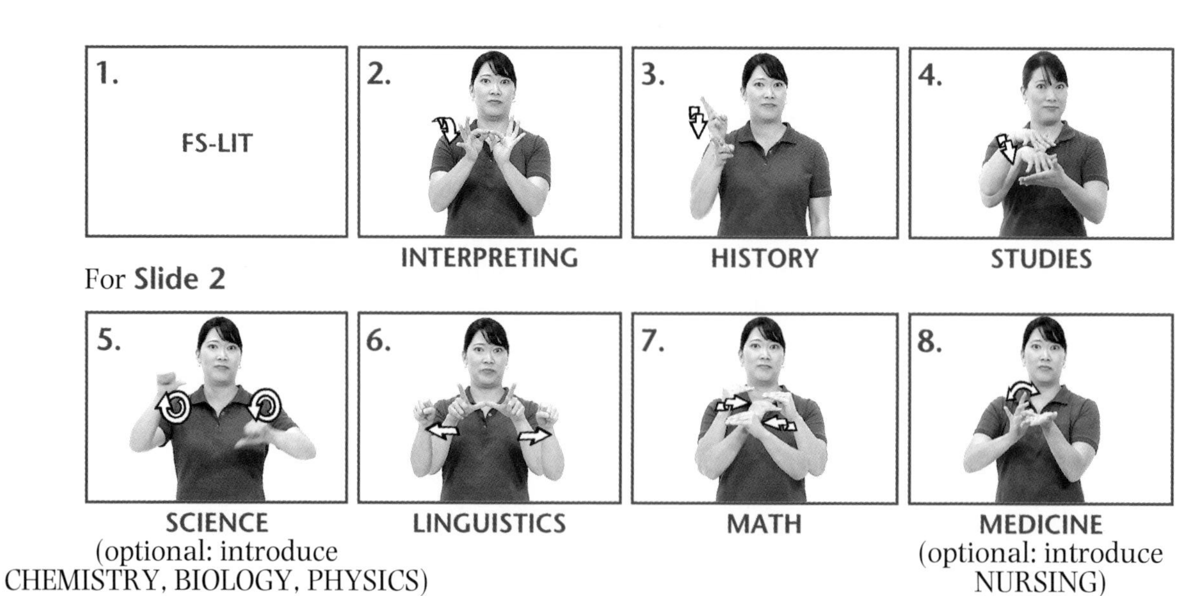

INTERPRETING

HISTORY

STUDIES

For **Slide 2**

SCIENCE
(optional: introduce CHEMISTRY, BIOLOGY, PHYSICS)

LINGUISTICS

MATH

MEDICINE
(optional: introduce NURSING)

Review. Show **Lesson Slides 11:1:1–4** again to review the vocabulary. Then, discuss college major(s). Begin with your own:

T: IN-PAST COLLEGE (t), ME **MAJOR** (subject). YOU **MAJOR** "what" (whq)

Have student tell their major(s):

S: IN-PAST COLLEGE (t), ME **MAJOR** (subject), or

S: NOW (t) ME MAJOR (subject)

For high school or new college students:

S: FUTURE COLLEGE, ME PLAN **MAJOR** (subject), or

neg

S: ME NOT+SURE, MAYBE ME **MAJOR** (subject).

Introduce signs for majors that students have or plan to have, which are not listed on the previous page.

NOTE: For these majors students can use signs they already know; English (ENGLAND), American Sign Language (fs-ASL), Spanish (SPAIN), French (FRANCE), Theatre/Drama (PERFORMANCE), Visual Arts (ART), Photography (PICTURE), and Computer Science (COMPUTER SCIENCE).

INTRODUCE *Knowledge and Abilities*

45 minutes

PRESENT
(LESSON SLIDE 11:1:5)

Definitions

1. Being well-informed about a subject area
2. having the ability, or training to perform a certain task well; to be skilled in
3. having a talent or unusual ability to perform tasks well

BE-KNOWLEDGEABLE-IN

Introduce the signs, and demonstrate using them in sentences:

T: MY SISTER IX*"sister"* **BE-KNOWLEDGEABLE-IN** FRANCE fs-LIT, FINISH READ !MANY! BOOK, KNOW WRITE+ER POSS-arc++ DIFFERENT++ fs-STYLE, fs-DATES

T: fs-JIM IX*"Jim"* **BE-KNOWLEDGEABLE-IN** CAR,

when

KNOW DIFFERENT++ NAME, LOOK-AT*"car"* CAR, KNOW WHICH YEAR KNOW++

BE-SKILLED-IN

T: MY NIECE IX*"niece"* **BE-SKILLED-IN** SPEAK FRANCE.
ME KNOW LITTLE-BIT

t (over MY COMPUTER); neg (over CAN'T FIND)

T: MY COMPUTER, PICTURE MIXED, CAN'T FIND.
MY FRIEND IX*"friend"* KNOW #HOW IN-GEAR++,
IX*"friend"* COME-TO, TEACH ME, ME PRACTICE-cont

t (over NOW)

NOW, ME **BE-SKILLED-IN**, EASY FIND PICTURE

neg (over NOT-KNOW #HOW COOK)

T: ME NOT-KNOW #HOW COOK. MY ROOMMATE
IX*"roommate"* **BE-SKILLED-IN** COOK, ME ENJOY EAT

BE-EXCEPTIONAL-IN

t (over MATH)

T: MATH, MY SON **BE-EXCEPTIONAL-IN** FAST RESPOND/
ANSWER++

T: KNOW fs-RUBIK'S ICL*"twisting cube,"* MY BOY+FRIEND
IX*"boyfriend"* **BE-EXCEPTIONAL-IN** ICL*"twisting cube"*
[(wh)ICL*"hold cube"*/SAME-AS-all over COLOR] LESS-THAN
30 fs-SEC

T: MY FRIEND IX*"friend"* **BE-EXCEPTIONAL-IN** COPY-arc.
DIFFERENT++ PEOPLE POSS-arc VOICE, FACIAL-
EXPRESSION, PERFORMANCE COPY-arc !PERFECT!
IX*"friend"* **BE-EXCEPTIONAL-IN**

T: MY COUSIN IX*"cousin"* **BE-EXCEPTIONAL-IN** TWO WORD
(wh)fs-DOG, fs-CAT, (2h)FINGERSPELL TIME+JUST-THE-
SAME. IX*"cousin"* **BE-EXCEPTIONAL-IN**

PRESENT
(LESSON SLIDE 11:1:6–7)

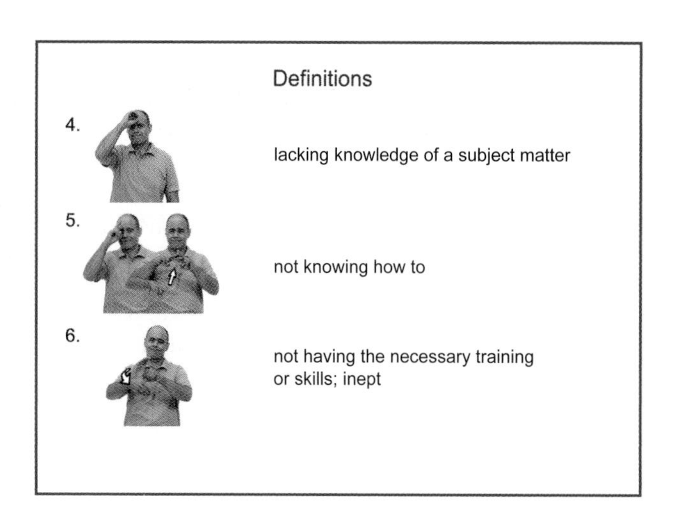

Definitions
4.
lacking knowledge of a subject matter
5.
not knowing how to
6.
not having the necessary training or skills; inept

Continue procedure for **Lesson Slide 11:1:6–7**, introducing signs and demonstrating them in sentences.

4.
ZERO-FOREHEAD

T: AMERICA HISTORY (t), ME KNOW SOME
CHINA HISTORY (t), ME **ZERO-FOREHEAD**

T: AIRPLANE. DIFFERENT++ fs-MODELS (2h)alt. POSS++
NAME (rhet), ME **ZERO-FOREHEAD**. YOU ASK-TO-me (cond),
ME NOT-KNOW (neg). YOU ASK-TO-father FATHER, IX*"father"*
BE-KNOWLEDGEABLE

NOTE: ZERO-FOREHEAD is the opposite of BE-KNOWLEDGEABLE-IN.

5.
BE-MIND-STUPID

T: ARCHITECTURE (t), ME **BE-MIND-STUPID**. BLUE+PRINT (t),
ME [(wh)LCL:B*"blueprint"*/LOOK-AT-over]
NOT+UNDERSTAND (neg).

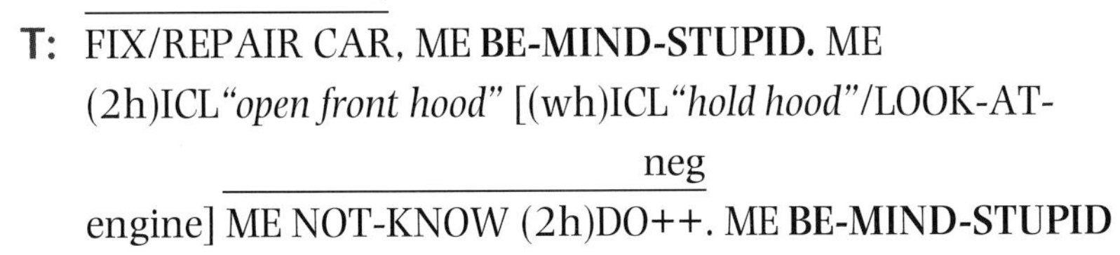

t

T: FIX/REPAIR CAR, ME **BE-MIND-STUPID.** ME (2h)ICL*"open front hood"* [(wh)ICL*"hold hood"*/LOOK-AT-

neg

engine] ME NOT-KNOW (2h)DO++. ME **BE-MIND-STUPID**

6.
BE-INEPT

t

T: MY PARTNER IX*"partner"* MAJOR MUSIC BUT DANCE **BE-INEPT**. ME TRY++ TEACH-partner DANCE. IX*"partner"* (2h)alt.WRONG++. BPCL:B*"feet stumbling."* IX*"partner"* **BE-INEPT** DANCE

t

T: ME GO-TO BAR. ICL*"throw darts,"* MY FRIEND IX*"mult"* BE-SKILLED ICL*"throw darts"* [(wh)DCL*"target"*/LCL:1 *"hit the bull's eye"*++]. ME **BE-INEPT**, ICL*"throw darts"* [(wh)DCL*"dart board"*/LCL:1*"miss the target"*++]. ME **BE-INEPT**

7.
AWKWARD/CLUMSY

t t

T: INTERPRETING IN-PAST ME **AWKWARD/CLUMSY**

t

LEARN++, NOW **ME BE-SKILLED-IN**

T: MY DAUGHTER IX*"daughter"* RECENT BUY NEW SHOE DCL*"high heels."* IX*"daughter"* ICL*"put on shoes"* WALK **AWKWARD/CLUMSY** BPCL:B*"wobbly feet."* IN-FUTURE IX*"daughter"* BE-SKILLED-IN BPCL:B*"feet sauntering smoothly"*

T: IN-PAST ME LEARN++ DRIVE WITH ICL*"use stick shift"*

when

AWKWARD/CLUMSY "wow." ICL*"use stick,"* (2h)BPCL:B*"feet manipulating clutch and gas pedals"* SCL:3*"car lurching forward."* ME PRACTICE+++, BE-SKILLED-IN

8.
CAN'T

T: MY FRIEND IX*"friend"* BE-EXCEPTIONAL-IN

neg

[(wh)LCL:B*"floor"*/SCL:V*"stand on head"*] ME **CAN'T**. [(wh)LCL:B*"floor"*/SCL:V*"trying to stand on head but keep falling down"*]

t
T: FAMOUS PERSON, MY FRIEND BE-EXCEPTIONAL-IN

neg
MEET-person, CHAT++. ME **CAN'T**. ME BASHFUL, BE-AFRAID++

neg
T: ME **CAN'T** DRIVE, ME NONE DRIVE LICENSE

Review. Describe **Situations A–I**. After each situation have students pick the sign that most appropriately describes the person in the situation.

Situation A

T: (describe situation) *Person has studied photography many years, knows names of different brands, lenses, and how to take pictures. Also knows names of famous photographers around the world. This person is...*

- BE-KNOWLEDGEABLE-IN
- BE-SKILLED-IN or
- BE-EXCEPTIONAL-IN

S: (answer) BE-KNOWLEDGEABLE-IN

Situation B

T: (describe situation) *Person, compared to other photographers, is a very good photographer, really knows how to take beautiful pictures. When you look at his or her pictures, you are very impressed with the framing, the color and the composition. This person is...*

- BE-KNOWLEDGEABLE-IN
- BE-SKILLED-IN or
- BE-EXCEPTIONAL-IN

S: (answer) BE-SKILLED-IN

Situation C

T: (describe situation) *Person whose paintings look very real, as if she or he has taken a picture and painted the scene. This person is...*

- BE-KNOWLEDGEABLE-IN
- BE-SKILLED-IN or
- BE-EXCEPTIONAL-IN

S: (answer) BE-EXCEPTIONAL-IN

Situation D

T: (describe situation) *Person has worked as a photographer for a long time, doing baby and wedding pictures, and family portraits. Knows how to adjust lighting for good effects, knows how to pick the right lens. This person is...*

- BE-KNOWLEDGEABLE-IN
- BE-SKILLED-IN or
- BE-EXCEPTIONAL-IN

S: (answer) BE-SKILLED-IN

Situation E

T: (describe situation) *Person wants to take pictures, but finds his lens is broken. This person is ....*

- BE-INEPT
- AWKWARD/CLUMSY
- CAN'T

S: (answer) CAN'T

Situation F

T: (describe situation) *Person has a camera that adjusts the aperture settings automatically. One day, their spouse gives him or her a new camera with manual settings. Person does not know how to adjust the settings. This person is...*

- BE-INEPT
- CAN'T
- BE-MIND-STUPID

S: (answer) BE-MIND-STUPID

Situation G

T: (describe situation) *Person wants to take pictures of children. But children either cry, look away or get restless. This person doesn't know how to make them sit and look at the camera. This person is...*

- BE-INEPT
- CAN'T
- BE-MIND-STUPID

S: (answer) BE-INEPT

Situation H

T: (describe situation) *You meet person and ask him or her if she knows Annie Liebovitz, Ansel Adams, and a couple of other famous photographers. This person says no they don't know any of them. This person is…*

- BE-INEPT
- BE-MIND-STUPID
- ZERO-FOREHEAD

S: (answer) ZERO-FOREHEAD

Situation I

T: (describe situation) *Person switches from an older camera model to a newer one with a different design. Struggles to use it, looks for a feature, but can't find it. Not sure how to use it properly. This person is…*

- CAN'T
- AWKWARD/CLUMSY
- BE-MIND-STUPID

S: (answer) AWKWARD/CLUMSY

PRACTICE *Compare Knowledge*

8–12 minutes

Students practice making statements comparing their knowledge of a subject matter with someone else's.

PRESENT
(LESSON SLIDE 11:1:8)

Compare a person's knowledge
of a subject matter to your own.

Demonstrate sentences comparing your own knowledge in a subject matter to someone else's. Then, have students give their own sentences using **BE-KNOWLEDGEABLE-IN** and **ZERO-FOREHEAD.**

t

T: WORLD HISTORY, MY COUSIN IX*"person"*
BE-KNOWLEDGEABLE-IN, ME ZERO-FOREHEAD

t

T: ARCHITECTURE, MY FATHER-IN-LAW IX*"person"*
BE-KNOWLEDGEABLE-IN, ME ZERO-FOREHEAD

t

T: FOOTBALL RULES, MY BROTHER IX*"person"*
BE-KNOWLEDGEABLE-IN, ME ZERO-FOREHEAD

t

T: BIBLE, MY MOTHER IX*"person"*
BE-KNOWLEDGEABLE-IN, ME ZERO-FOREHEAD

t

T: BIRD (2h)alt.POSS NAME, MY FRIEND IX*"person"*
BE-KNOWLEDGEABLE-IN, ME ZERO-FOREHEAD

Now, have students take turns comparing their knowledge in a subject matter with someone else's. Be sure they follow this structure:

t

S: (subject matter), (person) IX*"person"*
BE-KNOWLEDGEABLE-IN, ME **ZERO-FOREHEAD.**

TEACHER TO TEACHER

Students may give examples for knowledge that are really skills. Probe further to make sure. For example, if the student says

t

"CAR, MY BOY+FRIEND BE-KNOWLEDGEABLE-IN" and means the boyfriend has knowledge of the names, make, model of cars and their origin, the student's example is correct. But if the student means the boyfriend is good at figuring out the car problem and fixing it, then the correct sign to use would be BE-SKILLED.

PRACTICE *Describe Developed Skills*

8–12 minutes

Students practice telling about activities in which they have developed skills.

PRESENT
(LESSON SLIDE 11:1:9)

Tell about an activity that you have become skilled in.

Follow this sequence:
1. name activity you are not good at
2. tell what you did
3. describe current level of skill

Demonstrate the sequence to describe an activity that you have become skilled in, using **AWKWARD/CLUMSY** and **BE-SKILLED-IN**.

For "***1. name activity you are not good at***"

t t

T: INTERPRETING IN-PAST ME AWKWARD/CLUMSY

For "***2. tell what you did***"

t

T: TAKE-UP++ CLASS.

For "***3. describe current level of skill***"

T: NOW ME BE-SKILLED-IN

Demonstrate other sentences. Then, have students give their own sentences.

t t

T: fs-YOGA IN-PAST ME AWKWARD/CLUMSY

PRACTICE++. $\overline{\text{NOW}}^{t}$, ME BE-SKILLED-IN

T: $\overline{\text{CARPENTRY}}^{t}$ $\overline{\text{IN-PAST}}^{t}$ ME AWKWARD/CLUMSY

LEARN++. $\overline{\text{NOW}}^{t}$ ME BE-SKILLED-IN

Now, have students take turns telling about activities they have developed skills in. Be sure they follow the sequence on the slide:

S: $\overline{\text{(activity/skill)}}^{t}$ $\overline{\text{IN-PAST}}^{t}$ ME **AWKWARD/CLUMSY**.

LEARN++ (or PRACTICE++ or TAKE UP++ CLASS). $\overline{\text{NOW}}^{t}$,
ME **BE-SKILLED-IN**.

PRACTICE *Describe Unusual Skills and Abilities*

8–12 minutes

Students practice telling about an unusual skill or ability they possess.

PRESENT
(LESSON SLIDE 11:1:10)

Describe an unusual skill or ability you (or some person or animal you know) possess:
- speed
- number
- endurance
- problem solving
- extraordinary skills

Demonstrate describing an unusual skill or ability you have. Then, have students create their own sentences using **BE-EXCEPTIONAL-IN**.

For "• *speed*"

T: ME BE-EXCEPTIONAL-IN, RUN 100 fs-FEET LESS-THAN 6 fs-SEC, ME BE-EXCEPTIONAL-IN

For "• *number*"

t

T: ME BE-EXCEPTIONAL-IN, ICE CREAM 1 fs-GALLON DCL*"large container,"* ME EAT LCL*"from full to empty"* 15 MINUTE. ME BE-EXCEPTIONAL-IN

For "• *endurance*"

T: ME BE-EXCEPTIONAL-IN SIT, LOOK-AT MOVIE ALL-DAY, ME BE-EXCEPTIONAL-IN

For "• *problem solving*"

T: ME KNOW MAN IX*"man"* BE-EXCEPTIONAL-IN MANAGE EIGHT fs-DOG. IX*"man"* CAN ORDER #ALL DOG SIT (2h)SCL:V*"sit in a semi-circle"* QUIET. IX*"man"*

nodding

BE-EXCEPTIONAL-IN

For "• *extraordinary skills*"

t

T: MY #DOG BE-EXCEPTIONAL-IN, fs-REF DOOR, [(wh)LCL:B*"door"*/BPCL*"open fridge door with mouth"*]

t

fs-JELLO BOX, [(wh)LCL:B*"door"*/BPCL*"take jello box and put in fridge"*] IX*"dog"* BE-EXCEPTIONAL-IN

Now, have students take turns telling about an unusual ability or skill they (or someone/animal they know) possess. Be sure they follow this structure:

t t

S: ME (or person/animal) **BE-EXCEPTIONAL-IN** (describe skill), ME (or person/animal) **BE-EXCEPTIONAL-IN**

PRACTICE *Discuss Ineptness*

8–12 minutes

Students practice suggesting what other people should or should not do when they lack a certain ability or talent.

PRESENT
(LESSON SLIDE 11:1:11)

If someone lacks a certain ability or talent to do something, explain what they should or should not do.

Demonstrate describing what someone should or should not do when they lack a certain ability or talent. Then, have groups of 4 students create sentences using **BE-INEPT**.

cond
T: [SUPPOSE] IX*"person"* **BE-INEPT** COUNT MONEY,
neg
IX*"person"* SHOULD NOT WORK #BANK

cond
T: [SUPPOSE] IX*"person"* **BE-INEPT** fs-ASL, IX*"person"*
neg
SHOULD NOT INTERPRET

cond
T: [SUPPOSE] IX*"person"* **BE-INEPT** DANCE, IX*"person"*
SHOULD TAKE-UP CLASS

Now, have students take turns describing what someone should or should not do if they lack a certain skill or talent. Be sure they follow this structure:

cond

S: [SUPPOSE] IX*"person"* **BE-INEPT** (skill/talent), IX*"person"* SHOULD [NOT] (activity).

HOMEWORK

Tell students to do **Homework 11:1** (*Student Workbook*, page 316–322).

LESSON 11:2

Numbers Review 1

Lesson length: 55–80 minutes

LESSON GOAL Students review number types with numbers 1–15: cardinal, age, clock, money, year and lengths of time.

KEY SKILLS sign numbers quickly and accurately

NOTIONS

Grammar
cardinal number forms
age number forms
clock number forms
cent and dollar number forms
year number forms
number incorporation for lengths of time

PREPARATION

- Read and view **Number Types** and **Number Combinations** in *Student Workbook*, page 323.
- Make flash cards **11:2 Number Sets A, B, C and D** (for **Activity** on pages 629–630)

MATERIALS

11:2 Lesson Slides
11:2 Number Sets A, B, C and D

HOMEWORK 11:2 *Student Workbook*, pages 323–325

REVIEW *Forms for Numbers 1–15*

20 minutes

PRESENT
(LESSON SLIDES 11:2:1–5)

Review Number Types

Using number 3, sign these number types:

a) cardinal
b) age
c) dollars
d) cents
e) clock
f) minutes
g) hours
h) days
i) weeks
j) months

Show **Slides 1 and 2** and review number types with numbers 3 and 7. Give a letter that corresponds to a number type on the slide and have students use number type given on slide to form the number. For example:

T: fs-A (for "cardinal")
S: 3*"palm in"* (or 7*"palm out"*)

T: fs-B (for "age")
S: OLD-3 (or OLD-7)

T: fs-C (for "dollars")
S: 3-DOLLAR (or 7-DOLLAR)

T: fs-D (for "cents")
S: CENT-3 (or CENT-7)

T: fs-E (for "clock")
S: TIME-3 (or TIME-7)

T: fs-F (for "minutes")
S: 3-MINUTE (or 7-MINUTE)

Be sure students:

- use the "3" or "7" handshape with the correct palm orientation and movement for each number type.

Do the same with **Slides 3–5**, using numbers 10, 12 and 15. For example:

T: fs-A (for "cardinal")
S: 10 (or 12, 15)

T: fs-B (for "age")
S: OLD-10 (or OLD-12, OLD-15)

T: fs-C (for "dollars")
S: 10 DOLLAR (or 12 DOLLAR, 15 DOLLAR)

T: fs-D (for "cents")
S: CENT-10 (or CENT-12, CENT-15)

T: fs-E (for "clock")
S: TIME-10 (or TIME-12)

NOTE: There's no TIME-15.

T: fs-F (for "minutes")
S: 10 ONE-MINUTE (or 12 ONE-MINUTE, 15 ONE-MINUTE)

NOTE: For "10 minutes," the number can be incorporated with *MINUTE*, or signed separately like "12 minutes" and "15 minutes."

PRESENT
(LESSON SLIDE 11:2:6)

Review Number Combinations
Years

1212 1502 1911
2007 2014

Years: Have students sign each number on the slide.

Be sure students use these patterns and movements:
1212 = 12+12 (single, emphatic movement for both 12s)
1502 = 15+02 (single, emphatic movement for the 15; palm out for the 02)
1911 = 19+11 (single, emphatic movement for the 11)
2007 = 2+00+7
2014 = 20+14 (single, emphatic movement for both numbers).

PRESENT
(LESSON SLIDE 11:2:7)

Review Number Combinations
Money: dollars + cents

$1.05 $2.15 $6.11
$8.10 $9.09

Money: Have students sign each number on the slide.

Be sure students use these patterns and movements:
$1.05 (twist movement for $1; palm out for .05; no CENT sign)
$2.15 (twist movement for $2; single, emphatic movement for .15; no CENT sign)
$6.11 (twist movement for $6; single, emphatic movement for .11)
$8.10 (twist movement for $8; single, emphatic movement for .10)
$9.09 (twist movement for $9; palm out for .09; no CENT sign).

PRESENT
(LESSON SLIDE 11:2:8)

Review Number Combinations
Clock: hours + minutes

2:05 3:13 4:11
7:15 12:10

Clock: Have students sign each number on the slide.

Be sure students use these patterns and movements:
2:05 (palm out for both 2 and 05 parts)
3:13 (palm out for the 3)
4:11 (palm out for the 4)
7:15 (either repeated or single, emphatic movement for the 15
12:10 (use single, emphatic movement for both numbers)

PRACTICE *Number Forms*

35–50 minutes

Students practice forms for different number types: cardinal, age, clock, year, money and lengths of time.

Activity. Divide class into four groups and give each group a set of flash cards **11:2 Number Set A, B, C or D** (See **Materials**). One student in each group is to be the leader who pulls a card from the stack, shows it to the group and asks one student to sign the number. The group is to confirm (or correct) the number form. When done, rotate the sets of flash cards among the groups, select a new leader and repeat the activity.

Continue until groups have practiced with all four sets of flash cards.

PRESENT
(LESSON SLIDES
11:2:9–66)

Quick and Right
Number Challenge

Conclude. Show **Lesson Slides 11:2:9–66.**

Round 1—focus on students' sign forms for all numbers.

Round 2—go through the slides quicker, and focus on students giving the numbers quickly.

HOMEWORK

Tell students to do **Homework 11:2**
(*Student Workbook*, pages 323–325).

LESSON 11:3

Asking for Opinion about Someone

Lesson length: 50–65 minutes

LESSON GOAL

Students will sign this dialogue:

Dialogue

A: give name (from B's list); ask who

B: explain relationship

A: explain need[1],ask opinion about person as a potential...[2]

- travel companion
- roommate
- employee
- date
- babysitter

B: give opinion about him or her

- at least three personal quality signs
- example(s) to support your opinion
- at least one drawback about this person[3]

A: ask follow-up questions if necessary

B: reply

A: tell what you plan to do[4]

KEY PHRASES

[1] (travel companion) ME WANT SOMEONE WITH ME TRAVEL...

(roommate) ME NEED ROOMMATE, ME THINK-cont ASK-person
or
IX CONTACT-me IX WANT US-TWO ROOMMATE.

(employee) ME MULL-OVER INVITE/HIRE WORK
or
ME MULL-OVER ASK-TO-person IX*"person"* TRANSFER-TO-me WORK WITH ME.

(date)	ME MULL-OVER TAKE-FROM-person LEAVE-FOR fs-DATE
(babysitter)	ME NEED SOMEONE (2h)LOOK-AT, TAKE-CARE-OF MY CHILDREN.

q
[2] THINK IX*"person"* GOOD.

t
[3] [ONE] WARNING...

[4] ME IN-FUTURE CONTACT-person IX*"person"*
ME GO-AHEAD (contact person, take out for date or hire person)
ME IN-FUTURE LOOK-FOR OTHER PERSON

NOTIONS

Vocabulary
CONTACT-TO
BE-EXPERIENCED
(2h)PICK-UP++
BE-CREATIVE
TO-FLIRT
INVITE/HIRE-person
TRANSFER-TO

PREPARATION

- Come up with five names of people you know with various personalities (**Dialogue**, pages 637–638)

MATERIALS

11:3 Lesson Slides
11:3 Follow-up Slides
Exercise 1 (in *Student Workbook*, page 473)

HOMEWORK 11:3

Student Workbook, pages 326–335

WARM UP *Desirable and Undesirable Personal Qualities*

20–25 minutes

PRESENT
(LESSON SLIDE 11:3:1)

Roles

Group 1 – travel companion
Group 2 – roommate
Group 3 – employee
Group 4 – date
Group 5 – babysitter

In your group, discuss what personal qualities may be desirable and undesirable for the role.

Divide class into five groups. Assign each group a number 1, 2, 3, 4 and 5. Have students in each group discuss personal qualities that may be desirable and undesirable for the role.

Have each group share with the class the qualities they came up with. Supplement the group's lists with any additional useful vocabulary from the teacher's guide below.

Teacher's Guide

For ***"travel companion"***

DESIRABLE	UNDESIRABLE
TALK++, CHAT++, MEET-people++	BASHFUL+
BE-POSITIVE++, BE-HONEST, EASY GET-ALONG-WITH	BE-NEGATIVE++, LIE++, DISAGREE++, COMPLAIN++
LAID-BACK(mm)	WORRIED-char
FLEXIBLE	STUBBORN
(2h)FUNNY-char	QUIET++
TIME++	LATE++

For ***"roommate"***

DESIRABLE	UNDESIRABLE
BE-POSITIVE++, BE-HONEST, EASY GET-ALONG-WITH	BE-NEGATIVE++, DISAGREE++, COMPLAIN++
SHARE++, FLEXIBLE	BE-SELFISH++
PAY-TO++ MONTH++, GOOD+MONEY+EXCHANGE++	LATE++ PAY-TO++ BE-BROKE++
IN-GEAR++, !CLEAN!	MESSED-UP++
RESPECT-TO, LEAVE-ALONE++	NOSE-IN++, TOUCH+++

For ***"employee"*** (glosses in bold to be introduced)

BE-EXPERIENCED

(2H)PICK-UP++

DESIRABLE	UNDESIRABLE
BE-POSITIVE++, BE-HONEST, EASY GET-ALONG-WITH	BE-NEGATIVE++, DISAGREE++ COMPLAIN++
BE-EXPERIENCED, **(2h)PICK-UP++** BE-SKILLED-IN, BE-EXCEPTIONAL-IN,	AWKWARD/CLUMSY, BE-INEPT
serious WORK-char RESPONSIBLE++,	th (2h)alt.PLAY++ NOT+RESPONSIBLE,
IN-GEAR++, COMPLETE++	(2h)alt."pshaw," POSTPONE++
TIME++, ATTEND++	LATE++, SKIP-WORK++

For *"date"* (gloss in bold to be introduced)

TO-FLIRT

DESIRABLE	UNDESIRABLE
SMART, BE-KNOWLEDGEABLE-IN (subject)	NOT+SMART ZERO-FOREHEAD (subject)
OPEN-MINDED, (2h)alt.UNDERSTANDING	NARROW-MINDED
COOL/NEAT,	STRANGE/ODD
HUMBLE/MODEST	BIG-HEADED, TALK++, BOASTFUL
BE-POLITE, SWEET, CHEERFUL	RUDE++, MEAN, STUCK-UP/SNOBBISH **TO-FLIRT**
(2h)FUNNY-char	QUIET++

For *"babysitter"* (gloss in bold to be introduced)

BE-CREATIVE

DESIRABLE	UNDESIRABLE
BE-RESPONSIBLE++, TRUST	NOT+BE-RESPONSIBLE, FLICK-SHOULDERS
GOOD+BEAR-WITH	NONE+BEAR+WITH
BE-CREATIVE	NOT BE-CREATIVE
STERN/STRICT or HEART+SOFT, WARM, BE-POSITIVE++, SUPPORT++, ENCOURAGE	HEART+SOFT or STERN/STRICT, COLD, BE-NEGATIVE++, (2h)alt.INSULT, CRITICIZE/CORRECT++
BE-CAREFUL, GOOD+MIND+JUDGE	(2h)CARELESS

PRACTICE *Giving Opinions about a Person*

30–40 minutes

Students practice giving opinions about a person.

PRESENT
(LESSON SLIDE 11:3:2)

A: give name (from B's list), ask who
B: explain relationship
A: explain need, ask opinion about person as a potential...
- travel companion
- roommate
- employee
- date
- babysitter

B: give opinion about him or her
- at least three personal quality signs
- example(s) to support your opinion
- at least one drawback about this person

A: ask follow up questions
B: reply
A: tell what you plan to do

Begin with Signer A's lines. Demonstrate lines and have students copy.

For ***"A: give name (from B's list); ask who"***

whq
T: fs-ROSE-SMITH WHO
S(all): copy

For ***"A: explain need, ask opinion about person as a potential..."***

T: *(travel companion)* ME **WANT SOMEONE**

q
WITH ME TRAVEL-AROUND, **THINK IX*"Rose"* GOOD**
S(all): copy

CONTACT-TO

INVITE/HIRE

T: *(roommate)* ME NEED ROOMMATE, ME

q
THINK-cont ASK-person. **THINK IX*"Rose"* GOOD**
or
IX*"Rose"* **CONTACT-TO-me** IX*"Rose"*WANT US-TWO

q
ROOMMATE. **THINK IX*"Rose"* GOOD**
S(all): copy

TRANSFER-TO-ME

T: *(employee)* ME MULL-OVER **INVITE/HIRE**

q

WORK. **THINK IX"*Rose*" GOOD**

or

ME MULL-OVER ASK-TO-person IX*"person"*

q

TRANSFER- TO-me WORK WITH ME. **THINK IX"*Rose*" GOOD**

S(all): copy

T: *(date)* ME MULL-OVER TAKE-FROM-person

q

LEAVE-FOR fs-DATE. **THINK IX"*Rose*" GOOD**

S(all): copy

T: *(babysitter)* ME NEED SOMEONE (2h)LOOK-AT++ "children,"

q

TAKE-CARE-OF MY CHILDREN. **THINK IX"*Rose*" GOOD**

S(all): copy

For ***"A: tell what you plan to do"***

T: ME IN-FUTURE CONTACT-person IX*"person"*

S(all): copy

T: ME GO-AHEAD TAKE-person
LEAVE-FOR fs-DATE (or INVITE/HIRE-person)

S(all): copy

T: ME IN-FUTURE LOOK-FOR OTHER PERSON

S(all): copy

Demonstrate dialogue. Give five names of people you know with various personalities. You can write them on the board or add them to the slide.

Now, role play Signer B and call one student to role play Signer A and have him or her select one of your names and a role listed on the slide to begin.

NOTE: For *"B: give opinion about him or her (give at least one drawback about this person),"* use one or both of these signs as a transition to signal the drawback. Be sure to give examples to support your opinion of the person.

ONE

and/or

WARNING

Repeat procedure with a different student as Signer A. Make sure she or he selects a different name from your list and a different role.

EXERCISE 1 (*Student Workbook*, page 473).
Now, ask students to open their workbook, read instructions and write in the names of five people they know.

Mingle. Have students exchange workbooks with their partners so they can select a name and a role for that person to begin the dialogue.

Have students continue with different partners until all five names and roles have been checked off in their workbooks.

Conclude. Call pairs of students up front to go through the dialogue. Be sure each Signer B give examples to support their opinion and share a drawback about the person discussed.

HOMEWORK

Tell students to do **Homework 11:3** (*Student Workbook*, pages 326–335).

HOMEWORK FOLLOW-UP
10–15 MINUTES

PRESENT
(HOMEWORK SLIDES 11:3:1–30)

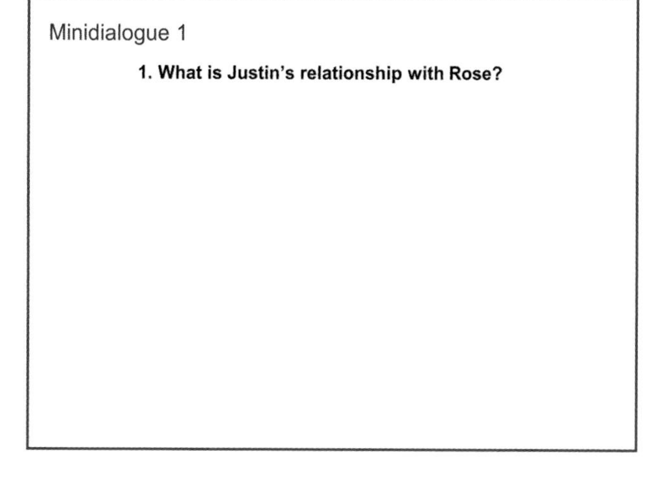

Check students' answers to **Minidialogues 1–5**. See **Introduction** pages xviii–xix for different ways to check answers.

LESSON 11:4

Describing Reactions

Lesson length: 60–80 minutes

LESSON GOAL

Students will sign this dialogue:

Dialogue

A: ask hypothetical question[1]
- use hypothetical sign
- state sequence of events
- ask the question

B: tell how you would react or feel

KEY PHRASES

cond: [1] SUPPOSE, (state sequence of events),

whq: HOW FEEL YOU or whq: YOU ANSWER/RESPOND HOW

NOTIONS

Grammar

conditional clause

Vocabulary

Positive Reactions	*Negative Reactions*	*Either*
BE-THRILLED	BE-SCARED	TOUCH-HEART
JUMP-JOY	BE-LET-DOWN	BE-PUZZLED
BE-RELIEVED	BE-DISAPPOINTED	BE-SHOCKED
	SQUEEZE-THROAT	JAW-DROP
	#UPSET	BE-EMBARRASSED
	BE-ANGRY	
	BE-DISGUSTED	

others

ELECTRIC	PIE	NUT
LAST++ (at the end)	LONELY	GROUND/SOIL
RUN-OUT-OF	PREACH+ER	FULL (space)
!ERASE!	APPLY	

PREPARATION Review **Exercises 2A–2D** in *Student Workbook*, pages 479, 482, 484 and 487

MATERIALS **11:4 Lesson Slides**

HOMEWORK 11:4 *Student Workbook*, pages 336–345

INTRODUCE *Reactions*

30–40 minutes

PRESENT
(LESSON SLIDES 11:4:1–15)

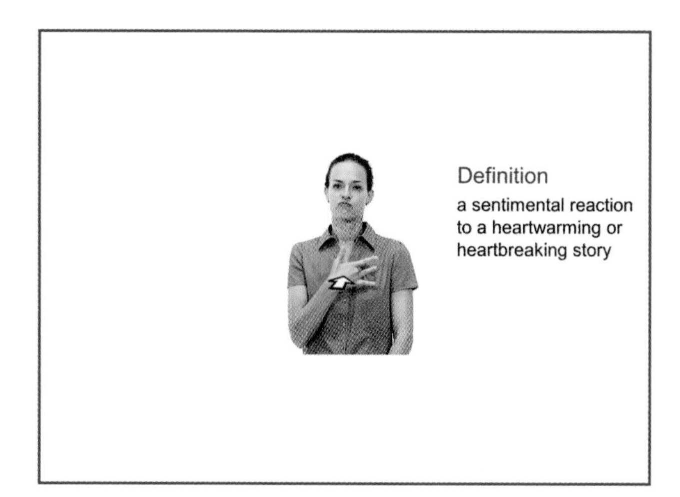
Definition
a sentimental reaction to a heartwarming or heartbreaking story

Introduce vocabulary for reactions on **Lesson Slides 11:4:1–15**. Have students read the definition. Then, demonstrate the sign and have students copy.

TOUCH-HEART

For **Slide 1**

definition: a sentimental reaction to a heartwarming or heartbreaking story

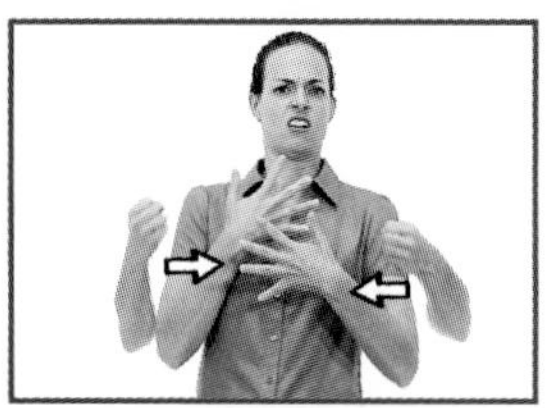
BE-SCARED

For **Slide 2**

definition: a frightened or alarmed reaction; to be scared

BE-THRILLED

For **Slide 3**

definition: a joyful reaction upon learning good news; to be thrilled

BE-LET-DOWN

For **Slide 4**

definition: a disheartened reaction; to feel let down

BE-DISAPPOINTED

For **Slide 5**

definition: a reaction to someone or something that has failed to meet one's hopes or expectations; to be disappointed

#UPSET

For **Slide 6**

definition: a reaction of anxious uneasiness or worry; to be disturbed or upset

BE-ANGRY

For **Slide 7**

definition: an angry or furious reaction

BE-PUZZLED

For **Slide 8**

definition: a puzzled reaction; uncertain of what's going on

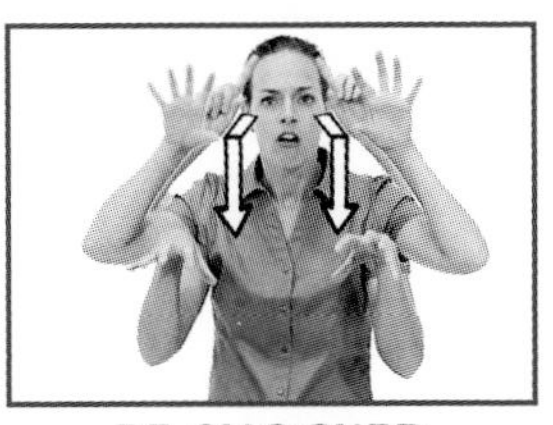

BE-SHOCKED

For **Slide 9**

definition: a shocked reaction; temporarily unable to react upon seeing or learning something surprising or tragic

JAW-DROP

For **Slide 10**

definition: a reaction of astonishment to something that is hard to believe

SQUEEZE-THROAT

For **Slide 11**

definition: a sheepish reaction after learning you made a fool of yourself

BE-DISGUSTED

For **Slide 12**

definition: an annoyed reaction toward yourself after realizing you should have known better

BE-EMBARRASSED

For **Slide 13**

definition: an embarrassed reaction upon realizing others have witnessed your predicament

JUMP-JOY

For **Slide 14**

definition: an elated reaction, with great joy

BE-RELIEVED

For **Slide 15**

definition: a relieved reaction; being freed from fear or worry

Review. Show **Lesson Slides 11:4:1–15** again and have students give the sign.

PRESENT
(LESSON SLIDES 11:4:16–30)

Now, show videos **Situations 1–15** (**Lesson Slides 11:4:16–30**). Have students answer using a reaction sign.

Teacher's Guide: *(recommended answers)*

Situation 1 BE-DISAPPOINTED
Situation 2 BE-SCARED
Situation 3 BE-LET-DOWN
Situation 4 BE-ANGRY
Situation 5* TOUCH-HEART
Situation 6 BE-PUZZLED
Situation 7 BE-SHOCKED or JAW-DROP
Situation 8 BE-THRILLED or JUMP-JOY
Situation 9 JAW-DROP
Situation 10 BE-DISGUSTED or SQUEEZE-THROAT
Situation 11 SQUEEZE-THROAT
Situation 12 BE-RELIEVED
Situation 13 #UPSET
Situation 14 BE-EMBARRASSED
Situation 15 JUMP-JOY

Make sure students understand these possible new signs from those videos.

Situation 1

PIE

Situation 5

LONELY

Situation 7

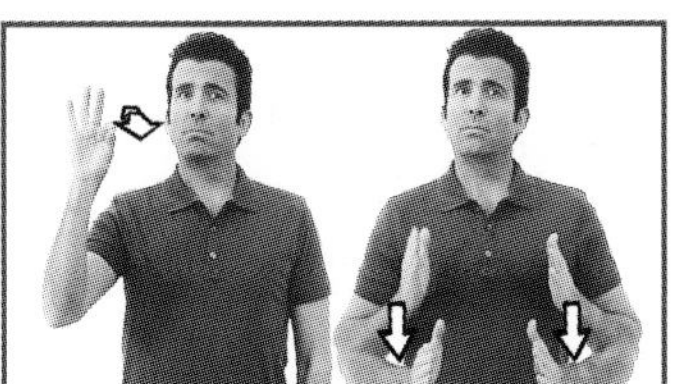

PREACHER+ER

Situation 8

APPLY

Situation 12

FULL (space)

* This question "HOW FEEL YOU" is another way to elicit a reaction sign.

TEACHER TO TEACHER

Take opportunities to clarify the usage of reaction signs. For example, some students might sign BE-EMBARRASSED instead of #UPSET to describe their reaction to their dress getting splattered with mud. #UPSET would be better to describe one's immediate reaction. BE-EMBARRASSED describes one's reaction to being observed by others, not to the incident itself.

PRACTICE *Asking Hypothetical Questions*

30–40 minutes

Students practice asking hypothetical questions with conditional clauses to elicit reaction signs.

PRESENT
(LESSON SLIDE 11:4:31)

To ask a hypothetical question,
- use hypothetical sign
- state sequence of events
- ask the question

Question: How would you react if upon returning home from a three month vacation, you received an $800 electric bill?

Demonstrate asking this hypothetical question using a conditional clause. Have students repeat.

ELECTRIC

T: (• ***use hypothetical sign***) SUPPOSE (cond)

(• ***state sequence of events***)
YOU LEAVE-FOR VACATION 3-MONTH,
FINISH, COME-here HOME, (when)
GET **ELECTRIC** fs-BILL,
ICL*"open bill statement,"* !800! DOLLAR.

whq
(• ***ask the question***) HOW FEEL YOU *or*

whq
YOU RESPOND/ANSWER HOW

S: (repeat)

Be sure students:

• raise brows with the conditional clause

• furrow brows with the wh-word question.

PRESENT
(LESSON SLIDE 11:4:32)

To ask a hypothetical question,
• use hypothetical sign
• state sequence of events
• ask the question

Question: How would you react if the adorable dog in the movie dies in the end?

Demonstrate asking this hypothetical question. Have students repeat.

LAST++

cond
T: (• ***use hypothetical sign***) SUPPOSE

(• ***state sequence of events***)
MOVIE YOU GO-TO WATCH,
#DOG IX-loc*"on screen"* CUTE,
MOVIE **LAST++**, IX*"dog"* DIE.

whq
(• ***ask the question***) HOW FEEL YOU *or*

whq
YOU RESPOND/ANSWER HOW

S: (repeat)

PRESENT
(LESSON SLIDE 11:4:33)

To ask a hypothetical question,
• use hypothetical sign
• state sequence of events
• ask the question

Question: How would you react if you were at a friend's birthday party and they ran out of birthday cake before you could get a piece?

Demonstrate asking this hypothetical question. Have students repeat.

RUN-OUT-OF

cond
T: (• ***use hypothetical sign***) SUPPOSE

(• ***state sequence of events***)
FRIEND POSS*"friend"* BIRTHDAY PARTY, YOU GO-TO,
NOW IX*"host"* (2h)GIVE-OUT-all fs-CAKE,
YOU GO-TO GET [fs-CAKE], !WRONG! **RUN-OUT-OF**

whq
(• ***ask the question***) HOW FEEL YOU *or*
whq
YOU RESPOND/ANSWER HOW

S: (repeat)

PRESENT
(LESSON SLIDE 11:4:34)

To ask a hypothetical question,
• use hypothetical sign
• state sequence of events
• ask the question

Question: How would you react if you pushed the wrong button and erased the pictures you were transferring to the computer?

Demonstrate asking this hypothetical question. Have students repeat.

!ERASE !

cond

T: (• ***use hypothetical sign***) SUPPOSE

(• ***state sequence of events***)

t

COMPUTER, PICTURE YOU TRANSFER-to-computer++ !WRONG! ICL*"press wrong button,"* PICTURE **!ERASE!**

whq

(• ***ask the question***) HOW FEEL YOU *or*

whq

YOU RESPOND/ANSWER HOW

S: (repeat)

EXERCISE 2A, 2B, 2C, 2D

Divide class into groups of four. Assign each student **Exercise 2A**, **2B**, **2C**, or **2D** (*Student Workbook*, pages 479, 482, 484 and 487).

PRESENT
(LESSON SLIDE 11:4:35)

Signer A: ask hypothetical question
• use hypothetical sign
• state sequence of events
• ask the question
B: tell how you would react or feel

Take turns asking your hypothetical questions and getting everyone's reactions.

Students take turns asking each other the questions on their assigned exercise page, and respond to the questions using a reaction sign.

Conclude. Call students up front to ask one of their hypothetical questions to the class and have the class share their reactions.

Be sure students:

- begin the conditional clause with SUPPOSE (raised brows) [cond marker over SUPPOSE]
- arrange information according to sequence of events
- furrow brow and lean head forward for the wh-word question: HOW FEEL YOU or YOU RESPOND/ANSWER HOW. [whq marker over each]

HOMEWORK

Tell students to do **Homework 11:4** (*Student Workbook*, pages 336–345).

LESSON 11:5

Fingerspelling: States and Provinces 1

Lesson length: 45–55 minutes

LESSON GOAL

Students will learn to name U.S. states and Canadian provinces using fingerspelling or signs.

KEY SKILLS

Movement and palm orientation in fingerspelled states and provinces

NOTIONS

Vocabulary

States that are signed

ALASKA
ARIZONA
CALIFORNIA
COLORADO
HAWAII
MAINE
MONTANA
NEW-YORK
OREGON
TEXAS
WASHINGTON

States and Provinces with fingerspelled forms
(refer to list on pages 657–658)

Provinces that are signed

ALBERTA
MANITOBA
NEWFOUNDLAND
ONTARIO
QUEBEC
optional: YUKON (territory)

Others

fs-US, fs-USA, or AMERICA
CANADA
STATE
PROVINCE (2 variations)

MATERIALS

11:5 Lesson Slides

HOMEWORK 11:5

Student Workbook, pages 346–352

INTRODUCE *States and Provinces*

25–30 minutes

PRESENT
(LESSON SLIDE 11:5:1)

Explain that ASL is used in the U.S. and Canada, and that the U.S. has 50 states and that Canada has 10 provinces (plus three territories). You can add that in Quebec, there's also LSQ (Quebec Sign Language or Langue des Signes Quebecoise). Also, explain that some of the states and provinces have signs, some are fingerspelled—either in full or abbreviated.

Introduce signs:
fs-US, fs-USA, or AMERICA
STATE or fs-STATE
CANADA
PROVINCE

STATE

CANADA

PROVINCE
(variation 1)

PROVINCE
(variation 2)

PRESENT
(LESSON SLIDE 11:5:2)

Show video introducing signs for eleven U.S. states. Have students copy:

ALASKA
ARIZONA
CALIFORNIA
COLORADO
HAWAII
MAINE
MONTANA
NEW-YORK
OREGON
TEXAS
WASHINGTON

PRESENT
(LESSON SLIDE 11:5:3)

Show video introducing signs for five Canadian provinces. Have students copy:

ALBERTA
MANITOBA
NEWFOUNDLAND
ONTARIO (2 variations)
QUEBEC (2 variations)

PRESENT
(LESSON SLIDE 11:5:4)

Show video introducing states and provinces with initials fingerspelled. Point out the movements and palm orientations used in the initials. Have students copy:

fs-NH	(New Hampshire)	**fs-SC**	(South Carolina)
fs-NJ	(New Jersey)	**fs-SD**	(South Dakota)
fs-NM	(New Mexico)	**fs-BC**	(British Columbia)
fs-NC	(North Carolina)	**fs-NB**	(New Brunswick)
fs-ND	(North Dakota)	**fs-NS**	(Nova Scotia) (2 variations)
fs-RI	(Rhode Island)	**fs-PEI**	(Prince Edward Island)

PRESENT
(LESSON SLIDE 11:5:5)

Show video introducing states and provinces with first and last letters fingerspelled. Point out the movements and palm orientations used in the abbreviations. Have students copy:

fs-FLA (Florida)	**fs-MO** (Missouri)
fs-GA (Georgia)	**fs-PA** (Pennsylvania)
fs-KY (Kentucky)	**fs-VA** (Virginia)
fs-LA (Louisiana)	**fs-VT** (Vermont)
fs-MD (Maryland)	**WEST+fs-VA** (West Virginia)

PRESENT
(LESSON SLIDE 11:5:6)

Show video introducing states and provinces with first few letters fingerspelled. Point out the movements and palm orientations used in the abbreviations. Have students copy:

fs-ALA (Alabama)	**fs-MINN** (Minnesota)
fs-ARK (Arkansas)	**fs-MISS** (Mississippi)
fs-COLO (Colorado)	**fs-NEB** (Nebraska)
fs-CONN (Connecticut)	**fs-NEV** (Nevada)
fs-DEL (Delaware)	**fs-OKLA** (Oklahoma)
fs-ILL (Illinois)	**fs-TENN** (Tennessee)
fs-IND (Indiana)	**fs-WIS or fs-WISC** (Wisconsin)
fs-KAN (Kansas)	**fs-WYO** (Wyoming)
fs-MASS (Massachusetts)	**#SASK** (Saskatchewan) (two variations)
fs-MICH (Michigan)	

PRESENT
(LESSON SLIDE 11:5:7)

Show video introducing the states for which names are fingerspelled in full. Point out the movements and palm orientations in each name. Have students copy:

fs-ALASKA	**fs-MAINE**
fs-ARIZONA	**fs-MONTANA**
fs-COLORADO	**fs-NEVADA**
fs-HAWAII	**fs-OHIO**
fs-IDAHO	**fs-OREGON**
fs-IOWA	**fs-UTAH**

PRESENT
(LESSON SLIDES 11:5:8–67)

Alabama

Review. Have students practice by giving the signs or fingerspelled forms for the states or provinces on the slides. The states and provinces are shown in alphabetic order.

Teacher's Guide

Alabama	fs-ALA
Alaska	ALASKA (signed), or fs-ALASKA
Arizona	ARIZONA (signed), or fs-ARIZONA
Arkansas	fs-ARK
California	CALIFORNIA (signed)
Colorado	COLOR+fs-ADO, or fs-COLORADO, or fs-COLO
Connecticut	fs-CONN
Delaware	fs-DEL
Florida	fs-FLA
Georgia	fs-GA
Hawaii	HAWAII (signed), or fs-HAWAII
Idaho	fs-IDAHO
Illinois	fs-ILL
Indiana	fs- IND
Iowa	fs-IOWA
Kansas	fs-KANSAS, or fs-KAN
Kentucky	fs-KY
Louisiana	fs-LA
Maine	MAINE (signed), or fs-MAINE
Maryland	fs-MD
Massachusetts	fs-MASS
Michigan	fs-MICH
Minnesota	fs-MINN
Mississippi	fs-MISS
Missouri	fs-MO
Montana	MONTANA (signed), or fs-MONTANA
Nebraska	fs-NEB
Nevada	fs-NEVADA
New Hampshire	fs-NH
New Jersey	fs-NJ
New Mexico	fs-NM
New York	NEW-YORK (signed)
North Carolina	fs-NC
North Dakota	fs-ND
Ohio	fs-OHIO
Oklahoma	fs-OKLA
Oregon	OREGON (signed), or fs-OREGON
Pennsylvania	fs-PA
Rhode Island	fs-RI
South Carolina	fs-SC

South Dakota	fs-SD
Tennessee	fs-TENN
Texas	TEXAS (signed)
Utah	fs-UTAH
Vermont	fs-VT
Virginia	fs-VA
Washington	WASHINGTON (signed)
West Virginia	WEST+ fs-VA
Wisconsin	fs-WIS, or fs-WISC
Wyoming	fs-WYO
Alberta	ALBERTA (signed)
British Colombia	fs-BC
Manitoba	MANITOBA (signed), or fs-MANITOBA
New Brunswick	fs-NB
Newfoundland	NEWFOUNDLAND (signed)
Nova Scotia	fs-NS (2 ways)
Ontario	ONTARIO (2 signed variations)
Prince Edward Island	fs-PEI
Quebec	QUEBEC (2 signed variations)
Saskatchewan	fs-SASK (2 variations)

PRACTICE *Naming the States in a Region*

20–25 minutes

Students practice naming states in different regions in the U.S.

PRESENT
(LESSON SLIDE 11:5:68)

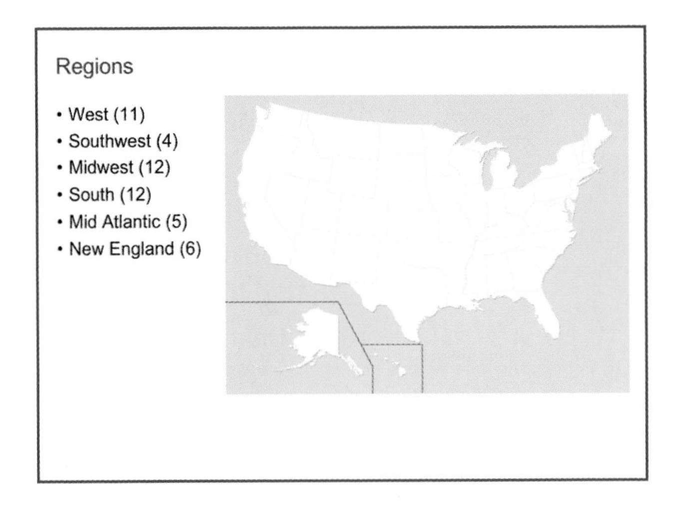

Regions
• West (11)
• Southwest (4)
• Midwest (12)
• South (12)
• Mid Atlantic (5)
• New England (6)

Divide class into six groups. Assign a region (West, Midwest, Southwest, New England, Mid Atlantic or South) to each group. Each group is to determine what states belong to their region.

When done, begin with the "West Region" group. Have the groups give you the names of states. Write the names on the board.

PRESENT
(LESSON SLIDES 11:5:69–74)

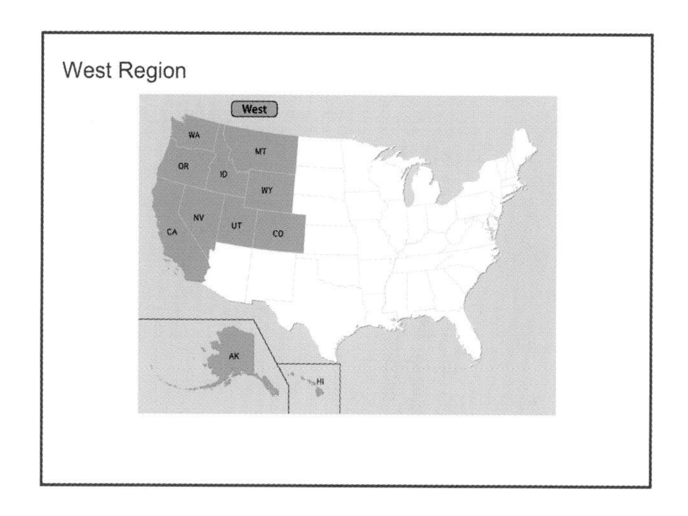

Show the **West Region** slide to confirm students' answers. Then, have the whole class review the signs or fingerspelling for the states in that region.

For the **West Region (Slide 69)**

ALASKA (signed), or fs-ALASKA
CALIFORNIA (signed)
COLOR+fs-ADO, or fs-COLORADO, or fs-COLO
HAWAII (signed), or fs-HAWAII
fs-IDAHO
MONTANA (signed), or fs-MONTANA
fs-NEVADA
OREGON (signed), or fs-OREGON
fs-UTAH
WASHINGTON (signed)
fs-WYO

Repeat the procedure for the remaining regions.

For the **Southwest Region (Slide 70)**

ARIZONA (signed), or fs-ARIZONA
fs-NM
fs-OKLA
TEXAS (signed)

For the **Midwest Region (Slide 71)**

fs-ILL
fs- IND
fs-IOWA
fs-KANSAS, or fs-KAN
fs-MICH
fs-MINN
fs-MO
fs-NEB
fs-ND
fs-OHIO
fs-SD
fs-WIS, or fs-WISC

For the **South Region (Slide 72)**

fs-ALA
fs-MISS
fs-ARK
fs-NC
fs-FLA
fs-SC
fs-TENN
fs-KY
fs-VA
fs-LA
WEST+ fs-VA

For the **Mid-Atlantic Region (Slide 73)**

fs-DEL
fs-MD
fs-NJ
NEW-YORK (signed)
fs-PA

For the **New England Region (Slide 74)**

fs-CONN
MAINE (signed), or fs-MAINE
fs-MASS
fs-NH
fs-RI
fs-VT

Conclude. Ask these questions to stimulate further discussion:

1. Which state is the largest?

    t whq
    STATE, LARGE+EST, WHICH
    Answer. Alaska

2. The smallest?

    t whq
    STATE, SMALL+EST, WHICH
    Answer. Rhode Island

3. Which state is the most populated?

    t whq
    STATE, HAVE !MOST! NUMBER PEOPLE, WHICH
    Answer. California

4. The least populated?

    t whq
    STATE, HAVE !SMALL+EST NUMBER PEOPLE, WHICH
    Answer. Wyoming

5. Which state is the 50th?

    t whq
    STATE, WHICH 50+fs-TH, WHICH
    Answer. Hawaii

6. Which state is the first?

    t whq
    STATE, WHICH FIRST-thumb, WHICH
    Answer. Delaware

HOMEWORK

Tell students to do **Homework 11:5**
(*Student Workbook*, pages 346–352).

LESSON 11:6

Making and Canceling Plans

Lesson length: 115–135 minutes

LESSON GOAL

Students will sign these dialogues and follow the narrative outline.

Dialogue 1

Signer A: invite B to join him or her[1]

B: respond

- accept invitation
- state problem with date[2]
- decline invitation[3]

A and B: finalize plans if B accepts

A and B: close conversation[4]

Dialogue 2

A: refer to the plan you made together (use relative clause)[5]

B: acknowledge

A: tell you must cancel the plans; explain why

A and B: close conversation

Narrative Outline

Narrating about Canceled Plans

1. tell what was planned with the other person
    - tell when (date and time)
    - tell who (use plural pronoun)
    - tell about activity planned
2. (conjunction) tell what came up that caused you to cancel
3. tell you informed the other person
4. describe their reaction
5. close with your reaction

KEY PHRASES

1 • IN-FUTURE+FRIDAY ME WANT LEAVE-FOR fs-BEACH,

q: WANT *you*-JOIN-*me*

• ME PLAN IN-FUTURE+FRIDAY, LEAVE-FOR fs-BEACH,

q: WANT *you*-JOIN-*me*

• IN-FUTURE+FRIDAY, ME THINK-ABOUT LEAVE-FOR fs-BEACH, (q: WANT *you*-JOIN-*me*)

• ME MULL-OVER IN-FUTURE+FRIDAY, LEAVE-FOR fs-BEACH, (q: WANT *you*-JOIN-*me*)

2 (q/t: IN-FUTURE+FRIDAY), CONFLICT ME MUST WORK
(or other commitments)
or
(q/t: IN-FUTURE+FRIDAY) (neg: BE-STUCK, CAN'T), (explain why)

3 (neg: NOT+CARE-FOR...)

4 • "close conversation" *(if plan works out for both)*
"thumb-up"
(2h)"perfect"
ME (2h)LOOK-AT*"forward"*
• "close conversation" *(if plan does not work out)*
SORRY
(wh)"pshaw" FINE++
IN-FUTURE ASK-TO-*another person* OTHER PERSON

5 (rel cl: REMEMBER US-TWO PLAN (activity)), ...

NOTIONS

Grammar

relative clause

Vocabulary

Inviting	*Canceling*
PLAN	CANCEL
JOIN-me	

Declining	*Comments*
BE-STUCK	SORRY
CONFLICT	"shucks"
NOT-CARE-FOR	(2h)PERFECT
	(2h)LOOK-AT*"forward"*

Others

MAYBE

Signs for Thinking	
THINK-ABOUT	MULL-OVER
THOUGHT-OCCUR	IDEA

PREPARATION

- Read and view **Key Grammar: Relative Clause**, *Student Workbook*, page 354
- Read and view **Narrating about Canceled Plans**, *Student Workbook*, page 357
- Modify calendar in **Slides 1**, **2** and **8** to reflect actual dates (See pages 666–667)

MATERIALS

11:6 Lesson Slides
11:6 Follow-up Slides
Exercise 3 (in *Student Workbook*, page 491)

HOMEWORK 11:6

Student Workbook, pages 353–361

REVIEW *Calendar Signs*

5–8 minutes

PRESENT
(LESSON SLIDE 11:6:1)

NOTE: Modify the slide to reflect actual dates.

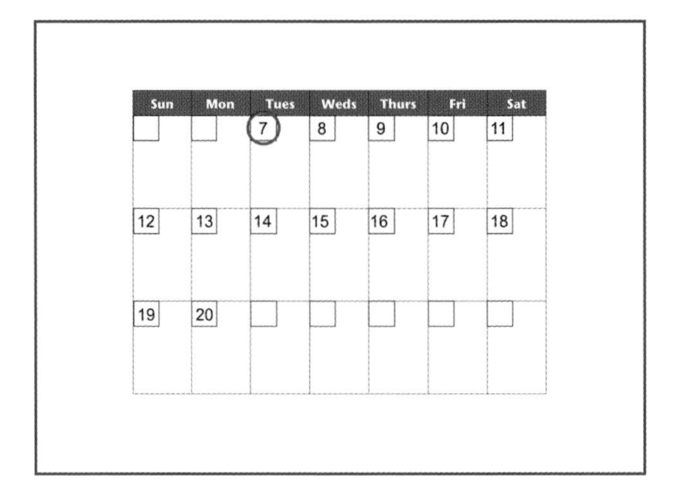

Show the dates for the next two weeks starting with today. The example above uses Tuesday, the 7th as the date for "today."

Point to dates for today, tomorrow and other days in the next two weeks and have students sign, for example,

T: (point to today's date) "what" (whq)
S: TODAY

Continue asking about the other dates to review these signs and phrases:

TOMORROW

IN-FUTURE+(day),
    for example, IN-FUTURE+TUESDAY

1-WEEK-IN-FUTURE+(day),
    for example, 1-WEEK-IN-FUTURE+WEDNESDAY

2-WEEK-IN-FUTURE+(day),
    for example, 2-WEEK-IN-FUTURE+MONDAY

PRESENT
(LESSON SLIDE 11:6:2)

NOTE: Modify the slide to reflect actual dates.

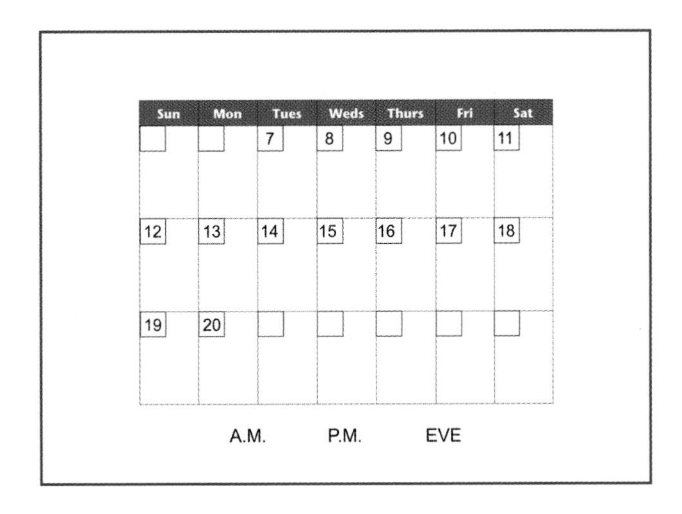

Point to a date on the calendar and then point to A.M., P.M., or EVE and have students sign the phrase, for example,

whq

T: (point to tomorrow's date then to "A.M.") "what"
S: TOMORROW MORNING

Continue pointing to other dates and parts of the day to review these phrases:

IN-FUTURE+(day) (part of day),
for example, IN-FUTURE+TUESDAY AFTERNOON

1-WEEK-IN-FUTURE+(day) (part of day),
for example, 1-WEEK-IN-FUTURE+WEDNESDAY MORNING

2-WEEK-IN-FUTURE+(day) (part of day),
for example, 2-WEEK-IN-FUTURE+MONDAY NIGHT

INTRODUCE *Making Plans*

30 minutes

PRESENT
(LESSON SLIDE 11:6:3)

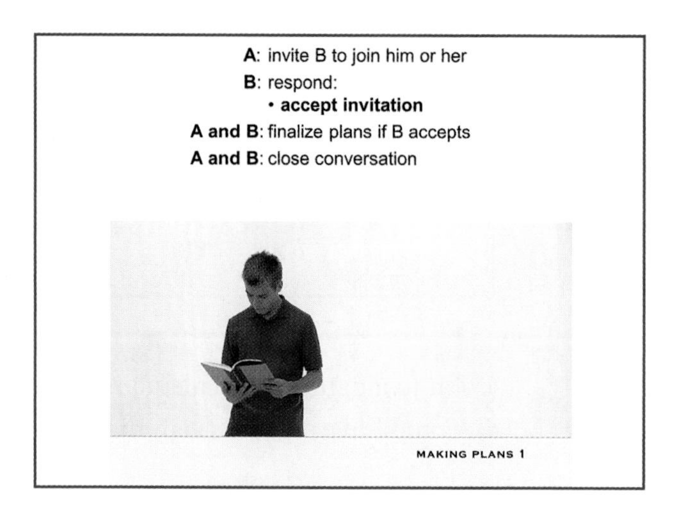

A: invite B to join him or her
B: respond:
• accept invitation
A and B: finalize plans if B accepts
A and B: close conversation
MAKING PLANS 1

Show video **Making Plans 1** and ask students what was signed for parts of the dialogue.

whq
T: (point to *"invite B to join him or her"*) SIGN "what"

q
S: ME WANT GO-TO SEE MOVIE, WANT **you-JOIN-me***

you-JOIN-me

whq
T: (point to *"respond"*) fs-DERRICK IX RESPOND/ANSWER HOW

nod
S: YES, FINE++, SURE...

whq
T: (point to *"finalize plans..."*) THEY-TWO GO-TO-SEE MOVIE, WHEN

S: FRIDAY TIME-7. fs-MELVIN PICK-UP fs-DERRICK TIME 6:45

whq
T: (point to *"close conversation"*) THEY-TWO SIGN "what"

S: (Melvin) (wh)SEE-you (wh)YOU (2h)"thumb-up"
(Derrick) "thumb-up" BYE

* If students ask about the sign **you-JOIN-me**, explain it means to COME-TO-here WITH ME.

PRESENT
(LESSON SLIDE 11:6:4)

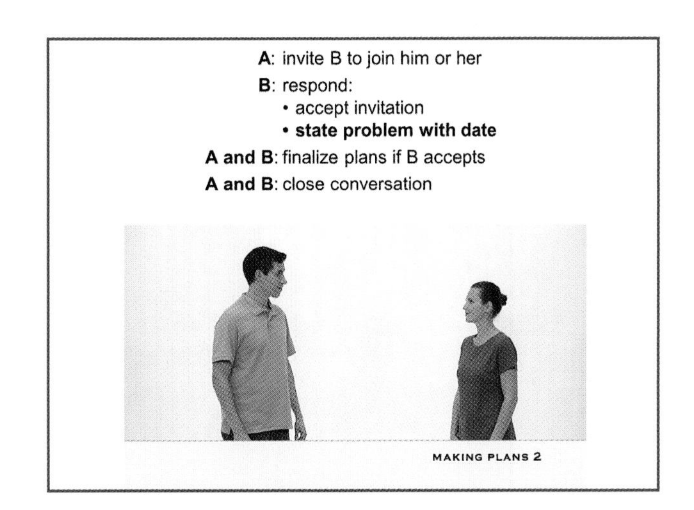

PLAN

CONFLICT

Show video **Making Plans 2** and repeat procedure.

T: (point to *"invite B to join him or her"*) SIGN "what" (whq)

S: ME **PLAN** NEXT-WEEK TUESDAY GO-TO SKIING, [YOU] WANT *you*-JOIN-*me* (q)

T: (point to *"respond"*) fs-AMBER IX RESPOND/ANSWER HOW (whq)

S: YES, ME WANT, (disappointed). TUESDAY, **CONFLICT** (neg) ME MUST WORK.

(2h)"perfect"

(2h)LOOK-AT *"forward"*

T: (point to *"finalize plans..."*) THEY-TWO DECIDE "what" (whq)

S: THEY-TWO DECIDE GO-TO SKIING 1-WEEK-IN-FUTURE WEDNESDAY MORNING. MEET IX-loc*"college"* COLLEGE TIME+8

T: (point to *"close conversation"*) THEY-TWO SIGN "what" (whq)
(JT) **(2h)"perfect"**
(Amber) ME **(2h)LOOK-AT*"forward"***
(JT) me-SAME-AS-you

PRESENT

(LESSON SLIDE 11:6:5)

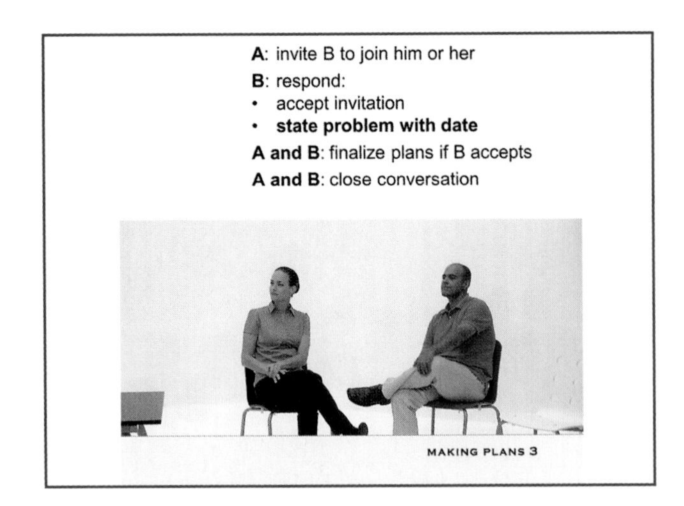

THINK-ABOUT

BE-STUCK

Show video **Making Plans 3** and repeat procedure.

whq
T: (point to *"invite B to join him or her"*) SIGN "what"
S: ME **THINK-ABOUT*** LEAVE-FOR PLAY BILLIARDS.
q
WANT *you*-JOIN-*me*

whq
T: fs-URSULA IX RESPOND/ANSWER HOW
q/t neg
S: TOMORROW, **BE-STUCK**, CAN'T, ME VISIT FAMILY

Ask what they decided on.

whq
T: THEY-TWO DECIDE "what"
S: MAYBE GO-TO ANOTHER TIME

whq
T: (point to *"close conversation"*) THEY-TWO SIGN "what"
(Ursula) FINE++, #OK. SORRY
(David) (wh)"pshaw" FINE++, "well"

* If students ask about the sign "**THINK-ABOUT**," explain it means "to give thought to, to consider."

PRESENT
(LESSON SLIDE 11:6:6)

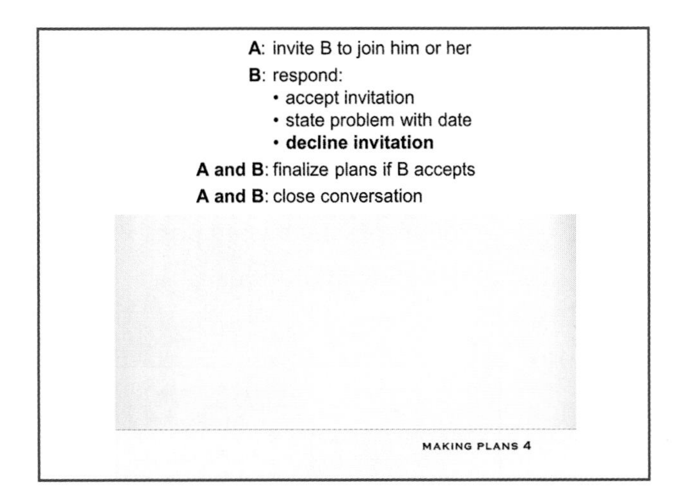

NOT-CARE-FOR

Show video **Making Plans 4** and repeat procedure.

whq
T: (point to *"invite B to join him or her"*) SIGN "what"
S: ME MULL-OVER GO-TO MUSEUM, SIGHTSEE,
q
WANT *you*-JOIN-*me*

whq
T: fs-MELVIN IX RESPOND/ANSWER HOW
q/t neg
S: MUSEUM "oh" ME **NOT-CARE-FOR*** "well" SORRY

Ask how Terrylene responded to Melvin.

whq
T: IX*"Terrylene"* WOMAN RESPOND/ANSWER "what"
q
S: REAL/TRUE "shucks," ME IN-FUTURE me-ASK-TO-*another person* OTHER PERSON.

whq
T: (point to *"close conversation"*) THEY-TWO SIGN "what"
S: (Melvin) SORRY
(Terrylene) FINE++

* If students ask about the sign NOT-CARE-FOR explains it's a polite way to say NOT+LIKE (something). If this sign is not used in your region, show what is used instead.

PRACTICE *Inviting Others*

50–60 minutes

Students practice using phrases to invite and phrases to accept and decline invitations.

PRESENT
(LESSON SLIDE 11:6:7)

A: invite B to join him or her (going to the beach)
B: respond:
- accept invitation
- state problem with date
- decline invitation

A and B: finalize plans if B accepts
A and B: close conversation

Demonstrate four phrases for Signer A's line. Have students copy.

For ***"A: invite B to join him or her"*** (4 phrases)

T: IN-FUTURE+FRIDAY ME **WANT** LEAVE-FOR fs-BEACH,
q
WANT ***you*-JOIN-*me***

T: ME **PLAN** IN-FUTURE+FRIDAY, LEAVE-FOR fs-BEACH,
q
WANT ***you*-JOIN-*me***

NOTE: The time phrase "IN-FUTURE+FRIDAY" occurs either in the very beginning or after the broaching phrase "ME WANT, ME PLAN, ME THINK-ABOUT, ME MULL-OVER."

T: IN-FUTURE+FRIDAY, ME **THINK-ABOUT** LEAVE-FOR
q
fs-BEACH, WANT ***you*-JOIN-*me***

T: ME **MULL-OVER** IN-FUTURE+FRIDAY, LEAVE-FOR
q
fs-BEACH, **WANT *you*-JOIN-*me***

S(all): (copy)

Have students as Signer A repeat the invitations to you. You as Signer B demonstrate possible responses. Have all students copy your responses.

For *"A: invite B to join him or her (going to the beach)"*
S(as Signer A): (repeat one of phrases to invite)

For *"B: respond • accept invitation"*

nod nod
T(as Signer B): YES, FINE++, SURE or YES, ME WANT
S(all): (copy)

For *"B: respond • state problem with date"*

q/t neg
T(as Signer B): IN-FUTURE+FRIDAY, CONFLICT, ME MUST WORK

or

q/t neg
T: IN-FUTURE+FRIDAY, BE-STUCK, CAN'T, MUST TAKE-*person*, GO-TO-*doctor* SEE DOCTOR
S(all): (copy)

For *"B: respond • decline invitation"*

t neg
T: fs-BEACH, ME NOT-CARE. "well" SORRY
S(all): (copy)

Demonstrate phrases for *"A and B: close conversation."*

plan works out for both

- "thumb-up"
- (2h)"perfect"
- ME (2h)LOOK-AT*"forward"*

plan does not work out

- SORRY
- (wh)"pshaw" FINE++
- IN-FUTURE/WILL ASK-TO-*another person* OTHER PERSON

PRESENT
(LESSON SLIDE 11:6:8)

NOTE: Modify to slide to reflect actual dates.

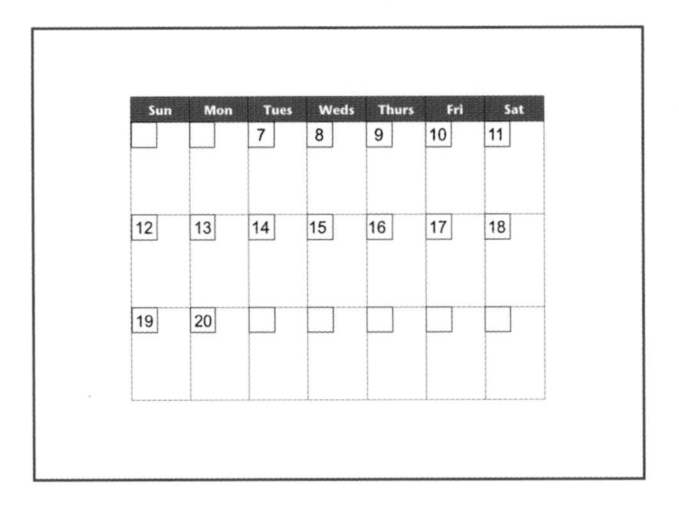

EXERCISE 3: Two-Week Calendar

Have students copy the calendar on **Slide 8** into their workbook (page 491), then fill in the activities they have already scheduled for the next two weeks, and come up with four additional activities they would like to do during their free time.

PRESENT
(LESSON SLIDE 11:6:9)

Follow this dialogue to complete Exercise 3.

A: invite B to join him or her
B: respond:
- accept invitation
- state problem with date
- decline invitation

A and B: finalize plans if B accepts
A and B: close conversation

Mingle. Have students use the dialogue on the slide to find other students, who are also free and available, to join them in their "free time" activities and write their names in the blanks.

PRACTICE *Canceling Plans*

15–20 minutes

Students practice using relative clause to recall original plans in order to cancel them.

PRESENT
(LESSON SLIDE 11:6:10)

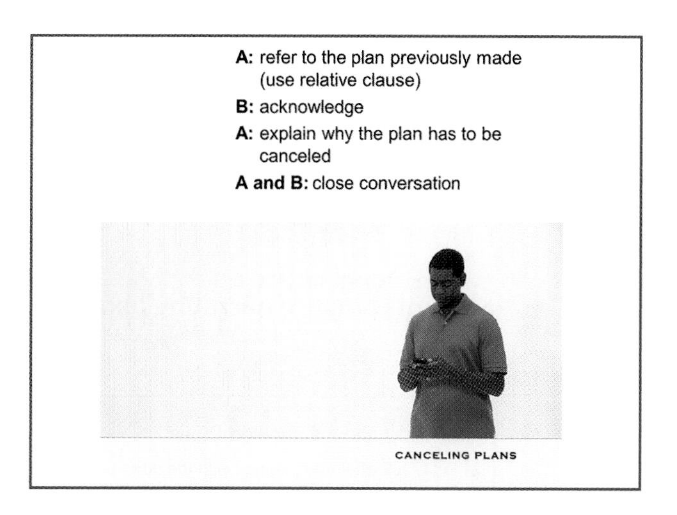

A: refer to the plan previously made (use relative clause)
B: acknowledge
A: explain why the plan has to be canceled
A and B: close conversation
CANCELING PLANS

Show video **"Canceling Plans"** and demonstrate Signer A's lines and have students copy.

For ***"A: refer to the plan previously made"***

rel cl
T: REMEMBER TONIGHT US-TWO PLAN SEE MOVIE
S(all): (copy)

For the relative clause be sure students raise brows and upper lip, and nod head.

CANCEL

For ***"A: explain why the plan has to be canceled"***

T: MUST **CANCEL**. MY FATHER MUST LEAVE-FOR HOSPITAL, ME MUST GO-TO WITH/TOGETHER.
S(all): (copy)

Mingle. Have students refer to **Exercise 3**, workbook page 491, to review the plans they made with others, and come up with reasons why they need to cancel those plans. When ready, have them approach each person (they had made plans with) to explain why they have to cancel.

Be sure students:

- raise brows and upper lip, and nod head with the relative clause.

PRACTICE *Narrating about Canceled Plans*

15–20 minutes

Students practice narrating about plans that have been canceled.

PRESENT
(LESSON SLIDE 11:6:11)

Narrating about Canceled Plans

1. tell what was planned with the other person
   - tell when (date and time)
   - tell who (use plural pronoun)
   - tell about activity planned
2. (conjunction) tell what came up that caused you to cancel
3. tell you informed the other person
4. describe their reaction
5. close with your reaction

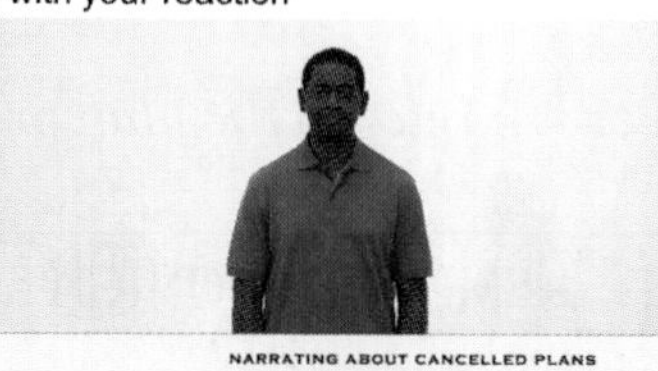

Show video **Narrating about Canceled Plans**, then refer to the narrative outline and have students provide information given in the video narrative.

Teacher's Guide

For ***"1. tell what was planned with the other person"***

- tell when: NOW+NIGHT,
- tell who: fs-DERRICK, US-TWO
- tell about activity planned:
  SHOULD LEAVE-FOR SEE MOVIE

For *"2. (conjunction) tell what came up that caused you to cancel"*

conj

!WRONG! MY FATHER MUST GO-TO*"left"* HOSPITAL, ME MUST GO-TOGETHER.

For *"3. tell you informed the other person"*

neg

ME *me*-INFORM-*right* fs-DERRICK, ME CAN'T GO-TO-right MOVIE, MUST CANCEL.

For *"4. describe their reaction"*

IX*"Derrick"* BE-DISAPPOINTED.

Demonstrate and/or elicit other possible signs for reactions from students. For example:

IX*"person"* #UPSET
IX*"person"* MAD
IX*"person"* BE-RELIEVED

For *"5. close with your reaction"*

regret

"well"

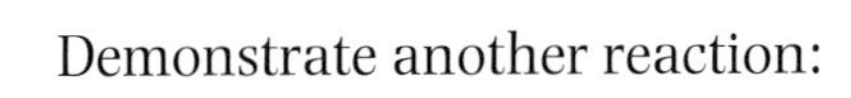

Demonstrate another reaction:

regret

"well," **SHUCKS.**

SHUCKS

Pair Up. Have students take turns signing Melvin's narrative to each other.

Be sure students:

- follow the narrative outline
- use the plural pronoun: US-TWO
- use conjunction !WRONG!
- give the other person's reaction IX*"Derrick"* BE-DISAPPOINTED
- regret
  close with "well."

HOMEWORK

Tell students to do **Homework 11:6** (*Student Workbook*, pages 353–361).

Also, students are to:

- develop a narrative about one of their canceled plans (See **Assignment**, workbook pages 357–358)
- identify the best signs for **Signs for Thinking** (See **Assignment**, *Student Workbook*, pages 358–359).

HOMEWORK FOLLOW-UP

20–30 MINUTES

PRESENT

(FOLLOW-UP SLIDES 11:6:1–12)

Minidialogue 1

1. What plans were made previously?
2. Why must the plans be canceled?

Check students' answers to **Minidialogues 1–3**. See **Introduction** pages xviii–xix for different ways to check answers.

Telling about Canceled Plans. Have students get into groups and tell their narratives about a canceled plan (See **Assignment**, *Student Workbook*, pages 357–358).

Conclude by calling on several students to share their narratives with the whole class.

Be sure students:

- use plural pronoun US-TWO
- use !WRONG! to tell why the plan had to be canceled
- tell about the other person's reaction
- close with "well" or "shucks."

PRESENT
(FOLLOW-UP SLIDES 11:6:13–24)

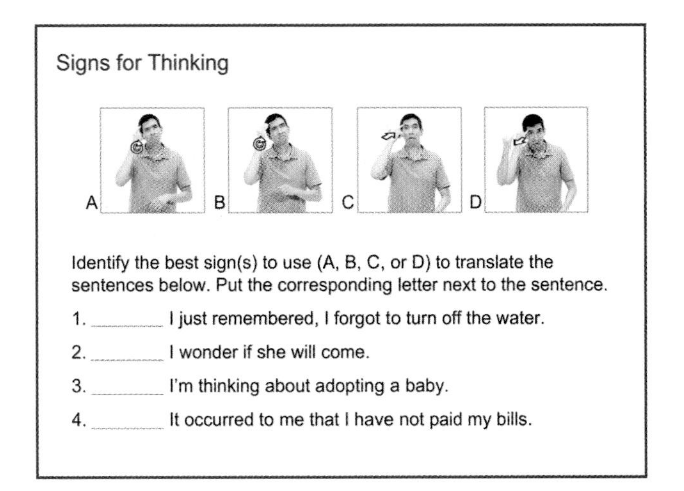

Signs for Thinking
A
B
C
D
Identify the best sign(s) to use (A, B, C, or D) to translate the sentences below. Put the corresponding letter next to the sentence.
1. ______ I just remembered, I forgot to turn off the water.
2. ______ I wonder if she will come.
3. ______ I'm thinking about adopting a baby.
4. ______ It occurred to me that I have not paid my bills.

Signs for Thinking. Have students give you their answers (A, B, C, or D) for the sentences on **Slide 13** and confirm with following slides. (See **Assignment**, *Student Workbook*, page 358–359). Continue for all sentences.

PRESENT
(FOLLOW-UP SLIDES 11:6:25–26)

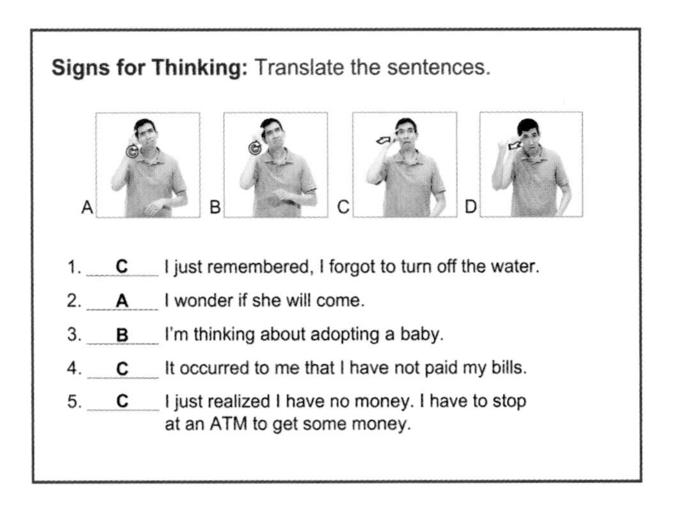

When done, have students translate the sentences.

Teacher's Translation Guide

t
1. ME THOUGHT-OCCUR, WATER [ME] FORGET #OFF

q
2. WOMAN IN-FUTURE COME-TO-here, ME THINK-ABOUT

3. US-TWO MULL-OVER ADOPT BABY

t neg
4. ME THOUGHT-OCCUR, fs-BILLS, ME PAY NOT-YET

t neg
5. ME THOUGHT-OCCUR, ME MONEY NONE.
ME MUST GO-TO fs-ATM, WITHDRAW MONEY

t
6. POSS *"woman"* IDEA, ME LIKE

t
7. ME THOUGHT-OCCUR, TODAY TIME+3 ME [HAVE] APPOINTMENT, SEE DOCTOR

8. "hey" [HAVE] !IDEA! WHY+NOT US-ALL LEAVE-FOR CAMPING

9. ME MULL-OVER (or THINK-ABOUT) IN-FUTURE+SATURDAY [ME] LEAVE-FOR fs-BEACH

mm
10. IN-PAST+NIGHT ME SEE MOVIE, ME STILL THINK-ABOUT

LESSON 11:7

First and Last Time You Did Something

Lesson length: 50–65 minutes

LESSON GOAL

Students will ask questions using "when" clauses asking about the first or last time someone did something, then:

- repeat information to another person
- summarize results of a survey

KEY SKILLS

- use spatial agreement with TELL-TO-person
- use horizontal listing to give results of the survey

NOTIONS

Grammar

"when" clauses

horizontal listing

Phrases

Ask when was the last time someone did something

when whq

LAST+TIME YOU (activity) WHEN

Ask how old someone was the first time she or he did something

when whq

FIRST-thumb+TIME (activity), HOW-OLD YOU

Repeat information, last time a person did something

when whq

ME ASK-TO*"partner"* LAST+TIME IX (activity), WHEN.
IX*"partner"* TELL-TO-me (when) (with whom) (what they did) (comment)

Summarize the survey results

10 PEOPLE, ME ASK-TO-all. FIRST-thumb+TIME (activity),
(t over "10 PEOPLE"; when over "FIRST-thumb+TIME (activity)")

HOW-OLD YOU
(whq)

(largest number), FIRST-thumb+TIME (activity), OLD+(#)
(t over "(largest number)"; t over "FIRST-thumb+TIME (activity)")

(next largest number), OLD+(#), etc.
(t over "(next largest number)")

Vocabulary

Last Time
LAST+TIME

First Time
FIRST-thumb+TIME

Wh-word Question
WHEN

PREPARATION Read and view **Using Horizontal Listing** in the *Student Workbook*, page 363.

MATERIALS **11:7 Lesson Slides**
11:7 Follow-up Slides

HOMEWORK 11:7 *Student Workbook*, pages 362–364

INTRODUCE *Last Time You Did Something*

10–15 minutes

PRESENT
(LESSON SLIDE 11:7:1)

When was the last time you drank water?

Possible answers in terms of:

minutes
hours
days
weeks
months
years

unspecified time:
recently
a long time ago
never

LAST+TIME

Review time signs with possible answers to the question on the slide. Demonstrate by beginning with this phrase and ending with the time information.

when (over LAST+TIME ME DRINK WATER)
T: **LAST+TIME** ME DRINK WATER,...

For *"minutes"*	FIVE-MINUTE+IN-PAST
For *"hours"*	TWO-HOUR+IN-PAST
For *"days"*	NOW MORNING or IN-PAST+MONDAY
For *"weeks"*	ONE-WEEK-IN-PAST
For *"months"*	ONE-MONTH+IN-PAST
For *"years"*	ONE-YEAR-IN-PAST
For *"recently"*	cs (over IN-PAST) IN-PAST
For *"a long time ago"*	puff cheeks (over IN-PAST) IN-PAST
For *"never"*	NEVER

WHEN

Now, ask students this question and check their answers:

when (over LAST+TIME YOU DRINK WATER), **whq** (over WHEN)
T: **LAST+TIME** YOU DRINK WATER, **WHEN**
S: (answer with a time sign or phrase)

Ask other questions to continue reviewing time signs:

when whq
T: **LAST+TIME** YOU GO-TO AMUSEMENT-PARK, **WHEN**
S: (answer with a time sign or phrase)

when whq
T: **LAST+TIME** YOU [EAT] ICE-CREAM, **WHEN**
S: (answer with a time sign or phrase)

when
T: **LAST+TIME** YOU LEAVE-FOR FOOD SHOPPING,
whq
WHEN
S: (answer with a time sign or phrase)

PRACTICE *Repeat Information— Last Time a Person Did Something*

20–25 minutes

Students practice repeating information about the last time a person did something.

PRESENT
(LESSON SLIDE 11:7:2)

A: ask when was the last time B did something
B: tell when, explain (where, with who, why)

Demonstrate three examples of Signer A's question. Have students copy.

when whq
T: **LAST+TIME** YOU GO-TO AMUSEMENT-PARK, **WHEN**
S(all): (copy)

when whq

T: **LAST+TIME** YOU [EAT] ICE-CREAM, **WHEN**

S(all): (copy)

when whq

T: **LAST+TIME** YOU LEAVE-FOR FOOD SHOPPING, **WHEN**

S(all): (copy)

Have students as Signer A ask you the questions. Demonstrate Signer B's answers:

when whq

S1: **LAST+TIME** YOU GO-TO AMUSEMENT-PARK, **WHEN**

T: (tell when) TWO-YEAR-IN-PAST.

(explain) IX-loc 6+FLAG. MY NIECE POSS *"niece"* BIRTHDAY, ME TAKE-FROM *"niece's location"* LEAVE-FOR "Six Flags" #FUN

when whq

S2: **LAST+TIME** YOU [EAT] ICE-CREAM, **WHEN**

T: (tell when) IN-PAST fs-APRIL.

(explain) MY fs-GRAND+CHILDREN COME *"here"* VISIT, ME TAKE-FROM *"children's location"* GO-TO fs-FENTON'S ICE-CREAM

when whq

S3: **LAST+TIME** YOU LEAVE-FOR FOOD SHOPPING, **WHEN**

T: (tell when) FEW-DAYS-AGO.

(explain) NIGHT, ME WATCH #TV, WANT COOKIES. ME RUN-TO *"store"* BUY MY FAVORITE CHOCOLATE fs-CHIP, COME-TO *"here"* HOME, ICL *"take from bag, put in mouth"*++, PCL *"cookies dwindling till bag empty"*

PRESENT
(LESSON SLIDE 11:7:3)

Instructions:
First Partner
Ask each other your "last time you did something" question.
Second Partner
Ask him or her your previous partner's question.
Third and Fourth Partner
Do the same with your third and fourth partners, each time asking your previous partner's question.

Give students a minute to come up with their own questions, then have them mingle asking and exchanging questions, following instructions on the slide.

PRESENT
(LESSON SLIDE 11:7:4)

Show the video **Repeat Information** Justin repeats Amber's information to Suzanne. Have students rehearse what Justin repeated.

S: (as Justin) ME ASK-TO*"Amber"* LAST+TIME TRAIN
when whq
IX*"Amber"* RIDE-TRAIN, WHEN. IX*"Amber"* Amber-TELL-TO-me IN-PAST-THREE-YEAR, WITH FAMILY, [(wh)IX-loc"left"/ CALIFORNIA], [(wh)IX-loc*"California"*/IX- dir*"from California to New York"*] NEW-YORK. ENJOY

Be sure students:

- establish and refer to a location for "Amber"
- match their me-ASK-TO-Amber and Amber-TELL-TO-me with the established location
- relay the information to you (teacher) as Suzanne, glancing away toward "Amber's" location with these signs; me-ASK-TO-Amber and Amber-TELL-TO-me.

Conclude. Have each student tell you about their last partner's answer. Be sure they follow this structure:

when whq

ME ASK-TO"-partner" LAST+TIME IX (activity), WHEN.
IX*"partner"* partner-TELL-TO-me (repeat information).

Be sure students:

- match their me-ASK-TO-partner and partner-TELL-TO-me with the partner's location
- relay the information to you (teacher), glancing away toward the partner's location with these signs: me-ASK-TO-partner and partner-TELL-TO-me.

PRACTICE *Summarize Survey— First Time a Person Did Something*

20–25 minutes

Students learn to summarize survey information using horizontal listing about the first time people did something.

PRESENT
(LESSON SLIDE 11:7:5)

A: ask how old B was the first time she or he did something
B: tell how old

Demonstrate two examples of Signer A's question. Have students copy.

<table><tr><td></td><td>when</td><td>whq</td></tr><tr><td>T:</td><td>FIRST-thumb+TIME YOU GET BICYCLE,</td><td>HOW-OLD YOU</td></tr></table>

S(all): (copy)

<table><tr><td></td><td>when</td></tr><tr><td>T:</td><td>FIRST-thumb+TIME YOU LEAVE-FOR fs-DATE,</td></tr><tr><td></td><td>whq</td></tr><tr><td></td><td>HOW-OLD YOU</td></tr></table>

S(all): (copy)

FIRST-thumb+TIME

Group. Put students in groups of three and have them practice asking each other "how old" questions. Possible topics for students to ask if they need ideas:

- age they first dated
- age they started using the telephone
- age they first drove a car
- age they first flew on an airplane
- age they first used a computer
- age they first opened a banking account
- age they first tried smoking a cigarette
- age they first had a pet.

PRESENT
(LESSON SLIDE 11:7:6)

Survey: "The first time…"

1. Create a question and ask ten people the question.
2. Summarize the results:
   - tell you surveyed ten people
   - tell the question you asked
   - tell the results (four groups using horizontal listing)

Survey. Demonstrate how to conduct the survey. First, ask 10 students the question you have created for your survey.

For example:

when
T: **FIRST-thumb+TIME** YOU LEAVE-FOR fs-DATE,
whq
HOW-OLD YOU
S1–10: (tell how old)

Put the ten given ages on the board (example: four students at 13 years old, three at 17 years old, one each at 14 years old and 16 years old, and one who hasn't dated yet).

Categorize the ages into four groups and demonstrate how to summarize the results. Have students repeat.

For "*• **tell you surveyed ten people***"

t
T: 10 LEARN+ER, ME ASK-TO-all
S: (repeat)

For "*• **tell the question you asked***"

when whq
T: FIRST-thumb+TIME LEAVE-FOR fs-DATE, HOW-OLD YOU
S: (repeat)

For *"• tell the results (four groups using horizontal listing)"*

t when

FOUR, FIRST-thumb+TIME fs-DATE, OLD+13

t

THREE, OLD+17

t

TWO, BETWEEN OLD+14, OLD+16

t neg

ONE, NOT-YET

S: (repeat)

Point out: When using horizontal listing, be sure to begin with the largest group on your non-dominant side and end with the smallest group on your dominant side.

1st group

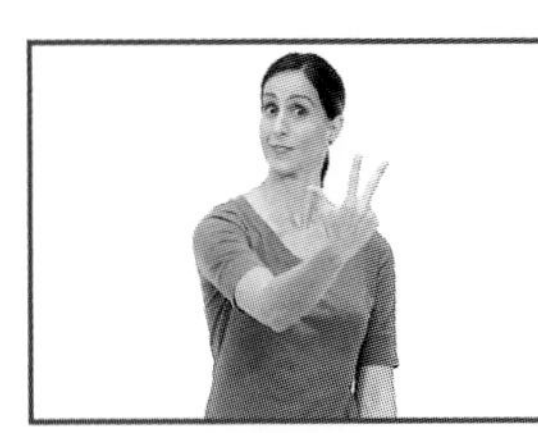

2nd group

3rd group

4th group

HOMEWORK

Tell students to do **Homework 11:7** (*Student Workbook*, pages 362–364).

Also, students are to survey 10 people with the same question and summarize the information using horizontal listing.

HOMEWORK FOLLOW-UP
15-30 MINUTES

PRESENT
(HOMEWORK SLIDE 11:7:1)

Summarize the results of your survey:

- tell you surveyed ten people
- tell the question you asked
- tell the results (four groups using horizontal listing).

Have students take turns sharing the results of their surveys, either before the whole class, or in small groups.

Be sure students:

- begin with this phrase

  ______t
  10 PEOPLE, ME ASK-TO-all. FIRST-thumb+TIME
  ____________when ______whq
  (person did something), HOW-OLD YOU
- categorize the results into four groups
- begin with the largest group on their non-dominant side
- end with the smallest group on their dominant side
- use topicalization with each number/result, for example,

  ____t
  THREE, OLD+17.

LESSON 11:8

Numbers Review 2

Lesson length: 25–40 minutes

LESSON GOAL Students will practice number combinations for money, clock and year numbers.

KEY SKILLS sign number combinations accurately and without hesitation

Dollar + cent combinations
the dollar sign for 1–9 is twisted before giving the cent number.

Clock: hour + minute combinations
clock numbers 1–9 face out before signing the minute number.

Year number combinations
year numbers are signed as a pair of two-digit numbers;
for example, 20+15 for year 2015, 19+86 for year 1986.

PREPARATION Make copies of **11:8 Number Set E**, one set for every five students (for **Activity** on page 694)

MATERIALS
11:8 Lesson Slides
11:8 Number Set E

HOMEWORK 11:8 *Student Workbook*, page 365

REVIEW *Number Combinations*

8–12 minutes

Students review combination forms for money, clock and year numbers.

PRESENT
(LESSON SLIDES 11:8:1–15)

money: dollars + cents		$3.50	$6.15	$4.49
$9.99	$1.76			
clock: hours + minutes		12:45	7:36	2:25
5:10	6:33			
year				
2015	1986	1998	2019	1776

Have students sign the numbers as they appear on **Slides 1–15**.

Be sure students:

For ***"money: dollars + cents"***

- twist their hand for the dollar ($1–9) part before giving the cent amount

For ***"clock: hours + minutes"***

- have their hand face the palm out for the hour numbers (1–9) before giving the minute information

For ***"year"***

- sign the year numbers as a pair of two-digit numbers; for example, 20+15 for year 2015, 19+86 for year 1986.

PRACTICE *Matching Number Combinations*

20–30 minutes

Students practice signing number combinations for money, clock and year by playing a game.

ACTIVITY

Divide class into groups of five students each and give each group a set of flash cards **11:8 Number Set E**. Each set has 30 matching pairs for a total of 60 cards (See **Materials**).

Give instructions to play the game (similar to the **Go Fish** game), then have students play the game.

Instructions

- One student deals out all the cards to the players.
- Players discard any matching pairs in their hand.
- Players take turn asking one of the other players if they have a matching card.
- If the player has a matching card, they surrender it to the player who requested it.
- Game ends when all the players run out of cards.

PRESENT
(LESSON SLIDES 11:8:16–45)

2001
$1.05

Conclude. Show **Slides 16–45** and have individual students sign both number combinations on the slides. Have the whole class practice any corrections.

HOMEWORK

Tell students to do **Homework 11:8** (*Student Workbook*, page 365).

LESSON 11:9

Discussing Personal Goals

Lesson length: 55–65 minutes

LESSON GOAL

Students will sign this narrative:

Narrative Structure

1. Broach subject [1]
2. State five goals [2]
   - travel
   - personal
   - learning
   - adventure
   - volunteer
3. Conclude [3]

KEY PHRASES

[1] BEFORE-EVENT ME DIE (t), 5 THING ME GOAL (nod), WANT (nod), TRY (nod), SEE (nod), EXPERIENCE (nod), TOUCH (nod), CHECKMARK (nod). [(wh)5/IX-mult]["what"] (rhet)...

[2] ME GOAL [or WANT] (state goal), ME GOAL [or WANT] ME (nod).

[3] [(wh)5/#ALL,] (t) ME GOAL MUST FINISH++arc BEFORE-EVENT ME DIE.

NOTIONS

Grammar

Repeating for emphasis

Vocabulary

Continents

WORLD (2 variations)
EUROPE
AFRICA (2 variations)
AUSTRALIA (2 variations)
ASIA
SOUTH AMERICA
NORTH AMERICA

Countries

COUNTRY
ENGLAND
FRANCE
SPAIN (2 variations)
MEXICO (2 variations)
ITALY (2 variations)
GERMANY (2 variations)
CHINA
JAPAN
INDIA
EGYPT (2 variations)

Time-Related

BEFORE-EVENT

Verbs

DIE
SIX-FEET-UNDER
BE-GONE (die)
TRY
CHECKMARK
EXPERIENCE
TOUCH
VOLUNTEER
STUDY-all
DECORATE
BECOME

Nouns

GOAL/AIM
LANGUAGE (2 variations)
DEGREE
(2h)THING

PREPARATION

- Read **Learn the Narrative and Assignment**, *Student Workbook*, pages 369–372.
- Make copies of **11:9 Evaluation** (for **Homework Follow-up**)

MATERIALS

11:9 Lesson Slides
Exercise 4A and 4B (in *Student Workbook*, pages 495 and 497)
11:9 Evaluation

HOMEWORK 11:9

Student Workbook, pages 366–376

INTRODUCE *Five Goal Categories*

20–30 minutes

PRESENT
(LESSON SLIDE 11:9:1)

Bucket List

goal categories
- travel
- personal
- lifelong learning
- adventure
- community service

Explain to the class you will discuss "bucket list" goals under these five categories on the slide.

PRESENT
(LESSON SLIDE 11:9:2)

Goals: Travel

1. World	7. North America	13. Mexico
2. Europe	8. England	14. China
3. Africa	9. France	15. Japan
4. Australia	10. Spain	16. India
5. Asia	11. Germany	17. Egypt
6. South America	12. Italy	

For the "travel" category, begin by introducing the signs for the destinations on the slide:

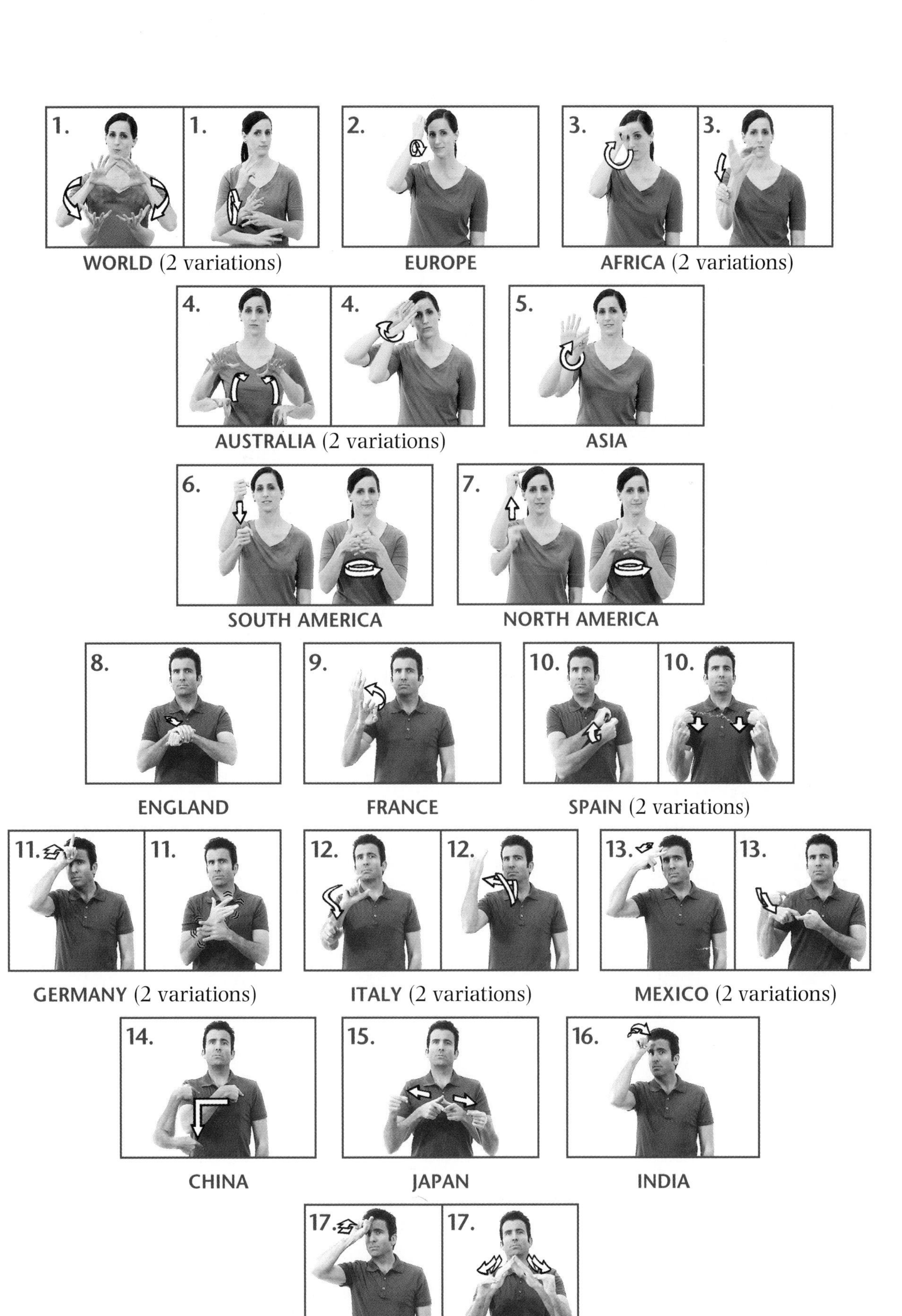
1.
1.
WORLD (2 variations)
2.
EUROPE
3.
3.
AFRICA (2 variations)
4.
4.
AUSTRALIA (2 variations)
5.
ASIA
6.
SOUTH AMERICA
7.
NORTH AMERICA
8.
ENGLAND
9.
FRANCE
10.
10.
SPAIN (2 variations)
11.
11.
GERMANY (2 variations)
12.
12.
ITALY (2 variations)
13.
13.
MEXICO (2 variations)
14.
CHINA
15.
JAPAN
16.
INDIA
17.
17.
EGYPT (2 variations)

Review. Give a number from the slide and have students give you the sign for the destination. For example:

whq
T: NUMBER 13, SIGN "what"
S: MEXICO (2 variations)

COUNTRY
(2 variations)

Introduce the category sign **COUNTRY** by naming the countries and tracing a circle around the sign space.

Conclude. Discuss goals for "travel" using TOUCH and TRAVEL-AROUND. For TOUCH, tell what two countries your goal is to visit and ask the students what two countries they want to visit. For example:

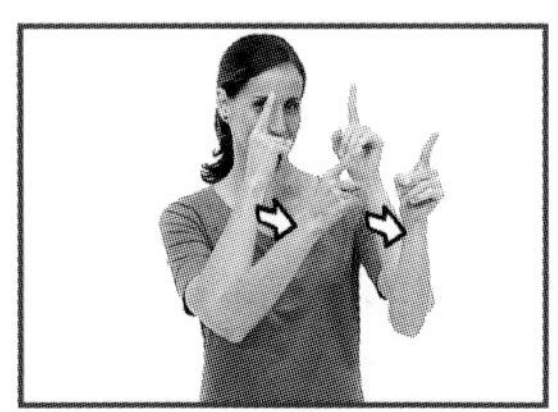
GOAL

nod
T: ME **GOAL** TOUCH ITALY, JAPAN, ME **GOAL**, ME.
t — whq
TWO **COUNTRY**, YOU GOAL TOUCH++ "what"
nod
S: ME **GOAL** TOUCH EGYPT, FRANCE, ME **GOAL**, ME.

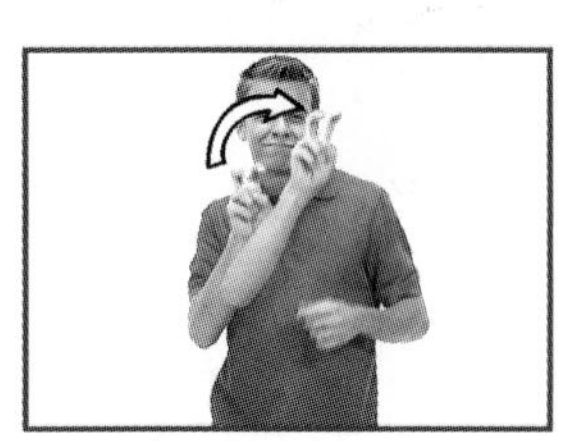
TRAVEL-AROUND

For **TRAVEL-AROUND**, tell where you would like to travel (in a continent or the whole world) and ask students about where they would like to travel:

nod
T: ME GOAL **TRAVEL-AROUND** WORLD, ME **GOAL**, ME.
whq
YOU GOAL **TRAVEL-AROUND**, WHERE.
S: ME GOAL **TRAVEL-AROUND** (continent, or the world),
nod
ME **GOAL**, ME

Be sure students begin the sentence with ME GOAL, and end with ME GOAL, ME with an emphatic nod.

NOTE: TRAVEL-AROUND is a sign that students should already know. Semantically, it means traveling around in a wide area such as a continent or the whole world. If within a single country, such as France, China, or South Africa, the sign means touring within that country visiting cities, attractions, and not traveling to that country. Make sure the students understand the difference between TOUCH and TRAVEL-AROUND.

PRESENT
(LESSON SLIDE 11:9:3)

Goals: Personal

1. get a college degree
2. have a family
3. own something
4. see something
5. join something
6. become something

For the "personal" category, introduce the following phrases and vocabulary. Then, ask a few students to share their goal for each category:

For ***"get a college degree"***

T: ME GOAL (or WANT) GET **DEGREE** [fs-BA, fs-MA,
nod
fs-PHD], ME GOAL (or WANT), ME.
t whq
YOU GOAL (or WANT) DEGREE, "what"

DEGREE

S: ME GOAL (or WANT) GET DEGREE, (type of degree),
nod
ME GOAL (or WANT), ME

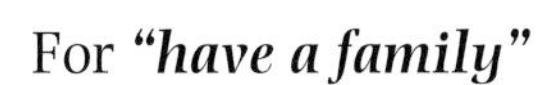

For ***"have a family"***

T: ME GOAL (or WANT) MARRY, HAVE 3 CHILDREN,
nod
ME GOAL (or WANT), ME.
t whq
FAMILY, YOU GOAL (or WANT), "what"

S: ME GOAL (or WANT) (kind of family),
nod
ME GOAL (or WANT), ME

For ***"own something"***

T: ME GOAL (or WANT) BUY MY #OWN HOUSE,

nod

ME GOAL (or WANT), ME.

or

ME GOAL (or WANT) GET MY #OWN HORSE,

nod

ME GOAL (or WANT), ME.

whq

YOU GOAL (or WANT), [YOUR] #OWN "what"

S: ME GOAL (or WANT) [MY] #OWN (or BUY, etc)

nod

(thing), ME GOAL (or WANT), ME

For ***"see something"***

T: ME GOAL (or WANT) SEE EGYPT DCL*"pyramids,"*

nod

ME GOAL (or WANT), ME.

whq

YOU GOAL (or WANT), SEE "what"

S: ME GOAL (or WANT) SEE (thing), ME GOAL (or

nod

WANT), ME

For ***"join something"***

T: ME GOAL (or WANT) JOIN PERFORMANCE #CO

nod

(theatre company), ME GOAL (or WANT) ME.

whq

YOU GOAL (or WANT), JOIN "what"

S: ME GOAL (or WANT) JOIN (activity), ME GOAL (or

nod

WANT), ME

BECOME

For ***"become something"***

T: ME GOAL (or WANT) **BECOME** DOCTOR, ME GOAL (or
nod
WANT), ME.

whq
YOU GOAL (or WANT), BECOME "what"

S: ME GOAL (or WANT) BECOME (role), ME GOAL (or
nod
WANT), ME

PRESENT
(LESSON SLIDE 11:9:4)

Goals: Lifelong Learning

For the "lifelong learning" category, introduce these vocabulary and phrases, and ask a few students about their goals.

DECORATE

T: ME GOAL [or WANT] LEARN #HOW [or HOW]
nod
DECORATE WEDDING fs-CAKE, ME GOAL [or WANT] ME.

or

ME GOAL [or WANT] LEARN #HOW (or HOW) MAKE
nod
FURNITURE. ME GOAL (or WANT), ME.
whq
YOU GOAL (or WANT), LEARN "what"

S: ME GOAL (or WANT) LEARN #HOW (or HOW) (skill),
nod
ME GOAL (or WANT), ME

PRESENT
(LESSON SLIDE 11:9:5)

Goals: Adventure

1. name vehicle or equipment (raised brows)
   (if no sign, describe it using DCLs or LCLs)
2. describe the activity using ICLs and SCLs

Kayaking Parachuting

For the "adventure" category, demonstrate the sequence to describe adventures.

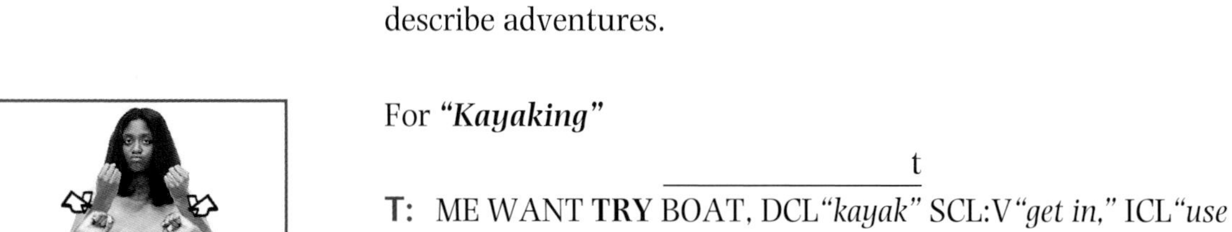
TRY

For ***"Kayaking"***

t

T: ME WANT **TRY** BOAT, DCL*"kayak"* SCL:V*"get in,"* ICL*"use*

nod

kayak oars," ME WANT **TRY**, ME.

For ***"Parachuting"***

t

T: ME WANT **TRY**, AIRPLANE [(wh)LCL:ILY*"airplane"*/
SCL:V*"jump from airplane"*], [(wh)LCL:claw*"parachute"*/

nod

SCL:V*"ride down"*], ME WANT **TRY**, ME.

whq

YOU WANT **TRY** "what"

nod

S: ME WANT **TRY** (adventure), ME WANT **TRY**, ME

PRESENT
(LESSON SLIDE 11:9:6)

Goals: Community Service

VOLUNTEER

For the "community service" category, introduce these vocabulary and phrases, and ask a few students about their goals.

T: ME GOAL **VOLUNTEER** [IX-loc] fs-PEACE-CORPS WORK

nod

WITH CHILDREN, ME GOAL ME.

or

neg

ME WANT JOIN GROUP HELP PEOPLE NONE HOME,

nod

BUILD HOUSE FOR THEY-ALL, ME GOAL ME.

whq

YOU GOAL (or WANT) VOLUNTEER HELP "what"

S: ME GOAL (or WANT) VOLUNTEER (community service),

nod

ME GOAL (or WANT), ME.

PRACTICE *Narrating about One's Bucket List*

25–35 minutes

Students learn the narrative structure for talking about one's bucket list.

PRESENT
(LESSON SLIDE 11:9:7)

Show video **Derrick's Bucket List**, then ask:

whq

T: fs-DERRICK POSS *"Derrick"* FIVE GOAL, "what"

Answer.

1. get married, and have 4–5 boys
2. get an M.A. in linguistics, then find a job studying signed languages
3. travel to Egypt to see the pyramids and ride a camel
4. volunteer delivering food to home-bound elderly
5. travel to all 50 states

Make sure students understand the possible new vocabulary from the list of goals:

STUDY-ALL

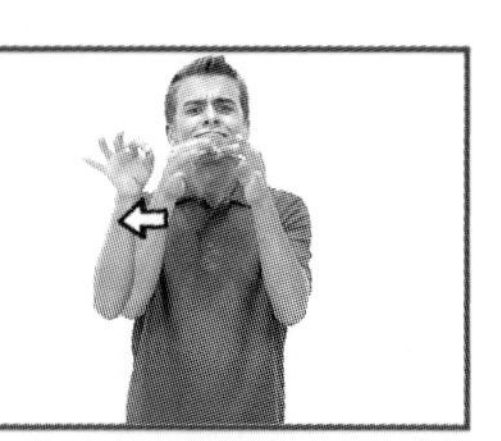
LANGUAGE

PRESENT
(LESSON SLIDE 11:9:8)

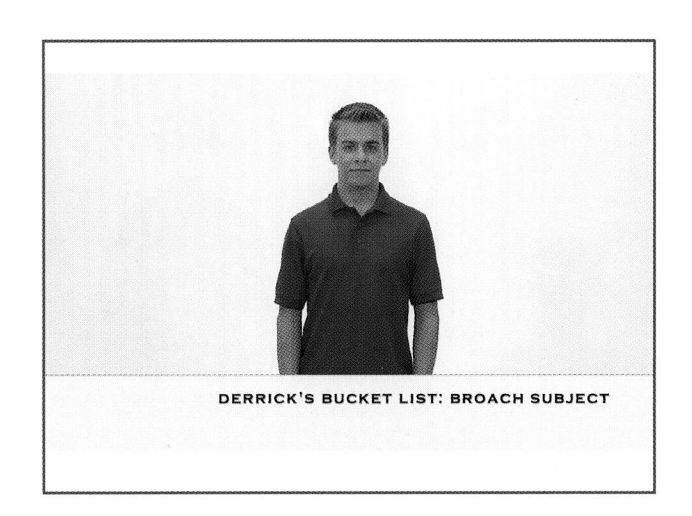

BEFORE-EVENT

DIE

EXPERIENCE

CHECKMARK

Show video **Derrick's Bucket List: Broach Subject** and have students rehearse this line:

t / nod / nod
S(all): BEFORE-EVENT ME **DIE**, 5 THING ME GOAL, WANT,

nod / nod / nod / nod / nod
TRY, SEE, **EXPERIENCE**, TOUCH, **CHECKMARK**.
[(wh)5/IX-mult]

Be sure when students nod their head as they sign each verb.

Introduce two other signs that mean "to die": **SIX-FEET-UNDER** or **BE-GONE**.

SIX-FEET-UNDER

BE-GONE

Have students repeat the "broach subject" phrase until they are comfortable signing it.

PRESENT
(LESSON SLIDE 11:9:9)

Show video **Derrick's Bucket List: Conclude** and have students rehearse this line:

S(all): [(wh)5/#ALL] GOAL !MUST! FINISH++arc BEFORE-EVENT ME DIE.

Have students repeat the sentence until they are comfortable signing it.

PRESENT
(LESSON SLIDE 11:9:10)

Derrick's Bucket List

1. Broach subject
2. State five goals
   - personal—*get married, and have 4-5 boys*
   - lifelong learning—*get an M.A. in linguistics, then find a job studying signed languages.*
   - travel—*to Egypt to see the pyramids and to ride a camel*
   - community service—*volunteer delivering food to home-bound elderly*
   - adventure—*travel to all 50 states*
3. Conclude

Pair off. Now have students repeat Derrick's narrative to each other. Make sure they follow the narrative structure and use [(wh)5/IX-(finger)] to list each of the five goals.

EXERCISE 4A and 4B

Assign half of the class **Exercise 4A** and the other half **Exercise 4B** (*Student Workbook*, pages 495 and 497). Have them rehearse their assigned narratives until they can give the information without looking at their paper.

Pair up. When ready, pair up students—one with **Exercise 4A** and the other with **Exercise 4B**. Have them sign their narratives to each other.

Conclude. Call upon a student with **Exercise 4A** and one with **Exercise 4B** to sign their narratives to the whole class.

Be sure students:

- use the phrases rehearsed for "broach subject" and "conclude"
- use their weak hand to list the five goals [(wh)5/IX-(finger)]
- repeat phrase at end of each goal stated, for example, "ME WANT, ME" or "ME GOAL, ME" with head nodding.

Give feedback on how they explain the five goals listed in the **Exercise 4A and 4B**. Have class rehearse the corrections.

HOMEWORK

Tell students to do **Homework 11:9** (*Student Workbook*, pages 366–376).

Also, students are to present their own narratives about their bucket lists (See **Assignment**, *Student Workbook*, page 372).

HOMEWORK FOLLOW-UP

Your Bucket List. Have students present their own narratives about their bucket lists (See **Assignment**, *Student Workbook*, page 372)

Two ways to approach this:

As fluency practice.

Have students get into groups and tell each other about their bucket lists.

Be sure students:

- use "broach subject" phrase
- list on their weak hand
- begin the sentence with ME GOAL (or WANT [TRY]) and repeat the phrase at the end with an emphatic nod
- use "conclude" phrase to end narrative.

Conclude. Ask each student to state one goal from their own list. Make sure they begin the sentence with ME GOAL (or WANT [TRY]) and repeat the phrase at the end with an emphatic nod.

As preparation for quiz.

If you want to use this narrative as a production quiz, have students present their narratives and you give feedback before recording their final versions. Rate with **11:9 Evaluation** (See **Materials**).

> **NOTE:** If you have a large class, divide class and focus on one group at a time.

LESSON 11:10

Fingerspelling: States and Provinces 2

Lesson length: 35–45 minutes

LESSON GOAL Students will review naming U.S. states and Canadian provinces using fingerspelling or signs.

KEY SKILLS use correct fingerspelling patterns for states and provinces

MATERIALS
11:10 Lesson Slides
Exercise 5 (in *Student Workbook*, pages 500–502)

HOMEWORK 11:10 *Student Workbook*, page 377

REVIEW *Naming States and Provinces*

15–20 minutes

PRESENT
(LESSON SLIDE 11:10:1)

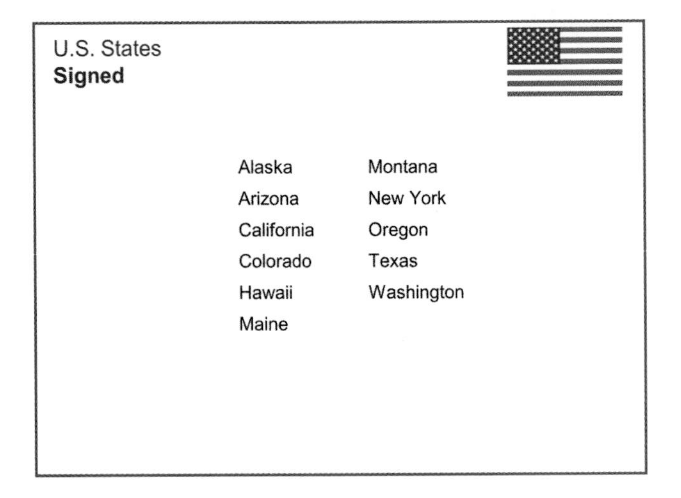

Have students give signs for the eleven U.S. states listed. Check sign forms.

PRESENT
(LESSON SLIDE 11:10:2)

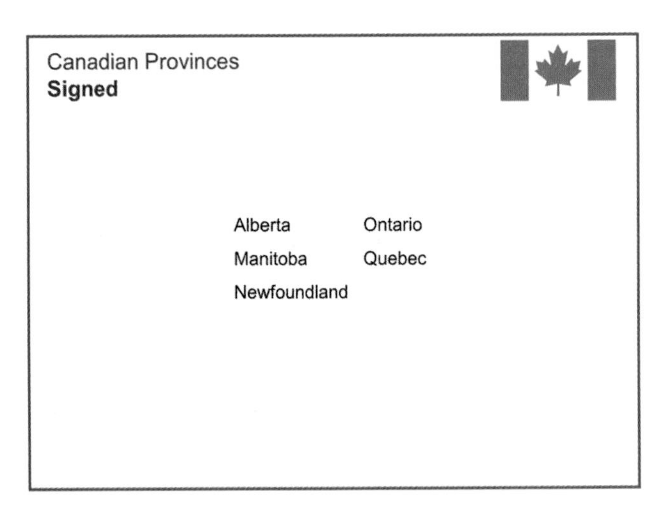

Have students give signs for the five Canadian provinces listed. Check sign forms.

PRESENT
(LESSON SLIDE 11:10:3)

States and Provinces
Initials Fingerspelled

New Hampshire	North Carolina
New Jersey	South Carolina
New Mexico	British Columbia
North Dakota	Rhode Island
South Dakota	Prince Edward Island
New Brunswick	

Have students fingerspell the initials for the states and provinces. Check forms.

For ***"New Hampshire"*** and ***"New Jersey"***
- twist hand toward the non-dominant side

For ***"Nova Scotia (2 variations)"***
- twist hand toward dominant side, or move forward

For ***"New Mexico, North Dakota, South Dakota"*** and ***"New Brunswick"***
- hand moves slightly forward

For ***"North Carolina, South Carolina"*** and ***"British Columbia"***
- palm faces sideways

For ***"Rhode Island"*** and ***"Prince Edward Island"***
- hand slides away from dominant side

PRESENT
(LESSON SLIDE 11:10:4)

States
First and Last Letters Fingerspelled

Georgia	Florida
Missouri	Maryland
Pennsylvania	Virginia
Louisiana	Vermont
Kentucky	West Virginia

Have students fingerspell the first and last letters for the states listed. Check forms.

For ***"Georgia, Missouri"*** and ***"Pennsylvania"***
- twist hand toward dominant side

For ***"Louisiana"***
- hand slides away from dominant side

For ***"Kentucky"***
- palm drops down

For ***"Florida, Maryland, Virginia, Vermont, West Virginia"***
- hand moves slightly forward

NOTE: Florida uses three letters (fs-FLA); West Virginia is done this way: sign WEST fs-VA, fs-VA starts where the movement for WEST ends.

PRESENT
(LESSON SLIDE 11:10:5)

States and Provinces
First Few Letters Fingerspelled

Arkansas	Massachusetts
Delaware	Mississippi
Kansas	Alabama
Nebraska	Nevada
Colorado	Indiana
Wisconsin (2 variations)	Illinois
Connecticut	Michigan
Wyoming	Saskatchewan (2 variations)
Minnesota	Tennessee
Oklahoma	

Have students fingerspell the first few letters of the states and provinces listed. Check forms.

For ***"Arkansas (fs-ARK), Delaware (fs-DEL), Kansas (fs-KAN), Nebraska (fs-NEB), Nevada (fs-NEV)"*** and ***"Wisconsin (fs-WIS or fs-WISC)"***

- hand moves slightly backward then forward

For ***"Connecticut (fs-CONN), Illinois (fs-ILL), Minnesota (fs-MINN)"*** and ***"Tennessee (fs-TENN)"***

- bounce hand forward for the double letters

NOTE: For Illinois (fs-ILL), the palm is oriented to the side.

For ***"Oklahoma (fs-OKLA)"***

- hand slides away from dominant side

For ***"Massachusetts (fs-MASS)"*** and ***"Mississippi (fs-MISS)"***

- hand slides sideways with the double letters

For ***"Alabama (fs-ALA)"*** and ***"Colorado (fs-COLO)"***

- hand moves up and down

For ***"Indiana (fs-IND)"*** and ***"Wyoming (fs-WYO)"***

- palm drops down, then bounces back up

For ***"Michigan (fs-MICH)"***
- twist hand (with "H") toward dominant side

For ***"Saskatchewan (fs-SASK or #SASK)"***
- move hand slightly forward or twist hand (with "A") toward dominant side

PRESENT
(LESSON SLIDE 11:10:6)

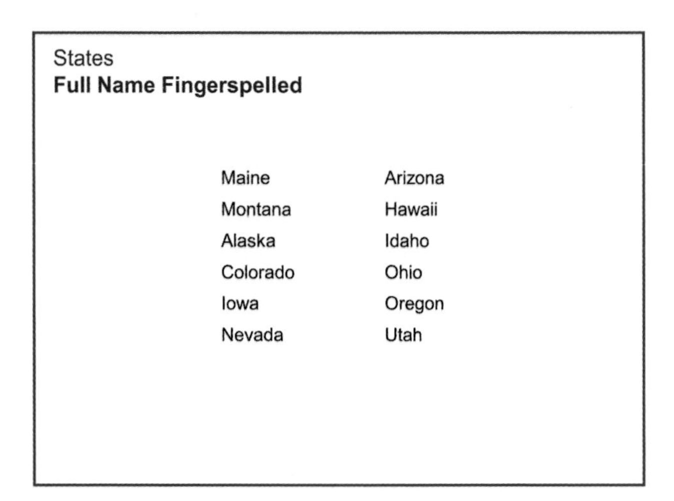

States
Full Name Fingerspelled
Maine
Montana
Alaska
Colorado
Iowa
Nevada
Arizona
Hawaii
Idaho
Ohio
Oregon
Utah

Have students fingerspell the names for the states in full. Check forms.

For ***"Maine"*** and ***"Montana"***
- hand moves slightly forward (fist letters only)

For ***"Alaska, Colorado, Iowa"*** and ***"Nevada"***
- hand bounces (up and fist letters)

For ***"Arizona"*** and ***"Hawaii"***
- hand slides away from dominant side

NOTE: For Arizona, fs-ONA starts where the movement of fs-Z ends.

For ***"Idaho, Ohio, Oregon"*** and ***"Utah"***
- hand twists to side ("g" and "h" letters)

PRACTICE *Identifying States and Provinces*

20–25 minutes

Students practice naming states and provinces and matching them to their locations on the maps.

EXERCISE 5

Divide class into groups of five. Assign each group a list, either Group A, B, C, D or E (*Student Workbook*, page 500). Students in each group work together to write in the names of states and provinces from their list in the correct locations on their maps (*Student Workbook*, pages 501 and 502).

PRESENT
(LESSON SLIDES 11:10:7–8)

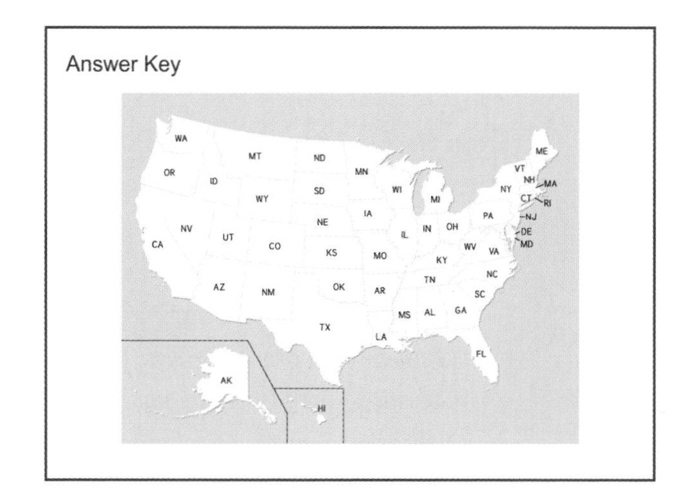

When all the groups are done, show **Lesson Slides 11:10:7–8** to confirm the groups' answers.

PRESENT
(LESSON SLIDE 11:10:9)

Trivia Time

1. Where was Ben and Jerry's Ice Cream established?
2. Chicago is in which state?
3. Which state is known for its motto "Live Free or Die"?
4. What two states are bordered by the most number of states (8)?
5. Name the first 13 states.
6. In which two states can you find places that are below sea level?

Conclude. Show **Lesson Slide 11:10:9** and have the same groups discuss the answers to the trivia questions. Then, call on each group to share their answers. Confirm or correct the answers.

Teacher's Answer Key

1. Vermont
2. Illinois
3. New Hampshire
4. Tennessee and Missouri
   (Tennessee bordered by Kentucky, Missouri, Mississippi, Alabama, Georgia, North Carolina and Virginia; Missouri bordered by Iowa, Nebraska, Kansas, Oklahoma, Arkansas, Tennessee, Kentucky and Illinois)
5. New Hampshire, Connecticut, Massachusetts, Rhode Island, New York, New Jersey, Pennsylvania, Delaware, Maryland, Virginia, North Carolina, South Carolina and Georgia
6. California and Louisiana

HOMEWORK

Tell students to do **Homework 11:10** (*Student Workbook*, page 377).

LESSON 11:11

Comprehension: Brother on the Roof

Lesson length: 30–35 minutes

LESSON GOAL

Students will develop comprehension and production skills through the story **Brother on the Roof**.

KEY SKILLS

For comprehension: Students will develop the ability to process larger chunks of information and figure out the meaning of a sign from context.

For production: Students will build fluency by re-telling the story or by asking questions about the story.

NOTIONS

Vocabulary

Possible new signs in the story

EXAGGERATE

SOMETHING/SOMEONE

BE-GONE/DISAPPEAR

"shh"

PREPARATION

- View the story **Brother on the Roof** on **Lesson Slide 11:11:1**
- Decide which **Comprehension** and **Production** activities to use for the lesson

MATERIALS

11:11 Lesson Slides

11:11 Follow-up Slides

HOMEWORK 11:11

Student Workbook, pages 378–380

INTRODUCE *Brother on the Roof*

6–7 minutes

PRESENT
(LESSON SLIDE 11:11:1)

Show the story. Then, do one of the options below.

Comprehension:
- quiz (page 720)
- answer questions (pages 721–722)

Production:
- develop questions to ask (page 723)
- re-tell the story (page 723)
- change details of the story. (page 723)

COMPREHENSION

15–30 minutes

Students will develop the ability to process larger chunks of information and figure out the meaning of a sign from context.

QUIZ (15–30 minutes)
Students write down the information given in the story. Collect papers and grade their papers using FC (full credit), PC (partial credit) or NC (no credit).

FC (full credit) = details are accurate and complete; one or two minor details may be missing, such as Suzanne winning the game twice

PC (partial credit) = sufficient details to show satisfactory comprehension of story, actions or cause and effect, but few significant details missing or incorrect, such as not mentioning how brother got up on the roof or which room Suzanne checked while looking for brother.

NC (no credit) = does not show sufficient comprehension of story, actions or cause and effect to follow along.

Return the papers. Pair off "FC" with "PC" or "NC" students.

- Give the "FC" students a minute to read their own papers and review the story.
- Have the "PC" students ask the "FC" students questions to find out what they got wrong or missed and make corrections on their papers.
- Have the "FC" students sign the story so the "NC" students can rewrite their papers.

Check the "PC" or "NC" students' corrected papers.

ANSWER QUESTIONS (20-30 minutes)

First, pair off students and have them fill each other in on what happened in the story. If there is anything in the story they don't understand, have them ask other students to get clarification.

Then, ask the following questions:

t rel.cl

1. **WOMAN IN-PAST IX"*woman*" DCL"*short*," IX"*woman*"**

   NOT+LIKE LEAVE-FOR EAT WITH POSS"*woman*"

   neg whq

   MOTHER +FATHER. WHY

   Answer. Because her parents take their time drinking and eating when she was ready to go home.

2. **MOTHER TELL-TO-girl IX*"girl"* CAN STAY HOME,**

cond ... whq

UNDERSTAND, MUST [(wh)3/IX-mult] "what"

Answer. 1) don't answer the door, 2) don't answer the phone, and 3) no cooking.

whq

3. **BROTHER BE-MAD SCL:1*"stormed off"* WHY**

Answer. Because he hated losing to his sister.

whq

4. **SISTER LOOK-FOR FIND BROTHER, WHERE**

Answer. Sitting on the ridge of the roof.

whq

5. **SISTER (2h)#DO**

Answer. She went to get a camera to take a picture of her brother on the roof.

EXAGGERATE

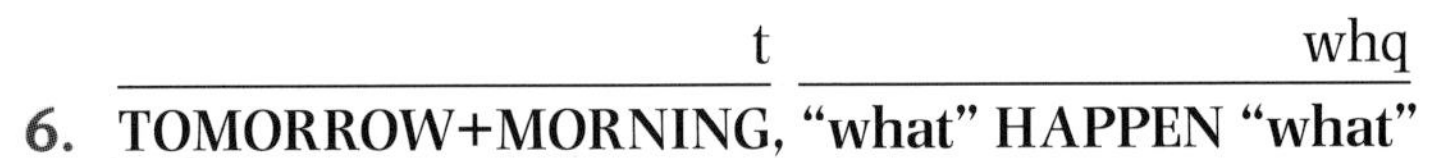

t ... whq

6. **TOMORROW+MORNING, "what" HAPPEN "what"**

Answer. The mother noticed the camera was on, checked to see what was on the display, saw the photo of the brother on the roof, got upset and asked the sister when it happened. When she found out it happened the night before, she reprimanded the girl and sent her to her room.

SOMETHING/ SOMEONE

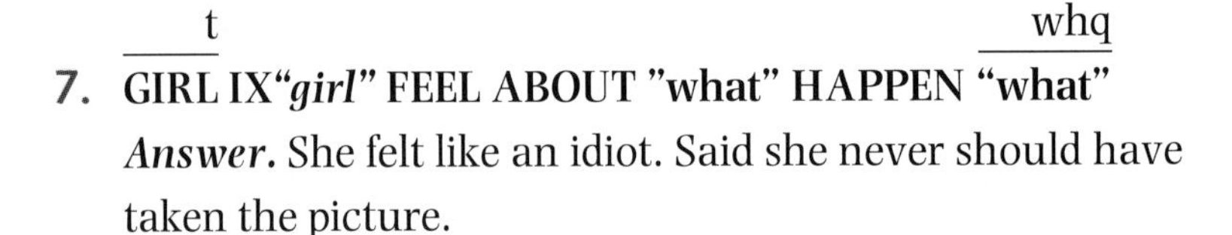

t ... whq

7. **GIRL IX*"girl"* FEEL ABOUT "what" HAPPEN "what"**

Answer. She felt like an idiot. Said she never should have taken the picture.

BE-GONE

Show video again. Make sure students understand those possible new signs, and if needed, use one of the strategies below to explain the meaning.

- list things in a category
- give the opposite sign if known
- describe or act out situation
- give definition using familiar signs

"shh"

PRODUCTION

15 minutes

Students will build fluency by re-telling the story or by asking questions about the story.

After showing the video, and making sure students understand the story and all the signs, choose one of these activities:

- **DEVELOP QUESTIONS TO ASK** (20–30 minutes)
  Pair up students and assign one student to develop true or false questions and the other wh-word questions. Have them ask each other questions.

- **RE-TELL STORY** (15–20 minutes)
  Pair up students and have them tell each other the story.

- **CHANGE DETAILS OF THE STORY** (30–40 minutes)
  Pair up students and have them collaborate to change the details of the story. For example, have the brother do something else he wasn't supposed to do, change how the mother found out, how she punished Suzanne, or how Suzanne reacted. Then, have students mingle and tell their versions of the story.

HOMEWORK

Tell students to do **Homework 11:11** (*Student Workbook*, pages 378–380).

HOMEWORK FOLLOW-UP

Review answers to **Busted** (*Student Workbook*, page 378).

Option 1: show answers on **Follow-up Slides 11:11:1–12** and have students check their answers in their workbook.

Option 2: for more language practice, sign the questions from the workbook and have students sign their answers. For example:

For "*1. What did Lauren say about her father?*"

t whq

T: **fs-LAUREN POSS"*father*" FATHER POSS"*father*"++ "what"**

Answer. Smart, clever, can find out stuff much like a cop.

For "*2. What did she get when she turned 16 years old?*"

when whq

T: **IX"*Lauren*" !OLD+16! IX"*Lauren*" GET "what"**

Answer. A driver's license.

For "*3. What did Lauren and her sister want to do?*"

t

T: **IX"*Lauren*" POSS"*Lauren's sister*" SISTER THEY-TWO WANT**

whq

"what" *Answer.* Go cruising down Main Street.

For "*4. Why did Lauren's father say they couldn't use the car?*"

neg whq

T: **FATHER SAY-NO-TO-girls, WHY**

Answer. It was a school night and they needed to go to bed early (implied).

For "*5. What did Lauren and her sister do after their parents went to bed?*"

t

T: **MOTHER+FATHER GET-IN-BED SLEEP, THEY-TWO**

whq

GIRL (2h)#DO

Answer. They got in the car, and without turning the headlights on (so parents couldn't see the car leaving), they backed out the car.

For "*6. How did their father know they were taking the car?*"

t nod whq

T: **THEY-TWO SCL:3"*backing car out,*" FATHER KNOW HOW**

Answer. He smelled the exhaust fumes when the car was started.

For “*7. What happened the night the parents went to church?*”

T: LATER-ON MOTHER+FATHER LEAVE-FOR CHURCH,

___________________whq

“what HAPPEN “what”

Answer. Lauren figured her parents wouldn’t be home from church until around 11 p.m. So she and her sister “dragged Main” until just before 11 p.m., then dashed home and jumped into bed just as their parents got home.

For “*8. How did the father know the girls had been out?*”

_____________________t _____________nod __whq

T: THEY-TWO LEAVE-FOR, FATHER KNOW HOW

Answer. He felt the car’s engine and it was hot, which meant Lauren had been driving the car.

For “*9. What did Lauren resolve to be from now on?*”

____whq

T: FROM-NOW-ON, GIRL IX“*Lauren*” (2h)#DO “what”

Answer. To be a good girl and do as she is told.

LESSON 11:12

Culture: ASL Student in the Community

Lesson length: 25–30 minutes

LESSON GOAL

Students will learn appropriate ways to interact in environments where Deaf people are present.

KEY BEHAVIORS

Offering to interpret for a Deaf person

- first let the Deaf person know you can sign, then let him or her decide if she or he needs help

Communicating in a Deaf environment

- avoid using spoken language; sign at all times
- leave the room if you need to speak

PREPARATION

Read and view **At the Cafe** and **At the Gallery**, *Student Workbook*, pages 381–382

MATERIALS

11:12 Lesson Slides
11:12 Follow-up Slides

HOMEWORK 11:12

Student Workbook, pages 381–383

INTRODUCE *ASL Student in the Community*

25–30 minutes

PRESENT
(LESSON SLIDE 11:12:1)

ASL Student in the Community

Explain to students you will show two videos of similar situations and that the students are to note the differences.

PRESENT
(LESSON SLIDES 11:12:2–3)

After showing the two videos **At the Cafe: Version 1 and 2**, ask students:

                                  t   whq
T: THEY-TWO *"videos"* DIFFERENT "what"

Answer. In **Version 1**, the ASL (Lauren) student proceeded to help the barista and Justin on her own before he was able to figure the best communication strategy with the barista.

In **Version 2**, the ASL student (Lauren) asked Justin if he needed help first, and Justin declined her offer. Justin then resorted to gesturing his order, then writing it down.

whq

T: WHICH YOU THINK DEAF COMMUNITY (or PEOPLE) IX-all PREFER WHICH

Answer. **Version 2**

whq

T: WHY

Discussion Notes:

In *Signing Naturally Units 1–6 Student Workbook* (Unit 1, page 23) "Ways of communicating with others," these were pointed out:

- let the Deaf person know you sign
- avoid spoken English or using voice without relaying information in ASL
- let the Deaf person set the communication mode which may be one of these: signing, gesturing, writing or typing, using a third person, or speaking and lipreading.

Lauren, as an ASL student, in **At the Cafe: Version 1** contradicted all these.

- She did not let the Deaf person know she could sign.
- She went ahead and used spoken English without relaying information in ASL.
- She prevented the Deaf person from setting his own preferred communication mode to use with the barista.

However, Lauren, again as an ASL student, in **At the Cafe: Version 2**, informed Justin she could sign by asking him directly, "I can sign a little. Do you need help?" This allowed the Deaf person to decide if he needed help. In this case, Justin declined. Lauren respectfully went back in line to let Justin continue. Notice also that Justin first signed directly with the barista, then switched to gesturing and when the barista still couldn't figure it out, he switched to writing and then successfully placed the order.

Point out that because Deaf people consist of a linguistic and cultural minority in the U.S. and Canada, opportunities to assure achieving equality in as many situations as possible is essential even if the situation is small and mundane as this one in the cafe.

T: SUPPOSE WOMAN WORK (barista) SPEAK, ASK-TO"all"
cond / whq
WHO KNOW SIGN, fs-LAUREN (2h)#DO++
Answer. It is best for the ASL student to inform the Deaf person of the barista's request and let him or her decide what role the ASL student will play in the exchange. The ASL student should not automatically start interpreting for the barista.

PRESENT
(LESSON SLIDES 11:12:4–5)

Do the same with the next two videos. After showing the two videos **At the Gallery: Version 1 and 2**, ask students:

t / whq
T: THEY-TWO*"videos"* DIFFERENT "what"
Answer. In **Version 1**, the ASL students are signing with each other. In **Version 2**, the ASL students are talking without signing to each other.

T: WHICH YOU THINK DEAF COMMUNITY (or PEOPLE) IX-all

whq

PREFER WHICH

Answer. **Version 1.**

whq

T: WHY

Discussion Notes:

In *Signing Naturally Units 1–6 Student Workbook* (Unit 3, page 152) "Speaking in the Presence of a Deaf Person Is Considered Impolite," we point out that:

- signing to the best of a person's ability in a Deaf environment (school, event, gathering) shows respect and courtesy to the Deaf people.

In **At the Gallery: Version 1**, both ASL students (Derrick and Terrylene) continually signed while they were in the presence of Deaf people and other signers. It implies "total inclusion" and respect for the language and culture. It also provides opportunities for Deaf people to approach them and chat with the students should they be interested and able to.

However, in **At the Gallery: Version 2**, when the students do not sign with each other, the students may imply to other people in the room they are not to be included. It may be interpreted as rude when it's revealed they know ASL. Although the students may think it's polite to stand off to the side and speak softly, their behavior will appear rude to the Deaf people because their behavior is still visible.

T: SUPPOSE LEARN+ER THINK IX"*student*" NOT BE-

cond

SKILLED-IN fs-ASL (or SIGN), CAN'T TELL POSS"*student*"

neg whq

FRIEND SOMETHING, IX"*student*" (2h)#DO++

Answer. She or he should go outside the room, to a place where nobody else sees them to communicate in whatever ways they need.

T: SUPPOSE LEARN+ER MUST BRING"here" POSS*"student"*

cond / neg

FRIEND, FAMILY, IX*"friend/family"* NOT-KNOW fs-ASL,

whq

IX*"student"*(2h)#DO++

Answer. The ASL student should tell his or her friend or relative prior to the event that:

- it is considered rude to use voice only in a Deaf environment
- even when talking with each other, they should use voice sparingly and only when necessary
- if they need to approach a Deaf person or ASL user, for example, to buy a ticket, to order refreshments, to ask for information, the ASL student will relay information for both parties. The friend or relative should be patient with the process since the student will not be talking and signing at the same time as it compromises both languages
- there may be times when she or he is engaged in an extended conversation in ASL. In this case, the friend or relative should not consider it rude if the information isn't relayed immediately.

HOMEWORK

Tell students to do **Homework 11:12** (*Student Workbook*, pages 381–383).

Also, students are to bring ideas or suggestions on how the ASL student (on the video) could have handled the situation better (See **Assignment**, *Student Workbook*, page 383).

HOMEWORK FOLLOW-UP
15–20 MINUTES

Have students share their ideas or suggestions on how Justin should have handled the situation with the AV technician to make it more acceptable to Melvin, the Deaf teacher. (See **Assignment**, *Student Workbook*, page 383).

PRESENT
(FOLLOW-UP
SLIDE 11:12:1)

Then, present video **In the Classroom 2** to demonstrate the way Justin should have handled the situation with the AV technician to make it more acceptable to Melvin.

Point out the following:

- By directing the AV technician to talk with Melvin directly, Justin puts the responsibility and authority in the teacher's hands where it belongs.
- Justin begins to interpret the exchange between the AV technician and Melvin, but when it becomes clear Melvin intended to address the technician directly through gesturing, Justin stops.

PRESENT
(FOLLOW-UP
SLIDE 11:12:2)

Key points to remember.

- Check with a Deaf person first before offering to help.
- Have the Deaf person determine how communication will be handled.
- Use ASL when Deaf people are around or in any Deaf space.
- Don't allow your help to usurp responsibility, authority and rights of a Deaf person to determine how to handle the situation.

Conclude. Show slide and summarize the key points of this cultural lesson.

LESSON 11:13

Culture: Focus on Chuck Baird, Deaf Artist

Lesson length: 45–60 minutes

LESSON GOAL

Students will learn what constitutes De'VIA art by discussing Chuck Baird's paintings.

KEY SKILLS

Identify and describe how an art work may or may not meet these criteria for De'VIA art:

- visual fine arts intended to express cultural or physical Deaf experience
- centralized focus on facial features or on the hands
- may incorporate contrasting or intense colors and values

PREPARATION

- Read **The De'VIA Manifesto** and **Assignment**, *Student Workbook*, pages 386–387. Decide if students will submit their reports written or signed on video
- Review pages 734–740 and think about how to sign the information

MATERIALS

11:13 Lesson Slides

HOMEWORK 11:13

Student Workbook, pages 384–387

INTRODUCE *Deaf Artist: Focus on Chuck Baird*

45–60 minutes

PRESENT
(LESSON SLIDE 11:13:1)

Lecture Notes:
Discuss what is De'VIA. Show **Field of Poppies** by Granville Redmond and **Double Arches** by Chuck Baird to introduce the concept of De'VIA by discussing the differences between the two paintings. Then, point out that artwork using Deaf symbols is called De'VIA.

For ***"Field of Poppies"***
Explain Granville Redmond was a Deaf impressionist painter in the early 1900s, known for his works featuring California landscapes of rolling hills of poppies. **Field of Poppies** is an example of his work that does not reflect his Deaf experience.

For ***"Double Arches"***
Explain Chuck Baird was a Deaf visual artist during the 1970s–2000s known for his works that reflect signing and Deaf experience. **Double Arches** here uses symbols for the Deaf experience or view. Examples are:

- hands—the cupped hands form the shape of the heart representing the Deaf community's solidarity.
- smoke—its movement is similar to the one in the sign SPIRIT/SOUL
- eye—it's the main way most Deaf people absorb the world
- arch—looks like two hands signing EQUAL for:
  "Deaf people = hearing people"
  "Deaf = nature" (being Deaf is natural)

PRESENT
(LESSON SLIDE 11:13:2)

De'VIA (Deaf View/Image Art)

Main points of their Manifesto (created in 1989):
- visual fine arts intended to express cultural or physical Deaf experience
- centralized focus on facial features or on the hands
- may incorporate contrasting or intense colors and values.

Characteristics of De'VIA. Discuss the following:

For ***"• visual fine arts intended to express cultural or physical Deaf experience"***
Deaf experience can be either positive or negative. For example:

Positive views related to Deaf
- Acknowledging signed languages are natural languages.
- Recognizing that being Deaf is fine and natural.
- Experiencing commonality, unity, and community.
- Viewing Deaf people as visual beings.

Negative views related to Deaf
- Experiencing language deprivation for example, ASL being denied.
- Experiencing denial of cultural identity, for example, separation from Deaf peers or adults.
- Seeing Deaf people as "broken" and needing to be fixed.
- Believing it's more important to hear and speak than to be happy and content as a Deaf person.
- Having an obsession with the ears and mouth.

For ***"• centralized focus on facial features or on the hands"***
- artwork focusing on mouth and ears usually more negative
- artwork focusing on eyes and hands usually more positive

For ***"• may incorporate contrasting or intense colors and values"***

- gray or dark colors = oppression, denial of language and cultural identity
- bright, bold colors = visual appeal and inspiration that happens when sign language, being Deaf and Deaf culture are respected and celebrated

PRESENT
(LESSON SLIDE 11:13:3)

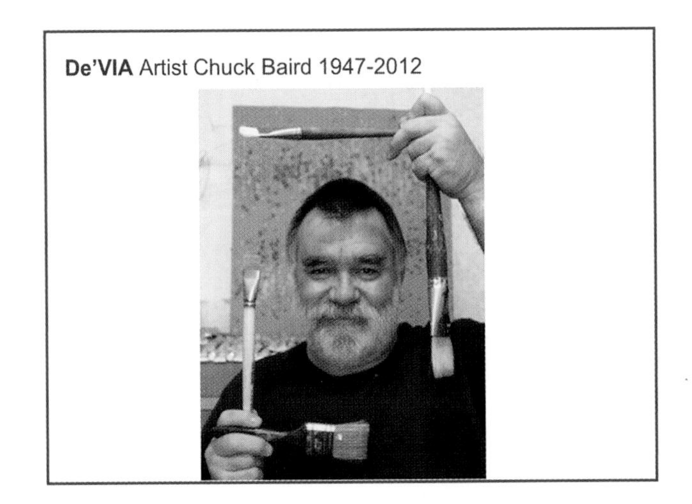

Featured De'VIA artist. Introduce Chuck Baird as one of the many De'VIA artists, and how his works reflect De'VIA characteristics.

Chuck Baird, one of the founders of De'VIA attended the Kansas School for the Deaf. He then attended Gallaudet and N.T.I.D. before receiving his B.F.A. in Painting from the Rochester Institute of Technology in 1974.

PRESENT
(LESSON SLIDE 11:13:4)

Art No. 2 (1993)

- visual fine arts intended to express cultural or physical Deaf experience
- centralized focus on facial features or on the hands
- may incorporate contrasting or intense colors and values

Art, No. 2. Examine the De'VIA characteristics in the self-portrait.

For "***• visual fine arts intended to express cultural or physical Deaf experience***"

- the ASL sign ART is incorporated in the painting
- the glow at the chest inplies the passion for art in his Deaf heart and soul

For "***• centralized focus on facial features or on the hands***"

- the hands are central to the painting's composition, showing Baird's bond with ASL

For "***• may incorporate contrasting or intense colors and values***"

- the illumination and the neon colors offsetting the dark background symbolizes the brightness that comes from sharing one's art, language and cultural identity despite misconceptions and denials

PRESENT

(LESSON SLIDE 11:13:5)

Njamala (1992)
(Ghanian word for "giraffe")

- visual fine arts intended to express cultural or physical Deaf experience
- centralized focus on facial features or on the hands
- may incorporate contrasting or intense colors and values

Njamala. Examine the De'VIA characteristics in the painting.

For "***• visual fine arts intended to express cultural or physical Deaf experience***"

- a Deaf man signing GIRAFFE is superimposed on the giraffe
- the man wears the robe worn only by a king in Ghana which elevates Deaf people and ASL to the level of royalty
- Deaf people are highly visual and tactile, which is also true of giraffes, the main symbol in this painting

For “• *centralized focus on facial features or on the hands*”

- the hands and head signing GIRAFFE is central to the painting

For “• *may incorporate contrasting or intense colors and values*”

- colors are vibrant in the painting

PRESENT
(LESSON SLIDE 11:13:6)

All American Breakfast (1992)

- visual fine arts intended to express cultural or physical Deaf experience
- centralized focus on facial features or on the hands
- may incorporate contrasting or intense colors and values

All American Breakfast. Examine the painting.

For “• *visual fine arts intended to express cultural or physical Deaf experience*”

- Deaf people making life richer or sweeter for America is symbolized by adding syrup to pancakes
- ASL should be considered as commonplace as having pancakes for breakfast. The Pop Art style reflects the movement’s tendency to use commonplace objects as subject matter

For “• *centralized focus on facial features or on the hands*”

- the hand with the sign POUR is superimposed onto the syrup being poured over the pancakes

For “• *may incorporate contrasting or intense colors and values*”

- the colors are bright and cheerful

PRESENT
(LESSON SLIDE 11:13:7)

Late Deafened Beethoven's Version

- visual fine arts intended to express cultural or physical Deaf experience
- centralized focus on facial features or on the hands
- may incorporate contrasting or intense colors and values

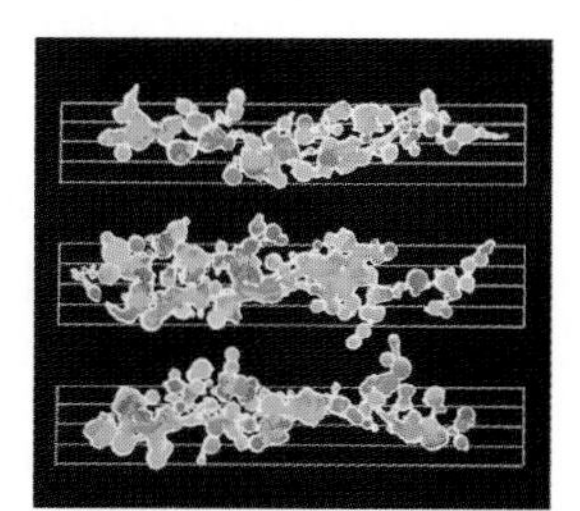

Late Deafened Beethoven's Version. Examine the painting.

For ***"• visual fine arts intended to express cultural or physical Deaf experience"***

- movement and colors, rather than sounds and instruments, are Deaf people's "music." This painting uses clouds moving in the sky in place of musical notes

For ***"• centralized focus on facial features or on the hands"***

- even though there is no specific reference to facial features or the hands, the subject alludes to contrasting hearing and seeing

For ***"• may incorporate contrasting or intense colors and values"***

- contrasting bold colors are used on a black background

PRESENT
(LESSON SLIDE 11:13:8)

Left and Right (2000)

- visual fine arts intended to express cultural or physical Deaf experience
- centralized focus on facial features or on the hands
- may incorporate contrasting or intense colors and values

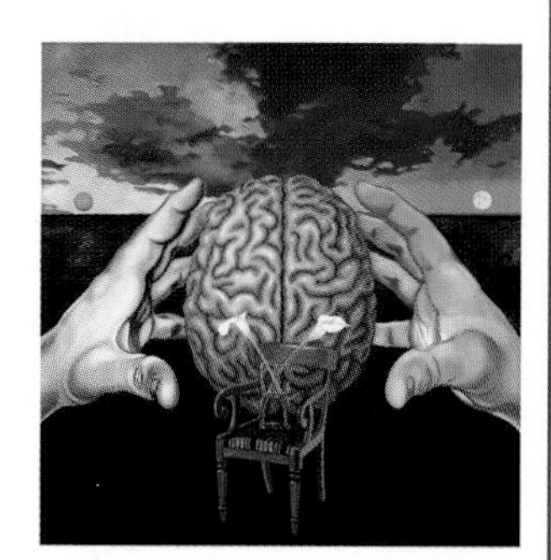

Left and Right. Examine the painting.

For "*• **visual fine arts intended to express cultural or physical Deaf experience***"

- hands: the colorful hand on the right epitomizes the warm and bright world of Deaf people. The gray hand on the left side represents the bleak and cold effects of Oralism, which perpetuates many hearing parents' grief over their Deaf children. Oralism is the ideology that undermines Deaf children's access to Sign Language and a healthy Deaf cultural identity
- brain: the left hemisphere of the brain is more linear, logical, and sequential, while the right hemisphere is more creative, holistic, intuitive, and visual. Research shows when a person signs he utilizes both hemispheres of the brain, whereas when a person speaks he uses the left hemisphere only
- calla lilies: the stems of the two calla lilies are crossed which symbolizes the signs CROSS and CONFLICT: the cross-cultural experience navigating both the hearing and Deaf worlds and the other, the conflict created by Oralism that he experienced growing up
- chair: the chair represents a witness stand, from which Chuck attests to his experience—one that is shared by many Deaf people
- suns: the red sun on the left implies impurities in the air, signifying unhealthy life and the yellow sun on the right implies all is healthy and good in the world

For "*• **centralized focus on facial features or on the hands***"

- the hands are used to represent the shape of brain and abstractly, the world
- the hands also reflect how central ASL is to Chuck's life and creativity

For "*• **may incorporate contrasting or intense colors and values***"

- colors are used as essential symbols (gray = desolation, versus rainbow colors = light and energy)

HOMEWORK

Tell students to do **Homework 11:13** (*Student Workbook*, pages 384–387).

Also, students are to describe how the artwork by one of the De'VIA artists meets the De'VIA criteria (See **Assignment**, *Student Workbook*, page 387).

Be sure to tell students how they should present their reports, written or signed on video.

HOMEWORK FOLLOW-UP
3–5 MINUTES

Report on a De'VIA artist. Collect students' reports (written or signed on video) on artwork by a De'VIA artist (See **Assignment**, *Student Workbook*, page 387). Make sure students include a picture of the artwork itself or at least a link to the site that shows the artwork in their reports.

UNIT 11 REVIEW

Putting It All Together

Lesson length: 55–65 minutes

LESSON GOAL

Students will...

- practice comparing themselves with their partners
- practice naming the states to answer questions
- practice vocabulary to discuss someone they know, covering various topics from Units 7–11

NOTIONS

Vocabulary

vocabulary previously learned

MATERIALS

11UR Lesson Slides

Exercise 6 (in *Student Workbook*, page 503)

HOMEWORK

Student Workbook, pages 388–389 (**Self-Assessment**)

PRACTICE *Similar and Different*

12–15 minutes

Students practice comparing themselves with their partners.

PRESENT
(LESSON SLIDE 11:UR:1)

Compare yourself with your partner.

- avoid telling the obvious (for example, you both are wearing pants)
- avoid telling something we already know about you (for example, you both are studying ASL)

Dig deeper and come up with something that surprises us!

Pair up. Give them five minutes to talk to each other and to find out ways they are similar and different.

Conclude. Go around the room and ask students to tell you what they learned from each other.

whq

T: YOU-TWO SAME-AS, DIFFERENT "what"

S1: US-TWO person-SAME-AS-me (describe the similarity).

S2: US-TWO DIFFERENT (describe the difference).

PRACTICE *State Trivia*

15–20 minutes

Students practice naming the states to answer questions.

EXERCISE 6 (*Student Workbook*, page 503)

Divide class into groups of three or four, have them follow instructions in the workbook, and discuss answers to the questions. After about 10–15 minutes, ask one group give their answer to a question. Check the other groups' answers to that question before confirming the answer from the Answer Key.

Teacher's Answer Key

1. ***Which state boasts of being the birthplace of the greatest number of Presidents of the U.S.?***
   Answer. Virginia (George Washington, Thomas Jefferson, James Madison, James Monroe, William Henry Harrison, John Tyler, Zachary Taylor and Woodrow Wilson)

2. ***The Grand Canyon is in which state?***
   Answer. Arizona

3. ***Yellowstone National Park is in which state?***
   Answer. Wyoming

4. ***Which state has the longest shoreline?***
   Answer. Michigan

5. ***Which is the only state in the Union with a pennant-shape flag?***
   Answer. Ohio

6. ***Which state does not have a natural lake?***
   Answer. West Virginia

7. The ***Alamo is in which state?***
   Answer. Texas

8. ***Which state is famous for its potatoes?***
   Answer. Idaho

9. ***The Salem Witch trials of 1692 occurred in which state?***
   Answer. Massachusetts

10. ***Mount Rushmore is in which state?***
Answer. South Dakota

11. ***Which state do you have to travel to find the L.L. Bean Flagship store?***
Answer. Maine

12. ***The Everglades are in which state?***
Answer. Florida

13. ***The NFL Giants football team plays in which state?***
Answer. New Jersey

14. ***The Gateway Arch is in which state?***
Answer. Missouri

15. ***In which state was the current President born?***
Answer. (get current information)

PRACTICE *Sharing Information about Someone*

25–30 minutes

Students practice vocabulary to discuss someone they know, covering various topics from Units 7–11.

PRESENT
(LESSON SLIDE 11:UR:2)

> Write down the names of two people you know well
> • one person you are fond of
> • one you don't care for

Have students write down the names of two people on a piece of paper and exchange names with a partner.

PRESENT
(LESSON SLIDE 11:UR:3)

Interview

1. Ask your partner a "which" question to select one of the two names on the paper they gave you. The question should be about an activity, tendency or personal quality.
2. Ask questions about the person your partner told you was "more" or "better":
   - relationship
   - where she or he grew up
   - age
   - physical description
   - marital status and family
   - education
   - job
   - hobbies
   - personal qualities
   - what about him her annoys you

Review how to ask the questions. First, ask students how to sign the questions.

Teacher's Guide

1. Ask your partner a 'which' question to select one of the two names on the paper they gave you

lf / rt
(person 1) (person 2), WHICH MORE (or BETTER)

whq
(skilled in an activity, tendency or personal quality), WHICH

2. Ask questions about the person your partner told you was "more" or "better."

For "• ***relationship***"

whq
(person), YOU-TWO RELATE-TO-person, HOW

For "• ***where she or he grew up***"

whq
IX*"person"* BE-RAISED WHERE

For "• ***age***"

whq
IX*"person"* HOW-OLD

For "• ***physical description***"

whq
IX*"person"* LOOK+SAME-AS "what"

For “• ***marital status and family***”

q
IX*“person”* HAVE BROTHER+SISTER

q
IX*“person”* HAVE CHILDREN

q
IX*“person”* BE-MARRIED

For “• ***education***”

q whq
IX*“person”* GO-TO COLLEGE. MAJOR “what”

For “• ***job***”

q whq
IX*“person”* WORK. “what”

For “• ***hobbies***”

whq
IX*“person”* ENJOY “what”

For “• ***personal qualities***”

q
IX*“person”* (personal quality)

whq
(if answer is no, ask) POSS*“person”* “what”

SICK-OF

For “• ***what about him or her annoys you***”

whq
POSS*“person”* TEND-TO, **YOU SICK-OF “what”**

Now, have students interview their partners.

Conclude. Write two names of people you know on the board—one person you are fond of, and one you don't care for. Have each student take turns asking you a question from the slide.

NOTES:

UNIT 12

Storytelling

LESSON 12:1

"The Tailor" Understanding the Story

Lesson length: 50–70 minutes

LESSON GOAL Students understand the story **The Tailor**.

NOTIONS

Vocabulary

DECIDE
COLD
[(wh)SCL:1*"person"*/SELF++]
SMOOTH
SEW++
USE-cont
WEAR-OUT
SCISSORS
COMFORTABLE

Grammar

- descriptive classifiers (DCLs)
- instrument classifiers (ICLs)
- locative classifiers (LCLs)
- transition

PREPARATION View the story **The Tailor** on **Lesson Slide 12:1:1**. Read "Special Information for Unit 12" in **Introduction**, pages xix–xxii.

MATERIALS **12:1 Lesson Slides**

HOMEWORK 12:1 *Student Workbook*, pages 394–396

INTRODUCE *"The Tailor"*

30–40 minutes

PRESENT
(LESSON SLIDE 12:1:1)

Show video **The Tailor** and have students fill in **The Tailor** activity sheet (*Student Workbook*, page 394). If needed, show the story again.

Check students' answers by asking the following questions:

USE-cont

t whq
T: MAN SEW (or MAKE) COAT, FACE+SAME-AS "what"
S: (describe long, blue, wool, double-breasted coat with ruffles on the sleeves with stand-up collars)

WEAR-OUT

conj whq
T: MAN **USE-cont** EVERYDAY, !WRONG!, "what" HAPPEN
S: (describe hem of coat dragging on ground, **WEAR-OUT**)

whq
T: MAN (2h)#DO++
S: (describe coat cut off at waist)

conj whq
T: MAN USE-cont EVERYDAY !WRONG! "what" HAPPEN
S: (describe man eating too much and coat getting too small)

whq

T: NOW, MAN (2h)#DO++

S: (describe changing coat from double-breasted to one row of buttons down front)

conj

T: MAN CONTINUE USE-cont EVERYDAY !WRONG!

whq

"what" HAPPEN

S: (describe holes emerging at elbows)

whq

T: NOW, MAN (2h)#DO++

S: (describe sleeves being cut off, and the coat is now a vest)

whq

T: NOW, COAT FACE+SAME-AS "what"

S: (describe coat now sleeveless, cut at waist, with single row of buttons, with stand-up collars, and color still blue)

PRESENT

(LESSON SLIDE 12:1:2)

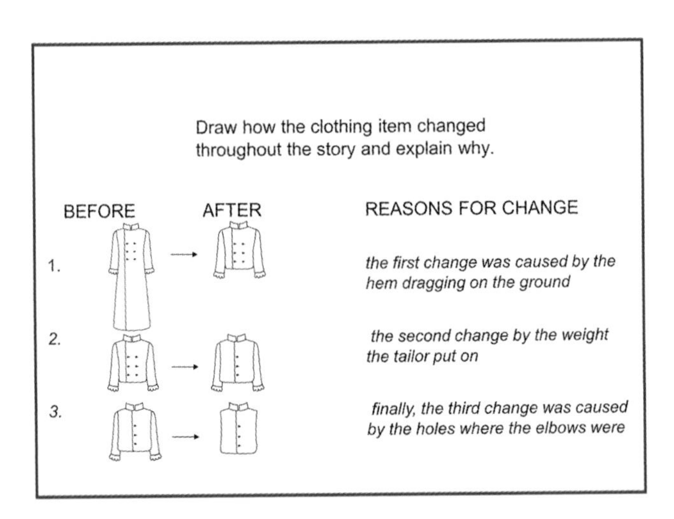

Conclude. Show **Slide 12:1:2** to confirm students' answers in their workbooks.

PRACTICE *Retelling the Story*

20–30 minutes

PRESENT
(LESSON SLIDE 12:1:3)

I. Background

- give relevant background—who, when, where
- tell how you got the clothing item
- describe the item (include the parts that change to in the story)

BACKGROUND

SEW++

COLD

DECIDE

[(wh)SCL:1 *"person"*/SELF++]

SMOOTH

SCISSORS

Show video **Background** and have students practice signing the information. Signs in bold may need to be introduced.

For **"• *give relevant background—who, when, where*"**

(2h)LONG-AGO MAN GOOD **SEW++**. IX*"man"* MAN MAKE++ BEAUTIFUL CLOTHES FOR PEOPLE IX*"people"*++-arc.

For **"• *tell how you got the clothing item*"**

t (over ONE-DAY)
ONE-DAY, **COLD**. IX*"man"* MAN **DECIDE** MAKE COAT FOR [(wh)SCL:1 *"person"*/**SELF++**]. MAN <rs:man DRAW-

when (over attentively>FINISH)
attentively>FINISH, LOOK-FOR FABRIC IX*"man"* PREFER BLUE. <rs: man LOOK-FOR, [(wh)LCL:B*"bolt of cloth on shelf"*/ BCL*"flipping through bolts of cloth"* !IX*"right bolt"*! DCL*"bolt on shelf"*]> BLUE fs-WOOL BEAUTIFUL, **SMOOTH**. <rs:man IX*"bolt"* (2h)F*"perfect,"* ICL*"pull out bolt"* ICL*"set bolt on table,*

t (over FABRIC)
FABRIC, ICL*"spread out cloth on table"* [(wh)LCL*"cloth on table"*/

t (over SCISSORS); when (over FINISH)
ICL:F*"sewing."* **SCISSORS**, ICL:V*"cutting patterns"*]. FINISH, PUT-ON-COAT>

For **"• *describe the item*"**

rhet

COAT FACE+SAME-AS "what" BEAUTIFUL, DCL*"front side"* BLUE, DCL*"long, to the ground,"* DCL*"long sleeve with ruffles at end,"*

t t

COLLAR, LCL:B*"flipped upward."* COAT, (2h)LCL:B*"overlapping sections in front,"* (2h)DCL:F*"two columns of buttons on front."* MAN (2h)F*"perfect."*

PRESENT
(LESSON SLIDE 12:1:4)

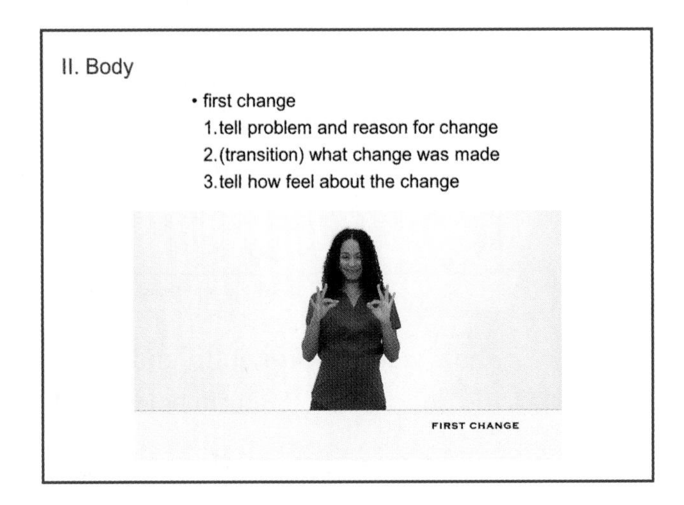

Show video **First Change** and have students practice describing the change.

For **"*1. tell problem or reason for change*"**

MAN USE-cont EVERYDAY USE-cont, COAT LAST++

t

IX-loc*"hem down there at feet"* WEAR-OUT.

For **"*2. (transition) tell what change was made*"**

MAN <rs:man LOOK-AT-down (nod)> GET SCISSORS <rs:man (2h)ICL:V*"use scissors, cut off coat across waist"* DCL*"coat length at waist level"*>

For **"*3. tell how feel about the change*"**

(2h)F*"perfect"*

NOTE: When signing the transition "MAN <rs:man LOOK-AT-down (nod)," be sure students **pause momentarily** after signing LOOK-AT-down, and then **nod** before signing GET SCISSORS.

PRESENT
(LESSON SLIDE 12:1:5)

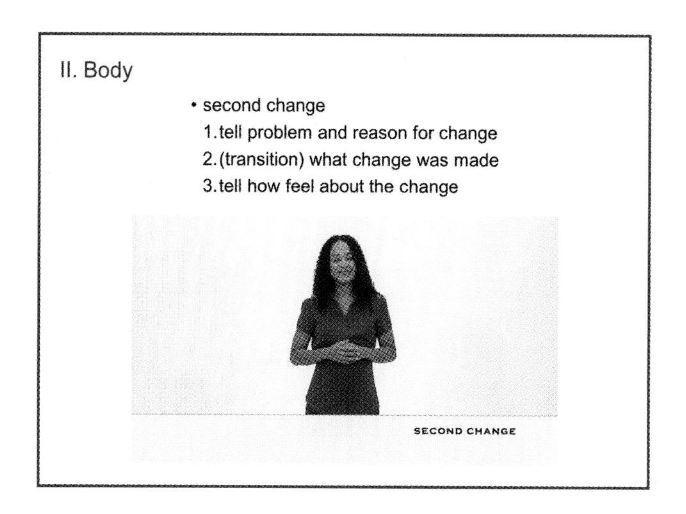

Show video **Second Change** and have students practice describing the change.

For ***"1. tell problem or reason for change"***

IX*"man"* MAN LIKE EAT, IX*"man"* (2h)alt.EAT++, BPCL*"body getting bigger, bigger,"* COAT DCL*"getting smaller, smaller"*

For ***"2. (transition) tell what change was made"***

whq nod
<rs:man "grimace" (2h)#DO++ "oh"> (2h)LCL:B*"overlapping sections front,"* (2h)DCL:F*"two columns of buttons on front,"* (shake head) (2h)ICL*"take off and discard,"* (2h)LCL:B*"sections changed from overlapping to touching each other at edges,"* ONE DCL:F*"one column of buttons on front"*

NOTE: whq nod
When signing the transition <rs:man "grimace" (2h)#DO++ "oh">, be sure students **pause momentarily** after signing "oh" and then **nod** before signing (2h)LCL:B*"overlapping sections front."*

For ***"3. tell how feel about the change"***

nod
"sigh" **COMFORTABLE.**

COMFORTABLE

PRESENT
(LESSON SLIDE 12:1:6)

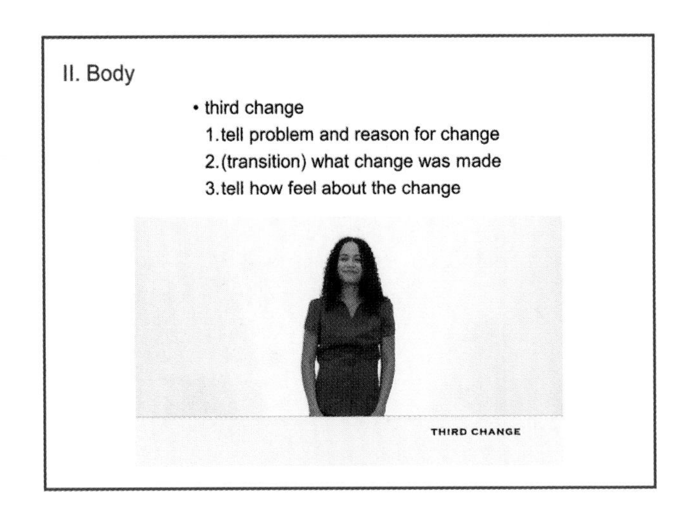

Show video **Third Change** and have students practice describing the change.

For ***"1. tell problem or reason for change"***
MAN IX-loc *"work"* WORK, USE-cont, EVERYDAY, USE-cont. WORK-cont. "ugh," DCL:S->F *"hole emerge on left elbow of coat,"* DCL:S->F *"hole emerge on right elbow of coat"*

For ***"2. (transition) tell what change was made"***
"well" <rs:man BCL *"looking at both elbows"* (shake head) "pshaw" ICL:V *"cut off sleeve at left shoulder,"* (wh)ICL:V *"cut off sleeve at right shoulder."* DCL *"sleeveless"*

NOTE: When signing the transition "<rs:man BCL*"looking at both elbows"* (shake head)," be sure students shake head before signing "pshaw."

For ***"3. tell how feel about the change"***
(not mentioned)

PRESENT
(LESSON SLIDE 12:1:7)

Show video **Conclusion** and have students practice the conclusion.

rhet (over: NOW, COAT FACE+SAME-AS)

NOW, COAT FACE+SAME-AS, fs-VEST.
DCL*"hip length,"*
DCL*"sleeveless,"*
DCL:F*"buttons down front,"*

t (over: COLLAR)

COLLAR, STILL (2h)LCL:B*"collar turned up."*

t (over: DCL"all over shirt")

DCL*"all over shirt"* STILL BLUE.

t (over: MAN IX"man")

MAN IX*"man"* STILL USE-cont.

Pair up. Have the students retell the whole story to each other.

HOMEWORK

Tell students to do **Homework 12:1** (*Student Workbook*, page 394–396).

LESSON 12:2

"The Tailor"
Telling One's Own Version

Lesson length: 70–95 minutes

LESSON GOAL

Students will sign this narrative:

Narrative Outline

I. Background

- give relevant background—who, when, where
- tell how you got the clothing item
- describe the item (include those parts that you will make changes to in the story)

II. Body

- First change:
  1. tell problem or reason for change
  2. (transition) what change was made
  3. tell how feel about the change
- Second change:
  1. tell problem or reason for change
  2. (transition) what change was made
  3. tell how feel about the change
- Third change:
  1. tell problem or reason for change
  2. (transition) what change was made
  3. tell how feel about the change

III. Conclusion

KEY SKILLS

To describe the change, use:

1. negative expression or headshake after telling the problem, and nodding to transition into describing the change
2. classifiers to describe removing, adding or replacing, signed in location where change is made

NOTIONS

Vocabulary

Removing

TAKE-AWAY-item, DROP-OFF-item

Adding

PUT-ON
ADD-ON

Reasons for Change

UGLY
!NEW!
OLD+FASHION
fs-STYLE
TOO-PLAIN
FRILLY

How Feel about the Change

BETTER
(2h)F*"perfect"*
PRETTY

Grammar

Descriptive classifiers (DCLs) to describe size of garment
Instrument classifiers (ICLs)

- ICL:V*"use scissors to cut off..."*
- ICL:F*"sew something on..."*
- ICL*"put glue on..."*

Locative classifiers (LCLs)

- LCL:B*"patched on"*

PREPARATION

View the story **My Favorite Leather Jacket** on **Lesson Slide 12:2:1**. Make copies of **12:2 Self-Evaluation** (for **Evaluation**, page 769). Be ready to video tape students (optional, see page 769).

MATERIALS

12:2 Lesson Slides
12:2 Evaluation

HOMEWORK 12:2

Student Workbook, pages 397–401

CHECK ANSWERS *My Favorite Leather Jacket*

15–20 minutes

PRESENT
(LESSON SLIDES 12:2:1–10)

My Favorite Leather Jacket

1. Explain why Justin rejected the first two jackets before finding the one he liked.

Show **Slide 12:2:1** and have students share their answers (in **Homework 12:1**, page 396). Confirm answer on next slide. Continue with **Slides 12:2:3–10**.

INTRODUCE *Reasons for Change*

10–15 minutes

PRESENT
(LESSON SLIDES 12:2:11–16)

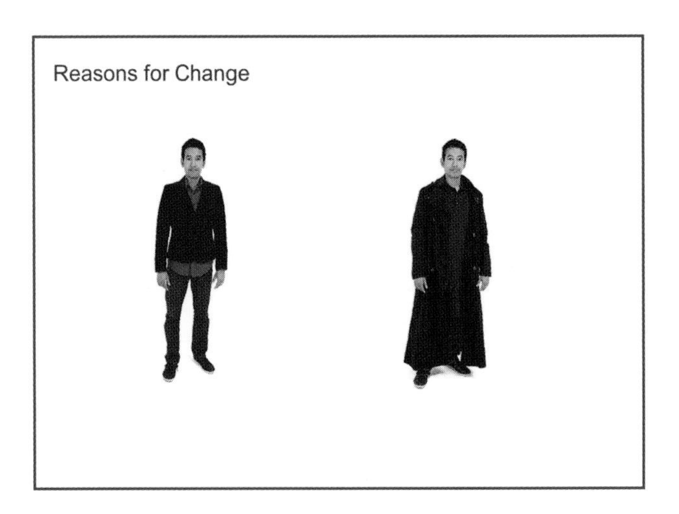

Introduce or review vocabulary to discuss reasons for changes in clothing items with **Slides 12:2:11–16**.

oo
DCL*"too short"*

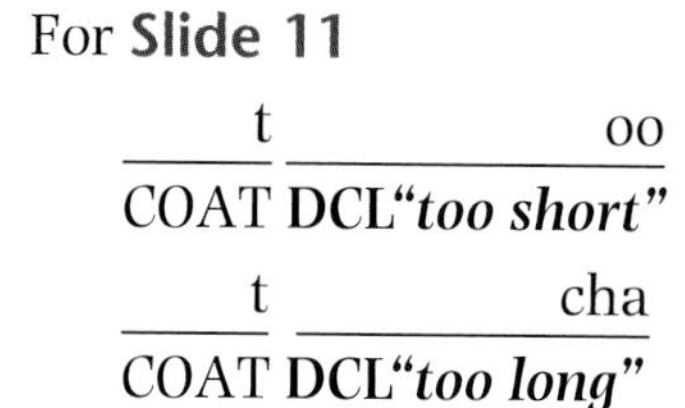

For **Slide 11**

t oo
COAT **DCL"*too short*"**

t cha
COAT **DCL"*too long*"**

cha
DCL*"too long"*

oo
DCL*"too tight"*

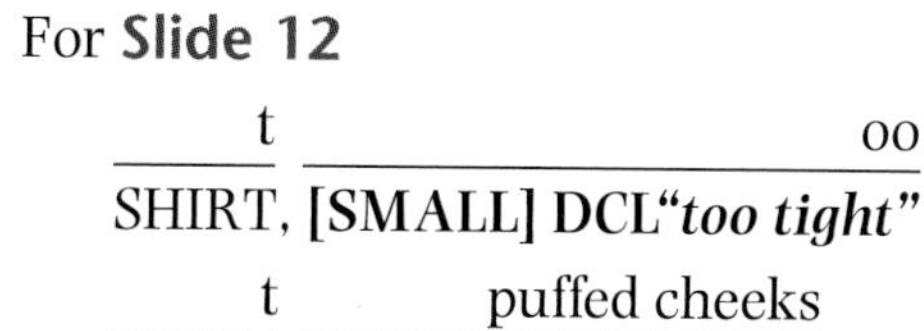

For **Slide 12**

t oo
SHIRT, **[SMALL]** DCL**"*too tight*"**

t puffed cheeks
SHIRT, **[BIG]** DCL**"*too loose*"**

puffed cheeks
DCL*"too loose"*

UGLY

For **Slide 13**

t
SHIRT, **UGLY**

t
SHIRT, **PRETTY**

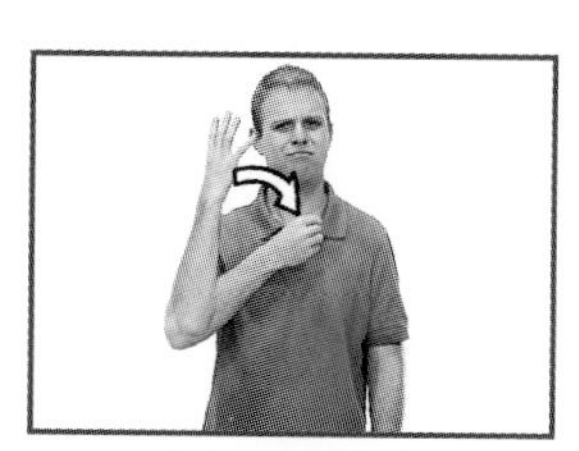

BEAUTIFUL

For **Slide 14**

t
SHIRT, OLD, WEAR-OUT

t
SHIRT, **!NEW!**

!NEW!

For **Slide 15**

t
SWIM CLOTHES DCL*"full length, striped swimsuit,"*
OLD+FASHION

t
SWIM CLOTHES DCL*"swim trunks with flower pattern,"*
NOW **fs-STYLE**

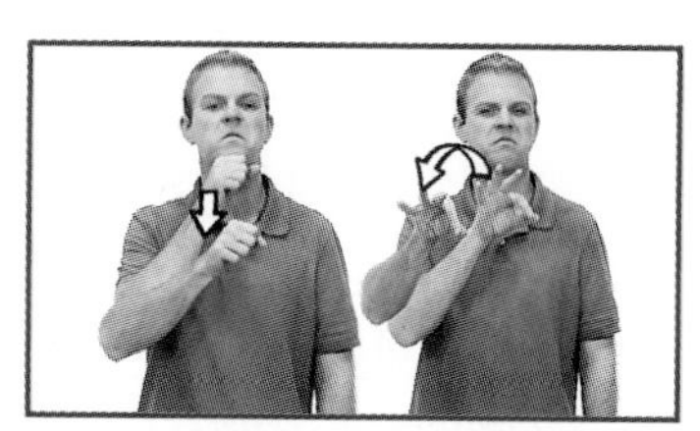

OLD+FASHION

FRILLY

For **Slide 16**

t

DRESS, **FRILLY**

t

DRESS, **!PLAIN!**

!PLAIN!

Review. Show **Slides 12:2:11–16** again and have students give you the signs.

INTRODUCE *Describing Changes to Clothing Items*

45–60 minutes

PRESENT
(LESSON SLIDE 12:2:17)

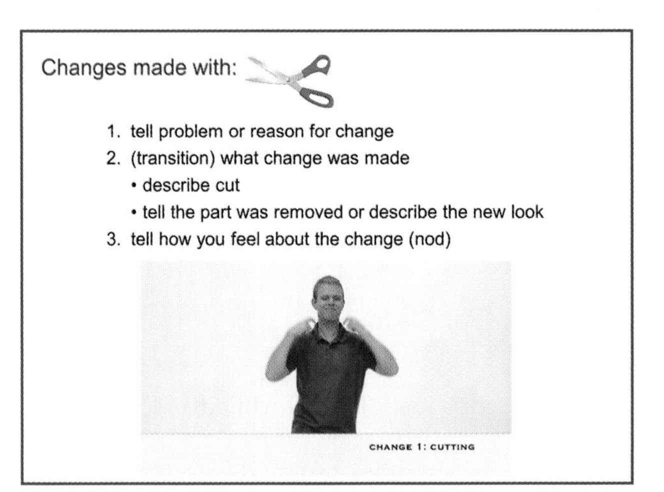

Changes made with:
1. tell problem or reason for change
2. (transition) what change was made
• describe cut
• tell the part was removed or describe the new look
3. tell how you feel about the change (nod)
CHANGE 1: CUTTING

Show video **Change 1: Cutting** and point out how to describe changes made with scissors and have students rehearse the whole segment.

For ***"1. tell problem or reason for change"***

"grimace" IX*"collar"* COAT, DCL*"collar"* (shake head)

For ***"2. (transition) what change was made"***

(nod) MOTORCYCLE, [(wh)LCL:C*"back of seat"*/ME LCL:B*"open seat,"* ICL*"pull out from seat"* SCISSORS], ICL:V*"cut off collar,"* ICL*"discard cut collar"*

For ***"3. tell how you feel about the change (nod)"***

ICL*"put helmet on"* (nod) BETTER

Be sure students:

- nod as the transition
- sign ICL:V*"cut collar"* around the neck
- use ICL*"discard cut collar"* to show part being removed
- nod before signing BETTER.

Other Changes with Scissors. Describe a problem, give a transition, then have students add a change and tell how they felt about it. For example:

t
T: SHIRT, DCL*"sleeves too long"* (shake head), (nod)...
S: (repeat, then add a change and tell how feel about it)
t
SHIRT, DCL*"sleeves too long"* (shake head), (nod)
GET SCISSORS, [(wh)BCL*"hand"*/ICL:V*"cut off cuff,"*
DCL*"sleeve shortened to wrist length"*]. (nod) BETTER

Continue with other examples:

t
T: COAT, DCL*"too long"* (shake head), (nod)...
S: (repeat, then add a change and tell how feel about it)

t
T: HAT, DCL*"brim too long"* (shake head), (nod)...
S: (repeat, then add a change and tell how feel about it)

PRESENT
(LESSON SLIDE 12:2:18)

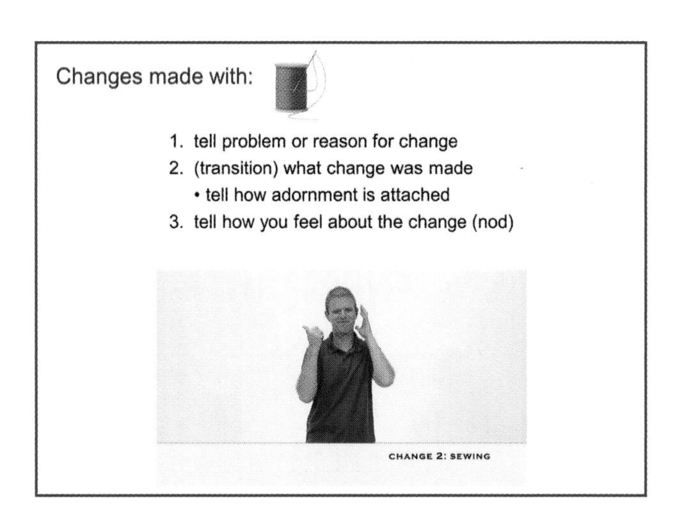

Show video **Change 2: Sewing** and point out how to describe changes made by adding on adornments and have students rehearse the whole segment.

For ***"1. tell problem or reason for change"***

BCL*"put hands in pockets"* "ugh" KEY CAN FALL-OUT

neg

"of pocket," "wave-no"

For ***"2. (transition) what change was made"***

nod

MUST PUT-ON*"pockets"* ICL*"zippers on pockets."*
ICL*"open and search kit,"* ICL*"select zippers from kit,"*
ICL*"sew zipper on both pockets,"* ICL*"use zippers"*

For ***"3. tell how you feel about the change (nod)"***

(nod) BETTER

Be sure students:

- for the transition, superimpose the nod with the sign phrase MUST PUT-ON*"pockets"* ICL*"zippers on pockets"*
- sign ICL*"zippers"* and ICL*"sew zipper"* in the locations of the pockets
- nod before signing BETTER.

Other Changes by Sewing. Describe a problem, give a transition, then have students add a change and tell how they felt about it. For example:

t

T: SHIRT, DCL:S-F*"hole developing on elbows"* (shake head),

nod

NEED LCL:B*"patches on both elbows,"*...

S: (repeat, then add a change and tell how feel about it)

t

SHIRT, DCL:S-F*"hole developing on elbows"* (shake head),

nod

NEED LCL:B*"patches on both elbows,"*
GET LCL:B*"patch on left elbow,"* ICL:F*"sew on elbow,"*
LCL:B*"patch on right elbow,"* ICL:F*"sew on elbow."*
(nod) BETTER

ADD-ON

Continue with other examples:

t neg

T: COAT, NONE HOOD, COLD ECL*"wind blowing on neck"*

nod

(shake head), MUST **ADD-ON** HOOD...

S: (repeat, then add a change and tell how feel about it)

t

T: SHIRT, !PLAIN! BORING (shake head),

nod

ME WANT **ADD-ON** BOW...

S: (repeat, then add a change and tell how feel about it)

t neg

T: TODAY, fs-ST-PATRICK DAY, MY CLOTHES NONE GREEN,

nod

BETTER ADD-ON GREEN...

S: (repeat, then add a change and tell how feel about it)

PRESENT

(LESSON SLIDE 12:2:19)

Changes made by gluing on adornment:

1. tell problem or reason for change
2. (transition) what change was made
   - tell how adornment is glued on
3. tell how you feel about the change (nod)

Show video **Change 3: Gluing** and point out how to describe changes made by gluing on adornments and have students rehearse the whole segment.

For ***"1. tell problem or reason for change"***

MY OLD COAT HAVE METAL LCL:B*"elbow cover on both*

t neg

elbows," NEW NONE

For ***"2. (transition) what change was made"***

nod (over: MUST PUT-ON"both elbows.")

MUST PUT-ON *"both elbows."*
ME ICL*"place metal sheet"* METAL [(wh)LCL:B*"metal sheet"*/ ICL:V*"cut out from metal sheet"*] fs-GLUE ICL*"put glue on metal shapes,"* LCL:B*"place on both elbows"*

For ***"3. tell how you feel about the change (nod)"***
(nod) BETTER

Be sure students:

- for the transition, superimpose the nod with the sign phrase MUST PUT-ON*"both elbows"*
- sign LCL:B*"place on both elbows"* in the locations of the elbows
- nod before signing BETTER.

Other Changes by Gluing. Describe a problem, give a transition, then have students add a change and tell how they felt about it. For example:

t (over: SHIRT)
T: SHIRT, DCL:S-F*"hole developing on elbows"* (shake head),
nod (over: NEED LCL:B"patches on both elbows.")
NEED LCL:B*"patches on both elbows."*...
S: (repeat, then add a change and how feel about it)
t (over: SHIRT)
SHIRT, DCL:S-F*"hole developing on elbows"* (shake head),
nod (over: NEED LCL:B"patches on both elbows")
NEED LCL:B*"patches on both elbows"*
GET FABRIC, [(wh)LCL:B*"fabric"*/ICL:V*"cut out from material"* fs-GLUE ICL*"put glue on fabric"*],
LCL:B*"place on both elbows."*(nod) BETTER

Continue with other examples:

t (over: BOWLING SHIRT); neg (over: NONE NAME DCL"label,")
T: BOWLING SHIRT, IX*"back of shirt"* NONE NAME DCL*"label,"*
nod (over: MUST ADD-ON)
MUST ADD-ON...
S: (repeat, then add a change and tell how feel about it)

t nod

T: HAT, !PLAIN! (shake head) SHOULD FRILLY,...

S: (repeat, then add a change and tell how feel about it)

PRESENT

(LESSON SLIDES 12:2:20–22)

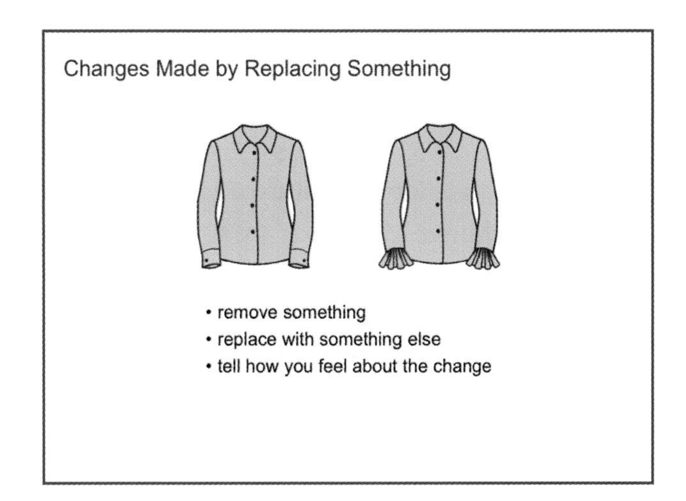

Changes Made by Replacing Something

Introduce phrases to describe the change to the shirt on **Slide 20**. Have students copy. Be sure students sign the verbs in the location where the adornment is removed or placed.

For "*• remove something*"

T: **TAKE-AWAY-item, DROP-OFF-item** or **ICL:V"*cut off,*" ICL"*discard*"**

S: (copy)

TAKE-AWAY-item, DROP-OFF-item

For "*• replace with something else*"

T: **PUT-ON, ICL:F"sew on"** or **ICL"*glue on adornment,*" LCL:B"*put on*"**

S: (copy)

For "*• tell how you feel about the change*"

T: (nod) BETTER

(nod) (2h)F"*perfect*"

(nod) PRETTY

(nod) COMFORTABLE

S: (copy)

Now, have students describe the change to the shirt on **Slide 20**.

t

S: SHIRT, [(wh)BCL*"arm"*/DCL"cuff"] (shake head), [(wh)BCL*"arm"*/ICL*"cut off cuff,"* **TAKE-AWAY-cuff, DROP-OFF-cuff**], GET fs-RUFFLE, [(wh)BCL*"arm"*/PUT-ON*"around wrist,"* ICL:F*"sew on around wrist"* DCL*"ruffles around wrist"*], (nod) !PRETTY!

Continue with **Slides 21** and **22.** Have students describe the changes.

t

S: (Slide 21) COAT, DCL:F*"buttons down the front,"* **TAKE-AWAY-buttons, DROP-OFF-buttons**, (2h)PUT-ON*"chest,"* ZIPPER ICL:F*"sew on chest"* ICL*"zip up front,"* (nod) COMFORTABLE

t

S: (Slide 22) HAT, FLOWER LCL:C*"flower on hat,"* **TAKE-AWAY-flower, DROP-OFF-flower**, GET PICTURE, fs-GLUE [(wh)LCL:B*"picture"*/ICL*"put glue on picture"*], LCL:B*"put on hat,"* (nod) (2h)F*"perfect"*

Optional: Have students create other descriptions of changes (removal and replace with) and show to the class. Be sure students:

- use **TAKE-AWAY, DROP-OFF** or **ICL:V*"cut off,"* ICL*"discard"*** to remove items
- use **PUT-ON, ICL:F*"sew on"*** or **ICL*"glue on,"* LCL:B*"put on"***
- sign the verbs in the location where the adornment is removed or placed.

HOMEWORK

Tell students to do **Homework 12:2** (*Student Workbook*, pages 397–401).

EVALUATION

Have students present their own versions about three changes to a clothing item (See **Guidelines**, *Student Workbook*, pages 397). To evaluate their presentations, you have two choices:

As a Fluency Assignment

Have students video themselves and evaluate themselves with **12:2 Self Evaluation** (See **Materials**). Collect their videos and self-evaluations and give feedback. Grading is optional.

As an Exam

Videotape students presenting their versions and grade using the **12:2 Evaluation** (See **Materials**).

LESSON 12:3

"One Fine Day" Understanding the Story

Lesson length: 30 minutes

LESSON GOAL

Students understand the story **One Fine Day**.

NOTIONS

Vocabulary

FOX
THIRSTY
FULL
BE-ANGRY
COW
CHEW
GRASS
THANK-you
BE-READY++
FROM-NOW-ON

PREPARATION

View the story **One Fine Day** on **Lesson Slide 12:3:1**.
Read "Special Information for Unit 12" in **Introduction**, pages xix–xxii.

MATERIALS

12:3 Lesson Slides

HOMEWORK 12:3

Student Workbook, pages 401–404

INTRODUCE *"One Fine Day"*

30 minutes

PRESENT
(LESSON SLIDE 12:3:1)

Show video **One Fine Day**. (This is an abbreviated version of the published story by Nonny Hogrogian)

PRESENT
(LESSON SLIDE 12:3:2)

Show the video segment **The Fox and the Woman**, and ask questions to review and to introduce vocabulary in bold.

FOX

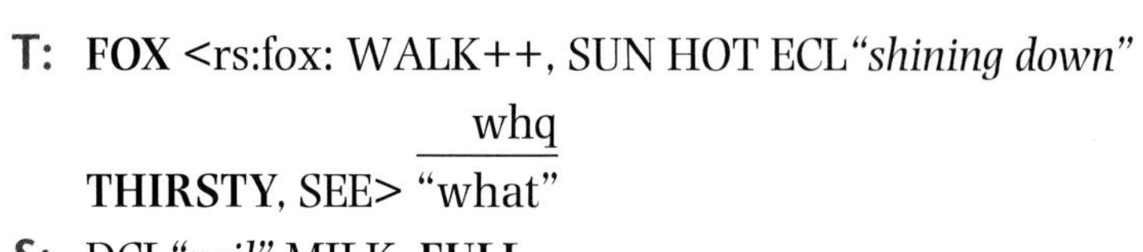

T: **FOX** <rs:fox: WALK++, SUN HOT ECL*"shining down"*

whq: "what"

THIRSTY, SEE> "what"

S: DCL*"pail"* MILK, **FULL**

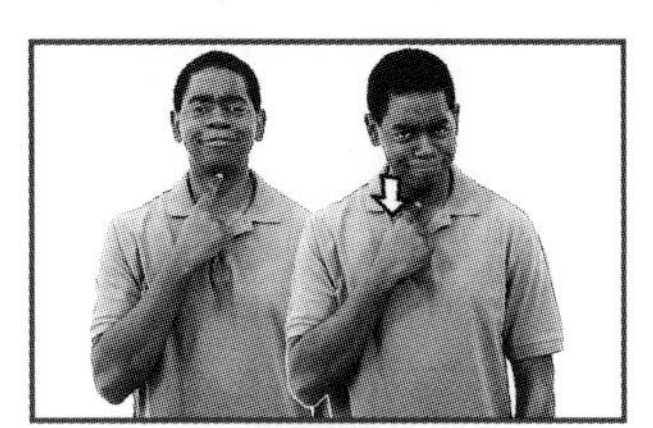

THIRSTY

whq: FOX (2h)#DO++

T: FOX (2h)#DO++

S: (describe fox picking up the pail and drinking the milk)

conj: WRONG; whq: "what" HAPPEN

T: FOX <rs:fox BCL*"wipe mouth,"* WRONG "what" HAPPEN

S: (describe the woman angrily **[BE-ANGRY]** approaching the fox and cutting his tail off)

FULL

cond: FOX WANT fs-TAIL; whq: FIRST MUST "what"

T: FOX WANT fs-TAIL, FIRST MUST "what"

S: (explain that fox needs to replace woman's milk)

BE-ANGRY

PRESENT

(LESSON SLIDE 12:3:3)

Show the video segment **The Fox and the Cow**. Continue asking questions to review and to introduce vocabulary in bold.

COW

CHEW

GRASS

whq

T: FOX <rs:fox: WALK++, SEE "what"

S: **COW [CHEW]**

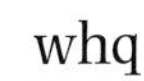

whq

T: FOX TELL-TO-cow "what"

S: (describe fox explaining he has no tail, and asking the cow for milk to give to the woman to get his tail)

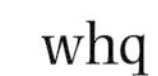

whq

T: COW TELL-TO-fox "what"

S: (explain the cow asking for grass **[GRASS]**, before it will give fox the milk)

PRESENT
(LESSON SLIDE 12:3:4)

Show the video segment **The Fox and the Grass**.
Continue asking questions to review.

whq

T: FOX <rs:fox: WALK++, SEE "what"

S: GRASS

whq

T: FOX TELL-TO-grass "what"

S: (describe fox explaining he has no tail, and asking for grass to give to the cow for the milk to give to the woman for his tail)

whq

T: GRASS TELL-TO-fox "what"

S: (explain the grass asking for water, before it will give fox the grass)

PRESENT
(LESSON SLIDE 12:3:5)

Show the video segment **The Fox and the Stream**. Continue asking questions to review.

whq

T: FOX <rs:fox: WALK++, HEAR IX-loc*"right"* "what"

S: WATER ECL*"flowing"*

whq

T: FOX TELL-TO-stream "what"

S: (describe fox explaining he has no tail, and asking for water to give the grass to get grass in return to give the cow for the milk to give to the woman for his tail)

whq

T: WATER ECL*"flowing"* TELL-TO-fox "what"

S: (explain the water asking for a jug before it will give fox the water)

PRESENT
(LESSON SLIDE 12:3:6)

Show the video segment **The Fox and the Girl**.
Continue asking questions to review.

whq

T: FOX <rs:fox: WALK++, SEE "what"

S: GIRL [(wh)TREE/SCL:V *"sitting on branch"*

whq

T: FOX TELL-TO-girl "what"

S: (describe fox explaining he has no tail, and asking for jug to collect water for the grass to give to the cow to get the milk for the woman so she will give back his tail)

whq

T: GIRL TELL-TO-fox "what"

S: "go-ahead"

HOMEWORK

Tell students to do **Homework 12:3** (*Student Workbook*, pages 402–404).

LESSON 12:4

"One Fine Day" Character Placement

Lesson length: 25–30 minutes

LESSON GOAL

Students practice placing characters alternatively on the left and right sides and maintaining agreement throughout **One Fine Day**.

KEY SKILLS

Students also practice indicating distance, location, and size of characters using eyes gaze and head positions.

To place each character:

- react first before pointing out the character
- point to show distance and location (head tilted back)
- look at audience when naming characters
- shift sign MEET and "waving" upward or downward to match the height and location of the characters

NOTIONS

Grammar

Spatial agreement to match placements of characters
Sign orientation to reflect location and height of the character

MATERIALS

12:4 Lesson Slides

HOMEWORK 12:4

Student Workbook, pages 405–406

CHECK ANSWERS *One Fine Day*

5–7 minutes

PRESENT
(LESSON SLIDE 12:4:1)

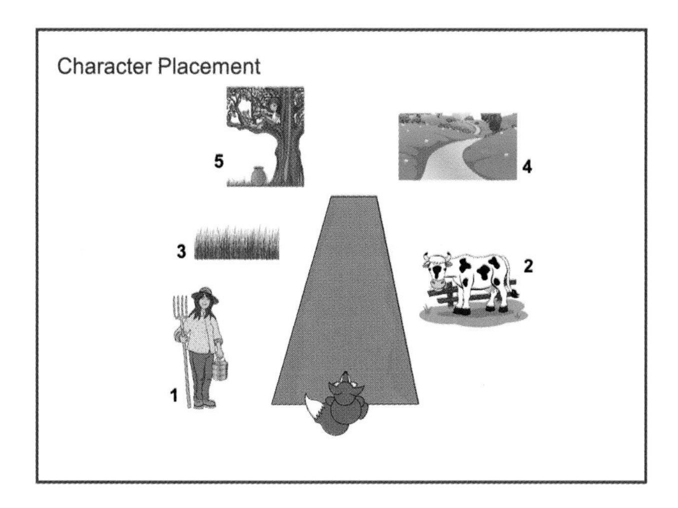

Verify students' answers to **Character Placement** in **Homework 12:3** with **Slide 1**.

INTRODUCE *Character Placement*

20–25 minutes

PRESENT
(LESSON SLIDE 12:4:2)

Show video **Placement 1: The Fox and the Cow** and have students rehearse the segment.

Be sure students as the fox:

- react first to seeing the cow before signing SEE
  - tilt their heads back when pointing to the cow down the road on their right
  - shift eye gaze back to the audience when signing COW
  - shift eye gaze and signs upward to the right when signing MEET and waving to get the cow's attention while showing the fox approaching the cow.

PRESENT
(LESSON SLIDE 12:4:3)

Show video **Placement 2: The Fox and the Grass** and have students rehearse the segment.

Be sure students as the fox:

- react first to seeing the grass before signing SEE
  - tilt their heads back when pointing to the grass down the road on their left
  - shift eye gaze back to the audience when signing GRASS
  - shift eye gaze and signs downward to the left when signing MEET and waving to get the grass's attention.

PRESENT
(LESSON SLIDE 12:4:4)

Show video **Placement 3: The Fox and the Stream** and have students rehearse the segment.

Be sure students as the fox:

- react first to hearing the stream before signing HEAR
  - tilt their heads back when pointing to the stream down the road on their right
  - shift eye gaze back to the audience when signing WATER ECL*"flowing"*
  - shift eye gaze and signs downward to the right when signing MEET and waving to get the stream's attention.

PRESENT
(LESSON SLIDE 12:4:5)

Show video **Placement 4: The Fox and the Girl** and have students rehearse the segment.

Be sure students as the fox:

- point to the left, with raised brows, at the location of the tree
  - shift eye gaze back to the audience when signing TREE
  - shift eye gaze back to the tree to sign [(wh)TREE/GIRL SCL:V*"girl sitting on branch"*]
  - look down to base of tree, react, and point to the jug
  - shift eye gaze back to the audience when signing DCL"jug"
  - shift eye gaze and signs upward to the left when signing MEET and waving to get the girl's attention.

PRESENT

(LESSON SLIDE 12:4:6)

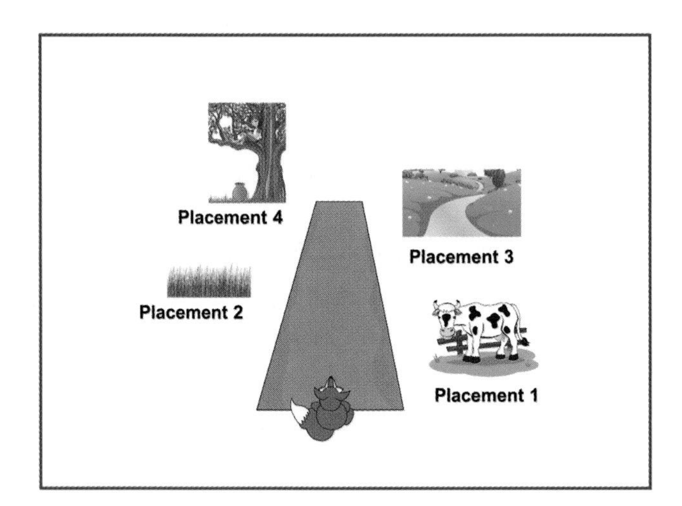

Pair Up. Have students retell **Placements 1–4** to each other.

Be sure students:

- react first before pointing
- point to show distance and location (head tilted back)
- look at audience when naming characters
- shift sign MEET and "waving" upward or downward to match the height and location of the characters.

Conclude. Have students take turns signing a segment to you.

HOMEWORK

Tell students to do **Homework 12:4** (*Student Workbook*, pages 405–406).

LESSON 12:5

"One Fine Day" Conditional Sentence and Agreement Verbs with Role Shift

Lesson length: 30–40 minutes

LESSON GOAL

Students practice using conditional sentences with role shift used in **One Fine Day**.

Students also practice using agreement verb GIVE-TO with role shift.

KEY SKILLS

For the conditional sentence:

- first, have the character react to the fox's request
- have the character tell what must happen first (conditional)
- then tell what it wants in return (nodding)

For the agreement verb GIVE-TO:

- maintain eye contact with the character they are addressing
- except to glance left or right when signing (2h)GIVE-TO
- orient (2h)GIVE-TO to match the locations and heights of the other characters
- end the requests by looking directly at the characters

NOTIONS

Grammar

Role shift
Conditional sentences
Agreement verb GIVE-TO
Spatial Agreement

MATERIALS

12:5 Lesson Slides

HOMEWORK 12:5

Student Workbook, pages 407–409

INTRODUCE *Conditional Sentence with Role Shift*

15–20 minutes

PRESENT

(LESSON SLIDE 12:5:1)

Show video **Conditional 1: The Fox and the Woman** and have students rehearse the segment.

Be sure students:

- as the fox, look up and orient their signs up to the left to the woman when making the request
- as the woman, look down and orient their signs down to the right when responding to the fox
- as the woman, shake head in response to fox's request
- then, sign the conditional clause with raised brows

  cond
  FIRST YOU you-GIVE-me MILK,
- and sign this with a nod

  nod
  me-(2h)GIVE-you fs-TAIL.

PRESENT
(LESSON SLIDE 12:5:2)

Show video **Conditional 2: The Fox and the Cow** and have students rehearse the segment.

Be sure students:

- as the fox, look up and orient their signs up to the right to the cow when making the request
- as the cow, look down and orient their signs down to the left when responding to the fox
- show the cow thinking while chewing, then checking the fox's missing tail
- then, sign the conditional clause with raised brows

  cond
  FIRST YOU you-GIVE-me GRASS,
- and sign this with a nod

  nod
  me-(2h)GIVE-you MILK.

PRESENT
(LESSON SLIDE 12:5:3)

Show video **Conditional 3: The Fox and the Grass** and have students rehearse the segment.

Be sure students:
- as the fox, look down and orient their signs down to the left to the grass when making the request
- as the grass, look up and orient their signs up to the right when responding to the fox
- show grass thinking while swaying in the wind
- then, sign the conditional clause with raised brows

  cond

  FIRST YOU you-(2h)GIVE-me WATER,
- and sign this with a nod

  nod

  me-(2h)GIVE-you GRASS.

PRESENT
(LESSON SLIDE 12:5:4)

Show video **Conditional 4: The Fox and the Stream** and have students rehearse the segment.

Be sure students:
- as the fox, look down and orient their signs down to the right to the stream when making the request
- as the water, look up and orient their signs up to the left when responding to the fox
- show water thinking while it's flowing by

- then, sign the conditional clause with raised brows

  cond
  FIRST YOU (2h)BRING-me DCL*"jug"*
- and sign this with a nod

  nod
  me-(2h)GIVE-you WATER.

INTRODUCE *Agreement Verbs with Role Shift*

15–20 minutes

PRESENT
(LESSON SLIDE 12:5:5)

Show video **Agreement 1: The Fox and the Cow** and have students rehearse the segment.

Be sure students as the fox:

- maintain eye contact with the cow on their right
- except to glance left and upward at the woman when signing (2h)GIVE-TO
- orient (2h)GIVE-TO upward to match the woman's height
- end request with looking directly at the cow.

PRESENT
(LESSON SLIDE 12:5:6)

Show video **Agreement 2: The Fox and the Grass** and have students rehearse the segment.

Be sure students as the fox:

- maintain eye contact with the grass on their left
- except to glance right and upward to the cow and then left and upward to the woman when signing (2h)GIVE-TO
- orient (2h)GIVE-TO upward to match the cow's and woman's heights
- end request with looking directly at the grass.

PRESENT
(LESSON SLIDE 12:5:7)

Show video **Agreement 3: The Fox and the Stream** and have students rehearse the segment.

Be sure students as the fox:

- maintain eye contact with the stream on their right
- except to glance left and downward to the grass, right and upward to the cow and then left and upward to the woman when signing (2h)GIVE-TO
- orient (2h)GIVE-TO downward and upward to match the grass', cow's and woman's heights
- end request with looking directly at the stream.

PRESENT
(LESSON SLIDE 12:5:8)

Rehearse these segments with your partner.

Agreement 1 – The Fox and the Cow
Agreement 2 – The Fox and the Grass
Agreement 3 – The Fox and the Stream

Pair Up. Have students take turns rehearsing **Agreements 1–3** with each other.

Be sure students as the fox:

- maintain eye contact with the character they are addressing
- glance left or right when signing (2h)GIVE-TO
- orient (2h)GIVE-TO to match the locations and heights of the other characters
- end the requests by looking directly at the character.

HOMEWORK

Tell students to do **Homework 12:5** (*Student Workbook*, pages 407–409).

LESSON 12:6

"One Fine Day" Instrument Classifiers with Role Shift

Lesson length: 30–40 minutes

LESSON GOAL

Students practice using instrument classifiers (ICLs) with role shift in **One Fine Day**.

KEY SKILLS

For each exchange:

- show the fox getting permission to begin the exchange (except with the girl and woman)
- use instrument classifiers to show how the object(s) are handled
- as the fox, thank the other character while holding the object with the other hand.

NOTIONS

Grammar

Instrument classifiers (ICLs) with Role Shift

Orienting eye gaze and signs to match the locations and heights of the characters

MATERIALS

12:6 Lesson Slides

HOMEWORK 12:6

Student Workbook, pages 410–414

REHEARSE *Agreement Verb*

15–20 minutes

Call on a student to sign the fox's request in **The Fox and the Girl** segment (See **Homework 12:5**, page 409).

Be sure students as the fox:

- maintain eye contact with the girl
- except to glance left or right when signing (2h)GIVE-TO
- orient (2h)GIVE-TO to match the locations and heights of the other characters
- end the request by looking directly at the girl.

Have the whole class rehearse any corrections you may give to the student. Then, divide the class into groups and have students take turns signing **The Fox and the Girl** segment to each other.

INTRODUCE *Instrument Classifiers with Role Shift*

15–20 minutes

PRESENT
(LESSON SLIDE 12:6:1)

Show video **Exchange 1: The Fox and the Girl** and have students rehearse the segment.

Be sure students:

- use role shift to show girl permitting the fox to take the jug
- use instrument classifier (ICL*"hold jug"*) with role shift to show the fox picking up the jug and holding it while thanking the girl for the jug
- show the fox running to the right side (toward the stream).

PRESENT
(LESSON SLIDE 12:6:2)

Show video **Exchange 2: The Fox and the Stream** and have students rehearse the segment.

Be sure students:

- use role shift to show the fox greeting the stream; then the stream giving permission for the fox to proceed
- use instrument classifier (ICL*"hold jug"*) with role shift to show the fox scooping water with jug; and holding it while thanking the stream
- show the fox running to the left side (toward the grass).

PRESENT
(LESSON SLIDE 12:6:3)

Show video **Exchange 3: The Fox and the Grass** and have students rehearse the segment.

Be sure students:

- use role shift to show the fox greeting the grass; then the grass giving permission for the fox to proceed
- use instrument classifier (ICL*"hold jug"*) to show the fox pouring water on the grass
- use role shift to show the grass growing, then telling it is ready for cutting
- use instrument classifier (ICL*"use blade"*) to show the fox cutting the grass
- use instrument classifier (ICL*"hold grass"*) to show the fox gathering and holding the cuttings while thanking the grass
- show the fox running to the right side (toward the cow).

PRESENT
(LESSON SLIDE 12:6:4)

Show video **Exchange 4: The Fox and the Cow** and have students rehearse the segment.

Be sure students:

- use *role shift* to show the cow giving permission for the fox to proceed
- use instrument classifier (ICL"*spread grass*") to show the fox spreading out the grass in front of the cow
- use role shift to show the fox asking the cow if it's ready and the cow replying yes
- use instrument classifiers to show the fox placing the items to milk the cow and to hold the pail while thanking the cow
  - (2h)ICL:C"*put down pail*"
  - (2h)ICL:A"*put down stool*"
  - (2h)alt.ICL:S"*squeeze teats*"
  - ICL:S"*pick up pail by handle*"
  - [(wh)ICL:S"*hold pail handle*"/ICL"*hold pail bottom*"]
- show the fox running to the left side (toward the woman).

PRESENT

(LESSON SLIDE 12:6:5)

Show **Exchange 5: The Fox and the Woman** segment and have students rehearse the segment.

Be sure students:

- use instrument classifier [(wh)ICL:S"*hold pail handle*"] with role shift to show the fox holding the pail while knocking on the woman's door
- use role shift to show the woman opening the door, and commenting that the fox has her milk

- use instrument classifiers [(wh)ICL:S*"hold pail handle"*/ ICL:B*"hold pail bottom"*] with role shift to show the fox handing the pail to the woman, and the woman taking the pail and setting it on the counter.

NOTE: Remember signs with role shift must match the heights and locations of the characters.

HOMEWORK

Tell students to do **Homework 12:6** (*Student Workbook*, pages 410–414).

LESSON 12:7

"One Fine Day" Story Cohesion

Lesson length: 45–65 minutes

LESSON GOAL

Students practice signing the opening and closing segments of **One Fine Day**.

Students also prepare to tell **One Fine Day** in its entirety.

KEY SKILLS

For the Opening:

- focus on the content
- focus on the expressions
- focus on tail cutting scene with emphasis on timing for dramatic effect
- focus on engaging the audience

For the Closing:

- maintain agreement among objects in the woman's space
- use ICLs to show how woman handle objects
- make direct eye contact with audience when giving final remarks

PREPARATION

Make copies of **12:7 Self-Evaluation** or **12:7 Evaluation** (for **Evaluation**, page 799).
Be ready to videotape students (optional, see page 799).

MATERIALS

12:7 Lesson Slides
12:7 Self-Evaluation
12:7 Evaluation

HOMEWORK 9:11

Student Workbook, pages 415–416

REHEARSE *The Exchanges*

15–20 minutes

Pair Up. Pair off students and have them sign the **Exchanges** to each other (See **Homework 12:6**, *Student Workbook*, pages 410–414).

Be sure students:

- role shift the fox greeting each character; then role shift the character giving permission to proceed
- adjust eye gaze and orient signs while role shifting to match the locations and heights of the characters
- use the correct instrument classifiers (ICLs) when giving and receiving the object
- hold the object in the other hand when saying "thank you"
- orient the sign RUN-TO to match the location of the next character.

NOTE: For a more detailed analysis of each segment, refer to *Student Workbook*, pages 410–416.

INTRODUCE *Opening and Closing*

15–20 minutes

PRESENT
(LESSON SLIDE 12:7:1)

Show video **Opening** and have students rehearse this segment four times. Each time show the video again and emphasize different aspects of the segment.

First time—focus on the content. Be sure students:

- role shift fox pointing to pail of milk in the distance (head tilted back)
- look at audience and tells what he sees (DCL*"pail"*)
- role shift fox walking to the pail, looking inside the pail, then looking at the audience to tell what is inside (FULL MILK), checking to see if anyone is around, drinking the milk, setting down pail, wiping his mouth.

Second time—focus on the expressions. Be sure students show:

- the fox feeling the sun rays (very hot)
- the fox feeling thirsty (parched)
- the fox walking toward the pail (excited)
- the fox realizing no one is around ("why not" attitude)
- the woman walking toward fox (angry)
- the fox apologizing (remorseful, with fear)
- the woman rejecting fox's apology (disgusted)
- the fox rubbing his rear after losing tail (painful)
- the fox asking woman for tail back (pleading).

Third time—focus on tail cutting scene with emphasis on timing for dramatic effect. Be sure students:

- show the woman shaking her head (to stretch the moment) before suddenly cutting off the tail
- show the woman quickly grabbing the fox's tail with her right hand and cutting the tail off with her left hand
- show the fox quickly reacting by rubbing his rear.

Fourth time—focus on engaging the audience. Be sure students make direct eye contact when signing these parts:

- ONE DAY FOX...
- each time FOX is signed
- introducing the pail
- FULL MILK
- shrugging (after looking in the pail)
- neg
NONE (after looking around)

conj
- WRONG (before woman comes).

Pair Up. Have students take turns signing the opening segment.

Be sure students:
- use facial expressions to convey attitude and feelings
- achieve effective timing in the "cutting tail" segment
- use eye contact with audience effectively.

PRESENT
(LESSON SLIDE 12:7:2)

Show video **Closing** and have students rehearse the segment.

Be sure students:
- role shift the woman
  - opening the cupboard and referring to the different tails on her left
  - getting and threading the needle on her left
  - turning to the right and instructing the fox to turn around with her right hand, while holding the needle in her left hand
  - using her right hand to sew while holding the tail in her left hand
- role shift the fox
  - receiving the tail (with left hand); and raising chest with each attempt to attach the tail
  - reacting with happiness and thanking the woman (looking up to the left) as he strokes his tail

- transition into closing remarks
  - use direct eye contact
  - FOX WALK++ SCL:1 *"walking down the road."* FROM-NOW-ON FOX NEVER STEAL MILK AGAIN.

Pair Up. Have students take turns signing this segment. Be sure students:

- maintain agreement among objects in the woman's space
- use ICLs to show how woman handles objects
- make direct eye contact with audience when transitioning into and giving final remarks.

PRACTICE *Rehearsing the Story*

15–25 minutes

PRESENT
(LESSON SLIDE 12:7:3)

Storyteller. Tell the story "One Fine Day" to two different students to get their feedback in writing.

Listeners. Write your feedback on the following (be sure to sign and date the paper):

- whether the story is clear, engaging, and easy to follow
- whether storyteller made good eye contact with the audience
- suggest two or three ways storyteller can improve.

Have students tell the story to two different students and get their feedback.

HOMEWORK

Tell students to do **Homework 12:7** (*Student Workbook*, pages 415–416).

EVALUATION

Have students present **One Fine Day** (See **Guidelines**, *Student Workbook*, pages 415–416). To evaluate their presentations, you have two choices:

As a Fluency Assignment

Have students video themselves and evaluate themselves with **12:7 Self Evaluation** (See **Materials**). Collect their videos and self-evaluations and give feedback. Grading is optional.

As an Exam

Videotape students presenting the story and grade using the **12:7 Evaluation** (See **Materials**).

LESSON 12:8

Fables: The Lion and the Mouse

Lesson length: 170–225 minutes

LESSON GOAL

Students learn to adapt **The Lion and the Mouse** into ASL.

KEY SKILLS

To describe characters' movements

- **role shift + BPCL***"feet and legs movement"*
- SCL:1 *"direction of character's movement"*
- combine ways to describe movement

To describe character interacting with object

- role shift+ ICL*"character handling object"*
- [(wh)classifier for object/SCL:V *"character interacting with object"*]

To describe contact between characters

- **use non-dominant hand to represent part of receiver's body, then show the initiator making contact with it**
- **role shift the receiver and show how the initiator makes contact**
- **role shift initiator making contact, then role shift receiver to show their response**

NOTIONS

Transition into moral

rhet

STORY POINT "what"...

Vocabulary

LION
MOUSE
LOOK-FOR

SLEEP
WAKE-UP
HUNGRY
ZOOM-AWAY
LATER-ON
ROPE
BE-STUCK
(2h)YELL++
!HEAR!
FLEE/ESCAPE
FROM-NOW-ON
BEST-FRIEND

PREPARATION

- Read **The Lion and Mouse** in the *Student Workbook*, page 417
- View the story **The Lion and the Mouse** on **Lesson Slide 24**.

It is recommended this lesson be divided into at least three class sessions.

Session 1 (60–85 minutes) pages 802–818
Focus:
Describing Characters' Movements
Describing Character Interacting with Object
Describing Contact between Characters

Session 2 (60–75 minutes) pages 818–824
Focus:
Translating Scenes

Session 3 (50–65 minutes) pages 824–828
Focus:
The Title, the Background and the Moral

MATERIALS **12:8 Lesson Slides**

HOMEWORK 12:8 *Student Workbook*, pages 417–432

INTRODUCE *Characters' Movements*

10–15 minutes

PRESENT
(LESSON SLIDE 12:8:1)

Adapting fables into ASL:
"The Lion and the Mouse."

Have students read **The Lion and the Mouse** in their workbook page 417. Introduce signs: LION, MOUSE

LION

MOUSE

PRESENT
(LESSON SLIDE 12:8:2)

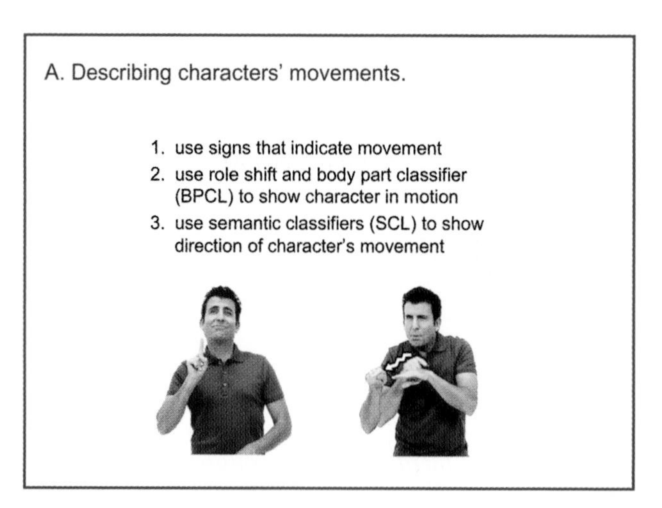
A. Describing characters' movements.
1. use signs that indicate movement
2. use role shift and body part classifier (BPCL) to show character in motion
3. use semantic classifiers (SCL) to show direction of character's movement

Introduce or review possible ways to describe the characters' movements.

FLEE/ESCAPE

For ***"1. use signs that indicate movement"***

Show signs:

WALK, RUN	**FLEE/ESCAPE**
COME-here	**ZOOM AWAY**
GO-TO	

ZOOM AWAY

For ***"2. use role shift and body part classifier (BPCL) to show character in motion"***

Explain that body part classifiers (BPCL) are classifiers that can be used to represent the character's leg or feet movements. Give examples:

(2h)BPCL:B(or fists)
"movement of front paws"

[LION] **(2h)BPCL:B(or fists)***"movement of front paws"*
(add manner, for example, sauntering)

[LION] **(2h)BPCL:V***"lying down"*

(2h)BPCL:V
"lying down"

[LION/MOUSE] **(2h)BPCL:V***"running"*

[MOUSE] **(2h)BPCL:X***"legs scurrying away"*

For ***"3. use semantic classifiers (SCL) to show direction of character's movement"***

(2h)BPCL:V
"running"

Explain that these semantic classifiers SCL:1 and SCL:1 (horizontal) represent the whole character (as opposed to parts), and show the direction the character is moving in. Give examples:

SCL:1*"moving forward"*

SCL:1(horizontal)*"moving from place to place"*

(2h)BPCL:X
"legs scurrying away"

SCL:1
"moving forward"

SCL:1(horizontal)
"moving from place to place"

PRESENT
(LESSON SLIDE 12:8:3)

Instruction. Identify which combination was used to show the character's movement—1, 2, or 3. Then rehearse the example.

1. use signs that indicate movement
2. use role shift and body part classifiers (BPCL) to show character in motion
3. use semantic classifiers (SCL) to show direction of character's movement

Review. Demonstrate the following and ask students which combination of 1, 2 or 3 was used. Then repeat the sentence and have students copy.

T: MOUSE RUN (2h)BPCL:X*"legs scurrying away"*
S: 1 and 2
T: (repeat the sentence)
S: (copy)

T: MOUSE RUN SCL:1(horizontal)*"moving from place to place"*
S: 1 and 3
T: (repeat the sentence)
S: (copy)

T: MOUSE (2h)BPCL:X*"legs scurrying away"* SCL:1(horizontal)*"moving from place to place"*
S: 2 and 3
T: (repeat the sentence)
S: (copy)

T: LION (2h)BPCL:B(or fists)*"movement of front feet"* (2h)BPCL:V*"lying down"*
S: 2 for both
T: (repeat the sentence)
S: (copy)

T: LION WALK SCL:1 *"down the road"*
S: 1 and 3
T: (repeat the sentence)
S: (copy)

PRACTICE *Describing Characters' Movements*

10–15 minutes

Students practice translating parts of the fable that involve characters' movements.

PRESENT
(LESSON SLIDE 12:8:4)

> *One day, a little mouse was busily searching for food.*

LOOK-FOR

Have students translate the underlined part of the sentence using at least two ways to describe the mouse's movement.

Possible Translation:

MOUSE [**LOOK-FOR** FOOD] RUN,
[or (2h)BPCL:V *"mouse running"*],
SCL1(horizontal) *"moving from place to place."*
or
MOUSE [LOOK-FOR FOOD] (2h)BPCL:V *"mouse running"*],
SCL1(horizontal) *"moving from place to place."*

PRESENT
(LESSON SLIDE 12:8:5)

….. (let) the little mouse escape.

Have students translate the sentence.

Possible Translations:

MOUSE, (2h)BPCL:X*"legs scurrying"* ESCAPE

or

MOUSE (2h)BPCL:V*"mouse running"* ZOOM-AWAY

PRESENT
(LESSON SLIDE 12:8:6)

The little mouse heard the lion's …roar and came to help.

Have students translate the sentence.

!HEAR!

Possible Translation:

MOUSE **!HEAR!** (glance at lion's location), RUN*"toward lion,"* (2h)BPCL:X*"legs scurrying,"* [or (2h)BPCL:V*"mouse running"*] SCL:1(horizontal)*"zigzagging toward lion"*

INTRODUCE *Characters Interacting with Objects*

10 minutes

PRESENT
(LESSON SLIDE 12:8:7)

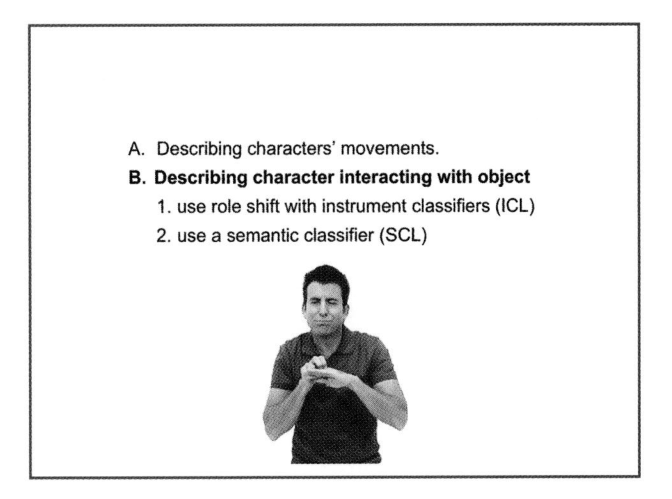

Review and introduce instrument and semantic classifiers.

For ***"1. use role shift with instrument classifiers (ICL)"***

Have students give examples of ICLs they may have learned in previous lessons. Be sure they use role shift with the ICL.

Examples:
from **Lesson 12:6 "One Fine Day"**
ICL*"holding jug"*
ICL*"cutting grass"*
ICL*"milking cow"*
ICL*"hold tail"*

from **Lesson 10:12 "The Missing Sandwich"**
ICL*"open refrigerator door"*
ICL*"opening drawers"*
ICL*"open car trunk"*
ICL*"open cabinet"*
ICL*"open purse, look in"*

For **"2. *use a semantic classifier (SCL)*"**

Demonstrate the classifier SCL:V used in conjunction with another classifier to show the character's interaction with the object.
Give examples:

"The dog sitting under the table"

- TABLE (t), #DOG **[(wh)LCL:B"*table*"/SCL:V"*sits under table*"]** (from **Unit 8, Lesson 10**, page 257)

"Do you prefer to sleep on your back or on your side?"

- SLEEP (t), YOU PREFER, **[(wh)LCL:B"*bed*"/SCL:V"*lie on back,*"** (lf) **SCL:V"*lie on side*"]** (rt), WHICH (whq) (from **Unit 10, Lesson 8**, page 559)

PRESENT
(LESSON SLIDE 12:8:8)

Instruction. Use the classifier(s) below to create different interactions between the character and the object.

1. use role shift with instrument classifier (ICL)
2. use a semantic classifier (SCL)

Review. Give students the pairs and have students create various possible interactions between the character and the object.

T: ***(Pair 4)* MOUSE, FENCE**

S: ***(possible interactions)***

FENCE, MOUSE ICL*"shaking fence"*

FENCE [(wh)LCL:4*"fence,"* MOUSE SCL:V*"climb over"*]

FENCE [(wh)LCL:4*"fence,"* MOUSE SCL:V*"walk on top"*]

FENCE [(wh)LCL:4*"fence,"* MOUSE SCL:V*"jump over"*]

FENCE [(wh)LCL:4*"fence,"* MOUSE SCL:V*"go through"*]

FENCE, MOUSE ICL*"grabbing and climbing up,"*
[(wh)LCL:4*"fence,"* SCL:V*"climb over"*]

T: ***(Pair 2)*** LION, TABLE

S: ***(possible interactions)***

TABLE, LION ICL*"move table to another location"*

TABLE, LION ICL*"shake table"*

TABLE, LION ICL*"put table on top of head"*

TABLE, LION [(wh)LCL:5*"table,"* SCL:V*"jump on top"*]

TABLE, LION [(wh)LCL:5*"table,"* SCL:V*"walk around on top"*]

TABLE, LION [(wh)LCL:5*"table,"* SCL:V*"lay under"*]

TABLE, LION [(wh)LCL:5*"table,"* SCL:V*"walk under"*]

T: ***(Pair 3)* MOUSE, CUP**

S: ***(possible interactions)***

CUP, MOUSE ICL*"drink from cup"*

CUP, MOUSE ICL*"pour out contents"*

CUP, MOUSE [(wh)LCL:C*"cup,"* SCL:V*"jump in"*]

CUP, MOUSE [(wh)LCL:C*"cup,"* SCL:V*"walk around top"*]

CUP, MOUSE [(wh)LCL:C*"cup,"* SCL:V*"jump over"*]

CUP, MOUSE [(wh)LCL:C*"cup,"* SCL:V*"bump into"*]

T: ***(Pair 4)* LION, fs-LOG DCL*"log"***

S: ***(possible interactions)***

DCL*"log,"* LION ICL*"lift log up"*

DCL*"log,"* LION ICL*"carry log on shoulder"*

DCL*"log,"* LION ICL*"drag on ground"*

DCL*"log,"* LION [LCL:1*"log"*/SCL:V*"jump over"*]

DCL*"log,"* LION [LCL:1*"log"*/SCL:V*"walk along on top"*]

DCL*"log,"* LION [LCL:1*"log"*/SCL:V*"jump up and down on top"*]

PRACTICE *Describing Character Interacting with Object*

10–15 minutes

Students practice translating parts of the fable where the lion and the mouse interact with an object (for example, the trap).

PRESENT
(LESSON SLIDE 12:8:9)

...the lion became caught in a trap. It roared and struggled...

Trap 1: net dropping down on the lion
Trap 2: net pulling lion up into the tree

Demonstrate translations for each of the two possible traps based on the written story. Have students copy.

Possible Translations:
For "***Trap 1: net dropping down on lion***"

DCL*"rope up front"*

LION <rs:lion BPCL ***"front legs walking"***

[(wh)LCL:1*"rope"***/ BPCL:fist***"paw touches rope"***]**

(2h)LCL:5*"net falls down on lion"*

[(wh)LCL:C*"net"***/ SCL:V***"lion struggling inside net"***]**

BCL*"lion struggling"*

(2h)alt.YELL++

For "***Trap 2: net pulling lion up into the tree***"

DCL*"net on ground"*

LION <rs:lion BPCL *"front legs walking"*

[(wh)ICL:C *"rope grab paw"*/ BPCL:fist*"paw"*]

(2h)LCL:5*"net folding up around lion"*

[(wh)LCL:C*"net"*/ SCL:V*"lion struggling inside net"*]

BCL*"lion struggling"*

(2h)alt.YELL++

PRESENT
(LESSON SLIDE 12:8:10)

[the mouse] saw the lion trapped in the ropes, and it busily went to work. It chewed on the ropes.

Trap 1: net dropping down on the lion
Trap 2: net pulling lion up into the tree

<rs:mouse ICL*"chew rope"*>

First, ask:

T: ROPE, MOUSE (2h)DO++ (t: ROPE; whq: MOUSE (2h)DO++)

S: MOUSE, **<rs:mouse ICL*"chew rope"*>** (t: MOUSE)

(2h)LCL:1 *"rope broke apart"*++

t whq

T: ROPE, "what" HAPPEN
S: **(2h)LCL:1*"rope broke apart"*++**

Now, have students translate the sentence on the slide.

Possible translations:
For "***Trap 1: net dropping down on lion***"

surprised

MOUSE LOOK-AT*"lion,"* RUN.

t

ROPE, **<rs:mouse ICL*"chew rope"*>**
(2h)LCL:1*"rope broke apart"*++

For "***Trap 2: net pulling lion up into the tree***"

surprised

MOUSE LOOK-AT*"lion,"* RUN.

t

[(wh)TREE/**SCL:V***"mouse scurrying up the tree, across the*

t

branch, and down the rope" ROPE, <rs:mouse ICL*"chew rope"*>
(2h)LCL:1*"rope broke apart"*++

NOTE: For Trap 2, the mouse must climb up a tree to get to the rope (trap) holding the lion—so the tree is added to the scene.

PRESENT
(LESSON SLIDE 12:8:11)

...the lion broke free from the trap and escaped.

Trap 1: net dropping down on the lion
Trap 2: net pulling lion up into the tree

Have students translate this sentence:

Possible translation (for both traps):

SCL:V *"lion jumps out"*

> [(wh)LCL:C*"net"*/LION SCL:V*"lion jumps out"*] FLEE/ESCAPE [or ZOOM-AWAY]

Be sure students' eye gaze is different for each trap:

- for ***Trap 1***—the eye gaze should be level with the ground as lion jumps up out of the trap
- for ***Trap 2***—the eye gaze should look down as lion jumps down to ground.

INTRODUCE *Contact between Characters*

10–15 minutes

PRESENT
(LESSON SLIDE 12:8:12)

A. Describing characters' movements.
B. Describing character interacting with object
C. Describing contact between characters (initiator and receiver).
Three ways to describe contact:

1. ***use non-dominant hand*** to represent part of receiver's body, then show initiator making contact with the body part
2. ***role shift*** the receiver and show how the initiator makes contact
3. ***role shift*** initiator making contact, then ***role shift*** receiver to show their response

Explain and give examples of the three ways to describe contact between characters.

For "***1. use non-dominant hand*** *to represent part of receiver's body, then show the initiator making contact with the body part*"

> Explain that the **non-dominant hand** can represent the receiver's back side, or body parts that are below the waist, for example, legs (or an animal's back legs), foot (or an animal's back paw), buttocks, or tail.

Also, explain that the initiator's contact can be shown with either BPCL or SCL:V. Give examples:

LION POSS*"lion"* fs-TAIL, (wh)BPCL:1*"tail on ground,"* [(wh) BPCL:1*"tail"*/MOUSE SCL:V*"lay on tail"*]

LION POSS*"lion"* fs-FOOT, (wh)BPCL:5*"foot off ground,"* [(wh)BPCL:5*"foot"*/MOUSE BPCL*"tickle bottom of foot"*]

For "***2. role shift** the receiver and show how the initiator makes contact*"

Explain that when you role shift the receiver, you can show the contact made to the receiver's head, face, chest, and arms (or an animal's front legs) only. Give examples:

LION SIT, MOUSE <rs:lion SCL:V*"mouse on lion's shoulder"*>

LION ICL*"brushing hair,"* MOUSE <rs:lion SCL:V*"mouse crawling into lion's mane"*>

For "***3. role shift** initiator making contact, then **role shift** receiver to show their response*"

Give examples:

t

MOUSE, LION <rs:lion (bending forward to kiss the mouse) BPCL:flatO *"lips puckered"*>, <rs:mouse (looking up) BPCL:flatO*"getting kiss on forehead,"* BPCL*"rubbing forehead"*>

MOUSE, <rs:mouse (looking up) BPCL:bentB*"tapping lion's leg,"* LION <rs:lion (looking away) BPCL:bentB*"feel tapping on leg,"* (looking down) *"wait a second"*

PRESENT
(LESSON SLIDE 12:8:13)

Instructions. Identify which way was used to show contact between characters—1, 2 or 3. Then rehearse the example.

1. ***use non-dominant hand*** to represent part of the receiver's body, then show initiator making contact with the body part
2. ***role shift*** the receiver and show how the initiator makes contact
3. ***role shift*** initiator making contact, then ***role shift*** receiver to show their response

Review. Demonstrate the following and students identify which way was used to show contact between characters. Then, repeat the examples and have students copy.

T: LION <rs:lion LOOK-AT*"other way,"* MOUSE BPCL:bentB *"lion's cheek being tapped"*>
S: 2
T: (repeat the sentence)
S: (copy)

T: LION POSS*"lion"* fs-FOOT, (wh)BPCL:5*"foot off ground,"* MOUSE [(wh)BPCL:5*"foot"*/BPCL:S*"head rubbing bottom of lion's foot"*]
S: 1
T: (repeat the sentence)
S: (copy)

T: LION <rs:lion READ, MOUSE SCL:V*"mouse jump off book and land on top of lion's head"*>
S: 2
T: (repeat the sentence)
S: (copy)

T: LION <rs:lion ICL:F*"pick up mouse and fling it"*>,
MOUSE <rs:mouse BPCL:arms*"waving arms as if trying to fly"*>
S: 3
T: (repeat the sentence)
S: (copy)

T: LION POSS*"lion"* fs-TAIL, MOUSE <rs:mouse ICL*"pull tail"*>, LION <rs:lion LOOK-AT*"behind at mouse,"* LAUGH>
S: 3
T: (repeat the sentence)
S: (copy)

T: LION (2h)BPCL:1*"legs outstretched,"* [(wh)BPCL:1*"leg"*/MOUSE SCL:V*"walk down one of lion's legs"*]
S: 1
T: (repeat the sentence)
S: (copy)

PRACTICE *Describing Contact between Characters*

10–15 minutes

Students practice translating parts of the fable that imply physical contact between characters.

PRESENT
(LESSON SLIDE 12:8:14)

...the mouse was running up and down and around a sleeping lion.....

Use the following to show the contact:

- ***use non-dominant hand*** to represent the lion's tail, then show the mouse getting on it
- ***role shift*** the lion sleeping and show the mouse moving around on the lion.

Have students translate the sentence.

Possible translation:

[(wh)BPCL:1 *"tail"*/ SCL:V *"walk up on lion's tail"*]

<rs:lion BCL *"head resting over paws"*/SCL:V *"mouse walk over lion's head and front paw"*>

Be sure students:

- use weak hand to represent lion's tail ((wh)BPCL:1) and use SCL:V to show mouse walking up the tail
- maintain lion's role shift when showing mouse (SCL:V) walking on lion's body.

PRESENT
(LESSON SLIDE 12:8:15)

The king of beasts grabbed the tiny mouse in its huge paw. The lion was about to swallow the poor mouse when the mouse said, "Please, let me go…"

Use the following to describe the contact between the mouse and the lion:

- ***role shift*** lion grabbing the mouse, then ***role shift*** mouse to show its response.

Have students translate sentence.

Possible translation:

LION WAKE-UP, <rs:lion **(wh)ICL:C→S*"clutch mouse and bring it closer"*>**

MOUSE <rs:mouse (2h)"wave-no" EAT ME. (2h)"wave-no">

NOTE: This translation "MOUSE <rs:mouse (2h)"wave-no" EAT ME. (2h)"wave-no"> for *"Please, let me go…"* makes the most sense as a response to the lion's attempt to swallow the mouse.

<rs:Lion (wh)ICL:C→S *"clutch mouse and bring it closer"*>

<rs:mouse (2h) *"wave no"*>

Be sure students:

- as the lion, use their weak hand to grab the mouse so the lion can sign to mouse before releasing it
- as the mouse, show its reaction.

PRACTICE *Translating "The Lion and the Mouse"*

60–75 minutes

Students examine the story scene by scene and practice translating the fable.

PRESENT
(LESSON SLIDE 12:8:16)

> **Scene 1**
> *One day, a little mouse was busily searching for food. It was running up and down and around a sleeping lion looking for scraps.*

Ask these following questions to help students develop the scene.

1. Why was the mouse looking for food?
   Possible answers. The mouse was hungry or the mouse has a family to feed
2. Why was the mouse not afraid of the lion?
   Possible answer. Probably because the lion was sleeping
3. Why did the mouse think the lion had food?
   Possible answer. The mouse smelled food coming from the lion or assumed the lion had food on its face and paws.

Pair up. Students practice translating the scene.

Possible translation:
ONE DAY, MOUSE !HUNGRY! LOOK-FOR FOOD, RUN SCL:1(horizontal)*"moving from place to place"*

SEE LION SLEEP, (2h)SCL:V*"lying down."* THINK MAYBE IX*"lion"* HAVE FOOD. RUN SCL:1(horizontal)*"running toward the lion"*

t t

fs-TAIL, MOUSE [(wh)BPCL:1 *"tail"*/SCL:V*"walk up lion's tail"*]
<rs:lion SCL:V*"mouse walk over lion's head and front paw"*>
<rs:mouse ICL*"pick up food scraps and eating"*>

PRESENT
(LESSON SLIDE 12:8:17)

Scene 2

Suddenly, the lion woke up. The king of beasts grabbed the tiny mouse in its huge paw. The lion was about to swallow the poor mouse when the mouse said, "Please, let me go and I will do something for you some day."

The lion was amused. "I don't know how you can help me," it said. "but I am not so hungry, you are only a tiny mouthful, and you have amused me."

And the lion let the little mouse escape.

Ask:

1. How would we translate ***"Suddenly..."***?
   Answer. !WRONG!

2. How would we translate ***"Please, let me go and I will do something for you some day."***?

   Possible translation:

   pleading

   <rs:mouse BCL*"pleading"* (2h)*"wave-no"* EAT ME (2h)*"wave-no."* MAYBE IN-FUTURE ME [IN-EXCHANGE], me-HELP-you>

3. How did the lion respond?

   Possible translation:

   q oo

   <rs:lion [(wh)ICL:S*"holding mouse"*/ YOU. DCL*"tiny thing"*

   laughing neg

   LAUGH. (pause) YOU !LUCKY!, ME NOT+HUNGRY>

4. What did the lion do?
Answer.
<rs:lion (wh)ICL*“release mouse”* GO-AWAY>

Pair up. Students practice translating the scene.

Possible translation:

!WRONG! LION WAKE-UP <rs:lion, (wh)ICL:C→S*“clutch mouse”* [or (wh)ICL:F*“grab by its tail”*]>

<rs:mouse MOUSE BCL*“pleading”* (2h)*“wave-no”* EAT ME (2h)*“wave-no.”* MAYBE IN-FUTURE ME [IN-EXCHANGE], me-HELP-you>

q oo
<rs:lion [(wh)ICL:S*“holding mouse”*/ YOU. DCL*“tiny thing”*
laughing neg
LAUGH. (pause) YOU !LUCKY!, ME NOT+HUNGRY,
ICL*“release mouse”* GO-AWAY>

MOUSE RUN, ZOOM-AWAY

Be sure students:

- hold mouse in their weak hands while role shifting the lion talking to the mouse with their dominant hands
- show characters’ emotions while role shifting.

PRESENT
(LESSON SLIDE 12:8:18)

Scene 3
Some time after that, the lion became caught in a trap.
It roared and struggled, but it could not escape.

Ask:

1. How do we translate ***"Some time after that"***?
   Answer. LATER-ON, NEXT+DAY, FEW-DAYS-LATER, or TOMORROW+MORNING

2. What are the two possible traps?
   Answer.
   Trap 1: net dropping down on lion
   Trap 2: net pulling lion up into the tree

3. Why did the lion get caught in the trap?
   Answer.

   ______________t ______neg
   for Trap 1: DCL*"rope up front,"* LION NOT+SEE

   ______________t ______neg
   for Trap 2: DCL*"net on ground,"* LION NOT+SEE

Pair up. Students practice translating the scene.

Possible translations:

For ***"Trap 1: net dropping down on lion"***

________t __t
LATER-ON, LION <rs:lion (2h)BCPL:fist*"sauntering"*

______________t ______neg
DCL*"rope up front,"* NOT+SEE <rs:lion (2h)BCL:fist*"sauntering"*
[(wh)LCL:1*"rope up front,"*/BPCL:fist*"paw touches rope"*],
(2h)LCL:5*"net drops down on lion"*>
[(wh)LCL:C*"net"*/SCL:V*"lion struggling on ground inside net"*]
BPCL*"lion struggling,"* (2h)alt.YELL++

______________neg
!BE-STUCK! CAN'T ESCAPE/FLEE

For ***"Trap 2: net pulling lion up into the tree"***

t t

LATER-ON, LION <rs:lion (2h)BCL:fist*"sauntering"* DCL*"net on*

neg

ground," LION NOT+SEE <rs:lion (2h)BPCL:fist*"sauntering"*
[(wh)LCL:C*"net"*/BPCL:fist*"paw got caught and pulled up"*]>,
(2h)LCL:5*"net folding up around lion"*
[(wh)LCL:C*"net"*/SCL:V*"lion struggling inside net"*].
BPCL*"lion struggling,"* (2h)alt.YELL++

neg

!BE-STUCK! CAN'T ESCAPE/FLEE

Be sure students:

- establish lion walking before describing how he got trapped
- role shift the lion struggling against the net.

PRESENT

(LESSON SLIDE 12:8:19)

Scene 4

The little mouse heard the lion's frightening roar and came to help. It saw the lion trapped in the ropes, and it busily went to work. It chewed on the ropes until the lion broke free from the trap and escaped.

Ask:

1. Where was the mouse?
   Answer.
   MOUSE IX-loc*"far away"*

2. How did the mouse know the lion needed help?
   Answer.
   LION (2h)YELL, MOUSE IX-loc*"far away"* !HEAR!

3. What did the mouse see?
Answer.
<rs:mouse: LOOK-AT-up,> SEE LION [(wh)LCL:C*"net"*/ SCL:V*"lion struggling inside net"*] <rs:lion BPCL*"lion struggling"*>

> **NOTE:** For the other trap that drops down, students need to keep the mouse's eye gaze and the sign LOOK-AT at eye level.

Pair up. Students practice translating the scene.
Possible translation:

Part 1:
MOUSE IX-loc*"far away"* LION (2h)YELL, MOUSE IX-loc*"far away"* !HEAR! RUN SCL:1(horizontal)*"toward the lion"*
rs:mouse: LOOK-AT(up or straight ahead), SEE LION [(wh)LCL:C*"net"*/ SCL:V*"lion struggling inside net"*] <rs:lion BPCL

surprised
"lion struggling"> MOUSE LOOK-AT*"lion,"* RUN-to-lion's lcoation

Part 2 for Trap 1:

t
ROPE, <rs:mouse ICL*"chew rope"*> (2h)LCL:1*"rope breaking apart"*++, (2h)LCL:C*"net opening up"* [(wh)LCL:C*"net"*/LION SCL:V*"lion jumps out"*] FLEE/ESCAPE [or ZOOM-AWAY]

Part 2 for Trap 2:

t
[(wh)TREE/SCL:V*"mouse scurrying up the tree, across the branch,*

t
and down the rope" ROPE, <rs:mouse ICL*"chew rope"*> (2h)LCL:1*"rope breaking apart"*++,(2h)LCL:C*"net opening up"* [(wh)LCL:C*"net"*/LION SCL:V*"lion jumps out"*] FLEE/ESCAPE [or ZOOM-AWAY]

Be sure students:

- name object (tree or rope) before describing action
- role shift character to show their actions (lion struggling and mouse chewing rope).

PRESENT
LESSON SLIDE 12:8:20)

Conclusion
Forever after, the lion and the mouse remained best friends.

Ask (and introduce signs if students are not familiar):

FROM-NOW-ON

1. How would we translate ***"forever after"***?
   Answer.
   FROM-NOW-ON

2. How would we translate ***"best friends"***?
   Answer.
   !BE-BEST-FRIEND!

!BE-BEST-FRIEND!

Pair up. Students practice translating the conclusion.

Possible translation:
FROM-NOW-ON, LION, MOUSE THEY-TWO !BE-BEST-FRIEND!

INTRODUCE *The Title, the Background and the Moral*

30–40 minutes

PRESENT
(LESSON SLIDE 12:8:21)

Title
The Lion and the Mouse

QUOTATION-MARKS

Explain and show how to present the title.

T: **QUOTATION-MARKS** fs-THE LION **AND** fs-THE MOUSE
S: (copy)

Have students rehearse the title. Be sure they:

- Sign or spell the title word for word starting from their non-dominant side to your dominant side.

PRESENT
(LESSON SLIDE 12:8:22)

Background
• establish setting
• character description
• other relevant information

Ask the following questions to help students expand on the written version by adding background to the fable.

For ***"• establish setting"***
Where did the mouse live?
Answer.
IX-loc*"there"* MOUNTAIN
or
IX-loc*"there"* TREE++ (recommended)

NOTE: The second character (lion) is usually described when it first appears in the story, which is during the body.

What did the mouse and lion look like?
Answer.
mouse—MOUSE DCL*"small"* GREY ALL-OVER,
BPSASS*"big ears, pointed face"* CUTE
lion—LION IX, YELLOW DCL*"body"* BROWN
DCL*"mane"* BIG-SHOULDERS, ARROGANT

For ***"• other relevant information"***
Why was the mouse looking for food?
Answer.
MOUSE HUNGRY, NEED FOOD

Pair up. Have students practice developing and signing the background.

Possible version:
For ***"• establish setting"***
IX-loc*"there"* TREE++, MOUSE LIVE IX-loc*"there"*
For ***"• character description"***
IX*"mouse"* GREY ALL-OVER, BPSASS*"big ears, pointed face"* [CUTE]
For ***"• other relevant information"***
MOUSE IX*"mouse"* HUNGRY, NEED ENOUGH FOOD.

PRESENT
(LESSON SLIDE 12:8:23)

Moral
Even the weak and small may be of help to those much mightier than themselves.

- begin with a transition
- give moral

Demonstrate phrase to use for ***"• begin with a transition"***

POINT

rhet
T: STORY POINT "what"

Have students share ideas for how to translate the moral, then you sign the translation below. Have students copy.

right-HELP-TO-left

rhet
T: STORY POINT "what," SUPPOSE PERSON IX*"left"*!STRONG!

BIG-SHOULDERS, OTHER PERSON IX*"right,"* SHORT-size,

cond
WEAK, IX*"left"* <rs:big person "pshaw"(*to weak person*),

neg nod
"wave-no." IX*"right"* CAN right-HELP-TO-left

S: (copy)

WRAP-UP *"The Lion and the Mouse" signed by John*

20–25 minutes

PRESENT
(LESSON SLIDE 12:8:24)

Show **The Lion and The Mouse.** Ask students to notice the details John adds to the story to make it more interesting.

For example:

- an animated description of the mouse's whiskers
- the lion's tail twitching (before the mouse jumped onto it)
- SCL:V*"mouse turning to look at the lion"* after being released and SCL:V*"mouse turning forward to run away"* after thanking the lion
- the mouse patting its tummy after eating
- the exaggerated response "wave-no" after mouse was caught by the lion

- used pauses for dramatic effect in dialogue (before the lion laughed at the mouse, and before the mouse made the proposition)
- described vividly how the lion was caught (turning around in the net as if in a vortex)
- described how wide the lion opened its mouth while roaring (BPCL*"showing its fangs"*)
- the lion's roar causing the trees to sway and the ground to shake
- the mouse feeling the vibrations of the roar, before hearing it
- when describing the mouse scurrying away, he used the "oo" expression (indicating smallness and quickness of the mouse)
- added the mouse's thoughts (lion may have food scraps on its mane and paws, and lion may need its help)
- added the dialogue between the lion and the mouse near the end (the lion thanking the mouse and the mouse saying "FINE++, GO-AWAY++").

HOMEWORK

Tell students to do **Homework 12:8** (*Student Workbook*, pages 417–432).

Also, have students tell the story to two different students and get written feedback from each. The feedback papers must have the students' signature. (See **Assignment**, *Student Workbook*, page 431.)

LESSON 12:9

Fables: The Fox and the Crow

Lesson length: 135–165 minutes

LESSON GOAL

Students learn to adapt **The Fox and the Crow** into ASL.

KEY SKILLS

For a character talking to themselves:

- **to describe a character's thoughts**, role shift that character looking at the subject of its thoughts, and externalize what it is thinking
- **to describe a character's intentions**, role shift that character and look at the audience while it describes its scheme

Integrate reactions after each comment by others

To describe an object passing between characters

- name character, tell what it was doing
- use conjunction
- name object, tell what happened
- name second character, tell what it did

NOTIONS

Transition into moral

rhet
LEARN LESSON "what"...

Vocabulary

BE-EXCEPTIONAL-IN
FLATTER
SHAMPOO
WEIGHT-DECREASE
SUPPOSE
NAME-you
QUEEN
BE-LET-DOWN
SOMETHING/SOMEONE
BELIEVE
TO-TRUST

PREPARATION

- Read **The Fox and the Crow** in the *Student Workbook*, page 433
- View the story **The Fox and the Crow** on **Lesson Slide 25**
- Make copies of **12:9A Evaluation** and **12:9B Evaluation** (for **Evaluation**, page 850)

It is recommended this lesson be divided into at least two class sessions.

Session 1 (75–90 minutes) pages 831–846

Focus:

Differences between **The Fox and the Crow** and **The Lion and the Mouse**

Describing a **Character Talking to Itself**

Translating Scenes in **The Fox and the Crow**

- role shift sequence (responses)
- object passing between characters

Session 2 (50–65 minutes) pages 846–849

Focus:

The Title, the Background and the Moral

MATERIALS

12:9 Lesson Slides
12:9A Evaluation
12:9B Evaluation

HOMEWORK 12:9

Student Workbook, pages 433–443

INTRODUCE *The Fox and the Crow*

10–15 minutes

PRESENT

(LESSON SLIDES 12:9:1–7)

Adapting fables into ASL

	The Lion and the Mouse	The Fox and the Crow
1. time frame:	two different days	________
2. characters:	Lion, Mouse	________
3. objects:	trap or rope	________
4. action or dialogue oriented?	action	________
5. physical contact?	yes	________
6. thoughts shared?	no	________

Have students read **The Fox and the Crow** on *Student Workbook* page 433. Then, have them tell how the story is different from **The Lion and the Mouse.** Confirm answers with **Slides 2–6.**

Teacher's Discussion Guide

For ***"1. time frame"*** (**Slide 2**)
Since the events in **The Fox and the Crow** all happened on the same day, there's no need for transitions like LATER-ON.

For ***"2. characters"*** (**Slide 3**)
Review the sign FOX. Since there is no specific sign for "crow," introduce it by fingerspelling fs-CROW, and/or describing it as BIRD, !BLACK! DCL*"big size of crow,"* then using only BIRD from there on.

For ***"3. objects"*** (**Slide 4**)
Review the sign CHEESE.

For ***"4. action or dialogue oriented?"*** (**Slide 5**)
If a character addresses the other character with a statement, comment or question, the storyteller must role shift the other character to show their response, reaction or action, to complete the role shift sequence.

For "*5. physical contact?*" (**Slide 6**)
In **The Fox and the Crow**, the characters do not have any physical contact with each other.

For "*6. thoughts shared?*" (**Slide 7**)
There are ways in ASL to show a character talking to itself as opposed to the character talking with someone else.

PRESENT
(LESSON SLIDE 12:9:8)

Describing a Character Talking to Itself

"Hey, I should have that cheese……he (the fox) said. …….I'll have it soon enough.

1. To describe a character's thoughts, role shift that character looking the subject of its thoughts and externalize what it is thinking.
2. To describe a character's intentions, role shift the character and look at the audience while the character describes its scheme.

For "*1. To describe a character's thoughts…*"
Demonstrate how to sign ***"'Hey, I should have that cheese…,' he (the fox) said"*** as a thought by:

- looking up at the crow in the tree
- simultaneously signing this phrase CHEESE IX*"cheese"* SHOULD !MINE! low and close to your body.

Then, demonstrate the same phrase but this time directly address the crow to point out the difference:

- look at the crow and lean toward it
- orient your signs higher and toward the crow while signing 'hey' CHEESE IX*"cheese"* SHOULD !MINE!

BE-EXCEPTIONAL-IN

NOTE: Be sure to glance at the crow with "GET" to agree with crow's location.

For "*2. To describe a character's intentions…*"
Demonstrate how to sign. ***"…I'll have it soon enough."*** as an intention by:

- looking at the audience with a scheming facial expression
- signing this phrase ME **BE-EXCEPTIONAL-IN** GET CHEESE. you-LOOK-AT-me

Pair up. Have the students practice both parts of the translation.

Be sure students:

- look up at the crow and sign low and close to body with CHEESE IX*"cheese"* SHOULD !MINE!
- look at the audience with a scheming look with ME BE-EXCEPTIONAL-IN GET CHEESE. you-LOOK-AT-me
- glance at the crow with the sign GET.

PRACTICE *Translating "The Fox and the Crow"*

65–75 minutes

Students examine the story scene by scene and practice translating the fable.

PRESENT
(LESSON SLIDE 12:9:9)

Scene 1
One day, while he was out walking, a fox saw a crow swoop down and pick up a piece of cheese in its beak. The crow then flapped its wings and flew up onto a high branch in a nearby tree.

Ask the following questions to help students develop the scene.

1. From the fox's perspective, where were the cheese, the crow and the tree located?

   Answer.

   - cheese on the ground in front of the fox (at a distance)
   - crow in the air swooping in from either side (or from behind)
   - tree located on the side opposite from where the crow entered the scene

2. How would we translate. ***"...a crow swoop down and pick up a piece of cheese in its beak"***

   Possible translation:

   BIRD <rs:crow BPCL*"flap wings"*>, SCL:1(horizontal)*"crow swoop down,"* BPCL:G*"beak clamping on the cheese,"* SCL:1(horizontal)*"go up"*

<rs:crow BPCL *"flap wings"*>

SCL:1(horizontal) *"swoop down"*

BPCL:G *"beak clamping on the cheese"*

SCL:1(horizontal) *"go up"*

Pair up. Students practice translating the scene.

Possible translation:

ONE-DAY, FOX WALK++ SCL:1(vertical)*"walk along"*

t

CHEESE IX-loc*"on ground in front of fox in the distance"*
BIRD BLACK <rs:crow BPCL*"flap wings"*> SCL:1(horizontal) *"crow swoop down,"* BPCL:G*"beak clamping on the cheese,"* <rs:crow BPCL*"flap wings"* SCL:1(horizontal)*"go up to tree"*

t

TREE, [LCL:arm*"tree"*/(wh)SCL:V*"crow alights on top of tree"*]

Be sure students:

- name object (cheese and tree) before telling what happened (the bird scooping up the cheese and landing on the branch).

PRESENT
(LESSON SLIDE 12:9:10)

Scene 2
"Man, that's a tasty looking piece of cheese," said the fox to himself.

Ask:

1. How would we translate ***"Man, that's a tasty looking piece of cheese"***?
   Possible translations:
   CHEESE IX*"cheese up in crow's beak"* FACE+GOOD
   CHEESE IX*"cheese up in crow's beak"* FACE+DELICIOUS
   CHEESE IX*"cheese up in crow's beak"* ME !WANT! EAT

2. How would we show the fox talking to himself?
   Best answer:
   Role shift the fox looking at the crow, and sign low, close to body to externalize what he is thinking.

PRESENT
(LESSON SLIDE 12:9:11)

Scene 3
"Hey, I should have that cheese. I'm the fox and I deserve it," he said. "I'm a sly, smooth talking fox too. I'll have it soon enough."

1. How would we translate ***"I'm the fox and I deserve it"***?
Possible translation:

rhet — arrogant

- <rs:fox WHY, ME FOX, ME "well">

> **NOTE:** It's important to show arrogant facial expression with "ME FOX, ME "well"" to give the impression of "I deserve it."

2. How would we translate ***"I'm a sly, smooth talking fox too. I'll have it soon enough"***?

Possible translations:

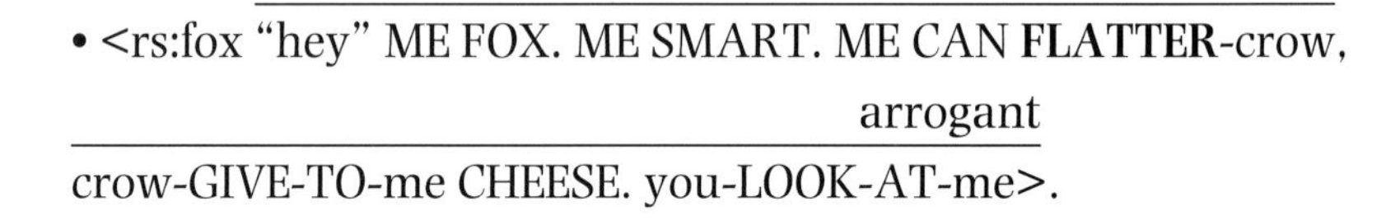

- <rs:fox "hey" ME FOX. ME SMART. ME CAN **FLATTER**-crow, crow-GIVE-TO-me CHEESE. you-LOOK-AT-me>.

arrogant

FLATTER

- <rs:fox "hey" ME FOX. ME fs-SLY. ME BE-EXCEPTIONAL-IN **FLATTER**-crow, crow-GIVE-TO-me CHEESE. you-LOOK-AT-me>

arrogant

> **NOTE:** It's important to show arrogant facial expression throughout this statement to establish the fox's arrogant character.

PRESENT
(LESSON SLIDE 12:9:12)

Scenes 2 and 3

"Man, that's a tasty looking piece of cheese," said the fox to himself. Hey, I should have that cheese. I'm the fox and I deserve it," he said. "I'm a sly, smooth talking fox too. I'll have it soon enough."

Pair up. Students practice translating the scene.

Possible translation:

<rs:fox CHEESE IX*"cheese up in crow's beak"* FACE+DELICIOUS.

"hey" ME FOX ME, "well." ME SMART. ME CAN **FLATTER**-crow,

arrogant

crow-GIVE-TO-me CHEESE. you-LOOK-AT-me>

Be sure students:

- as the fox, look up at the crow, and sign low, close to body when signing CHEESE IX*"cheese up in crow's beak"* FACE+DELICIOUS
- then, continue as the fox, look at the audience and maintain a arrogant and scheming attitude when signing <rs:fox "hey" ME FOX ME, "well." ME SMART. ME CAN **FLATTER**-crow, crow-GIVE-TO-me CHEESE. you-LOOK-AT-me.>

PRESENT
(LESSON SLIDE 12:9:13)

Scene 4

The fox walked over to the foot of the tree. "Hi ya, Miss Crow" cried the fox.

"How are you today?" asked the fox. "You're looking mighty fine. Is there something different about you? Have you changed shampoo?"

Ask:

1. How would we translate ***"'Hi ya, Miss Crow,' cried the fox"***?
   Answer.
   - exaggerate the sign '!HELLO!' to incorporate this meaning of "cried" (to call out loudly)
   - don't sign the part "Miss Crow." **Lesson 8:14** explains that name signs are not used in direct address.

2. How would we translate ***"You're looking mighty fine"***?
   Answer.
   YOU !FACE+GOOD! YOU FACE PRETTY

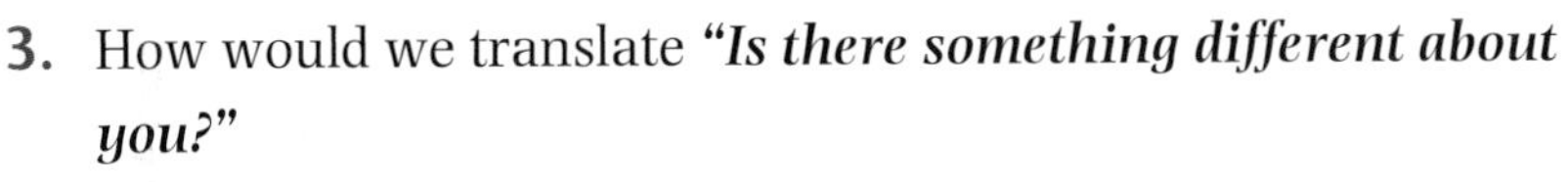

3. How would we translate ***"Is there something different about you?"***
   Answer.
   YOU LOOK !DIFFERENT!

SHAMPOO

4. How would we translate ***"Have you changed shampoo?"***
   Answer.
   q (over: YOU NEW SHAMPOO, YOU)
   YOU NEW **SHAMPOO**, YOU

> **NOTE:** The word "change" has several meanings in English. In this case, it means something new or different. So the best ASL translation would be NEW or DIFFERENT.

Pair up. Students practice translating the scene.

Possible translation:

whq (over: HOW YOU)
FOX WALK++, MEET-crow <rs: fox !HELLO! HOW YOU.
q (over: YOU NEW SHAMPOO, YOU)
YOU LOOK !DIFFERENT! YOU NEW **SHAMPOO**, YOU>

Be sure students:

- maintain a flattering attitude when role shifting the fox
- sign !HELLO! with an extremely big movement.

PRESENT
(LESSON SLIDE 12:9:14)

Scene 5
"Your feathers look so glossy and black and your eyes are sparkling like diamonds," said the fox, flattering the crow. "Hey, have you lost weight? Your figure looks great."

Ask:

1. How would we translate ***"Your feathers look so glossy and black and your eyes are sparkling like diamonds"***?
   Possible translation:
   <rs:fox YOU ALL-OVER*"body"* !BLACK!, **ECL*"shiny body,"*** !PRETTY!

   ______t

   YOUR EYES, **ECL*"shiny eyes,"*** SAME-AS **DCL*"big gem on ring"*** **ECL*"sparkling."*** !PRETTY!>

ECL*"shiny body"*

ECL*"shiny eyes"*

DCL*"big gem on ring"*

ECL*"sparkling"*

> **NOTE:** Exaggerate the facial expressions when signing PRETTY each time to show the fox is flattering and is not sincere.

Ask:

WEIGHT-DECREASE

2. How would we translate ***"Hey, have you lost weight? Your figure looks great."***?

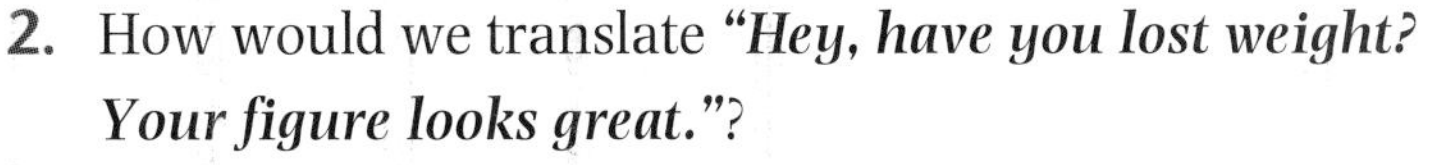

   ______________q ______________oo

   YOU **WEIGHT+DECREASE**. YOU DCL*"slim, shapely body"*

Pair up. Students practice translating the scene.

Possible translation:
<rs: fox YOU ALL-OVER*"body"* !BLACK!, ECL*"shiny body,"* !PRETTY!

______t

YOUR EYE, ECL*"shiny eyes,"* SAME-AS DCL*"big gem on ring"* ECL*"sparkling."* !PRETTY!

______________q ______________oo

YOU WEIGHT+DECREASE. YOU DCL*"slim, shapely body"*>

Be sure students:

- exaggerate their signs and facial expressions when role shifting the fox flattering the crow.

PRESENT
(LESSON SLIDE 12:9:15)

Scene 6
“Wow, if you can sing as good as you look then I'll have to call you Queen of all Birds” said the fox.

Demonstrate and have students copy:

exaggerated

T: <rs: fox“wow” YOU !PRETTY! “wow” **SUPPOSE** YOU

cond

CAN SING !PRETTY! EQUAL YOUR FACE, (nod)

exaggerated

FOR+SURE, ME **NAME-you** **!QUEEN!** ALL-OVER BIRD.

exaggerated

“come-on” SING BPCL:G*“open beak and sing”* “come-on”>

S(all): (copy)

SUPPOSE

NAME-you

!QUEEN!

Be sure students:

- exaggerate their signs and facial expressions when role shifting the fox flattering the crow
- raise brows when signing the conditional clause, then nod before signing what the fox will do.

PRESENT
(LESSON SLIDE 12:9:16)

Role Shift Sequence 1

1. *"How are you today?" asked the fox. "You're looking mighty fine. Is there something different about you? Have you changed shampoo?"*
2. ***(add Crow's reaction)***

[(wh)BCL *"fluff feathers"* / BPCL:G *"hold cheese in beak"*]

Have students sign the translation for Part 1 (the fox's line) to you. Then, you demonstrate the crow's reaction in Part 2.

S: (sign Part 1)
T: (demonstrate Part 2) [(wh)BCL*"fluff feathers"*/BPCL:G*"hold cheese in beak"*]

Switch roles. Role play the fox (Part 1) and have students practice the crow's reaction (Part 2).

PRESENT
(LESSON SLIDE 12:9:17)

Role Shift Sequence 2

1. *"Your feathers look so glossy and black and your eyes are sparkling like diamonds," said the fox, flattering the crow. "Hey, have you lost weight? Your figure looks great."*
2. ***(add Crow's reaction)***

Repeat procedure.

S: (sign Part 1)

T: (demonstrate Part 2) **[(wh)BPCL*"flutter eyelashes"*/**
BPCL:G*"hold cheese in beak"*] or **BPCL*"ruffle feathers"***

[(wh)BPCL*"flutter eyelashes"*/BPCL:G *"hold cheese in beak"*]

BPL*"ruffle feathers"*

Switch roles. Role play the fox (Part 1) and have students practice the crow's reaction (Part 2).

PRESENT
(LESSON SLIDE 12:9:18)

Role Shift Sequence 3

1. *"Wow, if you can sing as good as you look then I'll have to call you Queen of all Birds" said the fox.*
2. ***(add Crow's reaction)***

Repeat procedure.

S: (sign Part 1)

coyly/q

T: (Part 2) [(wh)ME"/BPCL:G*"hold cheese in beak"*]

or

coyly/nodding

[(wh)#OK/BPCL:G*"hold cheese in beak"*]

Switch roles. Role play the fox (Part 1) and have students practice the crow's reaction (Part 2).

PRESENT
(LESSON SLIDE 12:9:19)

Scenes 4-6

"How are you today?" asked the fox. "You're looking mighty fine. Is there something different about you? Have you changed shampoo?"

"Your feathers look so glossy and black and your eyes are sparkling like diamonds," said the fox, flattering the crow."Hey, have you lost weight? Your figure looks great."

"Wow, if you can sing as good as you look then I'll have to call you Queen of all Birds" said the fox.

Pair off students and have each student sign **Scenes 4–6**, role shifting between the fox and the crow.

Be sure students,
as the fox,

- maintain a flattering demeanor throughout

as the crow,

- maintain BPCL:G*"hold cheese in beak"* while gesturing or signing with the other hand
- limit the crow's reactions to one or two gestures or signs
- maintain a coy demeanor throughout.

PRESENT
(LESSON SLIDE 12:9:20)

Scene 7

Flattered by all the compliments from the fox, and wanting to be called Queen of all Birds, the crow lifted her head and began to sing.

But the moment she opened her mouth the cheese fell out, and the quick fox jumped and caught it before it hit the ground.

Object passing between characters

1. name character, tell what it was doing (*crow is about to sing*)
2. use conjunction
3. name object, tell what happened (*cheese falls out*)
4. name second character, tell what it did (*fox catches the cheese*)

Explain that for this part *"Flattered by all the compliments from the fox, and wanting to be called Queen of all Birds..."* it is an effective storytelling technique to integrate the crow's reactions earlier after each flattery (**Scenes 4–6**). The audience gets to experience the crow's growing pride, which brings into better focus the final act, which is the crow dropping the cheese.

Pair up. Students practice translating the rest of the scene following the sequence for "Object passing between characters."

For ***"1. name character, tell what it was doing"***

t (BIRD) / coyly (BPCL:babyO"open beak to sing")

BIRD, BPCL:babyO*"open beak to sing"*

For ***"2. use conjunction"***

conj (!WRONG!)

!WRONG!

For ***"3. name object, tell what happened"***

t (CHEESE) / open mouth/widen eyes (IX-dir"cheese falling out and falling to the ground")

CHEESE, IX-dir*"cheese falling out and falling to the ground"*

For ***"4. name second character, tell what it did"***

t (FOX) / determined (SCL:V"jumping high up in the air" ICL"catch the cheese")

FOX, SCL:V*"jumping high up in the air"* ICL*"catch the cheese"*

Be sure students:

- raise brows when naming the characters or the object
- open mouth and widen eyes while signing IX-dir*"cheese falling out and falling to the ground"*
- maintain a determined expression while signing SCL:V*"jumping high up in the air"* ICL*"catch the cheese."*

PRESENT
(LESSON SLIDE 12:9:21)

Scene 8
"Yes!!!" yelled the fox, holding the cheese up over his head as he did his victory dance. "I got what I wanted."

Ask:

1. How would we translate ***"Yes!!"***?
   Answer.
   (2h)"yeah" or any other gestures showing excitement (but ***not*** the sign YES)

2. How would we translate ***"...holding the cheese up over his head as he did his victory dance."***?
   Answer.
   excited
   ICL*"holding cheese up"* SCL:V*"hopping around"*

3. How would we translate ***"I got what I wanted."***?
   Answer. Since the idea is already shown when role shifting the fox being excited and holding the cheese proudly, there is no reason to state it again.

BE-LET-DOWN

4. How do you think the crow should respond as the fox hop around excitedly?
   Answer.
   looking down, feeling dejected
   BPCL:G*"beak,"* **BE-LET-DOWN.**

Pair up. Students practice translating the scene.

excited

<rs:fox [(wh)ICL*"holding cheese up"*/"yeah"] SCL:V*"dancing"*>

looking down, feeling dejected

<rs:crow BPCL:G*"beak,"* BE-LET-DOWN>

Be sure students:

- maintain demeanor of the fox (excited) and of the crow (dejected) while signing their lines.

INTRODUCE *The Title, the Background and the Moral*

25–30 minutes

PRESENT
(LESSON SLIDE 12:9:22)

Title
The Fox and the Crow

Review how to present the title.

- Sign or spell the title word for word starting from your non-dominant side to your dominant side.
- Begin with QUOTATION-MARKS.

Have students practice giving the title:

S: QUOTATION-MARKS fs-THE FOX AND fs-THE [BIRD] fs-CROW

NOTE: "Crow" does not have a specific sign, so use BIRD, then fingerspell fs-CROW to specify what kind of bird.

PRESENT
(LESSON SLIDE 12:9:23)

Background
- establish setting
- describe character
- other relevant information

Ask the following questions to help students expand the written version by adding background to the fable.

For ***"• establish setting"***
Where did the fox live?
Answer.
IX-loc*"far away"*
or
IX-loc*"there"* TREE++

For ***"• describe character"***
What did the fox and crow look like?
Answer.
fox—FOX GREY or RED ALL-OVER, BPSASS*"pointy ears,"* BPSASS*"snout,"* fs-TAIL DCL*"bushy tail"*
crow—BIRD BLACK DCL*"approx. 2 feet long"*

NOTE: Remind students that the second character (crow) is usually described when it first appears in the story, which is during the body.

For ***"• other relevant information"***
What are the fox's personal qualities?
Answer.
arrogant arrogant
SMART, BIGHEADED, MISCHIEVOUS

Pair up. Have students practice developing and signing the background.

Possible version:

IX-loc*"far away"* TREE++, FOX LIVE IX-loc*"there"*

IX*"fox"* GREY or RED ALL-OVER, BPSASS*"pointy ears,"*

BPSASS*"snout,"* fs-TAIL DCL*"bushy tail"* FOX IX*"fox"* SMART,

arrogant

BIG-HEADED, MISCHIEVOUS

PRESENT

(LESSON SLIDE 12:9:24)

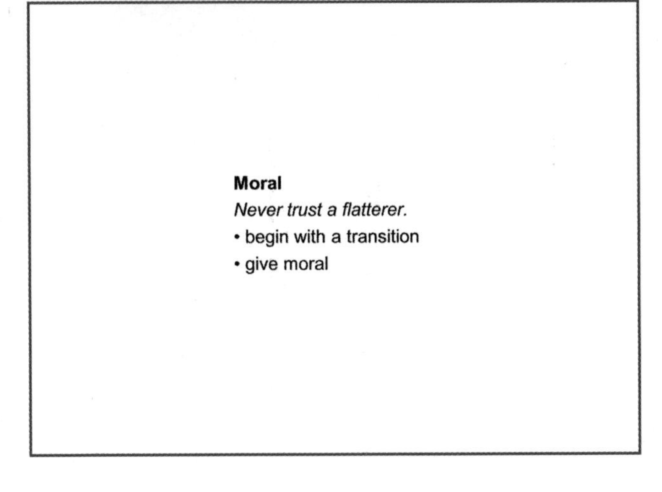

Moral
Never trust a flatterer.
• begin with a transition
• give moral

Introduce another phrase to use for "• begin with a transition".

rhet

T: LEARN LESSON "what"...

Have students share ideas for how to translate the moral, then you sign the translation below. Have students copy.

rhet cond

T: LEARN LESSON "what"... SUPPOSE PERSON FLATTER YOU,

nodding neg

[YOU] **BELIEVE TRUST-person**, "wave no"

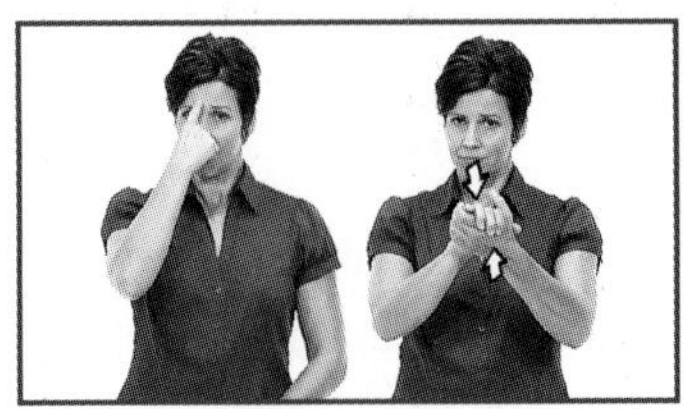

BELIEVE

TRUST

WRAP-UP *"The Fox and the Crow" signed by Terrylene*

20–25 minutes

PRESENT
(LESSON SLIDE 12:9:25)

Show **The Fox and The Crow**. Ask students to notice the details Terrylene adds to the story to make it more interesting.

For example:

- used facial expressions that enhanced the description of the fox
- described the fox seeing the cheese first, expressing desire to eat it
- used the sign !FINISH! to mean "for sure" or "there would be no question"
- added **BCL*"bow down"*** to describe what the fox will do when naming the crow the Queen of all Birds
- swayed her body when describing the fox's victory dance
- showed the fox eating the cheese (instead of holding it up in the air).

HOMEWORK

Tell students to do **Homework 12:9** *(Student Workbook*, pages 433–443).

Have students tell the story to two different students and get written feedback from each. The feedback papers must have the students' signature. (See **Assignment**, *Student Workbook*, page 442.)

Also have students prepare to tell either the **The Lion and the Mouse** or **The Fox and the Crow** for a grade (See **Evaluation** below).

EVALUATION

Videotape students signing either **The Lion and the Mouse** or **The Fox and the Crow**. Collect the videos, along with the student feedback papers, and grade them using the **12:9A Evaluation** for **The Lion and the Mouse**, or **12:9B Evaluation** for **The Fox and the Crow** (See **Materials**).

LESSON 12:10

Fables: Telling Your Assigned Fable

Lesson length: 145–195 minutes

LESSON GOAL

Students use language elements to adapt an assigned fable successfully.

KEY SKILLS

- describe characters
- describe movements
- describe interactions with objects or other characters
- describe character talking to self
- create relevant background to fable

NOTIONS

Grammar

- BPSASS*"part of body"* and BPCL*"part of body movement"*
- SCL*"whole body moving"*
- ICL*"handling object"*
- conditional or when clause (for Moral)

Vocabulary

BUG
FOX
BIRD
SCORPION
FROG
GOAT
#DOG
WOLF
BABY GOAT

PREPARATION

- Familiarize yourself with all worksheets, *Student Workbook*, pages 449–466
- Determine the date of students' presentations of their assigned fables (See *Student Workbook*, page 444)
- Make copies of **12:10 Student Feedback** and **12:10 Evaluation** (for **Evaluation**, page 877)

It is recommended this lesson be divided into five class sessions.

Session 1 (55–70 minutes) pages 853–859

Focus:

Titles for Assigned Fables

Character Descriptions

Characters' Movements

Session 2 (60–75 minutes) pages 860–868

Focus:

Interactions with Objects and Characters

Session 3 (50–75 minutes) pages 869–876

Focus:

Character Talking to Itself

The Background and the Moral

Session 4 and 5 (5–7 minutes per student) pages 876–877

Focus:

Rehearsing and Presenting the Fables

Be ready to videotape students.

MATERIALS

12:10 Lesson Slides

12:10 Student Feedback

12:10 Evaluation

Worksheet: The Ant and the Grasshopper, *Student Workbook*, pages 449–451

Worksheet: The Wolf and the Kid, *Student Workbook*, pages 452–454

Worksheet: The Fox and the Stork, *Student Workbook*, pages 455–457

Worksheet: The Dog and the Wolf, *Student Workbook*, pages 458–460

Worksheet: The Scorpion and the Frog, *Student Workbook*, pages 461–463

Worksheet: The Fox and the Goat, *Student Workbook*, pages 464–466

HOMEWORK 12:10

Student Workbook, pages 444–448

INTRODUCE *Titles for Assigned Fables*

15–20 minutes

PRESENT
(LESSON SLIDE 12:10:1)

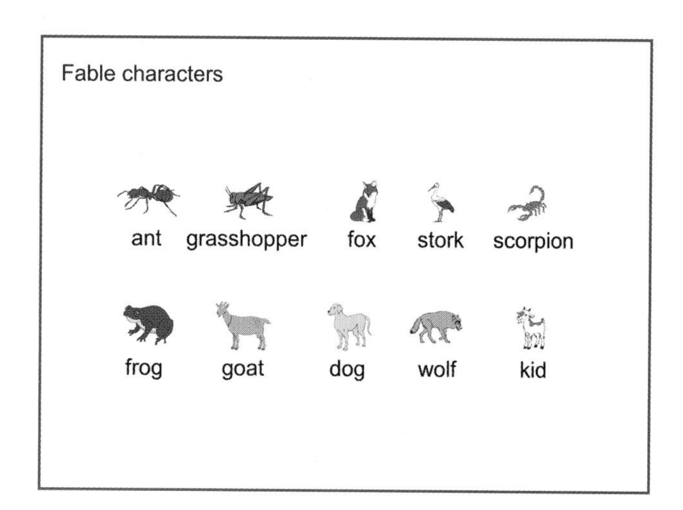

BUG

FOX

BIRD (stork)

SCORPION

FROG

GOAT

Introduce the signs for names of characters.
Use regional signs, if any.

Ant	sign BUG, spell fs-ANT to specify
Grasshopper	spell fs-GRASSHOPPER
Fox	sign FOX
Stork	spell fs-STORK, sign BIRD
Scorpion	sign SCORPION
Frog	sign FROG
Goat	sign GOAT
Dog	sign #DOG
Wolf	sign WOLF
Kid	spell fs-KID, sign BABY GOAT

#DOG

WOLF

BABY GOAT (kid)

PRESENT
(LESSON SLIDE 12:10:2)

1. The Ant and the Grasshopper, *Student Workbook,* pages 449-451
2. The Wolf and the Kid, *Student Workbook,* pages 452-454
3. The Fox and the Stork, *Student Workbook,* pages 455-457
4. The Dog and the Wolf, *Student Workbook,* pages 458-460
5. The Scorpion and the Frog, *Student Workbook,* pages 461-463
6. The Fox and the Goat, *Student Workbook,* pages 464-466

Divide class into six groups. Assign each group a fable and have them fill in the name and date of their presentations in Workbook, page 444. Have them go to the worksheet for their assigned fable and read the fable.

Giving the Title. Have students give the titles for their assigned fables. Be sure they translate the title word for word from their non-dominant side to their dominant side.

Go to each group and have one person from the group sign the title. Then, have the whole group practice the corrections, if any.

INTRODUCE *Character Description*

20–25 minutes

PRESENT
(LESSON SLIDE 12:10:3)

Character Description

- Name the character.
- Identify three or four distinctive physical features and order them from general to specific.

Features to consider:
- coloring
- facial or head features (ears, horns or antennas, eyes, muzzle or beak)
- size (large or small, husky or skinny)
- tail type (bushy, thin, stinger)
- characteristic movements (how character walks or moves its head or tail)

Demonstrate how to describe a character. Begin by describing one character from each of the assigned fables. Have students copy.

The Ant

T: ANT or BUG, DCL*"tiny size"* BPCL:1*"antennae"* BPCL:X*"mandible,"* BODY STRONG

S: (copy)

The Wolf

T: WOLF, IX*"wolf"* GREY BCL*"all over,"* BPCL*"pointy ears,"* EYE BPCL:F*"small eyes,"* TEETH BPCL:claw*"big teeth"*

S: (copy)

The Fox

T: FOX, DCL*"pointy ears,"* DCL*"pointed snout,"* fs-TAIL DCL*"bushy tail"*

S: (copy)

The Scorpion

T: SCORPION, BPCL:V*"claws,"* BPCL:4*"rows of legs,"* BPCL:X*"stinger moving"*

S: (copy)

EXERCISE 1: Character Description

Have students go to their assigned fable groups and develop the description for their second character (*Student Workbook*, pages 449, 452, 455, 458, 461 or 464). Make sure they incorporate the signs or classifiers from their worksheets.

Conclude. Have one person from each group describe their second character. Make suggestions if needed. Then, have the group practice the description again with the suggested changes.

Teacher's Guide

The Grasshopper **(The Ant and the Grasshopper)**

fs-GRASSHOPPER, GREEN DCL*"all over,"* BPCL:C*"bulging eyes"* (2h)BPCL:1*"antennae"*

The Kid **(The Wolf and the Kid)**
BABY GOAT, DCL*"small size,"* BPCL*"short horns,"* (2h)BPCL:V*"frolicking"*

The Stork **(The Fox and the Stork)**
BIRD WHITE BCL*"all over,"* BPSASS*"long neck,"* BPSASS*"long bill"*

The Dog **(The Dog and the Wolf)**

#DOG, BROWN DCL*"all over,"* BPSASS*"pointed ears"* CHUBBY (mm)

The Frog **(The Scorpion and the Frog)**
FROG SCL:V*"sitting on ground,"* (2h)BPCL:C*"bulging eyes,"* BPCL*"throat croaking"*

The Goat **(The Fox and the Goat)**
GOAT, BROWN DCL*"all over,"* BPCL*"horns"* BPCL*"long goatee"*

REVIEW *Character's Movement*

20–25 minutes

PRESENT
(LESSON SLIDE 12:10:4)

Character's Movement

Three ways to show a character's movement.

1. use signs that indicate movement
2. use role shift and body part classifier (BPCL) to show character in motion
3. use semantic classifiers (SCL) that show the direction of character's movement

Use a combination of at least two ways when describing a character's movement.

Pick one of the above ways to describe a movement. Have students create combinations by repeating and adding another way. For example.

T: SCL:1*"walking forward"*
S: SCL:1*"walking forward,"* ZOOM-AWAY*"slowly"*

T: RUN
S: RUN, SCL:1(horizontal)*"from place to place"*

T: BPCL*"flapping wings"*
S: BPCL*"flapping wings,"*
SCL:1(horizontal)*"swooping through the air"*

Continue with these:
FLEE/ESCAPE
DANCE
BPCL:X*"legs scurrying away"*
BPCL*"swimming with breast strokes"*
(2h)SCL:1(horizontal)*"2 animals walking side by side"*
SCL:V*"hopping on ground"*
(2h)SCL:V*"trotting along"*

EXERCISE 2: Character's Movement

Have students go to their assigned fable groups and translate the excerpts on their worksheets. (*Student Workbook*, pages 450, 453, 456, 459, 462 or 465). Make sure they incorporate the signs or classifiers from their worksheets.

Conclude. Have each group show you their translations. Make suggestions if needed (See guide below). Then, have the group practice the translations again with the suggested changes.

Teacher's Guide

From **The Ant and the Grasshopper**

For ***"a) a grasshopper was ...hopping about."***
fs-GRASSHOPPER PLAY++ [(wh)LCL:B*"ground"*/
SCL:V*"hop around"*]

For ***"b) He saw an ant who was busy gathering and storing grain..."***
SEE ANT BUSY BRING-TO++ FOOD SCL:1(horizontal)*"walking back and forth"*

For *"c) ...the grasshopper continued to dance..."*
fs-GRASSHOPPER *"pshaw"*(to ant), PLAY++ DANCE++

For *"d) ...and the ant continued to work."*
ANT LOOK-AT-grasshopper *"pshaw"*(to grasshopper), WORK++,
BRING-TO++ SCL:1(horizontal)*"walking back and forth"*

For *"e) He (grasshopper) went to the ant's house..."*
fs-GRASSHOPPER GO-TO ANT HOUSE, (2h)BPCL:X*"hopping,"*
BCL*"knocking on door"*

From **The Wolf and the Kid**

For *"a) A wolf was chasing a young kid"*

scared

WOLF CHASE, GOAT RUN++, (2h)BPCL:X*"legs running"*

For *"b) ...so it (the kid) turned to the wolf"*
[GOAT] (2h)BPCL:X*"legs running,"* STOP, LOOK-AT-behind

For *"c) ...and the kid danced"*
GOAT (2h)SCL:bentV*"hopping/dancing"* DANCE++

For *"d) (dogs) came after the wolf"*

lf

#DOG... RUN, PCL*"flock toward wolf"* WOLF <rs:wolf ICL
"playing the flute" SEE-dogs PCL*"dogs flock toward me(wolf)"*>

For *"e) ...the wolf escaped..."*
WOLF RUN, [FLEE/ESCAPE] BPCL:X*"legs running"*
ZOOM-AWAY

From **The Fox and the Stork**

For *"a) (stork) come to its (fox's) house"*
BIRD*"stork"* [BPCL"flapping wings"] GO-TO-fox's house FOX
POSS*"fox"* HOUSE

For *"b) ...stork...went home"*

angry

BIRD LEAVE-FOR HOME, [BPCL*"flapping wings"*]

For ***"c)...the fox received an invitation from the stork. (the fox went to the stork's house)"***
FOX [WALK] GO-TO-stork's house BIRD POSS*"stork"* HOUSE

From **The Dog and the Wolf**

For ***"a)...house-dog who was passing by (the wolf)."***
WOLF WALK++ SEE IX*"dog"* #DOG, SCL:1*"approach me"*

For ***"b)...the wolf and the dog went toward the town together."***
WOLF, #DOG WALK++ (2h)SCL:1horizontal*"go together"*

For ***"c)...the wolf quickly turned around and ran back to the forest."***
WOLF (2h)BPCL:X*"legs running,"* ZOOM-AWAY

From **The Scorpion and the Frog**

For ***"a)...meet on the bank of a stream"***
SCORPION SEE IX*"frog"* FROG, SCL:1*"approach frog"*

For ***"b)...and they set out."***
FROG SCL:bentV*"jump into water"* BPCL*"swim"*

For ***"c)...and starts to sink..."***
(2h)SCL:V*"both animals floating down together"*

From **The Fox and the Goat**

For ***"a) A fox one day fell into a well..."***
FOX [(wh)LCL:C*"well"*/SCL:V*"fall down"*]

For ***"b) A goat...came to the same well,"***
GOAT [WALK++] GO-TO [(wh)LCL:C*"well"*/LOOK-AT-inside well]

For ***"c) The goat... thoughtlessly jumped down"***
GOAT [(wh)LCL:C*"well"*/SCL:V*"jump inside"*]

For ***"d) fox...made off as fast as he could."***
(2h)SCL:bentV*"running"* FLEE/ESCAPE or (ZOOM-AWAY)

INTRODUCE *Interactions with Objects and Characters*

60–75 minutes

PRESENT
(LESSON SLIDE 12:10:5)

Interactions with Objects and Characters

Ways to describe characters interacting with an object.

1. character's "hands" interacting with object (ICL)
   - fox handling a basket
   - lion handling a pencil

Have students describe different ways for a ***"• fox handling a basket."***

Possible descriptions:

- fox carries basket by handles
- fox carries basket on head
- fox drags basket from behind
- fox hugs basket
- fox empties out basket

Do same for ***"• lion handling a pencil."***

Possible descriptions:

- lion takes pencil out of shirt pocket and writes
- lion takes pencil out from behind ear and breaks it
- lion takes pencil out of pants pocket and sharpens it
- lion picks up pencil and throws it

Be sure students:

- name the object or character before describing the action
- role shift fox or lion
- refer to object with eye gaze
- show handling object with appropriate "size and scale."

PRESENT
(LESSON SLIDE 12:10:6)

Interactions with Objects and Characters

Ways to describe characters interacting with an object.

1. character's "hands" interacting with object (ICL)
2. character's "mouth" interacting with object (BPCL)
   - bird or dog drinking out of a bowl
   - bird or dog eating off a plate

Demonstrate describing a character's mouth interacting with an object. Be sure to match your mouth's movements with the BPCL's movements.

For ***"• bird drinking out of a bowl"***

[(wh)LCL:C *"bowl"*/

BPCL:G *"bird*
mouth open/close
drinking from bowl"]

t

T: BOWL, [(wh)LCL:C*"bowl"*/WATER IX-loc*"inside bowl"*], BIRD [(wh)LCL:C*"bowl"*/BPCL:G*"bird scoops up water with beak, swallows it down"*]
S: (copy)

Be sure students' mouth movements match the movement of the bird's beak.

For ***"• dog drinking out of a bowl"***

t

T: BOWL, [(wh)LCL:C*"bowl"*/WATER IX-loc*"inside bowl"* #DOG BPCL:U*"dog licks water from bowl"*]
S: (copy)

(wh)LCL:C *"bowl"*/
BPCL:U *"dog licking water from bowl"*

Be sure students' tongue (licking) movements match the movement of the dog licking the water.

(wh)LCL:B *"plate"*/
BIRD BPCL:G *"picking up food from plate"*

For "• ***bird eating off a plate***"

t

T: PLATE, [(wh)LCL:B *"plate"*/FOOD DCL *"pile of food on plate,"*
BIRD BPCL:G *"picking up food from plate"*

S: (copy)

Be sure students' mouth movements match the movement of the bird's beak.

(wh)LCL:B *"plate"*/
#DOG BPCL:U *"eating off the plate"*

For "• ***dog eating off a plate***"

t

T: PLATE, [(wh)LCL *"plate"*/FOOD DCL *"pile of food on plate"*],
#DOG BPCL:U *"eating off the plate"*

S: (copy)

Be sure students' mouth (eating) movements match the movement of the dog eating the food.

PRESENT
(LESSON SLIDE 12:10:7)

Interactions with Objects and Characters

Ways to describe characters interacting with an object.

1. character's "hands" interacting with object (ICL)
2. character's "mouth" interacting with object (BPCL)
3. object being put on character, describe effect of removal
   - a crown placed on the frog's head
   - a piece of tape put on a goat's chest

Have students describe the objects being put on the character. Then, you describe the effect of removal. Have students repeat the complete description.

For **“• *a crown placed on a frog’s head*”**

S: DCL*“crown”* FROG, ICL*“put on head”* (nonmanual marker: t)

T: (**describe effect of removal** – red mark on forehead)

DCL*“crown”* FROG ICL*“put on head.”* FINISH, ICL*“take crown off,”* **RED DCL*“strip across forehead”*** (nonmanual markers: t, when)

S: (repeat complete description)

For **“• *a piece of tape put on a goat’s chest*”**

S: TAPE, GOAT, ICL*“put on chest”* (nonmanual marker: t)

T: (**describe effect of removal** – bare strip across chest)

TAPE, GOAT ICL*“put on chest.”* FINISH, ICL*“take tape off,”* (nonmanual markers: t, when)

ECL:open8 *“bare strip across chest”* (nonmanual marker: oo)

S: (repeat complete description)

PRESENT
(LESSON SLIDE 12:10:8)

Interactions with Objects and Characters

Ways to describe characters interacting with an object.

1. character’s “hands” interacting with object (ICL)
2. character’s “mouth” interacting with object (BPCL)
3. object being put on character, describe effect of removal
4. character getting in or on object (SCL:V)
   - bird and a fence
   - wolf and a chair
   - goat and a board leaning on the wall

Have students describe different possible ways the characters can get in or on their objects.

For **“• *bird and a fence*”**

- bird flies and alights on the fence
- bird flies over the fence
- bird flies and hits the fence
- bird hops along top of fence
- etc.

For "• *wolf and a chair*"

- wolf jumps up and down on chair
- wolf lies under the chair
- wolf goes under the chair
- etc.

For "• *goat and a board leaning on the wall*"

- goat walks up the board and jumps over the end
- goat goes under the board
- goat hops down the board to the ground
- etc.

Be sure students:

- name the object or character before describing the action
- role shift the character
- use weak hand to represent the object during the interaction.

PRESENT

(LESSON SLIDE 12:10:9)

Ways to describe contact between characters
(initiator and receiver):

1. use non-dominant hand to represent part of receiver's body then show the initiator making contact with the body part
2. role shift the receiver and show how the initiator makes contact
3. role shift initiator making contact, then role shift receiver to show their response

Sentence A.
"The lion set out with the mouse on its back..."
Sentence B.
"...the mouse got the lion's attention..."

Ask students to translate **Sentence A** using:

1. ***use non-dominant hand to represent part of receiver's body, then show the initiator making contact with it***

NOTE: This way presents the information from the narrator's point of view, meaning role shifting is not used.

t (over LION (2h)SCL:V"standing"), t (over [POSS] fs-BACK)

S: LION (2h)SCL:V"*standing*" [POSS] fs-BACK, MOUSE [(wh)BPCL:B"*lion's back*"/SCL:V"*mouse lands on lion's back*"]

Ask students to translate **Sentence A** again using:

2. ***role shift the receiver and show how the initiator makes contact***

t t

S: LION (2h)SCL:V*"standing"* MOUSE <rs:lion SCL:V*"mouse jumps on lion's back"*>

> **NOTE:** This way presents the information from the lion's point of view, using role shift as opposed to the narrator's view used with number 1.

Now, ask students to translate **Sentence B** using:

3. ***role shift initiator making contact, then role shift receiver to show their response***

t

S: LION WALK (2h)SCL:V*"walking,"* MOUSE <rs:mouse ICL*"mouse holds lion's mane,"* BPCL*"taps lion"*>

whq

LION <rs:lion LOOK-AT-mouse-on-its-back WHATS-MATTER>.

> **NOTE:** For every action or comment made by one character, a response from the other character is needed. It can be a comment or action.

EXERCISE 3:
Interactions with Objects and Characters

Have students go to their assigned fable groups and translate the excerpts on their worksheets. (*Student Workbook*, pages 451, 453, 456, 459, 462 or 465). Make sure they incorporate the signs or classifiers from their worksheets.

Conclude. Have each group show you their translations. Make suggestions if needed (see guide next page). Then, have the group practice the translations again with the suggested changes.

Teacher's Guide

From **The Ant and the Grasshopper**

For ***"• (ant)...gathering and storing grain for the winter"***

t

ANT GO-TO-left, FOOD <rs:ant ICL*"gather food,"* ICL*"carry food on its shoulder"*> WALK IX-dir*"from left to right"* DROP-OFF HOME. IX-dir*"left."* AGAIN, <rs:ant ICL*"gather food,"* ICL*"carry food on its shoulder"*> BRING-TO*"back and forth"* PUT-IN-SAVINGS-right++

From **The Wolf and the Kid**

For ***"• (wolf) thought it was a great flute player. It played..."***

[FLUTE] WOLF <rs:wolf ICL*"takes out flute from his pants pocket,"* ICL*"plays the flute"*>

From **The Fox and the Stork**

For ***"• It (fox) served the soup in a flat dish so the stork could only sip a little at a time with its long pointed beak. Meanwhile, the fox quickly lapped up the soup with its tongue."***

t

PLATE, FOX <rs:fox ICL*"take two plates from shelf"*> IX*"plates"* DCL*"thin and flat"*

t

SOUP <rs:fox ICL*"ladles soup into both plates,"* ICL*"carries plates to table,"* ICL*"places plates on table"* (to stork) ENJOY EAT>

frustrated

BIRD <rs:stork [(wh)LCL:B*"plate"*/BPCL:G*"stork sipping soup"*]>

mischievous

FOX <rs:fox [(wh)LCL:B*"plate"*/BPCL:H*"fox laps up soup"*>

NOTE: Be sure students' mouth movements match the movement of the bird's beak sipping and fox's licking.

For **"• *The stork served the dinner in a tall pot with a narrow mouth. The stork easily stuck its long beak into the pot and pulled out piece after piece of the meat. The fox with its shorter nose could not reach the food in the pot.*"**

t

DCL*"2 tall pots with narrow mouth"* BIRD <rs:stork ICL*"takes 2 pots from shelf"*>

t

MEAT <rs:stork [(wh)LCL:C*"mouth of pot"*/ICL*"ladles meat into both pots"*] ICL*"carries pots to table"* ICL*"puts pots on table"* (to fox) ENJOY EAT>

t

FOX <rs:fox [(wh)LCL:C*"mouth of pot"*/BPCL:H*"licks inside*

frustrated

trying to reach meat">

mischievous

BIRD <rs:stork BPCL:G*"pulls meat from pot repeatedly"*>

NOTE: Again, be sure students' mouth movements match the movement of the bird's beak sipping and fox's licking.

NOTE: Be sure to be consistent with the placement of the characters. For example, the fox stays on the left side and the stork on the right side. Now, to maintain the placement, at the fox's house, have the fox get the plates from its left. Likewise, have the stork get the pots from its right. It makes it less confusing for the audience.

From **The Dog and the Wolf**

For **"• *the hair on a certain part of the Dog's neck was very much worn away ...where the collar is put on at night to keep me chained up; it chafes a bit*"**

EVERY-NIGHT, COLLAR <rs:dog LCL:L*"collar put on dog's neck"* (2h)LCL:F*"chain from collar down to post,"* LCL:L*"collar*

oo

on neck rubs constantly," ECL:open8*"bald area"*>

Excerpts from **The Scorpion and the Frog**

For ***"• ...and they set out... (carry him across on its back)"***

t

FROG SCL:V *"sit on ground,"* THUMB-loc *"frog's back"* SCORPION [(wh)LCL:B *"frog back"*/SCL:V *"scorpion gets on frog back"*]. FROG [(wh)LCL:B *"ground"*/SCL:V *"frog jumps into river"*]...

or

FROG SCL:V *"sit on ground,"* SCORPION <rs:frog SCL:V *"scorpion gets on frog back"*>. FROG [(wh)LCL:B *"ground"*/ SCL:V *"frog jumps from ground into river"*]...

For ***"• ...the scorpion stings the frog..."***

<rs:scorpion ICL *"hold onto frog"* [WRONG] [(wh)ICL *"hold onto*

shocked/whq

frog"/BPCL:X *"stings the frog"*]> FROG <rs:frog !*"what"*! !WHY!

Excerpt from **The Fox and the Goat**

For ***"• 'you place your forefeet upon the wall and bend your head, I will run up your back to get out.' The goat readily assented and the fox leaped upon his back and made off..."***

<rs:fox YOU BPCL *"place hands on wall, head down,"*
ME [(wh)LCL:B *"goat's back"*/SCL:V *"run up goat's back and get out"*] *"well"*?>
GOAT <rs:goat FINE++. BPCL *"place hands on wall, head down"* SCL:V *"fox hop off goat shoulder and head"*> ZOOM-AWAY.

or

<rs:fox YOU BPCL *"place hands on wall, head down,"*
ME [(wh)LCL:B *"goat's back"*/SCL:V *"run up goat's back and get out"*] *"well"*?>
GOAT <rs:goat FINE++. BPCL *"place hands on wall, head down"*>
FOX [(wh)LCL:B *"goat's back"*/SCL:V *"run up goat's back and get out"*] ZOOM-AWAY.

REVIEW Character Talking to Itself

20–35 minutes

PRESENT
(LESSON SLIDE 12:10:10)

Describing a Character Talking to Itself

1. to describe a character's thoughts, role shift that character looking at the subject of its thoughts, and externalize what it is thinking by signing low and close to your body
2. to describe a character's intentions, role shift that character and look at the audience while the character describes its scheme

Review how to describe a character's thoughts or intentions by using parts from **The Lion and the Mouse** and **The Fox and the Crow** and have students copy.

For ***"1. to describe a character's thoughts..."***

From **The Lion and the Mouse**:

- as the mouse, look at the lion sleeping
- simultaneously sign low and close to your body
  MAYBE FOOD (2h)alt.IX-loc*"all over face"* (nod)

From **The Fox and the Crow**:

- as the fox, look up at the crow in the tree
- simultaneously sign low and close to your body
  CHEESE IX*"cheese"* SHOULD !MINE! (nod)

For ***"2. to describe a character's intentions..."***

From **The Lion and the Mouse**:

- as the mouse, after hearing the lion's roar, look at the audience
- and sign LION NEED MY HELP before describe mouse running to the lion

From **The Fox and the Crow**:

- as the fox, after looking at the crow, look at the audience
- and sign

ME BE-EXCEPTIONAL-IN FLATTER-crow, crow-GIVE-TO-me

arrogant

CHEESE. you-LOOK-AT-me, before signing HELLO to crow.

PRESENT

(LESSON SLIDE 12:10:11)

Describing a Character Talking to Itself

1. to describe a character's thoughts, role shift that character looking at the subject of its thoughts, and externalize what it is thinking by signing low and close to your body
2. to describe a character's intentions, role shift that character and look at the audience while the character describes its scheme

Activity

Add the character's thought or intention to this situation:

"The mouse sees the lion with some food in front of him."

Pair up students and have them add a thought and an intention to the mouse.

Possible descriptions:

For ***"describe character's thoughts"***

MOUSE SEE LION <rs:lion SLEEP, BPCL*"head resting on paws"*>
FOOD PCL*"in front of lion's paws"*
MOUSE <rs:mouse (looking at lion, sign low, close to body)
FOOD IX*"food,"* ME !WANT! (nod)> (2h)SCL:V*"running to lion"*

For ***"describe character's intentions"***

MOUSE SEE LION <rs:lion SLEEP, BPCL*"head resting on paws"*>
FOOD PCL*"in front of lion's paws"*
MOUSE <rs:mouse LOOK-AT*"lion"* (look at audience) LION SLEEP,
ME *"shh"* TAKE-FROM*"lion"* (nod)> (2h)BPCL:1*"tiptoeing to lion"*

EXERCISE 4: Character Talking to Itself.

Have students go to their assigned fable groups and translate the excerpts on their worksheets. (*Student Workbook*, pages 451, 454, 457, 460, 463 or 466). Make sure they incorporate the signs or classifiers from their worksheets.

Conclude. Have each group show you their translations. Make suggestions if needed (see guide below). Then, have the group practice the translations again with the suggested changes.

Teacher's Guide

From **The Ant and the Grasshopper**

For ***"• When winter came the grasshopper had no food and was starving."*** (intentions)

when
LATER-ON TIME !COLD! fs-GRASSHOPPER !HUNGRY!

neg
<rs:grasshopper LOOK-FOR FOOD NONE++, THOUGHT-

conj
OCCUR IX*"ant"* ANT IX*"ant"* PUT-IN-SAVINGS++ FOOD, me-ASK-TO-ant, ant-GIVE-TO-me. (nodding)>

From **The Wolf and the Kid**

For ***"• The poor kid realized it could not escape..."*** (intentions)

GOAT RUN, <rs:goat (2h)SCL:V*"legs running"* SCL:1*"wolf approaching me(goat)"*

whq
(gaze at audience) ME (2h)DO++. THOUGHT-OCCUR, HAVE

nod
IDEA "wait-a-minute" (turn to wolf) "halt."...>

For ***"• ...(wolf) said to itself, 'My purpose was to be a butcher, not a musician.'"*** (thoughts)

<rs:wolf (describe dogs coming) (look at kid) ME STUPID.

neg
SHOULD GO-AHEAD CAPTURE, EAT GOAT, NOT ICL*"play flute"* MUSIC, *"pshaw"*> RUN ZOOM-AWAY

From **The Fox and the Stork**

For ***"•...it (fox) decided to play a trick on its friend (stork)."*** (intentions)
FOX <rs:fox ICL*"stirring soup"* (gaze at audience) WHY+NOT ME TEASE-TO-stork...(nod) (look at shelf) PLATE, ICL*"get plates from shelf."*...>

From **The Dog and the Wolf**

For ***"• 'Is that all?' said the Wolf. 'Then good-bye to you, Master Dog.'"*** (thoughts)

q
<rs:wolf LOOK-AT-dog YOU BE-USED-TO, LCL:L*"collar on neck"* (2h)LCL:F*"chain from collar down to post"* (sign low and

neg
close to body) ME NOT-WANT (or REFUSE), "bye bye"> RUN, ZOOM-AWAY

From **The Scorpion and the Frog**

For ***"• A scorpion, desiring to cross the stream, meets a frog..."*** (intentions)

WATER ECL*"flowing past,"* SCORPION BE-STUCK CAN'T GO-

neg
ACROSS. <rs:scorpion SEE FROG IX*"frog"* (looks at audience) FROG CAN SWIM, IX *"frog"* CAN frog-BRING-TO-me*"across stream"* GO-ACROSS. LETS-SEE ASK-TO*"frog"* (nod)> SCL:1*"scorpion approaches frog."*...

From **The Fox and the Goat**

For ***"• Concealing his sad plight under a merry guise, the Fox indulged in a lavish praise of the water..."*** (intentions)
FOX <rs:fox LOOK-AT-goat> (gaze at audience) ME NEED

IX*"goat"* HELP-me EXIT. ME NOT WANT goat-LOOK-AT-me

neg
BE-PEABRAINED. THOUGHT-OCCUR (nod) "wait-a-sec" (to goat) !"hey"!...>

REVIEW *The Background and the Moral*

30–40 minutes

PRESENT
(LESSON SLIDE 12:10:12)

Background

- setting
- character description
- other relevant information

EXERCISE 5: Background

Have students go to their assigned fable groups and develop the background for their fables based on the questions in their worksheets. (*Student Workbook*, pages 451, 454, 457, 460, 463 or 466).

Conclude. Have each group share the background to their fable with you. Make suggestions if background is insufficient or not relevant to the fable. Then, have the group practice the background again with the suggested changes.

PRESENT
(LESSON SLIDE 12:10:13)

Moral

- begin with a transition
- give moral

Ask what are the two transitions to begin the moral in the fables.

Answer.

rhet
STORY POINT "what"...

or

rhet
LEARN LESSON "what"...

EXERCISE 6: Moral

Have students go to their assigned fable groups and refer to the worksheets to develop a translation for the moral to their fable. (*Student Workbook*, pages 451, 454, 457, 460, 463 or 466). Be sure they begin the moral with one of the two transitions.

Conclude. Have each group show you their translations. Make suggestions if needed (see guide below). Then, have the group practice the translation again with the suggested changes.

Teacher's Guide

Moral for **The Ant and the Grasshopper**

For "***• There is a time to work and a time to play.***"

rhet cond neg
(transition)... SUPPOSE ALWAYS WORK++, NOT+GOOD,
cond neg
ALWAYS PLAY+++ , NOT GOOD, !IMPORTANT! BOTH WORK, PLAY BALANCE

Moral for **The Wolf and the Kid**

For "***• Those who stray from their true business often lose the prize in hand.***"

rhet determined
(transition) ...SUPPOSE YOU GOAL-cont, [(wh)GOAL/SCL:1
th/cond nod
"stray from goal," IN-FUTURE !LOSE-OUT! !BE-CAREFUL!

Moral for **The Fox and the Stork**

For "• ***One bad turn deserves another.***"

rhet cond

(transition)...SUPPOSE YOU TEASE-all IX-mult*"people"* PEOPLE,

nod

IN-FUTURE SAME-AS IX-mult*"people"* TEASE-you YOU.

cond

SUPPOSE YOU NICE, SWEET, POLITE TO IX-mult*"people"* PEOPLE,

IN-FUTURE SAME-AS IX-mult*"people"* NICE, SWEET, POLITE

nod

TO+YOU

Moral for **The Dog and the Wolf**

For "• ***Better free than be a fat slave.***"

rhet

(transition) SOMETIME YOU HUNGRY, SOMETIME YOU NOT HAVE

neg

ENOUGH, BUT YOU !FREE! !THAT-ONE!, BETTER+THAN

neg

!COMFORTABLE! BUT STUCK, NOT+FREE "well"

Moral for **The Scorpion and the Frog**

For "• ***It's hard to change one's character.***"

rhet

(transition) [SUPPOSE] PERSON-on left, IX*"person"* LIE++, MEAN,

cond t

BIGHEADED++, BE-RAISED, NOW IX*"person"* TELL-you

nod

<rs:person ME !CHANGE!> YOU BELIEVE IX*"person"* (shake head)

neg

"wave no" THAT POSS-left NATURE. !HARD! CHANGE, [MAYBE]

neg

CAN'T "well"

Moral for **The Fox and the Goat**

For "**• *Look before you leap.***"

rhet — when

(transition) BEFORE-EVENT YOU DECIDE, YOU (2h)alt.LOOK-AT-over, MULL-OVER, POSITIVE-left, NEGATIVE-right, PROCEED (nod)

HOMEWORK

Tell students to do **Homework 12:10** (*Student Workbook*, pages 444–448).

REHEARSE *First Draft of Assigned Fables*

5–7 minutes per student

PRESENT
(LESSON SLIDE 12:10:14)

Storyteller. Tell your fable to two different students in your group to get their feedback.
Listeners. Give your feedback on the following (you may write notes too):
- whether the story is clear, engaging, and easy to follow
- whether storyteller made good eye contact with the audience
- suggest two or three ways the storyteller can improve.

Have students tell the story to two different students in their fable groups and get feedback from them.

EVALUATION

5–7 minutes per student

EXAM

Arrange the room according to the diagram below. Have the storyteller ***stand*** while presenting his or her fable. Remind the audience to be attentive throughout the presentation, and the storyteller to look at the audience.

PROCESS

- Videotape students telling their fables.
- After each presentation, have the audience members fill out the **12:10 Student Feedback** and give to the storyteller.
- While the audience fill out the **12:10 Student Feedback**, you fill in the **Overall Comments** section of the **12:10 Evaluation** based on the student's presentation.
- Fill in the rest of the **12:10 Evaluation** when you review the video later.

NOTES:

Index

M

N

STUDENT WORKBOOK TOPIC INDEX

NOTES:

NOTES: